The Donner Party Chronicles

A Day-by-Day Account of a Doomed Wagon Train 1846 – 1847

By Frank Mullen Jr.

Photos by Marilyn Newton

Foreword by Will Bagley

FROM A YEAR-LONG NEWSPAPER SERIES PUBLISHED IN THE RENO GAZETTE-JOURNAL, COMMEMORATING THE 150TH ANNIVERSARY OF THE DONNER PARTY'S TREK ACROSS THE CONTINENT AND ENTRAPMENT IN THE SIERRA.

The publication of this book was made possible through the generous support of the following donors:
John Ben Snow Trust
E. L. Cord Foundation
Pioneer Citizens Bank of Nevada
William and Moya Lear Charitable Foundation
Gaming Foundation for Educational Excellence

A HALCYON IMPRINT OF THE
NEVADA HUMANITIES COMMITTEE

Dedication

To my parents, who taught me to learn, and to my wife Susan, my inspiration

Book design by Nancy Peppin
Managing Editor, Stephen Adkison

© Copyright 1997
Nevada Humanities Committee

ISBN   1-890591-01-7

First Printing August 1997
Second Printing March 1999
Third Printing November 2001

**A Halcyon Imprint of the
Nevada Humanities Committee.**

Contents

Acknowledgments

I am a newspaperman, and I approached the Donner saga as a journalist rather than a historian. I have been a reporter, looking over the shoulders of the real detectives of Donner Party history.

To accumulate information for the year-long *Reno Gazette-Journal* sesquicentennial series on the Donner Party, I consulted more than a hundred books, including anthologies of primary sources and rare books such as *The Donner Miscellany* and *The Journal of Heinrich Lienhard*. I looked up other sources, published and unpublished, including diaries, letters, and newspaper accounts of 1846 – 47.

I traveled the Donner Party Trail in the summer of 1996, consulted scholars, historians, researchers, archaeologists, authors, wagon-builders, re-enactors, doctors, librarians, museum curators, archivists, and many other experts. In the endnotes of this book I sought to list them all, but there are some people I must thank at the outset:

The late Dale Morgan, whose books *Overland in 1846* and *West from Fort Bridger* (with J. Roderic Korns, updated by Will Bagley and Harold Schindler) supplied many of the scholarly references and insights reflected throughout my study of the Donner Party.

Authors Kristin Johnson (*Unfortunate Emigrants: Narratives of the Donner Party*) and Will Bagley, who were kind enough to endure many hours of discussions and interviews about the minutiae of the Donner saga. Their openness, willingness to share research, and encouragement made the newspaper series possible.

The newspaper readers who gave me much encouragement throughout the year, and the audiotext readers, listed in the endnotes, helped the series come alive.

Thanks as well to the students and teachers of Washoe County Schools, and my friend Glen Feighery, historian and copy editor, for his patience, support and skill in copy editing both the series and the book manuscript.

Reno Gazette-Journal Executive Editor Ward Bushee allowed me the budget and the time to research the project. Special thanks to photographer Marilyn Newton, graphics director Mark Bartley, artist Gabriel Moron, Mark Lundahl, John Smetana, Linda Dono, Sevil Omer, Tonia Cunning, George Petras, Kathy Novak, Angela Beard-Mann, Curt Seifert, Kenn Altine, and Edward Shur.

Rollan and Marilyn Melton of Reno, who encouraged a book version, and the Nevada Humanities Committee, a local chapter of the National Endowment for the Humanities, especially the executive director, Judith Winzeler. Thanks to managing editor Stephen Adkison, book designer Nancy Peppin, and editor Nick Cady.

The Oregon-California Trails Association was especially helpful, particulary members Don Wiggins, Paul Sawyer, and Martin Griffith; also educators Fred Horlacher, John Clark, and University of Nevada, Reno, professor Don Hardesty.

Thanks to Donner reenactor Bill Pugsley, who shared his experience in retracing the Donner Trail in 1996, as well as Sandy Sei, Elaine Lange, Dede Read, and Patsy

Colip who helped prepare the manuscript, and to Gayle Green of the Emigrant Trails Museum, who provided critical research help.

The late Gregory Lee Pearson, founder of the journalism department at Metropolitan State College of Denver, taught me that newspapers have the power to inform, entertain, educate, illuminate, and inspire.

And my wife, Susan Skorupa Mullen, shared me with the Donners for two years and never complained.

To these and all the others who helped me and thought the Donner story worth retelling, I give my heartfelt thanks.

Frank Mullen Jr.
Reno, July 1997

Many of the photographs in this book would not have been possible without the help of people in several different states. There were those who accompanied me along the trail, which is not always easy to find, and there were those who allowed me onto their property in my search of the ever elusive trail. I want to thank all of them for their support.

In Nevada, Don Wiggins spent many days away from his mapping of the trails through Nevada to take me on arduous hikes in the Sierra Nevada and the hills east of Reno so I could photograph little known areas. Martin Griffith's minutely detailed directions also allowed me to find much of the trail through Nevada by myself.

In Utah, Roy Tea showed me the trail from border to border. We were accompanied one day by Al Mulder and his wife, Laura, who provided support as we made our way from Twenty Wells across the salt desert.

In Wyoming, Mike Brown and his wife Mimi, married just three weeks, took one of their weekends to take me along the trail from Twin Mounds to the Big Sandy.

In California, Jack Steed took me to the Johnson Ranch and shared his knowledge of the area.

Without the help of these people many of the crucial photographs would never have been captured on film.

I also want to thank the following for allowing me access to the trail segments running across their property: Jay Anderson, who owns a ranch at Grantsville, Utah where many of the springs known as Twenty Wells are located and who took time to show me around. Mitch Walk of the Scull Valley Ranch where Hope Wells is located. Ruth Chesnovar, who owns the area where the Donner Party camped at the Little Sandy. And John Eachus, who allowed me to photograph the Johnson Ranch near Sacramento, California.

Marilyn Newton
Reno, July 1997

Foreword

Will Bagley
Historian and
Emigrant Trail Scholar
Salt Lake City, Utah
July 1997

History — like all memory — is selective. It overlooks the ordinary achievements of humankind in place of its awful crimes, and ignores good news in favor of the bad, just as newspapers favor tales of depravity and disaster over the commonplace triumphs of everyday heroism. So the story of our past often reads like a catalog of disasters, and the annals of war, famine, plague, and holocaust obscure the daily routine and simple endurance that have marked the lives of most people since time began.

In the late 1870s, newspaperman C. F. McGlashan began to look into a disaster that had taken place only a few miles from his home in Truckee, California, when the event was already thirty years in the past. McGlashan had made his mark as an investigative journalist in 1875 when he published a report on Utah's Mountain Meadows Massacre of 1857, and he now turned his attention to writing a *History of the Donner Party* that would forever enshrine the event among the legends of the American West.

Historians have sometimes complained about the dramatic liberties McGlashan took in telling the story and the occasional factual errors that pepper his narrative. More troubling was his willingness to suppress — and eventually destroy — evidence that reflected poorly on his subjects, many of whom became his dear friends. Yet McGlashan preserved a wealth of both lore and data, much of it valuable and all of it interesting, that otherwise would have simply disappeared. As the many editions of his book testify, he thoroughly captured the popular imagination.

On the sesquicentennial of the Donner trek, McGlashan's mantle fell on the shoulders of another journalist. In August 1996, I cornered George McKinstry at a Donner Party symposium in Reno, Nevada, and, dressed as gold rush impresario Sam Brannan, had the pleasure of meeting Frank Mullen, who was convincingly attired as McKinstry, the redoubtable 1846 emigrant and sheriff of Sutter's Fort. We spoke in character for a spell before I realized this was the Donner Party's latest chronicler. I'd already talked with Frank on the telephone and had followed his Donner series in the *Reno-Gazette Journal* with positive delight. It was clear that the history bug had bit Frank hard, and like many others I expressed the hope that he could publish his series in book form.

This work is proof that dreams come true, and Frank Mullen has joined the rank of Donner Party historians with a book that is not only good history, but one that delivers a whopping good story as well.

Professionally trained historians have avoided wrestling with the Donner Party legend, perhaps because it's about such odd particulars. The job has been left largely to amateurs — journalists, businessmen, dentists, English professors, librarians and poets. As a historian, I think the natural reluctance of my better-credentialed colleagues to deal with such a horrific story has led them to discount the larger significance of the disaster at Truckee Lake. The dead of the Donner Party were the first casualties of Manifest Destiny — a phrase coined in New York just as Lansford Hastings was departing for the West. Historians have spent surprisingly little time examining the political intrigue behind the 1846 emigration (aimed at the conquest of the Southwest) and most have failed — at least since Bernard DeVoto — to note how enmeshed the unfortunate emigrants were in the consequences of national politics.

The wealth of information we have on the Reed, Donner, Breen, Graves, and Murphy families has seldom been put to good use. The Donner Party opens a wide window into the complex details of overland migration and its complicated pioneers. Close to half a million emigrants crossed the plains before the completion of the transcontinental railroad in 1869, and while the trials and adventures of entire wagon companies have simply vanished from the historical record, we have a surprising amount of information about most members of the Donner Party, and the names of them all. The company included Mexican frontiersmen and Irish, English, and German emigrants; Catholics, Protestants, and Mormons; elders and infants; and a healthy majority of middle-class Americans. Though the emigrants believed they were going into the wilderness, the plains, mountains and deserts they crossed looked a lot like home to the Indians who inhabited them. The Donners and their comrades ran into exceptional problems near the end of their trek, but the story of their experiences on "the plains across" was close to typical. It gives us insights into the experiences of hundreds of thousands of other emigrants whose journeys are forgotten.

In hindsight, it's easy to see the catastrophe as both accidental and inevitable. Accidental in that it was an odd combination of circumstances — why did they believe Hastings, and why didn't they hurry? — and inevitable in that someday, the rearguard of the emigration was bound to face the wrath of a Sierra winter. There had been a drought in the mountains since Caleb Greenwood first brought wagons across them in 1844, and Hastings himself had crossed the summit in the previous December. Only the Indians and the *Californios* appreciated what the mountains could do.

People seldom learn anything from history, but the Donner saga became a cautionary tale in the annals of the emigration. Ragged frontier California would rally its slender resources in the following years to mount effective rescue efforts before the snow fell. (Since one of the rescued emigrants was historian Josiah Royce's mother, it was surely worth the public expense.) So the event had some impact on subsequent history, but more importantly, it became a remarkable popular legend with a life all its own.

Why has the public fallen in love with a story that historians have artfully avoided? The answer is simple: it's a compelling tale of people pushed to the limits of survival, overflowing with all the heroism and evil that attends such hard times. It is so awful in its particulars, so dramatic in its inescapable chronology, and so compelling in its personae that it is, simply, a great story. But the details are so troublesome — it's a witch's brew of excellent contemporary sources, confusing reminiscences, lies and legends — and the material so inherently dramatic, that perhaps it is a subject best left to novelists and dreamers.

That's why Frank Mullen's book is such a joy. He's attacked the story like the veteran newspaperman he is, and as an added bonus, he got the history as close to right as anybody might ever get it. We learn that the Donner Party was not made up of heroes and villains, but of ordinary people, just like you and me, trapped in extraordinary circumstances. As a bonus, this book makes a singular contribution to Donner Party lore — there is now a fascinating record of how the legend lived on during the years 1996 and 1997, its sesquicentennial. The legend is alive and well, and the level of public interest shows no signs of flagging.

The Donner Party Chronicles has it all — it's both good history and a well-written tale. Frank Mullen has created as compelling a Donner Party story as anyone has ever put on paper. Readers will enjoy it, and historians will be forever in his debt.

Preface

A welter of essential components are vital, if a historical book is to be unforgettable. For certain, a magnetic storyline is required. There must be a brew of solid research and writing, with compelling illustrations and/or photographs that are integral companions of text. Author Frank Mullen Jr. and photographer Marilyn Newton have given us such a rich, unbeatable blend of results. Their wonderful effort makes *The Donner Party Chronicles* a giant book.

Additional factors went into creating this memorable telling of an American tragedy.

First came Mullen's year-long, historically sound series of *Reno Gazette-Journal* articles that graphically humanize the agony, heroism, and misjudgments that made these overland migrants an indelible part of American history.

The newspaper gave unswerving commitment to the Donner series. From publisher Sue Clark-Johnson, to editor Ward Bushee and his newsroom, to many other *Gazette-Journal* colleagues, there came meritorious teamwork.

Marilyn Royle Melton, a senior trustee of the Nevada Humanities Committee, first approached the Committee's executive director, Judith Winzeler, suggesting the series be published as a book. The Humanities Committee, galvanized by Winzeler, set out to form a publishing team, whose members' efforts constitute still another vital contribution by the Nevada Humanities Committee in is distinguished 25-year existence.

Publishing a book takes paper, ink, and brains. However, without funding, there can be no happy ending, no matter how much talent supports a venture. Fortunately, *The Donner Party Chronicles* was blessed with contributors who supported the book with cash and in-kind support, including these major funders: Pioneer Citizens Bank of Nevada instantly grasped the significance of author Mullen's painstaking work. The publisher is in the debt of Pioneer's president, William Martin; executive vice president Leo Seevers, and talented marketing persons Susie Kapahee and Kathleen Kosman. E. L. Cord Foundation, long highly regarded for its wide-ranging charitable goodness, provided major financial support. Trustee William O. (Bud) Bradley was an especially significant Cord principal. The John Ben Snow Trust weighed in with a major grant, recognizing the careful research and writing that went into the book. The William and Moya Lear Charitable Foundation unhesitatingly offered funding support. Mike O'Callaghan and trustees of the Gaming Foundation for Educational Excellence deserve warmest thanks for a grant that helps carry *The Donner Party Chronicles* into a myriad of school classrooms. All these players deserve sincerest applause. It goes to them with lasting gratitude.

Rollan Melton,
distinguished Nevada journalist and
Reno Gazette-Journal columnist
Reno, Nevada
July, 1997

Introduction

Detail of Donner Party monument, Truckee, California — Tim Dunn photo

In the spring of 1846 the Donner and Reed families and hundreds of other emigrants stepped off into the wilderness for a two-mile-per-hour walk across the continent. They passed from the dirt roads of Independence, Missouri into history and legend.

These were not the mountain men and explorers who had opened the unmapped West. They were families with children — farmers, businessmen, homemakers, tradesmen, and hired hands who signed on in the hope of getting free land in California. They sold most of their possessions and loaded the remainder of their households into covered wagons aimed toward the setting sun.

They were looking for new life and wealth in California. Some of them wanted a shortcut to prosperity. They were Americans all — even though they or their forebears came from Ireland, Germany, Poland, Mexico, England, or Belgium. All those who took to the trail in 1846 were Americans by deed, if not by birth or law. They were expanding a nation.

In May of 1846 in Independence, the families that became the Donner Party could not foresee the suffering and the death it would cost to cross two thousand miles of prairie, mountain ranges, and salt deserts.

The picnic atmosphere of the first leg of the journey would give way to distrust, conflict, and incredible hardship. Only one day from crossing their last mountain pass the lead wagons would be trapped by Sierra snowstorms and the pioneers would face despair, murder, and cannibalism.

George Donner, like Moses, would lead his people to a mountaintop in sight of the Promised Land, yet never enter it himself. The families would suffer like characters in a Greek tragedy, and only about half would find deliverance.

Through the mist of fifteen decades, the ghosts of the Donner Party still speak to us. These people and their adventures during a year-long crossing of the continent branded the American imagination as surely as did the *Titanic* or the Battle of the Little Big Horn. The lurid tales of cannibalism first attracted the public's attention, but in a deeper sense, the emigrants' two-thousand-mile walk remains a metaphor of American history.

There was much suffering, and people are curious about that. There is romance in stepping off into a blank spot on the map and overcoming barriers. There is the drama of hope turning into desperation.

And there is the knowledge that these were real people, with families just like our own.

How could they have crossed mountains and deserts with those wagons? How did they dare?

The Donner Party struggles to cross the Sierra. — Emigrant Trails Museum

Terrible! Thrilling! True!

HISTORY OF THE DONNER PARTY

A TRAGEDY OF THE SIERRA

Price, Paper, - - $1.00.

Sent Prepaid to any Address on Receipt of Price,

By the Author, C. F. McGLASHAN, Truckee, Cal.

Truckee newspaper ad for C. F. McGlashan's book.

1846

The nation is turning seventy. Texas was admitted to the Union the year before, an act that will lead to a war with Mexico. Oregon Country is jointly occupied by the United States and Great Britain and the possibility of another war is simmering in the Northwest.

This is the America of Herman Melville, Henry David Thoreau, Henry Clay, and President James K. Polk. Other luminaries wait in the wings: Abraham Lincoln, 37, has just been nominated as Whig candidate for Congress. U.S. Army Capt. Robert E. Lee is in charge of the defensive fortifications of New York Harbor.

The first telegraph lines are two years old. Elias Howe has just invented the sewing machine. Canned goods are becoming available, but people are wary of their safety.

In New York, Walt Whitman is the editor of the *Brooklyn Eagle*. His eyes also turn westward: "Then there is California, in the way to which lovely tract lies Santa Fe," he wrote. "How long a time will elapse before they shine as two new stars in our mighty firmament?"

California, like most of what will become the southwestern states, is part of Mexico, but there are about 800 Americans there. This fall, there will be more.

The Donner Trail Today

Photographs by Marilyn Newton

From Independence Rock in Wyoming to Sutter's Fort in California, this photo essay traces the path of the Donner Party west of the Great Divide. The wagon trains faced arid lands, unknown country, and hostile tribes. After Hastings' Cutoff, the Donners were drawn into a whirlpool of events culminating in disaster.

These contemporary views of the trail illustrate both the physical influence of the emigrants on the western landscape and their enduring legacy to our history. On the eve of the 21st century, traces of the trail still remain, both on our land and in our imaginations.

Dates following the captions approximate the progress of the Donner Party in 1846 and 1847.

This soldier's name is one of the oldest still visible on Independence Rock. Although time and erosion have obliterated many names, including James Reed's, many names are visible around the base and on the summit. (June 12, 1846)

Independence Rock in central Wyoming as the emigrants would have seen it on their approach to the granite monolith. Westward travelers would try to reach this point by July 4, hence the name. More than a mile around its base and 136 tall, the formation is a directory of many who passed this way. (July 12, 1846)

A short distance east of South Pass looking back toward Twin Mounds, the emigrant wagons traveled side by side, two and sometimes three abreast. (July 17, 1846)

The Donner party stopped here at South Pass and ate lunch on the top of the continental divide. Here, the emigrants made the fateful decision to follow Hastings' route. (July 18, 1846)

After leaving South Pass, the emigrants passed Plume Rock, a landmark mentioned in many diaries and painted by many as they passed. (July 19, 1846)

Emigrants seldom traveled in a straight line, as is evidenced near the parting of ways as the trail snakes its way through the sagebrush. (July 18, 1846)

The parting of the ways. Here, wagon trains took separate routes west. The Donner Party followed the left-hand trail. The one on the right led to the already established route via Fort Hall. (July 19, 1846)

While most emigrants seeking different routes west separated at the parting of the ways, the Donner Party camped here at the Little Sandy some miles to the west before parting the next day. (July 18, 1846)

After crossing waters like the Dry Sandy, Little Sandy, and Big Sandy, the Green River proved formidable to the emigrants. The wagons had to be ferried across as the emigrants slowly made their way to Fort Bridger. (July 22, 1846)

The historical park at Fort Bridger boasts several structures built in the mid-to-late 1800s, as well as this reproduction of the original structure owned and run by Jim Bridger. (July 26, 1846)

After leaving Fort Bridger the party traveled through Echo Canyon, a long canyon of high red cliffs. After this canyon, the emigrants would face one of their toughest obstacles, the Wasatch. (August 4, 1846)

Hastings led his party through Weber Canyon with great difficulty, one wagon plunging over a cliff. He left word for the Donner Party to stay where they were so he might find another route. While the party avoided Weber Canyon, the Wasatch would be even worse.

The Donner Party traversed the low pass in the background and crossed Yellow Creek enroute to the Wasatch. (August 13, 1846)

After leaving Donner camp enroute to the east mouth of Emigration Canyon, the travelers passed over this road. (August 14, 1846)

The Donner Party camped on the east side of Emigration Canyon while all able-bodied men went ahead to the canyon and began cutting their way through. (August 14, 1846)

A tunnel cut through the dense growth of scrub oak and manzanita on the west side of Emigration Canyon in the Wasatch is a remnant of those traveling west. (August 16, 1846)

Just a short stretch of willows separated the Donner Party from the end of the Wasatch and the yawning valley beyond, with the great salt lake and the salt desert. But after days of hacking through the scrub, they were too tired to cut their way out, electing instead to double team the oxen and climb what is now Donner Hill, just about where the pines now grow. (August 22, 1846)

A few stones are all that is left of what is believed to be Luke Halloran's grave near present-day Grantsville, Utah. Although some historians dispute the actual location of the grave, this one was found using old photos and diaries noting that Halloran was buried next to another pioneer. A second grave was found at this site. (August 25, 1846)

All roads come together at Tempe Point west of Salt Lake City. From left is Interstate 80, U.S. 40, the Lincoln Highway, and, barely visible around the bowl area, the Donner trail. The road in the foreground is a frontage road.

As the Donner Party made their way to Hope Wells, the tired emigrants were probably oblivious to the petroglyphs atop a bluff overlooking the trail. The symbols were left by American Indians. (August 27, 1846)

One of the many huge trees at Hope Wells that were probably there when the Donner Party camped nearby. Tamsen Donner found a note left here by Hastings. Though it had been torn apart by birds, she carefully pieced the note back together. (August 28, 1846)

After leaving Hope Wells and crossing Hastings Summit, the emigrants saw the first view of Pilot Peak with its twin summits visible in the distance. (August 29, 1846)

Looking back across the salt desert, the trail the Donner Party followed is barely visible. From here, they still had a long way to go. (August 30 – September 5, 1846)

After crossing the dreaded 80 miles of the salt desert, the Donner Party finally arrived at Donner Springs at the base of Pilot Peak. The last portion of the desert can be seen in the distance. (September 4 – 10, 1846)

Set in a bowl, Flowery Springs was just one of many springs at which the emigrants camped while traveling through what is now Nevada. Surprisingly, the land which is believed by many even now to be dry desert, is dotted with many springs, many of which offer good water. (September 13, 1846)

After leaving Flowery Springs the emigrants crossed over Jasper Pass then camped at Mound Springs, so named because the springs are sheltered by mounds of earth and grasses. (September 14, 1846)

After leaving Mound Springs and Warm Springs the Donner Party entered the Ruby Valley, surrounded by magnificent mountains. From here the travelers would go south in search of a way across. (September 17, 1846)

The emigrants had little time to enjoy the beauty of Ruby Valley. Hastings' shortcut was becoming longer with each passing day. (September 17, 1846)

The members of the Donner Party, making their way along the Ruby Mountains, would have been greeted by scenes such as this dawn over the Ruby Marshes. (September 19 - 20, 1846)

Water gushes out of Cave Creek at the southern end of the Ruby Mountains. Water from snow melt cascades down the inside of the mountain and flows through a cave (the black opening at right) and down into the Ruby Marshes.

Finally, the emigrants reached the southern end of the Ruby Mountains and found a way over what is now the Overland Trail. (September 21, 1846)

After exiting this canyon at the fork of the Humboldt, the Donner Party was only a short distance from rejoining the California Trail. (September 26, 1846)

After rejoining the California Trail, one of the party's first campsites was near Carlin Hot Springs. (September 28, 1846)

A ribbon of trail near the area of Gravelley Ford still winds its way through the sagebrush near present-day Beowawe. (September 29, 1846)

As the oxen fought their way through deep sand up and over the right side of this low hill, James Reed and John Snyder argued and Reed stabbed Snyder to death. Snyder's grave lies somewhere on this hill, now know as Snyder Hill. (October 5, 1846)

The California and Oregon trails split near present-day Imlay. The Donner Party followed this trail west to the Fortymile Desert, while others went in a more northerly direction over the sunblasted Black Rock Desert to Oregon. (October 9, 1846)

A full moon rises over the Humboldt Sink while the desert playa, surrounding hills, and what appears to be wagon parts glow in the last light of the sunset. (October 12, 1846)

Steam rises from Boiling Springs in the early morning light. After leaving the Fortymile Desert, the Donner Party passed by here on their way to the Truckee River. (October 13, 1846)

The Truckee River at Painted Rock. After reaching the river, the Donner Party was forced to cross the twisting, turning river 22 times. (October 18, 1846)

According to trail scholar Don Wiggins, the Donner Party made their way to the top of this mountain range before descending into the valley below. Following the track, still visible in areas, shows a route over the small saddle in the foreground which continues into the valley. At the time the area was a lush green meadow surrounding a slough. The pioneers veered left and camped at the south end of the valley before making their way into the Sierra (October 20, 1846)

A wagon wheel rim, its origin unknown, lies near the trail on the steep decline into Dog Valley. (October 26, 1846)

These two rows of pines growing in the Hoke Valley area indicate a wagon trail according to some historians. They believe draft animals and wagons stirred up the seeds as they passed and trees grew where the seeds landed on either side of the trail. (October 27, 1846)

One of the few big pines left in the Hoke Valley area, this tree stood when the Donner Party passed.

Some historians believe some members of the Donner Party camped at what is now Prosser Reservoir, later crossing Prosser Creek at Station Creek and traveling up a small hill by this spring before heading back toward the Truckee River. (October 28, 1846)

Historians have followed this trail to the Truckee River which some say was used by the Donner Party and other emigrants. The trail is located east of present-day Truckee, California. (October 29, 1846)

Some members of the Donner Party camped at the extreme far end of Donner Lake. The campsites were spread out over a large area, and a second camp was miles away to the northeast. When rescued, the starved and exhausted emigrants made their way up this rugged summit. The rocks were under feet of snow. (October 30, 1846 – April, 1847)

The wagon road at Johnson's Ranch near Sacramento can still be seen winding away from the adobe building where the emigrants stayed after their rescue. (W. Eddy arrived here January 17, 1847; Keseberg, the last of the survivors, arrived April 25, 1847)

Cannon still guard the entrance of Sutter's Fort in Sacramento, California, the ultimate destination of the Donner Party.

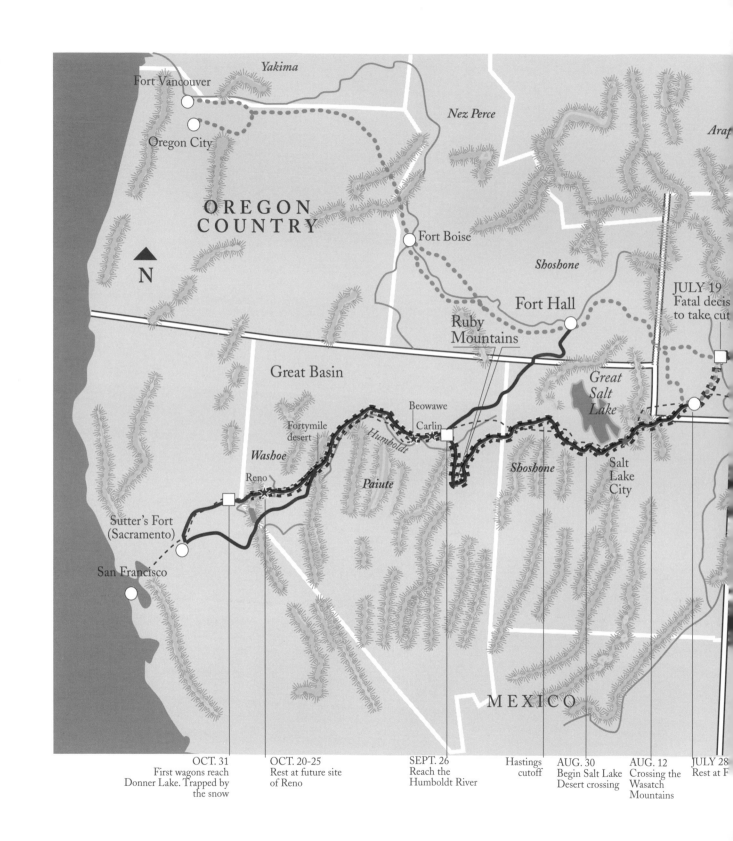

The Donner Party Trail

Fort Vancouver

Oregon City

Yakima

Nez Perce

Arap

OREGON COUNTRY

N

Fort Boise

Shoshone

Fort Hall

Ruby
Mountains

JULY 19
Fatal decis
to take cut

Great Basin

*Great
Salt
Lake*

Beowawe

Fortymile
desert

Humboldt

Carlin

Washoe

Reno

Paiute

Shoshone

Salt
Lake
City

Sutter's Fort
(Sacramento)

San Francisco

MEXICO

OCT. 31	OCT. 20-25	SEPT. 26	Hastings	AUG. 30	AUG. 12	JULY 28
First wagons reach Donner Lake. Trapped by the snow	Rest at future site of Reno	Reach the Humboldt River	cutoff	Begin Salt Lake Desert crossing	Crossing the Wasatch Mountains	Rest at F

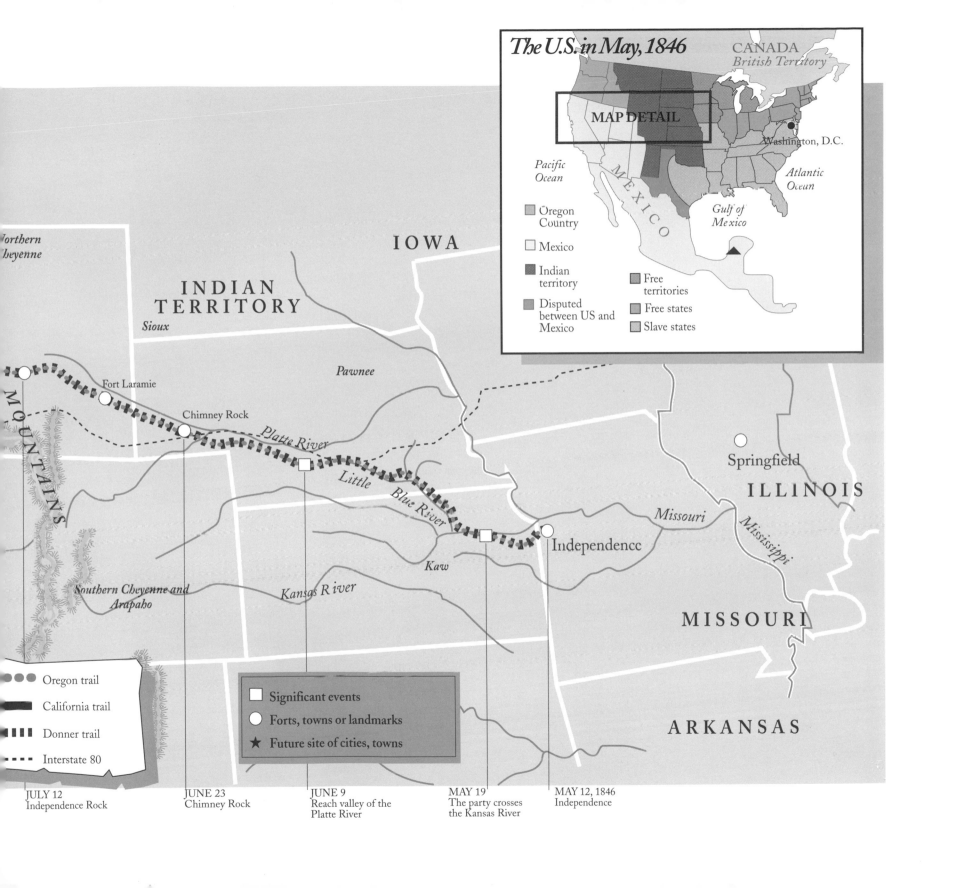

The U.S. in May, 1846

CANADA
British Territory

MAP DETAIL

Washington, D.C.

Pacific
Ocean

MEXICO

Gulf of
Mexico

Atlantic
Ocean

Oregon
Country

Mexico

Indian
territory

Disputed
between US and
Mexico

Free
territories

Free states

Slave states

Northern
Cheyenne

INDIAN
TERRITORY

Sioux

Pawnee

IOWA

Fort Laramie

Chimney Rock

Platte River

MOUNTAINS

Little

Blue River

Springfield

ILLINOIS

Missouri

Mississippi

Independence

Kaw

Southern Cheyenne and
Arapaho

Kansas River

MISSOURI

ARKANSAS

Oregon trail

California trail

Donner trail

Interstate 80

☐ Significant events

○ Forts, towns or landmarks

★ Future site of cities, towns

JULY 12
Independence Rock

JUNE 23
Chimney Rock

JUNE 9
Reach valley of the
Platte River

MAY 19
The party crosses
the Kansas River

MAY 12, 1846
Independence

MAY TO JULY 31, 1846

Part 1: The Picnic Missouri to Fort Bridger

I am seated on the grass, in the midst of my tent, to say a few words to my dearest, only sister . . . [Tomorrow] we go to California, the Bay of Francisco. It is a four-month trip. We have three wagons furnished with food and clothing and such . . . I am willing to go and have no doubt it will be an advantage to our children and to us.

— Tamsen E. Donner in a letter
dated May 11, 1846, at
Independence, Missouri

May 12, 1846

Donners and Reeds leave Independence for trail west

James F. Reed — Nevada Historical Society

Margaret Reed — Nevada Historical Society

This morning, pioneers leave their camps along the Missouri River. Rich or poor, educated or unschooled, they point their wagons west and seek a new life.

The families of George and Jacob Donner leave Springfield, Illinois, on April 15, 1846, along with their neighbors James and Margaret Reed. They are the genesis of the Donner Party, which will not become a single wagon train until late July.

George Donner, 62, a native of North Carolina, is a well-to-do farmer who has been to Texas, prospered in Illinois, and is now taking his younger children to a new, wide-open land. His third wife, Tamsen, 45, is a teacher who wants to write a book about the plants along the westward route. Her dream is to found a girls' school in California. Tamsen and George's children are Frances, 6; Georgia, 4; and Eliza, 3. His children from a previous marriage are Elitha, 13; and Leanna, 11. His family has three wagons.

George travels with his brother Jacob, 56, and Jacob's wife, Elizabeth, 45, who also have three wagons. The Jacob Donners have seven children along, including two from Elizabeth's former marriage. The brothers employ Noah James, about 16, and Samuel Shoemaker, about 25, as teamsters. Charles Stanton, a shopkeeper recently from Chicago, and John Denton, an English goldsmith and gunsmith from Sheffield, travel with the Donners.

Irish-born James Reed, 45, is a descendant of Polish nobility. A Protestant despite his Polish roots, he is a successful contractor and furniture maker in Springfield. Reed is well known in Sangamon County and fought alongside his neighbor Abraham Lincoln in the Black Hawk War of 1832.

He is the originator of this party. He wants to become an Indian agent in California. His family are wife, Margaret, 32, who suffers from "sick headaches" that she and her husband hope the western climate will ease; Virginia Reed, 12, Margaret's daughter from a previous marriage; daughter Martha, known as Patty, 8; sons, James Jr., 5, and Tommy, 3; and Mrs. Reed's mother, Sarah Keyes, 70, who is bedridden with tuberculosis but determined to make the trek.

Sarah Keyes is lying in a customized wagon outfitted for her comfort and drawn by four yoke (pairs) of oxen. The Reeds also have two supply wagons, cows, horses, and what they believe will be enough supplies to make the trip and provide provisions for their first winter in California.

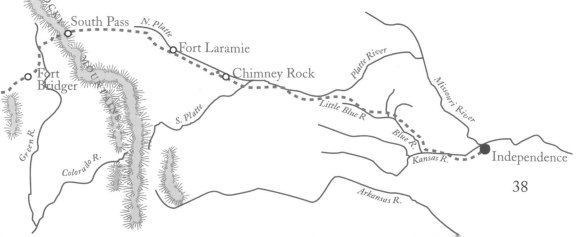

Independence is the "jumping-off place" for pioneers going west. Beyond it is Indian Country: the Great Plains, the Rockies, and the trackless deserts of what will become Utah and Nevada. In the years before 1846 other parties had blazed trails to California, but most of the pioneer traffic was bound for the Oregon Country. As the Donner and Reed families face the setting sun and push off to their great adventure, would they have gone if they had known what lay ahead? With hindsight, would anyone face such suffering?

But they are caught now in a wave of hope and ambition — and avarice — that sweeps the nation and will remain a trend for decades.

They are players in a folk movement because they are brave enough or desperate enough or romantic enough to pack up and look for something better and richer and grander than anything they have known.

It is time to leave, and one direction beckons.

They push off and don't look back.

INDEPENDENCE IS BOOMING.

The air clangs with iron ox shoes being hammered in the blacksmith shops. Mountain men, traders, Mexican cowboys from the Santa Fe Trail, teamsters, and mule skinners drink in the saloons and gamble in the muddy streets.

Flour, lead for bullets, cloth, ox yokes, sugar, lard, rifles, gunpowder casks, and Indian trade goods are stacked in shops. Children play in the dirt alleys. Indians gather in front of the courthouse to sell their crafts, and men frantically check provisions and grease wagon wheels.

Prices: Oxen at $21-$25 per pair; mules and horses from $30 to $40 per head; flour at $4 per barrel.

On May 12, a wagon train soon to be joined by the Donner and Reed families takes an inventory: Sixty-three wagons; 119 fighting men, fifty-nine women and 110 children; 58,484 pounds of flour; 38,080 pounds of bacon; 1,065 pounds of gunpowder; 2,557 pounds of lead for bullets; 144 rifles and shotguns and ninety-four pistols; and an estimated 750 head of cattle and 150 horses.

This is a migration of a people, of an army of families.

Since the first colonies on the Atlantic shore, Americans pushed west. Their internal compasses pointed that way when they needed elbow room, hope, and possibilities.

The Indians live there, but most tribes far west of the Mississippi River have not yet measured the greed of the European-Americans. The emigrants will soon learn, but in 1846, the trail has more pressing dangers than Indian raids.

The town was a first violent shock of the strangeness which was a primary condition of the emigration. The most powerful tension of pioneering began here at the jumping-off. Here was a confusion of tongues, a multitude of strange businesses, a horde of strangers — and beyond was the unknown hazard.
— Bernard DeVoto, *Year of Decision 1846*

Leaving the Old Homestead by James F. Wilkins
— *Missouri Historical Society*

SIGNATURE OF MARGARET W. REED

Employment agreement between the Reeds and their teamster Milt Eliott — *Emigrant Trails Museum*

May 15, 1846

Donners encamped on Heart Grove; they've already encountered heat and rain

From the Sangamo Journal *newspaper, Springfield, Illinois, March 26, 1846*

Tonight the Donner and Reed families are camped at "Heart Grove" on the Big Blue River, about twenty-two miles west of Independence, Missouri. Cottonwoods, oaks, maples, and hickory trees spread their arms above the wagons and tents. A river, swollen with recent rains, rushes past the idle company.

It was sunny — an "oppressive heat" — three days ago when they left Independence. The pilgrims were getting organized and the drivers were getting used to the wagons, the ox teams, the skittish cattle, and traffic along the road. That day, they made just over four miles through the prairie.

It rained the second day. The wagons slogged about sixteen miles through mud. The air was thick with the sound of rain and the crack of the oxwhips and the "whoa-haws!" of the teamsters. They set up camp in a downpour. The sky wept all night.

They remained encamped today. Mud is everywhere. The Donners' outfits have held up well, but in the other emigrant camps some canvas wagon bonnets and tents are already showing wet spots in the stitching.

The Donners and their companions are still in Jackson County, Missouri, at the Indian Country line. Other emigrants are encamped along the road to the east and west of them. It is like a great moving village.

They have passed through a prairie destitute of timber or shrubs and have seen grouse, which they call prairie hens, flushed by their movement across the plain.

They rest under cloudy skies. Tomorrow they will be on the move again, across deep road ruts with wet bottoms soft as featherbeds, gooey as molasses.

It's early in the season, but every delay now might haunt them later on. Motion is the rule. The direction: West.

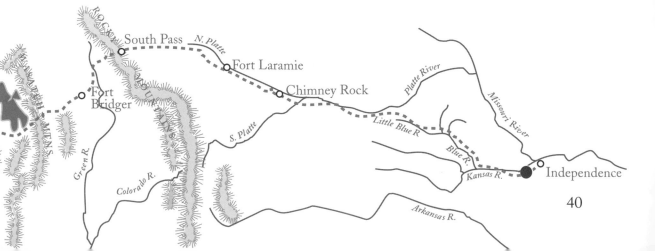

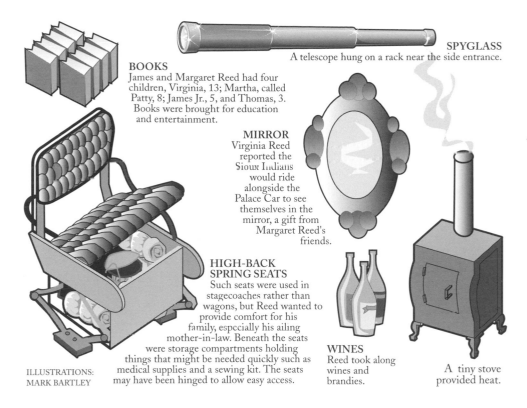

BOOKS
James and Margaret Reed had four children, Virginia, 13; Martha, called Patty, 8; James Jr., 5; and Thomas, 3. Books were brought for education and entertainment.

SPYGLASS
A telescope hung on a rack near the side entrance.

MIRROR
Virginia Reed reported the Sioux Indians would ride alongside the Palace Car to see themselves in the mirror, a gift from Margaret Reed's friends.

HIGH-BACK SPRING SEATS
Such seats were used in stagecoaches rather than wagons, but Reed wanted to provide comfort for his family, especially his ailing mother-in-law. Beneath the seats were storage compartments holding things that might be needed quickly such as medical supplies and a sewing kit. The seats may have been hinged to allow easy access.

WINES
Reed took along wines and brandies.

A tiny stove provided heat.

ILLUSTRATIONS: MARK BARTLEY

On our departure day [from Springfield] we Donner children were dressed in new traveling suits. Early in the day the first two wagons started off, each drawn by three yoke of oxen. The beef cattle and milk cows followed. Finally, about noon, the family wagon was ready to go. Eliza sat beside Mother up front on the wagon, the rest of us in back. When we left our home on its grassy knoll, and passed through the last pair of bars, I could see that my mother had tears in her eyes.

— Frances Donner, from *Pioneer Children on the Journey West*

Small lamp said to have been found at site of Donner camp at Alder Creek.
— Reno Gazette-Journal

THE TRAVELERS

George Donner, 62, a prosperous farmer from outside Springfield, Illinois, with three wagons; his third wife, Tamsen Donner, 44; and their three children: Frances, 6; Georgia, 4; and Eliza, 3. George's daughters from a previous marriage, Elitha, 13; and Leanna, 11. His teamster is Hiram Miller.

Jacob Donner, 56, farmer and George's brother, with 3 wagons and his wife, Elizabeth Donner, 45. Their five children and two of Elizabeth's children from a previous marriage. Three Donner employees: Noah James, 16; Hiram O. Miller, 30; and Samuel Shoemaker, 25.

Traveling with the Donners were Charles Stanton, 35, from Chicago; and John Denton, 35, a goldsmith from England.

James Frazier Reed, 45, Irish-born furniture maker from Springfield, Illinois, with three wagons; his wife, Margaret Reed, 32; with her mother, Sarah Keyes, 70. The Reeds' children: Virginia, 12; Martha "Patty" Reed, 8; James Jr., 5; and Thomas Reed, 3. Two servants — Eliza Williams, 31, the cook; and her brother Baylis Williams, 25, — and three teamsters: Milford Elliot, 28; Walter Herron, 27; and James Smith, 25.

May 17, 1846

War news hits camps: hostilities with Mexico

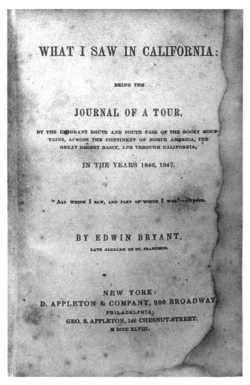

The cover of Edwin Bryant's book
— Marilyn Newton photo

In camp tonight is a rumor of war.

The Donners, Reeds, and their companions have recently heard of conflicts along the Rio Grande between a company of American dragoons and elements of the Mexican Army. General Zachary Taylor and his command are reported to be in a sticky situation in Texas.

Will President James K. Polk persuade Congress to declare war? California is Mexican territory. So is what will become New Mexico, Arizona, Nevada and Utah. Will the wagons be driven more than eighteen hundred miles over mountain and desert only to meet Mexican lancers beyond the Sierra? That's the concern in this camp on the Wakarusa River, sixty miles from Independence (by the reckoning of teamster Hiram Miller on the fifth day of travel). No one is panicked, it seems.

"None of the emigrants to California, as far as I could learn, manifested a disposition to turn back," writes Edwin Bryant, 41, a Kentucky newspaperman who travels the road just ahead of the Donners.

Bryant, a native of Massachusetts, studied medicine but later settled on journalism as a career. He'd been an editor of both the Louisville, Kentucky, *Courier* and the *Journal* when his health began to fail in 1845. He decided to go west to see if the climate and the exercise of the trek might improve his condition and to write a book while he was at it.

An educated man, Bryant is able to comment on botany, geology, medicine, and many other subjects. His companions are impressed with this Boston Brahmin who can ride a horse, shoot a gun, and who also knows the names of plants and stars. His journal, to be published as *What I Saw in California*, will provide a readable, in-depth report of his activities and a detailed snapshot of the emigration of 1846. The journal — which contains not only geographic notes but also stories about the immigrants and details of everything from mineral deposits to daily weather reports — will serve as a model for pioneer journals in the years after 1846.

The last two days on the trail have been clear, Bryant reports, with temperatures in the 70s — a pleasant drive. Indians — Shawnee, Kansas,

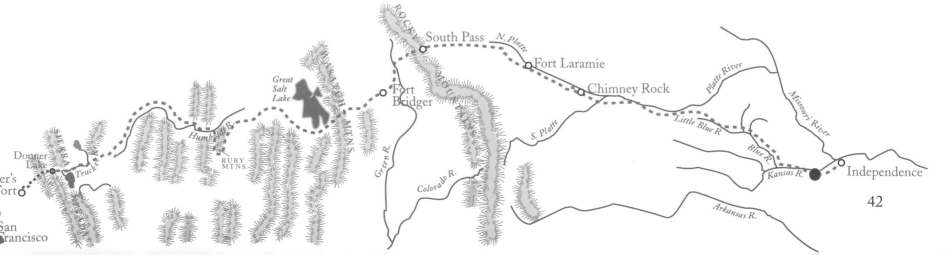

Potowatamie — have greeted the pioneers and offered to trade. Today, Bryant had a close call with a few Sac hunters when he wandered off exploring, but no harm came to him. In two days, he will meet the Donners and Reeds.

Tomorrow, they will travel across level plain, make another camp, and then cross the Kansas River.

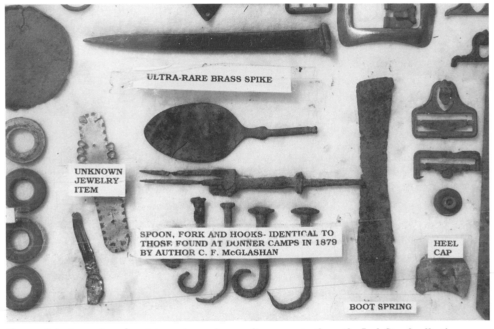

ULTRA-RARE BRASS SPIKE

UNKNOWN JEWELRY ITEM

SPOON, FORK AND HOOKS- IDENTICAL TO THOSE FOUND AT DONNER CAMPS IN 1879 BY AUTHOR C. F. McGLASHAN

HEEL CAP

BOOT SPRING

Some of the items found at Johnson's ranch near Sacramento, from the Jack Steed collection.
— Marilyn Newton photo

The morning was so delightful and the atmosphere so bracing, that I started on foot in advance of the train . . . six Indians, mounted on horses, came in sight at the top of the hill, and began to descend it . . . I was sufficiently near to see that one of them carried in his hand a broadsword, with a bright metal scabbard, which glistened with sunbeams. This Indian was leading a horse. When he saw me he gave the horse in charge of another. I had very carelessly, in order to be unincumbered by weight, left all my arms in the wagon, except my hachet. I was now several miles distant from our train and entirely concealed from them. There was no probability of any of our party passing this way . . . The leader spoke to me in English, and said "How do?" I re plied and reciprocated the inquiry in the usual manner. He then asked, in his broken English, if there were more white men with me. I replied there was a great number just behind. He nodded his head and looked at his companions with an expression of disappointed intelligence.
— Edwin Bryant, May 17, 1846,
What I Saw in California

MAY 19, 1846

Donners cross Kaw River and join Russell Party

A corral formed by wagons. — Mark Bartley

Today the Donners and Reeds cross the Kaw (Kansas) River and meet with a party of emigrants led by "Col." William Russell. The nine Donner-Reed wagons are brought across on boats manned by French-Indian ferrymen. The price: $1 a wagon. Women and children ride in the wagons. Men and boys stand with the boatmen. Oxen, cows, and horses swim.

On the other side of the Kansas, the Russell group — now down to thirty-five wagons after the departure of a party led by a Methodist minister — is waiting. The Russell party, including journalist Edwin Bryant, is awaiting stragglers, including Alfonso Boone, a grandson of Daniel Boone, and his group. Boone doesn't make it today, but there is excitement in camp, for last night Mrs. Hall gave birth to twins. One is named for the attending doctor, the other for Col. Russell.

The Donners and Reeds are welcomed in the camp at Soldier Creek. "We are joined today by nine wagons from Illinois, belonging to Mr. Reed and the Messrs. Donner [brothers]," Bryant wrote in his journal. "They are highly respectable and intelligent gentlemen with interesting families. They were received into the company by unanimous vote."

The Donners and Reeds make camp, giving Margaret Reed's 70-year-old mother, the consumptive Sarah Keyes, a chance to rest from the bone-jolting road.

The wagons are circled so they form a corral and the cattle are placed inside. The pioneers' tents are set up outside.

While waiting for Boone, Bryant and a companion carry trinkets to two nearby Kansas Indian villages. They imagine they'll be greeted by stern chiefs and beautiful Indian maidens. But the wigwams are deserted, perhaps because the Kansas are at war with the Pawnee.

The Donners and Reeds are happy to be traveling in a large company that will give them protection from Indians. The families are in high spirits. Even Grandma Keyes is feeling a bit better than usual, perhaps because she's been traveling with her grandbabies in a special wagon, which writers will dub "The Pioneer Palace Car."

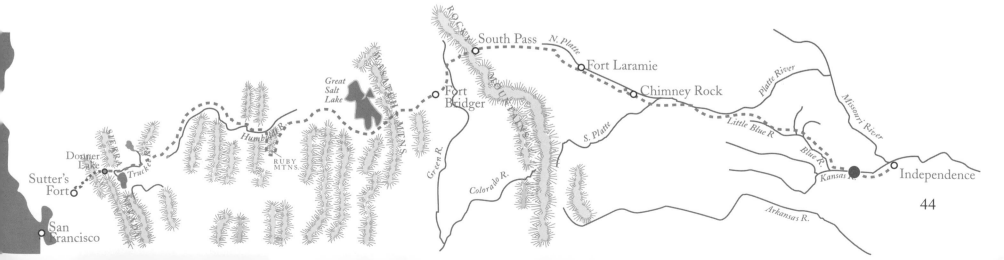

An illustration of an ox being hitched was drawn by William H. Jackson and appeared in the American version of Heinrich Lienhard's 1846 journal, From St. Louis to Sutter's Fort.

The company bound for California is composed of as much intelligence and respectability, certainly, as ever wended their way to a new country, and the integrals are representatives from almost every state in the union. I was just visited by a gentleman and a lady each, who came from the widely separated States of Louisiana and Pennsylvania. We have, also, clergymen, lawyers, physicians, painters, and mechanics of every trade, including some jolly printers.

— William H. Russell, in a letter to the *Missouri Republican*, Indian Country, twenty miles west of Independence, May 10, 1846

Grandma Keyes, who was seventy-five years of age, was an invalid, confined to her bed. Her sons in Springfield, Gersham and James W. Keyes, tried to dissuade her from the long and fatiguing journey, but in vain; she would not be parted from my mother, who was her only daughter. So the car in which she was to ride was planned to give comfort.

— Virginia Reed, *Across the Plains In The Donner Party.* (Her father and others wrote that Mrs. Keyes was 70, not 75.)

WILLIAM HENRY "OWL" RUSSELL, 43, is the prototype for the Kentucky Colonel character. He is nicknamed "Owl" because it is said that one time while walking through the woods an owl hooted, and Russell, hearing the "who? who?" in the darkness, answered: "Why it is I, Col. William Henry Russell of Kentucky, a bosom friend of Henry Clay!"

Russell is always ready to make a speech or take charge of things. Historians will describe him as a popular figure but an ineffective leader. "He was a good talker," 1846 pioneer Jacob Wright Harlan will remember. Russell will serve with John C. Frémont in California and return to Missouri in 1847.

MAY 22, 1846

Emigrants move across prairie; Daniel Boone's kin arrives at camp

A compass face, similar to those used by the Donner party, found at Johnson's Ranch near Sacramento. From the Jack Steed collection.
— Marilyn Newton photo

It's been slow going since the Kansas River crossing and the camp at Soldier Creek three days ago.

The Russell Party, including the wagons of the Donners and the Reeds, is only 116 miles from Independence, Missouri. They've been traveling the plains for twelve days.

Three days ago, they advanced over a flat prairie with wet and boggy sections and camped in a heavy rain and thunder. The family dogs that follow the caravan fight among themselves and while in camp rest in the shade of wagons. Most families have several dogs along. The Reeds have five: Tyler, Barney, Trailer, Tracker, and little Cash, Virginia's favorite. Each night the guards strain their eyes to see outside the pools of firelight and are alert to any disturbances communicated by the dogs.

"I was on watch tonight until one o'clock," writes Edwin Bryant. "The howls and sharp snarling barks of the wolves; the mournful hootings of the owl, and the rush of the winds through the tree-tops of the neighboring grove, are the only sounds disturbing the deep solitude of the night."

The next day they moved across an undulating plain and struggled four hours to get their wagons across a steep-banked stream. They camped in a bend of that stream and greeted the much-awaited Alfonso Boone, a grandson of Daniel Boone, who added his group's eleven wagons to the Russell train.

That evening the men amused themselves with target practice. "The distances were 80 and 200 yards," Bryant writes. "The day has been delightful, and a more cheerful spirit seems to prevail in our party."

The next day they moved eighteen miles across green prairie after thirteen wagons separated from the group elect to advance under their own captain. The group believes the Russell Party is too large and traveling too slowly. The Donners and Reeds remain with Russell.

Indians swarm the wagon train and Bryant says they were "troublesome" rather than hostile.

Tonight they camp at Black Paint Creek, with two Kansas Indian villages nearby.

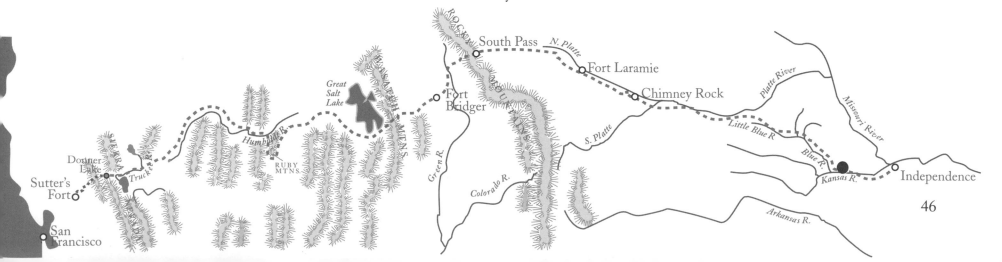

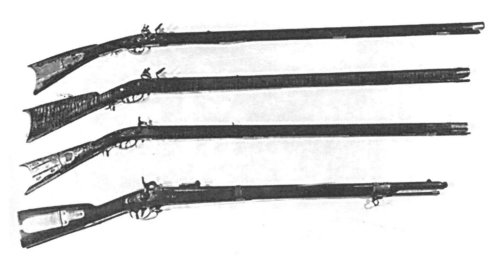

We carried many supplies, seeds, and implements that we would use on our farms in the new country. We had bolts of cotton prints and flannels, handkerchiefs, glass beads, and knickknacks to give to the Indians, and stores of laces, silks, satins and velvet, to use for trade in California. My mother brought books and school supplies to use in the young ladies seminary she hoped to establish.

— Frances Donner, from *Pioneer Children on the Journey West*

Pioneer type rifles using both flintlock and percussion firing systems similar to those used by the emigrants of 1846 — Photo by Roy Vogel

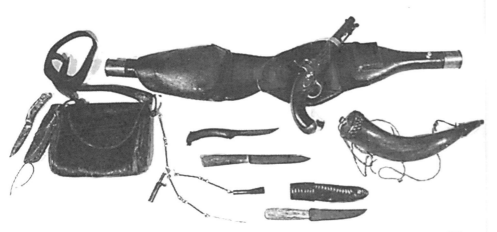

In the afternoon, near a small pond of water, we met four trappers from the Rocky Mountains, returning to the settlements. They were accompanied by several Delaware Indians, all of whom spoke English so as to be understood. There were suspended from the saddle of one of the trappers, a wild turkey, a raccoon and several squirrels, which they had taken last night . . . They were packing several large sacks of fur-skins. They reported that on the Platte, some one or two hundred miles in advance of us, there were large herds of buffaloes, and that we should experience no difficulty in this region in supplying ourselves with fresh meat.

— Edwin Bryant, May 23, 1846, *What I Saw in California*

Hunting pouch with a pistol circa 1842 and other accessories. — Roy Vogel photo, from The Donner Party Rescue Site: Johnson's Ranch on the Bear River *by Jack Steed*

MAY 24, 1846

Donners moving slowly westward; Bryant worries about progress

The Russell Party, which includes the Donner and Reed families, has traveled only twenty-two miles in the past two days.

That worries Edwin Bryant, the journalist. "Singular as it may seem, there are many of our present party who have no just conceptions of the extent and labor of the journey before them," Bryant writes. "They appear to be desirous of shortening each day's march as much as possible, and when once encamped, are reluctant to move, except for the benefit of fresh grass for their cattle, and a more convenient and plentiful supply of wood for cooking. There are several persons ill in camp of [stomach and intestinal] complaints."

They are about 138 miles from Independence, Missouri, and have about 1,700 miles to go.

Yesterday, the pioneers had to chop trees and stack brush to ford a small creek. The wagon train was strung out for several miles and Indians swarmed around the emigrants, asking for gifts. They were not disappointed.

Bryant has taken time to observe the plants blooming on the prairie. Surely Tamsen Donner, an aspiring botanist who is planning to write a book about the trek, has already sketched the flora and pressed flowers into the pages of her journal.

Tomorrow they'll roll through "broken country" and reach the Big Blue Earth River. They'll camp three-quarters of a mile from a beautiful spring, near three elm trees. A dead elm will be dragged into camp and the fires will burn bright.

The spring is "the finest water that we found on the plains thus far," observes George McKinstry, whose journal also provides a look at the Russell Party's journey. McKinstry, 35, a merchant from New York, fancies himself a writer — a talent that will resurface with much sensationalism later in the Donners' journey.

Bryant will dub the water source "Alcove Spring." McKinstry will carve the name on a rock. James Frazier Reed will scratch his initials nearby.

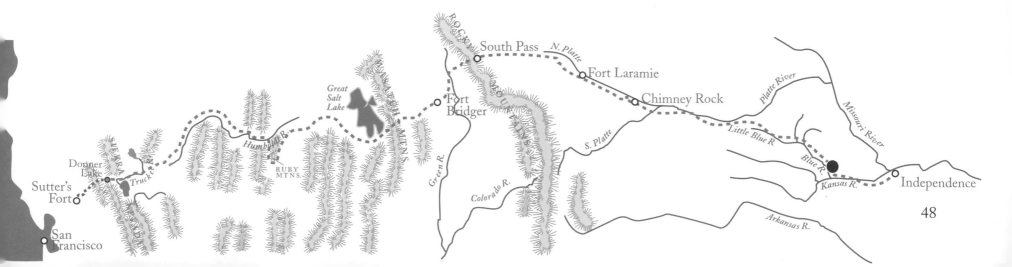

Emigrants move along the trail
— Charles Russell painting

Just as our wagons were forming a corral, a storm of thunder, lightning, rain and wind, burst upon us, drenching us to the skin, and nearly upsetting some of our wagons with furious violence. The cloud rose from the west, and soon passing over to the east, within a hundred yards of us the most brilliant rainbow I ever beheld was formed, the bases of the arch resting upon two undulations which we had passed. No Roman general, in all his gorgeous triumphal processions, ever paraded beneath an arch so splendid and imposing. The clouds soon cleared away, the rain ceased, and the brilliant meteor faded, leaving nature around us freshened and cleansed from the dust and impurities, which for two days past have been excessively annoying.
— Edwin Bryant, May 25, 1846,
What I Saw in California

James Reed took time to carve his initials and the date in a rock at Alcove Spring.
— Bancroft Library

MAY 26, 1846

Donners, Reeds reach Big Blue, do laundry, and hold meetings

Washday along the Big Blue Bluffs: Men, women, and children haul their mud-splattered clothes out of the prairie schooners and soak them in the Big Blue River.

Tallow soap is rubbed into the fabric of the gritty shirts, soil-caked dresses, blankets, canvas coats, and "unmentionables."

Travel has been slow for the Russell Party. They needed several hours to cross steep-sided Vermillion Creek, and when they cleared the obstacle, a sudden thunderstorm lashed the wagon train. The cloudburst gave way to a magnificent rainbow.

Today, they crossed broken country vacant of timber or water and reached the river. The Big Blue is now a hundred yards wide and rising by the hour. They've made 25 miles in two days — 163 miles from Independence, Missouri, in two weeks.

Now they'll wait for the river to fall.

After laundry is done, the emigrants hold a public meeting about "bylaws, and regulations heretofore adopted and rarely enforced." James F. Reed, George Donner (who has been elected a sub-captain under Col. Russell), and Edwin Bryant help run the meeting.

"We are a pure democracy," writes Edwin Bryant, who scribbles in his journal as the meeting takes place in the corral. "All laws are proposed directly to a general assembly and are enacted or rejected by a majority."

The pioneers play music beneath a crescent moon. A young man dances a jig on the end gate of a wagon. The girls giggle and the babies cry.

That night, thunder and rain return, and the storm rages through the night.

The Reed family is concerned: Consumption (tuberculosis) is again plaguing Margaret Reed's 70-year-old mother. Mrs. Keyes also might have had a stroke. No one has seen her this sick before.

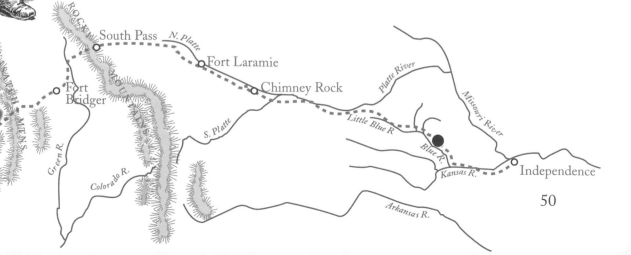

This clothing is typical of the attire worn by members of the Donner Party circa 1846.

[Besides the family wagon] we had two wagons loaded with provisions. Everything in that line was brought that could be thought of. My father started with supplies enough to last us through the winter in California, had we made the journey in the usual time of six months. Knowing that books were always scarce in a new country, we also took a good library of standard works. We even took a cooking stove.

—Virginia Reed, *Across the Plains In The Donner Party*

J. Quinn Thornton
— Marion County Historical Society

I came up with little Patty [Martha Reed, 8] and her brother, children of one of our company. She was busied in calling the attention of little Tom [Tommy Reed, 3] to a variety of objects that seemed to please and delight him. At the moment I came up, they were admiring a large butterfly, which like us, had ventured out after the storm. "You are a dear, sweet little girl," I said to Patty, as I approached them and tenderly put my hand on her cheek.

"Yes, and Tommy here is a dear, sweet little boy; so he is isn't he? He is my dear little brother," she continued, affectionately, as she threw her arms around his neck and drew him nearer to her.

"Oh! you. Patty, you, do quit," said Tom, somewhat fretfully and impatiently, as he stumbled; "you almost threw me down. You are always a–huggin' me, so you are."

—J. Quinn Thornton, May 25, 1846

May 29, 1846

Grandmother Sarah dies in camp

James Clyman — Utah State Historical Society

Styled after Frederic Remington, this drawing shows a mountain man of Clyman's time. — Mark Bartley

Mrs. Sarah Keyes, 70, is dead.

Her body is buried under an oak tree near a spring on the banks of the Big Blue River in Kansas. The grave is on the right-hand side of the Oregon-California Trail where hundreds of thousands more emigrants will pass. She is the first casualty of what will become known as the Donner Party.

Several weeks after Mrs. Keyes was laid to rest, a mountain man, James Clyman, will pause at her grave. He will be surprised to see the occupant is past her seventieth year. "All ages and sects are found to undertake this long, tedious and even dangerous journey for some unknown object never to be realized even by the most fortunate," Clyman will write. "And why? Because the human mind can never be satisfied, never at rest, always on the stretch for something new, some strange novelty."

Mrs. Keyes went on the trip west despite the pleadings of her family. She had wanted to see her son, who had gone to Oregon, once more before she died. So Reed made her as comfortable as possible in the family wagon, which was built for her comfort — the legendary "Pioneer Palace Car."

She was frail and ill, however, and had gotten worse during the last few days of storms. Yesterday, she could no longer speak.

Although her death was expected, it "cast a shade of gloom all over the encampment," writes Edwin Bryant. As the emigrants prepare to cross the swollen Big Blue River, "the construction of the ferry boat and all recreations are suspended, out of respect. At 2 p.m. a funeral procession was formed, in which nearly every man, woman and child of the company united."

A grave is prepared, a eulogy is given, a prayer is offered, and hymns are sung "with much pathos and expression." J. A. Cornwall, a Presbyterian minister, "conducted the burriel and delivered a sensible sermon at the grave takeing his text from Thessilonians 'Trouble yourselves not about those that sleep,' " George McKinstry writes.

The plot is covered with sod and Bryant predicts wildflowers will bloom. Virginia Reed will say the cemetery of Manhattan, Kansas will grow around this grave, but historians will report the gravesite near Alcove Spring is unknown.

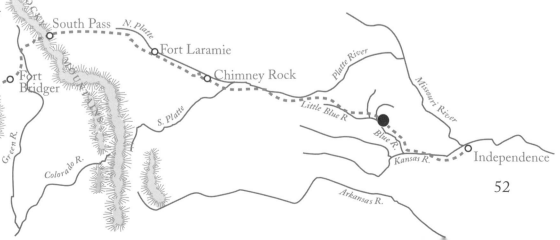

Martha "Patty" Reed, 9, has several keepsakes from her grandmother. They include a tiny doll made of wood, a small pincushion, and a lock of her grandma's hair.

The party goes to sleep under the crescent moon, with no noise but the rushing river, chanting whippoorwills, and hooting owls.

The Donners, Reeds, and the rest of the Russell Party will spend the next few days crossing the river. No one realizes that Mrs. Keyes died a merciful death — she will not have to face the horrors in store for her family.

We came to the blue [river] — the water was so hye we had to stay thare four days — in the mean time gramma died, she became spechless the day before she died. We buried her very decent We made a nete coffin and buried her under a tree we had a head stone and had her name cutonit and the date and yere verry nice, and at the head of the grave was a tree we cut some letters on it the young men soded it all ofer and put Flores on it We miss her verry much . . . every time we come into the Wagon we look at the bed for her.

    — Sarah Keyes's granddaughter Virginia Reed, in a letter written farther up the trail on July 12

And from there we traveled a Bout 10 miles and camped on the Big Blue and Remained their the 27 and the Twenty Eight and twenty ninth and thirtyeth thirty first day we crossed over the Big Blue and camped.

    — Hiram Miller's journal, May 26–31

The opening in the diary of James Clyman — Huntington Library

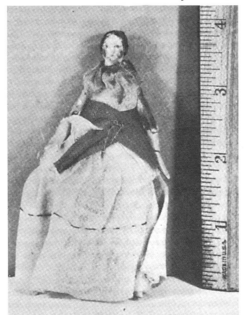

A replica of Patty Reed's doll —
Emigrant Trails Museum

The Pioneer Palace Car

The legendary Pioneer Palace Car is bound to the Donner Party saga by a thread of history and a chain of myth.

The wagon was described by Donner Party survivor Virginia Reed in a magazine article written forty-five years after her rescue. Although hers is the only description of the customized prairie schooner, the legend of the wagon has grown through the years.

It has been seen as a behemoth, and historians have blamed the wagon's size for many of the delays that led to the entrapment of eighty-one members of the Donner wagon train in the Sierra Nevada during the terrible winter of 1846–47.

A typical wagon
The giant Conestoga wagons seen in the movies were seldom used in the migration to the west. Standard square-boxed farm wagons drawn by two or three yoke of oxen were the vehicle of choice for pioneers. These were small, about four feet wide by nine or ten feet long. Although they sometimes carried passengers, usually they were used for freight and the pioneers walked to California or Oregon.

But if the wagon built for James Frazier Reed was so remarkable, asks historian Kristin Johnson, why was his stepdaughter the only one to remark upon it? Johnson, a librarian at Salt Lake Community College in Utah, is editor of *Unfortunate Emigrants: Narratives of the Donner Party* and many articles on the Donner saga. She combed the accounts of diarists in the emigration of 1846 and found no mention of the Palace Car.

Yet the prairie schooner looms large in the lore of the Donners.

Reed described a vehicle remarkably different from the average farm wagons used on the Oregon-California Trail in 1846. Amenities included: a side entrance like a stagecoach, a stove, a "second story," spring seats and a "ladies parlor." Her term "Palace Car" probably came from Pullman railroad palace cars, the standard of luxurious travel in the 1890s.

Writers of history and novels built on Virginia's account. George Stewart, author of *Ordeal By Hunger*, had members of the Donner Party complaining about Reed's heavy, clumsy prairie schooner. Stewart saw it as "a great wagon looming out over all the rest . . . gigantic." That angle has been followed ever since.

Historians and novelists concluded that the wagon's ostentation earned Reed some envy that turned into resentment. Writers have used the wagon to show why Reed's companions turned against him, Johnson said.

The published scenarios: The wagon got bogged down in the mud way back by the Blue River in Kansas, prevented the Donner Party from following an alternate route down Weber Canyon in Utah, delayed them in the Wasatch Mountains, and finally had to be abandoned on the salt flats.

"Or then again, maybe it was hauled out," Johnson said. She found dozens of examples in secondary sources of the wagon being described as huge, but none was borne out by historic evidence.

Not even Virginia Reed says it was very large. Chroniclers of the 1846 trek — like Edwin Bryant, J. Quinn Thornton, and Heinrich Lienhard — fail to mention the remarkable car. Significantly, however, Thornton noted that a wagon had been outfitted for Reed's ailing mother-in-law's comfort. No 1846 account mentions the Reed wagon except in general terms, Johnson said, and no source says it was exceptionally large or accuses Reed of slowing the company down.

Virginia said the wagon was drawn by four pairs of oxen — indicating a heavy vehicle. But her sister, Patty, decades after the trek, remembered only three yoke of oxen. Was it heavier than a standard farm wagon? Was Virginia correct that "nothing like our family wagon ever started across the plains"?

Plagued by such questions, Johnson began her search for the truth about the Palace Car. "You can say a lot of things about James Frazier Reed, but no one has ever accused him of being stupid," Johnson said. She believes that bringing an overly wide or tall wagon on the trail would have been the height and width of stupidity. Such a vehicle couldn't have kept up with the other rigs in the train. Road ruts would have been too narrow; tree branches would have blocked progress. The weight alone would have exhausted the oxen.

But Virginia Reed wasn't just using her imagination. What was the Palace Car?

Johnson might have found her answer in an article in the *Sangamo Journal* from September 5, 1845. The *Journal* was James F. Reed's hometown newspaper in Springfield, Illinois, and the piece was published just as Reed was preparing for his journey West.

The article, by William B. Ide, gives instructions on how to construct a passenger wagon. Ide's design includes a side entrance, extensions over the sides (a "second story"), and he uses the term "ladies' parlor." Virginia used the same term to describe the twin seats and the space in the middle of her family's wagon.

Wagon builder Anderson said the wagon described by Ide would have been unusual but would not necessarily stand out on the trail. Al Mulder, former president of the Utah Crossroads Chapter of the Oregon-California Trails

The entrance was on the side, like that of an old-fashioned stage coach, and one stepped into a small room, as it were, in the center of the wagon. At the right and left were spring seats with comfortable high backs, where one could sit and ride with as much ease as on the seats of a Concord coach. In this little room as placed a tiny sheet–iron stove, whose pipe, running through the top of the wagon, was prevented by a circle of tin from setting fire to the canvas cover. A board about a foot wide extended over the wheels on either side the full length of the wagon, thus forming the foundation for a large and roomy second story in which were placed our beds. Under the spring seats were compartments in which were stored many articles useful for the journey, such as a well filled work basket and a full assortment of medicines, with lint and bandages for dressing wounds. . . .

—Virginia Reed Murphy,
*Across the Plains
In The Donner Party*

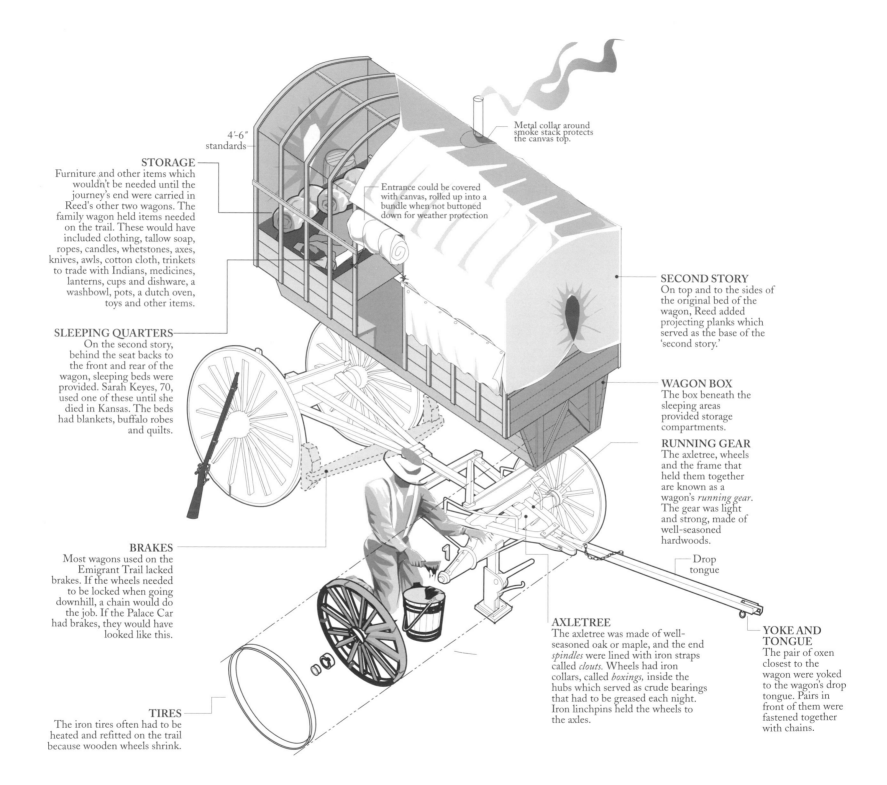

4'-6"
standards

Metal collar around
smoke stack protects
the canvas top.

STORAGE
Furniture and other items which
wouldn't be needed until the
journey's end were carried in
Reed's other two wagons. The
family wagon held items needed
on the trail. These would have
included clothing, tallow soap,
ropes, candles, whetstones, axes,
knives, awls, cotton cloth, trinkets
to trade with Indians, medicines,
lanterns, cups and dishware, a
washbowl, pots, a dutch oven,
toys and other items.

Entrance could be covered
with canvas, rolled up into a
bundle when not buttoned
down for weather protection

SECOND STORY
On top and to the sides of
the original bed of the
wagon, Reed added
projecting planks which
served as the base of the
'second story.'

SLEEPING QUARTERS
On the second story,
behind the seat backs to
the front and rear of the
wagon, sleeping beds were
provided. Sarah Keyes, 70,
used one of these until she
died in Kansas. The beds
had blankets, buffalo robes
and quilts.

WAGON BOX
The box beneath the
sleeping areas
provided storage
compartments.

RUNNING GEAR
The axletree, wheels
and the frame that
held them together
are known as a
wagon's *running gear.*
The gear was light
and strong, made of
well-seasoned
hardwoods.

BRAKES
Most wagons used on the
Emigrant Trail lacked
brakes. If the wheels needed
to be locked when going
downhill, a chain would do
the job. If the Palace Car
had brakes, they would have
looked like this.

Drop
tongue

AXLETREE
The axletree was made of well-
seasoned oak or maple, and the end
spindles were lined with iron straps
called *clouts.* Wheels had iron
collars, called *boxings,* inside the
hubs which served as crude bearings
that had to be greased each night.
Iron linchpins held the wheels to
the axles.

**YOKE AND
TONGUE**
The pair of oxen
closest to the
wagon were yoked
to the wagon's drop
tongue. Pairs in
front of them were
fastened together
with chains.

TIRES
The iron tires often had to be
heated and refitted on the trail
because wooden wheels shrink.

The Pioneer Palace Car

The Reed family wagon, brought west in the Donner Party, has gone into history and myth as the Pioneer Palace Car. Described only by Virginia Reed, the wagon nonetheless has become larger than life and blamed for delays that led to the death of many pioneers in the Sierra Nevada in the winter of 1846-47.

Yet, no detailed drawings of the wagon have ever been published. Here, after several months research, is what the Reed's prairie schooner might have looked like.

Association, used Ide's description to sketch a customized wagon using a standard wagon as a base. Those sketches and further research were used to compile the *Reno Gazette-Journal's* graphic of the Palace Car.

Ide's ideas weren't new. In the 1830s Washington-based scientist Ferdinand R. Hassler built a custom wagon called "The Ark." It had compartments for scientific instruments, a "bedroom" and office space, said Reno-based researcher Patricia McDowell Wing. "Modified wagons were known in England for quite some time," she said. But Ide apparently brought such thinking to the trail.

"We don't know how closely Reed may have followed Ide's instructions," Johnson said. But Reed was warned not to take too big a wagon on the trail.

So the Reed's wagon might not have been the dinosaur described in Donner lore. It might have been remarkable on the inside, but on the outside it might not have been very different from a standard wagon.

Johnson said she still isn't sure about how the wagon looked or how big it was. "I still can't make up my mind about it," she said. "But however big it might have been, it's been blown out of proportion by secondary historians."

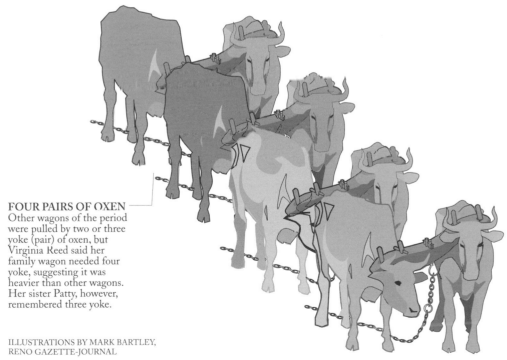

FOUR PAIRS OF OXEN
Other wagons of the period were pulled by two or three yoke (pair) of oxen, but Virginia Reed said her family wagon needed four yoke, suggesting it was heavier than other wagons. Her sister Patty, however, remembered three yoke.

ILLUSTRATIONS BY MARK BARTLEY,
RENO GAZETTE-JOURNAL

By working with historians, archaeologists, wagon makers and scholars, and researching published accounts, we attempted to cut through some of the mystery surrounding the Palace Car to show you how it may have looked and why it may have gone unnoticed by many of the pioneers who took the Overland Trail in 1846.

May 31, 1846

Donners cross the Big Blue; ferrying takes two days

Yesterday, work on a makeshift raft supported on pontoons was complete and the "Blue River Rover" was launched amid the cheers of the men of the Russell Party, including the Donner brothers and James F. Reed.

"She floated down the stream like a cork," writes Edwin Bryant. But it handled like a tree trunk and the polers had difficulty in getting the Rover, top-heavy with three wagons, across the raging torrent.

On the western shore, where the current is strong and the water only three or four feet deep, "one of the canoes was swamped" while unloading the third wagon. With damage repaired, six more wagons were ferried across the hundred-yard-wide stream.

Today they rose at dawn and worked until 9 p.m., when all wagons, contents, stock, and people formed a corral on the western side. A chill wind began in late afternoon as the temperature dropped to forty-eight degrees. A downpour pounded the camp.

"Our men, many of whom had been standing in water the whole day" shiver as though in convulsions, Bryant says. Tempers flare around the campfire. A fistfight follows in which knives are drawn. The two men are separated. Bad feelings remain.

Violent conflicts erupt on the prairie trail "for slight causes and provocations," Bryant observes. "Perpetual vexations and hardships . . . keep the nerves in a state of great irritability."

Tonight they rest at a spring beneath elms, oaks, walnuts, poplars, and cottonwoods about a mile from the river. Grapevines embrace the trees. The men are so exhausted that no guards are posted.

In some tents, resentment simmers.

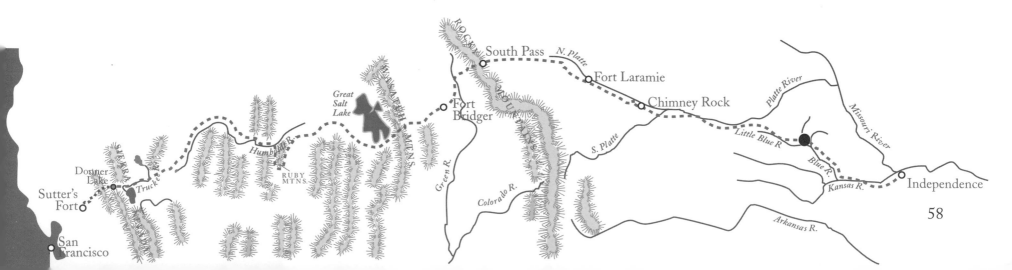

Emigrants ferry their wagons across a river.
— From Virginia Reed Murphy's Across the Plains In The Donner Party

Much difficulty, as had been anticipated, was experienced in working the boat on account of the rapidity of the stream and the great weight of many of the wagons. The current was so strong, that near the shore, where the water was not more than three feet deep, the strength of a man could with difficulty breast it. One of the canoes was swamped on the western side in drawing the third wagon from it. The damage, however, was soon repaired and the work resumed.

— Edwin Bryant, May 30, 1846,
What I Saw in California

Logs, about twenty-five feet in length, were united by cross timbers, forming rafts, which were firmly lashed to stakes driven into the bank. Ropes were attached to both ends, by which the rafts were pulled back and forth across the river. The banks of the stream being steep, our heavily laden wagons had to be let down carefully with ropes, so that the wheels might run into the hollowed logs. This was no easy task when you take into consideration that in these wagons were women and children, who could cross the rapid river in no other way.

— Virginia Reed Murphy,
Across the Plains In The Donner Party

June 2, 1846

Party advances against wind; while tempers flare, wagon train splits

Several unpleasant difficulties and altercations have occurred to-day, from the perverse obstinacy of some of the men, who refuse obedience to the orders of our captain . . . If a man is predisposed to be quarrelsome, obstinate or selfish, from his natural constitution, these repulsive traits are certain to be developed on a journey over the plains.

> — Edwin Bryant, June 1, 1846,
> *What I Saw in California*

Last night's courts were held to try a dutchman for insulting officers and to settle a disagreement between Col. Thornton and his partner in the wagon. Great confusion prevailed and the meeting broke up in a row . . . we met two Shawnee Indians this evening and stoped them in our camp until morn to enable the members of our company to write to the settlements as they live near Westport, Mo. [The Indians] are returning from the Platte river where they have been trapping and Buffalo hunting.

> — George McKinstry, June 3, 1846, journal

The Russell Party moves northwest as unseasonably cold weather continues.

It's cloudy with a cold, raw wind opposing them. The children, presumably including the broods of the Donners and Reeds, suffer greatly. They slept in wet tents and awakened to slog through mud. June feels like November.

Even crowned with gray skies, the wide, treeless plain is stunning. Edwin Bryant reports springs, grass carpeting the rich soil, and flowers in bloom. Bryant imagines villages, farms, and towns will sprout here in the land of the fierce Pawnee.

The men keep rifles and sidearms ready. The flintlocks and percussion-cap guns are loaded and half-cocked.

Yesterday, the company passed graves of children, apparently dug less than a week before. Bryant hopes the young pioneers will remain undisturbed until the final trumpets sound on Judgment Day. He does not know how they died. The party struggled to cross another creek and make camp, again forming a protective corral.

This morning it is cool again. Tonight they will camp with four Shawnee hunters who have been trapping and chasing buffalo in the Platte River country. When they leave, the Indians will take emigrants' letters to the Missouri settlements.

Trouble has come, but not from Indians. Two Oregon-bound pioneers, one owning a wagon and the other the oxen drawing it, have been feuding for days. They are at each other's throats, yet because each has something the other desperately needs, they are more joined than man and wife. A council was called last night to settle the dispute, but violence was the only result.

This morning, after another council, the Oregon-bound emigrants and their twenty wagons proceeded ahead of the group going to California. Tempers are strained, and perhaps splitting the party will help end conflict.

"The trip is a sort of magic mirror," Bryant writes, "and exposes every man's qualities of heart connected with it, vicious or amiable."

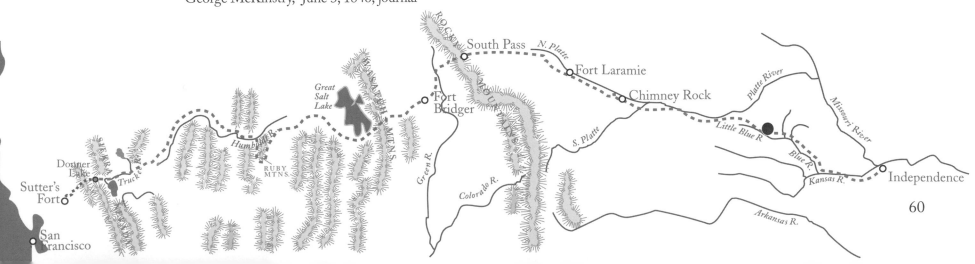

"The Oregon Trail." *The original is in the Butler Institute of American Art, Youngstown, Ohio.* — *Albert Bierstadt*

June 5, 1846

Donners, Reeds go northwest; weather cool; travel easier

Tonight the Russell Party, which includes the Donner and Reed families, is encamped along the Little Blue River.

They've been traveling on a sloping plain and have camped among good wood and water. The temperature remains in the forties and fifties but the wind from the north, although cool, is less bitter.

Yesterday, some of the men chased antelope, but the fleet animals easily outran their horses. Edwin Bryant today puts their distance since the Big Blue crossing at 88 miles — a total of 251 miles from Independence, Missouri.

Tempers are still on edge. Two days ago, two men fought with knives and were split up before anyone was killed.

The same day, Lewis Keseberg's wagon was upset. The accident broke the wagon's tongue and sent Keseberg's wife and baby into a pool of water and the wagon's contents into the mud. He is traveling with two wagons, his wife, and children. He's a 32-year-old German immigrant who speaks three languages and is among the most educated in the Russell Party.

Keseberg will stay with the Donners and Reeds until the end. Many on the trail do not like him and say he is cruel to his wife. Before the pioneers' ordeal ends, he'll be accused of selfishness, robbery, murder, and madness. People will say he bragged of cannibalism and killed people to use their flesh for food.

Today he is just an angry, mud-caked man with a broken wagon. Worse things await him in the West.

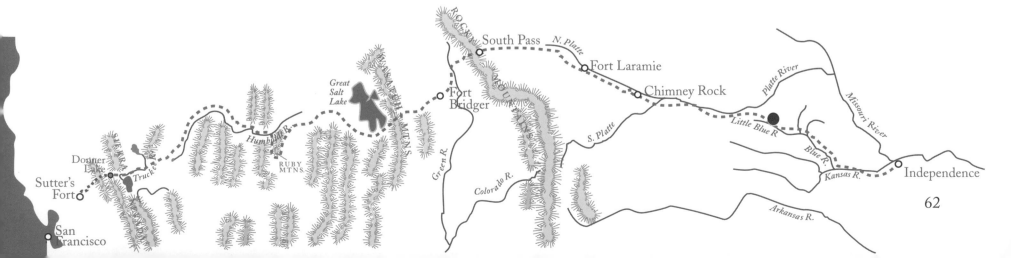

Heinrich Lienhard — West from Fort Bridger, *courtesy of Marta Lienhard Vincent.*

Lewis Keseberg — Bancroft Library

Keseberg was married to a young and pretty German girl, and used to abuse her, and was in the habit of beating her till she was black and blue. This aroused all the manhood in my father and he took Keseberg to task — telling him it must be stopped or measures would be taken to that effect. Keseberg did not dare to strike his wife again, but he hated my father and nursed his wrath.
— Virginia Reed Murphy, *Across the Plains In The Donner Party*

Keseberg's greatest weakness was his unbridled temper, and one day he confessed that it was the source of considerable embarrassment to him. After his anger had subsided, he always realized his mistake and was extremely penitent. He gave every indication of being an honorable person.
— Heinrich Lienhard, who came across the plains in 1846, part of the time with the Russell Party, and later became friends with Lewis Keseberg

My name is Lewis Keseberg. I was born in the city of Berleburg, Province of Westphalia, in the Kingdom of Prussia, on the twenty-second of May, 1814. . I was married June 22, 1842, came to the United States May 22, 1844, and emigrated to California in 1846 with the Donner Party.
— Lewis Keseberg in a statement to author C. F. McGlashan

June 7, 1846

Party stops corralling cattle; buffalo country is near

The emigrants no longer corral their animals at night. They are near the buffalo country along the Platte River and decide that Indians won't take an interest in cattle when bison are available.

There is sickness among the party. Rain, hard travel, and unseasonably cold temperatures continue to take their toll. Edwin Bryant, the journalist, is lagging behind. The axle trees of his wagon have broken, but he wisely brought spares. He gets help from William Eddy, 28, a wagon-maker from Belleville, Illinois, who is traveling near the Reed and Donner families. Eddy is accompanied by his wife, Eleanor, 25, and his children, James, 3, and Margaret, 1.

Eddy sets to work, Bryant says, with augers, saws, and a shaving knife as if he were in his own carriage shop at home. The wagon is fixed as strong, or stronger, as it was at the start of the journey.

Eddy is also entwined in the fate of the Donner Party. His accounts of the ordeal will form the basis of the most sensational stories. Was he a hero or a liar? both and neither? The next ten months will tell. Historians will argue such points forever.

Tonight the Russell Party waits for Bryant. They camp by good water and timber. Tomorrow they will reach the bluffs overlooking the Platte River, the banks of which provide a great road to the West.

Flowers bloom along the trail — foxglove, wild pea, and lupine. Bryant notices them, and Tamsen Donner has catalogued them in her journal.

"We feel no fear of Indians," Tamsen will write. "Our cattle graze quietly around our camp unmolested. . . . We have found the wild tulip, the primrose, the lupine, the ear-drop, the larkspur, and creeping hollyhock, and a beautiful flower resembling the bloom of the beech tree, but in bunches large as a small sugarloaf, and of every variety of shade, to red and green. I botanize and read some, but cook a 'heap' more."

Tonight they rest. The cattle are corralled on a "handsome lawn" of new grass. Skies are clear. A light wind from the west ruffles the leaves of the ash and elm trees above the tents. The moon is bright. Owls hoot. Peace reigns.

William Eddy.
— Emigrant Trails Museum

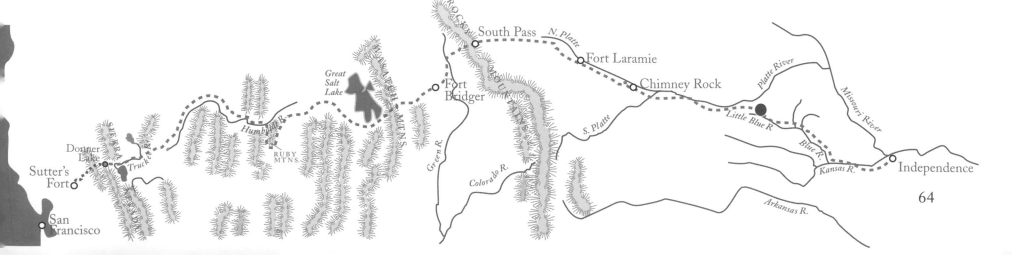

Oxen yokes used by pioneers grace the stables at Sutter's Fort. — Marilyn Newton photo

Our system of travel is thus: The whole encampment is roused by the sound of a trumpet at or before sunrise. Breakfast, which hitherto has consisted of bread, fried bacon, and coffee, is prepared and discussed as soon as possible. Usually by six o'clock in the morning when the morning cattle guard is summoned to drive the oxen into the corral preparatory to "catching up" or yoking. This occupies an hour or more, and at seven or half-past seven o'clock, our march commences. Between 12 o'clock and one o'clock the train is halted in the road for the oxen to breathe. There is a delay of an hour, during which each person partakes of such refreshment as has been provided for him before leaving camp in the morning. The march is then resumed, and continued according to circumstances in reference to grass, water and wood, until 5 or 6 o'clock in the afternoon, when our corral is formed, our tents pitched, and our evening meal provided.

— Edwin Bryant, June 6, 1846,
from What I Saw in California

JUNE 9, 1846

Pioneers reach Platte River, the road into the wilderness

A buffalo skull found on the plains — Emigrant Trails Museum

The emigrant party has reached the Great Platte River Road. This is the wide, shallow river — too thick to drink, too thin to plow — reaching into the heart of the American West. They've hit the main highway.

Yesterday they reached the bluffs above what will be known as Grand Island, Nebraska. A hunter killed the party's first antelope. The animal's meat is "coarser" but more "juicy and tender" than venison, Edwin Bryant remarks in his journal.

A group of Oregon emigrants in advance of the Russell Party reported an attack by Pawnee warriors, but no Indians were seen when Russell's reinforcements arrived.

Today they travel west of Grand Island where the river widens to two miles in breadth. Bryant writes that if he rolls up the legs of his pantaloons, he can cross the river without water reaching his knees.

In the afternoon, the bleached bones of buffalo are encountered every few yards. This must be a former hunting ground. The buffalo skulls have become a sort of post office for pioneers. People in the lead wagon trains write messages on the skulls to those who follow and the skull is placed at the side of the trail next to an upright stick. One such notice reports trouble with the Pawnee and much rain and mud.

Toward evening, a man returning from hunting reports that human bones, as if from a great battle, litter a nearby meadow. An Indian skull is brought to the train, but most consider the artifact bad luck.

Bryant estimates there are three thousand souls on the trail this year going to either Oregon or California. Bryant, as usual, is an excellent reporter. Historian Dale L. Morgan estimates that 2,700 people went west in 1846.

Tonight they camp on the banks of the Platte, a river with few trees. They begin using "buffalo chips" for fuel. They burn bright and hot.

They've traveled forty-three miles in the last two days, passing many small islands in the river. From a distance, the islands with their shrubs take on fantastic shapes, Bryant says, such as "ships, gondolas, elephants and camels."

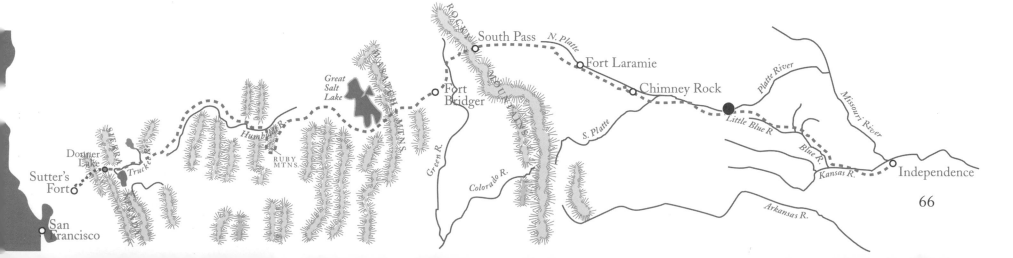

A painting by William Henry Jackson showing emigrants crossing the South Platte — Scotts Bluff National Monument

Monday, June 9 [actually Monday, June 8] — Started at 7 Oclock and struck the Platte River at Grand Island about 5 O'clock and traveling up three miles and camped we made 20 miles over good roads this day. Mr. Grayson killed an antelope to day the first one shot we found the meat better than the deer . . . our camp was formed on the river bank a beautiful place the river studed with small islands the river high and muddy.

— George McKinstry's journal

An ox yoke from the book The Donner Party Rescue Site *by Jack Steed — Roy Vogel*

GRAND ISLAND

On June 8, 1846, pioneer J. Quinn Thornton passed Grand Island, then in the country of the Pawnee tribe. Like explorer John C. Frémont before him, Thornton envisioned an Army fort at the site:

"This island is about 52 miles long . . . It is well-wooded, and has a fertile soil; and the annual rise of the stream does not overflow it. There are many circumstances which unite to make this a suitable point for the establishment of a military post in the lower Nebraska, if it be, indeed an object with our government to keep open a communication with the future Pacific states."

For Thornton and many other educated people of the time, the future "Pacific states" were an expected result of the westward migration.

JUNE 12, 1846

James F. Reed shoots elk; pleasant trail on river

Today James F. Reed shot an elk and shared it with others in the Russell Party.

The emigrants have made about fifty miles up the Platte River during the past two days of hot sunshine and cool breezes. The plain is flat and level. The only trouble comes from mosquitoes, which swarm around the animals and bite the travelers.

Hawks hunt above. Prairie dogs bark at the wooden schooners trundling past their vast cities, which are teeming with activity.

Yesterday the wagon train met up with eastbound trappers. These *voyageurs* were lunching on bread fried in filthy pots of buffalo fat, but the meal smelled delicious to the hungry, dusty pioneers. Some of the emigrants traded with the mountain men for buffalo hides. The going rates: sugar and coffee at $1 per pound; flour at 50 cents a pound, and $3 per buffalo robe.

Many mornings they awake to grass so wet with dew that it seems rain must have fallen during the night. The prairie stays soaked until 11 a.m. or noon. But this morning the grass is dry, and Bryant is told that from here west "we shall rarely witness the phenomenon of copious dew."

Already the wooden wagon wheels have shrunken, leaving the iron tires loose. There is some blacksmithing to do, and because this place has a good supply of wood, the train will lay over for a day to reset tires and do other minor repairs.

Tonight they feast on the "tender, fat and good flavor" of Reed's elk and gaze, contented, at clear skies mad with stars.

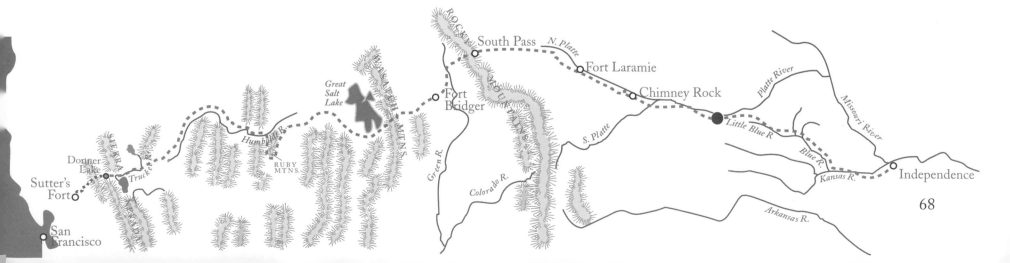

John Breen — Bancroft Library

THE BREEN FAMILY

Although they are unmentioned in any known pioneer journal, the Breen family — nine Irish souls from Keokuk, Iowa — traveled with the Russell Party and might have met the Donners and Reeds before joining them later on the trail.

John Breen will write: "Two of the wagons were loaded with provisions, etc. the third a light wagon carried the small children and some beds; We crossed the Missouri River at Glascow after a very tedious journey on account of high water as the spring of 1846 was exceedingly wet in that part of the country, in due time we arrived at a camp called the Lone Elm across the Missouri line. This place was thought to be the limit of civilization, at this camp were some hunters returning with furs & they gave us some dried buffalo meat and told us that we had no idea of what we would suffer before we reached California. . . ."

The Breens are traveling with their dog Towser, Patrick Breen's favorite. Their neighbor, Patrick Dolan, accompanies the family.

"We were only one family not having joined any other of the parties crossing the plains that year, still we were fairly on our way across the plains, and were afterwards joined by other parties, at one time the company consisted of about 1500 souls under the command of Co. Russel but after getting through what was called the Sioux Country the company began to break up, it being too large on account of wood and water."

June 14, 1846

Birth, pain, death, hope, all in space of two miles

Today Edwin Bryant has seen all of life and death condensed into two hours, within two miles.

Bryant, a Boston native, has built an unwanted reputation as a physician because he has some medical training. Today, while the Russell Party is encamped on the Platte River; the call for a doctor came from the emigrant train twenty miles behind, the Oregon party in which J. Quinn Thornton now travels.

Bryant rides to help. A boy about eight years old, who was run over by a wagon nine days ago, is in agony. Bryant sees that gangrene has set in. The feverish boy is doomed. The newspaperman refuses to amputate, saying it is cruel to subject the child to a painful operation that cannot possibly help him.

Another man heeds the mother's wailing. With a butcher knife, a carpenter's saw, and a shoemaker's awl to take up the arteries, the would-be Samaritan tries to amputate the boy's leg. He botches the job, cutting below the knee and then deciding the incision should have commenced above the joint.

"During these demonstrations, the boy never uttered a groan or complaint," Bryant writes. But he can see from the child's face that he is beyond pain and at the edge of eternity. Mercifully, the boy dies before the leg falls. Bryant walks away as the boy's family weeps and prays.

At 8 p.m., Bryant is invited to a wedding in the train. Prior to the ceremony, Mrs. Thornton receives him as though she were in her parlor at home. The wedding is a quiet affair without dancing or much celebration. After Bryant enjoys his unfrosted cake, he sets off to his guest tent. On the way, he passes the funeral procession of the little boy whose death he witnessed earlier.

As Bryant stands, hat in hand, another pioneer rides up and announces a woman has been safely delivered of a son. There is rejoicing this night.

Tomorrow this place of great events will be bare of all but a grave.

Bryant writes: "Such are the dispensations of Providence — such is the checkered map of human suffering and enjoyment!"

Tonight, gathering clouds flash with lightning, but the sky will not weep.

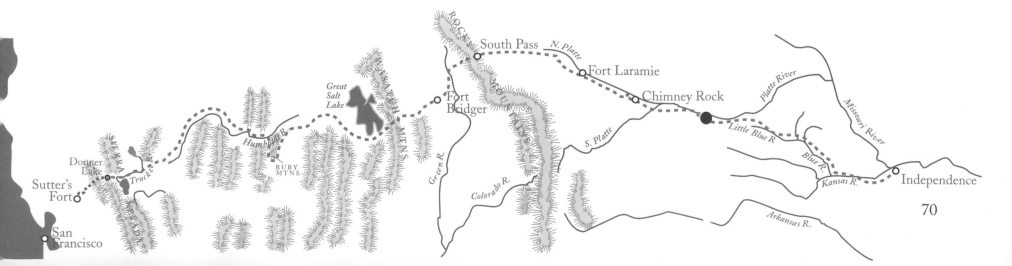

A mural by Frank Schwarz showing Oregon bound emigrants having a meeting within their wagon corral. — Oregon Department of Transportation

One boy fell and two wheels run over one leg and the other foot nearly cutting the leg off breaking the bone.

  —Nicholas Carriger, in a wagon train behind the Russell Party, June 6, 1846

The road at first was rough and led through a timbered country, but after striking the great valley of the Platte, the road was good and the country beautiful. Stretching out before us as far as the eye could see was a valley as green as emerald, dotted here and there with flowers of every imaginable color, and through the valley flowed the grand old Platte, a wide, rapid shallow stream. Our company numbered about 40 wagons . . . . Excercise in the open air under bright skies, and freedom from the peril combined to make this part of our journey an ideal pleasure trip.

  — Virginia Reed

Musical instruments, especially fiddles, were important on the trail. — Marilyn Newton photo

June 16, 1847

Sickness hits Russell Party; buffalo blanket the plains

Emigrants cooking over a buffalo chip fire.
— courtesy of the Huntington Library

Many emigrants in the Russell Party — including Col. William "Owl" Russell — have fallen ill as the wagon train nears the confluence of the north and south branches of the Platte River.

Great herds of buffalo are nearby and hunters supply plenty of meat. For the last two days they've traveled through mild temperatures over level road bordered with primrose, tulips, larkspur, and cacti.

Both Edwin Bryant and Tamsen Donner, a schoolteacher with an interest in botany, write about the wildflowers.

Today a party of men returning to the East from Oregon report counting 470 wagons, including the Russell company, on the trail West. Some emigrants in advance of the Donners and Reeds have had cattle and horses stolen by Indians, the men report. But for the Russell Party, contacts with Indians have been very friendly. It's been a picnic so far.

"How I enjoyed riding my pony, galloping over the plain, gathering wild flowers," Virginia Reed will write forty-five years later. "At night the young folks would gather about the camp fire chatting merrily and often a song would be heard, or some clever dancer would give us a barn-door jig on the hind gate of a wagon."

Virginia's stepfather, James F. Reed, is also having fun. He can afford to hire teamsters to do his work, leaving him free to hunt and gallop over the prairie.

Mrs. Margaret Reed also has a servant, Eliza Williams, to cook, mend clothes, and watch her children. Eliza's half brother, Baylis, is nearly blind in daylight but has excellent night vision. He tends to slumber in a wagon by day and watches the cattle at night.

Having hired hands sets the Reeds apart from the others. Even the Donner brothers, prosperous farmers in their 60s, and their wives, do much of their own work.

In camp tonight, Tamsen Donner takes time out from chores to write a letter to a friend in Springfield, Illinois. She reports the party is about 450 miles

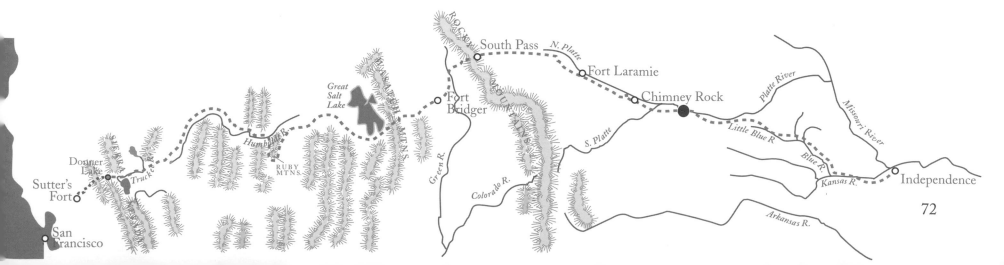

from Independence, Missouri, beginning their sixth week of travel. They are 200 miles from Fort Laramie, an important way station.

She tells her friend it's been an easy trip.

"Indeed, if I do not experience something far worse than I have yet done, I shall say the trouble is all in getting started."

Hunting buffalo on the Great Plains — Piercy's The Route from Liverpool to the Great Salt Lake

We are now on the Platte, 200 miles from Fort Laramee. Our journey, so far, has been pleasant. The roads have been good, and food plentiful. The water for a part of the way has been indifferent — but at no time have our cattle suffered for it. Wood is now very scarce, but "Buffalo chips" are excellent — they kindle quick and retain heat surprisingly. We had this evening Buffalo steaks broiled upon them that had the same flavor they would have had on hickory coals. We have no fear of Indians. Our cattle graze quietly around our encampment unmolested. Two or three men will go hunting twenty miles from camp — and last night two of our men lay out in the wilderness rather than ride their horses after a hard chase.

— Tamsen Donner, in a letter to a friend in Springfield, Illinois, from "Near the Junction of the North and South Platte," June 16, 1846

June 15—Accompanied by two men, I started back on the trail to meet the train to which I was attached . . . As we advance up the Platte, the soil becomes less fertile. The vegetation is thin and short. The river to-day has generally been eight or ten miles from us on our right . . . The heat of the sun during the day's march has been excessively oppressive.

— Edwin Bryant, 1846, *What I Saw in California*

June 19, 1846

Russell, Donner resign leadership; Bryant to advance on mules

A cooking pot found along the Donner Party trail on the salt desert, now on display at the Donner-Reed Museum in Grantsville, Utah — Marilyn Newton photo

William Russell has quit his post as captain of the wagon train, and his sub-captains, including George Donner, have also resigned. The actions took place yesterday. Russell, who has been sick for several days, blames his resignation on his health. His sub-captains quit to make way for another administration.

The party, which crossed the South Platte River two days ago, is now encamped at "Ash Hollow," where a trapper's cabin stands. The shack is used as a post office for emigrants. Notes describe lost cattle and horses. Letters addressed "to every corner of the globe" are stacked up waiting for eastbound travelers to take them to the settlements.

Edwin Bryant, long worried about the slow pace of a large wagon train, has decided to go forward on mules as soon as possible. Bryant's diary doesn't indicate how George Donner felt about losing his leadership position, but in a letter to a friend, Tamsen Donner writes that her husband woke up the party each morning with a yell of " 'Chain up, boys!' with as much authority as though he was 'something in particular.' "

George Donner now has experience as a wagonmaster. He will need these skills. The Donner brothers and James F. Reed can't go ahead by mule train — they have families and tons of goods. But they'd like to get to California faster.

The current way to California is to follow the Oregon route west from South Pass to Fort Hall in what will become Idaho, then to travel south to meet the Humboldt River near what will become Wells, Nevada. It seems wasteful to go northwest when many of the pioneers plan to go to California, which lies southwest of the Rocky Mountain pass.

George Donner, George McKinstry, and others in the party have a guide book, *Emigrants' Guide, to Oregon and California*, by Lansford Warren Hastings, an Ohio lawyer who traveled to California. Hastings' book reports on the main trail to Fort Hall and mentions the possibility of a nearer route, south of the Great Salt Lake.

Future authors will make much of Hastings' early speculation on a new

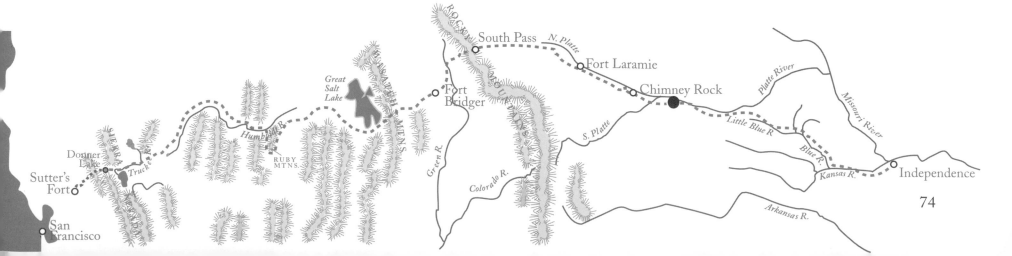

and nearer route, but others, including explorer John C. Frémont, have also reported this possibility. For those in a hurry, such rumors of a shortcut are tempting. James F. Reed, for one, is especially interested in shaving miles and time off the trek to the Promised Land.

The interior of the typical emigrant wagon was often overcrowded.
— Emigrant Trails Museum

Our preparations for the journey, in some respects, might have been bettered. Bread has been the principal article of food in our camp. We laid in 150 lbs. of flour and 75 lbs. of meat for each individual, and I fear bread will be scarce. Meat is abundant. Rice and beans are good articles for the road — cornmeal, too, is acceptable. Lindsey dresses are the most suitable for children. Indeed if I had one it would be comfortable. There is so cool a breeze at all times in the prairie that the sun does not feel so hot as one would suppose.
— Tamsen Donner, in a letter to a friend in Springfield, Illinois, from "Near the Junction of the North and South Platte," June 16, 1846

The most direct route, for the California emigrants, would be to leave the Oregon route, about 200 miles east from Fort Hall; thence bearing west southwest, to the Salt lake; and thence continuing down to the bay of St. Francisco.
— Emigrants' Guide, to Oregon and California

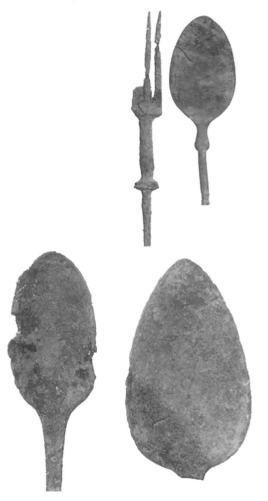

Fork and spoons found at Johnson's Ranch near Sacramento. From the Jack Steed collection — Marilyn Newton photo

June 21, 1846

Bryant leaves for Fort Laramie; Donners, Reeds move into arid land

The wagons are passing over sandy soil as they follow the North Fork of the Platte River.

The country begins to change to semi-desert, with blowing sand, cacti, and rock outcroppings. Yesterday's thunderstorm was a welcome visitor, keeping down the dust.

Yesterday, Edwin Bryant and nine other men left the train to press on to Fort Laramie, where they hope to secure mules and hasten their travel to California.

"Our design was to abandon our oxen and wagons, and all baggage not absolutely necessary to the journey," Bryant wrote two days ago. "This would enable us to proceed with much greater expedition to the point of our destination."

George McKinstry is with Bryant; that means two of the main diarists have left the party. Hiram O. Miller is still keeping his journal, but Miller is the soul of brevity, if not grammar:

"June 21 . . . traveled up the plat a Bowt 12 miles and Camped near the plat," Miller writes. "By a fine spring no timber off to left of the spring is a beautiful Pine ridge first I have Seen on the Rout."

The personal comment on the "Pine ridge" is uncharacteristically verbose for Miller, who usually just jots down distances and notes camps. But Miller is of great importance to Donner Party history: Soon he will turn over his diary to James F. Reed, who will keep it until the day he kills a friend.

A painting of pioneers resting at midday. This painting, "Nooning on the Platte," hangs in the St. Louis Art Museum, gift of J. Lionberger Davis. — Albert Bierstadt

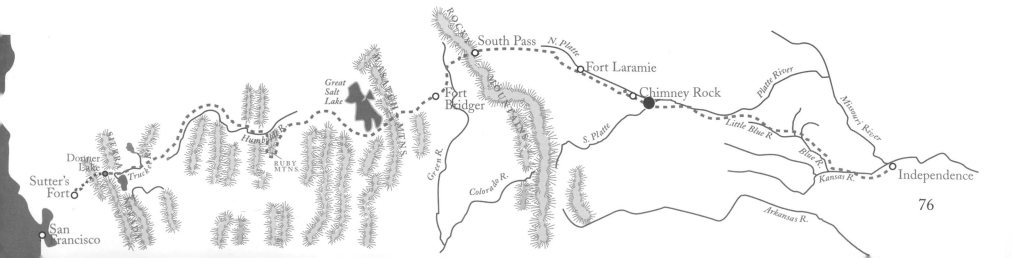

The soil is poor, the grass and other vegetation is thin and short. The bloom of the lupin in many places gives a blue coloring to the undulations of the prairie. No trees or shrubs are visible.

— Edwin Bryant, commenting on the twenty-two-mile dry drive between the north and south forks of the Platte River

Castle Rock near the North Platte River in Nebraska. — Charles Simmons painting from the Susan Skorupa Mullen collection

Lithograph of James F. Reed — Nevada Historical Society

JAMES REED SHOOTS A BUFFALO

In a letter to his brother-in-law James W. Keyes written on June 16, James Frazier Reed describes a buffalo hunt in which he sought to prove his prowess as a hunter and the speed of his purebred horse Glaucus. Reed was considered rather arrogant and haughty by some of his companions on the trail and the letter is a window into Reed's personality. He is driven to be the best in everything he attempts. He complains that as a greenhorn, the other hunters believe him to be "a sucker" and brags he will "remove the stars" from his critics' brows.

"[My purpose is] that they might see that a Sucker had the best horse in the company, and the best and most daring horseman in the caravan," Reed writes. He dashes among the herd with a pistol in hand and selecting a young calf, he fires, bringing his prey tumbling to the ground.

His companions are left in his dust. While waiting for them, Reed counts 597 buffalo. After more forays into the herd, and another calf shot, Reed butchers the animals and carries meat back to camp.

"An hour or two's ride found us safely among our friends, the acknowledged hero of the day, and the most successful buffalo hunter on the route," Reed wrote. "Glaucus was closely examined by many to-day and pronounced the finest nag in the caravan."

JUNE 23, 1846

Emigrants pass Chimney Rock as they cross Nebraska wilderness

Chimney Rock State Historic Site near Bayard, Nebraska, as it appears today — Marilyn Newton photo

Today the Donners and Reeds pass a monument that will become familiar to 500,000 pioneers who take the Trail.

Chimney Rock — dubbed the Eighth Wonder of the World by passersby — stands 450 to 500 feet above the river, pioneers note. Its spire can be seen for miles and is the most famous landmark on the wagon road to California and Oregon.

(The rock still stands 150 years later and is a Nebraska State Historic Site. Because of weathering, the landmark's height is now 350 feet.)

The forty-wagon train is now led by Lilburn Boggs, ex-governor of Missouri. This news would come as a shock to some of his former constituents. On June 6, a Saint Louis newspaper reported Boggs's death in a battle between the Russell Party and Mormon emigrants. The story was a hoax, but made sense to some readers because Boggs kicked the Mormons out of Missouri when he was governor. In the spring of 1846, the Latter-day Saints were moving west.

Boggs — who will see few Mormons this trip, yet live in fear of them — will lead the party to Fort Laramie in place of William "Owl" Russell, former captain of the train. Russell resigned June 19 due to "ill health." At Laramie, the Kentucky Colonel, "drunk as a pigeon," will tell traveler Francis Parkman that his men mutinied and deposed him. But he brags he is smarter than his former followers and is still leader in all but name.

Pride and politics, it seems, travel with the pioneers every step of the way west.

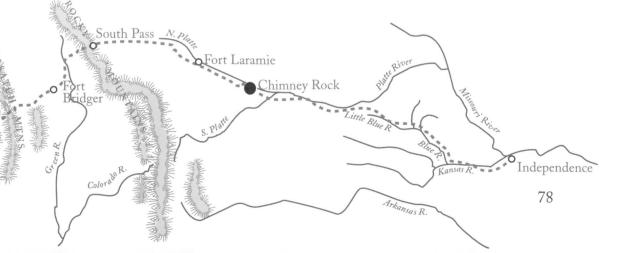

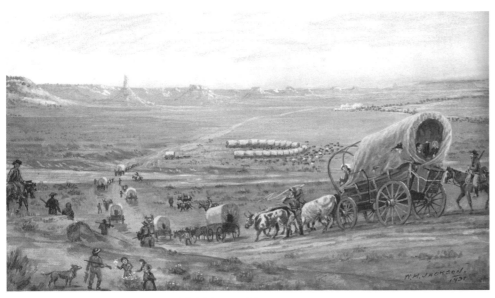

A painting by W. H. Jackson entitled "Approaching Chimney Rock" — Nebraska Historical Society

June 22: and from their wee traveled up the plat a Bout 20 miles and camped near the Court house on the Plat.

23 and from their wee traveled up the plat a Bout 10 miles and came to the Chimney Rock and from their wee traveled a Bout 8 miles and camped near the plat."

— Hiram Miller, journal

The Chimnies about 100 feet composed of soft rock and hard white earth the hills in the vicinity resemble old forts the river studed with small islands cov'd with grass the Scenery beautiful.

— George McKinstry, now traveling two days ahead of the Donners

Chimney Rock, sketched by J. Goldsborough Bruff in 1849.
— Huntington Library

Chimney Rock State Historic Site near Bayard, Nebraska, as it appears today

NEBRASKA NATURAL MONUMENTS

This morning, the atmosphere being clear, we saw distinctly the "Chimney Rock" at a probable distance of 35 or 40 miles. Some 10 or 12 miles to the side of it we also saw an elevated rock, presenting an imposing and symmetrical architectural shape. At this distance its appearance was not unlike that of the capitol at Washington; representing, with great distinctness of outline, a main building, and wings surmounted by domes. This, I believe, has been named by the emigrants the "Courthouse."

— Edwin Bryant's journal, 1846

June 26, 1846

Donners reach Fort Bernard near Fort Laramie, Wyoming

Emigrants crossing the plains by F. O. C. Darley. The original hangs in the Denver Public Library. — Emigrant Trails Museum

In the past few days the emigrants have passed Scotts Bluff and are now camped near Fort Bernard on the Platte River.

Scotts Bluff, which will become a National Monument, is another major landmark on the Oregon-California Trail in Nebraska. The party is camped at Frémont Spring near a ridgeline.

At Fort Bernard trading post, bands of Sioux are encamped and 206 more lodges are expected. The Indians are preparing for war with the Crow tribe. They are friendly to the pioneers, who write of their noble manner and magnificent attire of deerskin, colored bark, bone breastplates, shells received in trade from the Pacific coast, beads, feathers, and scalps taken in battle.

"Sioux indians are the best-dressed Indians there is," 12-year-old Virginia Reed writes.

"The Indians speak friendly to us," George Donner writes in a letter to a friend in Springfield, Illinois. "Two braves breakfasted with us. Their ornaments were tastefully arranged."

The high plain is giving way to arid country, but there is still plenty of grass and water, Donner writes. The weather is warm and the skies clear.

This place, or Fort Laramie on the trail ahead, would be a good spot to stay and rest. The summer is new, however, and winter is on their minds.

There is no time to waste.

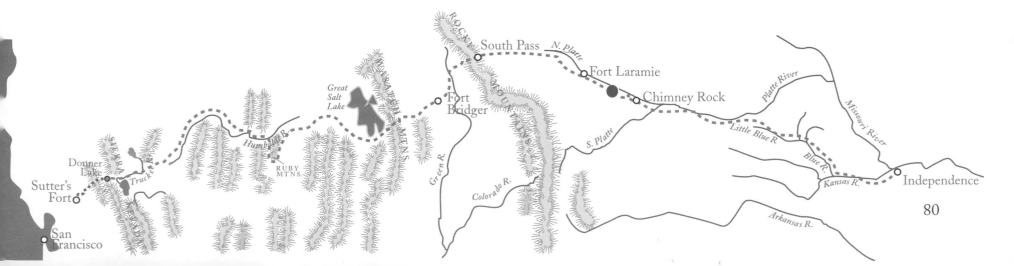

Emigrants make their way through a pass at Scotts Bluff.
— Scotts Bluff National Monument

We arrived here yesterday without meeting any serious accident. Our company are in good health. Our road has been through sandy country, but we have as yet plenty of grass for our cattle and water. Our fires have been kept up, but they burn feebly though we have had enough to cook every meal. Our journey has not been as solitary as we feared, and we have seen several on their return to the States. Several companies are just ahead . . . . I can say nothing except bear testimony to the correctness of those who have gone before us. Please show this letter to our Springfield neighbors and friends and to our children. Our provisions are in good order, and we feel satisfied with our preparations for the trip. Our wagons have shed the rain as yet.
— George Donner, June 27, 1846, in a letter from Fort Bernard to a friend

HASTINGS' NEW ROUTE

While emigrants are moving West, Lansford W. Hastings, the author of a guidebook to California and Oregon, has been going east from California. He is eager to promote a new, more direct way to California.

James Clyman, a mountain man and one of Hastings' companions on the trip, is not impressed with the route blazed by explorer John C. Frémont:

"[May 21] we encamped this being the point whare Mr. Freemant intersected the wagon Trail last fall on his way to california and Mr. Hastings our pilot was anxious to try this rout but my beleef is that it is veery little nearer and not so good a road as that by fort Hall."

But Hastings and Clyman press on. Clyman had been to the Salt Lake as a trapper twenty years earlier and helped push the Hastings party north to Fort Bridger. The fort had been a way station on the California Trail, but with the opening of Caleb Greenwood's cutoff to Fort Hall in 1844, the Bridger trading post had been effectively bypassed.

Hastings' idea of a new route, going right by the trading post, will appeal to Jim Bridger and his partner, Louis Vasquez.

FORT WILLIAM, 1837
From a sketch by A. J. Miller

Ft. Laramie, formerly known as Fort William —
Nevada Historical Society

JUNE 28, 1846

Reed warned about shortcut, but won't heed his friend

*James Clyman
— Utah Historical Society*

Today, Virginia E. B. Reed becomes a teenager.

She was born June 28, 1833, although later accounts will mistakenly list the year as 1834. In following years she will make no public reference to celebrating her thirteenth birthday on the trail, but it would be unlike the Reed family to allow such an occasion to pass unnoticed. There must have been cake and presents at Fort Laramie yesterday or this morning as the Reeds and Donners prepared to leave the post.

Yesterday, James Fraizer Reed did something notable: He got a warning about a shortcut to California through Utah and Nevada, and he ignored it, even though the advice came from a man who should know what he's talking about.

Mountain man James Clyman is Reed's friend. Clyman, Reed and Abraham Lincoln served together in the Black Hawk War in 1832. Clyman, who is heading back east, has just traveled with Lansford W. Hastings, who sought a more direct way to California than the usual path to Fort Hall. Hastings believes he has found it and awaits emigrants farther up the trail.

Clyman — who has traveled in the salt desert — sees Hastings' idea as foolish. The mountain man warned Reed that the new route could be fatal. "I told [Reed] to take the regular wagon track and never leave it — it is bearly possible to get through if you follow it — and may be impossible if you don't," Clyman said.

Reed wasn't afraid: "There is a nigher route, and it is of no use to take a roundabout course."

Clyman admits a shortcut might exist, but it is unproven for wagon travel and involves some of the roughest, most waterless country on the continent. "[I] told him about the great desert and the roughness of the Sierras, and that a straight route might turn out to be impracticable," Clyman said.

Reed is not swayed. Logic dictates that if you want to go southwest, it is a waste of time to go north to Fort Hall. He is not yet subject to Hastings' siren's song; the pilot is not at Fort Laramie. Yet Reed already believes in a route where no wagons have rolled.

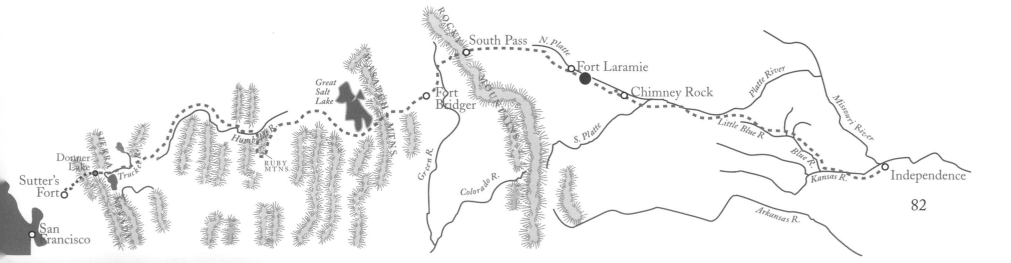

When word of Hastings' endorsement of this route later reaches the pioneers, many of them will be impressed. The lawyer, after all, is author of *The Emigrants' Guide, to California* and an "explorer" to boot. He is a man to be believed. Here at Laramie, absent of Hastings' salesmanship, Reed already favors the vague "new route." He will continue to talk to the Donner brothers about the matter. Not all the pioneers will want to take such a risk: It seems too good to be true.

It's not too late to take the proven path. There is time to reconsider and make a final decision.

John Sutter. The original drawing is from History of the Donner Party, a Tragedy of the Sierra by C. F. McGlashan. — Emigrant Trail Museum

Captain [Lansford] Hastings is leaving this place [Sutter's Fort] in a few days, to cross the mountains again, with the party which is going from here to the U. States, if he is going to the U.S. or not, or go, and meet the Emigrants, nobody knows for certain, perhaps nobody will see him here again, as his life will be in danger about his book, making out California a paridise, even some of the Emigrants in the Valley, threatened his life, and by his impudent writing, he made himself the Country people to his enemy.
— John Augustus Sutter, in a letter written April 3, 1846

A sketch of Fort Laramie in 1842
— From sketch accompanying John Frémont's report

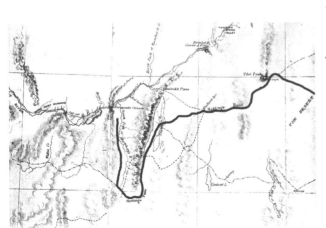

Hastings' cutoff, referred to as Hastings' Road, is enhanced as a solid line. Notice how the route goes to the south end of what was once called the Humboldt Mountains, turning west for a ways then heading north again. The dotted lines are other routes. — UNR Special Collections

J. Quinn Thornton, who had a bad experience on another "shortcut" — the Applegate Cutoff in Nevada from the Humboldt River northwest through the Black Rock Desert — also had a low opinion of Hastings:

"Lansford W. Hastings, who, if an opinion may be formed of him from the many untruths contained in his 'Emigrants' Guide to Oregon and California,' is the Baron Munchausen of travelers in these countries," he writes in *Oregon and California in 1848*.

Lansford W. Hastings

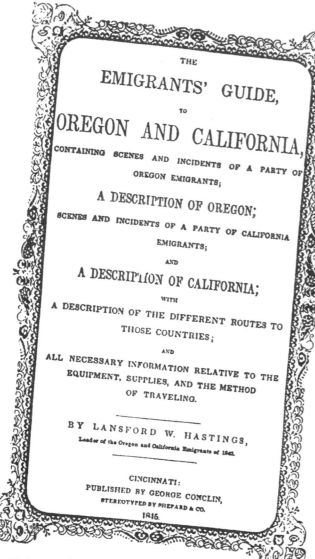

THE

EMIGRANTS' GUIDE,

TO

OREGON AND CALIFORNIA,

CONTAINING SCENES AND INCIDENTS OF A PARTY OF
OREGON EMIGRANTS;

A DESCRIPTION OF OREGON;

SCENES AND INCIDENTS OF A PARTY OF CALIFORNIA
EMIGRANTS;

AND

A DESCRIPTION OF CALIFORNIA;

WITH

A DESCRIPTION OF THE DIFFERENT ROUTES TO
THOSE COUNTRIES;

AND

ALL NECESSARY INFORMATION RELATIVE TO THE
EQUIPMENT, SUPPLIES, AND THE METHOD
OF TRAVELING.

BY LANSFORD W. HASTINGS,
Leader of the Oregon and California Emigrants of 1842.

CINCINNATI:
PUBLISHED BY GEORGE CONCLIN,
STEREOTYPED BY SHEPARD & CO.
1845.

*Title page of
Lansford W. Hastings' book, The Emigrants'
Guide to Oregon and California.*

Some historians will say Lansford Warren Hastings wanted to rule an empire but had two problems: He needed subjects and land to put them on.

Hastings — who will be painted as someone whose lies about a shortcut for California-bound wagons doomed the Donner Party — is moving eastward while the Donners and hundreds of other families and individuals are emigrating west. He will wait for the pioneers like "a spider in a web," historian George Stewart will write.

Stewart will say that Hastings, like Moses, wanted to lead his people through the desert and into the promised land. Like Joshua, he would take the land away from its "indolent" current rulers (the Mexicans) and occupy it with his own followers; like King David, he would take his empire into a golden age.

That kind of talk will annoy Thomas Franklin Andrews, whose doctoral dissertation on Hastings in 1971 will state: "A Hastings stereotype has been handed down to students of Western history that depicts the man variously as . . . 'a Frémont in miniature,' the 'Baron Munchausen of travelers' and the 'Sam Houston of California.' After researching Hastings' life, Andrews will see him as a misunderstood visionary, a dreamer who was a better leader than most will give him credit for and a victim of the Donner debacle, which allowed historians to slander him without fear of contradiction.

Good or evil, Hastings didn't think small.

In 1846, Hastings is about twenty-seven years old. A confident, dashing, handsome figure in buckskins and plucked beaver fur, he is "an ideal representative of the mountaineer," says emigrant John McBride.

He could be charming, but some of his fellows don't like him. They see him as selfish, arrogant, and a troublemaker. He was the first American lawyer in California and during his four months there he gathered material for his *Emigrants' Guide, to Oregon and California.* The book isn't a guide at all, merely thirteen chapters about Hastings' own experiences, along with propaganda about the wonders of the Mexican province and two chapters with bare-bones advice on getting there. To Hastings, the trip west apparently is a minor detail.

Many 1846 emigrants, including the Donners and Reeds, are familiar with Hastings' book. His notion that there is a faster way to California via a shortcut is mentioned in a single sentence — hardly enough to blame Hastings for James F. Reed's enthusiasm. Favorable reports from John C. Frémont, whose third expedition explored the route in the fall of 1845, reached the Missouri frontier about the time the emigrants set out.

As the Donners move west, Hastings positions himself to divert the stream of migration toward the route no wagons have ever taken. He proposes to guide families over trackless country, through deserts without water and over mountains with unscouted passes.

Historian Will Bagley of Salt Lake City will research Hastings' life and also set out to discover if the man was really a scoundrel or a misunderstood visionary. Unlike Andrews, Bagley will conclude that Hastings' bad press is justified. He will see Hastings as a con man, a liar, and a self-promoting inventor of wild schemes.

Hastings, Bagley will write, "bears out what the ancient Greeks believed: Character is fate."

Lansford Warren Hastings.
— Utah Historical Society

History likes a scapegoat and I believe Lansford Hastings has become that scapegoat for the Donner Party. His vision was much broader than the one his contemporaries shared. He saw limitless possibilities in the West . . . .[In California] he intended not to prosper, but to serve and be of help.

I don't think he had any malice; he just bit off more than he could chew. He clearly saw the mountain peak in the distance but neglected looking at the miles of obstacles between him and the peak. He sought to bring civilization to California. . . .

History and truth are somewhere in the middle, somewhere between a man who did everything he could for people and a villain who schemed to use people for his own ends.

— William Chrystal, minister of the First Congregational Church of Reno, who performs in character as Hastings

---

HASTINGS' OTHER CAREER

Pioneer John Bidwell told the story of how Lansford Hastings, desperate to finance his book, became a temperance lecturer in Ohio. While railing against the horrors of strong drink, and presumably collecting donations from the faithful, he met a "Methodist minister" named McDonald who was collecting funds for his missionary efforts.

On reaching California in 1846, Hastings stepped up to the bar in Jean Voiget's Saloon in San Francisco and ordered a brandy. The bartender was McDonald, but the lawyer didn't recognize him.

McDonald leaned over the bar and extended his hand.

"My good temperance friend, how are you?" he asked.

Hastings, surprised, recognized his former brother-in-prayer and said, "My dear brother, how do you do?"

June 30, 1846

Pioneers camp near Laramie Peak as they make slow progress

The Donners are encamped near a spring within sight of Laramie Peak.

Their party has traveled just thirty-two miles since they left Fort Laramie three days ago. As they near the backbone of the continent, the country turns rough and rocky. Sagebrush is the dominant shrub.

The weather has been clear for a week, with temperatures in the sixties — pleasant for travel. Sioux are everywhere, talking big about their coming war with the Crow. Nothing will come of it, historians will write.

Edwin Bryant has traded for pack mules and he and William Russell visit their former wagon train, containing the Donner and Reed families. George McKinstry also stops by and tells his former companions of the two thousand Sioux at Laramie, resplendent in their finest white buffalo skins decorated with beads and feathers. They ride like an army.

It's a relief that they tolerate the emigrants.

Tamsen Donner has made many friends on the road and has written about the fine folks in the company, and "some too, who are not so good."

Bryant and the others are glad they will advance on muleback. Compared to mules, wagon trains crawl. The families, disagreements, and mechanical and organizational problems of a wagon caravan will be left in their dust.

Meanwhile, the wagons press on.

The pioneers will soon celebrate the nation's seventieth birthday in the mountains to the west.

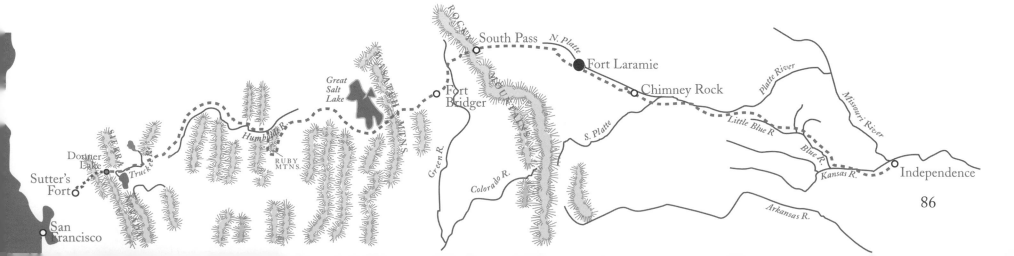

Ft. Laramie and Laramie Peak along with the North Fork of the Platte River — Nevada Historical Society

A reenactment wagon train moves through sagebrush. — David B. Parker

[June] 28: and from [Fort Laramie] we traveled up the Larome fork a Bout 2 miles and camped

29: and from their we traveled a Bout 16 miles and camped on willow creek timber.

30: and from their we traveled a Bout 14 miles and camped near a Spring on the Road and a Bout Eight miles from Lairomes peak.

[July] 1: and from their we traveled a Bout 15 miles and camped near a Creek their is a fine spring and timber plenty We are now in the Red mouns.

2: and from their we traveled a Bout 15 miles and camped on a Creek their is plenty of water and timber.

3: We made this day 18 miles and camped on Beaver Creek here is a natural Bridge 1 1/2 miles above camp.

4: we Celebrated the glorious 4th in camp and remained here to the morning of the 6th.

— Hiram Miller's diary

July 4, 1846

Donners, Reeds camp near Platte, celebrate nation's 70th birthday

Replica of a 28 star flag used during 1846 and 1847

Today the Donners and Reeds are encamped on La Prele Creek in Wyoming, where they celebrate Independence Day.

Old comrades who left the wagon train — J. Quinn Thornton, Edwin Bryant, William Russell, and others — are all reunited. Caravans are camped east and west of the Donners' train.

At dawn today, a guard in one company fires his rifle to welcome the holiday. A flag run up a staff softly flutters. The day is warm; the mood merry.

Pistols are fired and the emigrants shout "harrah" and parade around the corral. In a grove, the Declaration of Independence is read and Col. Russell stands on a log and makes a speech.

The celebrants feast on buffalo meat, bread, beans, and greens. Children sip lemonade made from dried lemon rinds and plenty of sugar. Adults raise cups of wine and liquor, with each toast punctuated by musketry and cheers. The revelers sing songs, both patriotic and sentimental. James F. Reed breaks out brandy and, facing east, makes a prearranged salute to friends in Illinois.

"Some of my father's friends in Springfield had given him a bottle of good old brandy," Virginia Reed will remember, "which he had agreed to drink at a certain hour of this day looking to the east, while his friends in Illinois were to drink a toast to his success from a companion bottle with their faces turned west, the difference in time being carefully estimated."

Bryant writes today in his journal, "I thought, on the whole, that the 'glorious fourth' was celebrated here in this remote desert with more spirit and zest, than it usually is in the crowded cities of the States. The pageantry, of course, was not so imposing."

In the afternoon, Bryant and Russell advance on mules with teamster Hiram Miller. Miller gives his diary to Reed.

Boggs's train (although it might no longer be Boggs's train; in his last journal entry of Tuesday, June 30, George McKinstry writes that Boggs has resigned his office) remains encamped for rest and repairs. The people remaining say goodbye to those they have traveled with earlier on the trail and believe they will soon see again in California.

For many, it is a final farewell.

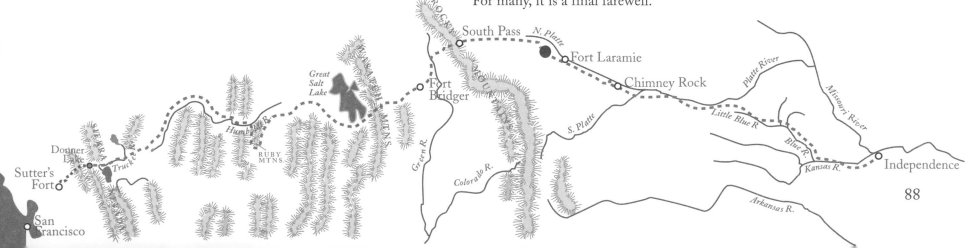

Titled "The Halt," this photo by Ben Wittick shows a family resting near a spring. Note: this is a later wagon train. — Museum of New Mexico

Mr. Reed had preserved some wines and liquors especially for this occasion — an anniversary, by the way, which in this remote and desert region crowded our memories with reminiscences of the past, pleasurable from the associations they recalled, and painful from the position we now occupied.
— Edwin Bryant, July 4, 1846

Monday, June 29: left [Fort Laramie] about 3 O'clock p.m. on pack mules with Messrs Ames, Wells & McCleary traveled 20 miles & camped at a large spring —
Tuesday June 30th Started before breakfast travelled 12 miles and camped on a creek for the day to repair packs & passed Dunbars company two miles from the camp and also our old company under way at the crossing of the creek Capt Boggs just resigned.
— George McKinstry, final diary entries of his 1846 trek west

July 6, 1846

After two-day rest, Donners cross high country toward pass

Yesterday the pioneers remained in camp near a creek by a natural bridge across the North Platte River.

Children ran and played games. Adults visited friends and made repairs. Some emigrants nursed hangovers from the July 4 celebration.

Cows, horses, and oxen grazed on plentiful grass. Dogs slept in the shadows of wagons. Women sewed. Men fixed harnesses and rearranged freight.

Today, James F. Reed, now the keeper of Hiram Miller's diary, writes that they are "much rested." They travel sixteen miles through rocky country along the river, passing hillsides shaggy with sage and wild with clumps of bunch grass. Cactus flowers bloom crimson and yellow.

The Sioux are on the move. Mounted warriors pass the caravan all day long. This makes the emigrants nervous and rifles are kept at the ready. If there were hostilities, however, the people in the wagon train would not stand a chance. "They could have massacred our whole party without much loss to them selves," Virginia Reed will write.

James F. Reed will make Virginia ride in the family wagon, because the Indians have taken too great an interest in her horse, Billy. Virginia hates riding in the wagon, but she takes harmless revenge on the curious Sioux by scaring them with a telescope.

Buffalo gnats and mosquitoes will plague them as they ride in wagons or walk beside the oxen. Box elders, willows, and alders will dot their course. They climb through green country. Insects hum. Birds dart and sing through the morning.

Tonight, they camp by a creek about a quarter mile from the Platte. There is a deposit of coal nearby, but it doesn't burn well. Wolves howl under a bright three-quarter moon. Saturn and Venus shine close together and low in the southeastern sky.

In the morning, frost clings to the buffalo robes they use for bedding. They continue their climb.

They aim to cross the Continental Divide at South Pass.

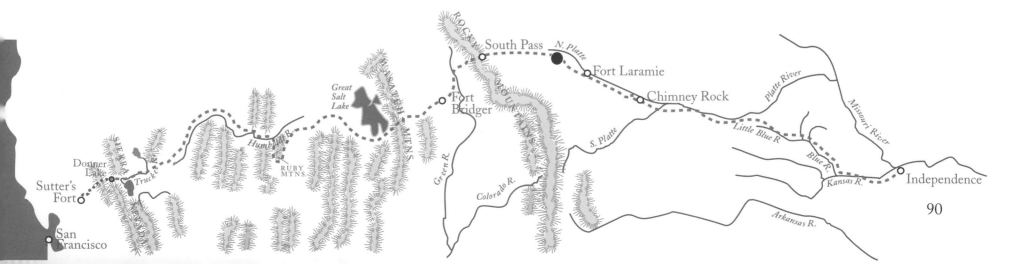

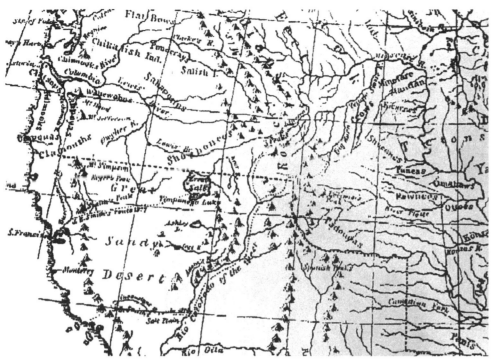

This map of the western United States predates the 1846 emigration.
— Fort Bridger Historic Site

[The Sioux warriors] curiosity was annoying, however and our wagon with its conspicous stove-pipe and looking glass attracted their attention. They were continuosly swarming about (the side door) trying to get a look at themselves in a mirror . . . in order to see how far back the line of warriors extended, I picked up a large field-glass which hung on a rack, and as I pulled it out with a click, the warriors jumped back, wheeled their ponies and scattered. This pleased me greatly, and I told my mother I could fight the whole Sioux tribe with a spyglass, and as revenge for forcing me to ride in the wagon, whenever they came near trying to get a peep at their war paint and feathers, I would raise the glass and laugh to see them dart away in terror.
— Virginia Reed, July 6, 1846, *Across the Plains In The Donner Party*

July 10, 1846

Party leaves North Platte River; hunters shoot eight buffalo in two days

The pioneers feast on buffalo again tonight; hunters have killed eight of the beasts in forty-eight hours.

Two days ago the wagons crossed the North Platte River and left the familiar stream the next day. Tonight they camp at Willow Springs, where there is little grass but good water. If they make twenty miles tomorrow they'll reach Independence Rock, a well-known landmark on the route to California and Oregon.

On the trail ahead, Wales B. Bonney, an east-bound traveler from Oregon, is visiting emigrants and sharing an open letter from Lansford W. Hastings, author of *The Emigrants' Guide, to Oregon and California*. The letter warns pilgrims they may expect trouble from the California (Mexican) government and advises pioneers of a new shortcut to the promised land by way of Fort Bridger, then southwest past the Great Salt Lake. Hastings suggests travelers go to Fort Bridger and he will guide them along the new route he blazed.

For some travelers, Hastings' letter is seen as the work of a man with his own ax to grind. Many ignore the epistle and take the proven road. Edwin Bryant, ahead on the trail, reads the letter today and likes the idea of a quicker way to California. But Bryant is traveling on mules, without wagons or families.

For others who will read the letter, this piece of paper will be a death warrant.

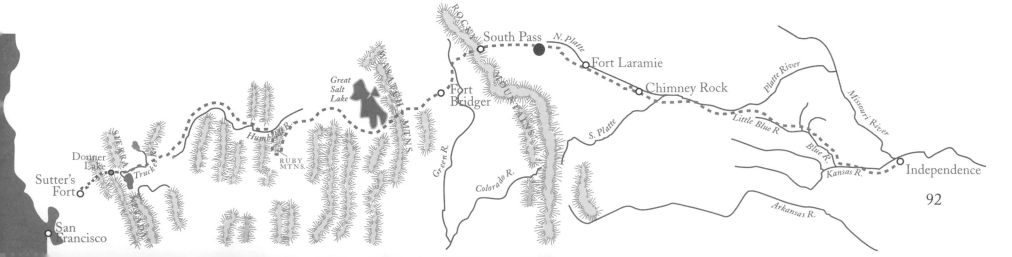

Emigrants crossing the Platte River. The Donner Party was three days from Independence Rock at this point on the trail. — *Emigrant Trails Museum*

CHARLES PUTNAM'S OPINION OF HASTINGS' CUTOFF

Pioneer Charles F. Putnam, a bachelor with his own wagon, travels on the road ahead of the Donners.

In a letter to his father dated July 11, he remarks that there are 510 wagons bound for Oregon and California on the trail and that most of them contain families.

Putnam received Hastings' letter before the Donners and Reeds would read it, but he didn't believe the lawyer's claims that the shortcut would be "a new route to California which would make a difference of 300 miles nearer."

Putnam correctly believes Hastings wants allies in California for a revolution against the Mexican government.

"If it is his design to aid in Revolutionizing the country and immortalizing himself, he will find himself vastly mistaken," Putnam writes.

July 12, 1846

Donners reach Independence Rock, 820 wagon miles from Independence, Missouri

The emigrants spend today resting at the great guest register of the Overland Trail — Independence Rock. Names and dates, carved in rock or painted with axle grease, cover the whale-shaped monolith. Tonight they'll sleep near its base.

Today they let the cattle graze, take care of chores, and patch worn equipment. It's a chance to write letters and act like tourists.

Tamsen Donner has time to write in her journal, examine wildflowers or prepare meals from the ample stores in her family's wagons. Virginia Reed begins a letter to her cousin in Springfield, Illinois. "We are all doing well and are in hye sperits," she writes, innocent of spelling.

Tomorrow, as his hired men chain up the oxen, James Fraizer Reed will study the writings on the stone. He'll read the names of mountain men and pioneers who came through this place. It's an easy climb to the top for a look at the valley below, with the Sweetwater River snaking through the plain. Reed sees alkali flats. That means bad water.

But it's only a hundred miles to South Pass across the Rockies — which many pioneers considered the halfway point to Sutter's Fort. In just over two months, they will have put half a continent behind them and crossed its backbone.

There have been hardships and illnesses and the death of an old woman, but hurts and sadness are forgotten once the river is forded, the deep sand is left behind, or the bad road evens out.

Soon they will leave the buffalo country of the Sioux and enter desert lands. But as they face the Wind River Range to the west, there is every reason for optimism.

And there's still talk of a shortcut that could save them hundreds of miles. Some members of the party have the book by Lansford W. Hastings which briefly mentions an easier way to California — a "cutoff" which will reduce the mileage and the trouble of the regular route.

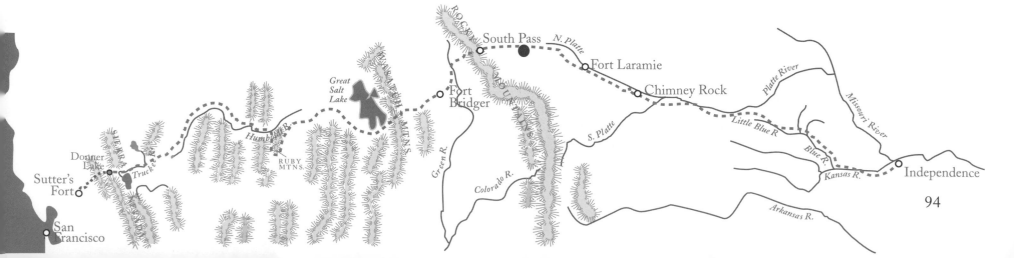

94

Rain clouds hover off Independence Rock in south central Wyoming. Those who would become the Donner Party wouldn't reach here until July 12. The monolith is known as a directory of some of those who passed this way. Emigrants would camp and many would carve their names and the dates they were there. — Marilyn Newton photo

[Eliza Williams, the Reed's servant] is a first-class cook . . . nice pickled pork and beans baked in a dutch oven, fresh bread and butter, cold ham, pickels & cheese & dried fruit of some kind with tea coffee and milk to drink.

— Virginia Reed, *Across the Plains In The Donner Party*

We have come [through] several tribes of indians the Caw [Kansas] Indians the soux the shawnees, at the caw village paw counted [250] Indians We diden see no Indians from the time we lefe the caw till we come to Fort Laramy the [Sioux] Indians are going to war with the crows we have to pass throw ther Fiting grond, the Soux Indians are the pretest drest Indians thare is, paw goes buffalo hunting most every day paw shot an elk some of our companions saw a grisly bear We hve thermometer 102 [degrees] — average for the last six days.

— Virginia Reed, in a letter to her cousin Mary C. Keyes from Independence Rock, July 12, 1846

Devil's Gate can be seen from Independence Rock and was one of the trail guides used by the emigrants who made their way around the left side of the granite ridge. The Sweetwater River has, over time, cut a chasm 330 feet deep. At the top it is 400 feet wide but at the base it is only 30 feet wide. — Marilyn Newton photo

JULY 14, 1846

Hastings' letter arrives, claims a new route will save time, trouble

Prairie dogs have found a home along the trail near between Twin Mounds and South Pass.
— Marilyn Newton photo

The letter is addressed: "At the Headwaters of the Sweetwater: To all California Emigrants Now On the Road."

The document is carried by Wales B. Bonney, who rides a horse and leads a mule. Unbelievably, Bonney is traveling alone from Oregon to the East.

Lansford Warren Hastings, the lawyer and adventurer, gave Bonney the epistle and asked him to share it with emigrants on the trail. The letter warns travelers to concentrate their numbers to protect themselves against attack by the Mexicans. It also tells of a new, shorter route blazed by Hastings that will cut hundreds of miles off the trip to Sutter's Fort.

The kicker: Hastings, the author of *Emigrants' Guide, To Oregon and California*, will wait for the emigrant trains at Fort Bridger and guide them across mountains and deserts in Utah and Nevada.

It seems a perfect plan to James Frazier Reed. The Donner brothers — George, who has a copy of Hastings' book, and Jacob — also are impressed. Tamsen Donner is worried, however. The deal sounds too good to be true. Should they gamble their lives on Hastings' schemes?

The road will fork: West to Greenwood's Cutoff to Fort Hall (named for mountain man Caleb Greenwood) and the proven route, or southwest to Fort Bridger and the new shortcut. A decision must be made within a week.

Today Bonney, with letters written by the emigrants at Independence Rock safe in his pack, is heading eastward to meet more pioneers and tell them of Hastings' scheme.

The Donners and Reeds are again moving west.

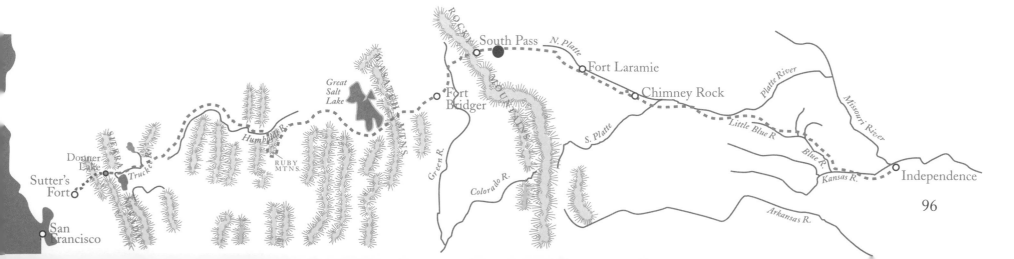

Two sets of tracks lead away from Twin Mounds. This is the view the emigrants would have if they looked back. — Marilyn Newton photo

C.T. Stanton. The original is from the History of the Donner Party, a Tragedy of the Sierra *by C.F. McGlashan. — Emigrant Trail Museum*

The whole region of country from Fort Laramie to this place is almost entirely barren. There is no grass except in the valleys, which in some few places only, is found luxuriant. One seems at a loss how to account how the buffalo can live on hills over which they range — only a few blades of grass can be seen, and that of a low, stunted growth. Over the whole region the wild sage or artemisia grows in abundance. Seen at a distance, it looks like the greenest, richest meadow, but, when you come to it, you are disappointed, as you see nothing but the wild sage in patches, and a barren soil in between.

The sage is not like the sage of the garden. It has more the smell of lavender, and an Englishman [John Denton?] of "our mess" sticks to it that it is nothing else. We are now in a country where there is little wood, the dry roots of [sagebrush] being only about the size of an ox whip, constitutes our only fuel.

— Charles T. Stanton, in a letter to his brother Sidney Stanton from "the banks of the Sweet Water," July 12, 1846

July 17, 1846

Donners crossing Great Divide; cattle sick from poisoned water

Tomorrow the Donners, Reeds, and their companions will have lunch on the roof of the continent — the summit of South Pass.

They have come about 920 miles from Independence, Missouri. They believe they are at the halfway point to their new home in California.

In the past few days the party has made its way up the Sweetwater River to the passage through the Rockies. Although the pass isn't steep, deep sand and other barriers have slowed their progress. "Bad, bad road," James Frazier Reed writes in his diary for July 14.

Water, standing in pools, is poisoned with alkali, and cattle have been sick. By July 19, Reed will report that the Donner brothers have lost two oxen and that he has lost a steer, "Old George." Referring to animals by name is characteristic for Reed, a trait relatives will say indicates his affection for them.

Tomorrow, as the Donners and the other emigrants — who split from Lilburn Boggs's party on July 12 — spend noon on the pass, Edwin Bryant and his mule-back party are at Fort Bridger.

Bryant decides to follow the advice of mountain man Jim Bridger and his partner, Louis Vasquez, and go over Lansford Hastings' new route to California through what will become Utah and Nevada. Bryant's party is on mules and the men have no wagons or families. Bryant writes letters to the travelers behind him — including his friend Reed — warning them not to take the shortcut.

"We could afford to hazard experiments, and make explorations. They could not," Bryant writes in his journal. In his letter, he advises Reed and the others to take the old trail to Fort Hall. Bryant gives the letters to Vasquez, who assures him he will pass them on to Reed and others.

Vasquez and Bridger have a stake in popularizing the new trail. When the Greenwood (later called Sublette's) Cutoff to Fort Hall was blazed, the route bypassed Fort Bridger. The life of their trading post depends on Hastings' route being used.

Reed and his companions will be at Fort Bridger in a week. They will ask the partners for advice.

Vasquez has their fate in his pocket.

Louis Vasquez
— Fort Bridger Historic Site

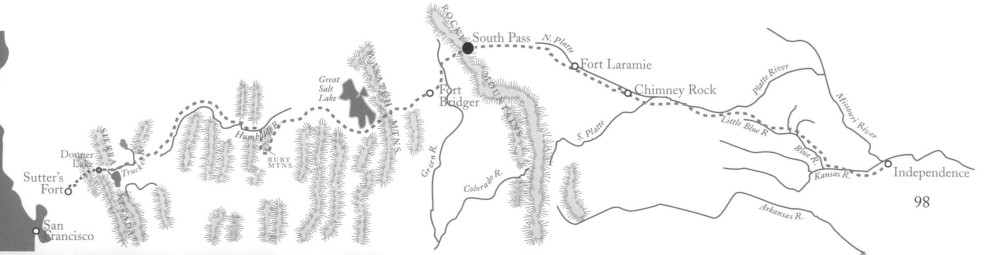

The well worn wagon road up to South Pass where the emigrants stopped and had lunch. On the left is Pacific Butte. — *Marilyn Newton photo*

We determined, this morning, to take the new route, via the south end of the great Salt Lake . . . I wrote several letters to my friends . . . advising them NOT to take this route, but to keep to the old trail via Fort Hall. Our situation was different from theirs.
— Edwin Bryant, July 18, 1846

A week's hard travel from the date of my last letter [July 12] on the Sweet Water, has brought us to this most interesting point in our route. Yesterday at noon we arrived at the "culminating point" or dividing ridge between the Atlantic and Pacific. This evening we are encamped on the Little Sandy, one of the forks of the Green river, which is a tributary of the great Colorado, which flows into the Gulf of California. Thus the great day-dream of my youth and of my riper years is accomplished. I have seen the Rocky Mountains — I have crossed the Rubicon, and am now on the waters that flow into the Pacific! It seems as if I had left the old world behind, and that a new one is dawning upon me. In every step thus far there has been something new, something to attract. — Should the remainder of my journey be as interesting, I shall be abundantly repaid for the toils and hardships of this arduous trip.
— Charles T. Stanton in a letter written at South Pass to his brother Sidney Stanton, July 19, 1846

A painting by William Henry Jackson shows wagons traveling abreast on the approach to South Pass. — *Utah State Historical Society*

July 19, 1846

The Donner Party is born; emigrants take left turn to "shortcut"

Hastings' cutoff. Notice how the route goes to the south end of what was once called the Humboldt Mountains, turning west for a ways then heading north again. The dotted lines are other routes. — UNR Special Collections

The fatal decision is made. Tamsen Donner is sick with worry.

The Donners, Reeds and others, joined by the Breen family, have reached a fork in the road. The right lane leads to Fort Hall and the proven trail; the left road leads to Fort Bridger and the start of the Hastings' Cutoff — a "shortcut" to California.

George Donner, 62, the solid farmer, will be their leader, even though James F. Reed, 45, the aristocratic businessman, is more suited to the task. People apparently resent Reed for his haughty manner and his affluence which allows him to hire others to do his labor. Donner, although rich, does not flaunt his wealth and is seen as "Uncle George."

Tomorrow the party will bear left and leave other families who will take the Fort Hall road. The new route is a gamble, but so was the overland journey. They cast the dice in Independence when they entered the wilderness. Why not roll again?

It doesn't seem like much of a risk. Lansford W. Hastings, the author who says he opened the new road, will lead them through deserts and mountains. He'll cut three hundred miles off their trip.

Tamsen Donner, 45, a teacher who wants a better life for her children and who plans to start a school in California, isn't convinced, however. She doesn't know Hastings and fears the man is a "selfish adventurer." There is a proven way; why not take it? Why chance their lives on the word of a man who might be a liar?

But she can't convince her husband, George, or her brother-in-law, Jacob, 65, or the brash Reed not to take the new road. They want to move faster. They say all will be well; what does a woman know of such matters?

Tamsen is gloomy and dispirited tonight as she sits by the campfire with her children at the Little Sandy River, where the mosquitoes are fierce and tenacious. Perhaps her husband will reconsider the decision at Fort Bridger, where a road — the old trail — branches northwest to Fort Hall.

Yet, the die is cast.

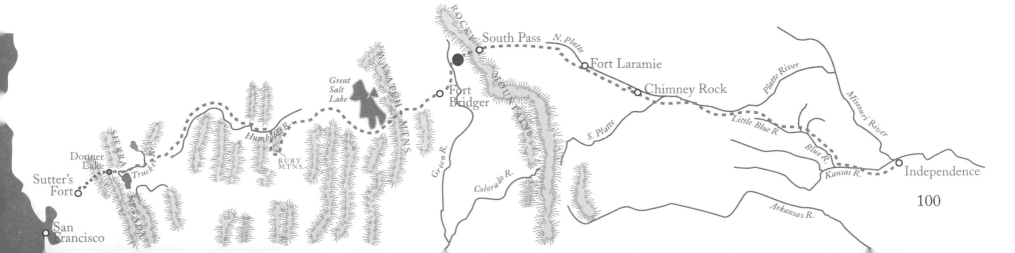

The parting of the ways. The road to the right leads to Fort Hall, a known route, the one to the left to Fort Bridger and the unknown Hastings Cutoff. The decision has been made and the Donners along with the Reeds and others have chosen the one to the left. George Donner has been selected as their leader. They will spend one more night together at the Little Sandy before parting. — Marilyn Newton photo

The newly formed Donner Party and the others who had chosen to follow the established trail to Fort Hall spent their last night together at the Little Sandy River before going their separate ways on July 20. — Marilyn Newton photo

J. Quinn Thorton — Marion County Historical Society

The greater number of the Californians, and especially the companies in which George Donner, James F. Reed, and William H. Eddy, and their families traveled, here turned to the left, for the purpose of going by way of Fort Bridger, to meet L.W. Hastings, who had informed them by a letter he wrote, and forwarded from where the emigrant road leaves the Sweet Water, that he had explored a new route from California, which he had found better than the old one

The Californians were generally much elated, and in fine spirits, with the prospect of a better and nearer road to the country of their destination.

Mrs. George Donner was, however, an exception. She was gloomy, sad, and dispirited, in view of the fact that her husband and others could think for a moment of leaving the old road, and confide in the statement of a man of whom they knew nothing, but who was probably some selfish adventurer.

— J. Quinn Thornton

The emigrant trail known as the "Greenwood's Cut-off" leaves the old trail via Fort Bridger to Fort Hall at this point. It is said to shorten the distance on the Fort Hall route to Oregon and California some fifty or sixty miles.

— Edwin Bryant, on the Big Sandy River, July 14, 1846

July 24, 1846

Road is rough, water poison on the start of road to Fort Bridger

The Donner Party is encamped at the Big Sandy River, where lupines bloom, grass is plentiful, and mosquitoes bite like jackals.

It's been hard going to get there. By James F. Reed's reckoning, they've traveled about twenty miles since turning left and taking the road to Fort Bridger and the Hastings Cutoff.

They've lost at least four oxen to poisoned water, which stands in puddles in Dry Sandy Creek. By the time the party reaches Fort Bridger, they'll buy more than a dozen oxen.

The Breen family, Irish Catholics and naturalized American citizens, are traveling with them: Patrick Breen, 51, and his wife, Margaret Breen, 40, have three wagons and seven children — John, 14; Edward, 13; Patrick Jr., 11; Simon, 9; Peter, 7; James, 5; and Isabella, six months.

Patrick Dolan, 35, the Breens' friend, has one wagon. The children like Dolan, a natural storyteller and singer. With him around the campfire, the green hills of Ireland are never far away; pixies dance around circles of mushrooms and banshees inhabit every storm.

The Breens and Dolan have been traveling together since leaving Missouri. At one time, they traveled with the Russell train, but being "foreigners" and "papists" they were not welcome in the same social scene open to the Donners and Reeds. About June 16, they might have been at the confluence of the North and South Platte. They probably spent Independence Day at Fort Laramie.

The group — history will not report how many people took the Fort Bridger road or even how many now consider themselves under the captaincy of George Donner — will reach the gates of the trading post in four days.

Some families will have second thoughts and take the old road from Bridger to Fort Hall. They'll bet on the proven route from Fort Hall south to the Humboldt River.

Others will join the Donner Party and take their chances on the new way.

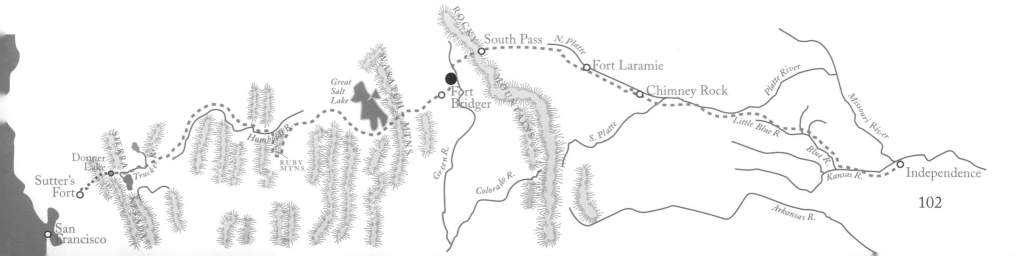

Fort Bridger, as it is called, is a small trading-post, established and now occupied by Messrs. Bridger and Vasquez. The buildings are two or three miserable log cabins, rudely constructed, and bearing but a faint resemblance to habitable houses. It's position is in a handsome and fertile bottom of the small stream on which we encamped . . . . There are a number of traders from the neighborhood of Taos, and the headwaters of the Arkansas, who have brought with them dressed buckskins, buckskin shirts, pantaloons and moccasins, to trade with the emigrants. The emigrant trade is a very important one to the mountain merchants and trappers. The countenances and bearing of these men, who have made the wilderness their home, are generally expressive of a cool, cautious, but determined intrepidity. In a trade, they have no consciences, taking all the advantages, but in a matter of hospitality or generosity are open-handed — ready, many of them, to divide with the needy what they possess.

— Edwin Bryant, July 17, 1846

After camping a few miles back at the Big Sandy, the Donner Party faced ferrying their wagons across the formidable Green River enroute to Fort Bridger. — Marilyn Newton photo

We arrived here on [July 16] and are now waiting for a sufficient number of waggons, in order to take a nearer route crossing the country on the south end of the great salt lake. This route will cut off at least 250 miles, and is the one through which Capt. Frémont passed last season. It is proposed by Mr. Hastings (who has been with us for some time;) he came through on horseback and reports the route perfectly practicable for wagons.

— Dr. T. Pope Long, in a letter from Fort Bridger, July 19, 1846

July 26, 1846

Donner Party camps in green meadow; will rest at Fort Bridger for five days

The Donner Party is encamped in a beautiful meadow about a half-mile from the Fort Bridger trading post. There's good grass and a cold, pure stream filled with fish and shaded by cottonwood trees. It's a welcome sight after the alkali water and sandy roads they traveled during the past week.

This is the country of the Northern Shoshone, whom the emigrants call the Snake Indians. There were about five hundred Shoshone here nine days ago when Edwin Bryant reached the post. But when told by the pioneers about the maneuvers of the Sioux in the east, the warriors and their families left the fort.

The Shoshone are known to be friendly to emigrant parties. They approach wagons and shout "Gee!," "Haw!" and "Gaw!" to show they are familiar with these strange bearded men who drive beasts that look like stunted, humpless buffalo. The Indians want to trade and willingly help the emigrants, but some will make off with a horse or a blanket if the pioneers aren't wary.

It's time to rest at the fort, where partners Jim Bridger and Louis Vasquez seem friendly and honest. The Donners and others must repair wagons and gear, wash clothes, prepare trail food, and replenish oxen and supplies.

Prices are high. Edwin Bryant saw a pint of whiskey traded for a pair of pants worth $10 and another trade where a man gave $2 for a half-pint bottle. But most pioneers have trade items and money and are glad to have a respite in a place where all manner of goods are available.

Vasquez and Bridger eat off English stoneware and their quarters contain things that would not be out of place in the finest Eastern homes.

This is the last outpost. Beyond this fort is untracked wilderness. The next "civilization" they'll see will be Johnson's Ranch on the far side of the Sierra Nevada, and then Sutter's Fort, in what will become Sacramento, California.

By using the "shortcut" beyond Bridger, James F. Reed believes Sutter's is about seven hundred miles away. The members of the Donner Party calculate they will reach their goal within two months. They figure they are seven weeks from paradise.

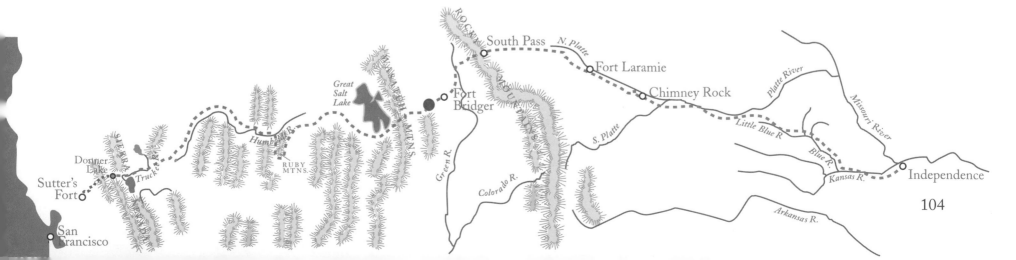

The new road, or Hastings Cut-off, leaves the Fort Hall road here, and is said to be a saving of 350 or 400 miles in going to California, and a better route. There is however, or thought to be, one stretch of 40 miles without water . . . . On the new route we will not have dust, as there are about 60 waggons ahead of us. The rest of the Californians went the long route feeling afraid of Hastings Cut-off. Mr. Bridger informs me that the route we design to take, is a fine level road, with plenty of water and grass, with the exception before stated. It is estimated that 700 miles will take us to Capt. Sutter's Fort, which we hope to make in seven weeks from this day.

— James F. Reed, in a letter from Fort Bridger, July 31, 1846

The Donner Party traveled near the bluffs as they made their way to Fort Bridger just a couple of miles away. — Marilyn Newton photo

Fort Bridger

Jim Bridger
— Fort Bridger Historic Site

FORT BRIDGER, Wyo. — Each morning after breakfast, Martin Lammers visits the Donner Party, trapper Jim Bridger, Pony Express riders, long-dead soldiers, and the ghosts of the Mormon pioneers. He walks where they walked, handles pottery that graced their tables, and, with trowel and whiskbroom, pieces together the history of Fort Bridger.

The site, which dates to 1843, served as a trading post, a Mormon outpost, a U.S. military fort, a Pony Express station, and a dairy operation. It's now a museum, an archaeological dig, and a living history memorial.

"Most people didn't believe we'd find any remains of the old fort due to all the changes over the years," Lammers said. "But we've got sixty to eighty percent of the original outline of the trading post."

Lammers, a contract archaeologist, is assistant to Dudley Gardner, who is in charge of the program. The project is conducted by Archaeological Services, Western Wyoming Community College. The dig delves through the layers of the fort's incarnations.

The log walls of Bridger's trading post, a rock wall built by Mormons who were preparing to defend the strategic site, later walls and foundations built by the Army, and support beams for a milk barn co-exist in the same plot of ground. They share space, but are decades apart in time. The archaeologists piece the clues together like a Rubik's Cube. Even the smallest shard or pollen grain tells them something.

"You can see the pottery there," said Lammers, who has one foot on a floor treaded by George Donner and James F. Reed, the leaders of the Donner Party, and by Jim Bridger and Louis Vasquez, the trappers who ran the post between 1843 and 1855. Lammers's other foot rests on the floor of a military building put up a decade and a half later, when the Pony Express followed the trail to the post. "This pottery tells us that Bridger and Vasquez didn't lack for the finer things," he said. "This is English stoneware, as fine as you would have seen in the best homes in the country in

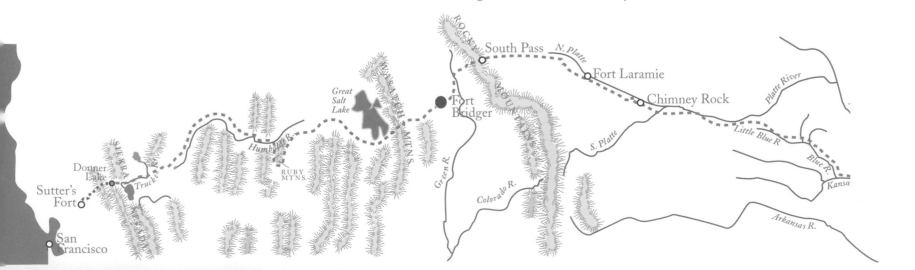

Martin Lammers, assistant archaeologist at Fort Bridger tells the history of Fort Bridger as discovered by their excavation. — Marilyn Newton photo

These brass shoulder scales used as epaulets by soldiers were left behind when Fort Bridger was abandoned by the U.S. Army in the late 1800s. — Marilyn Newton photo

the mid-1800s. They were isolated geographically, but not culturally." he said.

Another part of the old fort is rich in worked and unworked iron and has a door leading outside. This year, the scientists uncovered a spot anchored in charcoal and glass slag. The conclusion: The room was the trading post's blacksmith's shop.

Across the sides of the excavated site is a black line that looks like a seam of coal cutting across a canyon wall. "That's the layer of ash from the Mormon burn," Lammers said. "The Mormons knew an army was heading their way. First they prepared their defenses and then they found out the troops had large cannon."

The Mormons burned the site before retreating to Salt Lake City along the road through the Wasatch Mountains. It was the same road used by Brigham Young's wagon train in 1847 — a track blazed by the Donner Party the year before.

The scientists spend four hours in the lab for every hour spent digging. They examine pollen grains to get a look at the plants at the site over a 150-year period. They catalogue and study bones and rifle cartridges, Indian beads, buttons and bottles, thimbles and gun flints.

"These are shoulder scales," said Lammers, showing a pile of brass objects that were epaulets on the uniforms of noncommissioned officers and enlisted men. "They were obsolete in the late 1800s, so they may have piled them up and forgot about them."

Even the reconstructed fort/trading post on the monument's grounds holds answers to the past. "People using the replica fort do the same things people did 150 years ago," he said. "The earth floors get packed the same way. The wood weathers the same way."

"This may be the oldest continuously used site in Wyoming," Lammers said. "And we use it now for research and people use it to learn about the past." He said Fort Bridger is not dead. All who come to it contribute to its rich history. In fact, when Bill Pugsley, a Nevada history buff, walked the Donner route in commemoration of the 150th anniversary of the Donner tragedy, he lingered here waiting for the date of the Donner's departure.

The archaeological site will soon be opened as an interpretive center.

July 31, 1846

Donner Party leaves Fort Bridger, goes down the path to "shortcut"

The Donner Party camped about a half a mile from Fort Bridger. It was a time to repair wagons, wash clothes and buy more oxen for the long journey ahead. This would be the last outpost until they reached Sutter's Fort. — Marilyn Newton photo

It all comes down to money.

Jim Bridger and Louis Vasquez, the partners at Fort Bridger, know the new route is unsafe, unproven, and possibly deadly. Vasquez has letters, left by Edwin Bryant, warning James F. Reed and others not to take the Hastings Cutoff.

Instead of warning emigrants, however, the traders rave about the new road. They paint it as a near paradise of grass with only forty miles of waterless desert.

Vasquez and Bridger hope the "shortcut" will save their trading post, now bypassed by the Greenwood cutoff. With more than sixty wagons in the lead, why wouldn't things go as planned? Once a road is cut through the Utah mountains and the great drive across the salt desert is completed, why wouldn't the new road be as practical as the existing trails? After all, somebody has to go first and why not these people who made their own decisions to go west and face the dangers of the wilderness?

It is probable Bridger and Vasquez see nothing wrong with promoting a route that not only will reverse their own sagging fortunes but also will be a boon to travelers to California. They see themselves as honest men helping the pilgrims. Yet Vasquez keeps the letters in his pocket.

After the ordeal, James F. Reed, who today in a letter to his in-laws praised the partners' honesty, will make no bones about what happened: "Vasquez being interested in having the new route traveled, kept these letters."

But today, hope and comradeship prevail.

Wagons are repaired and stuffed with fresh supplies. New oxen have been purchased. The cattle are well-fed and rested. The laundry is done. Butter is churned. A fresh breeze blows from the west.

This morning, they set off on the shortcut. Tamsen Donner gazes at the old road branching off northwest to Fort Hall, the proven way. Dogs bark. Teamsters crack their whips above the oxen. Small children laugh and brace themselves in wagons. Wooden spokes turn.

The caravan moves on into unknown country.

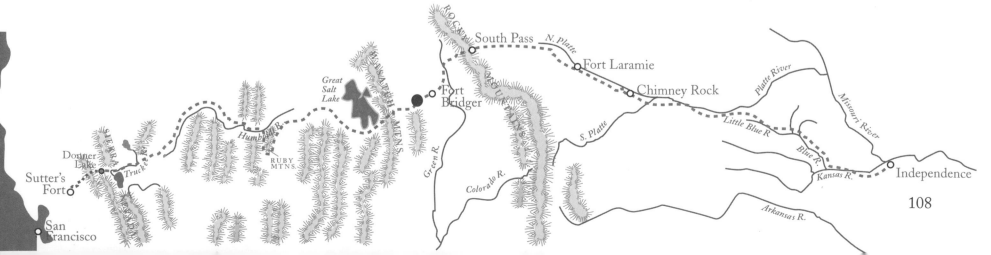

The Donner Party members at Fort Bridger:

George Donner, 62*, a prosperous farmer from near Springfield, Illinois, with three wagons, his third wife, Tamsen Donner, 44*, and their three children: Frances, 6; Georgia, 4; and Eliza, 3. George's daughters from a previous marriage, Elitha, 13, and Leanna, 11.

Jacob Donner, 56*, farmer and George's brother, with three wagons, and his wife, Elizabeth Donner, 45* Their five children and two of Elizabeth's children from a previous marriage. Two Donner employees: Noah James, 16*, and Samuel Shoemaker, 25*.

Traveling with the Donners were: Charles Stanton, 35*, from Chicago; John Denton, 28*, a goldsmith from England; Antonio, 23*, a sheepherder from Mexico whom they met along the trail; Luke Halloran, 25*, who had been ill, was left behind by another party and taken in by the Donners at the Little Sandy River; and Jean Baptiste Trudeau, 16, who claimed to be a mountaineer and joined the party at Fort Bridger.

James Frazier Reed, 45, an Irish-born furniture maker from Springfield, Illinois, with three wagons, and his wife, Margaret Reed, 32. Their children: Virginia Reed, now 13; Martha "Patty" Reed, 8; James Jr., 5; and Thomas Reed, 3. Two servants: Eliza Williams, 31, the cook, and her brother Baylis Williams, 24*; and three teamsters: Milford Elliot, 28*; Walter Herron, 27*; and James Smith, 25* (Sarah Keyes, Mrs. Reed's mother, died earlier on the trip).

Patrick Breen, 51, with three wagons and his wife, Margaret Breen, 40, and their seven children: John, 14; Edward, 13; Patrick Jr., 11; Simon, 9; Peter, 7; James, 5; and Isabella, six months. Patrick Dolan, 35*, the Breens' friend, with one wagon.

William H. Eddy, 28*, a carriage maker, with one wagon, and Eleanor, 25*, his wife, and two children: James, 3*; and Margaret, 1*.

Lavinah Murphy, 36*, a widow with two wagons, and children: John Landrum, 16*; Mary, 14; Lemuel, 12*; William, 10; Simon, 8; Sarah, 19, and her husband, William M. Foster, 30*, with one child, George, 1*; Harriet, 18, and her husband William Pike, 25*, and their children, Naomi, 2, and Catherine, 1*.

Lewis Keseberg, 32, an Ohio settler from Germany, with two wagons, his wife, Philippine, 23, and their two children, Ada, 3; and Lewis Jr., under age 1.

Mr. Wolfinger, with one wagon, with Doriss, 19, his wife, both German-born.

Others are: Charles Burger, 30*; Augustus Spitzer, 30*; Joseph Reinhardt, 30*; and Mr. Hardcoop, 60*; from Belgium.

William McCutchen, 30, from Jackson County, Missouri, with his wife Amanda, 25*, and infant daughter, Harriet. No wagon.

TOTAL: 74 people and 19 wagons. Other families and individuals will join them on the trail. Ages with asterisks (*) are approximate.

August to December 31, 1846

Part 2: The Shortcut
Fort Bridger to Donner Lake

There is a nigher route, and it is of no use to take a roundabout course.

— James F. Reed

August 2, 1846

Emigrants find water, grass at start of Hastings' Cutoff

These are some of the oldest ruins at Fort Bridger.
Even these postdate the Donner Party.
— Marilyn Newton photo

So far, Lansford Hastings' promises have come true.

Tonight, the Donner Party is encamped at Bear River. They have passed a creek jumping with trout and camped at fresh, clear springs. Pink and purple wild geraniums border their camp along a stream called the Little Muddy.

Yesterday, while crossing a rough road over a ridge, they marveled at the stunted cedars, twisted by the winds into fantastic shapes.

They fought their way through tangled sagebrush to reach this camp, where there's plenty of grass. Blue wild flax flowers nod in the breeze. The valley is rich and fertile. Aspen, clumps of hawthorn, and willow have taken root. Wild strawberry vines snake along the river bank, but animals have harvested the fruit.

Nearby rest the bones of buffalo, which now no longer range this far west.

The Donners, Reeds, and others who have traveled together since April or May are getting to know the newer members of their party. They are glad to have more able-bodied men to lend a hand.

One newcomer, Luke Halloran, doesn't fit that description. Although he is only about 25 years old, he's very sick with consumption — a disease that will later be called tuberculosis. Tamsen Donner took pity on the man, who had been left behind as a burden by his former wagon train, and the Donners agreed to take him with them through the "shortcut" out of Fort Bridger.

He has been called "a waif" by some writers, but Halloran, who is a former shopkeeper, showed a lot of spunk in getting this far. He's also traveling with a good deal of money.

Halloran rests in one of the Donners' wagons. Perhaps the California climate will do him good.

As the pioneers camp, they are surrounded by views of snow-crowned mountains. In the mornings, frost forms on buffalo robes and canvas.

Even in August, winter is not far from this place.

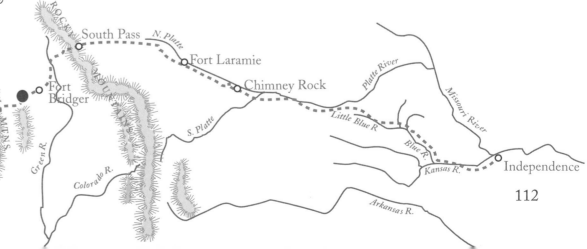

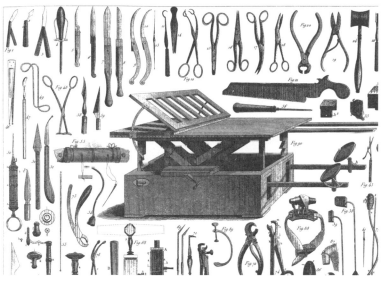

These medical instruments were typical of those in use during the Donner Party's era.

After leaving Fort Bridger, the Donner Party will reach and camp in Echo Canyon.
— *Marilyn Newton photo*

EDWARD BREEN'S ACCIDENT

A short distance from Fort Bridger, Edward Breen, 13, and Virginia Reed, 13, are running their horses when Edward's animal steps into a prairie dog hole and throws the boy, who breaks his leg.

It is a compound fracture: The jagged bone pokes out of the skin.

A rider is sent back to the fort to fetch help. A grizzled mountain man arrives, examines the boy's leg and then unwraps a small leather-covered bundle.

Edward Breen
— *Bancroft Library*

"Out of this came a short meat saw and a long-bladed knife," Harry Breen, Edward's son, will write. "The boy of course set up a loud cry when he sensed what was to be done."

Edward is so upset that his parents agree he may keep his leg, even though they fear gangrene might set in and threaten his life.

The disappointed mountain man, who wanted to show his skill with the saw, is given five dollars. Muttering to himself, he mounts his mule and rides back to Fort Bridger.

"[Margaret Breen] fashioned splints from wood strips," Harry Breen will recall.

The boy rides in the jolting wagon, gritting his teeth against the pain.

August 4, 1846

Donners west of Bear River, following Hastings' tracks

Today the Donner Party is encamped by grass and water at Echo Canyon. They are following a rough road carved by more than sixty wagons, which left Fort Bridger before the Donners arrived at the trading post.

Hastings' scout, James Hudspeth, is leading the advance caravan, while Hastings refines the route from Fort Bridger and encourages the wagons bringing up the rear. Apparently unaware of Hastings' plans, Hudspeth took the lead wagons down Weber Canyon. Historian Dale Morgan would show that Hastings intended to open a road across the Wasatch via today's East Canyon, Big Mountain, and Emigration Canyon. This route would offer a much better wagon road than Weber Canyon. Hudspeth's improvised route would have disastrous consequences for the Donner Party.

"After we had traveled about 5 miles, we encountered Captain Hastings, who had returned to meet us. By his advice we halted here," Heinrich Lienhard wrote in his journal yesterday. "He was of the opinion that we, like all the companies who had gone in advance of us, were taking the wrong road. He advised the first companies that on arriving at the Weber River they should turn to the left which would bring them on a shorter route to the Salt Lake; this advice they had not followed, but trusting to their luck had taken the road down the river."

The advance group set out without knowing exactly how they'd get through the Wasatch Mountains — a barrier no wagons had ever crossed. The lead group will hack and fight its way through steep-sided Weber Canyon, "doing things with wagons that wagons were never meant to do." Each party, upon seeing where the others have gone, attempts to find an easier way through. One wagon, with all its oxen, has tumbled 75 feet down a cliff.

It is a testament to Hastings' charisma that those in the lead wagons do not hang him from the nearest tree and return to the proven road to Fort Hall, George Stewart will observe. Hastings realizes Weber Canyon is a mistake, but it's too late for the lead wagons to turn back. He backtracks his route and today reaches the eastern mouth of the canyon, where he leaves a note for the Donner Party stuck in a clump of sagebrush.

They will find it in two days.

114

The steep sided Echo Canyon with its lush grass and water made an ideal camp site for the Donner Party. — Marilyn Newton photo

THE GRAVES FAMILY JOINS PARTY

The Donners will soon be joined by the Graves family, which left Marshall County, Illinois, for California on April 12, 1846.

"My father, Franklin Ward Graves, started with his family, consisting of my mother [Elizabeth], and [sisters] Sarah, Mary Ann, and myself," William Cooper "Billy" Graves will write in "Crossing the Plains in '46," a narrative written for *The Russian River Flag* newspaper in 1877. "Eleanor, Lavina, Nancy, Jonathan, Franklin and Elizabeth, the latter only about nine months old. . . ."

"My oldest sister, Sarah, had been married to Jay Fosdick a few weeks before we started; he and a hired man by the name of John Snider [Snyder] completed our company."

The Graves family joined a large wagon train about May 25 — which historians have identified as the Smith Company — and survived an attack by Pawnee Indians in which one emigrant was killed and another captured.

The Smith Company "was the hindmost party of the emigration of 1846, until the Donner Party was belated" author Kristin Johnson will write in *Unfortunate Emigrants: Narratives of the Donner Party*.

Reason P. Tucker, who will become one of the Donners' rescuers, also traveled with this group.

Several summer songsters were warbling their loves or chirping amongst the small willows which skirted the little brook as we passed along.
— James Clyman, as he and Hastings came through Echo Canyon June 5

Mary Graves

Lovina Graves

Sarah Graves Fosdick
All above from Emigrant Trails Museum

William Graves
— Bancroft Library

Eleanor Graves
— Bancroft Library

AUGUST 7, 1846

Donner Party finds Hastings note; Reed investigates Wasatch Range

On August 6, we ventured upon this furious passage, up to this point decidedly the wildest we had ever encountered, if not the most dangerous . . . In places, we unhitched from the wagon all the oxen except the wheel-yoke, then we tied one drove at both hind wheels, and the rest steadied the wagon; we then slid rapidly down into the foaming water, hitched the loose oxen again to the wagon and took it directly down the foaming riverbed, full of great boulders, on account of which the wagon lurched from one side to the other; now we had to turn the wheels by the spokes, then again hold back with all our strength we had, least it sweep upon a low lying rock and smash itself to pieces.

— Heinrich Lienhard in Weber Canyon,
August 6, 1846

The note from Lansford Warren Hastings is stuck in a split sagebrush stalk near the mouth of a canyon. James F. Reed and his fellow pioneers are bewildered by its contents.

Although Hastings has led more than sixty wagons through Weber Canyon, he advises the Donner company to camp where they are and send a messenger to him. Hastings wrote that he would put them on a new route, which would avoid the canyon and lessen the distance to the Great Salt Lake.

To go back to Fort Bridger and the old route would waste time. They decide to send three men through the canyon to examine its difficulty and find Hastings. James Reed, William Pike, and Charles Stanton set out. The others will camp and wait.

Stanton is a relatively small man, five feet five inches tall, with brown eyes and brown hair. He is the seventh child in a family of nine children. "He was rather slender in his youth," his brother Sidney will recall, "But at the age of fifteen he became strong and could endure as much hardship as any of his brothers." His talent for endurance will serve him well.

Reed will later say Will McCutchen was among the three — a mistake to be repeated in many books — but most historians will peg Pike as the third man.

The three ride as fast as they can.

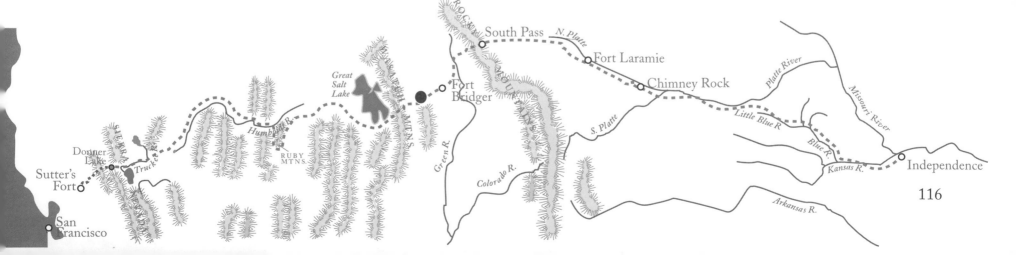

116

After getting a note from Hastings to camp where they are, three men set out through Weber Canyon to find the reasons Hastings had advised against their progressing up the canyon. — Marilyn Newton photo

AUGUST 9, 1846

Reed finds Hastings at Salt Lake; pilot points to another "shortcut"

Weber Canyon — Marilyn Newton photo

James F. Reed has seen why Lansford Hastings advised the Donner Party not to use Weber Canyon, where more than sixty wagons already have gone. Weber Canyon is a nightmare of cliffs with a boulder-littered river bottom and many dead ends. A tangle of elderberry bushes, willow, alder, and cottonwood clogs the bottoms.

"Our conclusions were that many of the wagons would be destroyed in attempting to get through," writes Reed, who traveled through the defile the day before with Charles Stanton and William Pike.

Yesterday, Reed caught up with Hastings and members of the advance party which crossed through Weber Canyon with the loss of one wagon. Reed finds them south of the Great Salt Lake.

"By this time, it would seem Hastings was losing what little judgment he ever had, and possibly his nerve had broken," historian George Stewart will write years later. "Hastings would not make good on his word to go back and point out the new route."

Defenders of Hastings will note that the pilot had his hands full with the advance party (which took a route he would not have taken) and could not abandon them to the Salt Desert while helping the Donners blaze a new trail.

Tomorrow the "guide" will take Reed to the top of a mountain and gesture towards a "better route" through the Wasatch Mountains, the route, presumably, through which he would have led the Harlan-Young wagons.

Hastings apparently gives no warnings about the difficulty of cutting a new road through the underbrush and tree-clogged canyon. If his own group of more than sixty wagons had difficulty in Weber Canyon, then what will happen to nineteen wagons with far fewer men to swing an ax or heft a shovel?

Reed, with a fresh mount, will ride back to the Donner camp alone. Pike and Stanton, their horses exhausted, will return later.

On the way back, Reed uses a hatchet to blaze trail markers on trees. He travels a route he hopes wagons can navigate once the brush is cleared.

With Hastings' wagon tracks now useless, it's up to Reed to find a new way west.

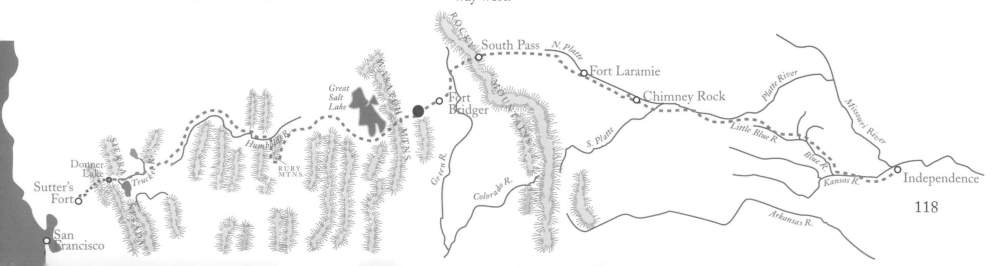

The Donner Party crossed this stream short of the mouth of Weber Canyon and headed west toward the nightmare of the Wasatch Mountains which was clogged with scrub oak trees. — Marilyn Newton photo

The Donner Party crossed Yellow Creek, near the present Wyoming and Utah borders. From here they would go camp at the eastern side of Emigration Canyon while the men would begin the arduous task of hacking and chopping their way through the dreaded Wasatch. — Marilyn Newton photo

We were compelled, as heretofore, to climb along the side of the precipitous mountains, frequently passing under, and sometimes scaling, immense overhanging masses and projections of rock. To thus be safely enlarged from this natural prison-house, locked in at every point, was an agreeable, if not an important event in the history of our journey.

> — Edwin Bryant on muleback, July 26, in Weber Canyon

When McCutchen [actually Pike], Stanton and myself got through Webber canon on our way to overtake Mr. Hastings, our conclusions were that many of the wagons would be destroyed in attempting to get through the canon. Mr. Stanton and McCutchen [Pike] were to return to our company as fast as their horses would stand it, they having nearly given out. I reached the company in the evening and reported to them the conclusions in regard to Weber canon, at the same time stating that the route that I had blazed that day was fair, but would take considerable labor in clearing and digging.

> — James F. Reed, *Pacific Press* account

August 11, 1846

Reed leads as party seeks way through Utah's Wasatch Mountains

James F. Reed leads the Donner Party onward.

They break camp at the place where Henefer, Utah will someday stand and follow Reed's horse to another canyon. Reed blazed trees on his way back to camp. He traveled along a route over which Hastings might have led the advance wagons if they had not turned down Weber Canyon. Had the lead wagons taken the route that the Donner Party is now entering, history would have been re-routed.

Had Hastings and the men of the Harlan-Young Party and others cut through what will become Emigration Canyon, the Donners could have followed their tracks with comparative ease. In 150 years, only scholars ever would have heard of the Donner Party, because they would have caught up with the others and cruised into California in September.

This was not to be.

Instead of following a new-made road, the men of the party must hack their way through the Wasatch Mountains to the Great Salt Lake.

The Wasatch, a range of high peaks and deep canyons, is the eastern wall of the Great Basin. Its snowcapped peaks crown the horizons. The sides of canyons are clogged with willow, dense berry bushes, thick cottonwoods, box elder, and alder trees. The riverbeds are narrow and full of boulders.

By Reed's reckoning, they travel five miles this day and camp at springs at what will be called Dixie Hollow, where Hastings and mountain man Jim Clyman had camped on their return from California.

From here, they can see there will be no easy route. There is hard work ahead.

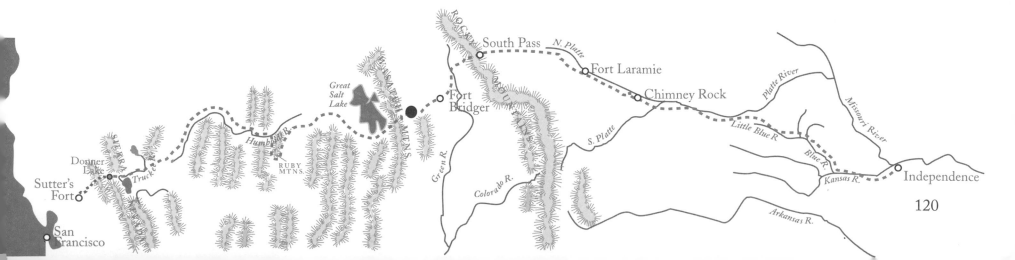

After realizing the folly of trying to get through Weber Canyon, the emigrants turned west and traveled over Hogsback Summit. The trail is still visible there. — Marilyn Newton photo

At night, it froze solid just out of Echo Canyon. There's a road through it now. It still echoes in there. It's a steep-sided crumbly canyon. During the day it was hot, very hot, with lots of water running through it.

— Bill Pugsley, Donner Party reenactor

Some three or four days ahead of us Bridger and Vasquez had hired L.W. Hastings to pilot a company on a new route by their Fort (or camp, for it was only a camp then) and the south side of Salt Lake, thence striking the Humboldt River ... he took them through Weber Canyon and left them close to where Ogden is now located; but he was dissatisfied with the Canon road, because it was so terribly rough and dangerous, so he hastened back to meet the Donners.

— W. C. Graves, *Russian River Flag* account

AUGUST 14, 1846

Party fights through Wasatch, hacking trees and making road

All the men and older boys in the Donner Party are clearing a road while the women and children wait in camp.

Among those waiting are Luke Halloran, 25 and ill with consumption, who is being nursed by Tamsen Donner, and Edward Breen, 13, suffering with a broken leg bound in splints and nursed by his mother Margaret, who is pleased to see infection has not visited the boy's wound. The medical kits of the time don't offer much help. Contents include bandages, castor oil, camphor, peppermint, patent-remedy alcohol mixtures and a kind of liniment.

The workers are making a pathway for wagons over an Indian trail where James F. Reed blazed trees on his way back from the valley of the Great Salt Lake. With typical modesty, he calls the canyon "Reed's Gap." The Mormons will first call it "Pratt's Pass" and then settle on Big Mountain.

Armed with axes, hatchets, spades, and chains, they fight their way through willow, cottonwoods, quaking aspen, box elder, and alder trees tangled with wild rose vines and service berries.

Two days ago they left Dixie Hollow and traveled two miles to "Bosman Creek," which will someday be called East Canyon Creek. Yesterday, they hacked through willow thickets and by late afternoon by Reed's reckoning had made only two more miles along the creek. Historians will find his mileage estimates too short, saying he made eight miles the second day.

For two nights, a meteor shower has sparkled in the sky, but no one has time for stargazing.

Tonight, in a camp above the mouth of what the Mormons will dub Little Emigration Canyon, the men fall, exhausted, on their buffalo robes and quilts. The women nurse their husbands' blisters and scrapes. At least they have water here and grass for the cattle. They also have mosquitoes and biting flies. They expected hardship; it has arrived. Perhaps their worries will be over once they cross these mountains and complete the hard drive across the desert that Lansford Hastings told them includes a forty-mile stretch without water.

Maybe this road, measured in feet instead of miles, will be the worst of the trip.

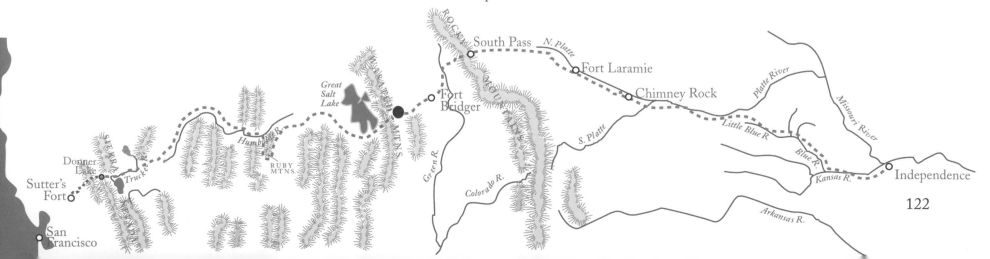

This is where they started up the hill and started hacking. Off the road that's there now, it's thick, real thick, just branches and brambles. It's hot in there in August, real hot.
— Bill Pugsley, Donner Party reenactor

We followed the dimly traced wagon tracks up this stream for eight miles, crossing the same 13 times. The bottoms of this creek are thickly covered with willows, from five to 15 rods wide, making an immense labour in cutting a road through for the emigrants last season. We still found the road almost impassable, and requiring much labour.
— Orson Pratt, with the Mormon emigration in East Canyon, July 17, 1847

The Donner Party camped at a spring about a mile from here. — Marilyn Newton photo

The eastern mouth of Emigration Canyon. From here the emigrants would cut and hack their way through scrub sak and willows to reach the salt lake valley. It would take them 18 days. — Marilyn Newton photo

AUGUST 16, 1846

Graves family overtakes party; wagon train now at its full strength

The Graves family has overtaken and joined the Donner Party.

They are a welcome addition.

Their strength will help the emigrants fight their way through the Wasatch.

The Graves group of thirteen, with three wagons, left Sparland, in Marshall County, Illinois, in April. They include: Franklin Ward Graves, about 57; his wife, Elizabeth, about 45; and their dependent children Mary Ann, 19; William C., 17; Eleanor, 14; Lovina, 12; Nancy, 8; Jonathan, about 7; Franklin Ward Jr., about 5; and Elizabeth, nine months.

With them are Graves's daughter, Sarah, 21, and her husband, Jay Fosdick, about 23, who are newlyweds. Teamster John Snyder, about 25, drives one of the Graves' wagons. Snyder, it will be said, is engaged to Mary Ann Graves.

Franklin Graves, the clan's leader, is a native of Vermont who came to Illinois in 1831. He served as a drum major in the Black Hawk War of 1832 while his family remained behind in his cabin on the frontier.

A big man, he has the reputation of a backwoodsman who "despised the trammels of civilization, and loved the unshackled freedom of the red man." Good-natured and hospitable, it is said he'd go out of his way to do a favor. His wife, Elizabeth, is tall and thin, with "a sunburnt face wraethed in smiles."

"She wore a blue calico frock, an old sun bonnet and a faded shawl," researcher Spencer Ellsworth will write. "... There was not a woman in the place but knew her and loved to see her kind face make its appearance."

The family's outfit consists of three wagons, a small herd of cows and oxen, and plenty of supplies. In one of the wagons, within holes drilled for the purpose, stacks of silver coins await the family's arrival in California.

The Donner Party now consists of eighty-seven people in twenty-two wagons. The company is at full strength. They'll need all of it.

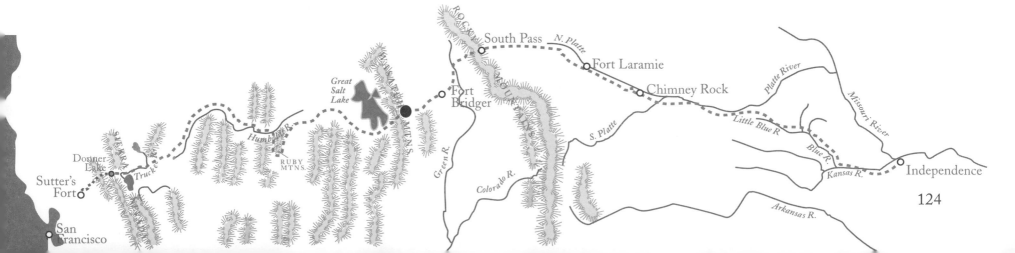

[Two pages of handwritten diary text from the Reed diary]

Two pages from the Reed diary — Sutter's Fort Museum

Sat. [Aug.]15: in Camp all hands Cutting and opning a road through the Gap.

Son. 16: Still Clearing and making Road in Reed's Gap.

— James F. Reed, journal

The party camped near this grove after leaving Little Emigration Canyon. — Marilyn Newton photo

---

GRAVES' HINDSIGHT

In his later account of the Donner tragedy, William C. Graves will remark:

"Here is what caused our suffering, for Reed told us if we went the [Weber] Canon road we would be apt to break our wagons and kill our oxen, but if we went the new way, we could get to Salt lake in a week or ten days."

Graves will always blame Reed for the delays that caused the Donner Party to be trapped by snow.

"There had been over a thousand wagons come a head of us except in the one place that we were fools enough to leave the old road and suffer the consequence," Graves will write in a letter to C. F. McGlashan. "But that was Reed's fault. Oh I get mad every time I think it."

But as Kristin Johnson will remark in *Unfortunate Emigrants: Narratives of the Donner Party*, the Graves family already had left the old road by the time they caught up with the Donners in the Wasatch.

AUGUST 18, 1846

Emigrants break camp, start across "Reed's Gap"

After three days of chopping, sawing, and digging, the twenty-two wagons of the Donner Party cross "Reed's Gap" through the Wasatch Mountains of what will become the state of Utah. Their goal: the Valley of the Great Salt Lake.

The wagons are making slow headway across the newly carved road, which leads over what will be called Big Mountain and into Mountain Dell Canyon. The Donner and Reed wagons, somewhat heavier than the others, lag behind. Reed's "two-story" family wagon — which will become famous as the Pioneer Palace Car — is the heaviest vehicle, yet no survivor will complain that it inordinately slowed them through the Wasatch.

James F. Reed estimates they have gone five miles today, but historians will figure the distance at eight miles. In his journal, apparently written for friends and family who might later wish to take the trip west, Reed refers to himself in the third person and concentrates on daily mileages and camping spots near springs rather than personal information.

Occasionally an accident or event will be noted, as it is today when he writes, "JF Reed broke an axletree." In an 1847 account of the tragedy, J. Quinn Thornton will write that the axle incident happened closer to the lake. Perhaps Reed broke an axletree here in the Wasatch, which is highly possible given the steepness of the mountains, and another later at the lake.

William Eddy, the carpenter who had done such a crackerjack job on Edwin Bryant's broken wagon earlier on the trail, and Samuel Shoemaker, a teamster for the Donners, help Reed make repairs.

They will camp here tomorrow and the men will go forward to do more road-clearing in what the Mormons will call Emigration Canyon.

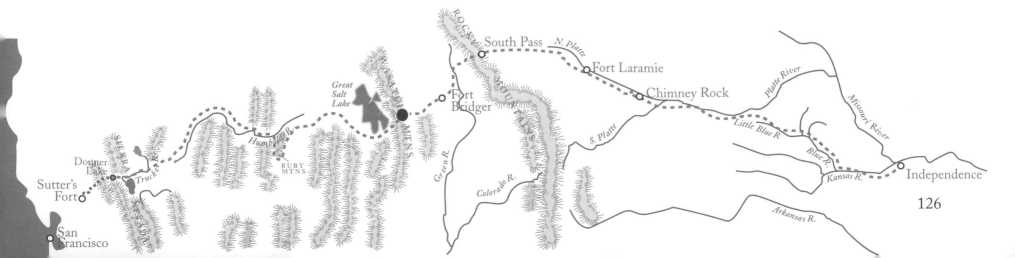

A tunnel can still be seen where emigrants carved their way through the tangled growth of trees and bushes that clog the Wasatch. Always resourceful, the emigrants used whatever they had including chains, spades and axes to hack their way through. — Marilyn Newton photo

Wagon ruts can still be seen where emigrants cut their way through the Wasatch.
— Marilyn Newton photo

Mon. 17: Still in camp and all hands working on the road which we finished and returned to Campe.

Tus. 18: this Morning all started to cross the Mountain which is a natural easey pass with a little more work and encamped making this day   5 [miles] J F Reed Brok an axletree

— James F. Reed, journal

AUGUST 21, 1846

Donner Party in Emigration Canyon; find exit blocked by thick timber

Weds 19 this day we lay in Camp in a neat little valley fine water and good grass the hands ware this [day] on the West Side of Small mountain in a Small Valley Clearing a road to the Valley of the Lake we have to Cross the outlett of the Utah Lake on this Rout near the Salt Lake.

Thurs 20 Still in Camp and hands Clearing road

Frid 21 this day we left Camp Crossed the Small Mountain and encapd in the vally running into the Utah Outlett making this day 4 [miles]

— James F. Reed, journal

The company today travels their new road only to find the mouth of Emigration Canyon blocked by dense willows. They fear they might have to abandon wagons. There's no enthusiasm for more road-building. Later accounts of the trip through the Wasatch Mountains will state that the emigrants slowed their road work as they continued up the canyons. Today, they decide to doubleteam the oxen and bring the wagons over what will be called Donner Hill, then descend to the Great Salt Lake.

The slow trip through the canyons has been tough on all the emigrants, especially two people traveling on sickbeds. Edward Breen, 13, with his badly broken leg in a splint, is recovering and seems to be out of danger from gangrene. Luke Halloran, 25, is continuously coughing in one of the Donners' wagons. He is very sick with consumption and nothing Tamsen Donner can do seems to help.

Two days ago, Charles Stanton and William Pike rejoined the train, after parting from Reed on his trip to meet with Lansford Hastings. Their absence during the bulk of the roadwork has made things harder on the others.

Hastings, the guide, is ahead with a group of more than sixty wagons which include the Harlan-Young Party and the Hoppe Company, which in turn includes "five German boys," diarist Heinrich Lienhard among them. Today, wagons of the Harlan-Young train are camped at the springs at the foot of Pilot Peak on the western edge of the Great Salt Lake Desert. They had to abandon about a third of their wagons on the desert and go back for them after reaching the springs on the western side. They lost several oxen.

It took the Harlan-Young Party three days of day-and-night travel to cross the barren salt flats, which proved to be eighty miles wide — double the forty-mile waterless stretch Hastings had predicted.

Today, Lienhard and others leave the springs at the base of Pilot Peak on the western edge of the Great Salt Lake Desert.

With this deadly obstacle still ahead of them, the Donner Party is falling farther behind by the day.

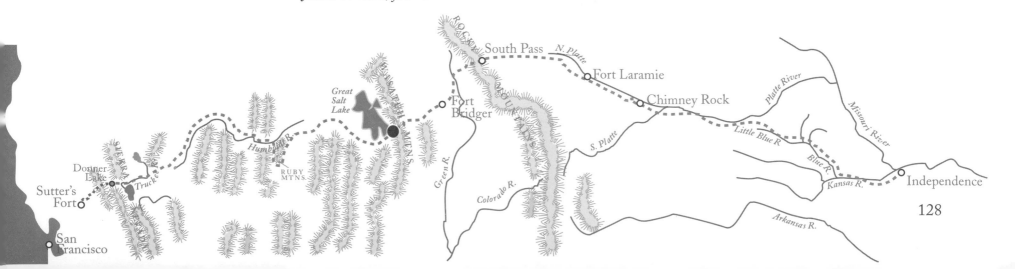

In spite of the long-sustained fatigue everyone was animated and happy; the young girls gathered together and sang, while the young Americans danced to the squeaky sounds which a man named Rhoadies coaxed from his old fiddle, so that the dust eddied up in clouds; in short, one might have supposed the whole journey completed.
— Heinrich Lienhard's journal, August 19, 1846, upon crossing the Great Salt Lake Desert

As the emigrants neared the Great Salt Lake they continued to encounter dense growth such as this a short way from the mouth of the canyon.
— Marilyn Newton photo

August 23, 1846

Reed: eighteen days to go thirty miles; pioneers free of the Wasatch

The tribulations of the Donner Party are depicted in a relief on the Mormon memorial near the mouth of Emigration Canyon. — Marilyn Newton photo

Yesterday the Donner Party went over what will be named Donner Hill.

In his journal, James F. Reed barely remarks on the ascent, even though almost all the oxen were needed to pull each wagon up. It's a testament to how Herculean tasks have become commonplace.

Tomorrow, Reed will write that it took eighteen days (from the time they found Lansford Hastings' letter) to go thirty miles. Historians will find Reed's estimates low and will say they should be doubled.

When they left Fort Bridger on July 31, they believed they were only seven weeks from Sutter's Fort. In more than three weeks they have yet to hit the south end of the Great Salt Lake — more than 720 miles from Sutter's, future site of Sacramento.

Today the party descends into the Valley of the Great Salt Lake and crosses marshland. Tomorrow they'll find tracks of wagons led by Hastings.

Several of those wagons already have crossed the waterless, eighty-mile Great Salt Lake Desert.

Next year, Mormons led by Orson Pratt will follow the Donner's mountain trail. Had the Wasatch road not been cut, the Saints would have arrived in the valley too late to plant crops. The history of the West, and certainly the history of Utah, would have been quite different, though the crops Pratt's Mormon Pioneer Company planted didn't amount to much.

The Mormons will acknowledge their debt to the Donners on a panel of the "This Is The Place" monument in Salt Lake City.

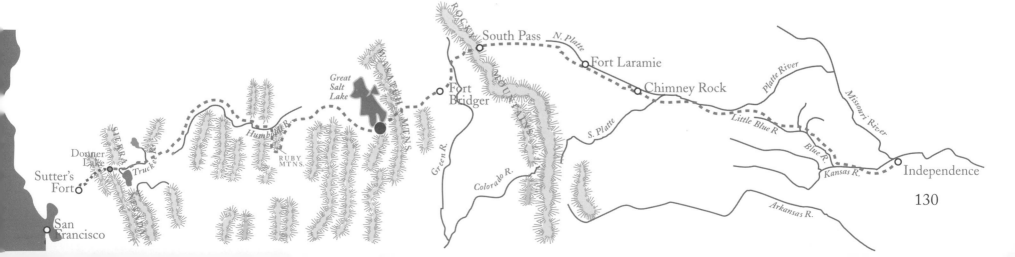

Only those who have passed through this country horseback can appreciate the situation. There was absolutely no road, not even a trail. The canon wound around among the hills. Heavy underbrush had to be cut away and used for making a road bed ... Finally we reached the end of the canon where it looked us through our wagons would have to be abandoned. It seemed impossible for the oxen to pull them up the steep hill and the bluffs beyond, but we doubled teams and the work was, at last, accomplished, almost every yoke in the train being required to pull up each wagon. While in this canon Stanton and Pike came into camp; they had suffered greatly on account of the exhaustion of their horses and had come near perishing. Worn with travel and greatly discouraged we reached the shore of the Great Salt Lake.
— Virginia Reed Murphy, *Across the Plains In The Donner Party*

Donner Hill is still a hard pull. I climbed it, but not my horse Patches. He had a hard enough time in Emigration Canyon. When the Mormons got here in 1847, they followed Reed's road to the hill and then cut their own road to the end of the canyon rather than go over it.
— Bill Pugsley, Donner Party reenactor

The emigrants were finally through the Wasatch — almost. There was just a short stretch of willows to hack through. But they opted instead to double team the oxen and pull the wagons up the grassy hill in the foreground near where the pine tree now stands. The next year, the Mormons, with more able-bodied men, will spend just four hours cutting their way through. The hill will be named after the Donners. — Marilyn Newton photo

AUGUST 25, 1846

Man dead in Donner wagon; party halts for burial

Luke Halloran was buried a few miles east of here at 20 Wells. Springs dot the landscape in and around presentday Grantsville. — Marilyn Newton photo.

Luke Halloran, 25, is dead.

"Left camp early this morning," James F. Reed writes in his journal. "Fair water. In the evening, a gentleman by the name of Luke Halloran died of Consumption having been brought from Bridger's Fort by George Donner a distance of 151 miles. We made him a Coffin."

The Donner wagons had lagged behind the party and rejoined the others about 8 p.m. Halloran died with his head resting in Tamsen Donner's lap. Reed will remember that his wagon train lost time for humanitarian reasons, as the sick man could not make the regular drives.

Another delay: J. Quinn Thornton will write that Reed broke an axletree on one of his three wagons and that William Eddy and Samuel Shoemaker backtracked fifteen miles for timber. They work all night to make repairs.

Tomorrow, Halloran, placed in his coffin, will be brought to the "Upper Wells" and buried next to John Hargrave, a member of one of the forward parties on Hastings Cutoff. Halloran, a former shopkeeper, was a Master Mason, as is Reed, who travels with his full Masonic regalia. Reed will preside at the funeral.

The dead man willed his property, including $1,500, to George Donner.

The location of Utah's first pioneer graves will soon become a mystery. But 150 years to the month of Halloran's demise, the Utah Crossroads Chapter of the Oregon-California Trails Association will commemorate the event at Grantsville, Utah. OCTA will hold a ceremony on August 10, 1996. A bearded man walking with a dog and an old horse will wander into the area, interrupting speeches.

The man, Bill Pugsley of Reno, will be the first person in more than 140 years to attempt to walk the original trail from South Pass to Donner Lake. He'll come to see Halloran's monument, lost for nearly fifteen decades, and will arrive at the site on the day it is re-commemorated.

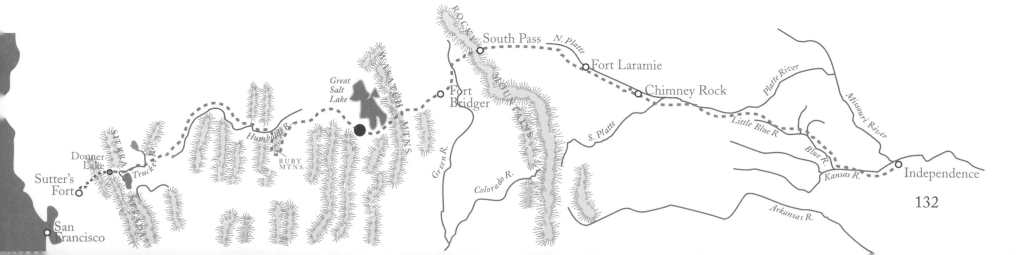

After taking time to bury Luke Halloran, the party made their way to Hope Wells along this trail. — Marilyn Newton photo

One of our company, a Mr. Halloron being in a dying condition from consumption. We could not make regular drives owing to his situation. He was under the care of Mr. Geo. Donner, and made himself known to me as a Master Mason. In a few days he died. After the burial of his remains we proceeded on our journey, making our regular drives, nothing occurring of note until we arrived at the springs where we were to provide water and as much grass as we could for the purpose of crossing the Hastings desert, which was represented as 40 or 45 mile in length (but we found it at least 70 miles).

— James F. Reed, *Pacific Press* account

On the Hastings Cut-off we were twenty-eight days in going twenty-one miles. Difficulty and disaster hovered about us from the time we entered this cut off.

— Lewis Keseberg to C. F. McGlashan

August 28, 1846

Party finds Hastings' note ripped to pieces by birds

At a spring in western Utah, the Donner Party has found another note from their "guide" — but it can't be read in its current condition. Birds have apparently been tearing at the paper, and pieces of it are blowing in the sagebrush.

The note from Lansford W. Hastings was left on a board in a meadow on the eastern side of the Great Salt Lake Desert. The party has reached the future site of Iosepa, where they are taking on grass, wood, and water for what they believe will be a forty-mile trek across the salt flats.

Tamsen Donner, the teacher, collects the scattered pieces and places the board in her lap. While her companions crowd around her as though watching a magic trick, Tamsen presses the scraps flat and fits them together like a puzzle. "The tedious process was watched with spellbound interest by the anxious group around her," her daughter, Eliza Donner, will write.

It is Hastings' handwriting: "2 days — 2 nights — hard driving — cross — desert — reach water."

The distance must be greater than forty miles!

That's beyond the limit a thirsty ox can travel, even if the emigrants carry water and bathe the steers' tongues with wet towels.

But there's no turning back.

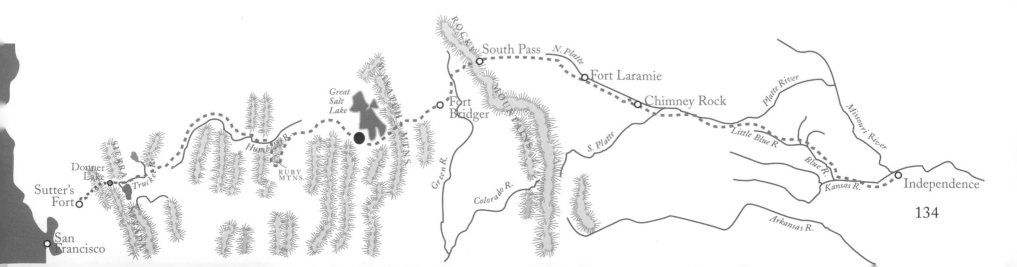

When the emigrants arrived at Hope Wells they found another note from Hastings. These trees might be old enough to have been there when the emigrants camped nearby. — *Marilyn Newton photo*

Eliza Donner
— Bancroft Library

Close by the largest well stood a rueful spectacle — a bewildering guide board, flecked with bits of white paper, showing that the notice or message which had recently been pasted and tacked thereon had since been stripped off in irregular bits. In surprise and consternation, the emigrants gazed at its blank face, then toward the dreary waste beyond. Presently my mother [Tamsen Donner] knelt before it and began searching for fragments of paper, which she believed crows had wantonly pecked off and dropped to the ground.

Spurred by her zeal, others also were soon on their knees, scratching among the grasses and sifting the loose soil through their fingers. What they found, they brought to her and after the search ended she took the guide board, laid it across her lap, and thoughtfully began fitting the ragged edges of paper together and matching the scraps to marks on the board. The tedious process was watched with spellbound interest by the anxious group around her. The writing was that of Hastings, and her patchwork brought out the following words: "2 days — 2 nights — hard driving — cross — desert — reach water.

— Eliza P. Donner Houghton

A tree growing horizontally with vertical branches at Hope Wells. — Marilyn Newton photo

135

AUGUST 30, 1846

Pioneers begin crossing deadly salt flats in Utah

After leaving Hope Wells and before crossing the salt flats, the emigrants first had to cross a low but steep range of hills.
— *Marilyn Newton photo*

Now the Donner Party begins the trek across the Great Salt Lake Desert.

Hastings said the desert was a "dry drive" of forty miles, but even the dumbest greenhorn is able to tell that Pilot Peak, above the nearest spring, is far more distant across the barren lake bed. Such dry, treeless flats are called *playa*s in Spanish because they resemble a beach.

They must walk this beach, this playa, day and night. It is death to stop.

No other companies are in sight. The others they knew are on the plains are well ahead.

Today, Edwin Bryant's mule-back party reaches Johnson's Ranch west of the Sierra, a day's ride from Sutter's Fort. Bryant, William Russell, and the others eat cheese, drank milk, and read war news in a two-week-old newspaper.

Northern California is in the hands of the Americans. Volunteers are forming companies to fight the Mexicans in the south.

Today, the advance wagons led by Lansford Hastings are making their way through Ruby Valley in what will become Nevada.

Companies bound for Oregon and California on the old trail have passed Fort Hall in Idaho. The California groups are making their way south to the Humboldt River.

Today the Donner Party is entering a new hell, where their eyes can't be believed and the oxen will go mad from thirst.

They are the stragglers of the 1846 emigration. The sun pounds the playa, but summer is dying.

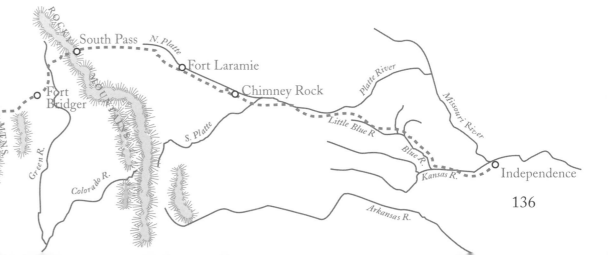

Clouds shroud the tops of Pilot Peak in this view of the trail.
— Marilyn Newton photo

The desert had been represented to us as only forty miles wide but we found it nearer eighty. It was a dreary, desolate alkali waste; not a living thing could be seen; it seemed as though the hand of death had been laid upon the country. We started in the evening, traveled all that night, and the following day and night — two nights and one day of suffering from thirst and heat by day and piercing cold by night.
— Virginia Reed, *Across the Plains In The Donner Party*

Son 30 [August] Made this day 12 [miles] to a Silphur Spring in the Mountain which ought to be avoided water not good for Cattle . . . Commencd the long drive through the Salt desert
        Mon 31 in dessert drive of Sixty 60 miles
        Tusdy Sept 1 in dessert
— James F. Reed, journal

SEPTEMBER 1, 1846

Party crossing salt flats; Reed rides ahead for water

A lone marker indicates the route the Donners took as they got closer to Silver Island and the spring at the base of Pilot Peak. But they still had a long way to go. — Marilyn Newton photo

On the eighty-mile Great Salt Lake Desert every family fends for itself.

The caravan of twenty-two wagons is in segments. William Eddy's outfit is ahead. His steers are giants when seen through magnifying heat waves.

The George Donner and Reed families, with three heavy wagons each, bring up the rear. The other families are in the middle of the migration.

They've been walking a day and a night and all day today. They aim for Pilot Peak, with trees and a spring at its base, but it stays far away.

"We struck a vast white plain, uniformly level, and utterly destitute of vegetation or any sign that shrub or plant had ever existed above its snow-like surface," Edwin Bryant wrote after crossing the flats a month before the Donners. "It was a scene so entirely new to us, so frightfully forbidding in its aspects, that all of us, I believe, though impressed with its sublimity, felt a slight shudder of apprehension.

"For 15 miles the surface of this plain is so compact, that the feet of our animals, as we hurried them along over it, left but little if any impression for the guidance of the future traveller. It is covered with a hard crust of saline and alkaline substances combined."

The salt flats are as hard and dusty as Bryant described until the wagons reach the center of the desert, where a shallow lake has turned the alkali into mush. It is like walking through deep oatmeal mixed with glue. The gunk covers their feet like cement casts. It clumps around the wagon rims. Oxen stumble.

The mountains ahead seem to float on air. They see sky below the Silver Island range. Corners of the ranges float, vanish, and reappear. The midday sun is a hammer. At sunset shadows stretch for miles. The night air is cold tongs reaching through blankets. Children cry. Cattle moan.

James F. Reed rides ahead for water. He instructs his teamsters to unchain oxen and drive them ahead when they get too exhausted to pull.

His wife and children stay with the wagons.

The options: Move or die.

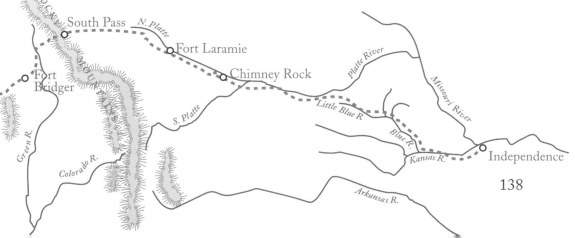

138

Time has all but obliterated the trail even though other conveyances had followed the trail after the Donner Party. This view looks west. — *Marilyn Newton photo*

About 11 o'clock at night I met my teamsters with all my cattle and horses. I cautioned them particularly to keep the cattle on the road, for that as soon as they would scent the water they would break for it. I proceeded on and reached my family and wagons. Some time after leaving the men one of the horse gave out and while they were striving to get it along, the cattle scented the water and started for it. And when they started with the horses the cattle were out of sight, they could not find them or their trail, as they told me afterward. They supposing the cattle would find water, went on to camp.
— James F. Reed, *Pacific Press* account

[We saw] an object so enormously large, considering its apparent distance, and its movement forward, parallel with ours, so distinct, that it greatly excited our wonder . . . [Some thought] it might be some cyclopian nondescript animal, lost upon the desert; others that it was the ghost of a mammoth or Megatherium wandering on 'this rendezvous of death'; others that it was the devil mounted on an Ibis.
— Edwin Bryant, describing a mirage
on the salt desert

September 4, 1846

Emigrants reach Pilot Peak; Reeds left on salt desert

Pioneers of the Donner Party have reached the spring at the base of Pilot Peak, but most of their wagons and the Reed family are left in the desert.

James F. Reed arrived at the spring two days ago. William Eddy already was there and the two men went back to revive some of the oxen collapsed on the salt flats.

As Reed went back to rejoin his family, he passed his teamster, Milford Elliot, who had unhitched the oxen from the Reed's three wagons and was driving them ahead to the spring. Reed cautioned him that the cattle would stampede when they smelled water.

Reed got back to his family at daylight yesterday. They waited for the teamsters all day, then began walking to the spring with their five dogs. Last night the children became exhausted and as a fierce wind came up Reed covered them with blankets and the dogs.

"Very soon one of the dogs jumped up and started out barking, the others following making an attack on something approaching us," Reed will remember. "Very soon I got sight of an animal making directly for us; the dogs seizing it changed its course, and when passing I discovered it to be one of my young steers."

Reed remarks to his wife and children that the animal seems mad, provoking his family to their feet, "scattering like quail." It takes Reed a while to calm them, but he remarks "There was no more complaining about being tired or sleepy the balance of the night."

At daylight, they arrive at Jacob Donner's wagons marooned on the playa. Reed leaves his family with the Donners, who will bring them to the spring today.

Meanwhile, Reed's teamsters have lost his cattle. They scented water and ran into the desert. Reed, now down to a cow and a steer, will begin a search for thirty-eight head of cattle.

They must also rescue wagons left on the barren desert if they are to survive.

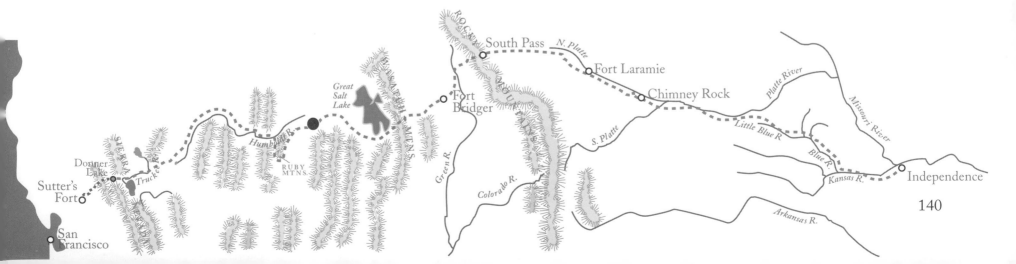

The final miles across the last of the salt desert with the base of Pilot Peak in the distance. The spring at the base of the mountain would be named after the party. — *Marilyn Newton photo*

Wed 2 in do [desert] Cattle got in Reeds Cattle lost this night

 Thurdy 3 in do some teams got in

 Fridy 4 lost Reeds cattle 9 Yok by not driving them Carefule to water as directed by Reed —
Hunting Cattle 9 Yok by not driving them Carefule to water as directed by Reed — [in margin]
Hunting cattle 3 or 4 days rest of teams getting in and resting Cattle all nearly given out

 Sat 5 Still in camp in the west side of Salt Dessert

    — James F. Reed, *journal*

Can I ever forget that night in the desert, when we walked mile after mile in the darkness, every step seeming to be the very last we would take!
   — Virginia Reed, *Across the Plains In The Donner Party*

Finally, the last of the emigrants reached the welcome spring at the base of Pilot Peak, in the background. Here they will rest while Reed and others search for lost cattle. — *Marilyn Newton photo*

September 6, 1846

Reed's oxen can't be found; four wagons abandoned in desert

Patty Reed — Emigrant Trails Museum

In one day, James F. Reed has gone from being the richest man in the Donner Party to being the poorest in possessions.

Reed's teamsters lost all but two of his cattle when the loose animals smelled water and stampeded on the Great Salt Lake Desert.

They have not been found. Goshute Indians will feast on some of them.

Today Reed, Franklin Ward Graves, and others go back into the salt flats to retrieve their rigs. The wagons, drawn by the remaining horses and mules, will be brought to Pilot Springs tomorrow.

Graves, William Pike, and Patrick Breen will loan oxen to Reed, who has one pair of his own left. Reed will save his "family wagon" — probably the Pioneer Palace Car. He will leave his other two wagons on the playa. George Donner and Lewis Keseberg each abandoned wagons.

Patty Reed wants to take some of her toys, but is told to say good-bye to her dolls. In the sand, Patty spies the tiny wooden doll possibly made for her by her grandmother Sarah Keyes, who died in Kansas. Patty hides the doll, a lock of her grandmother's hair, a pincushion, and a few other keepsakes in the hem of her apron. She mentions this to no one for fear her parents will learn she has disobeyed them.

Reed's provisions are divided among the other families. What's left is cached in the desert. *Cache* is a French term meaning to hide. Donner Party members, like those in most pioneer trains, hide goods they no longer can carry. They intend to come back for them someday.

The Graves family has shown kindness to the Reeds. Franklin loans them cattle. W. C. Graves, 17, helps James F. Reed look for his lost animals. But in recalling the salt desert crossing three decades later, Billy Graves will remark that the haughty Reed was too good to drive his own wagons and instead gave orders from horseback.

It may be here, in the crucible of the Great Salt Lake Desert, that Graves's dislike for Reed is born. His prejudice against the man he sees as "an aristocrat" will grow stronger. It will continue for the rest of his life.

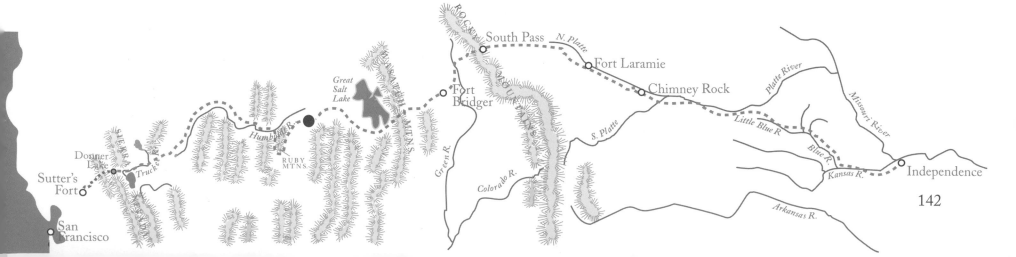

142

James Reed and William C. Graves went back into the salt desert to retrieve wagons.
— Marilyn Newton photo

On the next day, or day following, while I was out hunting my cattle, two Indians came to the camp, and by signs gave the company to understand that there were so many head of cattle out, corroborating the number still missing; many of the people became tender-footed at the Indians coming into camp, thinking that they were spies. Wanted to get clear of them as soon as possible. My wife requested that the Indians should be detained until my return, but unfortunately before returning they had left. The next morning, in company with young Mr. [W. C.] Graves, he kindly volunteering, I started in the direction the Indians had taken; after hunting this day and the following, remaining out during the night, we returned unsuccessful, not finding a trace of the cattle. I now gave up all hope of finding them and turned my attention to making arrangements for proceeding on my journey.
— James F. Reed, *Pacific Press* account

Another view of Donner Springs at the base of Pilot Peak.
— Marilyn Newton photo

As I can remember it took us about 40 days to get to Salt Lake. Here, at the crossing of the river Jordan, we struck the other road and had no trouble till we got to the Salt Lake desert, on the southwest side of the lake, which is about seventy-five miles without water. Reed, being an aristocratic fellow, was above working, so he had hired hands to drive his teams and he gave orders, although no one much paid attention to him; but his wife was a lady and the company humored him a good deal on that account.
— William C. Graves, account in the
Russian River Flag, April 26, 1877

143

SEPTEMBER 8, 1846

Emigrants rest at Pilot Springs to prepare for trek across Nevada

The next morning they [the cattle] could not be found, and they never were, the Indians getting them, except one ox and one cow. Losing nine yoke of cattle here was the first of my sad misfortune[s]. I staid with my family and wagons the next day, expecting every hour the return of some of my young men with water, and the information of the arrival of the cattle at the water. Owing to the mistake of the teamsters in turning the cattle out so soon the other wagons had drove miles past mine and dropped their wagons along the road, as their cattle gave out, and some few of them reaching water with their wagons.

— James F. Reed, *Pacific Press* account

Sond 6 [September] Satrted for Reeds waggons lying in the Salt Plains 28 miles from Camp Cached 2 waggs and other effects

Mond 7 Cam in to Camp on the Night and the waggon Came in on Tuesdy morng

Tudy 8 Still fixing and resting cattle

Weds 9 Mr. Graves Mr. Pike & Mr. Brin [Breen] loaned 2 Yoke of Cattle to J F Reed with one Yoke he [hired?] to bring his family waggon along

— James F. Reed, journal

The Donner Party rests at the base of Pilot Peak at springs that will someday be named for them.

Two of James F. Reed's wagons are abandoned on the flats and nearly all of his cattle are missing in the desert. Goshute Indians have come to camp and made signs about the lost oxen, but the pioneers are unable to locate Reed's eighteen animals or twenty more belonging to other members of the party.

George Donner and Lewis Keseberg also have abandoned a wagon each, but Reed has taken the worst beating.

The other families — the Breens, Dolans, Graveses, Wolfingers, the Murphys clan, and the Eddys — still have their wagons. The Breens have gotten through unscathed. Edward Breen, still nursing his broken leg, is safe from gangrene and his bone is healing nicely. Soon, he'll be walking again.

Everyone wants to press on. The entire party has lost days in the fruitless search for lost oxen. A clock is ticking against them and they know it. They still have to cross the sagebrush desert of what will become Nevada and are hundreds of miles behind the next nearest wagon taking the Hastings Cutoff.

Summer is waning. Snow is crowning nearby peaks. Provisions are low. They worry they won't have the food or the time needed to cross the Sierra Nevada before winter.

Something must be done.

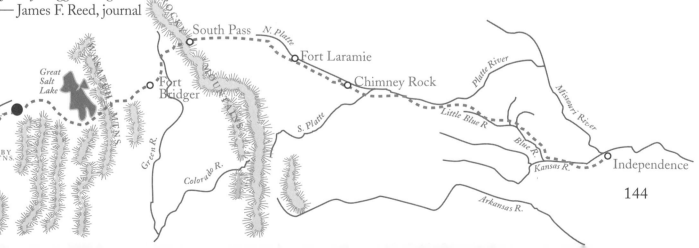

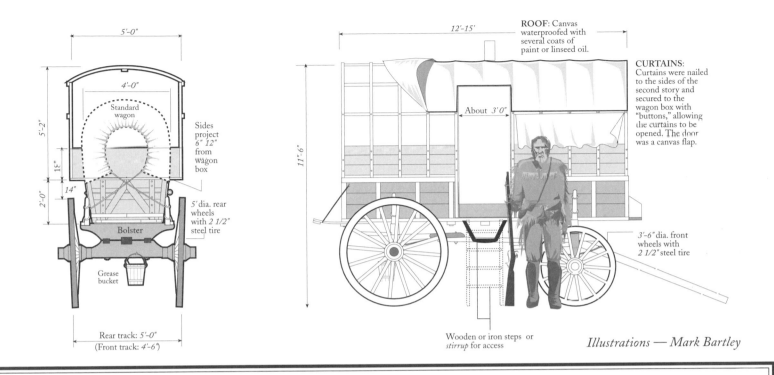

5'-0"

4'-0"

5'-2"

Standard wagon

13"

14"

2'-0"

Bolster

Grease bucket

Sides project 6"-12" from wagon box

5' dia. rear wheels with 2 1/2" steel tire

Rear track: 5'-0"
(Front track: 4'-6")

12'-15'

ROOF: Canvas waterproofed with several coats of paint or linseed oil.

CURTAINS: Curtains were nailed to the sides of the second story and secured to the wagon box with "buttons," allowing the curtains to be opened. The door was a canvas flap.

About 3'-0"

11'-6"

3'-6" dia. front wheels with 2 1/2" steel tire

Wooden or iron steps or *stirrup* for access

Illustrations — Mark Bartley

FATE OF THE PIONEER PALACE CAR • WAGON "FOUND" A FEW TIMES

Several people have claimed to find parts of the Reed family wagon and other Donner Party wagons on the Great Salt Lake Desert in Utah, but their evidence never has been verified.

In a Spring 1994 article in *Crossroads*, the newsletter of the Utah Crossroads Chapter of the Oregon-California Trails Association, author Robert K. Hoshide laments the tradition of attributing "every ox yoke and wagon wheel found on the salt flats to the Donner-Reed party."

A 1990 book, *Excavation of the Donner-Reed Wagons: Historic Archaeology Along the Hastings Cutoff* by Bruce R. Hawkins and David B. Madsen, documented excavations in the Salt Desert that began in 1986. The authors concluded that Reed dragged the Palace Car off the desert.

Others have found wagon parts and artifacts, including oversized wagon tires, in the area.

Pottery from salt desert wagon sites were compared with shards found at the Donner Party camps excavated by teams under the direction of Professor Donald Hardesty of the University of Nevada, Reno.

The samples didn't match.

So many wagons were abandoned in the desert that it's not possible to associate any find with the Donner Party in the absence of positive proof.

Even survivors' accounts of where the Palace wagon was abandoned differ. Virginia Reed wrote the rig was left "standing like a monument" on the Great Salt Lake Desert. Her stepfather, James F. Reed, maintained "the family wagon" was retrieved. If that's true, the Palace Car was the wagon later abandoned along the Humboldt River in Nevada.

The fate of the famous custom carriage remains uncertain.

"Each point that can be made in favor of one version can be countered by another," Kristin Johnson said. "Unless the bits and pieces brought out of the desert are examined and proven to be the Palace Car, or the remains of a large wagon with a side entrance are miraculously discovered in central Nevada, the end of the Reed family wagon will be the subject of dispute."

September 11, 1846

Two men leave Donner Party, ride to Sutter's for help

After leaving Donner Springs, the emigrants made their way across Silver Zone Pass enroute to Big Springs.
— Marilyn Newton photo

Charles T. Stanton and William McCutchen, who volunteered to go for supplies, are riding ahead to California.

They left the party yesterday, after a snowstorm blanketed the hills around Pilot Peak, near what will become the Nevada-Utah border. The emigrants took inventory of their provisions and confirmed what they already knew: They don't have enough food to reach the Sierra Nevada.

Stanton, 35, a bachelor, was among the three men who rode ahead to find Lansford Hastings in Utah in August. He's been traveling with Jacob Donner's family. A native of Onondaga County, New York, he decided to come West after his mercantile business failed in Chicago.

Missourian William McCutchen, 30, is without a wagon. He and his wife, Amanda, 25, and daughter, Harriet, 1, joined the party at Fort Bridger. It is no accident that one of the men who went on ahead has left his family behind with the wagon train. A bachelor like Stanton might be tempted to stay at Sutter's, but McCutchen is sure to hurry back from the fort.

Today, the Donner Party makes its way to another spring, later to be known as Johnson's Ranch and Big Springs. They arrive after a dry drive of about twenty-three miles. More exhausted oxen die. Nearby, James F. Reed and others bury whatever non-essential possessions they have to lighten loads. Books and clothing are left in a wagon bed, which is covered with dirt. Their hopes now ride with letters, asking for provisions, carried by Stanton and McCutchen.

They are facing hundreds of miles of Nevada desert where, as Horace Greeley will remark, "famine sits enthroned."

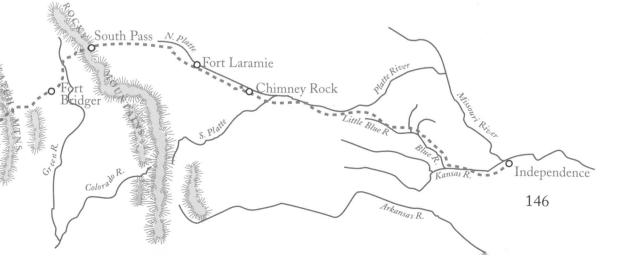

This short stretch of playa was the last the Donner Party would see of the dreaded salt desert after leaving Donner Springs to enter what would become Nevada. — Marilyn Newton photo

After leaving Donner Springs and crossing Silver Zone Pass, the Donner Party would camp here at Big Springs. — Marilyn Newton photo

Thu 10 left Camp and proceeded up the lake bed
* Frid 11 left the Onfortunate lake and mad[e] in the night and day about 23 [miles] Encamped in a Vally wher the is fine grass & water.*

   — James F. Reed, journal

Broken plates, pottery, a metal pin holding a yoke to an oxbow, and wagon parts found in the Salt Desert are in the Donner-Reed Museum in Grantsville, Utah. — Marilyn Newton photos

147

September 13, 1846

Party at "Mad Woman Camp"; all the women are angry

Tonight, the Donner Party is encamped at Flowery Springs, where James F. Reed reports in his journal that all the women are angry.

All the women are "mad with anger," he writes. He doesn't say why, but it's possible the strain of the last few weeks has finally boiled over around the sagebrush-fed campfires.

Coincidentally, two members of the Bryant-Russell Party, who went ahead to Sutter's Fort on muleback, had a near-fatal altercation at this grassy oasis on August 7. Bryant reports the argument was over "a trivial matter," but the two men aimed cocked rifles at each other and would have fired if not for his intervention.

Flowery Springs is "an oasis of about 50 acres of green grass, reeds, and other herbage, surrounding a number of springs, some of cool fresh water, others of warm sulphur water," Bryant wrote at this spot. "These waters rise here and immediately sink into the sands."

An examination of the site by journalists 150 years later will reveal a possible reason why pioneers might have been a bit testy: The springs swarm with mosquitoes, gnats, and biting flies.

But no 1846 account available mentions insects. Bryant — who previously has noted biting insects at many springs along the trail — writes about wolves, ducks, jackrabbits, and antelope there, but not bugs.

The Donner Party has crossed mountains into a valley and have found more mountains, the Pequops, to the west.

They can see a wagon trace snaking up Jasper Pass. There's another long, hard pull ahead.

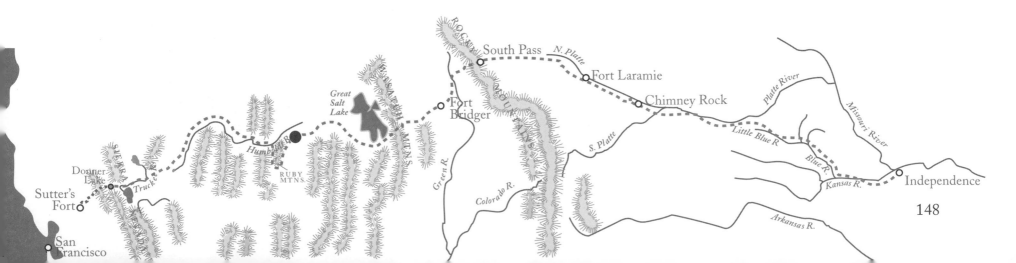

148

A disagreeable altercation took place between two members of our party about a very trivial matter in dispute, but threatening fatal consequences . . . . I rushed between the two parties and ordered them to hold up their pieces, and cease their causeless hostility towards each other . . . . It was truly a startling spectacle, to witness two men, in this remote desert, surrounded by innumerable dangers, to guard against which they were mutually dependent, so excited by their passions as to seek each other's destruction.

— Edwin Bryant, Aug. 7, 1846, at Flowery Springs, which James F. Reed would call Mad Woman Camp

They found an old stage coach up here on Jasper Pass that had been pushed off to the side of the road and forgotten for seventy years. The pass is steep; lots of shale and lots of dust. The OCTA [Oregon-California Trail Association] folks told me to watch out for snakes up here, but I didn't see any.

— Bill Pugsley, Donner Party reenactor

(Top) From Big Springs, the emigrants made their way along the trail toward Flowery Springs, their next camp. — Marilyn Newton photo

(Bottom) Boards form some sort of monument atop one of the springs at Flowery Springs. Several springs can be found here and the Donner Party camped here enroute to the Ruby Mountains. — Marilyn Newton photo

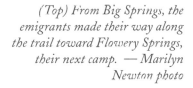

September 15, 1846

Party crosses Jasper Pass, faces more mountains

Leaving Flowery Springs, the Donner Party headed for Jasper Pass. From the summit in the background, the Donner Party could look back and see both of their previous camps. The trail has been used by wagons and cars over the years and is still plainly visible.
— Marilyn Newton photo

Today the party leaves camp at Mound Springs, which they reached yesterday after making about fourteen miles over the Pequop Mountains via Jasper Pass.

From the top of that pass, the emigrants can see two of their former campsites behind them and another desert valley, crossed by earthquake faults, in front of them. Beyond that valley is another mountain range, with another valley of dancing sandstorms, more faults, and the imposing Ruby Mountains farther west.

This is the texture of what will become Nevada: a rhythm of basin and range, basin and range, stretching from the salt desert to the Sierra. Each basin is a desert; each range is a wall.

They can't see any sign of wagons in the distance ahead.

At Fort Bridger, they were told the Hastings Route offered level roads. They were told there would be grass and water and that Sutter's Fort was only seven weeks away. They were told there would be little dust.

Thus far, in six weeks, they have not even reached the Ruby Mountains. In six weeks, they have lived in alkali dust and fought their way over rugged terrain.

The wagons in advance of them have already joined — or are just about to join — the old California Trail at the Humboldt River.

The Donner Party is alone on the "shortcut." There is nothing to do but put one foot in front of the other and hope the oxen hold out.

Tomorrow they'll travel from Mound Springs across the Spruce Mountain range to what will become Clover Valley.

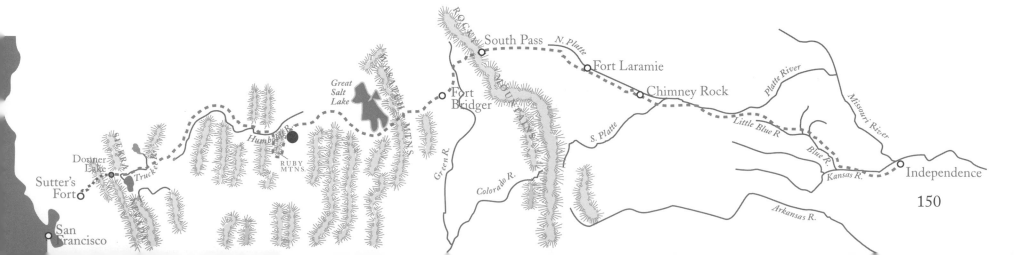

150

The Donners came out of Jasper Pass and it's a straight shot to Mound Springs. You can still see the wagon ruts there. They complained about the dust and I don't blame them. Rolling hills, soft sand, and alkali dust. Jump on the mounds and you are standing on Jell-O; the mounds go up and down.
— Bill Pugsley, Donner Party reenactor

Mond 14 left the Bason Camp or Mad Woman Camp . . . to the Two mound springs — 14 [miles]
Tus 15 left the 2 mound Spings and Crossed the Mountain as usual and Camped in the West Side of a Valley and Made this day about 14 [miles]
— James F. Reed, journal

The bleached bones of a cow lie near Mound Springs, the dark mounds in the upper center of the photo.
— Marilyn Newton photo

September 18, 1846

Caravan reaches Ruby Valley, goes south around mountains

The Hastings Cutoff has led to the Ruby Mountains — a barrier that stretches south as far as the emigrants can see.

They have been living in dust clouds since leaving the camp at Pilot Springs. Today they'll rest with water and grass nearby. They want to go west, but they've been walking south with the mountains on their right without knowing where they will get through. James F. Reed calls this basin Mineral Valley; it will be named Ruby Valley by the Mormons. It is a place of grassy oases around hot springs, antelope, mountain sheep and Shoshone Indians.

Two days ago the party made their way south from Clover Valley and aimed for an ancient cottonwood that will still stand 150 years later. This place will be known as Thompson Creek. Here, Reed writes, George Donner loses two horses, a little gray and a cream-colored mare named Margret. Presumably, the Western Shoshones have helped themselves to the animals.

Tonight they remain father south at "50 Springs," where water — hot and cold, acid and pure — flows from the ground. There is water, grass and game. But how far is Sutter's Fort?

They are fragmenting. Each segment travels beneath its own dust cloud. Germans stay with Germans. Irish stay with Irish. The rich among them — the two Donner families and the Reeds — keep to themselves. The tedium and the worries about time wear on their tempers. They should be back on the main trail by now. They want to go west again.

They follow the wagon tracks of the advance parties. When will the mountains let them pass?

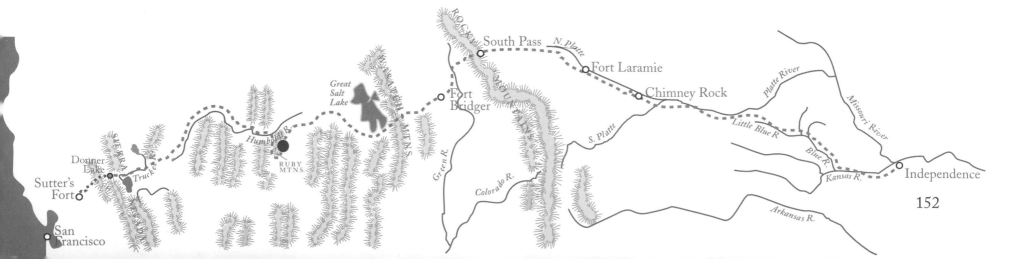

152

Wed 16 left Camp Early this morning Crossed flat Mounten of Hills and encamped on the east side of a Ruged Mountain plenty of grass & water here 18 (miles) here Geo Donner lost a little gray & his Cream Col mare Maggret.

Thu 17 made this day South in the Mineral Vally about 16

Frid 18 this day lay in camp

— James F. Reed, journal

(Upper left) Warm Springs at dawn. After crossing the last low summit, this was the last spring before they reached the formidable Ruby Mountains. — Marilyn Newton photo

(Above left) The Ruby Valley similar to the way the Donner Party saw it. (Above) Following the Rubies east, the Donner Party camped here at Thompson Creek. (Below left) The Donner Party camped near here where a number of springs dot the landscape, some visible on side of this hill. The area would become known as 50 Springs.
— Marilyn Newton photos

September 20, 1846

Donners in Ruby Valley, making slow progress south

Water gushes from Cave Creek toward the Ruby Marshes just as it did 150 years ago. The water from melted snow comes from a cave which extends about 300 feet into a mountain. — Marilyn Newton photo

Today, the wagon train made ten miles up Ruby Valley and reached forty-two springs of fresh water.

Historians will mark this site on what will become the Davis Ranch.

"Sat 19 this day [made] in Mineral Valley 16 [miles] and encamped at a large Spring Breaking out of from the and part of large Rock Stream lage enough to turn one pr Stone . . ." James F. Reed writes in his journal. This spot will be identified as Cave Creek. Reed's nearly incoherent notations in his diary are perhaps another indication of the stress facing the party.

"Son 20," he writes today, "this day made 10 [miles] up the Mineral Vally passed last evening and this day 42 beautiful springs of fresh water."

In the margin of today's journal entry, Reed adds up his estimated mileages and figures the party is 384 miles from Fort Bridger. His arithmetic is another confirmation of what he now sees as Lansford Hastings' lies.

The Donner Party is no longer a cohesive company. The families travel at their own speeds and regroup at each evening's camp. The anvil of the Great Salt Lake Desert has fractured them. The long, hard drives and the uncertainty of the Hastings Cutoff hasn't allowed them the luxury of becoming a company. Almost since the day they formed their group they have been under the pressure of the elements and the unknown trail.

This is their last camp in Ruby Valley. Tomorrow, the mountains will open to the west.

Heinrich Lienhard — Marta Lienhard Vincent

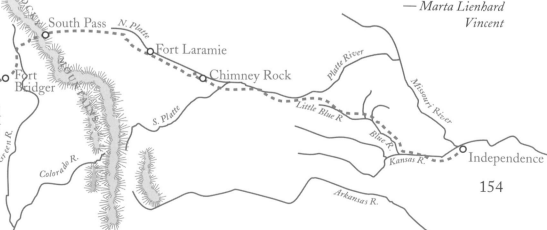

Shoshone Indians — Nevada Historical Society

Unlike the salt desert where the Donner Party traveled more than 80 miles before reaching water, the Ruby Valley offered many springs. —Marilyn Newton photo

The Indians here were not so shy as those in the vicinity of our previous encampment. Some 30 Shoshannees made their appearance at our camping place . . . The two eldest Indians were fat old fellows, one of whom had hair perfectly red, the only red-haired Indian I have seen. His hair, by the way, was coarse, but in his whole bearing and figure he was like the rest of his companions. A sour, doltish Englishman was smoking his clay pipe. The Indians gave him to understand by means of signs that they would find it most agreeable to be permitted a few puffs also. The Englishman, however, reflected their pleas, answering that these filthy Indians should not smoke from his pipe. Although the Indians did not understand his words, they recognized his forbidding mien as unfriendly to them, and we could immediately perceive an unpleasant expression on their dark faces.

The unfriendly behavior of the Englishman, however, was also disapproved by his fellow travelers; we regarded his action as rude, and under the circumstances, very unwise . . . An elderly American woman, the mother of five grown children, who like her husband were members of the company encamped near us, sought to allay the angry feelings of the Indians. Quickly filling her own pipe with tobacco, she lighted it and handed it to one of the fat old Indians. He accepted it with every sign of the greatest satisfaction, took 10 or 12 large puffs, letting the smoke escape through his nose with obvious pleasure, and then gave it to his equally fat companion at his side. He, after having gratified himself similarly, handed it on to the next, and so it was repeated, without exception, until the last had had his turn . . . though earlier they had favored the unkind, rude Englishman with malignant, vengeful looks, the countenances they turned upon the woman without exception were friendly and smiling. Had the American woman stayed on here, the red-haired chief could perhaps out of sheer gratitude have raised her up to be the 'Lady Chief.'

— Heinrich Lienhard, *The Diary of Heinrich Lienhard*

September 22, 1846

Party crosses Overland Pass, cuts north along Ruby Mountains

Yesterday, the wagons crossed west via Overland Pass and struck another beautiful valley of meandering streams. They reached Huntington Creek, making about fifteen miles all day. They camped on soggy soil near the creek with lots of grass and water for the cattle.

Today, they move north in Huntington Valley. In nine days, they have traveled only thirty miles west. It is frustrating to know they are only a little nearer to Sutter's Fort than they were last week. They walk north, with the Rubies on their right side, to get to the Humboldt River and the California Trail.

The wagon wheels turn slowly in the muddy ground along the creek banks. Today they made only ten miles. Tonight they encamp on land that will become the Sadler Ranch.

Each group goes at its own pace. Everyone understands the necessity of hurrying along.

Provisions are low but there is grass, water and game. More deserts are ahead and the nights are cold. They've already passed through snow.

They know that they are racing against time.

They know they are losing.

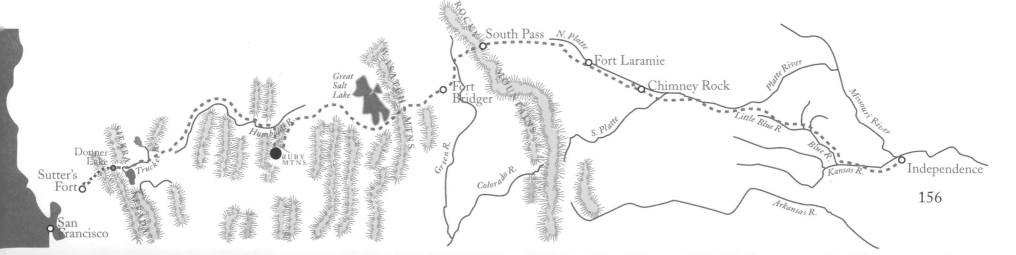

Finally, after completing their journey around the southern end of the Ruby Mountains, the emigrants began snaking their way north. — Marilyn Newton photo

Mond 21 [Sept.] Made 4 miles in Mineral Vally due south turned to the west 4 miles through a flatt in the mounton thence W N W. 7 miles in another vally and encamped on a Smal but handsome littl Branch or Creek making in all 15 miles

Tus 22 Made this day nearly due North in Sinking Creek Valy about 10 miles owing to water.

Wed 23 Made this day owing to water about Twelve 12 miles Still in Sinking Creek Valley

Thu 24 this day North west we mad[e]down Sinking Creek valley about 16 [miles] and encamped at the foot of Red earth hill good grass and water wood plenty in the Vallies Such as sage greace wood & ceder&C

— James F. Reed, journal

Overland Pass is a windy road through the trees. The trail is still visible in places. Lots of wild horses run here now. It's dusty, like everything else. By this time the Donners couldn't have had any clothes that weren't gray. The pass has a sampling of everything they've already been through to get this far. No water, steep cuts, bad road, dust, dust, dust. And then they get to the top of the pass and what do they see? The same damn thing that they've already been through. At that point they'd covered almost as many miles and more time than if they'd gone from Fort Bridger to take the Fort Hall route to the Humboldt River. At this pass, they had to be thinking: 'When are we going to see the Sierra?'

— Bill Pugsley, Donner Party reenactor

SEPTEMBER 25, 1846

Crossing Huntington Valley, party reaches canyon's mouth

For three days the company has crawled north "owing to water."

First there was not enough water and now there is too much. The soggy bottoms slow their progress and mud cakes the wagon wheels and the feet of the tired oxen. Today they follow what will be called Huntington Creek into a canyon. James F. Reed describes the defile as "a perfect snake trail." They travel for miles before the canyon — someday to be called South Fork Canyon — is wide enough to make a camp.

In his journal, Reed has ceased to mention the other families.

Resentments are simmering. Lewis Keseberg, on the trail with his wife and two small children, is nursing a grudge. Way back on the Platte River, it will be said, Keseberg was forced to travel behind the company, but no survivor will mention this.

Virginia Reed will say her father confronted Keseberg about his cruel treatment of his wife. She will say Keseberg was afraid to beat her again after Reed's warning, but that the German always held the incident against her father.

One 1878 account by a pioneer on the California Trail will say Keseberg and another man removed a buffalo robe from an Indian grave, potentially exposing the emigrants to the wrath of the Sioux.

"The company compelled him to take them back and wrap the body in the buffalo robes again and to put it up on the poles," pioneer Antonio B. Rabbeson will write. "It satisfied the Indians, however, when we made him do that."

The robe story might be a myth. Rabbeson will refer to the robe thief as "Boonhelm the Cannibal" of the Donner Party, but won't use Keseberg's name.

Members of the Graves family, including W. C. "Billy" Graves, also seem to resent Reed for the delays. Reed has a friend in John Snyder, the Graves's teamster. Snyder, about 25, is a good-natured fellow liked by just about everyone, but even Snyder is worn down by the trail.

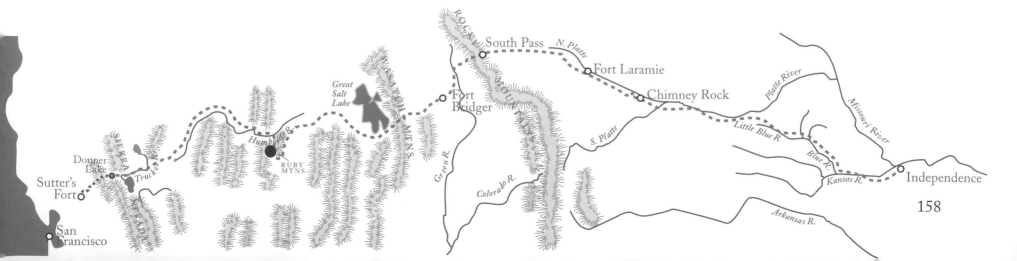

The emigrants traveled up this valley on their way to the south fork of the Humboldt River. In the distance is the west side of the Ruby Mountains. — Marilyn Newton photo

Frid 25 September This day we made about Sixteen miles 16 for Six miles a very rough Cannon a perfect Snake trail encamped in the Cannon about 2 miles from its mout

— James F. Reed, journal

The closer they got to the mouth of the canyon, the narrower it became.

Continuing northward, the party camped where Smith and Huntington Creeks met. — Marilyn Newton photo

159

September 27, 1846

Party reaches trail on Humboldt; shortcut is Hastings' "long tripp"

This special one-day postmark was issued by the Carlin, Nevada post office in commemoration of the sesquicentennial of the Donners' passing. More than five thousand were issued to collectors from as far away as Sweden and Japan.

Yesterday the emigrants came out of a twisting canyon and hit the Humboldt River — the California Trail at what will become Moleen, Nevada. The Hastings Cutoff was supposed to shave 300 miles off the trip to Sutter's Fort. Instead, the "shortcut" added 125 miles to the trek. Heinrich Lienhard, who reached this point on September 7, remarked that the cutoff should be renamed "Hastings' Long Tripp."

Lansford Hastings, after guiding advance parties to the river, has ridden ahead to assist in the liberation of California from the Mexicans. At Sutter's Fort an American flag already is flying. Hastings, as writer George Stewart will observe, failed as Moses and arrived too late to be Joshua.

Today, the Donners came through a short canyon (Susie Creek, below the future site of Carlin, Nevada) and camped. Tomorrow they will pass Carlin Spring.

Exactly 150 years later Carlin Postmaster Carolyn Rose and the Carlin Post Office will host a special event at Carlin Spring, commemorating the sesquicentennial of the Donners passing. A special one-day postmark will be issued, showing the California Trail through Nevada. More than 5,000 of these postmarks honoring the Donner Party will be ordered by history buffs and stamp collectors, with some orders coming from as far away as Sweden and Japan.

Bill Pugsley, the Donner reenactor, will speak to the crowd. Charles Greenhaw, the former dean of Great Basin College, will tell the crowd that the Donners' experience "enlarges and intensifies the experience of being alive ... It is saved from depravity by some genuine heroes and heroines." Paul Sawyer and Bob Pearce of Elko, Nevada, members of the Oregon-California Trails Association, will talk about the state's place in the history of the West.

"History is all around us here," Rose will say.

As the speakers talk about history, hardship, and the Donners passing by this place 150 years before, the mists of Carlin Spring will rise and waft above the yellow flowers of the sagebrush and rabbitbrush. The wind takes the mist north toward a highway — Interstate 80. Cars passing this place 150 years after the Donner Party will take seven hours to get to Sacramento.

Today in 1846, the Donner Party, with the same destination, face about six or seven weeks to go the same distance — if the weather holds.

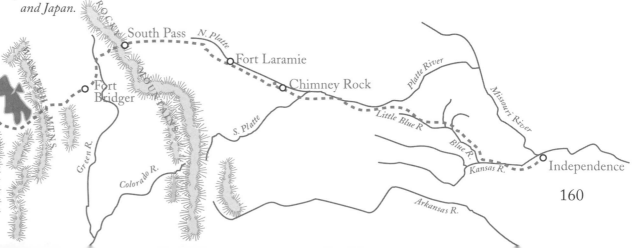

Sat 26 this day made 2 miles in the Cannon and traveled to the junction of Mary's River [the Humboldt] in all about 8 [miles]

Mary's River Son 27 Came through a Short Cannon and encamped above the first Creek [after the Cannon] on Mary's River

Mond 28 this day after leaving Camp about 4 miles J F Reed found Hot Springs one as hot as boiling water left the River Crossed over the Mounta[in] to the west Side of a Can, and encamp in Vally 12 [miles]

— James F. Reed, journal

By the 26th of September, the members of the Donner Party reached the mouth of the canyon the California Trail. The shortcut, instead of saving 300 miles, added more than 100. This view looks back the way they came. — Marilyn Newton photo

Hastings' "Long Tripp" is ended as the emigrants passed through the mouth of this canyon and reached the Humboldt River. — Marilyn Newton photo

September 29, 1846

Donner Party reaches Beowawe, near Gravelly Ford

Today the caravan, split into two groups, reaches what will become Beowawe, Nevada, near Gravelly Ford, where they cross to the south side of the Humboldt.

Yesterday they camped at what will be called Emigrant Springs, which pioneer T. H. Jefferson, traveling in advance of the Donners, noted on his 1846 map.

The company was joined by two Shoshone Indians, one of whom they called "Thursday" in imitation of Robinson Crusoe's "Friday" and because some of the party believed it was that day of the week when the Indian approached them. At last night's camp, a grass fire swept toward three of their wagons and would have consumed them had not the Indians helped beat out the flames. The Indians were fed and given blankets for sleeping.

When the pioneers awoke this morning the Shoshones were gone and so was a fine shirt and a pair of Franklin W. Graves's oxen.

The Donner families — led by George and Jacob — are ahead on the trail. The Reed, Graves, Murphy, Eddy, and Breen families follow.

Notes from other emigrants are posted, and now there is no question about the folly of the Hastings Cutoff. Parties that left Fort Bridger for Fort Hall passed this place so long ago that they already are over the Sierra's granite walls.

The first of the companies that followed the Hastings road in advance of the Donners are on the Truckee River, more than two hundred miles ahead.

Years later people will point out "Donner graves" at Gravelly Ford. They'll be wrong. The graves are of pioneers from other wagon trains.

Death is waiting a few days more up the trail.

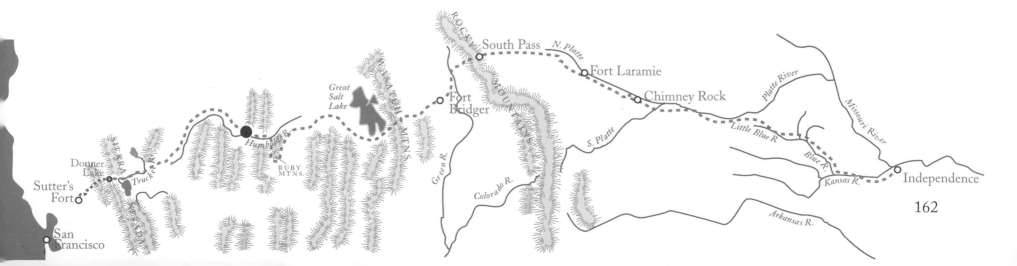

*Tus 29 This day 11 O.Clock left camp and went
about 8 mils to the river again 2 grave had two
oxen taken by 2 Indians that Cam with us all day*
*Wed 30 left Camp about 10 oclock and made
this day 12 miles down the River*
— James F. Reed, journal

*The pioneer trail winds its way toward present day
Beowawe, Nevada.*
— Marilyn Newton photo

October 2, 1846

Donner Party moves up river past present-day Battle Mountain

The party has made about forty miles west on the Humboldt in three days.

The river is alive with sage hens and sandhill cranes. Small birds of all descriptions dart in and out of the willows and reeds. Antelope can sometimes be seen leaping in the sagebrush in the distance.

The party members keep their eyes alert in this country, but not for wildlife. Franklin Graves, who already has lost two horses and two oxen to the Indians, lost another mare yesterday when the party came out from between the Shoshone Mesa and Shoshone Range into the wide plain below what will be called Argenta.

Tonight, the emigrant train is encamped on the north bank of the river midway between the future site of Battle Mountain, Nevada, and a place that will be called Stonehouse.

During the emigrants' time in Shoshone country, the Indians took just a few animals. That will change when the Donner Party continues into Paiute territory. They post guards on the horses and cattle. Weak as they are, alone as they are, they know they will make easy pickings for Indians looking for a quick meal of beef.

The other wagon trains are far ahead. The first of the parties that followed Hastings are on the west side of the Sierra this very day.

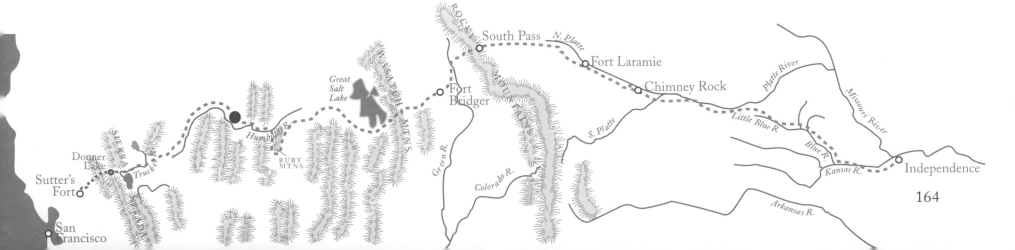

A view such as this would have been seen by the Donner Party as they passed this way in the Battle Mountain area. — Marilyn Newton photo

Oct Thur 1 left Camp about 10 oclock and made this day 12 Miles down the River encampe on a Rich bottom this night M. Graves lost a fine mare by the Indians

Frid 2 Still down the River Made to day 12 miles

— James F. Reed, journal

From Carlin, we followed wagon ruts up the spine of the hill. It's where they drove. The Oregon-California Trails Association marked this trail for their convention in Elko, Nevada. Then we went down into Emigration Pass in the vicinity of Primo, where there's three or four springs. Then we turned southwest into the canyon, back to the river where the graves are.

That was my third encounter with rattle-snakes, but nobody got bit.

When we reached Battle Mountain, I was a guest of the Te-Moak Band of the Western Shoshone. It was the second night I'd stayed on their reservation land — the first was in Ruby Valley. They just saw me walking and invited me to stay. They were real friendly folks and happy to help out. They told me when the first emigrants came, their ancestors thought the English word for mule was 'godamnits.'

— Bill Pugsley, Donner Party reenactor

October 4, 1846

Reed ends his journal with one enigmatic word

"Still"

With that one-word entry, James F. Reed today ends his diary of the trek.

What interrupted him? Was he going to write "Still down the River" as he did two days before? We will never know. He will never write in the journal again.

Yesterday the wagons reached what will be known as Stonehouse after going ten miles down the Humboldt. Today, they travel more than ten miles and camp near the future site of Redhouse.

Tonight, a lunar eclipse occurs, but the moon doesn't rise early enough here for it to be seen by the emigrants. Observers elsewhere see the moon covered with a scarlet shroud.

The party sleeps on the banks of a river under a full moon. A sandy hill is ahead.

The Donners remain in the lead, about a day or a little more ahead, with the Reeds, Breens, and Graves behind. Tomorrow, the fractured company will be torn forever in a flash of steel.

For the first time in the emigration west, one pioneer will kill another in a place far from law and beyond the borders of the United States. Lynching will be proposed.

Decades later, witnesses will still disagree on the facts of the homicide.

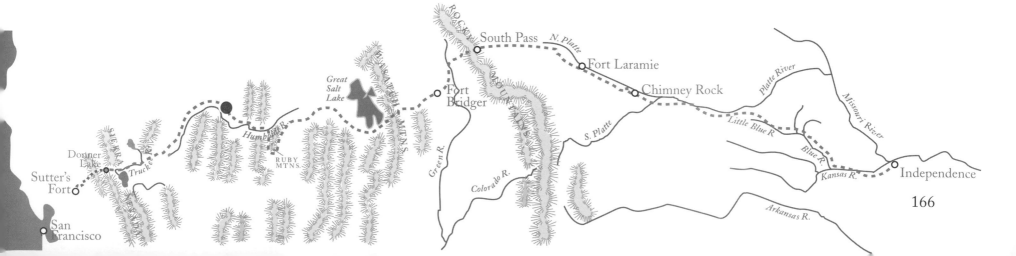

Sat 3 left Camp early mad a this day 10 miles
Son 4 Still
— James F. Reed , journal

The emigrants made their way along this valley to camp at a site that will be called Red House. — Marilyn Newton photo

October 6, 1846

Snyder killed in fight with Reed

My father [F.W. Graves] was in the lead, Jay Fosdick second, John [Snyder] third, and Reed fourth . . . Reed had gotten another team to double his wagon, and started to pass Snider's wagon, but the leaders did not want to pass, and tangled in with Snider's oxen. [Reed said to Snyder] "you have no business here in the way!" Snider said, "it's my place." Reed started toward him, and jumping over the wagon tongue, said "you are a damned liar and I'll cut your heart out!" Snider pulled his clothes open on his breast and said "cut away." Reed ran to him and stuck a large six-inch butcher's knife into his heart and cut off two ribs. Snider then turned the butt-end of his whip stock and struck at him three times, but missed him the third and hit Mrs. Reed, who had in the meantime got hold of her husband. Snider then started up the hill and went about 10 steps when he began to stagger . . . he died in five minutes.

— W. C. "Billy" Graves

John Snyder lies in a shallow grave where the wagons will roll today to remove the signs of the gravesite.

His killer, James F. Reed, is banished from the party.

The wagon train, which ceased being a company (if it ever was a company) after the hell of the Great Salt Lake Desert and the dusty roller coaster of the Hastings Cutoff, is now shattered beyond repair. From this point on, they will be like a defeated army, retreating before the wrath of their enemies. Their real leader, Reed, will be forced to ride for his life.

One hundred fifty years later, the circumstances of the Snyder killing will remain in dispute. A descendant of the Franklin Ward Graves clan, which employed Snyder as a teamster, will confront a descendant of Reed at a California Trail Days reunion in 1996. He'll say Reed was a coward who killed a man for the slightest of reasons. After fifteen decades, the anger will still burn. The facts will still be clouded. One thing is sure — it was a traffic altercation. Here is what most witnesses say happened:

Yesterday, October 5, 1846, the section of the Donner Party containing the Reed, Graves, and Breen families approached a sandy hill in the vicinity of what will be known as Iron Point near Golconda, Nevada. They had to doubleteam the wagons to get them over the obstacle.

After lunch, they got all the wagons up the hill except three: Reed's family wagon (the Pioneer Palace Car), William Pike's wagon, and one of the Graves family wagons driven by John Snyder. As the Reed wagon, driven by Milton Elliot, passed the Graves wagon, the two teams of oxen became entangled. Snyder argued with Elliot and whipped the oxen. Reed told Snyder to calm down. Snyder threatened to whip Reed and Reed drew his "butcher knife." Reed told Snyder they could settle things once they got the wagons up the hill.

Snyder, who was Reed's friend, turned the butt of his whip and smashed Reed over the head, drawing blood. Snyder struck out with his whip again, this time hitting Reed's wife, Margaret, who had run up to make peace. Snyder hit Reed twice more, then Reed lashed out with his blade, stabbing Snyder in the left chest over the heart. Snyder sank to the ground.

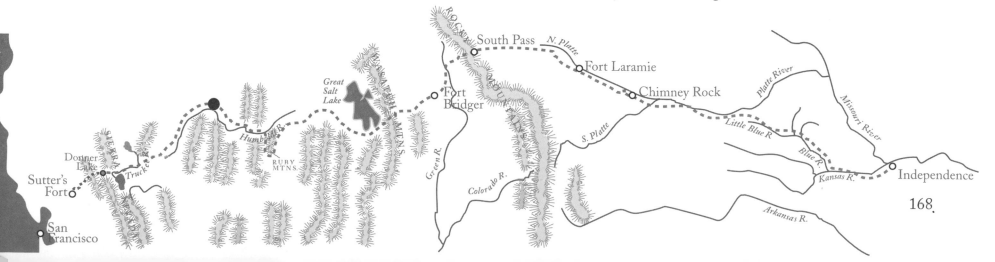

"Uncle Patrick, I am dead," Snyder said as Patrick Breen ran to his assistance. Snyder died in minutes.

Reed, blood streaming down his face, threw his knife away. He offered boards from his wagon for Snyder's coffin. The Graves family refused. The funeral was held as the Reed children helped dress their parents' wounds.

Lewis Keseberg, who long had held a grudge against Reed, put his wagon tongue in the air and suggested hanging Reed on the spot. The Graves family was screaming for justice, if not vengeance.

Reed, Elliot, and William Eddy were armed to the teeth and said they'd fight rather than abide by a death sentence. So it was decided that Reed be exiled — without horse, supplies, or rifle — to die in the desert. His daughter, Virginia, however, brought a mount, a gun, and food to her pa.

Eyewitness accounts will differ: Billy Graves will blame Reed for the altercation; John Breen will say Snyder never hit Mrs. Reed because "he was too much of a man for that." Many historians will reject Graves as biased and point out that even those who disliked Reed say that Mrs. Reed was hit during the struggle.

Today, Reed rides up the trail to overtake the Donners, who are two days in the lead. He'll tell them he's going for supplies. His employee, Walter Herron, traveling with the Donners, will volunteer to go with him.

Even decades later, Reed won't mention the killing. Self-defense or not, the fatal act of violence will haunt him until the end of his days.

As oxen struggled over this low, sandy rise now known as Snyder Hill, James Reed and John Snyder fought, resulting in Reed stabbing Snyder to death.
— Marilyn Newton photo

The team was stalled on a sand bank on the Humboldt River. It was Reed's team, Snyder was driving Greaves team next to Reed's behind, Reed was on the off side of his team assisting his man to get the team to pull Snyder came up on the nigh side also to assist. Soon there was an altercation between Reed and Snyder when Snyder called Reed some name and attempted to strike him across the tongue between the oxen and the wagon, Reed jumped across the tongue and stabbed him, Snyder died in a couple of hours. Mrs. Reed had nothing to do with the affair and if she had Snyder would not strike her for he would not strike a woman at all, he was too much a man for that. Snyder's loss was mourned by the whole company still Reed was not blamed by many.

— John Breen, Pioneer Memoirs

This stretch of low, sandy trail is where the Reed-Snyder fight occurred. — Marilyn Newton photo

OCTOBER 9, 1846

Reed family wagon abandoned; Old Hardcoop is left to die

Today the leaderless emigrants have reached the future site of Imlay, Nevada, where the new Applegate Cutoff to Oregon branches off from the California Trail.

J. Quinn Thornton took the Applegate "shortcut." The memory of the desolate desert drive will help form his opinions about Lansford Hastings.

Today, a party of emigrants is safe in Bear Valley after crossing the Sierra pass that will be named for the Donners and waking up to snow at the summit. The Donners are about a month behind them.

The party is still split in two groups, with the Donner and Murphy families a day or two in the lead and the Breens, Reeds, Graves, and others behind. Reed's heavy family wagon, probably the "Pioneer Palace Car," has been left behind. In 150 years, no one will be able to account for its fate. The wagon probably might not have been abandoned if James F. Reed were still with them, but he is exiled and has left a note on the trail warning of hostile Indians ahead.

The wagon and William Eddy's carpentry tools have been hidden in the desert soil. The Reeds now use one of the Graves wagons, driven by Reed employee Milt Elliot, about 28, who Virginia will say was like a big brother to her.

When Eddy and William Pike went out hunting two days ago, arrows flew at them from the sagebrush. None of the arrows found it's mark, but neither did the men find game.

Yesterday at camp, they noticed that Mr. Hardcoop, a Belgian in his sixties who had been traveling in Keseberg's wagon, was missing. Keseberg had thrown him out to walk, but the old man's feet had given out. Two boys driving cattle last saw him sitting at the side of the trail. His feet had swelled until they burst. Eddy and Elliot kept a fire going all night to guide Hardcoop, but he never arrived. This morning they and Mrs. Reed beg Keseberg, Breen, and Graves for a horse, but all refuse.

At noon today, they ask again for a horse, but their requests are angrily denied. Eddy, Elliot, and Pike offer to go back on foot, but the other men say they won't wait.

Old Hardcoop, they argue, is already dead.

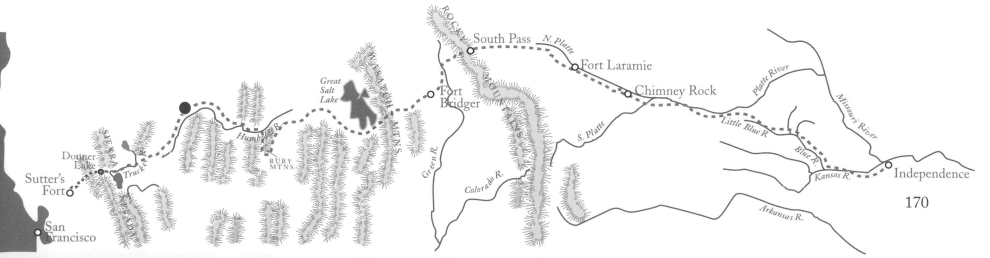

The wagon trail continues west in the Rose Creek area, west of present-day Winnemucca.
— *Marilyn Newton photo*

Virginia Reed, as an adult — Bancroft Library

My father was sent out into an unknown country without provisions or arms — even his horse was at first denied him . . . I had cried until I had hardly the strength to walk, but when we reached camp and I saw the distress of my mother, with the little ones clinging around her and no arm to lean upon, it seemed suddenly to make a woman of me. I realized I must be strong and help momma bear her sorrows.
— Virginia Reed, *Across the Plains In The Donner Party*

I would do all again that I did do in the company, except two things: First, leaving my family and wagons in the desert to hunt water to gratify the desire of a number of the company, when there was a plain road traveled by companies before us. Second: No inducement could persuade me to leave my family to the tender mercies of a company.
— James F. Reed, *Pacific Press* account

OCTOBER 11, 1846

Party passes present-day Lovelock; Paiutes steal horses, cattle

The Paiutes are depleting the company's livestock as the road gets harder and supplies dwindle.

Two days ago, the emigrants reached a bed of deep, loose sand at 4 p.m. and didn't make it across until 4 a.m. yesterday.

They halted at a place where a man named Sallee was buried, and they found the bones disinterred and gnawed by coyotes. Sallee, killed in a Paiute raid, had been buried, exhumed by Indians, and reburied by many of the 1846 emigrants. "Sallee's Grave" will become a notable landmark of the emigration of 1846.

As the Donner Party encamped on the Humboldt yesterday, the two groups again came together. They abandoned another wagon and all of Franklin Graves's horses were stolen by Indians.

Today, near the future site of Lovelock, Nevada, the Paiutes kill or seize eighteen head of cattle belonging to the Donner brothers and a German named Wolfinger. Graves loses another cow.

Tonight, they camp near bad grass and worse water. Patrick Breen's horse gets stuck in the mud and he asks William Eddy for help pulling him out. Eddy, reminding Breen of his refusal to lend a horse to retrieve the abandoned Hardcoop, won't lift a finger. The horse dies.

As they sleep, arrows whistle through the camp, but the night guard can't find a target.

The Paiutes have marked them as disorganized, ill-supplied stragglers. They will have no mercy on them.

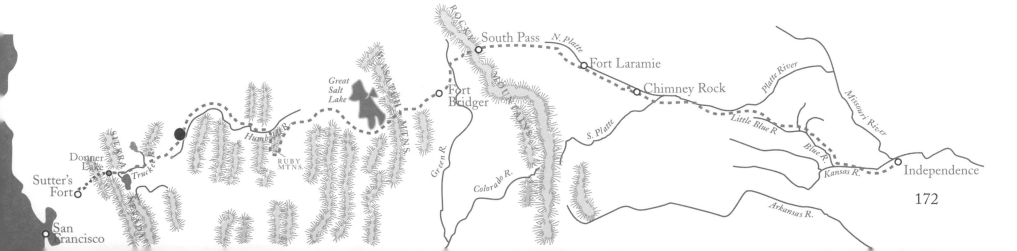

The Donner Party traveled across flat stretches of desert similar to this one as they neared present-day Lovelock. — Marilyn Newton photo

From Snyder Hill to Lovelock, it was hot and dusty as usual. I camped at Button Point near Winnemucca. I was on the south side of the river, the mighty Humboldt. The water was nasty, maybe because of the agriculture; it was brown and hardly flowing. I was to be resupplied in Winnemucca and was running real short on rations.
— Bill Pugsley, Donner Party reenactor

Our wagon was found to be too heavy, and was abandoned with everything we could spare, and the remaining things were packed in part of another wagon. We had two horses left from the wreck… they managed to carry my two little brothers.
— Virginia Reed Murphy, *Across the Plains In The Donner Party*

The trail winds through the desert as it leads from where Rye Patch reservoir stands now toward present-day Lovelock. — Marilyn Newton photo

October 13, 1846

Two more wagons abandoned as Donners reach Humboldt Sink

The Humboldt River has vanished into its sink.

Today the families begin their hike across the Fortymile Desert to reach the Truckee River.

Their bad luck is holding. Yesterday morning one of William Eddy's oxen gave out and was left on the trail.

At midnight, they camped at the Humboldt Sink and at dawn today they drove their cattle to grass and put them under guard. When the guard came into camp for breakfast, however, Paiute arrows killed twenty-one head, including nearly all of Eddy's and Jacob Wolfinger's teams. The two men must abandon their wagons and gear.

Eddy, 28, now down to what he can wear and some lump sugar and bullets in his pockets, begins walking. He carries his son, James, 3, while his ailing wife, Eleanor, 25, holds Margaret, 1.

Wolfinger, who is rumored to have a great deal of gold coin, wants to bury his wagon bed with his goods inside, but the others want no more delays. Two other Germans, Augustus Spitzer and Joseph Reinhardt, volunteer to stay behind and help. Wolfinger's wife, Doriss, 19, goes ahead with the others.

She will never again see her husband.

After leaving the water of Mary's River, now known as the Humboldt, the Donner Party traveled first along the Humboldt Sink , then traversed this northern portion of the Fortymile Desert before reaching the Truckee River.
— *Marilyn Newton photo*

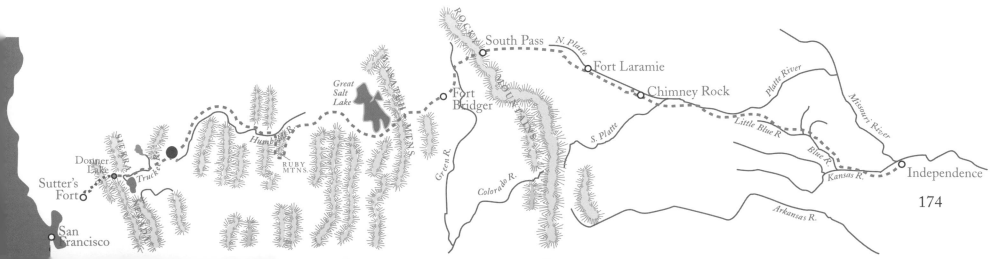

174

Wood slats, possibly from a wagon, lie abandoned on the Humboldt Sink. —Marilyn Newton photo

The guard came in to breakfast, and in their absence the Indians killed twenty-one head, including the whole of Mr. Eddy's team, except one ox; and the whole of Wolfinger's except one. Wolfinger wished to cache his goods at the sink, but the company refused to wait. Rianhard and Spitzer, who were traveling with him, remained behind to assist him.

— J. Quinn Thornton, *California in 1848*

October 16, 1846

Companions murder Wolfinger; Eddy denied water and food

The pioneers have reached the Truckee River but the Fortymile Desert turned resentment into hatred and greed into murder.

Jacob Wolfinger, the German who stayed behind to cache his wagon, is missing. Augustus Spitzer and Joseph Reinhardt, who had volunteered to stay behind to help him, return alone. They claim he was killed by Indians, but murder is suspected. The motive: Wolfinger's gold coins.

Two days ago, the party reached what will be called Brady's Hot Springs, where William Eddy asked Patrick Breen for food for his wife and two small children. Breen, who has a wife and seven children, says his water is spoken for. Eddy, gripping his rifle, says he will have the water or Breen's life. Eddy fills a bucket from the cask.

Yesterday, the party reached the future site of Wadsworth, Nevada, after losing three pairs of oxen to the Fortymile Desert.

Eddy asked Mrs. Breen and Mrs. Graves for food for his children. They refused. He took his gun and walked to the sounds of geese, returning with nine fat birds. He shared the bounty with the Graves, Breen, and Keseberg families. The children feast.

Today they begin their walk up the winding Truckee River. They're weak and malnourished and they do not know they are passing food the Paiutes have subsisted on for centuries — cattails, for example, are a rich source of protein.

In a few days, at a place that will become Tracy-Clark power plant, they'll finally see the Sierra Nevada. The range is crowned with dark clouds.

MR. EDDY AND FAMILY SETTING OUT.

An illustration from Camp of Death *by J. Quinn Thornton depicts the wagonless Eddys continuing their trek. — courtesy of the Emigrant Trails Museum*

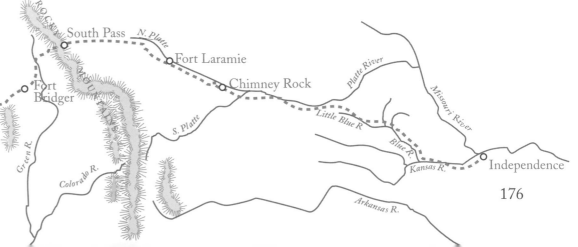

[Reinhardt and Spitzer] came up to the company at Truckee River, and said that the Indians came down from the hills upon them, and after killing Wolfinger, drove them from the wagons, which they burned, after taking the goods out. Wolfinger had a considerable amount of money.
— J. Quinn Thornton, *California in 1848*

After the desert I was just taking one day at a time. It was a relief to finally get to the Truckee River. For some reason I looked at the Truckee as downhill from there. Truckee River Canyon was like a hothouse. Lots of wildlife down here in September . . . The trail is every bit the killer today that it was a hundred years ago. It whupped me. It tests you mentally and physically. I've seen the elephant, as the pioneers used to say.
— Bill Pugsley, Donner Party reenactor

The emigrants stopped here at Boiling Springs on October 14, 1846. —Marilyn Newton photo

The Pass, about twenty miles east of present-day Wadsworth. —Marilyn Newton photo

A gold rush-era lettersheet depicts "seeing the elephant," slang for experiencing overland travel. — courtesy of the California Historical Society

OCTOBER 18, 1846

Party follows Truckee, crosses bends in river

The emigrants struggled up the Truckee River.
— Marilyn Newton photo

Today the emigrants advance upriver like wounded prey fleeing wolves.

Two groups are about a day apart. The remaining cattle are gaunt and stumbling over river rocks. Some have arrow wounds. Supplies are very low.

Two days ago, in a separate party, Samuel Young and his wagons arrived at the approach to the Sierra summit. Snow was falling "at a fearful rate," Young said, and one wagon was lost in an abyss. They were the last of all the 1846 emigrants except the Donners.

Today, Young's train descends the pass. The Donner Party is now alone on the California Trail east of the Sierra divide.

Can they even reach the mountains?

Where are William McCutchen and Charles Stanton, the two men sent ahead for supplies on September 10? Have they fallen to Indian arrows? Have they deserted after reaching Sutter's Fort?

Today at Sutter's, the bearlike McCutchen, with a wife and infant daughter left in the wagon train, is too ill to travel. Stanton has secured supplies, mules, and the services of two of John Sutter's Indian *vaqueros*. The cowboys are Catholic Miwoks named Luis and Salvador. They are on their way to resupply the emigrants.

The diminutive Stanton tells a fellow emigrant he will reach the Donners or die in the attempt. He is a bachelor without family or goods left on the trail and has no reason to return.

No reason but honor.

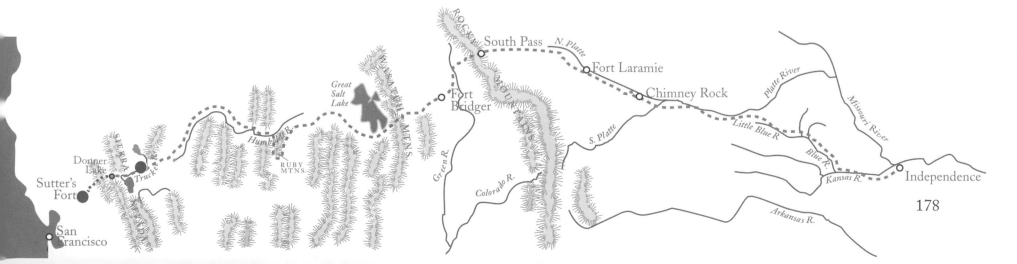

SARAH WINNEMUCCA REMEMBERS DONNERS

Sarah Winnemucca Hopkins was a teacher, Indian activist, and granddaughter of the great Paiute leader Captain Truckee, who was the first known Paiute leader to greet the white settlers.

She was only a toddler in 1846, yet she commented about the Donner Party and the emigrants of that year in her memoirs *Life Among the Piutes: Their Wrongs and Claims.*

Because she was so young at the time and must have gotten her tales from older tribal members, many historians dispute the accuracy of her stories about John C. Frémont, the Donners, and other historical characters and events.

The cannibalism motif adopted by Hopkins has the feel of being a product of hindsight. However, her tale of hiding out when emigrants came through has the ring of truth:

"There was a great excitement among my people on account of fearful news coming from different tribes, that the people whom they called their white brothers were killing everybody that came in their way, and all the Indian tribes had gone into the mountains to save their lives.

"So my father told all his people to go into the mountains and hunt and lay up food for the coming winter. Then we all went into the mountains. There was a fearful story they told us children. Our mothers told us that the whites were killing everybody and eating them. So we were all afraid of them. Every dust that we could see blowing in the valleys we would say it was the white people.

Sarah Winnemucca
Nevada Historical Soc.

"Oh, what a fright we all got one morning to hear some white people were coming. Everyone ran as best they could. My poor mother was left with my little sister and me. Oh, I never can forget it. My poor mother was carrying my little sister on her back, and trying to make me run; but I was so frightened I could not move my feet, and while my poor mother was trying to get me along my aunt overtook us, and she said to my mother: 'Let us bury our girls, or we shall all be killed and eaten up.'

"So they went to work and buried us, and told us if we heard any noise not to cry out, for if we did they would surely kill us and eat us. So our mothers buried me and my cousin, planted sage bushes over our faces to keep the sun from burning them, and there we were left all day."

OCTOBER 20, 1846

Wagons reach Truckee Meadows; party will reunite, rest

Tonight the lead wagons of the Donner Party reach the Truckee Meadows, the broad valley where Reno, Nevada, someday will stand.

Stragglers are still on the trail, making their way through twenty-two crossings of the river and struggling through Truckee Canyon.

More than a hundred years later, the Donner Trail will be marked from the sewer plant in Sparks, Nevada, east of Reno, to a camp near Rattlesnake Mountain, just south of town.

In the 1980s the Donner Springs development will rise on the site and bulldozers will bury the springs in rubble. A trail marker will be returned to a nearby park and a monument will be dedicated.

In 1996, Don Wiggins' research will indicate the 1846 wagon trains might not have gone that far south and instead camped along the river.

Wherever they are in the Truckee Meadows in 1846, the mountains look frightening. The Sierra are veiled in snow. The sky is the color of gun metal.

Here, there is grass, water, and game. They will rest, and why not?

In 1844, the Townsend-Stephens-Murphy Party, under Elisha Stephens, blazed the Sierra trail in late November. Last year, Hastings made it across the pass just before Christmas.

The road from Fort Bridger is littered with furniture, trunks of clothing, tools, crates of books, and buried wagon beds. Essentials and a few empty flour barrels are left.

In camp, William Pike and his brother-in-law, William Foster, volunteer to go to Sutter's Fort for supplies. Stanton and McCutchen, sent ahead on September 10, have not returned.

Today, near Johnson's Ranch in Bear Valley, California, Charles Stanton writes a note to Sutter about a lame mule. He pushes ahead to rejoin the Donners.

On the summit, snow swirls among the pines.

Elisha Stephens

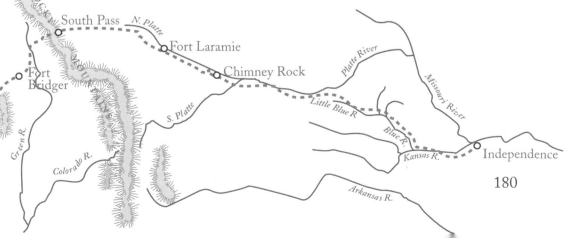

180

Tracks lead up a hill in the Lagomarsino Canyon area, which some historians say is the route the Donner Party followed before entering the Truckee Meadows. — Marilyn Newton photo

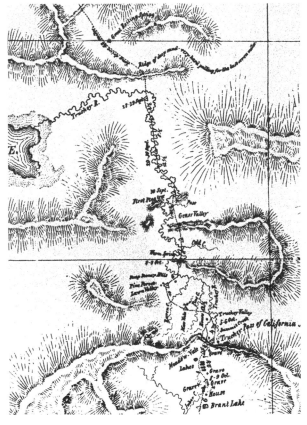

Old Jefferson map showing the Truckee River (then Truckey River) from the Sierra to its end at Pyramid Lake — University of Nevada, Reno Special Collections

Tamsen Donner, the teacher who planned to start a school in California had her 150-year-old dream come true in Reno with the dedication of Donner Springs Elementary School.

The school is located in Donner Springs in Reno, where the Donner Party may have encamped before going west into the mountains. Speakers at the dedication included Fred Horlacher, a retired Reno teacher and Donner historian, and Frank Mullen Jr., a *Reno Gazette-Journal* writer who spoke in costume as 1846 pioneer George McKinstry. Other speakers included students Britton Griffith and Wade McElroy, Principal June Gronert, architect Charles Grundy, Washoe Schools Superintendent Mary Nebgen and school board president Bob Bentley.

Ghost Trails Controversy

Those who walk with the specters of the Donner Party follow a road that vanishes in sagebrush and is swept away by machines.

But here and there are traces of ruts and road swells and artifacts in shallow sand.

For twenty years, Don Wiggins has traveled those ghost trails.

"At first I did the same thing everybody else did, find out where the trails were marked and explore them," said Wiggins, a retired electrical engineer.

After his move to Mogul, Nevada, he began trying to reconcile pioneer diaries with the marked routes.

"They didn't match," he said, so he set out to compare the written record with what he could see on the ground.

Among his theories: the Donner Trail marked in Sparks and east Reno may be the traces of emigrants of the 1850s and 1860s, not 1840s pioneers like the Donners.

That's heresy to folks who helped mark that route and have taught its lore for decades.

The trail markers were laid out by Walt Mulcahy of Sparks, a well-respected Nevada history buff. Mulcahy was the god of the ghost trails, friends said, and it will take a lot of proof to change his gospel.

Mulcahy, Jim Anderson, Ed Harris

Don Wiggins

and the other members of the Trail Marking Committee smelled of sage and wore boots covered with alkali dust. Their goals: Identify and protect the last traces of the pioneers.

According to Mulcahy's findings, the Donner Party and other 1846 emigrants followed the Truckee River to the area now occupied by the sewer treatment plant in Sparks. He identified nearby ruins as the remains of Jamison's Station, the first settlement in the Truckee Meadows.

The emigrants then went south, he said, along the east edge of steep-sided Steamboat Creek, through what is now Hidden Valley and camped at Rattlesnake Mountain.

Why go that far south away from the river?

"They had to avoid a swamp," said Fred Horlacher, a retired history teacher and instructor at Truckee Meadows Community College. Horlacher walked trails with Mulcahy in the 1970s.

The swampland is outlined on Mulcahy's map of the trail in the Truckee Meadows.

Mulcahy and others found old campsites and artifacts around Rattlesnake Mountain, at what is now Donner Springs. To the east are wagon ruts. Trail markers now stand on this path and a memorial at Donner Springs identifies the Donners' camp.

It was at Rattlesnake Springs that the Donners lingered too long and later became entrapped in the Sierra snow, the monument at the site reads.

"Walt was the most knowledgeable person on trails who ever lived," said John Clark, a friend of Mulcahy who is now the principal at Echo Loder Elementary School. Clark and other trail buffs helped convince the Reno City Council to designate a park at Donner Springs.

"Walt did his research well. He was positive the trail was there."

Wiggins agrees a trail did go as far as Donner Springs and that the area was used as a campsite — but in the 1850s and 1860s, not in 1846.

Like many trail buffs, Wiggins sometimes slips into the present tense while describing past events and people long dead.

"They're down there in that ravine," he said while riding through the hills of Storey County east of Reno. "Then they're over yonder following that ridgetop."

For people like Wiggins and Mulcahy, the wagons still roll in imagination and the past is as alive as the juniper trees.

Wiggins theorizes the Donners and

other 1846 emigrants left the Truckee at what is now Lockwood and followed Long Valley Creek, described by one emigrant as "an insignificant stream." The wagon trains then cut west through Storey County, he said, arriving at the top of a steep hill.

He cites a passage in the diary of Heinrich Lienhard, who traveled the road about a month ahead of the Donners. Lienhard writes about the small creek and the steep hill, which he describes as a "sleighride" for the wagons.

"Then they came through this canyon," Wiggins said, while walking through defile behind Hidden Valley. Along the route he describes are traces of pristine wagon trail, as yet untrammeled by bulldozers, graders or four-wheel-drive vehicles.

After emerging from Hidden Valley Canyon, he said, the Donners and others crossed Steamboat Creek, behind where Hidden Valley School is today, and went north to meet a southern bend of the river on what is now University of Nevada, Reno property.

What about the swamp?

An 1862 survey map of the Truckee Meadows shows the same sort of oval area marked as a marsh on Mulcahy's map. But this map and the accompanying surveyor's notes define the oval as a "meadow" and clearly shows "tule swamps" outside the boundary.

Some of those swamps are shown in the path of the trail.

"So it seems he had it 180 degrees wrong in this area," Wiggins said. "He has them going through swamp to avoid a swamp."

In addition, Wiggins said the first map of the California Trail — made in 1846 by T. H. Jefferson, who traveled weeks ahead of the Donners — also supports his theory.

One-hundred-fifty-year-old maps and diaries can be interpreted in different ways and the authors can't be cross-examined.

"One man's swamp is another man's meadow," said Horlacher.

Harold Curran of Reno, trails expert and author of *Fearful Crossing: The Central Overland Trail Through Nevada*, said he thinks the established trail through this area is "pretty well set."

"Why would they leave the river [at Lockwood]?" he asked. "There's no logic in it. I'd bet my last dollar on the way it's laid out now."

Clark said Mulcahy claimed to have found artifacts marked with George Donner's name near Rattlesnake Mountain, but those have never surfaced. Clark helped convince the Reno City Council to acquire a park at the site and helped get a monument placed there.

"The Donners came through so long ago," he said, while walking the small park containing several ancient cottonwoods and hemmed in by homes and Rattlesnake Mountain's slope.

"Who can say anything for sure?"

In Reno, Clark examined the last eighty yards of pristine pioneer trail in the Truckee Meadows, fenced off years ago, and wondered if the full truth about the Donners will ever be known.

Perhaps diaries or letters will surface or artifacts will be uncovered that will sway scholars one way or the other. He believes in Mulcahy's interpretation of the Reno-Sparks route, but is thrilled that Wiggins has identified more trail remains that may survive into the 21st century.

Such traces are a national treasure, he said.

Connie Stathes of Hidden Valley near Reno, a co-founder of the Nevada Historic Trails Association, agrees. She said it doesn't matter whether the Donners used a certain trail or not: "The pioneers came through here; their few remaining traces are the last legacy." In 1997, for example, plans called for a school on the site of the last remaining trail ruts and other proposals included a highway which would eradicate the last vestiges of the pioneers' route.

"The houses are coming this way," Clark said, while examining a bullet-scarred trail marker set next to those Hidden Valley ruts.

"Will there be anything left? So much of our past is already buried under concrete."

October 23, 1846

Pike accidentally killed; Breens ready to leave meadow

Pepperbox revolver, typical of the time.
— *Roy Vogel photo*

Today William Pike lies in a shallow grave near the Truckee Meadows camp of the reunited Donner Party.

Two days ago, Pike and his brother-in-law, William Foster, were preparing to go ahead to Sutter's Fort for supplies. Pike loaded his pepperbox pistol and handed it to Foster when he got up to get more wood for the morning campfire.

The pistol, a type known as being unreliable, fired, sending lead into Pike's back. "[Pike] lived only two hours," Eliza W. Farnham will write. "Death did not startle them now."

Back in Kansas, old Sarah Keyes was laid to rest with a funeral and a headstone. In Utah, Luke Halloran was buried in a coffin and honored with Masonic ceremonies. Along the Humboldt, John Snyder's body was wrapped in a shroud and put in the earth with a board beneath and a plank above.

Pike, Farnham will write, "was buried literally dust to dust, with nothing to separate his clay from that of the great parent." He was buried as snow fell on the meadow.

Today the Breens, always better prepared than the rest, ready their outfit for the assault on the summit.

After almost two thousand miles and more than five months, there's one more mountain to cross. It's about sixty miles to the other side and safety.

On that mountain, Charles Stanton and two Indians ride to resupply the emigrants. Their mules' hoofbeats are muffled by fresh snow.

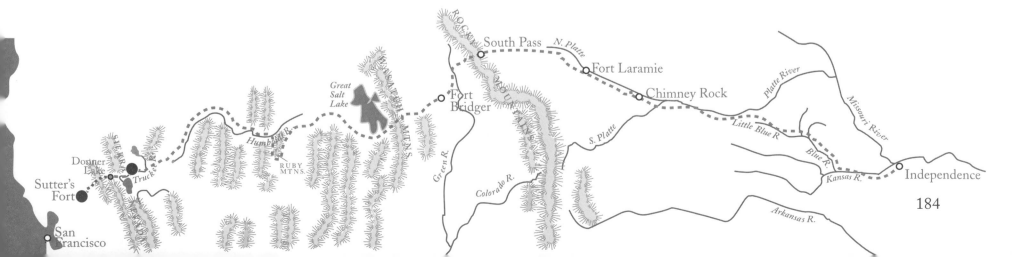

184

It was from here, some historians say, the emigrants took a hair raising ride down this canyon. The Truckee Meadows is in the distance.
— Marilyn Newton photo

At the last encampment on Truckee river, another life was lost, by the accidental discharge of a pistol. Two men, brothers-in-law [Foster and Pike], had been handling their arms by the camp fire in the morning. Wood to replenish it was called for, when one said to the other, 'Hold my pistol while I go for some.' In the transfer, by some means it went off, and the contents lodged in the body of the unfortunate man [Pike], who lived only two hours.
— Eliza Farnham, in her *Narrative of the Emigration of the Donner Party to California.*

One morning we were encamped near where Reno now is; two men, Wm. Foster and Wm. Pike, had agreed to get a head to Sutter's, get provisions and meet us as far back as possible. Foster was loading a pistol, which was accidentally discharged, shooting Pike in the back and killing him in about twenty minutes; so that is the end to their journey.
— Virginia Reed, *Across the Plains In The Donner Party*

October 25, 1846

Party follows river to Sierra; Stanton returns with supplies

An illustration of a Miwok Indian of the 1840s
— The Californians *Magazine*

The Breens are in the lead as the emigrants climb the Sierra, the western wall of the Great Basin.

They are the first to meet Charles Stanton and his two Miwok Indian helpers, Luis and Salvador. Stanton brings flour, jerked beef, sugar, and beans on seven mules borrowed from John Sutter. He also brings news that James F. Reed is alive and also will bring supplies from the fort.

With the Breens are Patrick Dolan, the Kesebergs, and the wagonless Eddys. Miles behind are the Reed, Graves, and Murphy families.

The Donners are the last to leave the meadow. Each group now acts independently.

The trail will take them along the river and through the future site of Verdi, Nevada. They'll leave the Truckee and go northwest through Dog Valley. At the second summit, the road cuts southwest through Hoke Valley, through what will become Stampede and Prosser reservoirs. It will rejoin the river at the future site of Truckee, California. Then they must pass a mountain lake and cross the summit.

North of Crystal Peak, an Indian shoots arrows into nineteen head of cattle. William Eddy, with a borrowed rifle, kills the man with one shot.

Today, Stanton continues east to bring relief to the emigrants in the rear.

For the Breen group, their bellies full, the promised land is days away. They ascend towards gray clouds as a gentle rain soaks the trail.

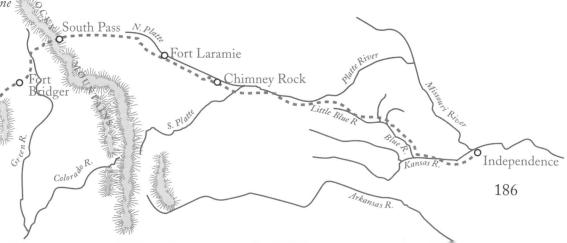

186

On Truckee river, the weather was already very cold, and the heavy clouds hanging over the mountains to the west were strong indications of an approaching winter. This of course alarmed several people, while others paid no attention to it. My family's family, among the former, used every effort to cross the mountains if possible before the snow should become too deep. We traveled up the river a few days, when we met the excellent Stanton, returning with five or six mules, packed with flour and meat. Capt. John A. Sutter had given him the mules and provisions, for the mere promise of compensation, an act for which he deserves the love of every soul of that suffering company. He will always be remembered by me, with gratitude and reverence, for that generous act.

— John Breen, personal letter

Wagon wheels west of Verdi — Nevada Historical Society

A wagon rut is still visible in the Dog Valley area. Reno is off in the distance.
— Marilyn Newton photo

OCTOBER 27, 1846

Breens cross Dog Valley; Donners break an axle

Wagon wheel remnants found along the trail in the Sierra.
— *Nevada Historical Society*

Amid ponderosa pines dusted with snow, the Donner Party climbs the last mountain.

Charles Stanton, 35, has reached all the emigrants with his supplies. He now travels with the destitute Reeds. Margaret Reed, 32, holding Tommy, 3, in her lap, mounts a mule. Virginia, 13, rides behind Stanton. Luis and Salvador hoist Patty, 8, and Jimmy, 5, on to their saddles.

The party's barking dogs follow the pioneers. Men and older boys and girls herd the surviving cattle.

The families of George, 62, and Jacob Donner, 56, are miles in the rear. While crossing a steep pitch, an axle breaks and a wagon overturns. Adults pull out Georgia, 4, and frantically search for Eliza, 3, who is nearly smothered by the jumble of quilts and clothing in the wagon box.

They will not abandon goods after coming this far. They fell a tree. As they shape an axle shaft, a chisel slips and blood pours from a gash in George's hand.

Tamsen Donner, 44, binds the wound in cloth strips. George jokes about the injury. He has more to worry about than a scratch.

More than they know.

Late tomorrow, in the Gulf of Alaska, clouds will whirl and a great storm will build its strength. It will move south, then punch eastward.

At Sutter's Fort for less than a week, James F. Reed is already trying to secure land for himself and his family. In a document dated October 29, 1847, Reed, Edwin Bryant, and the Reverend Jas. G. T. Dunleavy petition the magistrate of San Francisco for rights to the land on a "20 to 30 mile-long" island (Long Island) in the Sacramento River.

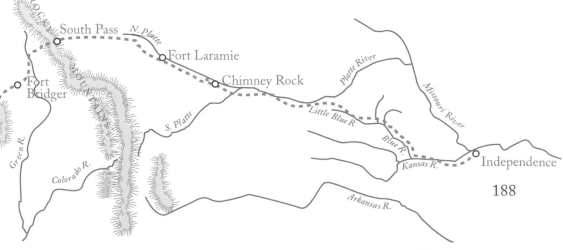

Some historians believe trees lined up like these indicate the trail where no trail can be seen today. This and other anomalies can be found in many places in the second summit area between Dog Valley and Hoke Valley where the Donner trail is believed to be. — Marilyn Newton photo

Our five Donner wagons were a day or more behind the train ... when an accident happened which nearly killed Eliza. Our mother and Frances were walking on ahead; Eliza and Georgia were asleep in the wagon, and father was walking beside it down a steep hill. It had almost reached the base of the incline when the axle to the fore wheels broke, and the wagon tipped over on the side, tumbling its contents upon the two children. Father and uncle, in great alarm, rushed to the rescue. Georgia was soon hauled out safely through the opening in the back of the wagon. Eliza was nowhere in sight, and father was sure she was smothering. Finally uncle came to Eliza's limp form, and just in time, she could not have lasted much longer.

— Elitha Donner, *The Expedition of the Donner Party* by Eliza Donner Houghton

Swales from where wagons passed 150 years ago on their way to crossing the Little Truckee River. — Marilyn Newton photo

189

October 30, 1846

Breen group nears lake as storm slams California

I took one day to walk from Reno through Dog Valley. That was the first time they were ahead of me on the day I walked it. It gave me a weird feeling. It was cold. It started to snow between Reno and Dog Valley. That's OK. It's easier to camp in the snow than the rain. It's quite a pull going up that hill.

It snowed all day the next day, big wet flakes. Then it cleared up and we camped in the snow the second night near Stampede Reservoir, which wasn't there in 1846.

— Bill Pugsley, Donner Party reenactor

Today the Breen group is just forty-eight hours away from safety.

The snow is an inch or more deep, and the Breens, Dolan, Eddys, and Kesebergs in the advance group are in the valley to the east of what will become Donner Lake. As they ascend toward the lake, grass becomes scarce and the men cut pine boughs to feed the cattle.

As they march, the high mountains to their right are wreathed in clouds. Every once in a while the clouds break and the pass reveals itself as an impossibly high wall of snow.

At Sutter's Fort, James F. Reed is preparing to depart with more provisions for the party which banished him for killing teamster John Snyder. The generous Sutter gives him supplies, mules, and Indian guides. William McCutchen, with a wife and infant daughter left with the party, has recovered from his illness and will go with Reed.

A great storm will soon hit the California coast. Its strength will not be spent on the coastal ranges. Dark clouds will bring rain to Sutter's as the front sweeps toward the Sierra, where rain will turn to snow.

The Breen group camps tonight as the middle group — Stanton, the Reeds, and others — struggle to catch up. The two Donner brothers and their families, delayed by the wagon accident, are far in the rear.

All pray the weather holds.

Tomorrow, the Breen wagons will reach just east of the lake. The Breens, Eddys, Kesebergs, and Dolan will sleep on snowy ground. The next day will dawn cold cold and clear. The party will pass a deserted cabin, built by pioneers in 1844, and roll along the north bank of the lake until they lose the trail in the drifts. They will retreat as night falls. The nine Breens will crowd into the cabin. The others will sleep in the wagons.

Mist will ring the moon, a prediction of rain which will melt the snow, someone will say. Near midnight, a downpour will soak the camp.

Panic will crouch just beyond the firelight; despair will sleep among them.

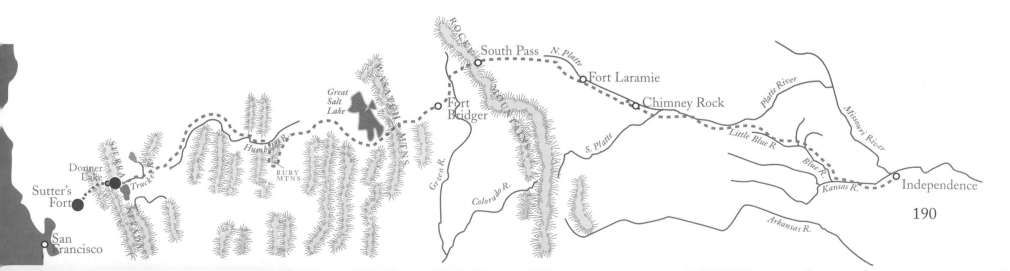

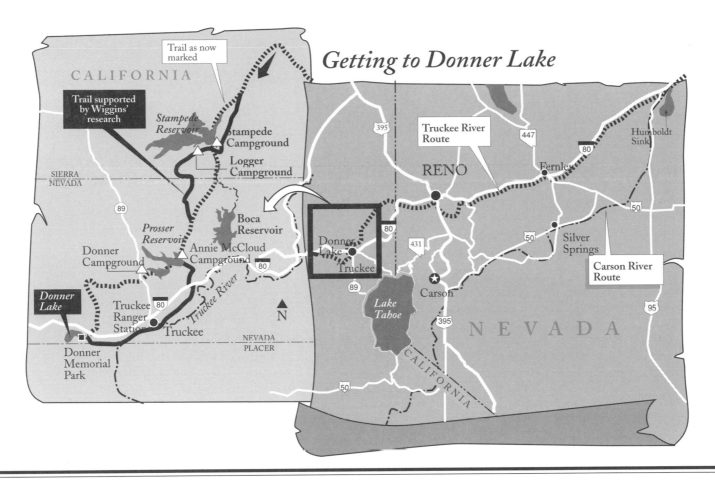

Getting to Donner Lake

SARAH WINNEMUCCA COMMENTS

Sarah Winnemucca Hopkins, the teacher, author, and Indian activist, told the following story about the Donner Party in her biography, *My Life Among the Piutes: Their Wrongs and Claims.*

Winnemucca's comments are repeated in several Donner-related books, but it is unlikely the Donner Party burned the Paiute's supplies on their way up the mountain. No wagon train survivor mentions anything like her story, although William Eddy admits to killing an Indian at about the site of Verdi, Nevada.

Winnemucca writes: "Well, while we were in the mountains hiding, the people that my grandfather called our white brothers came along to where our winter supplies were. They set everything we had left on fire. It was a fearful sight. It was all we had for the winter, and it was all burnt during that night. My father took some of his men during the night to try and save some of it, but they could not; it had burnt down before they got there.

"These were the last white men that came along that fall. My people talked fearfully that winter about those they called our white brothers. My people said they had something like awful thunder and lightning, and with that they killed everything that came in their way.

"This whole bank of white people perished in the mountains, for it was too late to cross them. We could have saved them, only my people were afraid of them. We never knew who they were, or where they came from. So, poor things, they must have suffered fearfully, for they all starved there. The snow was too deep.

"We shall no longer be a happy people, as we now are; we shall no longer go here and there as of old; we shall no longer build our big fires as a signal to our friends, for we shall always be afraid of being seen by those bad people.

"Surely they don't eat people?

"Yes, they do eat people, because they ate each other up in the mountains last winter."

November 3, 1846

Fresh snow thwarts attempt to cross Donner Pass

Up to the summit, Across the Plains with the Donner Party

Now they know what any mountain man could have told them: Rain in a Sierra valley means more snow at the pass.

Yesterday, they remained in camp in a downpour as Charles Stanton and the middle group reached the lake. The Donner families are in the rear — no one knows exactly how far. The emigrants hoped the rain would beat down the drifts, but this clear morning they see the snow ahead is deeper.

Panic springs on them. Some of the pioneers are in such despair they refuse to make further effort to cross the mountain wall, a few miles away.

The Breens and others yoke up their teams and travel west on the lake's north side. Oxen are weak from a diet of pine branches. At the lake, the snow is three feet deep.

They must abandon wagons, pack what goods they can on the animals and make a dash for safety. Decisions about what to take drag on: One wants a crate of tobacco; another argues for a bale of calico. The oxen are difficult to pack and become unruly beneath unfamiliar loads. Every adult must carry children. Lewis Keseberg, who has hurt his leg, rides a horse. One of the Indians coaxes his mule to break a trail, as Patty Reed, 9, clings to the animal's tail.

The party wallows in drifts for two or three miles. The lead mule is plunging into gullies and nearly drowning in snow. The party halts. Stanton and an Indian scout move ahead. Chest-deep in snow, the two men reach the summit. For a minute they gaze at safety, and then they turn back for the others. When they rejoin the party, the pioneers are camping beside a dead pine tree consumed in flames. Nothing Stanton says can move them.

"We'll cross in the morning," most answer. They stay as darkness creeps over the children and adults bundled beside the fire. A storm has passed, but another lurks behind.

Tonight, in the makeshift camp a few miles west of the lake and a mile or two short of deliverance, the vanguard of the Donner Party rests under blankets. Logs, rich in pitch, explode in the fire.

A blanket-wrapped Miwok Indian leans against a tree trunk. Stanton smokes his pipe.

It begins to snow.

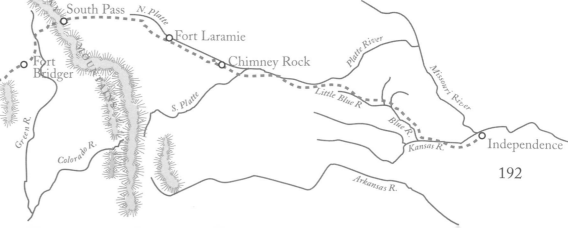

A storm moves over the Sierra near Donner Lake.
— Marilyn Newton photo

When it was seen that the wagons could not go through the snow, the goods and provision were packed on oxen and another start was made . . . men and women walking in the snow up to their waists, carrying their children in their arms and trying to drive their cattle . . . we camped within three miles of the summit. That night came the dreaded snow. We children slept soundly on our cold bed of snow . . . every few moments my mother would have to shake the shawl — our only covering — to keep us from being buried alive. In the morning the snow lay deep on mountain and valley. With heavy hearts we turned back.
— Virginia Reed, *Across The Plains In The Donner Party*

In the early days of November, the Donner Party members apparently have pinned their hopes on Milt Elliot, the Reed's teamster, to get over the mountains for help. The *Donner Miscellany*, a collection of documents saved by the Reed family, contains two notes written on the "River Trucky" and asking that supplies be given to the bearer, Millford Elliot.

A note dated November 1, 1846, is apparently signed by William M. Foster and asks that "four work mules" and three yoke of oxen be purchased or hired in California. Foster will be responsible for the cost once he arrives at the settlements.

Another note is dated November 2, 1846, and authorizes Elliot to buy six yoke of oxen and three steers, "for which I will pay the cash or Goods on my arrival in California." [Signed] Jacob Donner.

Donner Lake in snow
— Tim Dunn Photo

November 6, 1846

Pioneers make shelters as storms bury Sierra

The Donner party struggles to cross the Sierras.
— Emigrant Trails Museum

Two days ago the lead group of the Donner Party awoke surrounded by snow drifts ten feet deep.

All night, mothers brushed snow off children's blankets. The Miwok Indian who slept against the tree remained there all night, awakening periodically to shake snow off his shoulders.

The next morning, the pass was a white wall. To go forward would have been suicide.

They retreated to the lake. Even going downhill they did not reach it until 4 p.m. The Breens again took possession of the deserted cabin. The others struggled to construct shelters.

It's been snowing for three days.

Lewis Keseberg builds a lean-to on the side of the Breen cabin. William Eddy, a carpenter, takes borrowed tools and builds another cabin. The Graves family, with the Reeds, Stanton and Mrs. McCutchen, build a shack.

The roofs of all the structures are covered in pine branches, wagon canvas, and hides.

About six miles farther east, the two Donner families have made camp in a sheltered nook at the junction of Prosser and Alder creeks. Two days ago, they tried to build cabins but there was no time. Instead, they used branches to reinforce tents.

On the other side of the Sierra, James F. Reed, William McCutchen, a mule, and their horses are floundering in drifts. They can't get through with supplies. They can't bring relief to their wives and children trapped on the mountain.

Tomorrow evening, the two fathers will turn their backs on the Sierra's western slope while the entrapped emigrants prepare for a long wait.

Tomorrow night, another storm will sweep eastward.

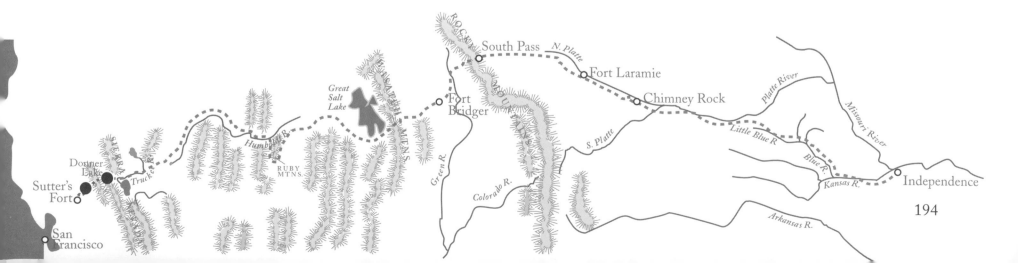

LOCATION OF THE MOUNTAIN CAMPS

There is no doubt about the general location of the lake camp itself, but since the 1930s questions have been raised about the site of the Donner camp on Alder Creek.

Don Wiggins, a member of the Oregon-California Trails Association, questions aspects of accepted Donner Party lore, including the locations of trail remains from Verdi to Donner Lake and the location of the Alder Creek campsite. The Donner family remained at Alder Creek, miles away from the other families, while the rest of the entrapped party stayed at camps around the lake. The U.S. Forest Service manages a campsite on Alder Creek identified as the original Donner camp.

Wiggins, however, suggests the real Donner family camp lies under the waters of Prosser Reservoir, about a mile from the site where archaeologists have been digging for the camp's remains. When Prosser Reservoir was flooded in the 1960s, articles in Reno newspapers said the waters would cover the site of the Donner camp. Old-time residents of the area recalled the foundations of cabins attributed to the 1846 emigrants.

"That controversy goes back to the 1930s," said Don Hardesty, an archaeologist at the University of Nevada, Reno.

He said the spot where his crew dug in the 1980s was identified by C. F. McGlashan, a Truckee newspaper editor and author of the first Donner Party history in the 1870s.

In the 1930s, Edwin Johnson and others argued for the Prosser site.

Hardesty's digs at Alder Creek have discovered some artifacts. Those pieces — including two coins and some ceramic tableware fragments — date the site to the 1840s.

He agreed there are many inconsistencies for the accepted site, such as its distance from the trail and the lake camps, but he said if the matter were brought before a jury in a civil trial, "the preponderance of evidence says that this is the place." In a criminal trial, however, there would be enough "reasonable doubt" to prevent a jury from deciding for either site. "If you look at diaries you come to one conclusion and if you look at artifacts you come to another," Hardesty said.

If the campsite is underwater, he said, it would take a lot of money and time to investigate it. Not that he wouldn't like to try. "I'd be willing to change my mind in an instant if we found better evidence at another location."

All plans for log cabins had to be abandoned. There was no sheltered nook for us shivering children, so father lifted Leanna and me on to a log, and mother tucked a buffalo robe around us, saying, 'Sit here until we have a better place for you.' There we sat, snug and dry, chatting and twisting our heads about watching. The men constructed tents on each side of the creek, with poles propped diagonally against a tree. Canvas, quilts, and buffalo robes were draped over the wood. They erected three shelters — one for our family, a second for Uncle Jacob's family, and a third for the single men.

— Georgia Donner, *Pioneer Children on the Journey West*

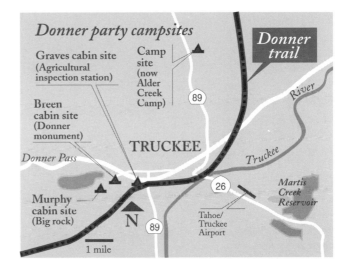

Artist's rendering of the Murphy cabin site, based on a rough sketch by Craig Meacham. The drawing appeared on the cover of The Archaeology of the Donner Party *by Professor Donald L. Hardesty.* — John Betz

November 8, 1846

Breens secure Schallenberger cabin; Kesebergs camp next door

THE DONNER PARTY IN CAMP.

Illustration of the Donner Party at Alder Creek from "Camp of Death" — Emigrant Trails Museum

Today the Breen family butchered cattle and stacked the beef like cordwood in the snow around their cabin. The snow has been falling five days.

Ox hides are stretched over the roof of the squat cabin built by a member of the 1844 Townsend-Stephens-Murphy Party. In this shack, which stands at the site where a Donner Party monument will be erected, are Patrick Breen, 51, and Margaret Breen, 40. Their children: John, 14; Edward, 13; Patrick, 11; Simon, 9; Peter, 7; James, 5; and Isabella, 1. Patrick Dolan, who is in his late twenties or early thirties, their neighbor from Keokuk, Iowa, shares the twelve-foot by fourteen-foot structure. The floor is thick with feathers. Moses Schallenberger, who wintered here in 1844 and stayed alive by trapping small game and shooting geese and ducks.

Lewis Keseberg, 33, and his wife, Philippine, 23, have built a lean-to against the side of the cabin. The Keseberg children, Ada, 3, and Lewis Jr., 1, share the space with Augustus Spitzer.

The Breens, naturalized Americans, are Irish-born and Catholic in an age of "Know Nothingism," when foreigners and Catholics are the targets and scapegoats of a national political movement.

When they joined the party in Wyoming, they were poor compared to the Reeds and Donners. Now in the mountains, the richest families have become destitute after Indians shot their cattle along the Humboldt River and they were forced to leave possessions on the trail.

The Breens, who have managed to retain most of their cattle and goods, now are better off than all the others. Even if the family were to hold onto everything, however, there's not enough food even for the people in and around the Breen cabin to survive the winter.

Tonight, the snow keeps falling.

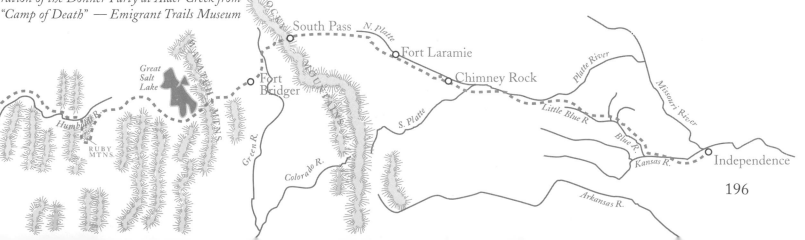

This is the site marked as the Donner camp at Alder Creek. Historians now disagree whether they stayed here, or at an area that is now covered by the waters of Prosser Reservoir. This tree's stump still stands at Alder Creek. — Nevada Historical Society

It rained and snowed so hard that the few animals we had were covered by the snow, and very few were found by feeling for them with a long pole. Families shared with one another as long as they had anything to share, making each one's portion very small.

— Georgia Donner, *Pioneer Children on the Journey West*

A 1914 photo shows a cross at the purported site of the Graves cabin. — Nevada Historical Society

The Murphy cabin site at Donner Lake — Marilyn Newton photo

November 10, 1846

Murphy, Eddy families already low on food

In the Murphy and Eddy camp, a cabin built against a rock about two hundred yards west of the Breen family, the occupants face the specter of a quicker death than their neighbors.

In the future, a bronze plaque affixed to this rock will list the names of the Donner Party, and archaeologists will dig for clues to what is happening there now.

Fires are burning. People huddle. In the flat-roofed shack with an oxhide for a door are: Lavinah Murphy, 36; William Foster ; the widow Harriet Murphy Pike, 18; Sarah Murphy Foster, 19; William Eddy, 28; Eleanor Eddy, 25; and nine children, ages sixteen to one year old.

The Murphy/Foster families have few provisions or livestock left. The Eddys, with an infant daughter, have one ox, a few items of clothing and some powder and shot.

Each day, William Eddy, with a rifle borrowed from William Foster, walks through snow drifts near the camp. Five days ago he killed a coyote and the tough, gamy meat was shared by all. The next day he shot an owl, a scant, stringy repast. He hasn't found targets since then. The deer have gone to lower elevations.

About a half-mile up the stream (Donner Creek) from the Murphy cabin, on land that will become a California Agricultural Inspection Station on Interstate 80, the Graves family built a cabin. In it are Franklin, 57; his wife, Elizabeth, 45; Sarah Graves Fosdick, 21; her husband, Jay Fosdick, 23; and eight Graves children, ages 19 to one year old. Margaret Reed, 32, and her four children are with the Graves. At night, the Reed children cuddle with the dogs, including Cash, Virginia's favorite.

The Reeds' employees, Milford Elliot, 28; Baylis Williams, 24; and his sister Eliza, 31, share the Reeds' area. Charles Stanton, 35, and the two Miwok Indians, Luis and Salvador, stay with the Reeds. Stanton's supplies are almost gone. The Graves family has some scrawny cattle. The eight-member Reed group is destitute. Deals must be made.

Tomorrow, eighty-one entrapped emigrants at the three lake cabins and the Alder Creek camp will awaken to their eighth straight day of snow.

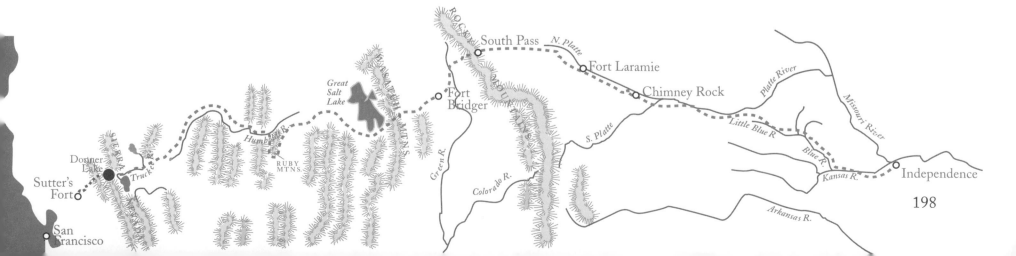

Donner Lake area in winter — Tim Dunn photo

November 13, 1846

Weather finally clears; 15 make break for pass

After eight days of snow, the sun came out yesterday.

In dawn's blinding whiteness, the emigrants thought only of escape.

On foot, the fifteen strongest people in the lake camps made a break for the mountain pass. They dressed in layers and packed dried beef in makeshift knapsacks.

Among them were three fathers — William Eddy, 28; Franklin "Uncle Billy" Graves, 57; and William Foster, 30. They left their wives and children in the hope they could get provisions in the California settlements and return.

Two young women, Sarah Fosdick, 21, and her sister, Mary Ann Graves, 19, took their chances with the men.

The group was led by Charles Stanton, 35, and the two Miwok Indians, Luis, 19, and Salvador, 28.

They waded through drifts along the north side of the lake. Beyond the lake the snow was ten feet deep. They waddled forward, pitching ahead, nearly swimming in powder, floundering in ravines.

Before dark, however, they returned to the lake camps, exhausted and in despair. They can't advance and they can't retreat east to the Truckee Meadows. As author George Stewart will say, the trap had closed in front and then "clicked shut" behind them.

The storms have built prison walls.

This morning, William Eddy arises before dawn. He shoulders Foster's gun and follows the path to the lake. Two shots awaken other members of the lake camps.

Eddy returns with two ducks, their necks tied together and resting over his shoulder. He gives one to Foster for the loan of the gun.

Tonight, the Eddy, Foster, and Graves families eat roast fowl and gaze at a clear sky. They begin making deals for the remaining cattle. Breen, Graves, and Dolan are the richest in beef. Others will have to pay dearly for meat.

There's talk of fishing in the lake. Each time they pass it, they see fish jump. But Eddy, with a wife and infant daughter to feed, is no patient fisherman.

Tomorrow, he'll borrow a rifle again.

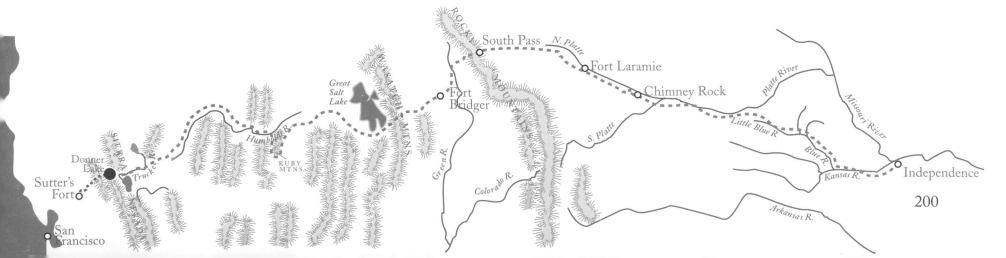

Donner summit in snow — Nevada Historical Society

The east shore of Donner Lake in winter — Emigrant Trails Museum

November 15, 1846

Eddy kills a grizzly bear in two-shot showdown near lake

Today, William Eddy and others at the lake camps feast on bear meat.

Yesterday, Eddy took William Foster's rifle and waded through drifts in the pine woods. In the snow were the fresh footprints of a large bear. Eddy thinks it's a grizzly.

Seldom would a man with a muzzle-loading gun want to face a bear alone, but Eddy is driven by his family's hunger. He cocks the rifle and puts his only other rifle ball in his mouth to make for faster reloading. He follows the tracks a few minutes and freezes in place. About ninety yards ahead, a huge bear is digging in the snow. Eddy crouches behind a tree, takes careful aim and fires. The bear rears up and roars, looking toward the tree where a puff of smoke betrayed Eddy's position.

The bear charges. Eddy pours his powder and rams home the lead ball, but can't level his rifle — the beast is nearly on him. He swings around the tree as the wounded bear lunges past him. As the enraged animal turns, Eddy shoves the rifle barrel into the beast's armpit and pulls the trigger. The bear roars and falls. Eddy grabs a fallen tree branch and beats the animal over the head. The bear is finished, but at eight hundred pounds, it's too heavy to carry.

"Uncle Billy" Graves and Eddy return with oxen to retrieve the bear. Graves confides that perhaps he is doomed to die in the mountains. God, he believes, might be punishing him for not rescuing the old man, Hardcoop, who was left to die on a Nevada desert trail last month.

The oxen drag the carcass to camp and within minutes bear meat is sizzling over the fire. Foster gets half the animal for the use of his gun. Graves gets a portion for the loan of oxen. Eddy gives Margaret Reed a share for her family.

In years to come, historians will wonder if Eddy's heroic story — one of many he told — is true. In the 1980s, the University of Nevada, Reno team led by anthropology professor Donald L. Hardesty will dig at the site of the Murphy-Eddy cabin at Donner Lake. Burnt bones will be found and identified in a laboratory. Among those artifacts will be bone fragments of a bear — probably a grizzly — roasted long ago.

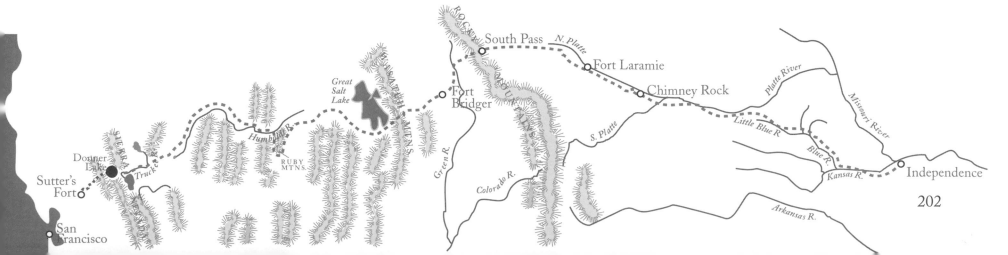

202

An illustration from J. Quinn Thornton's Camp of
Death *of William Eddy's encounter with a bear*
— Emigrant Trails Museum

NOVEMBER 17, 1846

Sutter says rescue impossible; Donners must wait three months

As soon as we arrived at Capt. Sutter's, I made a statement of all the circumstances attending our attempt to get into the mountains. He was no way surprised at our defeat. I also gave the Captain the number of head of cattle the company had when I left them. He made an estimate, and stated that if the emigrants would kill the cattle, and place the meat in the snow for preservation, there was no fear of starvation until relief could reach them. He further stated that there were no able bodied men in that vicinity, all having gone down the country with and after Frémont, to fight the Mexicans. He advised me to proceed to Yerba Bueno, now San Francisco, and make my case known to the naval officer in command.

— James F. Reed, *Pacific Press* account

At Sutter's Fort, James F. Reed is joining the California Battalion in the war against Mexico.

When Reed returned to the fort last week after his unsuccessful attempt to break through to the Donner Party, Sutter wasn't surprised. Winter will prevent Sierra travel until February, he said.

Sutter isn't concerned about the people imprisoned in the mountains. When Reed last saw them they had plenty of cattle and Charles Stanton must have reached them with more provisions.

They will be fine until spring, Sutter told Reed. Neither man knows the terrible toll the Indians took on the cows and oxen along the Humboldt River in what will become Nevada.

At the lake camps, hard bargains have been made. Mrs. Reed receives two oxen from Franklin Graves and two from Patrick Breen, promising to pay two-for-one when they get to Sutter's. She uses them to feed her children, Virginia, Patty, James and Tommy, and her family's three employees.

One of Graves's animals dies of starvation and Eddy buys it for $25, an exorbitant price even for a live, fat animal. In Independence, for example, a pair of oxen costs $25; in the California settlements, cattle are plentiful and a cow can be had for about $5. Breen sold Bill Foster two cows, taking a gold watch and goods in security. In this desperate commerce, the poorest have bought a few more weeks of life.

At the Donner Camp on Alder Creek less than six miles from the lake cabins, food is low but they still have some cattle. The two Donner families and the others are huddled in two tents and a hastily-built wigwam for the single men. The days are clear; the nights freezing.

There are fifty-six people at the lake camps and twenty-five in the Donner camp. Of eighty-one people, forty-four are children. Every day they look west hoping to see men and mules breaking through from California. But there's a war on. All able-bodied men have gone south to fight. Spring is months away.

Starvation is much closer.

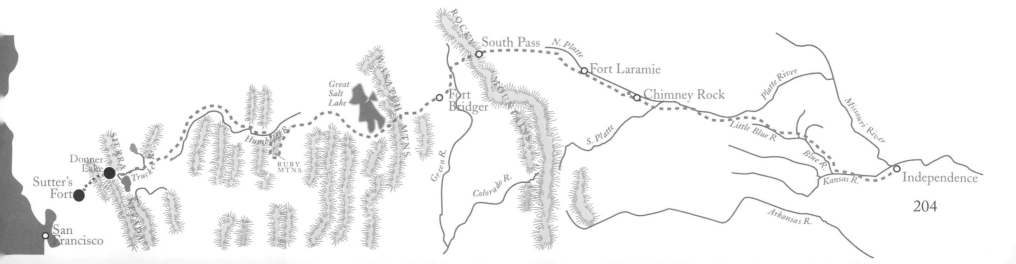

LITH. BY C.L. SMITH & CO. OAKLAND. CAL.

CAMP AT DONNER LAKE,
Nov. 1846.

A fanciful lithograph of the camp at Donner Lake — Nevada Historical Society

NOVEMBER 20, 1846

Patrick Breen begins his diary of the entrapment

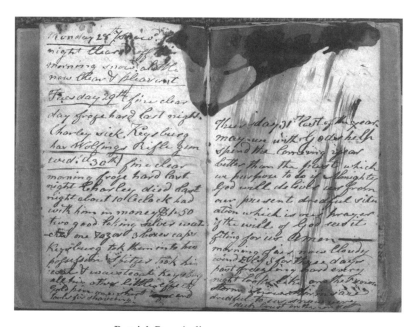

Patrick Breen's diary
— Bancroft Library

On this day Patrick Breen, 51, takes eight sheets of letter paper, trims and folds them into a little thirty-two-page book.

In the firelight, he begins a diary:

"Friday, Nov. 20, 1846: Came to this place on the 31st of last month that it snowed we went on to the pass the snow so deep we were unable to find the road when within three miles of the summit then turned back to this shanty on the lake Stanton came one day after we arrived here we again took our teams and wagons and made another unsucessful attempt to cross in company with Stanton we returned to the shanty it continuing to snow all the time we were here we now have killed most part of our cattle having to stay here until next spring and live on poor beef without bread or salt it snowed during the space of eight days with little intermission, after our arrival here, the remainder of time up to this day was clear and pleasant freezing at night the snow nearly gone from the valleys."

He writes as twenty-two others at the lake prepare to make a break for the pass after nine days of clear weather. Breen will stay with his family.

At Alder Creek, George and Jacob Donner are giving away clothes and tobacco to others in exchange for a promise to be paid in California at California prices. They make note of their agreements.

Tamsen Donner continues to write in the journal she began in Illinois, but the book won't be found.

Breen's journal of events, written as they happened, will speak to generations.

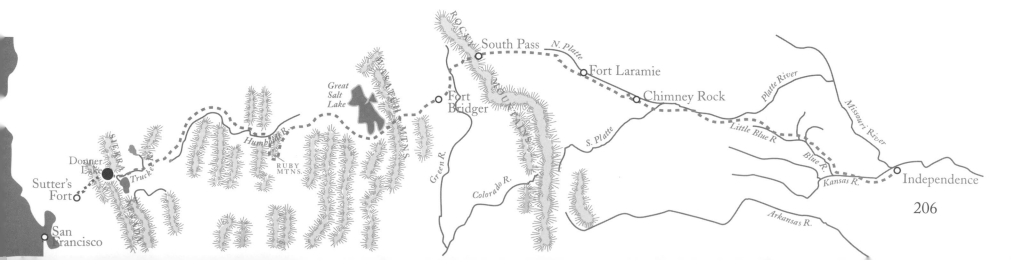

Brass military emblem found at the Alder Creek campsite by archaeologists led by Professor Donald Hardesty

A button found at the Murphy cabin site, manufactured probably between 1836 and 1847. It was found by Professor Donald Hardesty's team.

Salt and pepper shakers at the Emigrant Trails Museum
— Marilyn Newton photo

During the evening a meeting was held, in which I participated, adopting a memorial to the commander of Sutter's Fort, to raise one or more companies of volunteers, to proceed to Los Angeles, we being at war with Mexico at this time. The companies were to be officered by the petitioners. Being requested to take command of one of the companies, I declined, stating that it would be necessary for the Captain to stay with the company; also, that I had to return to the mountains for the emigrants; but that I would take a Lieutenantcy. The was agreed to, and I was on my return to the emigrants to enlist all men I could between there and Bear Valley. On my way up I enlisted twelve or thirteen.

— James F. Reed, *Pacific Rural Press* account

ANOTHER DIARY

As Breen writes in his new diary, someone is making notations in the journal that will become known as the Miller/Reed Diary.

James F. Reed ceased writing in the book on October 4, the day before he killed teamster John Snyder. But his family has kept the journal and today someone (Charles Stanton?) writes:

"Donner's Camp, Nov. 20, 1846 [Bought] of George Donner — one blanket coat — to be paid California @ California price ... [Bought] Jake Donner, 9 yards check, 1 cot flag on the same terms as the above. [Also bought of J. Donner] 1 pair brogans for Jim Smith — on the same terms which I am bound to see paid. Bought of George Donner, 1 pair pantaloons 1 pr socks 4 small plugs 6 large of Tabacco."

NOVEMBER 22, 1846

Another dash for safety ends in failure, irony

Donner Lake in snow — Nevada Historical Society

Today, twenty-two people have broken free of the lake camps and awake west of what will be called Donner Pass.

Yesterday morning, on the dawn of the tenth day without snowfall, the people and seven mules began a trek to safety. Much of the snow was melted and even the higher drifts at the summit were covered with a thick crust. They made good time.

The party includes almost all the men at the lake, except the ailing Lewis Keseberg and Patrick Breen, and six women, including Lavinah Murphy, 36, and three of her older children. John Baptiste Trudeau, 16, is the only member of the Donner camp at Alder Creek to join them.

Last night, at seven thousand feet above sea level in six feet of snow, they struggled to kindle a fire.

Then the argument — which will have dire consequences — began.

The mules, too heavy to travel on top of the snow, are more exhausted than the people. William Eddy tells Charles Stanton they must leave the mules and go down the mountain quickly.

Stanton's honor is his best quality and his fatal flaw. He will not leave Sutter's mules to die. Eddy threatens the two Indians if they do not lead them forward, but Luis and Salvador fear Sutter will hang them if they return without his mules.

Eddy argues that Sutter would place human life first above all. He offers to take financial responsibility for the animals.

This morning, Stanton won't be moved to proceed, and the others can't go west without him or the Indians as guides.

"We could see nothing but snow [ahead] and the tops of pine trees sticking out of it," William Graves will remember.

At midnight tonight, they and the mules stumble back to the cabins. They'll try again soon.

Tonight in the Gulf of Alaska, a storm is busy being born.

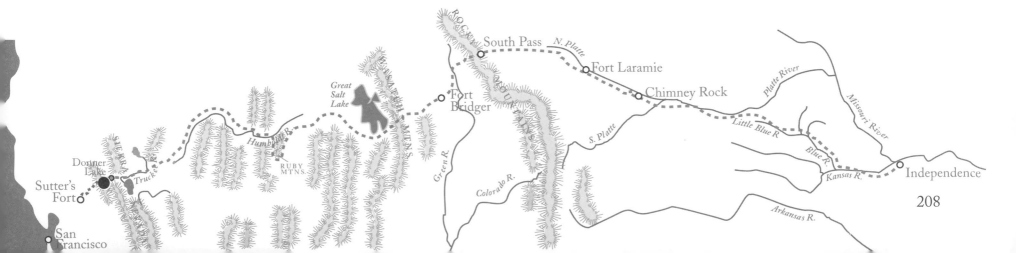

The mountains around Donner Lake in winter
— Emigrant Trails Museum

Sat. 21st Fine morning wind N:W 22 of our company are about starting across the mountain this moring including Stanton & his indians, some clouds flying thawed to day wnd E.

Sunday 22nd Froze hard last night this a fine clear morning, wind E.S.E. no account from those on the mountains.

— Patrick Breen, diary

November 24, 1846

Men and women preparing for another hike to the pass

The strongest are almost ready for another attempt at the pass. They must try again before a storm hits.

Margaret Reed is rationing beef and bear meat to her children, and her family's three employees. Baylis, who early on the trail slept in a wagon during the day and watched the cattle at night, is weak and sick from exposure and the hard labor of the last two months.

Even Breen is down to less than ten oxen and cows, emaciated from a diet of pine boughs. They rapidly consume that reserve.

Communication has been established between the lake camps and the Donner camp about six miles away at Alder Creek. There is no good news.

George Donner is still suffering from the gash in his hand caused when he fixed an axle on the way up the Sierra trail. Jacob Donner is also under the weather. John Baptiste Trudeau, 16, chops wood.

At the lake camps, all thoughts are of breaking out of the trap. The near-success of the last attempt has given them hope. They plan to start in two days, November 26 — declared Thanksgiving Day by George Washington in 1789.

Tonight, rain soaks San Francisco as a hard freeze envelops the Sierra. Clouds race above the camps.

1879 lithograph of Donner Lake
— Nevada Historical Society

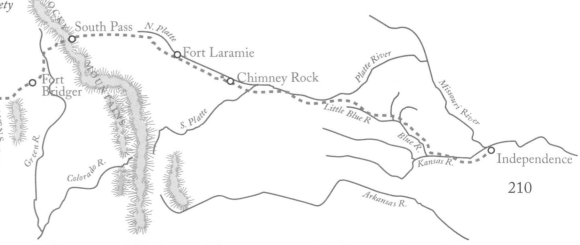

Monday 23rd Same weather wind W the expedition across the mountains returned after an unsuccsful attempt.

Tuesday 24th Fine in the morning towards eveng cloudy & windy wind W looks like snow freezeing hard.

Wendsday 25th Wind about W N W Cloudy looks like the eve of a snow storm our mountainers intend trying to cross the mountain tomorrow if fair froze hard last night.

Thurssday the 26th Began to snow yesterday in the evening now rains or sleet the mountaniers dont start to day the wind about W. wet & muddy.

— Patrick Breen, diary

Donner Lake is shrouded in fog at dawn.
— Marilyn Newton photo

November 27, 1846

Series of storms sweeps Sierra; climbers can't escape camps

Snow is falling at a fearful rate.

The storms began two days ago, first as flurries, then as a wind-driven blizzard. A party of men and women planned an escape attempt yesterday — the day celebrated as Thanksgiving in some northern states — but they won't risk it now.

"Began to snow yesterday evening, now rains or sleet" Patrick Breen wrote in his diary last night, noting that "the mountaineers," as he calls those trying to break free, were held up by the weather.

Today he writes: "Continues to snow, the ground not covered, wind W[est]. Dull prospect for crossing the mountains."

Tomorrow, Breen will note the snow falling faster — at 10 o'clock, it'll be eight or ten inches deep.

Still they hope. In the East, even a great blizzard that covered Illinois lasted only nine days.

The seven mules that Charles Stanton brought from Sutter's Fort stand with their backs to the west wind and bray from cold and hunger. A few of the emigrants move about outside their shelters looking for wood. The pine branches are hard to ignite. Dry wood gets scarcer by the day.

The snow is covering caches of meat and the scattered goods from the wagons.

The ground around the camps, where snow had accumulated and then melted, is again turning into a pure white landscape.

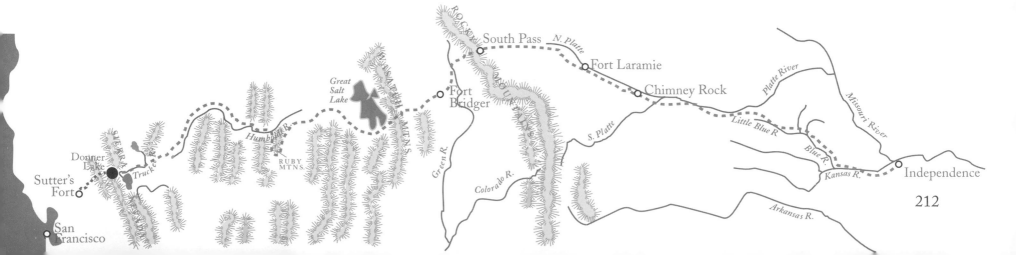

Donner Lake is frozen during a record winter in 1968-69. — Emigrant Trails Museum

Friday 27 Continues to snow, the ground not covered, wind W dull prospect for crossing the mountains.

Saturday 28th Snowing fast now about 10 o clock snow 8 or 10 inches deep soft wet snow, weather not cold wind W.

— Patrick Breen, diary

On November 28, George Donner takes pen in hand and writes a note under the dateline, "Donners Camp." The document authorizes Milford Elliot to be Donner's agent and purchase at the settlements any property "he may deem necessary for my distress in the mountains for which on my arival in California I will pay cash or Goods or both."

The list that follows includes five pack mules, two horses, "2 gallons salt, $3 worth of sugar," 150 pounds of flour, three bushels of beans, and fifty pounds of cake tallow.

Once again, the Donners have put their hopes in Elliot's ability to reach the settlements and come back with relief.

November 29, 1846

Indians know Donners trapped as snow storms rake Sierra

Trapped by storms, the pioneers in the camps think no one knows their plight, but many eyes watch them.

The Washoe people know what goes on in their own country. The Indians move freely. They invented snowshoes centuries ago. They won't help the unfortunate emigrants. They've been shot at too many times.

The pioneers look foolish, pitiful, and helpless but the Indians will not harm them. The mules and cattle are another matter.

Today, Patrick Breen gives Bill Foster a pair of oxen. Foster agrees to pay him in California.

Breen, suffering from an ailment he calls "the gravels" (kidney stones), kills his last few cattle today. His wife, Margaret, will butcher them tomorrow.

There are still a few head of cattle left at the lake and at the Donner Camp on Alder Creek. A few horses and Sutter's seven mules also remain.

The wind is westerly and snow continues without relief. "Hard to get wood," Breen writes today. The snow is more than three feet deep.

Tomorrow, in his shanty at the lake, Patrick Breen will write: "Monday, 30th Snowing fast wind W[est] about 4 or 5 feet deep . . . looks as likely to continue [now] as when it commenced.

"No liveing thing without wings can get about."

Except the Washoe Indians.

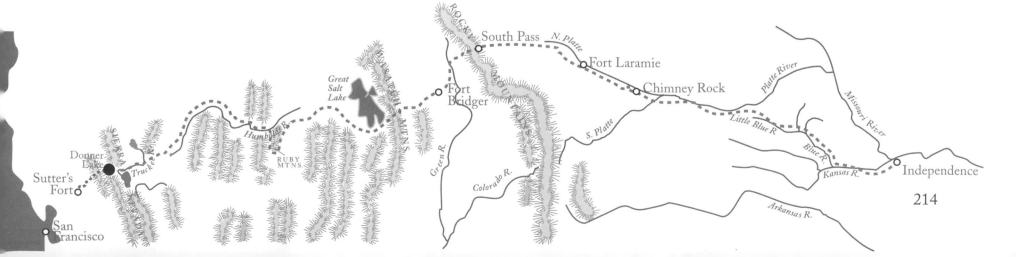

214

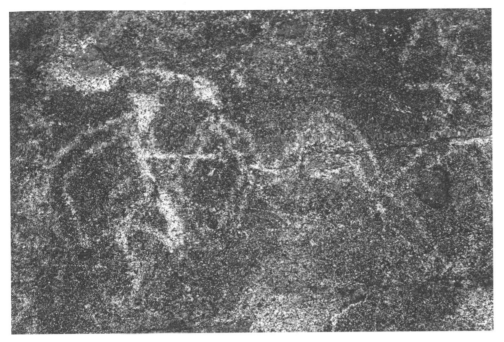

Indian petroglyphs at the summit of Donner Pass. The age of the drawings is unknown.
— Emigrant Trails Museum

Sunday 29th Still snowing now about 3 feet deep, wind W killed my last oxen to day will skin them tomorrow gave another yoke to Fosters hard to get wood.

Monday 30th Snowing fast wind W about 4 or 5 feet deep, no drifts looks as likely to continue as when it commenced no liveing thing without wings can get about.

— Patrick Breen, diary

Snow blankets trees near Donner Lake.
— Emigrant Trails Museum

DECEMBER 1, 1846

Cattle, horses, mules gone as snow piles up in camps

After being holed up in the cabins and tents for the last twenty-four hours, the pioneers look outside today to find their world covered in almost six feet of pure, untracked snow. It takes them a few moments to realize that all their remaining cattle, horses and mules are missing.

"Still snowing," Patrick Breen writes in his diary today. "Snow about 5 or 6 feet deep difficult to get wood no going from the house completely housed up looks as likely for snow [now] as when it commenced, our cattle all killed but three or four of them, the horses & Stantons mules gone & cattle suppose[d] lost in snow no hopes of finding them alive."

Survivors will say the mules were stolen by Indians. The loss increases resentment against Charles Stanton. He refused to abandon the animals during their hike to escape and now they are gone anyway.

This second series of storms has lasted six days. When will it end?

Many in the camps have read Lansford Hastings' *Emigrants' Guide to Oregon and California* but probably do not remember one of the few pieces of useful information in that book:

"[In California] December is as pleasant as May," Hastings wrote. "The remarks here made, in reference to the climate, are applicable only to the valleys and plains, for the mountains present one eternal winter."

Hastings, meanwhile, is still taking part in the Mexican War. He's a captain — attaining the rank he has claimed for years. Some of those who elected him, including Heinrich Lienhard, took his "shortcut."

They bear him no ill will. They arrived safely in California.

The members of the Donner Party wish they could say the same.

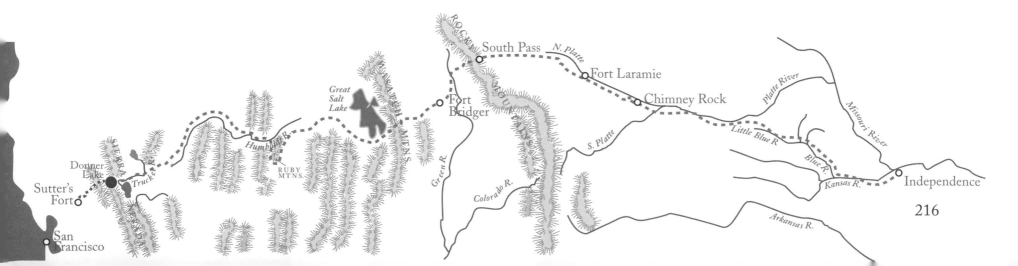

Donner Lake from summit — Nevada Historical Society

December 1st Tuesday Still snowing wind W snow about 5 feet or 6 deep difficult to get wood no going from the house completely housed up looks as likely for snow as when it commenced, our cattle all killed but three or four them, the horses & Stantons mules gone & cattle suppose lost in the snow no hopes of finding them alive

Wedns. 2nd. Continues to snow wind W sun shineing hazily thro the clouds dont snow quite as fast as it has done snow must be over six feet deep bad fire this morning.

Thursd. 3rd Snowed a little last night bright and coudy at intervals all night, to day cloudy snows none wind S.W. warm but not enough so to thaw snow lying deep allround expecing it to thaw a little to day the forgoing written in the morning it immediately turned in to snow & continued to snow all day & likely to do so all night.

— Patrick Breen, diary

Today in the Pueblo de San Jose de Guadalupe, U.S. magistrate John Burton approves a petition for land near the Fox River in San Jose signed by "Bailos" (Baylis) Williams. But the signature is a forgery. The handwriting is that of James F. Reed, who, with the probable complicity of the authorities, is securing land grants for his entrapped employees.

December 4, 1846

Snow storms end; search for lost cattle begins

High clouds race above the camps today as the temperature plunges below freezing.

A few emigrants have made attempts to find the lost cattle, horses, and mules by driving poles into the six-foot-deep snow. The activity is frantic but fruitless.

Neither the occupants of the lake cabins nor the Donner camp at Alder Creek have been able to find any trace of their remaining livestock beneath the snow. The Breen and Graves families and Patrick Dolan still have some larger sections of beef left. All the rest are down to scraps.

Starvation, which had seemed weeks away, now stares them in the face.

At the lake, Patrick Breen still suffers from "the gravels," but his family has the most stores. In the lean-to next door, the Keseberg family has little and their two children cry in the night. Augustus Spitzer, who is staying with the Kesebergs, is weak and sick.

The Murphys and the others at the lake camps are not much better off. In the Graves camp, Reed family employee Baylis Williams is in the worst condition. The Reed family is rationing their meager supply of meat.

At Alder Creek, Jacob Donner, James Smith, Joseph Reinhardt, and Sam Shoemaker are very weak from poor rations and illness. George Donner's "scratch" has infected his hand and lower arm. If a mountain man were around, an amputation would be insisted upon.

At the Donner camp, only John Baptise Trudeau can work searching for wood and chopping branches.

When the occupants of the cabins and camps speak to one another, there is only one topic: escape. When the weather breaks they must find a way to get down the mountains.

The weaker they become, the more they will be likely to face a death by starvation in the snow.

They pray for a thaw to take hold.

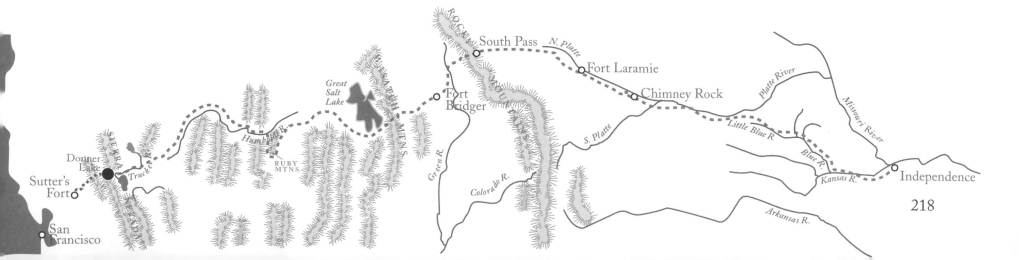

Friday 4th Cloudy that is flying clouds neither snow or rain this day it is a relief to have one fine day, wind E by N no sign of thaw freezeing pretty hard snow deep.

—Patrick Breen, diary

Mist rises from Donner Lake. — Emigrant Trails Museum

December 6, 1846

Sun shining on camps as emigrants plan snowshoe escape

It's a sunny, beautiful morning.

The snow ceased yesterday and the sun has turned the high camps into a glistening world of white mounds. In every direction are snowy vistas with green trees poking through the pure powder.

Patrick Breen, writing in his diary, is moved by the beauty: "Fine clear day," he wrote yesterday. "Beautiful sunshine thawing a little looks delightful after the long snow storm." Today he notes another clear morning and efforts by two companions to escape. "Stanton & Graves [are making] snow shoes for another mountain scrabble," he writes.

The mules, thought to have been buried in the snow along with the remaining cattle, have probably been stolen by Indians while the emigrants were holed up in shacks and tents. The Washoe people, well accustomed to snowshoe travel, can move in the snowbound mountains.

Most of the Donner Party members are flatlanders. Only Franklin Ward Graves, who spent his youth in the Green Mountains of Vermont, and Charles Stanton, from New York, have any knowlege of snowshoes. They and carpenter William Eddy are splitting and shaving oxbows and using the pieces as the frames for the snowshoes, cross-hatched with strips of rawhide. Stanton and his two California Miwok guides, Luis and Salvador, will again lead the expedition.

Stanton and the Miwoks, who brought supplies to the Donner Party in late October, are very low on food. The mules that Stanton refused to abandon were lost anyway. That hasn't endeared him to the emigrants who were so close to safety when Stanton refused to proceed. Yet Stanton remains their best hope.

Since the last escape attempt fifteen days ago, the people at the lake have seen no one from the Donner camp at Alder Creek, about six miles away. No one from the Donner camp will join the next expedition.

As Graves and the others work on the snowshoes they pray for a spell of fair weather. If the strongest of them can just get beyond the pass again, the shoes will take them to safety. Then they can assemble a rescue effort for the others. If they are quick and the weather holds, they reason, no one needs to die here.

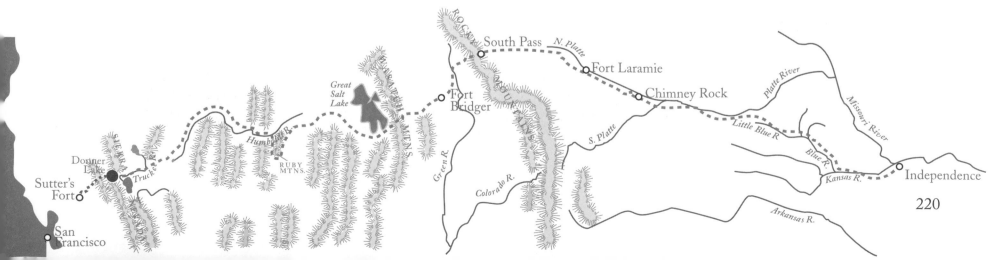

Saturday 5th Fine clear day beautiful sunshine thawing a little looks delightful after the long snow storm.

    Sund. 6th The morning fine & clear now some cloudy wind S-E not much in the sunshine, Stanton & Graves manufactureing snow shoes for another mountain scrabble no account of mules.

    Mond. 7th Beautiful clear day wind E by S looks as if we might some fair weather no thaw.

          — Patrick Breen, diary

Donner Lake from mountains to the south — Emigrant Trails Museum

December 8, 1846

Donners worse off than those at the lake camps

Good weather is holding. The recent storms, which Eliza Donner will say "made fires unsafe, froze the water and shut out all the light," are over.

Charles Stanton, Franklin Ward Graves, William Eddy, and others are making snowshoes for the next assault on the pass. The shoes, hickory frames laced with rawhide, are heavy and clumsy, but will do the job.

They try to work quickly, for their strength is waning. Although many of the fifty-six people at the lake still have meat, the diet of beef without bread, salt, vegetables, or fruit has many suffering the weariness of malnutrition. The week of storms has kept them breathing the fumes of smoky fires.

Today, Patrick Breen, 51, takes Augustus Spitzer, 30, into his cabin. Spitzer has been staying in a lean-to with the Keseberg family. He's so sick he can't sit up without help.

Breen writes: "Tues. 8th Fine weather clear & pleasant . . . deep snow the people not [stirring] round much hard work to get [get] wood."

Baylis Williams, 24, nursed by Margaret Reed, 32, remains very ill. Her four children, however, are well.

Things are worse at the Donner camp six miles away on Alder Creek, where John Baptise Trudeau, 16, climbs a tree and searches for signs of rescue. There is no movement on the wall of snow.

Trudeau climbs down into the camp where the storms have crushed tents and soaked the occupants. He and others search in vain for lost cattle. Little food is left.

The twenty-five people at Alder Creek already have eaten mice, scorched over coals, and some are boiling hides to skim and eat the glue that forms in the pots. Someone boiled parts of a moldy buffalo robe, but the result was too disgusting to eat.

Jacob Donner, 65; Joseph Reinhardt, 30; Sam Shoemaker, 25; and James Smith, 25, are fading fast. The sunshine might give them a respite.

Tonight, rain sweeps the California coast as the Jet Stream rushes like a river above the high camps.

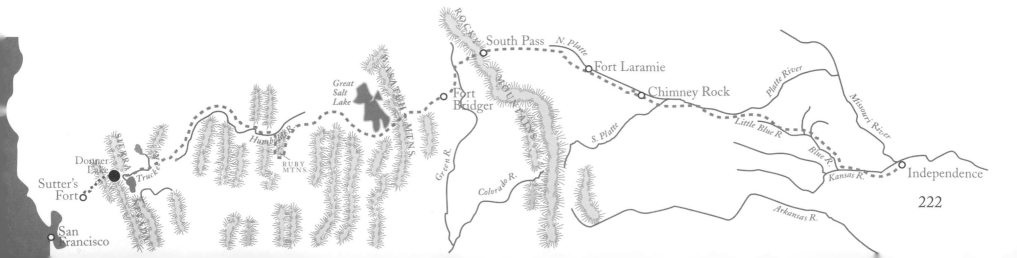

Patrick Breen
— Emigrant Trails Museum

C.T. Stanton
— Emigrant Trails Museum

William Eddy
— Emigrant Trails Museum

Margaret Reed
— Nevada Historical Society

Tues 8th Fine weather clear & pleasant froze hard last night wind S.E. deep snow the people not stirring round much hard work to wood sufficient to keep us warm & cook our beef.

— Patrick Breen, diary

December 11, 1846

Reinhardt confesses murder as more storms hit Sierra

In the Donner camp at Alder Creek, twenty-seven people are now huddled in soaked tents and brush shelters as more storms sweep the Sierra.

The snow began about 11 a.m. two days ago, shortly after Noah James and Milt Elliot left the lake camps to find out what's happening to the twenty-five people six miles away. They reached the Donner camp and took shelter as the snow continued all night and through the next day.

The situation is already critical. Jacob Donner, Sam Shoemaker, James Smith, and Joseph Reinhardt are deep in fever. George Donner, still suffering from an infected wound, isn't much better.

Reinhardt, believing he is dying, tells George Donner and others he had a hand in the mysterious disappearance of Karl Wolfinger at the Humboldt Sink in October. Wolfinger was rumored to have a lot of money and Rheinhardt and Augustus Spitzer stayed to help Wolfinger bury his goods. The pair returned without him, carrying his rifle, and told the others Indians attacked and killed him.

"[Reinhardt] was taken sick in our tent," Leanna Donner will remember. "When death was approaching and he knew there was no escape, then he made a confession in the presence of Mrs. Wolfinger that he shot her husband; what the object was I do not know."

At the lake camps, Franklin Ward Graves and others continue making snowshoes. Charles Stanton, Luis, and Salvador make the rounds of the cabins asking for food to take with them in the coming escape attempt. Stanton is "not likely to get much," Patrick Breen observed in his diary two days ago.

Margaret Reed, nearing the end of her own meager stores for her family, gives him some dried meat. She remembers how he helped her family.

Today the sun peeks in and out of clouds as slow flurries start and stop.

When the weather breaks the strongest must flee. It has become a choice between leaving and possibly dying in days or staying and probably dying in weeks.

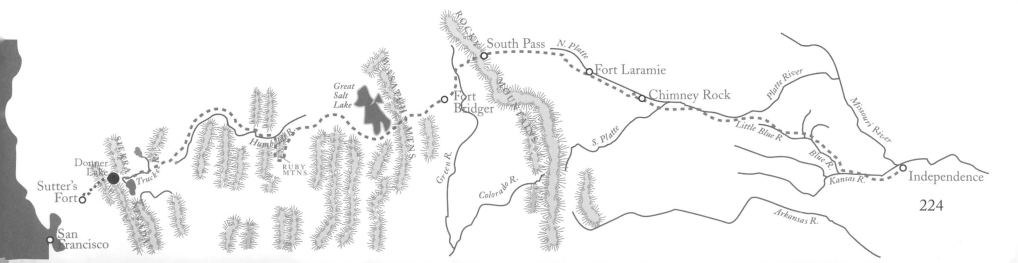

A man sits among the remnants of trees cut by members of the Donner Party during their ordeal in the Sierra. — Bancroft Library

Wedns. 9th Commenced snowing about 11 o clock wind N:W snows fast took in Spitzer yesterday so weak that he cannot rise without help caused by starveation all in good health some having scant supply of beef Stanton trying to make a raise of some for his Indians & self not likely to get much.

Thursd. 10th Snowed fast all night with heavy squalls of wind Continues still to snow the sun peeping through the clouds once in about three hours very difficult to get wood to day now about 2 o clock looks likely to continue snowing dont know the debth of the snow may be 7 feet.

Friday 11th Snowing a little wind W Sun vissible at times not freezeing.

— Patrick Breen, *diary*

I was informed by Mr. Eddy that George Donner, with whom Rianhard subsequently traveled, told him that Wolfinger had not died [at the hands of Indians] — that this fact he learned from a confession made by Rianhard a short time previous to his death; and that he would make the facts public as soon as he arrived in the settlements.

— J. Quinn Thornton, *California in 1848*

December 13, 1846

Jacob Donner, three other men, dead or dying at Alder Creek

Jacob Donner, 56, and three other men are on their deathbeds at the Alder Creek camp.

Sam Shoemaker, 25; James Smith, 25; and Joseph Reinhardt, 30; are breathing their last on the fifth day of the latest series of snowstorms to blanket the Sierra. They are malnourished and suffering from cold and dampness. They cry out in fever, but no one can help.

The young men, Eliza Donner will write, "were so light-hearted on the plains and so brave when they faced the snows," but in camp "they became dispirited and said they were too weak and hungry to gather wood, and did not care how soon death would end their miseries."

They will be buried in the snow.

Today at the lake camps, Patrick Breen, 51, writes in his diary: "Snows faster than any previous day . . . Stanton & Graves with several others [making] preparations to cross the mountains on snow shoes. "

Wood is difficult to find and food stores are dwindling.

For the last few days seventeen entrapped pioneers have made preparations to escape once the weather breaks and a crust forms on the powdery snow.

The snowshoers — ten men, two boys and five women — will be known as the Forlorn Hope.

They will soon earn the name.

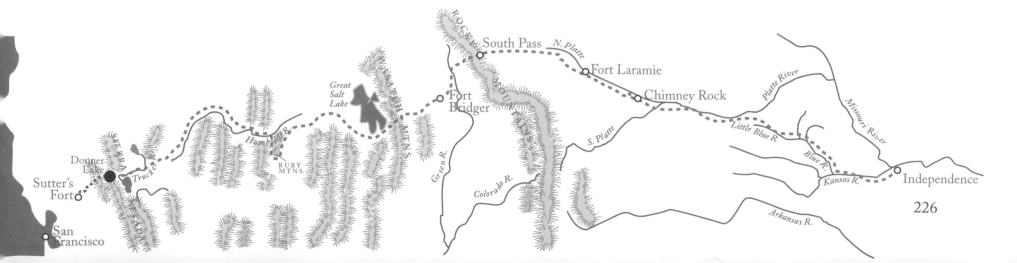

Donner Lake frozen over and covered in snow. — Emigrant Trails Museum

Satd. 12th Continues to snow wind W weather mild freezeing little.

Sunday 13th Snows faster than any previous day wind N:W Stanton & Graves with several others makeing preparations to cross the mountains on snow shoes, snow 8 feet deep on the level dull.

— Patrick Breen, diary

December 15, 1846

Snowshoers prepare escape; Baylis Williams dies at lake

The sun came out yesterday as work was completed on fourteen pairs of snowshoes.

Today the weather continues fair as the seventeen members of the Forlorn Hope Party prepare to leave tomorrow. They have some dried meat — minimal rations for six days. This allows each person a strip of beef, about the size of two fingers, three times a day. They have coffee and some sugar.

Fourteen will wear showshoes, with the other three plodding along behind. Other supplies include: one rifle, a few pistols, a blanket or quilt for each, a hatchet, and tobacco for smoking or chewing. They bring no extra clothing.

Four fathers and three mothers will leave their children. One of them is William Eddy, 28, who hopes to return for his wife, Eleanor, 25; his son, James, 3; and daughter, Margaret, 1; who are staying in the Murphy cabin. Mrs. Eddy packs her husband's knapsack and puts a surprise package inside along with a note. The other party members include Charles Stanton, 35; the Miwok Indians, Luis and Salvador; Franklin Ward Graves, 57, his daughters, Mary Ann Graves, 19, and Sarah Fosdick, 21, with her husband, Jay Fosdick, 23; Amanda McCutchen, 25, whose husband, Bill, is in California; Antonio the Mexican, 23; Karl "Dutch Charlie" Burger, 30; Lemuel Murphy, 12, and his brother, Bill, 11.

William Foster, his wife, Sarah, 19, and Harriet Pike, 18, will take their chances with the group.

Patrick Dolan, a bachelor in his late twenties or early thirties, with no family in camp and more food than the others, also joins the snowshoers, saying there will be one less mouth to feed when he leaves. He gives the Breens and Reeds some beef.

Tomorrow will come tearful goodbyes. Some of those farewells will be the last for people of the Forlorn Hope party and those left behind.

The snowshoers estimate the first American outpost, Johnson's Ranch, to be thirty to forty miles away. The ranch is actually seventy miles to the west.

Tonight, Baylis Williams, 24, crazy with fever, cries out and dies. He is buried in snow. Death, author George Stewart will reflect, bids these mountaineers godspeed.

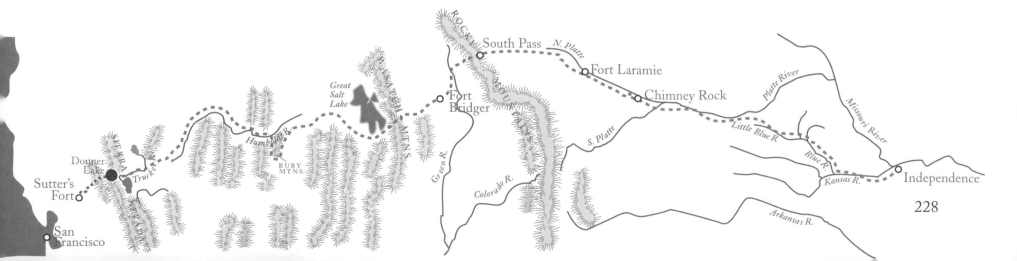

Monday 14 Fine morning sunshine cleared off last night about 12 o clock wind E:S:E dont thaw much but fair for a continueance of fair weather.
Tuesday 15th Still continues fine wind W: S:W.
— Patrick Breen, diary

Snowshoers attempt escape in this portion of a larger painting by Robert Lebron.
— Emigrant Trails Museum

December 18, 1846

Snowshoers cross Donner Pass; two return to lake camps

The Forlorn Hope party of snowshoers now numbers fifteen and is camped west of what will become Donner Pass.

They left the lake three days ago. The first day they made about four miles and rested on a hill beside a fire built on a platform of logs. They could see the smoke from the lake camp. Parents among them imagined they could hear babies crying.

The first day, Karl "Dutch Charley" Burger, almost 30, and Bill Murphy, 10, who were without snowshoes, could not follow in the tracks of the others and returned to the lake. Lemuel Murphy, 12, also without snowshoes, pressed on.

The second day, the escapees reached the pass. They reminded Mary Ann Graves, 19, struggling in the rear, of engravings she had seen of Norwegian fur company trappers on an icepack. As they climb the pass, someone grimly observes that they are "as close to heaven as we can get."

Last night, they camped, exhausted, west of the pass. They built another fire on a log platform over snow twelve feet deep. They boiled coffee and ate strips of dried beef.

The sun has been shining since they left the lake and they face another horror — snow blindness. Stanton, bringing up the rear, did not arrive in last night's camp until hours after the others were settled. He is weak from malnutrition and nearly blind. Their guide has become a straggler.

Today they flounder down the mountain, with Stanton far behind. Snow flurries and high winds come up in the afternoon. Tonight they camp six miles farther west. Stanton arrives late and sits near the fire like a man in a trance.

Tomorrow will repeat today — Stanton lagging behind while fierce snow squalls slap their faces as they move west. Mary Graves will see mist in a valley and insist it is smoke. The others don't believe it, but they fire a gun to attract attention.

It is only mist.

Today, at the lake, Patrick Breen comments on the beauty of the sunshine, but no one is moving about. Flurries arrive but clear by nightfall.

By midnight tonight, snow falls in earnest and continues into the morning.

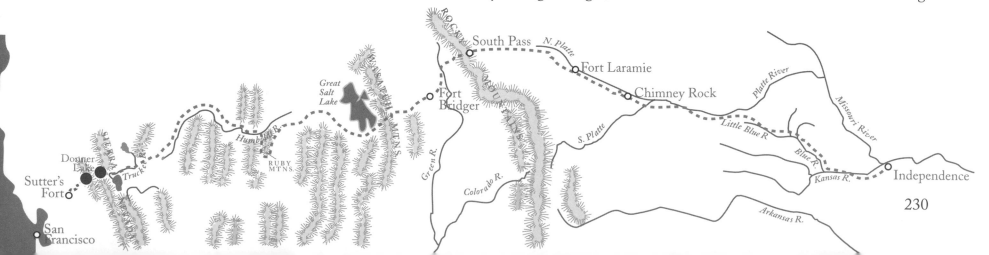

The Forlorn Hope Party escaping on snow shoes in a painting by Robert Lebron.
— Emigrant Trails Museum

Wed'd 16th Fair & pleasant froeze hard last night so the company started on snow shoes to cross the mountains wind S.E looks pleasant.

Thursd. 17th Pleasant sunshine to day wind about S.E Bill Murp returned from the mountain party last evening Bealis died night before last Milt. & Noah went to Donnos 8 days since not returned yet, thinks they got lost in the snow. J Denton here to day.

Frid'd. 18 Beautiful day sky clear it would be delightful were it not for the snow lying so deep thaws but little on the south side of shanty saw no strangers to day from any of the shantys.

Satd. 19 Snowd. last night commenced about 11 o clock . . . Squalls of wind with snow at intervals this morning thawing wind. N by W a little singular for a thaw may continue, it continues to snow sun shining cleared off towards evening.

— Patrick Breen, diary

December 20, 1846

Four deaths confirmed at Donner camp on Alder Creek

Today at the lake camp, the morning dawns clear and bright after a day of steady snowfall.

Karl "Dutch Charley" Burger tries to reach the Donner camp, six miles away at Alder Creek. He wants to learn the fate of the twenty-seven people there, including Milt Elliot and Noah James, who left for a visit on December 9 and haven't returned.

Burger can't get through. Tonight Patrick Breen writes: "Tough times but we are not discouraged, our hopes are in God, Amen."

Elliot and James return late tonight and bring news of deaths at Alder Creek: Jacob Donner, Sam Shoemaker, Joseph Reinhardt, and James Smith.

Today, the fifth day of the escape attempt by the Forlorn Hope party, the snowshoers are exhausted. Tonight they camp a near a cache of food buried by James F. Reed when he turned back to Sutter's Fort a month ago. They do not know salvation lies beneath the drifts.

They expected to be below the snow line by now, but even the valleys wear a deep white cloak. Charles Stanton is so weak he can hardly stand.

One day's ration of beef is left.

Tomorrow is Monday, December 21, the shortest day of the year. At the lake, Breen will suffer a severe attack of kidney stones. The Forlorn Hope party will awaken to cloudy skies and Charles Stanton sitting on a log close to the fire.

"Are you coming, Mr. Stanton?," Mary Graves will ask as the snowshoers shoulder their packs.

"Yes, I am coming soon," Stanton will reply. He will look in her direction, but he is snowblind.

Tomorrow, another storm will arrive.

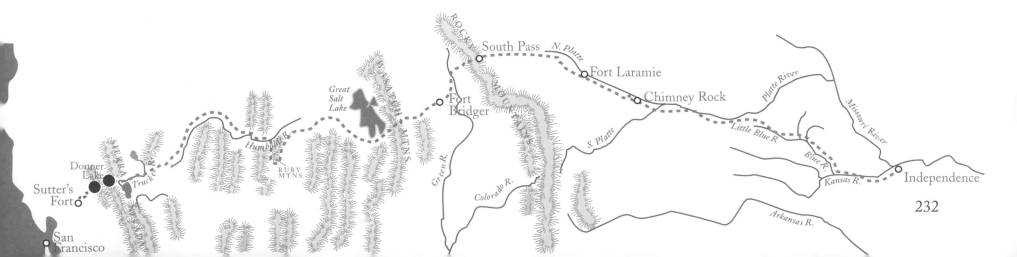

*Sund. 20 Night clear froze a little now clear &
pleasant wind N W thawing a little Mrs Reid here,
no account of Milt. yet Dutch Charley started for
Donoghs turned back not able to proceed tough
times, but not discouraged our hopes are in God.
Amen.*

*Mond. 21 Milt. got back last night from
Donos camp sad news. Jake Donno Sam Shoemaker
Rinehard, & Smith are dead the rest of them in a
low situation Snowed all night with a strong S-W
wind to day cloudy wind continues but not snowing, thawing sun shineing dimly in hopes it will
clear off.*

— Patrick Breen, diary

Painting by Robert Lebron on display at the museum
— Emigrant Trails Museum

DECEMBER 22, 1846

Stanton dies in the snow; snowshoers' food is exhausted

Charles T. Stanton — small and brave — is dead at age 35.

Twice the bachelor reached safety and twice he returned to help others. Honor demanded it.

Yesterday, as fourteen of the Forlorn Hope party left camp, Stanton, weak and snow-blind, sat on a log near the fire. He lit a pipe and smoked calmly, as though he were in his house in Brooklyn or sitting at the counter of his failed mercantile business in Chicago.

"I am coming soon," Stanton told them. Rescuers will find his bones next spring.

Yesterday, the sixth day of the escape attempt, rations ran out. In his pack, William Eddy found a small package of bear meat and a note from his wife, signed "Your Own Dear Eleanor."

Today the Miwok Indians, Luis and Salvador, guide the party through tangled watersheds. Bear Valley and safety are a day away, but with no landmarks, they are lost.

Tonight at the lake camp, Patrick Breen — recovered from an attack of kidney stones — thanks heaven. Tomorrow he will begin the Thirty Days Prayer of the Roman Catholic faith.

By noon today, another storm hits and the Forlorn Hope party makes camp. They pray for Stanton's return. They pray for good weather.

Their answer: bitter wind, blinding snow.

From this day on, cannibalism will be their only hope and their greatest horror.

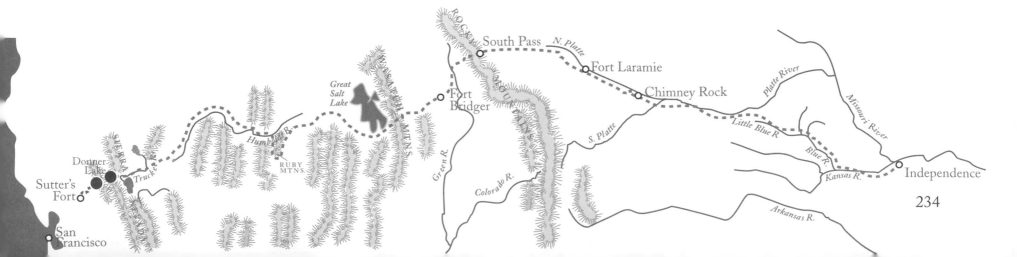

234

Mid–19th-century map showing the western United States.
— Nevada Historical Society

Tuesd. 22nd Snowd. all last night Continued to snow all day with some few intermissions had a severe fit of the gravel yesterday I am well to day, Praise be to the God of Heaven.

Wend. 23rd Snowd. a little last night clear to day & thawing a little. Milt took some of his meat to day all well at their camp began this day to read the Thirty days prayer, may Almighty God grant the request of an unworthy sinner that I am. Amen.

Thursd. 24th Rained all night & still continues to rain poor prospect for any kind of comfort spiritual or temporal, wind S: may God help us to spend the Christmass as we ought considering circumstances.

— Patrick Breen, diary

They then wrapped their blankets about them and slept upon the snow till the morning light recalled them to their weary travel. On the morning of their fifth day out, poor Stanton sat late by the camp-fire. The party had set off, all but Miss G., and as she turned to follow her father and sister, she asked him if he would soon come. He replied that he should, and she left him smoking. He never left the desolate fireside. His remains were found there by the next party who pased.
— Eliza Farnham, *California Indoors and Out*

And Mr. Stanton, who sacrificed his life to assist his companions — for he had no family or relations in the company — should be held in honored remembrance by every one who can appreciate a noble act. [As we ascended the Sierra] the clouds on the mountains looked very threatening, but he naturally looked at the bright side of things, and assured us there was no danger, little thinking that the next summer's sun would bleach his unburied bones, not far from that spot.
— John Breen, *Pioneer Memoirs*

December 25, 1846

Donner Christmas

Christmas dinner in the Reed cabin in a painting by William Henry Jackson — Emigrant Trails Museum

In the Reed family cabin at Donner Lake, the Christmas spirit is alive.

For weeks the Reeds and the others at the lake and Alder Creek camps have been boiling strips of oxhide and eating the gluey mess that results. A few have hoarded scraps of dried beef, but they will save them for a last meal.

Today is different.

In the Reed family's half of the Graves cabin, Margaret Reed has a Christmas surprise for her children.

"My mother had determined weeks before that her children should have a treat on this one day," Virginia Reed will remember. "She had laid away a few dried apples, some beans, a bit of tripe, and a small piece of bacon."

On Christmas morning, the family — Margaret Reed, 32; Virginia, 13; Patty, 8; James Jr., 5; and Thomas, 3 — has oxhide "soup." This evening, a feast is presented.

"The delight of the little ones knew no bounds," Virginia will remember. "The cooking was watched carefully."

"It was simply grand!" Patty will recall.

The family sits down to dinner in the flickering light of a pine stick fire as a blizzard howls.

"Children, eat slowly," Mrs. Reed says, "for this one day you can have all you wish."

Even thirty years later, the memory of that starved Christmas will burn in Virginia's mind: "So bitter was the misery relieved by that one bright day, that I have never since sat down to a Christmas dinner without my thoughts going back to Donner Lake."

The Graves children also eat beans, rice, and tripe, but in the other two cabins at the lake the day is almost unobserved.

"Rained all night and still continues to rain," Patrick Breen wrote yesterday. "Poor prospect for any kind of

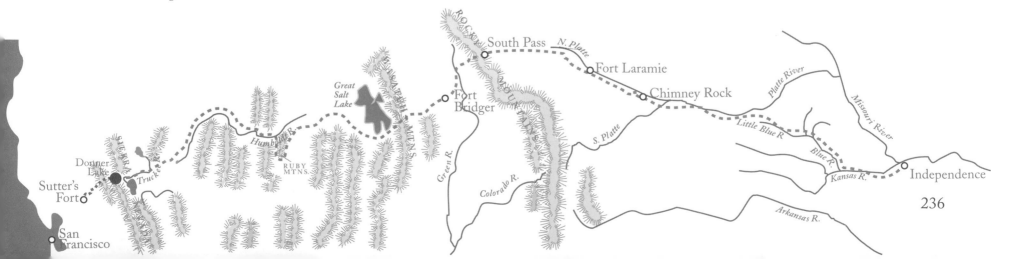

comfort . . . may God help us to spend the Christmass as we ought considering circumstances."

It began to snow yesterday about noon, snowed all night and still snows rapidly today, he notes in his diary. He's too sick to get wood. His sons search for some.

"Offerd. our prayers to God this Christmas morning the prospect is apalling but hope in God Amen," Breen writes.

At the Alder Creek camp, the holiday passes as any other day. The struggle to keep the snow from crushing the tents is a full-time job for the few people in the Donner camp who can still move.

The rest, soaked to the bone and wrapped in blankets, quilts and stinking buffalo robes, barely stir.

Even they are not in the worst circumstances.

Today, in the makeshift camp of the Forlorn Hope party, southwest of what will become Donner Pass, the snowshoers are reeling from one disaster after another.

Charles Stanton, their guide, was left behind four days ago.

Two days ago the storm caught them in the open and they hurriedly made camp.

Antonio, the 23-year-old Mexican herder, was the first to die. His hand fell into the fire, was removed once, and when it fell back into the flames no one moved him.

Patrick Dolan, 35, gone mad with hunger, and Franklin "Uncle Billy" Graves, 57, are also dead.

The eleven remaining members of the Forlorn Hope party decide they will eat the dead. With his last breath, Graves begged his daughters to use his flesh for nourishment.

The fire has gone out and can't be rekindled. The blizzard lashes them. Prayers become screams, then moans.

William Eddy gathers the party under blankets as the wind tugs at frozen hands.

Cannibalism will wait. Today, mere survival is the first priority.

Christmas Eve came, no stockings to hang, no Santa Claus to come down our chimney in that cold starving camp. No Papa to come home to his children . . . Christmas morning came and our breakfast was a pot of glue, it was stewed ox hide, but we were pleased to have even that to eat. But as soon as we had gone through this . . . our mother's face began to brighten . . .she had a surprise awaiting us.

— Patty Reed, Pioneer Children on the Journey West

Friday 25th Began to snow yesterday about 12 o clock snowd. all night & snows yet rapidly wind about E by N Great difficulty in geting wood John & Edwd. has to get I am not able offerd. our prayers to God this Christmas morning the prospect is apalling but hope in God Amen.

— Patrick Breen, diary

His wife and seven children were at the cabins, and he had pressed forward, feeling in that effort the only hope of saving them. But now, all power to serve them was gone, and, perfectly conscious of their own and his condition, he laid down under the relentless storm to die. In that desolate hour of death, he called his youngest daughter to his side, and bade her cherish and husband every chance of life, in the fearful days which he knew awaited them. They were still far from habitation or help, except such as God gave them, and their own courageous hearts. She must revolt at nothing that would keep life in her till she could reach some help for those whom they both loved. He clearly foreshadowed the terrible necessity to which, within a few hours, he saw they must come, and died, leaving his injunction upon her, to yield to it as resolutely as she had done everything else that had been required of her since their sufferings began.

— Eliza Farnham, California In-doors and Out

My mother had determined weeks before that her children have a treat on this one day. She had laid away a few dried apples, some beans, a bit of tripe and a small piece of bacon. When this hoarded store was brought out, the delight of the little ones knew no bounds. The cooking was watched carefully and when we sat down to our Christmas dinner, mother said, 'Children eat slowly, for this one day you can have all you wish.' So bitter was the misery relieved this one bright day, that I have never since sat down to a Christmas dinner without my thoughts going back to Donner Lake.

— Virginia Reed, Pioneer Children on the Journey West

December 27, 1846

Starving snowshoers eat the dead, avoid one another's eyes, and cry

In later remembrances, this place will be known as the Camp of Death.

On Christmas day, the eleven surviving members of the Forlorn Hope party huddled under blankets as a storm roared around them. The bodies of Antonio, Patrick Dolan, and Franklin Graves were nearby.

They dreamed of food. Some accounts will say they awoke to sink their teeth in one another's arms.

Yesterday, William Eddy attempted to start a fire under the blankets but he exploded his powder horn instead. He's badly burned.

The clouds broke yesterday afternoon. They used flint, steel, and cotton from Harriet Pike's coat to spark a flame. They set fire to a pine tree.

Beneath this blaze they cut the flesh from Patrick Dolan's arms and legs. A survivor will remember they "roasted it by the fire and ate it, averting their faces from each other and weeping."

William Eddy, who recently ate bear meat, and the Indians, Luis and Salvador, refused the meal. The Miwoks moved away from the others.

Lemuel Murphy, 12, delirous with hunger, was offered food, but couldn't be roused. The group slept on pine boughs under the burning tree while flaming branches fell around them.

As the quarter-moon set this morning, Lemuel Murphy died.

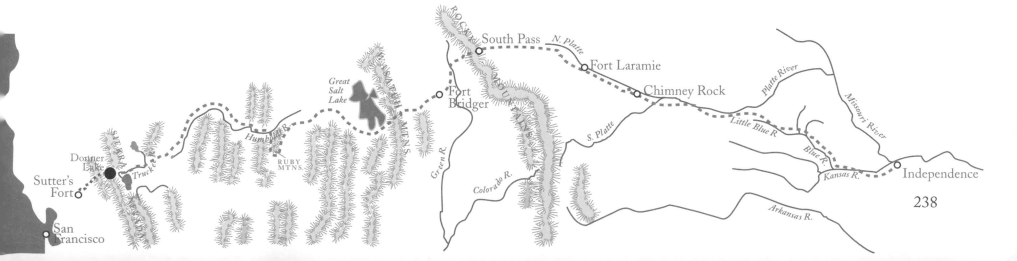

THE CAMP OF DEATH.

"Camp of Death," lithograph
— Emigrant Trails Museum

*Satd. 26th Cleared off in the night to day clear &
pleasant Snowd. about 20 inches or two feet deep
yesterday, the old snow was nearly run soft before it
began to snow now it is all soft the top dry & the
under wet wind S. E.*

*Sund. 27th Continues clear froze hard last
night Snow very deep say 9 feet thawing a little in
the sun scarce of wood to day chopt. a tree dow it
sinks in the snow & is hard to be got.*

— Patrick Breen, diary

December 29, 1846

"Dutch Charlie" dies at lake; snowshoers butcher the dead

At the lake cabins, the snow is nine feet deep.

Patrick Breen's sons have chopped down a tree, but the timber sinks in the snow and they have trouble getting at the branches.

Today is fine and clear, Breen writes in his diary. He reports "Dutch Charlie" Burger is very sick. Burger dies at 10 p.m.

His body joins others in snowy graves.

At the Donner camp six miles away at Alder Creek, fires are started but hardly anyone stirs. More hides are boiled. More snow is shoved off the tents' roofs. More water and more vermin invade their beds.

Miles to the southwest, the ten surviving members of the Forlorn Hope party are methodically carving up the bodies of four dead people, including Lemuel Murphy, 12.

They roast and eat some of the flesh. The rest is dried for their journey.

There is one rule: Family members are prohibited from touching their kin.

Still, author George Stewart will write, the attempt at propriety hardly reduced the horror.

"As she sat by the fire, [Sarah Murphy Foster, 19] suddenly realized that spitted upon a stick and broiling over the coals she saw the heart of her cherished younger brother."

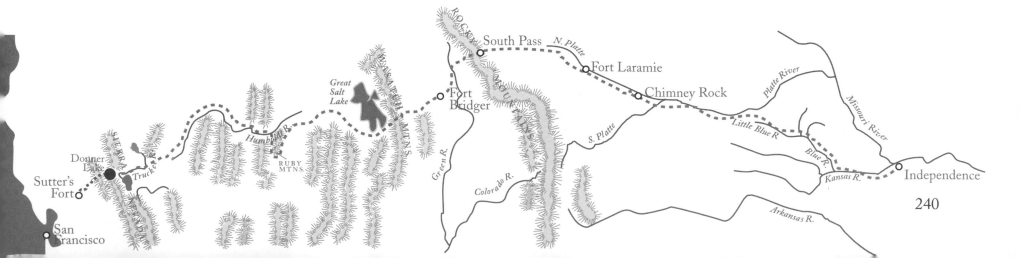

Members of the Donner Party attempt to make their way across the pass in a painting by Robert Lebron. — Emigrant Trails Museum

Monday 28th Snowd. last night cleared off this morning snowd. a little now clear & pleasant.

Tuesday 29th Fine clear day froze hard last night. Charley sick. Keysburg has Wolfings Rifle gun.

Wedsd. 30th Fine clear morning froze hard last night Charley died last night about 10 o clock had with him in money $1.50 two good loking silver watches one razor 3 boxes caps Keysburg tok them into his possession Spitzer took his coat & waistcoat Keysburg all his other little effects gold pin one shirt and tools for shaveing.

Thursday 31st Last of the year, may we with Gods help spend the comeing year better than the past which we purpose to do if Almight God will deliver us from our present dredful situation which is our prayer if the will of God sees it fiting for us Amen. morning fair now cloudy wind E by S for three days past freezeing hard every night looks like another snow storm Snow Storms are dredful to us snow very deep

— Patrick Breen, diary

More cut trees found near the camps of the Donner Party — Nevada Historical Society

JANUARY 1 THROUGH MAY, 1847

Part 3: The Calamity
Donner Lake to California

January 1, 1847

Forlorn Hope survivors see safety on horizon

*John Trudeau
— Emigrant Trails
Museum*

A new year has dawned on despair in the high camps and renewed hope for the snowshoe party trying to escape the Sierra.

At the Donner camp at Alder Creek, John Baptiste Trudeau, 16, again climbs a tree and peers westward. He sees plumes of blowing snow and smoke from the lake cabins, but no men or mules.

Last night at the lake camp, the Breen family observed New Year's Eve with prayers for deliverance.

Today in his diary, Patrick Breen writes: "Commenced snowing last night does not snow fast . . . sun pops out at times provisions getting scant dug up a hide from under the snow yesterday for Milt [Elliot]. . . ."

Those at the lake camps wonder about the fifteen people who escaped seventeen days ago. The nearest settlement was calculated to be six days' walk. Have they reached Sutter's? Is help on the way?

Miles to the southwest, the Forlorn Hope party is again on the move. The ten survivors of the snowshoe party — five women and five men, including the two Miwok Indian guides — left the Camp of Death two days ago. They packed dried human flesh carved from four of the five dead men, and moved west through twisting canyon country.

Luis the Miwok, who speaks some English, tells the pioneers he is lost without landmarks. Yesterday, they crossed a high ridge and saw snowless hills in the distance and a wide valley beyond. Is it the Sacramento Valley? It seems far.

This morning, their feet bloody and cracked from repeated frostbite, they slide down a canyon and cross a snowbridge over a stream. Then they grasp bushes and roots to make their way up a steep slope.

Jay Fosdick is in the rear, weak and nearly unable to walk. Should the stronger people wait for him when delay might mean their own lives are forfeit? What will happen when the food runs out?

Tonight, the ten survivors, who are without an ax, light a pine tree ablaze. Crouched around the light, they eat the last of their grisly provisions.

Tomorrow, starvation will stalk them again.

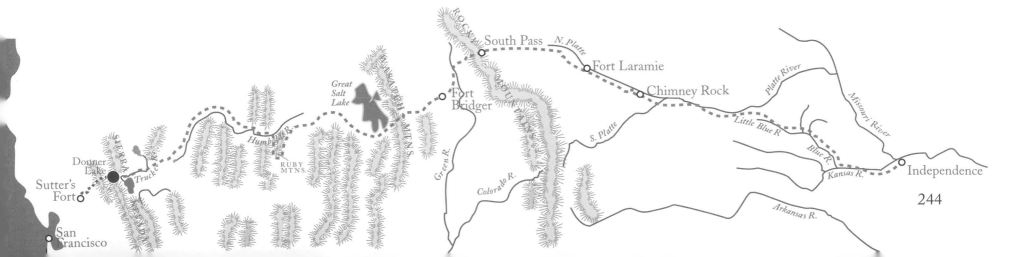

Winds blow off the peaks in the Sierra above Donner Lake. — Nevada Historical Society

Jany. 1st 1847 We pray the God of mercy to deliver us from our present calamity if it be his Holy will Amen. Commenced. snowing last night does not snow fast wind S:E sun peeps out at times provisions geting scant dug up a hide from under the snow yesterday for Milt. did not take it yet.

Sat. 2nd Fair & thawey snow got soft wind S-E look thawey froze pretty hard last night.

— Patrick Breen, diary

WAR NEWS, 1847: Tomorrow, James F. Reed, an officer in the California Battalion, will fight in the battle of Santa Clara.

The skirmish will be an American victory. Having done his duty in the Mexican War, his efforts will soon turn to the rescue of his wife and four children, entrapped in the Sierra with no food but ox hides.

January 3, 1847

Luis and Salvador flee to avoid being eaten

In the Donner Lake camps, the sun is shining again.

The Breen family is boiling hides. Margaret Reed, now out of all food stores, has nothing but hides left.

Today Reed plans a desperate escape attempt with Virginia, 13, her oldest daughter, and her two employees. They will leave tomorrow. Maybe they can cross the pass and meet rescuers coming the other way. Surely some members of the snowshoe party have alerted Sutter's Fort to their plight by now.

But the Forlorn Hope party is lost beyond the pass. Today, Jay Fosdick, 23, staggers, half-blind, in drifts as the other nine members of the party plod in front of him. As the snowshoers descend, oak trees begin to appear among the pines and cedars. All suffer from frostbite and some have blackened toes as they struggle along ridges and ravines. Blood oozes from their boots and moccasins.

Tonight they camp in three feet of snow. They bake the oxhide thongs of their snowshoes and eat the crisp strings. Without real food, they can't go much farther. Tomorrow they will make only two miles, but it's enough to reach the snowline. They will camp on bare ground in a grove of oak trees.

Odds are Fosdick will be the next of the ten survivors to die. But William Foster, 30, has another idea: Kill and eat the two Miwok Indians, Luis and Salvador. Foster's suggestion is shaped by generations of warfare between settlers and native populations. Are the "savages" not less than people? William Eddy, 28, argues against the plan. He says the party should draw lots to determine who is to die. But the others favor killing the Christian Miwoks, despite the fact they risked their own lives to save people they do not know and have done no harm.

"[Eddy] could not convince the others," George Stewart will write, "but forestalling them he warned Luis. "The Indian stood for a minute in mute amazement . . . He and Salvador disappeared from camp."

The eight whites — three men and five women — remain together. Eddy and Mary Ann Graves, 19, the two strongest, will go ahead while the others lag behind. Eddy takes their only rifle. Unless he finds a target soon, more will die so close to safety.

The others strain their ears for the sound of a gunshot.

Sund. 3rd Continues fair in day time freezeing at night wind about E Mrs. Reid talks of crossing the mountains with her children provisions scarce.
— Patrick Breen, diary

Donner Lake seen from the pass in winter — Emigrant Trails Museum

January 5, 1847

Mrs. Reed attempts escape; William Eddy shoots a deer

Mond. 4th Fine morning looks like spring thawing now about 12 o clock wind S:E Mrs. Reid Milt. Virginia & Eliza started about (an) hour ago with prospect of crossing the mountain may God of Mercy help them left ther children here Tom's with us Pat with Keysburg & Jas with Gravese's folks, it was difficult for Mrs Reid to get away from the children.

Tuesday. 5th Beautiful day thawing some in the sun wind S–E snow not settling much we are in hopes of the rainy time ending.

Weds. 6th Find day clear not a cloud froze very hard last night with S:E Eliza came back from the mountain yesterday evening not able to proceed, to day went to Graves, the other kept ahead.

— Patrick Breen, diary

It's a beautiful day in the high camps and in the mountains to the west.

Yesterday, Margaret Reed, 32; her daughter, Virginia, 13; Milt Elliot, 28; and Eliza Williams, 31; left the camp and attempted a walk to safety.

The other Reed children — Patty, 8; James Jr., 5; and Thomas, 3 — are left with the Breen family. Mrs. Reed cries and hugs her children close. It is torture to leave them here. This is the first of many instances where the Breens' charity will save the family of the absent James F. Reed.

Williams, exhausted and frostbitten, returned to the Graves cabin today. The other three keep going, armed with a compass and a few matches. They climb mountains to find more peaks beyond. Virginia weakens and begins to crawl behind her mother, who plods in the tracks of Elliot's homemade snowshoes.

"The nights were made hideous by the screams of wild beasts," Virginia will remember. "We would be lulled to sleep by the moan of the pine trees."

Miles ahead below the snowline, the eight white members of the Forlorn Hope party today follow the trail left by Luis and Salvador, the two Miwoks who fled the party rather than become their next meal.

William Eddy, 28, will tell this story: He and Mary Ann Graves, 19, are well in the lead. They notice a nest of crushed grass where a deer spent the night. As they make their way downhill, they spot a doe eighty yards away.

Eddy is too weak to raise the rifle. Finally, he lifts the flintlock straight up and swings it downward. He pulls the trigger as the muzzle tracks past the deer.

"Oh, merciful God, you've missed it," screams Graves as the deer bolts.

The two stagger after the animal and find it wounded. Eddy cuts its throat and they drink hot blood as it spurts like a fountain. They build a fire and roast its liver.

With the rest of the party still far in the rear, Eddy and Graves curl up under a tree and sleep.

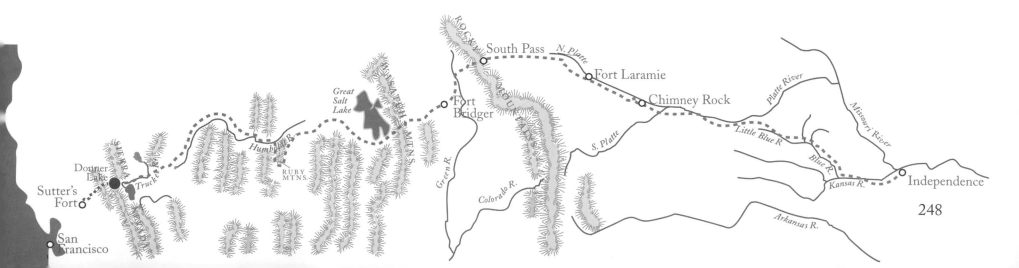

Aerial view of Donner Lake in winter. — Marilyn Newton photo

JANUARY 8, 1847

Reeds return to lake camp;
Fosdick dies with snowshoers

"Mrs. Reid [Reed] & company came back this [morning] could not find their way on the other side of the mountain they have nothing but hides to live on," writes Patrick Breen today at what will be named Donner Lake.

"Martha [Patty Reed] is to stay here [in the Breen cabin]," he writes. Milt Elliot and Eliza Williams are going to the Donners'; Margaret Reed and two sons will find shelter with daughter Virginia. "[P]rospects dull may God relieve us all from the difficults if it is his Holy will Amen."

Virginia's toes are frozen. She and the others had walked for five days in cold, sunny weather but could not escape the snowy trap. They returned just in time. Tonight, snow will fall again.

Miles to the west, Jay Fosdick, 23, has been dead four days. He expired shortly after hearing shots fired by William Eddy, who was trying to attract the other members of the party to the site where he and Mary Ann Graves had killed a deer.

Historians will debate the deer tale because Eddy is the only survivor who mentions the incident. Mary Ann Graves, who later wrote an account of the escape, is frank about cannibalism but omits the deer story.

The day after Fosdick's death, his wife, Sarah, 21, William Foster, 30, and his wife Sarah, 19, goes back to the body. Foster carves away the arms and legs and removes the heart and liver for food.

Sarah Fosdick's pleas to leave her dead husband alone go unheeded. Others will eat his flesh.

Today, with William Foster weak and stumbling, the seven white survivors climb a steep rock slope. They eat dried meat [deer or human?] at the top and fall asleep under a rain-laden sky.

Foster is raving like a madman. Eddy will later say Foster proposed to kill and eat Amanda McCutchen, 30. Eddy will say he protected the woman by threatening Foster with a knife.

Others will say Eddy was suspected of trying to lead Mary Ann Graves away from the party so he could kill and eat her.

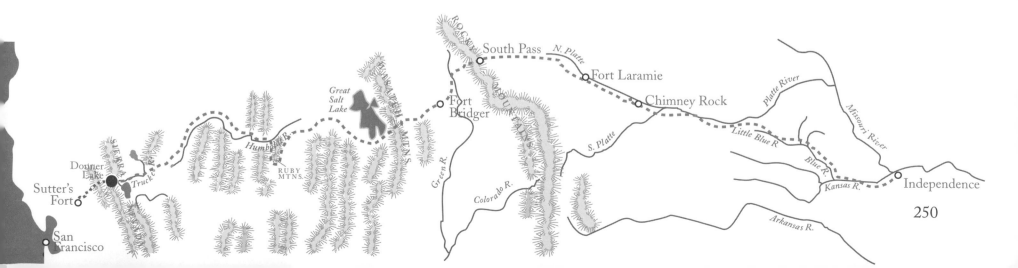

The time of desperation has arrived. Starving, frozen, and exhausted, their old taboos shattered, the last members of the Forlorn Hope party are shedding the mantle of civilization.

Tomorrow they will march with bleeding feet and come upon bloody footprints in the mud. These are the tracks of the Miwoks — Luis and Salvador — who fled their white companions rather than be eaten.

Foster will follow these prints the way a hunter tracks an animal. And for the same reasons.

Thursd. 7th Continues fine freezing hard at night very cold this morning wind S.S.E dont think we will have much more snow not thawing much not much dineinished in debph.

Friday 8th Fine morning wind E froze hard last night very cold this morning Mrs. Reid & company came back this moring could not find their way on the other side of the mountain they have nothing but hides to live on Martha is to stay here Milt. & Eliza going to Donos Mrs. Reid & the 2 boys going to their own shanty & Virginia prospects dull may God relieve us all from the difficults if it is his Holy will Amen.

Satd 9th Continues fine freezeing hard at night this a beatiful morning wind about S.S.E Mrs. Reid here Virginias toes frozen a little snow settleing none to be preceivd.

— Patrick Breen, diary

A survivor prays over one of the unfortunate ones in a painting by Robert Lebron.
— Emigrant Trails Museum

January 10, 1847

Foster kills Luis and Salvador while others turn away

Today Luis and Salvador lie dead and butchered for their flesh by people they risked their lives to save.

The seven white survivors of the Forlorn Hope party, again out of food, followed the Indians' bloody footprints in the mud. William Eddy will say the two men and five women came upon the Miwoks as they were lying, exhausted and near death, by a stream.

Foster, who earlier had proposed killing the Indians for food, took his rifle and approached them. Eddy and the five women walked away, faced the woods, and heard two gunshots. Foster will tell Eddy that Luis understood the terrible need to die so that others may eat. Captain John Sutter, who sent "his two good boys," as he called the *vaqueros*, to help the pioneers, will say the pair were gathering acorns when Foster shot them.

The crime is double murder, but no court will ever hear the case. In 1847, Indians are casually killed in punishment of theft or just for sport. It will be said that Lansford W. Hastings, among others, shot Indian passersby for target practice. Some emigrants and settlers consider peaceful "Diggers" fair game.

Nearly fifteen decades later, author Joseph King will look for records of the two unsung heroes. He will find baptismal documents at Mission San Jose. His theory: Luis was Eema of the Ochehamne group of Miwoks and would have been 19 years old in 1847. Salvador was QueYen of the Cosumne group and would have been 28.

Their murders will remain unpunished because many whites considered them less than human beings. The name Miwok comes from the tribe's word "Miwu," which means person.

One hundred and fifty years after their deaths, they will have no monument, except their tribe, which will endure.

Meanwhile at the high camps, snow falls. Life has settled down to days of half-sleep and meals of boiled hides and bone soup, which always simmer on fires. In the Graves/Reed cabin, families are at odds over food and space.

Tonight, the snow falls faster.

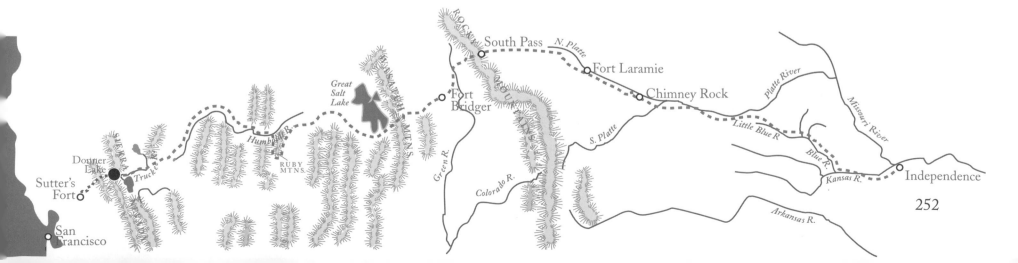

Northern California Indian boys are shown in this undated sketch — Emigrant Trail Museum

Sund. 10 Began to snow last night still continues wind W N W.

Mond. 11th Still continues to snow fast, looks gloomy Mrs Reid at Keysburgs Virg. with us wood scarce difficult to get any more wind W.
— Patrick Breen, diary

JANUARY 12, 1847

Miwoks help survivors of the Forlorn Hope party

Tuesd 12th Snows fast yet new snow about 3 feet deep wind S:W no sign of clearing off.

Wens. 13th Snowing fast wind N.W snow higher than the shanty must be 13 feet deep dont know how to get wood this morning it is dredful to look at.

— Patrick Breen, diary

After more than twenty miles of travel since the killings of Luis and Salvador, the seven survivors of the Forlorn Hope party have reached a haven among brethren of men they murdered.

This morning, walking over grassy hills and through sparse forests in a rainstorm, the haggard pioneers came upon an Indian trail. This afternoon, they reach a Miwok village.

The Indians are astounded at these walking skeletons. They feed them acorn bread. William Eddy can't tolerate the meal and eats grass. The survivors will stay the night in the Indians' shelters.

In the high camps, the snow falls fast. Margaret Reed has left the Graves cabin and is staying with the Kesebergs. Virginia Reed has moved in with the Breens, who already shelter her sister Patty.

"Poor little children were crying with hunger, and mothers were crying because they had so little to give their children," Virginia will remember decades later. "We seldom thought of bread, we had been without it so long. Four months of such suffering would fill the bravest hearts with despair."

The air is full of the stink of boiling oxhides.

Early on, Virginia passed her time at the camps by reading the same books over and over. She read *The Life of Daniel Boone*, and was cheered by the description of this hero of the wilderness. But now the books are burned and their covers have been consumed for food.

Wood is impossible to find. The snow at the lake is thirteen feet deep — higher than the cabin roofs.

"It is dredful to look at," Patrick Breen will write in his diary tomorrow.

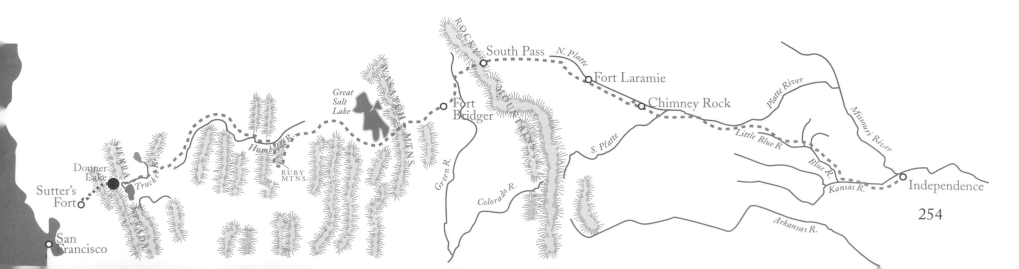

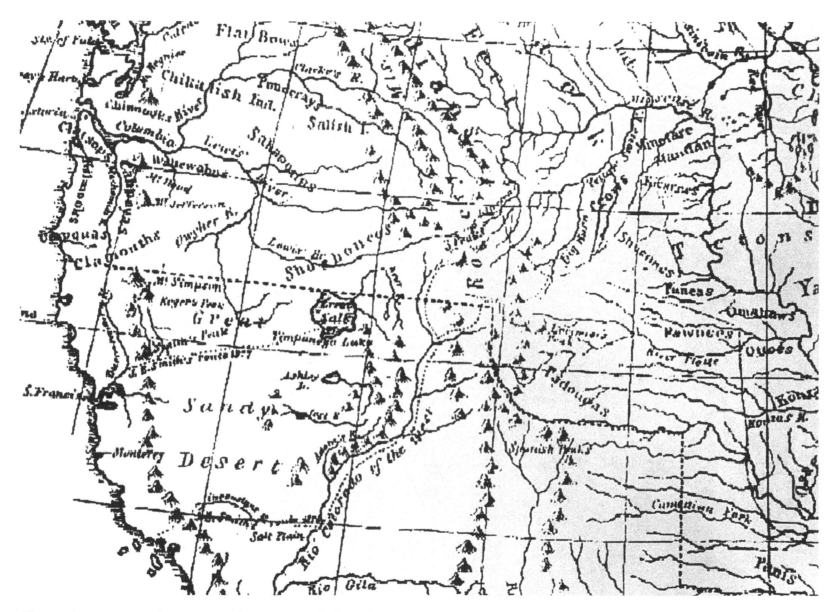

Nineteenth-century map of western area of country names Indian tribes known to the mapmakers. — Marilyn Newton photo

January 15, 1847

Miwoks guide survivors; snow buries lake camps

Today, the Miwoks' generosity and care protects the starving survivors of the Forlorn Hope escape party.

William Eddy, William Foster, Amanda McCutchen, Mary Ann Graves, Sarah Fosdick, Harriet Murphy Pike, and Sarah Murphy are eating acorn bread and pine nuts supplied by their Indian hosts.

Everyone in the Miwok communities, from the elders to little children, displays concern for these lost, emaciated whites.

The party reached a second village two days ago and rested before resuming their trek today.

The ragged pioneers are so weak they can barely lift their feet over logs or go a hundred yards without resting. The Miwok guides take them down trails and through canyons towards Bear Valley and the American settlements.

The Indians' rations do little to offset the survivors' malnutrition. They are fading fast.

For the last few days rain has continued to sweep the valleys and snow has covered the high camps. Today, the sun shines on the Sierra.

"Fine clear day," writes Patrick Breen in his diary. Mrs. Murphy, however, has gone snowblind. Her son, John, is unable to get to the trees buried in the drifts. He has only one ax between him and Lewis Keseberg, who moved in with the Murphys yesterday, Breen reports.

"Looks like another storm [coming] expecting some account from Suiters soon." Breen spells Sutter's as "Suiters" — the way it was pronounced in 1847.

There will soon be rescue activity at Sutter's Fort, but not in time to save the lives of all entrapped in the Sierra camps.

For now, their lives depend upon seven living skeletons making their way into Bear Valley.

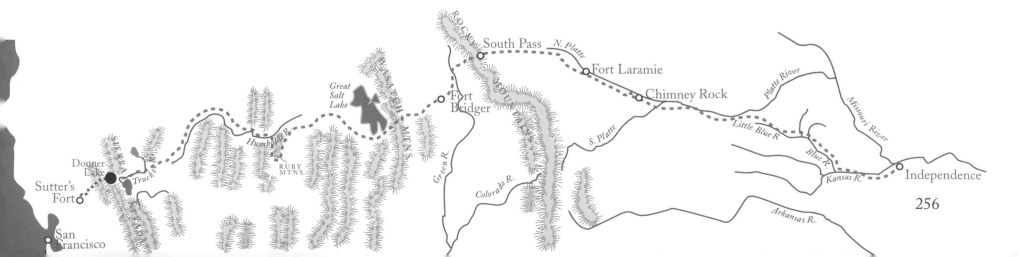

Snow in the Sierra near Donner Lake. — Tim Dunn photo

Thursd. 14th New moon Cleard. off yesterday evening snowd. a little during first part of night Calm but a little air from the North very pleasant to day sun shineing brilliantly renovates our spirits prais be to God, Amen.

Frid. 15th Fine clear day wind N W Mrs. Murphy blind Lanth. Not able to get wood has but one axe betwist him & Keysburg, he moved to Murphys yesterday looks like another storm expecting some account from Suiters soon.

Satd. 16th Wind blew hard all night from the W. abated a little did not freeze much this is clear & pleasant wind a little S of W no telling what the weather will do.

— Patrick Breen, diary

JANUARY 17, 1847

William Eddy reaches settlement in Johnson's Ranch area

William Eddy
— Emigrant Trails
Museum

Just before sunset, Harriet Ritchie goes to the door of her parents' cabin in Bear Valley and is startled by three visitors.

She sees a ghostly white man, haggard as a cadaver, supported between two Indian boys.

The specter speaks. "Bread," it croaks. "Bread."

Weeping, Harriet leads the skeletal man inside and gives him biscuits. Wrapping him in a quilt, she puts him in a bed. He seems near death. His name is William Eddy.

He tells her there are more — six others — behind him. They have walked out of the Sierra. They are members of the Donner Party.

The neighborhood is alerted. Food, in short supply in this emigrant camp, is prepared. Coffee is boiled, beans cooked, bread baked.

Many miles to the east in the lake camp, Patrick Breen has no such relief. "Fine morning sun shining clear wind." he writes in his diary. "Eliza came here this morning, sent her back again to Graves [cabin].

"Lanthrom [John Landrum Murphy] crazy last night so Bill [Murphy] says, Keyburg sent Bill to get hides off his shanty & carry thim home this morning

"Provisions scarce hides are the only article we depend on, we have a little meat yet, may God send us help."

In Bear Valley tonight, four men with packs, guided by the two Miwoks, retrace Eddy's trail by the light of the new moon's sliver.

They follow bloody footprints a half-dozen miles to where six exhausted people lie in the mud.

After thirty-three days, the Forlorn Hope party's journey is over. Of the fifteen snowshoers, all five women and two men survived. Eight men are dead. All but one was eaten by the others.

The survivors will soon tell the tale.

The news will shake California.

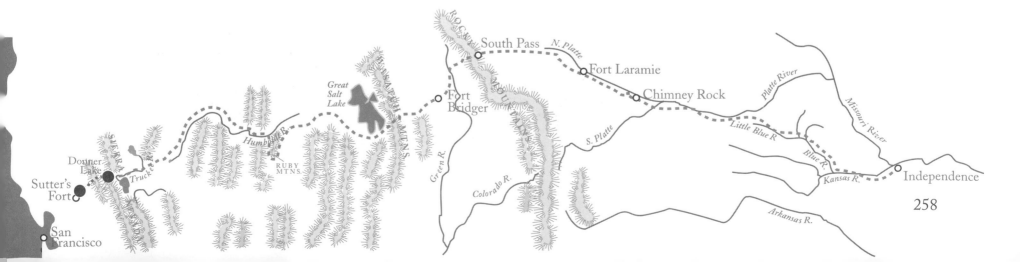

Dirt now covers the foundation of the adobe building at the Johnson's Ranch where the emigrants stayed after their rescue from the Sierra. The ranch is near Sacramento.
— Marilyn Newton photo

Sund. 17th Fine morning sun shineing clear wind S.S.E Eliza came here this morning, sent her back again to Graves Lanthrom crazy last night so Bill says, Keyburg sent Bill to get hides off his shanty & carry thim home this morning, provisions scarce hides are the only article we depend on, we have a little meat yet, may God send us help.

Mond. 18th Fine day clear & pleasant wind W, thawing in the sun Mrs. Murphy here to day very hard to get wood.

— Patrick Breen, diary

Artifacts of the 1840s were found at Johnson's Ranch — from the Jack Steed collection

JANUARY 19, 1847

Eddy sends letter for help; thaw begins at high camps

Daniel Rhodes
— Bancroft Library

Eliza Donner
— Bancroft Library

This morning, William Eddy awoke to a beautiful day in Bear Valley.

He has rested and had a meal. He's thinking of his wife, three-year-old son, and infant daughter still trapped in the Sierra snow. The Bear Valley settlements don't have the men or the expertise to mount a rescue party.

Daniel Rhodes, who was among the men who brought in the other Forlorn Hope survivors yesterday, will write that there "wasn't more than 14 men in the Sacrament Valley." Rhodes and his brother, John, Mormons and men of conscience, will vow to get the Donner Party to safety or die in the attempt.

Sutter's Fort, forty miles to the south, is Eddy's best hope. He sits up in bed and dictates a letter outlining the plight of the entrapped party. He sends the message with a Miwok runner to John Sinclair, who owns a ranch near Sutter's. The war with Mexico has made government authority uncertain, but Sinclair is the designated *acalde* (mayor) of northern California.

Yesterday at Mission San Jose, Lt. R. F. Pinkley of the U.S.S. *Savannah* handed over the keys to the mission to Capt. James F. Reed, who spent the day planting grapes, barley, and fruit trees on his land claim.

At the Alder Creek camp high in the mountains, however, the Donner family is starving.

"John Baptiste [Trudeau] and Noah James went forth in anxious search for marks of our buried cattle," Eliza Donner will write. "They made excavations, then forced their handpoles deep, deeper in snow, but in vain their efforts — the nail and hook at the points brought up no sign of blood, hair or hide." Oxhides and mice are their diet.

Tamsen Donner, still nursing her sick husband, writes in her journal each day. She wants to remember what happened here.

At the lake shanties, Patrick Breen writes that his wife and son Edward became ill last night by eating some tobacco-tainted meat, but today they are recovered. Landrum (John) Murphy seems near death. "In danger if relief dont soon come." Tomorrow Breen will write, "Expecting some person across the mountain this week."

All eyes look to the west.

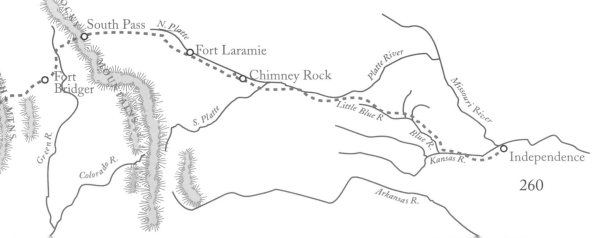

A lithograph of snow covered Donner summit looking east to Donner Lake
— Nevada Historical Society

Tuesd. 19th Clear & pleasant thawing a little in the sun wind S.W Peggy & Edward sick last night by eating some meat that Dolan threw his tobacco on, pretty well to day (praise God for his blessings,) Lanthrom very low in danger if relief dont soon come hides are all the[y] go[t], not much of any other in camp.

Wed. 20th Fine morning wind N froze hard last night. Expecting some person across the mountain this week.

— Patrick Breen, diary

I provided for the little children. It was I who brought in the wood, kept the fires going and tried to find food for the starving people of the Donner camps. The Donner family depended on me a great deal and even though I wanted to leave with the first relief, Mr. Donner talked to me and said, "I need you to take care of my family . . . you can have a home with us always, you will be a part of the family . . . you must stay and take care of them."

I would take the girls out of the huts to sit on the snow while I chopped the wood. I would take my old Navajo blanket and wind the girls up in it, one to each side, with their heads sticking out like the heads of pins in a roll of pin paper, and entirely rolled in its warm folds they would sit and watch me work. That old blanket was a great comfort to the little girls. Sometimes I would stretch it on poles above their heads to keep the rain off, or I would hang it as a shelter to keep the wind from piercing through them. At night I would put the big kettle over the fire coals and the little girls could hold their hands over the kettle to get some warmth before going to bed. We are true friends . . . without me they could not have lived to reach the valley.

— John Baptiste Trudeau

JANUARY 22, 1847

Rescue effort begins slowly; food critical in high camps

The rescue meeting at Sutter's Fort has yielded little result.

Capt. Kern, the fort's American commander, received William Eddy's appeal for help today. He offers $3 a day for men willing to rescue the Donners from their Sierra trap. The few men remaining at the fort during the war with Mexico are unimpressed. The pay is good, but the offer sounds like a suicide mission.

Three volunteers step forward: Joseph Sels, who had been a sailor and probably jumped ship; Aquilla Glover, an 1846 emigrant who had known the Donners on the plains; and Sept Moutry, another recently-arrived pioneer. These men, along with the two Rhodes brothers and a few others, should have "their names inscribed in letters of gold," Sheriff George McKinstry will later write. Three men aren't enough. In any case, John Sutter will have to wait until the *alcalde* returns from Yerba Buena (San Francisco). No official action can be taken without him.

And where is James F. Reed, who failed to get through to the Donner Party in November? His wife and four children remain entrapped in the mountains. He was last heard of in the south, fighting with the California Battalion.

There is much to be done before a rescue can commence.

At Donner Lake, the situation continues to worsen. Yesterday, John Baptiste Trudeau, 16, and the Englishman John Denton, 28, brought Eliza Williams, 31, from the Alder Creek camp back to the lake cabin of Patrick Breen. Williams can't digest boiled hides and she's come to beg meat from the Breens and Margaret Reed.

"Mrs. Reed sent her back to live or die on [hides]," Patrick Breen writes.

Breen reports that the Donners, encamped at Alder Creek about six miles away, "are all well." But that is a relative phrase. They are in worse shape than the lake camps and have less food. All are sick to some degree and George Donner is still in agony from a cut hand that hasn't healed.

This morning, snow again falls on the Sierra after eight days of sunshine.

"Likely to snow a good deal," Breen writes. He has learned the weather signs. By this afternoon, the snow is driven by a perfect gale from the west.

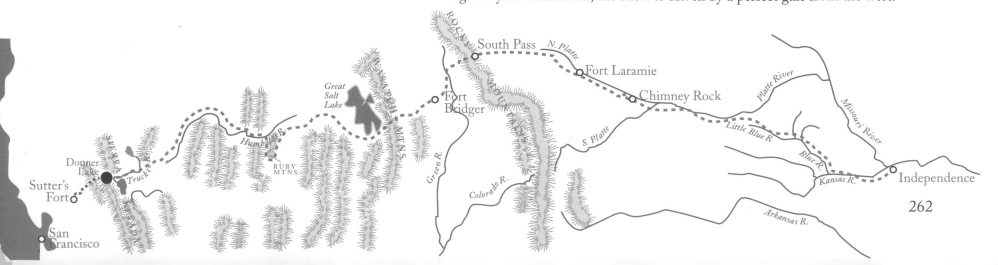

Sutter's Fort in 1846 — Sutter's Fort Museum

REED PREPARES HIS FUTURE

James F. Reed, a captain in the California Battalion, is now in charge of Mission San Jose where in December he made land claims for his family and forged the signature of his wife. Today, John Stark and William Daniels sign a statement that on January 18 they helped Reed plant "pear and apple trees together with a number of grape cuttings, for the purpose of raising an orchard, and vineyard," and also helped Reed plant barley. This statement will satisfy the homestead provisions for improving the land upon which a claim is filed.

Thursd. 21 Fine morning wind W did not freze quite so hard last night as it has done, John Battice & Denton came this morning with Eliza she wont eat hides Mrs Reid sent her back to live or die on them. Milt. got his toes froze the Donoghs are all well.

Frid. 22nd Began to snow a little after sunrise likely to snow a good dale wind W came up very suddenly, now 10 o clock.

Satd. 23rd Blew hard & snowd. all night the most severe storm we experienced this winter wind W sun now 12 oclock peeps out.

       — Patrick Breen, diary

January 24, 1847

Keseberg's infant son dies; Reed plans a rescue

Lewis Keseberg Jr. is dead at Donner Lake at the age of one year.

The baby died of multiple complications of being entrapped in the Sierra. Who can say if malnutrition, starvation, exposure, or sickness claimed his life?

The boy's father, Lewis Keseberg, is inconsolable. The child will be buried in the snow.

At the high camps the snow — which yesterday fell harder and faster than anyone at the lake had ever seen — has ceased but high clouds indicate more wet weather is coming.

"All in good health, thanks be to God," writes Patrick Breen, 51, referring to his own family of nine. He hasn't heard from the Murphys since the blizzard hit, but expects "to hear they suffered some."

Breen will hear of baby Keseberg's death in three days, when Philippine Keseberg comes to visit and ask for food. During this sixth storm, many people at the high camps have become so weary they don't even have the strength to search for wood and boil hides.

At Sutter's Fort, talk of a rescue attempt is still the hot topic, but the mayor still hasn't returned from San Francisco. Some of the men at the fort are saying that they might join the rescue party if the pay — already set at the exorbitant rate of $3 a day — were boosted to $5. Until the mayor returns, however, there's no one in authority to guarantee any payment at all.

James F. Reed has been busy as a military officer in the south. The land grants for his family and employees are guaranteed by forging the names of those held prisoner by the snow. The documents were signed with the probable complicity of the local authorities.

Today Reed is preparing to leave for San Francisco, which the Californians call Yerba Buena. He plans to gather support for a rescue.

He doesn't know of the activities at Sutter's or that seven haggard members of the Forlorn Hope snowshoe party have escaped the mountains.

Tonight, high in the Sierra camps, snow begins to fall.

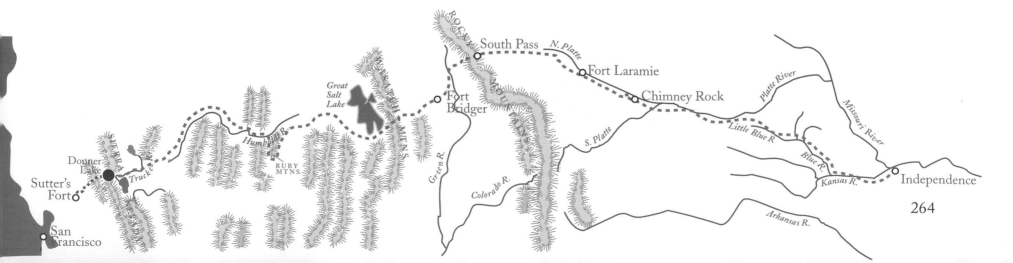

The Donner area blanketed with snow — Tim Dunn photo

If I believe in God Almighty having anything to do with the affairs of men, I believe that the misfortune which overtook the Donner Party, and the terrible part I was compelled to take in the great tragedy, was predestined.

— Lewis Keseberg, in a statement to C. F. McGlashan published in McGlashan's *History of the Donner Party*

Sund. 24th Some cloudy this morning ceased snowing yesterday about 2 oclock Wind about S. E all in good health thanks be to God for his mercies endureth for ever, heard nothing from Murphys camp since the storm expet to hear they sufferd some.

Mod 25th Began to snow yesterday evening & still continues wind W.

— Patrick Breen, diary

Philippine Keseberg
— Bancroft Library

Lewis Keseberg
— Bancroft Library

265

JANUARY 26, 1847

Officials will pay for rescue; men and supplies readied

Virginia Reed (Murphy),
— Bancroft Library

After a day of snow, the sun shines on the high camps as the sixth in a series of storms takes a respite.

"People geting weak," Patrick Breen notes today. Each night, Virginia Reed, 13, says prayers with the Catholic Breens in the dancing light of blazing pine twigs split like kindling wood.

"I was very fond of kneeling by the side of Mr. Breen and holding these little torches," Virginia will later write. "One night ... it was a fearful night and I felt the hour was not far distant when we would go to sleep never to awake again. All at once I found myself on my knees with my hands clasped, looking up through the darkness, making a vow that if God would send us relief and I would see my father again, I would be a Catholic."

Today, a relief party is assembling at Sutter's Fort. Captain John Sutter and the *alcalde*, John Sinclair, have guaranteed payment to volunteers who will risk their lives to get the survivors out of the Sierra. Four men join the original three.

Sutter and Sinclair donate horses and supplies and the men prepare to leave the fort.

Seven men are not enough to ride against the mountain. Sutter sends his launch, the *Sacramento*, downriver to Yerba Buena (San Francisco) to rally more support. He is also seeking James F. Reed and William McCutchen, who failed to get through the snow to reach their families in November.

Today Patrick Breen writes, "Hope we are done with snow storms."

Outside his cabin, snowflakes begin falling, and the white silence grows deeper.

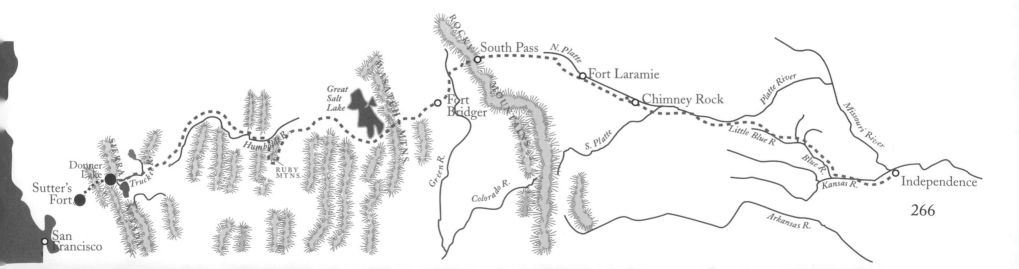

Donner Lake is frozen and covered in snow. — Emigrant Trails Museum

*Tuesd 26 Cleared up yesteday to day fine &
pleasant, wind S. in hope as we are done with snow
storms, those that went to Suitors not yet returned
provisions geting very scant people geting weak
liveing on short allowance of hides.*
— Patrick Breen, diary

*We now had nothing to eat but raw hides and they
were on the roof of the cabin to keep out the snow.
When prepared for cooking and boiled they were
simply a pot of glue. When the hides were taken off
our cabin and we were left without shelter Mr.
Breen gave us a home with his family, and Mrs.
Breen prolonged my life by slipping me little bits of
meat now and then when she discovered that I could
not eat the hide. We had to kill our little dog Cash ...
and eat him . . . we ate his head and feet and hide
and everything about him.*
— Virginia Reed, in a letter to her cousin

January 29, 1847

Murphy boys sick at lake; storm cycle ends

William McCutchen
— *from* History of the Donner Party
by C.F. McGlashan

At the Murphy cabin — where someday a plaque will record the names of the Donner Party — three boys are dreadfully ill.

The series of storms ended yesterday. Today the sun is shining.

The Murphy boys, John, also called Landrum, 16; William, 10; and Simon, 8; are huddled in the squat, hide-covered cabin. Their mother, Lavina, will go to the Breen cabin to beg a bit of meat.

John Murphy seems near death.

In all the cabins and in the tents at Alder Creek, the emigrants pray relief will come soon.

Today, James F. Reed is on his way to San Francisco and William McCutchen has been at Yount's Ranch in Sonoma trying to get help for the entrapped pioneers. Two days ago he wrote a letter to Reed:

"I am at Mr. Younts this morning with [Trapper Caleb] Greeenwood. The citizens are making a subscription to [help?] us into our Familys. We will start the first of February. If you come to Younts and we are gone you can over take us at Sutters we will go that way you had better come in fast as there is no time to delay your compliance will much oblige yours and mine."

Sutter's launch is also bound for San Francisco with the news of the Forlorn Hope survivors.

When all these people come together, relief will begin in earnest.

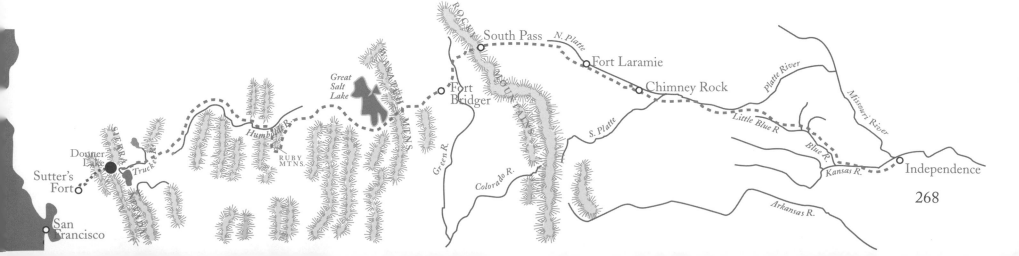

The only thing still remaining from the Donner party's stay at Donner Lake is this boulder used as a support for the Murphy cabin, pictured in summer. — Marilyn Newton photo

Weds 27th Began to snow yesterday & still continues to sleet thawing a little wind W Mrs. Keyber here this morning Lewis Suitor she says died three days ago Keysburg sick & Lanthrom lying in bed the whole of his time dont have fire enough to cook their hides. Bill & Sim. Murphy sick.

Thursd. 28th Full moon cleared off last night & froze some to day fine & warm wind S.E looks some like spring weather birds chirping qute lively full moon today.

— Patrick Breen, diary

JANUARY 31, 1847

First relief party leaves Sutter's; John Murphy dies at lake

Sixteen-year-old John "Landrum" Murphy is dead at the lake camp.

"My mother went to the Breens [yesterday] and begged a little meat," John's brother, William, 10, will say years later. "I remember well that little piece of meat! My mother gave half of it to my dying brother; he ate it [and] fell asleep with a hollow death gurgle.

"When it ceased I went to him — he was dead — starved to death in our presence. Although starving herself, my mother said that if she had known that Landrum was going to die she would have given him the balance of the meat."

Landrum died last night, under a full moon, at the same time Patrick Breen was recording grim events at the Graves cabin.

Elizabeth Graves, 45, has seized goods and oxhides belonging to Margaret Reed, 32. She took the property, Breen writes, "until they would be paid ... took hides that she and family had to live on."

Both women have small children. Reed had received meat from the Graves months ago, but Mrs. Graves now feels payment of the debt can't wait for safety in California. John Breen and Mrs. Reed go to the Graves cabin today "to look after her goods," Breen writes.

"You may know from these proceedings what our fare is in camp," Breen writes. He laments that the even with the thaw there are no animals about for hunting but he hopes there will soon be targets for his gun. "God send it Amen," he writes.

Today at Sutter's Fort, seven men on horseback with pack animals ride through the gates. They cross the swollen American River and slog north through the mud of recent rains.

Today, as a thaw begins in the high camps, the first rescue party is on its way.

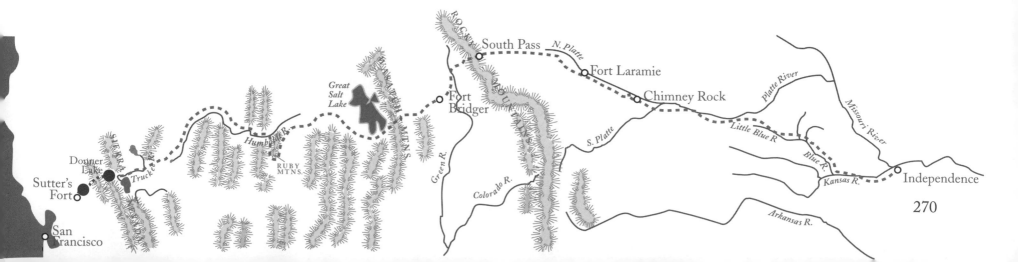

Donner Lake frozen and covered with snow
— Nevada Historical Society

Frid 29th Fine morning began to thaw in the sun early. Wind S.W froze hard last night there will be a crust soon God send Amen.

Satd. 30th Fine plasant morning wind W begining to thaw in the sun John & Edwd. went to Graves this morning the Graves seized on Mrs Reids good untill they would be paid also took the hides that she & family had to live on, she got two peices of hides from there & the ballance they have taken you may know from these proceedings what our fare is in camp there is nothing to be got by hunting yet perhaps there soon will. God send it Amen.

Sund. 31st. The sun dont shine out brilliant this morning froze prtty hard last night wind N.W. Lantron Murphy died last night about 1 o clock, Mrs Reid & John went to Graves this morning to look after her goods.

— Patrick Breen, diary

Sutter's Fort, the destination of emigrants bound for California
— Marilyn Newton photo

February 2, 1847

Another infant dies at lake; others sick as storms resume

At the high camps, a grim arithmetic of subtraction is continuing.

Harriet McCutchen, the infant daughter of William and Amanda McCutchen, is dead. Other nursing mothers — such as Margaret Eddy — are sick and starving and unable to supply milk for their babies. Other children, such as John Breen, are very ill. Among the adults, sickness is also taking a toll: George Donner and Augustus Spitzer have been bedridden for weeks.

Patrick Breen notes a snowfall began yesterday and continues, on and off, into today. His diary entries for the next four days include the same weather report.

Of the eighty-one people who reached the high Sierra on October 31, fifteen have died and seven have reached safety in California. The remaining fifty-nine, mostly children, are in the camps by Donner Lake or six miles away at Alder Creek.

Martha "Patty" Reed might say there are sixty "individuals" left at the high camps. In her dress, she has concealed a tiny doll, which she took from her family's wagon after it was abandoned in the desert.

This week, a meeting in San Francisco will mobilize California even as the first rescuers reach Johnson's Ranch in Bear Valley and press through to the mountains beyond.

This week, the race against time begins.

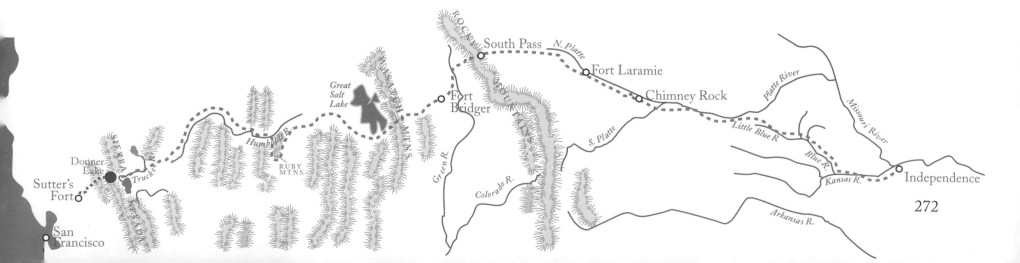

272

Items belonging to Patty Reed on display at the Emigrant Trails Museum in Truckee. The doll is a replica. — Marilyn Newton photo

I made a grave in the snow, and Mrs. Murphy and I laid him in and covered him with the snow again. I then got some wood, as they had very little fire and no one in the house was strong enough . . . they were so weak from starvation. Death had become so common an event that it was looked upon as a matter of course, and we all expected to go soon.
— John Breen, *Pioneer Memoirs*

Mond. February the 1st Froze very hard last night cold to day & cloudy wind N W. sun shines dimly the snow has not settled much John is unwell to day with the help of God & he will be well by night Amen.

Tuesday 2nd Began to snow this morning & continued to snow untill night now clear wind during the storm S.W.
— Patrick Breen, diary

FEBRUARY 5, 1847

Eddy's baby dies at lake; rescuers on the way

Reason Tucker
— from C.F. McGlashan's
History of the Donner Party

Margaret Eddy, the infant daughter of William and Eleanor Eddy, lies buried in the snow at the lake camp of the Donner Party.

The baby died last night. Mrs. Eddy, herself starving, is beyond grief. She is so weak that even with the help of the Breens, it is doubtful she'll survive.

The entrapped emigrants are all failing. Even Patrick Breen, who allowed bright hope to creep into his journal during these past weeks, is near despair.

"Peggy [Mrs. Breen] is very uneasy for fear we will all perish with hunger," Breen writes today. "We have put a little meat left and only part of three hides [We have] to support Mrs. Reid [Reed] she has nothing left but one hide and it is on Grave's shanty . . . Milt [Elliot] is living there and likely will keep that hide."

Tonight, another series of storms slams the high camps as the first rescue party leaves Johnson's Ranch in Bear Valley. Seven more would-be-rescuers have joined the seven men who rode from Sutter's Fort on January 31.

William Eddy, 28 — the father of a child he doesn't know is dead and the husband of a wife now dying — is with them.

The rest are: Adolph Bruheim, a German known as "Greasy Jim," who came to California in 1842; Edward Coffeemire, a sailor; William Coon, 30, an 1846 emigrant; Jotham Curtis, an 1846 emigrant; Aquilla Glover, who knew the Reeds on the trail; Sept Moutry, an 1846 pioneer; John, 27, and Daniel Rhodes, 25, Mormons who vowed to save the Donner Party or die; M. D. Ritchie, who settled at Johnson's Ranch; Joseph Sels, a sailor known for his good humor; Reason P. Tucker, 40, an 1846 emigrant; Tucker's son, George, 16; and Joseph Verrot, 36, a French Canadian who came west with John Frémont's party.

They travel in a valley soaked with recent rains. In thirty miles, at Mule Springs, the snow will be three feet deep, then five feet, then ten, then deeper.

The rain that falls tonight will be snow at higher elevations, adding to the frozen mountain.

They know this. They hurry on.

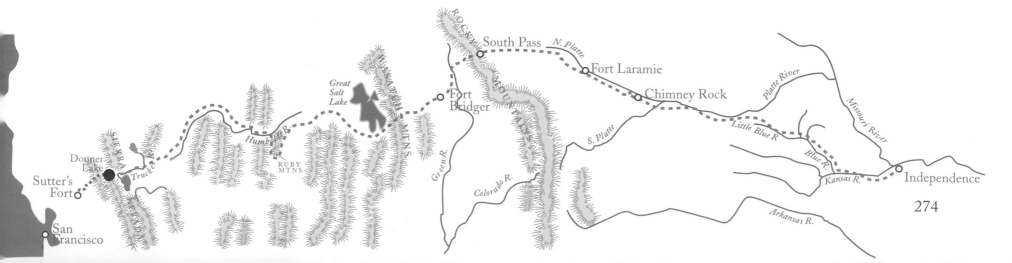

A portion of the old trail crosses Johnson's Ranch near Sacramento.
— Marilyn Newton photo

Wend. 3rd Cloudy looks like more snow not cold, froze a little last night wind S.S W. it was clear all last night sun shines out at times.

Thurd. 4th Snowd. hard all night & still continues with a strong S: W. wind untill now abated looks as if it would snow all day snowd. about 2 feet deep now.

Frid. 5th Snowd. hard all untill 12 o'clock at night wind still continud to blow hard from the S. W: to day pretty clear a few clouds only Peggy very uneasy for fear we shall all perrish with hunger we have but a little meat left & only part of 3 hides has to support Mrs. Reid she has nothing left but one hide & it is on Graves shanty Milt is livig there & likely will keep that hide Eddys child died last night.

— Patrick Breen, diary

Feb. 5, 1847: First day traveled 10 miles bad roades often miring down horses & mules.
— first entry from the diary
of the first relief party

FEBRUARY 7, 1847

Second relief party leaves city; two more dead at lake

JAMES F. REED.

Lithograph of James F. Reed — Nevada Historical Society

Caleb Greenwood, 83, a trapper, explorer, and guide who has traveled the Sierra "since they were sandhills" knows he's a legend.

When he arrived in Yerba Buena (San Francisco) yesterday, the grizzled mountain man wasn't surprised that the would-be rescuers of the Donner Party solicited his advice.

The second relief effort got underway four days ago after James F. Reed appeared at a public meeting in a saloon. The organizers collected several hundred dollars from the crowd and were preparing to leave for the Sierra.

Two days ago a launch from Sutter's brought news of the seven Forlorn Hope party survivors. The accounts shocked the citizens. The trapped emigrants are in worse shape than anyone imagined. The volunteers now know where the party is stranded. More preparations must be made.

Then Greenwood — who was dressed in buckskin so weathered that journalist Edwin Bryant said he must have "worn the same suit all his life" — offers to join the expedition. Greenwood predicts marchers might reach the high camps if they drive horses in front of them and use them for food on the way.

Reed and others leave San Francisco at 1:30 p.m. today on the launch *Dice Mi Nana* bound for Fort Sonoma. A schooner under the command of Selim E. Woodworth, a naval officer, will ferry supplies to a spot on the Feather River about twenty miles from Johnson's Ranch. Today the would-be rescuers leave the town on the bay.

Today at the high camps, death claims Augustus Spitzer, the German who had a hand in the death of Jacob Wolfinger on the trail, and Eleanor Eddy, who lost her only child three days ago.

This morning the sun came out on four feet of new snow. The remaining survivors make their way through the slush to each other's camps.

The Murphys and Kesebergs say they can't eat hides, Patrick Breen notes in his diary. "I wish we had enough of them," he writes. They know they'll all die unless help arrives soon.

Miles to the west, the men of the first rescue party are bogged down in

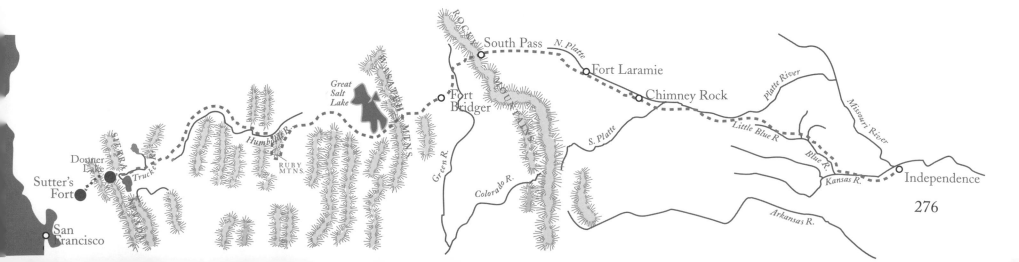

rain and mud, having made just twenty-five miles in three days. Tomorrow, they will stay in camp and dry their soaked clothing. Many miles farther west, the two groups of the second relief aim for the Sierra.

Old Caleb Greenwood knows about the first rescue party. He's willing to bet that the sailors and greenhorns will all die before they reach the lake.

Nobody takes the wager.

Yerba Buena (later called San Francisco) in 1847. — Emigrant Trails Museum

Satd. 6th It snowd. faster last night & to day than it has done this winter & still continues without an intermission wind S. W Murphys folks or Keysburgs say they cant eat hides I wish we had enough of them Mrs Eddy very weak.

Sund. 7th Ceasd. to snow last after one of the most severe storms we experienced this winter the snow fell about 4 feet deep. I had to shovel the snow off our shanty this morning it thawd so fast & thawd. during the whole storm. to day it is quite pleasant wind S. W.Milt here to day says Mrs Reid has to get a hide from Mrs. Muuphy & McCutchins child died 2nd of this month.

Mond. 8th Fine clear morning wind S. W. froze hard last. Spitzer died last night about 3 o clock to we will bury him in the snow Mrs Eddy died on the night of the 7th.

— Patrick Breen, diary

FEBRUARY 9, 1847

Milt Elliot dies in camp; rescuers battle up Sierra

Milford Elliot, 28, loyal employee of the Reed family, is dead tonight at the Murphy cabin.

"Milt Elliot died," Virginia Reed will remember. "Our faithful friend who seemed so much like a brother. My mother and I dragged him out of the cabin and covered him up with snow. Commencing at his feet, I patted the pure, white snow down softly until I reached his face.

"Poor Milt! It was hard to cover his face from sight forever, for with his death our best friend was gone."

Today, Patrick Breen writes: "Mrs. Murphy here this morning . . . Pike's child is all but dead. Milt at Murphys not able to get out of bed [he would die at 9 p.m.]." Lewis Keseberg stays in bed, saying he's too weak to get up, Breen reports.

What happened to the Forlorn Hope party? Is relief on the way? Or will they all suffer the fate of Elliot and the rest?

Today the men of the first relief effort ferry their provisions across a creek on a log. Tomorrow they will reach the snow line and struggle belly-deep through the drifts. In four miles they'll camp at Mule Springs.

Their plan is to set up provision points along the route. They'll mark trail with burned logs and make fires on platforms made of pine saplings to keep the blazes from sinking in the snow.

It will be slow, tiring work. At this rate, even if nothing goes wrong and good weather holds, it will take more than a week to reach the high camps.

They wonder if anyone will be alive when they get there.

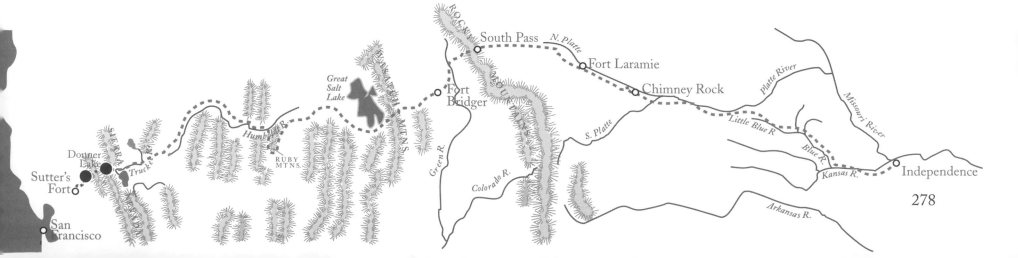

Twentieth-century snowshoers at the top of Donner Pass, looking east.
— Emigrant Trails Museum

Tuesd. 9th Mrs. Murphy here this morning Pikes child all but dead Milt at Murphys not able to get out of bed Keyburg never gets up says he is not able. John went down to day to bury Mrs Eddy & child heard nothing from Graves for 2 or 3 days Mrs Murphy just now going to Graves fine moring wind S.E. froze hard last night begins to thaw in the sun.

Wednsd. 10th Beautiful moring wind W: froze hard last night, to day thawing in the sun Milt Elliot died las night at Murphys shanty about 9 o'clock P: M: Mrs Reid went there this moring to see after his effects. J Denton trying to borrow meat from Graves had none to give they have nothing but hides all are entirely out of meat but a little we have our hides are nearly all eat up but with Gods help spring will soon smile upon us.

— Patrick Breen, diary

Donner Lake and the present-day Donner pass highway (Interstate 80) in the distance. — Emigrant Trails Museum

FEBRUARY 12, 1847

Clear weather brings visits, pleas for meat at high camps

The clear weather holds at the high camps. With it comes a sea of dripping water and slush by day and ice by night.

In bright sunlight people visit neighbors and beg for meat. John Denton, the Englishman at the Donner camp at Alder Creek, comes to the Graves cabin to ask for food, any food. They have none to give; "nothing but hides," Patrick Breen wrote in his diary two days ago. "All are entirely out of meat but a little we have our hides are nearly all eat up but with Gods help spring will soon smile upon us." There are nine people in the Breen family plus Margaret Reed and her four children. Denton came to the Breen cabin today. He's "very delicate," Breen reports.

Today the thaw continues. Breen hopes "with the assistance of almighty God to be able to live to see the bare surface of the earth once more."

Yesterday, on the west side of the mountains, William Eddy and Joe Verrot were assigned to bring exhausted pack animals back to Johnson's ranch. Young George Tucker and Billy Coon remained near Mule Springs to guard supplies.

The other ten men of the rescue party, who today stop to make snowshoes, try them on, "find them of no benefit [and] cast them away," according to the diary of the rescue party. They will make their way on a ridge between Steephollow Creek and Bear River. The snow is soon ten feet deep. Tonight, rain and snow lash their camp near an emigrant wagon where a cache of food has been pillaged by bears.

As the men of the first rescue party battle up the western slope of the Sierra, a printer's devil in San Francisco is setting a story in type today for tomorrow's *California Star* newspaper. The announcement, printed under the headline "Distressing News," outlines the plight of the emigrants on the mountain and the travails of the Forlorn Hope party that experienced such difficulty that "Napoleon's fete on the Alps was child's play compared with it . . . [they arrived] entirely naked, their feet frostbitten." The report, apparently written by George McKinstry, notes that the emigrants "made meat of the dead bodies of their companions" and that a rescue party of seven men is on the way.

Word of the disaster is getting around, but those who gaze at the wall of snow doubt a rescue can succeed until spring.

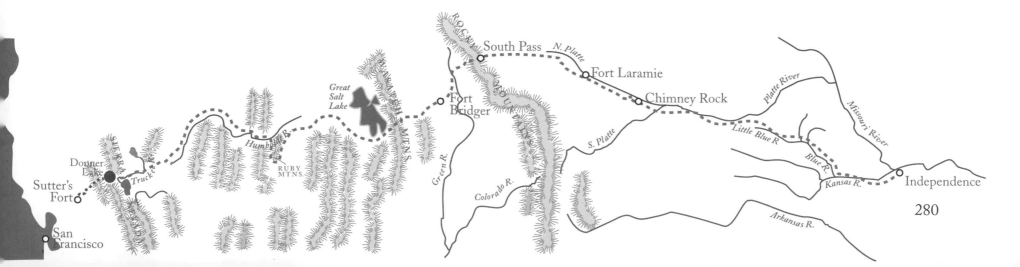

Donner Lake in snow, an old photograph. — Nevada Historical Society

Thursd 11th Fine morning wind W. Froze hard last night some clouds lying in the E: looks like thaw John Denton here last night very delicate. John & Mrs Reid went to Graves this morning.

Frid. 12th A warm thawey morning wind S.E. we hope with the assistance of Almighty God to be able to live to see the bare surface of the earth once more. O God of Mercy grant it if it be thy holy will Amen.

— Patrick Breen, diary

A company of twenty men left here on Sunday last for the California mountains with provisions, clothing &c. for the suffering emigrants now there. The citizens of this place subscribed about fifteen hundred dollars for their relief, which was expended for such articles as the emigrants would be most likely to need. — Mr. Greenwood, an old mountaineer, went with the company as pilot. If it is possible to cross the mountains they will get to the emigrants in time to save them.

— *California Star*, Yerba Buena, February 13, 1847

FEBRUARY 14, 1847

First relief party down to seven men; caches of food left behind

Edward Breen
— Bancroft Library

Margaret Reed
— Nevada Historical Society

In fine weather; relief is on the way.

By walking in one another's footsteps, ten men fight their way up the Sierra. By tomorrow, only seven will continue.

The rescuers have abandoned their snowshoes and walk on frozen crust, with the lead man breaking through to his knees or thighs. It is exhausting. The leader changes swiftly as another takes his place only to tire out and take up the rear. Every time they pass a dead pine tree they set it afire, hoping the trail of charred posts will lead them home even if another blizzard hits.

At night they cover themselves with blankets and huddle around a fire. If they sleep, they do it sitting up on logs — to lie down would mean freezing.

They're making caches of food as they work their way up the mountain. They will return and dig up these supplies or haul them down from bundles suspended by ropes from tree branches. They'll need the food for the survivors — if there are any.

These are the seven men who keep walking: Aquilla Glover, Reason P. "Dan" Tucker, Sept Moutry, Ned Coffeemeyer, Joseph Sels, Daniel Rhodes, and his brother, John. Tucker offered the men who stayed $5 per day to see the adventure through.

These men's names "ought to be recorded in letters of gold," Sheriff George McKinstry of Sutter's Fort will write.

At the lake camps, Margaret Reed has one of her migraine headaches. John Denton remains at the lake and seems as though he could die at any moment. The snow has melted off the body of Milt Elliot. Today John and Edward Breen bury him deeper in the drifts.

Tonight the rescuers are less than twenty miles from the lake. In summer, they'd be a day away.

This winter, with the steep wall of snow still before them, the distance seems like the abyss between the Earth and the Moon.

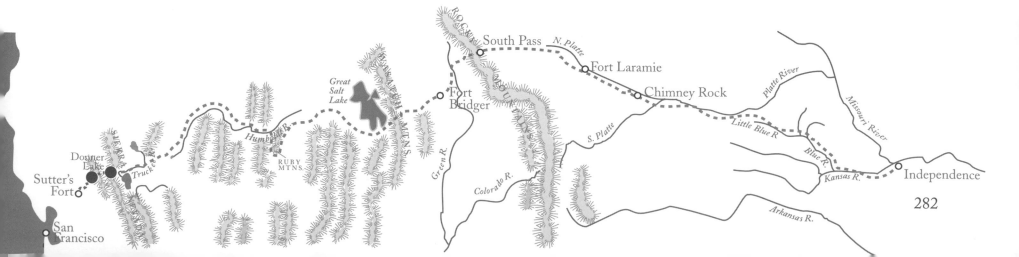

Ice crystals at Donner Lake — Emigrant Trails Museum

Sat. 13th Fine morning clouded up Yesteday evening snowd a little & continued cloudy all night, cleared off about day light wind about S: W Mrs Reid has headacke the rest in health.

Sund 14th Fine morning but cold before the sun got up, now thawing in the sun wind S E Ellen Graves here this morning John Denton not well froze had last night John & Edwd. E buried Milt. this morning in the snow.

— Patrick Breen, diary

PROVISIONS LIST

A list of provisions for the second Donner relief party includes 15 barrels of flour, 1 barrel of pork, 400 pounds of sugar, 17 pounds of tobacco, 6 frying pans, four camp kettles, 24 blankets, 48 pairs of woolen stockings, two pounds of thread, 84 yards of flannel, 30 yards of calico, 6 pairs of shoes, 30 yards of shirting, 24 pairs of pantaloons, 11 pairs of flannel drawers, 30 red flannel shirts, 15 pairs of children's' shoes, 2 axes, 2 hatchets, 1 shovel, 12 iron spoons, 100 pounds of cocoa and 20 tins of ground coffee. These and other items are paid for by $1,300 raised by the people and military personnel of San Francisco.

February 16, 1847

Mrs. Graves feels the strain; first relief party nears lake

Margaret Breen
— Bancroft Library

Patty Reed
— Emigrant Trails
Museum

Mrs. Graves is acting crazy, Patrick Breen says.

Elizabeth Graves, 45, has put three of Sutter's hides on her cabin. These are from animals brought to the lake by Charles Stanton and given to Margaret Reed. Graves won't give them to Mrs. Reed, who has no food for her four children.

Mrs. Graves also bickers with Breen: "[She] says if I say it will thaw, then it will not," Breen writes in his journal today. "She is a case."

He remarks that everyone feels weak as a snowstorm again covers the camps. With typical understatement he writes that the snow is "not getting much less in quantity."

The Breens share their hides with the Reeds, but the few scraps of meat remaining are reserved for the Breen children. Mrs. Breen sneaks pieces of meat to Patty Reed when her husband is not looking. Patty will say Mrs. Breen saved her life.

Except for the Breens, all at the high camps are days away from a choice: Cannibalism or starvation.

West of the camps, the storm has forced the seven members of the first relief party to again construct snowshoes out of pine boughs. Today they struggle three miles through snow fifteen feet deep.

Tomorrow, the men who have been climbing the mountain for two weeks will travel five miles. The day after they will cover eight miles and make camp in snow thirty feet deep at Summit Valley near the head of the Yuba River. They will be about a mile from Donner Lake and five hundred feet below the camps.

In two days, the prayers of the entrapped pioneers will be answered.

But it will be time for new appeals to heaven.

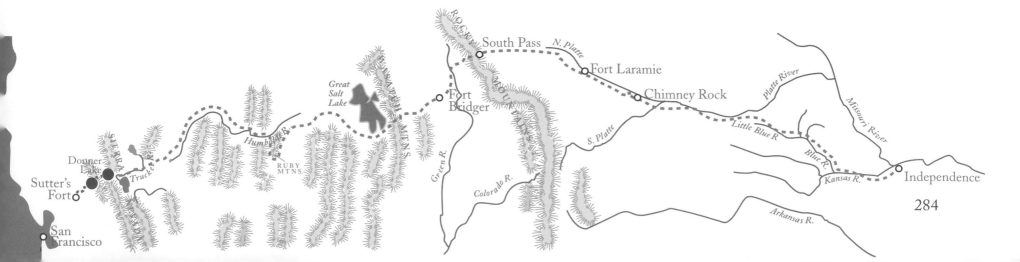

284

Snowy Donner Lake — Marilyn Newton photo

Mond.. 15. Moring cloudy untill 9 o clock then cleared off wam & sunshine wind W. Mrs Gaves refusd. to give Mrs. Reid any hides put Suitors pack hides on her shanty would not let her have them says if I say it will thaw it then will not, she is a case.

Tuesd. 16th Commencd. to rain yesterday evening turned to snow during the night & continud untill after daylight this morning it is now sun shine & light showers of hail at times wind N.W by W. we all feel very weakly to day snow not geting much less in quantity.

Wedsd. 17th Froze hard lst night with heavy clouds running from the N. W. & light showers of hail at times to day same kind of weather wind N.W. very cold & cloudy no sign of much thaw.

— Patrick Breen, diary

FEBRUARY 19, 1847

Rescuers arrive, are asked: "Do you men come from heaven?"

Reason Tucker — from C.F. McGlashan's History of the Donner Party

(February) 19: At sundown we reached the Cabins and found the people in great distress such as I have never witnessed there having been 12 deaths and more expected every hour the sight of us appeared to put life into their emaciated frames.
— Reason "Dan" Tucker, diary of the Donner relief party

Seven rescuers arrived at Donner Lake yesterday evening and walked on snowshoes over the icy crust to the east side of the lake.

From William Eddy's description, this is where the cabins are. The men see nothing but white mounds and tall drifts.

"Hello!" they yell. "Hello!"

A woman's head pops up from the snow like a prairie dog from a burrow. She sees the snowshoers. "Are you men from California or are you from heaven?" she asks.

"Other human figures, ghastly and horrible sights, begin to appear," author George Stewart will write. "It was as if the rescuers' halloo had been Gabriel's horn raising the dead from their graves. Their flesh was wasted from their bodies. They wept and laughed hysterically."

Joy rules the lake camp as food — as much as is thought safe — is passed around. Reason "Dan" Tucker moves on to the Alder Creek Camp and the Donner family.

In their happiness, the entrapped emigrants don't notice the seven men seem to need rescue themselves. They have little food with them and are exhausted from their trek.

James F. Reed's party, meanwhile, crosses the flood-swollen Sacramento River today at the mouth of the Feather River. They discover that their provisions haven't arrived to meet them and ride to Johnson's Ranch, twenty-five miles distant. They have no idea that the first relief has reached the camps.

Up at the lake, the rescuers put a guard on their packs and try to sleep. Their job isn't over; it has just begun.

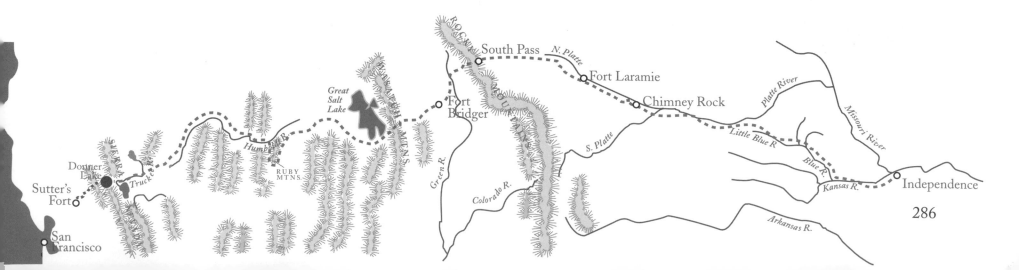

San Francisco · Sutter's Fort · Donner Lake · Truckee R. · SIERRA · Humboldt R. · RUBY MTNS. · Great Salt Lake · Fort Bridger · Green R. · Colorado R. · WASATCH MTNS. · ROCKY · South Pass · N. Platte · Fort Laramie · Chimney Rock · S. Platte · Platte River · Little Blue R. · Blue R. · Kansas R. · Missouri River · Arkansas R. · Independence

*Thrsd 18th Froze hard last night to day clear &
warm in the sun cold in the shanty or in the shade
wind S.E all in good heath Thanks be to Almighty
God Amen.*

*Frid. 19th Froze hard last night 7 men
arrived from Colifornia yesteday evening with som
provisions but left the greater part on the way to
day clear & warm for this region some of the men
are gone to day to Donnos Camp will start back on
Monday.*

— Patrick Breen, diary

A lithograph depicts a relief party arriving at Donner Lake on Feb. 18, 1847. — Bancroft Library

February 21, 1847

Twenty-three entrapped emigrants ready to leave with rescuers

Simon Breen
— Bancroft Library

The joy at the high camps is short-lived.

Yesterday, Harriet Pike's infant daughter, Catherine, never awoke from her slumber. The baby's suffering is over. For the rest, the arrival of the seven men of the first rescue party three days ago means another round of hardships if they are to escape the Sierra alive.

The relief party members are shocked at the emaciated condition of the emigrants and their unbalanced mental states. Some of the pioneers curse constantly; others mumble prayers over and over.

Three rescuers return from the Alder Creek camp, bringing with them Doris Wolfinger, 19; teamster Noah James, 16; and four of the older Donner children. Tamsen Donner is strong enough to leave, but she won't abandon her dying husband or younger children. John Baptiste Trudeau, 16, reluctantly remains at camp. He's the only one strong enough to chop wood or care for others.

The rescuers leave a felled tree, a few cups of flour and scraps of dried beef for the twelve people who stay at Alder Creek. They tell the sufferers that more help will be coming. Unknown to them, James F. Reed and others are at Johnson's Ranch, where Indians are working day and night to dry beef for the relief party.

Tamsen Donner tells the rescuers at Alder Creek that cannibalism is their only choice if Trudeau can't find the cattle buried in snow.

When the meager rations are gone, she says, the youth will dig up the bodies of the dead.

From the lake camps, seventeen people will brave the mountain in an escape attempt. They include: John Denton, 28, the Englishman who has been ill for weeks; Phillipine Keseberg, 23, and her daughter Ada, 3; Eliza Williams, 31; Naomi Pike, 3, whose mother escaped with the Forlorn Hope party; Margaret Reed, 32, and her four children; Billy Graves and two of his sisters; Edward Breen, 13, and Simon Breen, 9; Mary Murphy, 15, and her brother William, 11. Seventeen people will be left at the lake cabins: two men, three women, and twelve children.

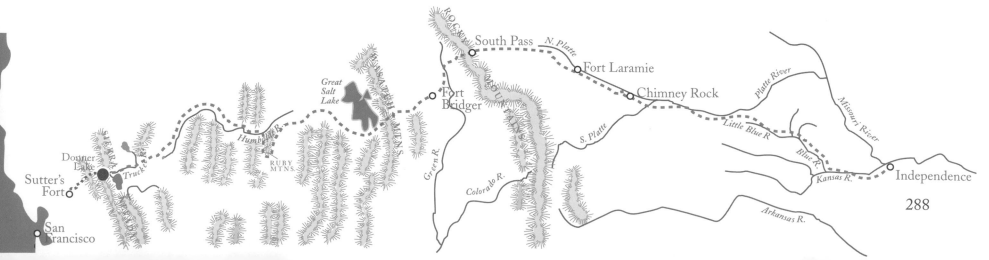

The rescuers keep the tragic news of the Forlorn Hope Party to themselves. They say only that Charles Stanton and the rest were too frostbitten to return to the camps.

They do not say Stanton and six other men died while walking to Sutter's Fort. They do not remark that perhaps those men had a better chance at survival then they have now — making the same journey with starving children and weak, sick adults.

Tomorrow, their trek begins.

Snow covered mountains around Donner Lake, on an old postcard.
— Nevada Historical Society

Saturd. 20th Pleasant weather.
Sund 21st Thawey warm day.
— Patrick Breen, diary

[February] 20: Myself [R. P. Tucker] and two others went to the Donnors camp 8 miles and found them in starving condition the most of the men had died one of them leaving a wife and 8 children, the two families had but one beef head amonst them, there was two cows buried in the snow but it was doubtful f they would be able to find them we left them telling them they would soon have assistance if possible on the road back I gave out but struggled on until sundown when I reached the other cabins.
— Diary of the Donner relief party

February 23, 1847

Misfortune dogs tracks of group trying to make escape

Fresh snow in the Sierra
— Tim Dunn photo

Yesterday, thirty people left the high camps and walked west toward the safety of Johnson's Ranch.

Today, twenty-eight are left.

Martha "Patty" Reed, who will be 9 in three days, and her brother, Tommy, 3, were too weak to go on and returned to the lake camp. Again Margaret Reed, 32, must be parted from her children. She walks with her son, James, 5, while her daughter, Virginia, 13, walks beside her. She is heartbroken — again. She wanted to return to the lake camp with them but has the other two to think about. Sending the boy and girl back seems a death sentence.

She asks rescuer Aquilla Glover if he is a Mason, as is her husband, James F. Reed. Glover says he is. "Promise me on the word of a Mason when you arrive at Bear River you will return and bring out my children," she asks. Glover gives his word.

"Good-bye, Ma," Patty said as she left. "If I don't see you again, do the best you can." Sept Moutry and Glover took the two children back to the lake. Patty told them she expects to die there. The men fought tears.

Patrick and Margaret Breen — with seven mouths to feed and no food left but rotted hides — were upset at seeing the Reed children again, but they took them in. Moutry and Glover returned to the escape party as they camped last night.

The men built platforms for fires. One ounce of smoked beef and two spoonfuls of flour are each person's rations. After dark, some of the rescued emigrants stole Ned Coffeemeyer's snowshoes and ate the rawhide thongs.

At the lake today, Breen shoots his dog, Towser, the last canine in camp, to provide food for his children. Elizabeth Graves comes to the Breen cabin to ask for meat, but Breen has none to spare.

To the west, the escape party's trek continues as high clouds soar above.

The four Donner children, walking near Reason P. Tucker, see that his soaked buckskin pants are tattered and they keep trying to tear pieces off so they can eat them.

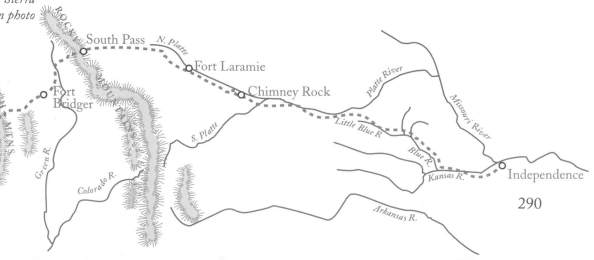

By noon, Phillipine Keseberg is too exhausted to carry her daughter, Ada, 3. She offers $25 and a gold watch to any man who can carry the child. She offers $50. There are no takers. The men are weary from breaking trail for the others. The smaller children are climbing from one deep footprint to the other.

John Denton, the Englishman, has fallen behind. Two men go back for him. Tonight they make camp at the spot where they had left a bale of food hanging from a tree. The bag is broken open on the snow. The tracks of a bear and other animals tell the story. Now they are four days away from the next cache with twenty-eight starving people to feed.

All eat rawhide and make a plan: four men — Daniel Rhodes, Moutry, Coffeemeyer, and Glover — will leave at dawn and advance as quickly as possible to get food and return for the others.

Tomorrow, Denton will tell the others he can't go on. They'll leave him wrapped in a quilt near a fire. Little Jimmy Reed will beg to stay with him.

The others will look at Denton, warm, comfortable, and doomed, and almost envy him.

All of them want to simply lie down and sleep in the soft, beautiful, and deadly snow.

Mond 22nd The Californians started this morning 24 in number some in a very weak state fine morning wind S. W. for the 3 last days Mrs Keyburg started & left Keysburg here unable to go I burried Pikes child this moring in the snow it died 2 days ago, Paddy Reid & Thos. came back Messrs [?] Graves & Mutry [?].

Tuesd. 23 Froze hard last night to day fine & thawey has the appearance of spring all but the deep snow wind S:S.E. shot Towser to day & dressed his flesh Mrs Graves came here this morning to borrow meat dog or ox they think I have meat to spare but I know to the contrary they have plenty hides I live principally on the same.

Wend. 24th Froze hard last night to day cloudy looks like a storm wind blows hard from the W. Commenced thawing there has not any more returned from those who started to cross the mts.

— Patrick Breen, diary

Leaving the weak to die, the death of John Denton. — from Virginia Reed's Across the Plains In The Donner Party

FEBRUARY 26, 1847

Cannibalism planned at camps; relief party escaping Sierra

Georgia Donner
— Emigrant Trails Museum

Slowly, the first relief party is working its way down the Sierra.

Not without casualties: John Denton has been left behind and is surely dead. "I made him a fire and chopped some wood for him when I very unwillingly left him telling him he should soon have assistance but I am afraid he would not live to see it," Reason P. Tucker wrote two days ago.

Denton, dying in the snow, takes his journal and composes a poem. The Englishman's verse will be found by a rescue party.

Yesterday, Ada Keseberg, 3, died in her mother's arms and was buried in the snow.

Today, two men sent ahead for supplies return to the escaping pioneers with provisions. They are now two days away from the head of Bear Valley and safety. The sun has cooperated — another storm could have finished them all.

The first relief party doesn't know that James F. Reed and the members of the second relief expedition are now leaving Bear Valley and making tracks across the snow towards them. Behind the second relief, a third group led by a Navy passed midshipman is also on its way.

Reed's group started with eleven horses and mules loaded with eighty-pound packs. One mule fails and the other animals battle through deep powder. Today they leave their camp in early morning, thinking the snow's crust will be thick enough to support the horses.

"Proceeded 200 yards with difficulty," Reed reports in his journal, "when we were compelled to unpack the horses and take the provisions on our backs for a few minutes."

Later in the day, Reed's group meets Aquilla Glover and Dan Rhodes, who were sent ahead by the first rescue party. They tell Reed of the situation on the mountaintop. The second relief leaves some supplies and presses ahead with renewed urgency.

At the high camps, cannibalism is practiced.

John Baptiste Trudeau is digging up dead bodies at Alder Creek, where the Donner survivors are starving. At the lake camps, Martha "Patty" Reed, who turns 9 today, is suffering a toothache, Patrick Breen notes. He writes: "Hungry

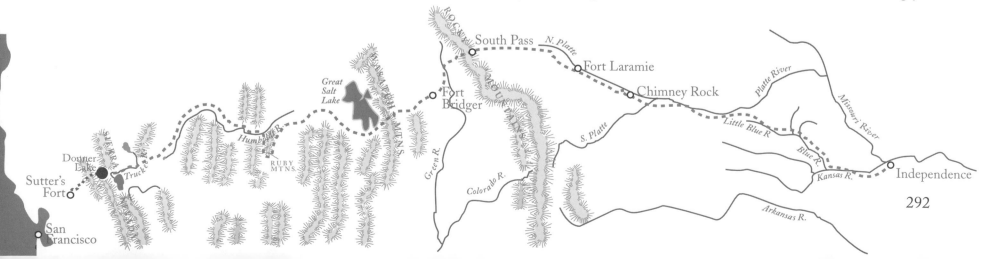

times in camp ... plenty hides but the folks will not eat them we eat them with a tolerable good appetite.

"Mrs. Murphy said here yesterday that [she] thought she would commence on Milt [Elliot, who died on February 9] & eat him. I don't [think] she has done so yet, it is distressing. [The Donners] told the California folks that they commence to eat the dead people 4 days ago. I suppose they have done so ere this time."

Alder Creek. For years it was believed that members of the Donner party camped at the foot of ths big tree. Some historians argue that this was not the site. — Marilyn Newton photo

Thursd. 25th Froze hard last night fine & sunshiny to day wind W. Mrs. Murphy says the wolves are about to dig up the dead bodies at her shanty, the nights are too cold to watch them, we hear them howl.

Frid 26th Froze hard last night today clear & warm Wind S: E: blowing briskly Marthas jaw swelled with the toothache; hungry times in camp, plenty hides but the folks will not eat them we eat them with a tolerable good apetite. Thanks be to Almighty God. Amen Mrs Murphy said here yesterday that thought she would commence on Milt. & eat him. I dont that she has done so yet, it is distressing The Donnos told the California folks that they commence to eat the dead people 4 days ago, if they did not succeed that day or next in finding their cattle then under ten or twelve feet of snow & did not know the spot or near it, I suppose they have done so ere this time.
— Patrick Breen, diary

When I spoke of human flesh being used at both tents, I said it was prepared for the little ones in both tents . . . Jacob Donner's wife came down the steps one day saying to mother, "What do you think I cooked this morning?" Then answered the question herself, "Shoemaker's arm."'
— Georgia Donner, in a letter to C. F. McGlashan, 1879

[February] 25: This day a child died and was buried in the snow traveled 5 miles and there met with some provisions half of a cash small allowance

[February] 26: at noon had a small divide of shoe strings roasted and eat them and then proceeded about half mile when we met two of our men with provisions we struck fire and feasted on our dry beef.
— Reason Tucker, diary of the Donner relief party

FEBRUARY 28, 1847

James Reed and wife, reunited; two of his children still trapped

Virginia Reed — Bancroft Library

James Reed — Bancroft Library

Four members of the first relief party remain encamped after the joyous reunion of James F. Reed with his wife and children.

Reed, Bill McCutchen, mountain men, and others have traveled east since leaving Johnson's Ranch on February 22. In the recent thaw, they made better time than the first rescuers and met the twenty-two-member first relief group yesterday.

Jimmy Reed, 5, was failing and no one could carry him. "Every step takes you closer to your father," his mother, Margaret, and his sister, Virginia, told him. As the two groups converged and Mrs. Reed heard her husband was near, she fainted in the snow. Virginia stumbled ahead to greet her father, whom she last saw when he was banished from the Donner Party on October 6 for killing John Snyder during an argument.

"Your mother, where is she?" asks Reed as he gathers Virginia into his arms. Husband and wife reunite. Tears fall on snow.

"Here I met Mrs. Reed and two children," Reed writes in his formal style, "two still in the mountains, I cannot describe the death like look they all had Bread Bread Bread was the begging of every child and grown person except my wife. I gave what I dared and left for the scene of desolation."

Reed forges ahead to the camps where his two other children remain trapped. Three children eat too much of the food brought by Reed and are left behind with an adult as nineteen others continue west to Bear Valley, where they camp at the head of the valley and feast on their cached provisions.

Cannibalism continues at the high camps, where today a solitary Indian (a Washoe?) walks through the wasteland. He motions Patrick Breen to stay away as he places tubers on the snow — a gift of food for the destitute whites.

The Indian hefts his pack and moves on, his snowshoes making barely a sound. He does not seem surprised. White people are an enigma.

The roots "taste like sweet potatoes," Breen writes. Above the camps, the sun shines and Canada geese honk. Can spring be far behind?

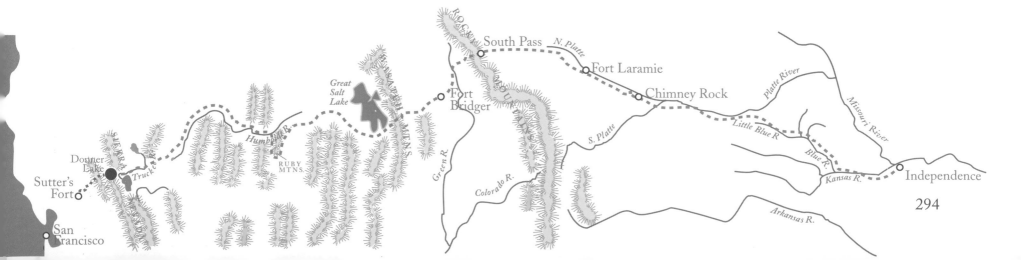

Miwok woman preparing acorn flour. — photographer unknown, Emigrant Trails Museum

One evening, as I was gazing around, I saw an Indian coming from the mountain. He came to the house and said something which we could not understand. He had a small pack on his back, consisting of a fur blanket, and about two dozen of what is called California soaproot, which, by some means, could be made good to eat. He appeared very friendly, gave us two or three of the roots, and went on his way. Where he was going I could never imagine. He walked upon snow-shoes, the strings of which were made of bark. He went east; and as the snow was very deep for many miles on all sides, I do not know how he passed the nights.

— John Breen, diary

We camped that night and ate the bread my father had brought for us. We were out of the snow, could see the blessed earth and green grass again. How beautiful it looked. We stayed a day or so, getting the horses and mules ready to ride. No more dragging over the snow, when we were tired, so very tired, but green grass, horses to ride, and plenty to eat.

— Virginia Reed, *Across the Plains In The Donner Party*

[February] 27: Mr. Reed met with his wife and two children the meeting was very affecting.

— Reason P. Tucker,
Diary of the Donner relief party

Satd. 27th Beautiful morning sun shineing brilliantly, wind about S.W. the snow has fell in debth about 5 feet but no thaw but the sun in day time it freezeing hard every night, heard some geese fly over last night saw none.

— Patrick Breen, diary

295

MARCH 2, 1847

Reed arrives at high camps; first relief party makes Bear Valley

Yesterday James F. Reed arrived at the lake camp to find his daughter, Patty, 9, sitting on a cabin roof with her feet dangling in the snow. His son Tommy, 3, is also safe with the Breen family.

"10 men arrived . . . with provisions," Breen wrote in the final entry of his journal. "We are to start in two or three days and [cache] our goods here . . . they say the snow will be here untill June."

Reed finds filthy conditions at the cabins and discovers the mutilated body of his employee, Milt Elliot, lying in the snow. He and Bill McCutchen wash the children. Reed bathes Lewis Keseberg, who in October wanted to hang Reed from a wagon tongue. Keseberg, later accounts will say, was shamed by the kind treatment he receives from his former enemy.

"[We] rendered every assistance in our power," Reed writes in his journal. "I left with Keseberg's people Mr. Stone to cook." and to make sure Keseberg, Mrs. Murphy, and the children do not gorge on food and become sick.

Nick Clark and Charles Cady are the first to visit the Donners at Alder Creek. They report butchered bodies, cannibalized to save the survivors. The camp looks like a battlefield. The survivors look like the living dead. They report John Baptise Trudeau was carrying a human leg to the George Donner tent — a limb they believe belonged to Jacob Donner. Their story, later to be repeated in J. Quinn Thornton's account and George Stewart's *Ordeal by Hunger*, has the Donner children sitting on a log with their faces smeared with the blood of their kin.

Reed, however, mentions none of the Alder Creek horrors in his diary, but will refer to it in a letter that will be published in the *Illinois Journal* on December 9, 1847. In his *Pacific Rural Press* account, he will again omit mention of the cannibalism but will remark on the state of the survivors: "We found Mrs. Jacob Donner in a very feeble condition . . . We removed the tent and placed it in a more comfortable condition."

Meanwhile, the first relief party has reached Bear Valley and safety. Yesterday they passed Mule Springs, where the third relief party is encamped.

The first relief has had one more casualty — William Hook, 12, who died two nights ago. He was one of the children who overate and was left behind to

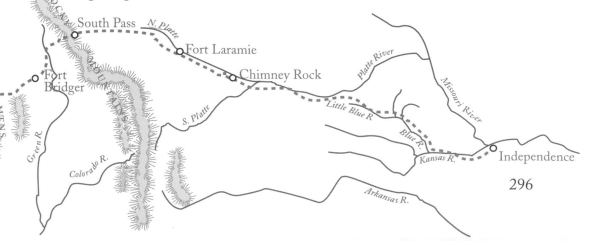

recover. Still, the weather holds and prospects are good that all survivors will soon escape.

Tonight, in the Gulf of Alaska, great clouds are churning. Whitecaps riot on the ocean.

Above the Sierra, the Jet Stream races eastward.

J.F. Reed and his daughter Patty Reed meet at Lake Camp.
—from Camp of Death *by J. Quinn Thornton*

Mond. March the 1st. So fine & pleasant froze hard last night there has 10 men arrived this morning from Bear Valley with provisions we are to start in two or three days & cash our goods here there is amongst them some old they say the snow will be here untill June.

— Patrick Breen, diary

Mr. Reed and party, after removing the tent to another place, retired for the purpose of being relieved for a brief period from sights so terrible and revolting. They had not gone far when they came to the snow-grave of Jacob Donner. His head was cut off, and was lying with the face up, the snow and cold having preserved all the features unaltered. His limbs and arms had been severed from the body which was cut open the heart and liver being taken out. The leg and thigh which the boy, John Baptiste, had obtained, had been thrown back, upon the party coming up with relief.

— J. Quinn Thornton, *Camp of Death*

About the middle of the next day we arrived at the first Camp of Emigrants, being Mr. Breen's. If we left any provisions here, it was a small amount. He and his family not being in want. We then proceeded to the camp of Mrs. Murphy, where Keysburg and some children were. Here we left provisions.

— James F. Reed, *Pacific Press* account

March 5, 1847

Reed leads second escape party; first relief group reaches fort

Two days ago James F. Reed and eight men of the second relief party left the camps with seventeen Donner Party survivors.

Two of the escorts — Big Bill McCutchen and old mountain man John Turner — punctuate their steps with so much swearing that author George Stewart will say their cursing should have melted the snow in front of them.

Two rescuers — Charles Cady and Nicholas Clark — were left behind to care for the nine Alder Creek residents who could not leave. Those still entrapped include Tamsen Donner, who again refused to leave her dying husband and younger children. They remain amid the carnage at Alder Creek waiting for Midshipman Selim Woodworth's relief party, which Reed says should arrive in a few days.

The late Jacob Donner's goods were auctioned off to the rescuers for a total of $181.31. Reed and Hiram Miller took about $600 of Jacob's money for safekeeping.

Elizabeth Graves had Reed remove a metal plate or cleat from her wagon. Beneath it was, Reed said, about $800 in gold and silver coins stored in holes drilled into the wagon box. Graves also took a violin belonging to Jay Fosdick, the son-in-law she does not know is dead.

Rescuer Charles Stone remains at the lake camp to care for the two adults, Lewis Keseberg and Lavina Murphy, and three children left behind. In all, fourteen people remain in the high camps.

Today at noon, the escaping pioneers struggle across Donner Pass. Mrs. Graves, overhearing the mountain men joking about her money and fearful of theft, will hide her money near a stump. She intends to come back for it in better weather.

Tonight they camp in Summit Valley, believing they are only five miles from a cache of food. They've sent three men ahead for provisions.

At tonight's campfire, Patrick Breen happily plays Graves's violin. He thinks the worst is over. As he fiddles the temperature drops and clouds race above the camp. Snow begins to fall.

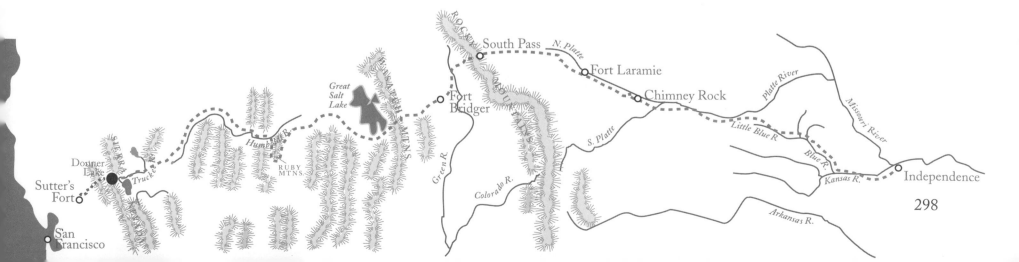

Ahead at Mule Springs, Woodworth's relief group has not budged from their camp. Woodworth's lack of motion will upset Reed, who will later speculate the man was too incompetent or cowardly to do his job. Author Joseph King will later write that Woodworth had good reasons not to proceed and that he did his duty to the best of his ability.

Yesterday, the eighteen survivors who escaped the mountains with the first relief reached Sutter's Fort. It was the end of the journey into the wilderness which began on May 12. Today, as those survivors rest, rain pounds the fort's rooftops.

Margaret Reed looks out a doorway tonight and stares eastward. Her husband and two children are still in the mountains. She knows rain at Sutter's becomes snow in the Sierra.

She knows what another storm will mean.

I requested Mrs. George Donner to come out with us, as I would leave a man to take care of both Mr. George Donner and Mrs. Jacob Donner. Mrs Geo. Donner positively refused, saying that as her children were all out she would not leave her husband in the situation he was in. After repeatedly urging her to come out, and she as positively refusing, I was satisfied in my own mind that Mrs. Geo. Donner remained with her husband for pure love and affection, and not for money, as stated by Mrs. Curtis [another writer].

— James F. Reed, *Pacific Press* account

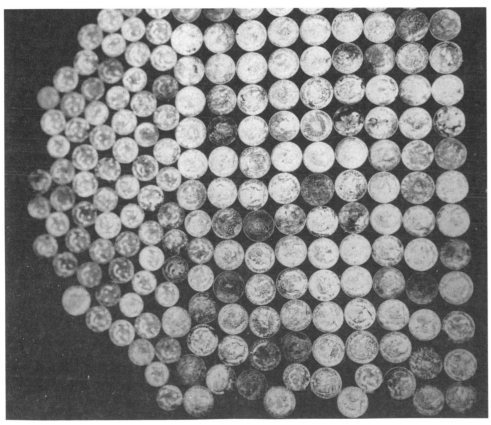

Some of Mrs. Graves money found at Donner Lake in 1891.
— Bancroft Library

MARCH 7, 1847

Reed's group trapped by storm; Breens decide to stay behind

The mountain will not release its death grip on the emigrants. Two nights ago the snow fell like a curtain as the party camped on fifteen feet of snow.

"March 5: Still in camp the last of our provisions gone," James F. Reed wrote in his diary. ". . . Dreaded storm now on us . . . a perfect hurricane in the night. A great crying with the children and with the parents praying crying lamentations on acc[ount] of the cold and dread of death from the Howling storm."

The men stay up at night to feed fires. Reed goes snowblind and can't even see the campfire. John Breen, 15, fell into a pit next to the fire and was hauled out delirious and shivering. His mother, Margaret, forced sugar lumps into his mouth.

"It has snowed already 12 inches, still the storm continues the light of Heaven, as it [were] shut in from us the snow blows so thick that we cannot see 20 feet looking against the wind. I dread the coming night."

The men gather what wood is available. The fire pit gets deeper as the blaze melts the snow. "Freesing was the cry of the mothers ... to their little starving freezing children," Reed wrote, "night closing fast and with it the Hurricane increases."

The cries and prayers continue all night. Reed reports "of all the crying I ever heard nothing ever equaled it." All might have perished had not Bill McCutchen kept the fire going.

Yesterday morning, Isaac Donner, 5, was found dead on a blanket between his sister, Mary, 7, and Patty Reed, 10. With the dawn more wood is piled on the fire and that's all the children can talk about. "Oh how good it feels," they say. "Oh it is good our fire did not go out. I'm glad, I'm glad we got some fire."

Margaret Breen becomes hysterical. She demands the rescuers work harder. She accuses Reed of foolishly taking her family away from the camp only to be murdered by the storm. Her children have survived so much pain and now it seems they will all die. The wind drowns her screams.

The next day and night repeated the first. McCutchen and Hiram Miller keep the fire going. Just after noon today, the snow ceased.

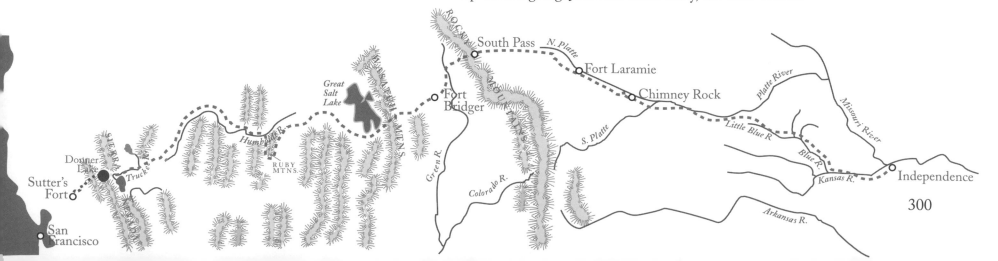

Reed's sight returns and he moves ahead with his two children and others. Miller carries Tommy Reed. Patty Reed walks. Left behind are the seven Breens, Elizabeth Graves and four of her children, Mary Donner and the body of little Isaac. Reed tells Breen if his children die, "the blood will be on his head, not ours." But Breen believes another relief party, which unknown to him has not left Mule Springs, will be along soon. Reed leaves a three-day supply of wood but no food. He has none to give.

The pioneers huddle around a fire platform sinking in the snow. The pit keeps getting deeper.

This place will be known as "Starved Camp."

John Breen
— Bancroft Library

I remember the time that I fell into the hole in the snow . . . I was about dead at that time. The reason that I fell was that I fainted or was overcome from weakness, and as I sat on a log my mother told me that she though I was dying. She had a few ounces of lump sugar in her pocket, and she put a small piece in my mouth which appeared to revive me.

— John Breen, diary

When my provisions gave out, I remained four days before I could taste human flesh. There was no other resort—it was that or death. My wife and child had gone on with the first relief party. I knew not whether they were living or dead. They were penniless and friendless in a strange land. For their sakes I must live, if not for my own. Mrs. Murphy was too weak to revive. The flesh of starved beings contains little nutriment. It is like feeding straw to horses. I can not describe the unutterable repugnance with which I tasted the first mouthful of flesh. There is an instinct in our nature that revolts at the thought of touching, much less eating, a corpse. It makes my blood curdle to think of it!

— Lewis Keseberg

MRS. BREEN IN TRIBULATION.

Mrs Breen in Tribulation. — from Camp of Death *by J. Quinn Thornton*

MARCH 9, 1847

All suffer at Starved Camp; "heroes" cheat Tamsen Donner

Nicholas J. Clark, one of the rescuers who stayed at Alder Creek to care for the Donners — Emigrant Trails Museum

At Starved Camp, Elizabeth Graves, 45, and her son, Franklin, 5, are dead since yesterday and their bodies lie at the edge of a pit melted in the snow by the campfire.

In the hole, the seven-member Breen family; Mary Donner, 7; and the three surviving Graves children shiver in a circle, their feet pointed at the blaze. Margaret Breen's baby, Isabella, nurses beneath her mother's shawl, but can get no milk.

Starving, they all weep and moan and pray. The fire and the forlorn people sink deeper into the snow and finally reach bare ground. The pit is more than fifteen feet deep. John Breen, 15, scoops steps into the icy walls of the pit. James Breen, 5, seems near death.

"Let him die," said Patrick Breen. "He will be better off than any of us."

Margaret Breen takes the lump sugar hidden in her pocket and with snow water gives some to the boy. She also gives some of the nectar and the last of her tea to Elizabeth Graves, 1. Now there is nothing left.

Two days ago, Reed's party, their feet frozen, camped near what will become Kingvale, California. Yesterday, they reached what will become Cisco, where they were met by food brought by men of the third relief group under Midshipman Selim Woodworth.

William Eddy and William Foster, who escaped in the Forlorn Hope, are on their way to join the third relief. The fathers hurry: Their young sons are still trapped at the lake.

Today, George Foster, 4, and James Eddy, 3, lie cold and motionless in the Murphy cabin.

Rescuer Charles Stone, who was left with the lake survivors, quickly moved to the Donner camp at Alder Creek. That's where the gold is.

At Alder Creek, Stone meets Charles Cady, who tells him Nick Clark, left to guard Alder Creek, is off hunting a bear. Stone and Cady make a deal with Tamsen Donner: For $500, they will carry three of her children to safety.

Tamsen combs the hair of Frances, 6; Georgia, 4; and Eliza, 3. She dresses

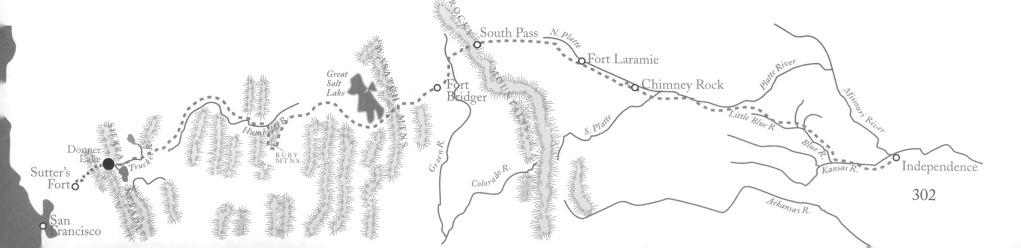

them in layers of their warmest clothes and gives them silver spoons, which Cady and Stone add to their packs.

Lewis Donner, 3, has been dead for days. His mother, Elizabeth, is hysterical. Tamsen takes comfort that her children will be safe.

The girls say good bye to their mother; their dying father, George, and the tearful Aunt Betsy.

Cady and Stone walk six miles to the lake camp and give the children to Lavina Murphy. They take up residence in the former Breen cabin and weather the storm.

Today the two men are fleeing the lake without the children. They soon will pass Starved Camp, but will ignore it.

The "heroes" move quickly over the snow, even though their packs are stuffed with booty.

I think my little brother James was the smallest child that walked across . . . Poor little fellow, he would have to place his knee on the hill of snow between each step of the snowshoes and climb over . . . We were afraid that he would give out, so we encouraged him every step of the way, telling him that with each step he was getting closer to Papa . . . At night we would go asleep with our clothes all dripping wet from dragging over the snow all day. In the morning they would be frozen stiff as a board . . . I only wonder that we did not freeze to death.
— Virginia Reed, *Across the Plains In the Donner Party*

Cover of Joseph King's Winter of Entrapment *showing Starved Camp.* — K&K Publications

MARCH 12, 1847

Cannibalism at Starved Camp; Reeds safe in Bear Valley

The second relief party under James F. Reed has reached Bear Valley.

All six members of Reed's family are now safe. In the warmth of Johnson's Ranch, Patty Reed reaches into her apron hem and takes out a tiny wooden doll. Months ago, her parents told her to take nothing from the abandoned wagon but she disobeyed them, taking this toy and a few other keepsakes of her grandmother: a lock of the old woman's hair and a small pincushion.

In old age, Patty Reed will look into the box containing the artifacts and say, "Here in this box is me." Even 150 years later, the tiny doll displayed at Sutter's Fort will remain a poignant witness to the Donner Party's suffering.

At Starved Camp, the eleven survivors eat the bodies of Elizabeth Graves, her son, Franklin, and tiny Isaac Donner. Margaret Breen will later tell author Eliza Farnham that Mary Donner, 7, suggested the desperate measure.

"Oh, child," the horror-stricken woman exclaimed, "sure you would not eat your own brother." But the girl already has experienced the cannibalism of her father at Alder Creek. Patrick Breen climbs to the top of the pit where the bodies lie and returns with the forbidden meat.

The nine children eat. Farnham will later write that the adults did not consume the meal, but most authors will not believe it. Mr. and Mrs. Breen cast their Catholic prayers to heaven.

Today, seven men, a new third relief effort, set out for the high camps led by the bearlike John Stark. With this group are William Eddy and William Foster, who are intent on saving their young sons, and Charles Stone, who made it back to safety after telling Tamsen Donner that he and his partner, Charles Cady, would save her daughters.

They lied. Stone is apparently going back for more booty.

At Alder Creek camp, Elizabeth "Aunt Betsy" Donner, 45, died yesterday. Her body will provide food for survivors. At the lake camp, the bodies of children serve the same purpose. The last adults left living at the lake have crossed the brink of madness.

Georgia Donner, 4, will say in later years that the tiny body of Georgie Foster was hung on a wall like a portion of beef.

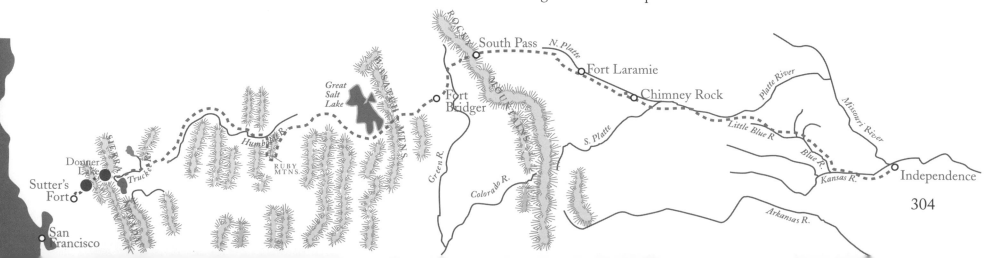

Replica of Patty Reed's doll at the Emigrant Trails Museum in Truckee.
— Marilyn Newton photo

I took "Dolly" out from where I had hidden her in my dress, and what a pleasant little hour we had, after all that we had gone through, but now happy we were at that camp of plenty. We knew that mama, sister and brother had plenty to eat and drink and we would see them soon.
— Patty Reed, from *The Tragedy of Donner Lake*

MARCH 14, 1847

Third relief party reaches Breens; some go on to high camps

Eleanor Graves — Bancroft Library

Lovina Graves — Emigrant Trails Museum

Mary Graves — Emigrant Trails Museum

William Graves — Bancroft Library

Sarah Graves — Emigrant Trails Museum

Things have happened quickly.

Yesterday, the third relief party reached Starved Camp, where eleven people have been living in a snow pit since March 6. They survived by eating the corpses of two children and an adult.

Rescuer William Eddy, 28, will later describe Starved Camp along with lurid details of the cannibalism. He'll be critical of the Breens for "sunning themselves" and ignoring the children, one of whom, Elizabeth Graves, 1, was trying to get the attention of her dead mother.

For a week, however, the couple kept seven youngsters alive in that hellhole, including four who are not their own.

Three rescuers go down the mountain: Big John Stark, 30, carries Jonathan Graves, 7, and leads the seven Breens and Nancy Graves, 9; Howard Oakley carries Mary Donner; Charles Stone, who cheated Tamsen Donner, carries Elizabeth Graves.

William Foster, Hiram Miller, and Bill Thompson press on to the high camps. By afternoon they reached the lake. "Bodies were laying in and around the camps," J. Quinn Thornton will write. "A body with half the flesh torn from it was lying near the door. Upon turning over a head which was severed from a body, Mr. Eddy instantly recognized the familiar face of an old friend and traveling companion."

Eddy and Foster are fathers no more and they have nothing to bury. Their tiny sons' bodies have been eaten by Lewis Keseberg and others. Keseberg says he's still unable to travel.

Eddy, suspecting Keseberg of murder, wants to kill him, but vows to do it later if Keseberg ever gets to California.

Lavina Murphy, 37, blind and sick, will also stay. She knows she is doomed and can't face the children when they try to say good-bye. The children she protected weep to leave her. Lying on a blanket, she turns her face to the wall.

"She seemed to realize her work was finished," Georgia Donner, 4, will remember.

Tamsen Donner, 45, also remains behind. She still refuses to leave her

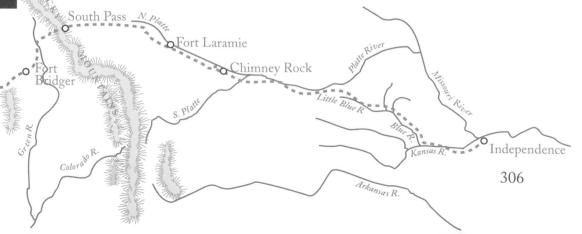

dying husband. Sammy Donner, 4, is too sick to move. Tamsen's three daughters will leave with the rescuers, as will Simon Murphy, 9; John Baptiste Trudeau, 16; and Nick Clark.

In two hours, the third relief heads back.

By tonight the survivors and rescuers have crossed Donner Pass. They will be the last party on this trail for a month. Then, salvage and booty, not relief, will be the travelers' goal.

Donner Lake and surrounding landscape as winter snows begin to melt
— Emigrant Trails Museum

I would without hesitancy express the opinion, that Kiesberg was at the time insane, had he not, long after his subsequent arrival in the settlements of California, shown himself to be a wild beast, by declaring with a profane explitive, that 'a man is a fool who prefers poor California beef to human flesh.' But the closing scenes of the mountain camp will more fully show that this man is perhaps without a parallel in history.
—J. Quinn Thornton, *Camp of Death*

What is the use of my making a statement? People incline to believe the most horrible reports concerning a man, and they will not credit what I say in my own defense. My conscience is clear. I am an old man, and am calmly awaiting my death. God is my judge, and it long ago ceased to trouble me that people shunned and slandered me.
— Lewis Keseberg to C.F. McGlashan, 1879

MARCH 16, 1847

Five left alive at high camps; relief party descends Sierra

Frances Donner — Emigrant Trails Museum

With five survivors left behind at the Donner Lake and Alder Creek camps, the scattered members of the third relief party battle their way down the Sierra.

Yesterday, Frances Donner, 6, was carried in a blanket on the back of Bill Thompson. She cries, but he quiets her up by promising he'll give her a book when they reach Bear Valley. Frances, the daughter of Tamsen, the teacher, is pleased.

Thompson stopped to pick up a bundle left on the trail. Last night at the campfire they opened it. The Donner sisters recognized silk dresses, silver spoons and other keepsakes their mother, Tamsen Donner, had entrusted to Charles Cady and Charles Stone.

The pair had promised to bring the Donner sisters to safety after Tamsen paid them $500, but instead left them at the lake camp and escaped.

Eliza Donner, 3, is being carried by Hiram Miller, a veteran of the second rescue, who promises her sugar if she walks for a while and then tells her there is none after she complies. In camp, Eliza cries and pouts.

Today Thompson, Miller, William Eddy, and the others pass John Stark, a native of Indiana, who is leading the seven Breens, carrying blankets and supplies and sometimes hoisting James Breen, 5; Jon Graves, 7; and others on his broad back.

Stark carries two children ahead, leaves them, and returns for others. In a one-man relay, he brings his charges down the mountain, telling them they are so skinny from their ordeal he could carry them all at once and not notice.

Later, Eddy's party passes Stone and Howard Oakley, who also are carrying children.

With Eddy are Nick Clark, who carries a forty-pound pack filled with booty and two guns picked up at the Alder Creek camp; and John Baptiste Trudeau, 16, who is too weakened by malnutrition to carry anything.

Tonight the forward party camps at the Yuba crossing. The fire is warm; safety is near.

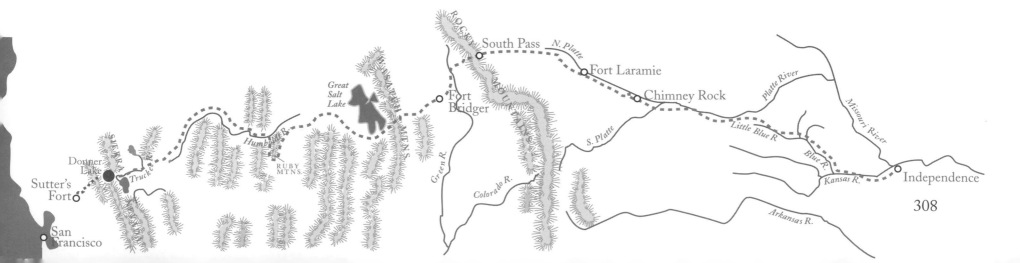

*John Stark
— Winter of
Entrapment by
Joseph King*

[John] Stark remained and had he not done so probably not one of them would have got out of the snow as the other men were not willing to wait for the weak children to get along as they feared another snow storm. But Stark was brave and intelligent and of great bodily strength, he said he would take them all to Bear Valley if they would only live long enough.

From the start he cheered the children telling them that they would soon be out of the snow and have all the fat meat they could eat and when one of the children would fall unable to go farther he would carry it until it was a little rested, in fact he carried some one of them almost constantly while traveling and sometimes had two at a time along with a heavy load of provisions, still he never uttered a word of complaint or got out of temper.

He would laugh and say it was no trouble to carry the children as they were so thin that they were very light — that we would soon be out of the snow where we would have enough to eat and take a long rest.

In this way he succeeded in getting all into Bear Valley where there was but little snow and some provisions and in a day or two we got to a camp called "Mule Springs" where there was no snow and here there was a pack train in charge of Selim E. Woodworth, a government officer. Here was an end to hunger and cold and here the great task of noble Stark was at an end.

Were it not for him I would probably not be here today. Few men have the resolution and physical strength that he had and if he had less of either he could not have done what he did. He was what I will call a perfect man, perfect in both body and mind . . . All honor to your memory brave generous honest Stark.

— John Breen, *Pioneer Memoirs*

Rescuer on snowshoes guides a survivor in this detail from Robert Lebron's painting — Emigrant Trails Museum

MARCH 18, 1847

Mrs. Murphy dead at lake; Breens, others, reach safety

I started with shoes that were too large for me and they would come off in the snow when I pulled my feet out. Mr. Thompson, who took charge of me to assist me out to California, got tired of pulling them out so often, so at last he left them where they pulled off. Then I traveled in my stocking feet for a time, then he took his mittens and made me a pair of moccasins and he went bare handed.

— Frances Donner, letter to C. F. McGlashan

Lavinah Murphy is dead.

The woman who cared for her children and other children during the ordeal died today. When the third rescue party left the camp five days ago, she turned her face to the wall rather than allow the children to see her hopelessness.

In later years both survivors and writers will debate her sanity at the end and call her "old Mrs. Murphy." She was 37.

Lewis Keseberg, 32, is now alone at the lake camp. Tamsen Donner, 45; her husband, George, 62; and nephew Sammy Donner, 4; remain at Alder Creek camp.

Today the third relief party reaches Johnson's Ranch and safety. The Breens are caring for their frostbite and eating bread, beef, and beans.

The survivors brought out by the second relief — including the Reed family — are being cared for at ranches near Sutter's Fort. Capt. John Sutter and Alcalde John Sinclair are generous.

The Breens and Reeds are the only families in the Donner Party to survive intact. Virginia Reed, 13, already has received a marriage proposal from a man who met her during her trek to Sutter's. She finally sees the paradise she's been dreaming about for more than a year.

"California is a beautiful country," Virginia will write to a cousin in Illinois. "It ought to be a beautiful country to pay us for our trouble getting here. . . . Oh, Mary I have wrote you half of the trouble we have had but I have wrote you enough to let you know that you don't know what trouble is but thank the Good God we have all got through and the only family that did not eat human flesh.

"We have left everything but I don't care for that — we have got through."

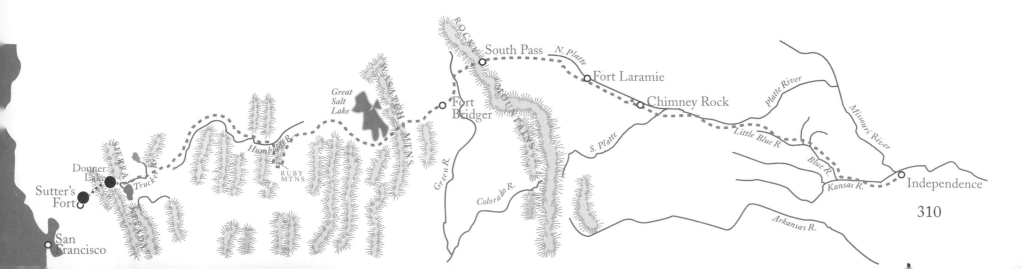

We were taken on horseback to Johnson's ranch, the first settlement in California; here we were left to look for ourselves, but the people were very kind to us and we got along very well, but our flesh swelled up as if we had been stung all over by bees, and it was equally as sore.
— William C. "Billy" Graves, *Russian River Flag* account

An old sign protrudes from the stump of a tree at Johnson's Ranch near Sacramento. The tree grew around the sign which originally said Emigrant Trail. Only a portion of the lettering is still visible today. — Marilyn Newton photo

March 21, 1847

Three left at high camps: Keseberg, Tamsen, and George

Sammy Donner, 4, is out of his long misery.

The boy, ill for weeks, died at Alder Creek camp. Tamsen Donner buried her nephew's emaciated body in the snow. She went back into her tent and sat at the side of her husband, George, whose infection has turned his arm blackish-green from his hand to his shoulder.

In the last week of October when George gashed his hand with a chisel while repairing a wagon, he had joked about the "scratch." For many weeks, Tamsen has known George will not recover. She refused each rescue party's offers of escape. She will not let him die alone. Tamsen holds his good hand and speaks to him.

She plans to keep her vigil — staying alive by cannibalism — until George's last breath. Then she will fight to rejoin her daughters, now safe at Johnson's Ranch in Bear Valley. She has more than enough reasons not to surrender to the ordeal.

At the lake camp Keseberg, his leg injury still hurting, limps among the bodies of his former companions. He cuts a piece and boils the flesh. He eats. He weeps and screams curses.

At night, wolves devour bodies outside his cabin door and then scratch on his roof. He covers his ears to stifle their howls.

Inside the cabin, five bodies remain, including that of Lavina Murphy. The third relief party, which spent two hours at the lake camp before departing for Bear Valley, was in too much of a hurry to remove them. Keseberg is too weak to drag them out.

"Their stark and ghastly bodies lay there day and night," he will remember, "seemingly gazing at me with their glazed and staring eyes.

"I endured a thousand deaths. To have one's suffering prolonged inch by inch, to be deserted, forsaken, hopeless, to see that loathsome food ever before my eyes, was almost too much for human endurance."

Keseberg loads his pistol and stares at what might be his only escape from horror.

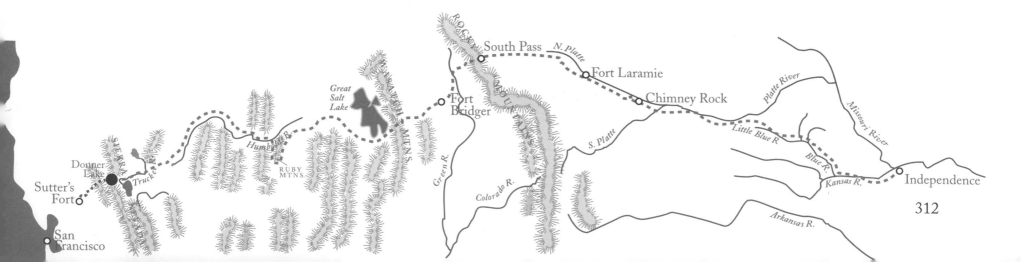

A painting by Frederic Remington entitled "End of the Trail"
— Emigrant Trails Museum

Each day allowances were cut short and shorter, until we received each for our evening meal two small pieces of jerked beef, the pieces not being larger than about the size of a finger. Finally the last ration was issued in the evening, for the evening and the next morning meal. I received my portion with the rest, but I was so famished that I could not resist the temptation to eat it all. Next morning, I had nothing for breakfast. Now comes an incident I shall never forget. My sister, seeing my distress, looking at the others eating their morsel of meat, divided her picnic with me, how long we went on without food after that I do not know.
— Leanna Donner, letter to C. F. McGlashan

March 23, 1847

Keseberg mulls suicide; fourth rescue party leaves Sutter's Fort

Snow covered mountains around Donner Lake.
— Nevada Historical Society

In his cabin at the lake camp, Lewis Keseberg puts the barrel of a pistol in his mouth.

"Suicide would have been a relief, a happiness, a godsend," Keseberg will tell author C. F. McGlashan thirty years after the events at Donner Lake.

"Many a time I had the muzzle of my pistol in my mouth and my finger on the trigger, but the faces of my helpless, dependent wife and child would rise up before me and my hand would fall powerless. I was not the cause of my misfortunes, and God Almighty had provided me with only this one horrible way for me to subsist."

He speaks, reads, and writes in four languages, but none gives him the words to describe the self-loathing and horror cannibalism has caused.

The days are still sunny at the high camps. The nights are bitter cold.

At Alder Creek camp, George Donner is surely at the close of his life. Tamsen Donner wipes the sweat from his feverish brow. She prays her husband will soon be delivered from his pain.

Today the Donner children and others brought out by the third relief party reach Sutter's Fort. James Breen's leg is badly frostbitten and a doctor is sent for to perform an amputation. Luckily, the doctor can't be found and Breen, 5, will recover and live out his life on both legs.

At Sutter's, a new rescue party, including survivors of the Donner Party and veterans of previous relief efforts, is organized today. They are: Reason P. Tucker, John Rhodes, W. C. "Billy" Graves, Joseph Sels, Edward Coffeemeyer, William Foster, and big John Stark, who requires little rest before going back up the mountain.

They are good men and not out for booty. Their goal is to bring the last five survivors — or as many as remain — down from the Sierra.

The party must hurry. Although the thaw has continued for weeks, John Sutter warns winter is not done and March is a fickle month.

Far west in the Pacific, thunderstorms beget more thunderstorms. A parade of clouds is building and begins to move east.

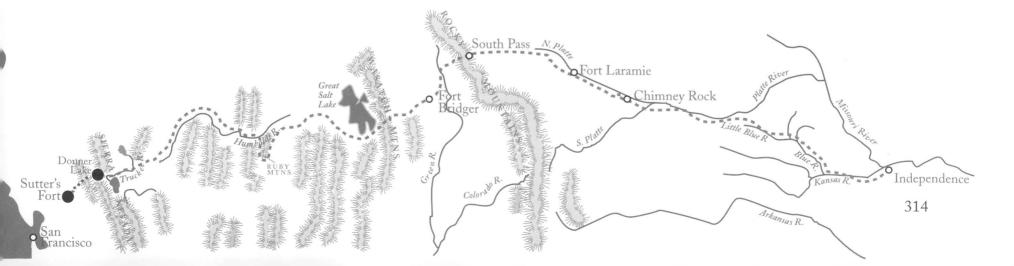

A double-barreled pistol circa 1844. — Marilyn Newton photo

Lewis Keseberg — Bancroft Library

I endured a thousand deaths. To have one's suffering prolonged inch by inch, to be deserted, forsaken, hopeless; to see that loathsome food ever before my eyes, was almost too much for human endurance. I am conversant with four different languages. I speak and write them with equal fluency; yet in all four I do not find words enough to express the horror I experienced during those two months, or what I still feel when memory reverts to the scene.
— Lewis Keseberg, to C. F. McGlashan

MARCH 26, 1847

George Donner, 62, dies with Tamsen at his side

George Donner, 62, is dead. His third wife, Tamsen, 45, weeps at his side.

He lingered five months with his infected wound sapping his life. Twice Tamsen refused offers of rescue because she would not abandon him.

The captain of the Donner Party had been called "Uncle George," owing to his age as well as his kindness and compassion. He was born to German parents in North Carolina. He moved west with the frontier to Kentucky, Indiana, and Illinois. He spent a year in Texas.

Just a year ago he was enticing teamsters to drive his wagons in exchange for free land in California. He was so proud last summer, Tamsen wrote in a letter, when he was a captain of wagons and his yells of "chain up, boys!" shattered the morning calm.

That was in June, a continent away and a lifetime before.

Tamsen washes her husband for the last time and wraps his body in a sheet as though he were to be laid out in a parlor in Springfield, Illinois. There is no time for mourning. Dark clouds fly. Tamsen must rejoin her daughters. She must travel at least six miles to the lake and then over the mountains.

Far to the west in Bear Valley, the latest rescue party is bogged down in slush, mud and the torrents of streams. Their horses are useless; their packs, heavy. They too look at the sky.

At the lake camp, Lewis Keseberg shivers in his cabin as the wind whistles through cracks in logs. The lone survivor lies among butchered bodies and considers them lucky.

Wolves howl. Keseberg, half-mad, his pistol ready, listens for their scratchings at his door.

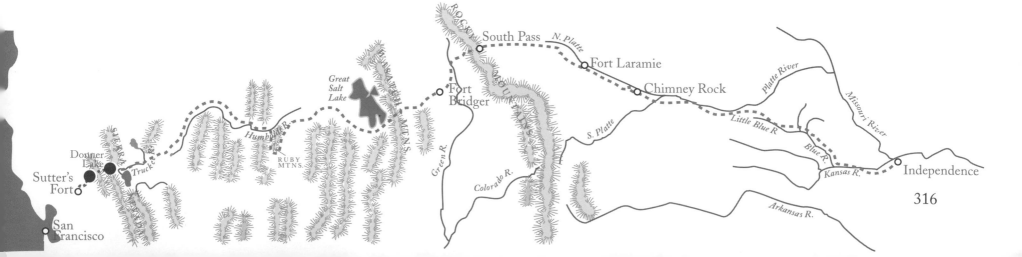

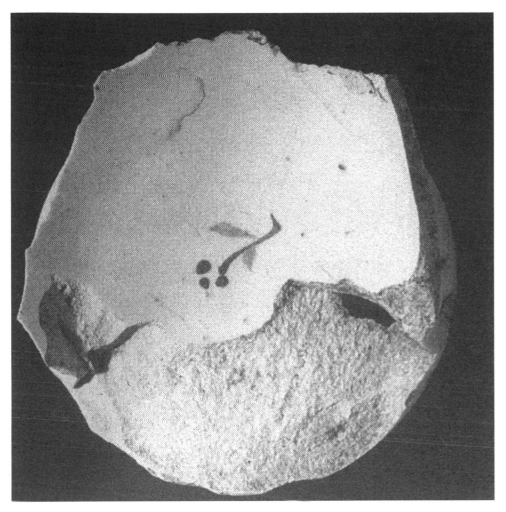

A cup, painted with a sprig, was found at the site on Alder Creek believed to have been the Donner family camp. — from The Archaeology of the Donner Party *by Donald L Hardesty*

March 28, 1847

Tamsen Donner dies at lake; Keseberg is sole witness

The body of Tamsen Donner, 45, has joined the other corpses on the floor of Lewis Keseberg's cabin at Donner Lake.

Keseberg, the only witness, will say: "At midnight, one cold bitter night, Mrs. George Donner came to my door. It was about two weeks after Reed (Does he mean Eddy and Foster?) had gone, and my loneliness was beginning to be unendurable. I was most happy to hear the sound of a human voice.

"Her coming was like that of an angel from heaven. But she had not come to bear me company. Her husband had died in her arms. She had remained by his side until death came, and then had lain him out and hurried away.

"He died at nightfall, and she had traveled over the snow alone to my cabin. She was going, alone, across the mountains . . . without food or guide."

"My children," Tamsen said. "I must see my children," Keseberg will report.

Keseberg will say Tamsen told him she had money in her tent and asked him to look after it and take it to her daughters in case she died before reaching safety. He says he promised her "sacredly."

He will say Tamsen had apparently fallen into a stream (Donner Creek?). Her clothes were frozen and her skin was like ice. She said she was hungry, but refused Keseberg's offer of human flesh, although it's unlikely the five-foot-tall, ninety-pound woman could have survived so long at Alder Creek without joining the cannibalism that kept her daughters and others alive.

"She finally lay down, and I spread a feather-bed and some blankets over her. In the morning she was dead. I think the hunger, the mental suffering, and the icy chill of the preceding night caused her death."

Today, snow falls on the lake camp. In Bear Valley, seven would-be rescuers, driven back by mud, slush and the coming storm, are returning to Sutter's Fort.

Keseberg is now the lone survivor. There will be no more rescuers until spring. But he has food, loathsome food.

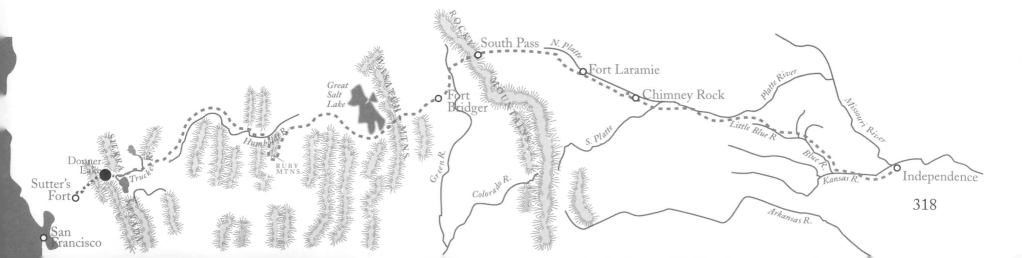

Donner Creek — Emigrant Trails Museum

MARCH 30, 1847

Tamsen's demise debated: mishap, hypothermia, or murder?

Lewis Keseberg is eating Tamsen Donner's body.

The circumstances of her demise will remain a matter of debate for 150 years.

Keseberg, now the lone survivor at the Sierra camps, will say she came to his cabin door at midnight the day her husband, George, died at the Alder Creek camp. She was soaked from a fall in a creek and frozen. Despite his efforts at keeping her warm she was dead by morning.

The last rescue party to leave the lake two weeks ago described Tamsen as strong, healthy, and determined to survive. Keseberg will be suspected of murdering her in revenge for some injury, or for food, or as a result of madness.

The accusation soon to be leveled against him will echo for fifteen decades. He'll be a suspect the rest of his life, but never be formally charged with anything.

Some people will revile him as a monster; children will throw things at him in the streets. Others who will know him — such as John Sutter, Heinrich Lienhard, and Jacob W. Harlan — will say he could not have killed anyone.

In his novel *Tamsen*, author David Galloway will provide another theory: When Tamsen came scratching at Keseberg's cabin at midnight, he mistook her for a wolf and shot her through the oxhide door.

Author Joseph King in *Winter of Entrapment* also will make a case for Keseberg's innocence. Although the ordeal might have unhinged the man's mind, King will speculate, he had no reason to kill Tamsen. He will believe Keseberg's account.

At the 1996 California Trail Days event, 150 years after the Donner tragedy, a mock inquest will be held to determine Keseberg's role in the matter. With University of Nevada, Reno English instructor David Fenimore as Keseberg, a cast of scholars, authors and actors will testify as witnesses.

For more than an hour, the participants at the Peppermill Hotel-Casino in Reno will review the facts of the case. The verdict: not guilty.

Fifteen decades later, there is no shred of hard evidence indicating Keseberg killed anyone.

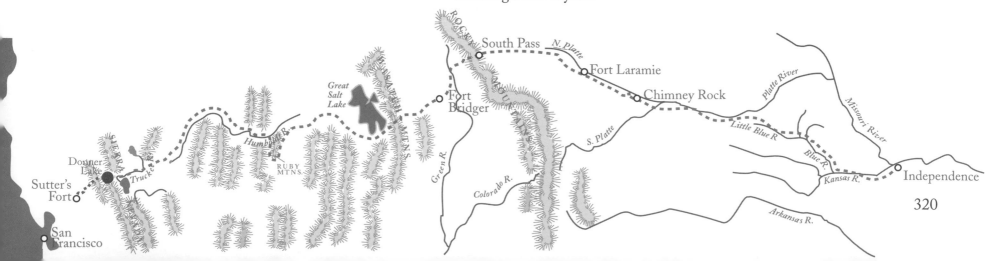

David Galloway's novel about Tamsen Donner

At midnight, one cold, bitter night, Mrs. George Donner came to my door. It was about two weeks after Reed had gone, and my loneliness was beginning to be unendurable. I was most happy to hear the sound of a human voice. Her coming was like that of an angel from heaven. But she had not come to bear me company. Her husband had died in her arms. She had remained by his side until death came, and then had laid him out and hurried away. He died at nightfall, and she had traveled over the snow alone to my cabin. She was going, alone, across the mountains. She was going to start without food or guide. She kept saying, 'My children! I must see my children!' She feared she would not survive, and told me she had some money in her tent. It was too heavy for her to carry. She said, "Mr. Keseberg, I confide this to your care." he made me promise sacredly that I would get the money and take it to her children in case she perished and I survived. She declared she would start over the mountains in the morning. She said, 'I am bound to go to my children.' She seemed very cold, and her clothes were like ice. I think she had got in the creek in coming. She said she was very hungry, but refused the only food I could offer. She had never eaten the loathsome flesh. She finally lay down, and I spread a feather-bed and some blankets over her. In the morning she was dead. I think the hunger, the mental suffering, and the icy chill of the preceding night, caused her death. I have often been accused of taking her life. Before my God, I swear this is untrue! Do you think a man would be such a miscreant, such a damnable fiend, such a caricature on humanity, as to kill this lone woman? There were plenty of corpses lying around. She would only add one more corpse to the many!
— Lewis Keseberg

APRIL 2, 1847

Mary Donner, Sol Hook get medical attention

Mary Donner
— Emigrant Trails Museum

Yesterday, Passed Midshipman Selim E. Woodworth arrived in the city by the bay.

He brings Mary Donner, 7, suffering from a burned and frozen foot, and her half brother, Solomon Hook, 14, who is also frostbitten. Also with Woodworth are two of his men, Henry Dann and Charles Cady, with feet black from frostbite. John Baptiste Trudeau, 16, and rescuer Howard Oakly are with the men and serve as nurses to the children.

"[At Starved Camp] Mary Donner fell in the fire and burned her foot so severely that amputation will be necessary in order to save her life," Woodworth writes in an article for tomorrow's edition of the *California Star*, which now has San Francisco instead of "Yerba Buena" on its front-page masthead.

The report outlines recent rescues. It is self-serving to Woodworth and makes only passing reference to John Stark, the man who single-handedly saved the Breens and others.

Woodworth predicts that the next rescue party might be able to save Lewis Keseberg and Tamsen Donner, but "Mrs. Murphy, Mr. Donner and the child could not survive many days when left." Even if they remain alive when the next rescuers reach them, he wrote, they would surely be too feeble to make the trip down the mountains.

Tamsen Donner and Keseberg, he wrote "could subsist on the remaining bodies yet some ten days. The snow at the cabins was going off rapidly; but in Bear Valley and the Juba River it was yet 20 feet deep on the level."

He doesn't mention he never made it to the cabins but claims, "Since the 28 day of February I have been twenty-four days in the snow, I may say without seeing land — have traveled over 140 miles on the snow, on foot, carrying a pack on my back, — have crossed Bear River Mountains four times, — been twice over on the Juba River, and can say that I never enjoyed better health. ..."

At Sutter's Fort and California ranches, other survivors are recovering.

The Reed family has left the post and are now guests of the Yount family at their Napa Valley ranch. Today they celebrate Tommy Reed's fifth birthday.

Virginia Reed has decided she's not interested in marrying a man

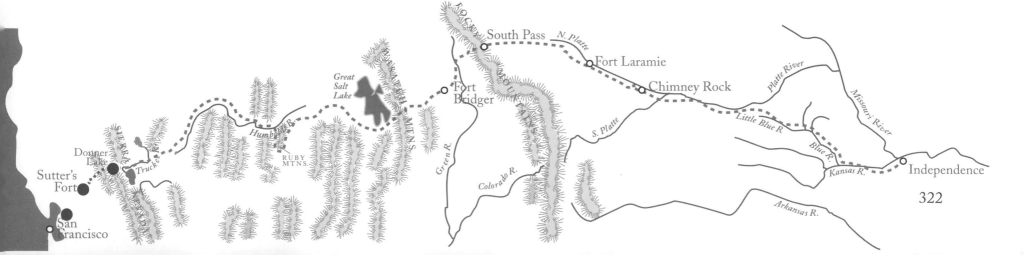

who proposed to the emaciated 13-year-old as she was traveling to the fort. Instead, she will get an education. She yet hasn't told her parents of her decision to become a Catholic. Her father, James, a Protestant and a dedicated Mason, would rage at her proposed conversion.

Rain sweeps California. There is talk of another rescue, but no action. Those who hear the reports of the last relief party assume Sammy and George Donner must be dead.

They say there's still hope for Tamsen and Keseberg. But both had elected to stay in the camps, so there is no pressing argument for another expedition as the storms spend their fury against the Sierra.

There are, however, valuable goods — and gold — left on the mountain. Some of the men at Sutter's talk of these things with great passion.

California Star *newspaper for April 3, 1847, uses* San Francisco *on the masthead instead of Yerba Buena*

April 4, 1847

Keseberg waits out storms; more will die after rescue

Lewis Keseberg, the last survivor in the high camps, is confined to his cabin as snowflakes swirl outside.

Another series of storms is marching across the mountains. They will end tonight.

Keseberg sits in his stinking, smoky room where the floor is littered with corpses. In the cabin are two kettles that rescuers will later say contain the blood of Tamsen Donner.

His sanity gone, his loneliness complete, Keseberg eats boiled flesh.

"To go into details, to relate the minutiae, is too agonizing," Keseberg will tell Truckee newspaper editor C. F. McGlashan thirty years after his ordeal.

"The necessary mutilation of the bodies of those who had been my friends, rendered the ghastliness of my situation more frightful."

Keseberg, who was lame for months, is now nursing his most recent injury: While chopping wood an ax slipped and sliced off the heel of his foot. No longer expecting rescue, he does what he can to survive for as long as he can.

Rain continues to sweep the California settlements.

The Donner Party's roster of death is not yet closed: Elizabeth Graves, 1, will soon join the roll, as will Jonathan Graves, about 7. The girl was carried out of the Sierra by Charles Stone, one of the men who cheated Tamsen Donner. At Johnson's Ranch in Bear Valley Stone gave the child to her sister Mary Ann, 19.

The toddler was ill, frostbitten, and malnourished. No one believed she would recover. However, these two deaths aren't usually counted as casualties of the Sierra.

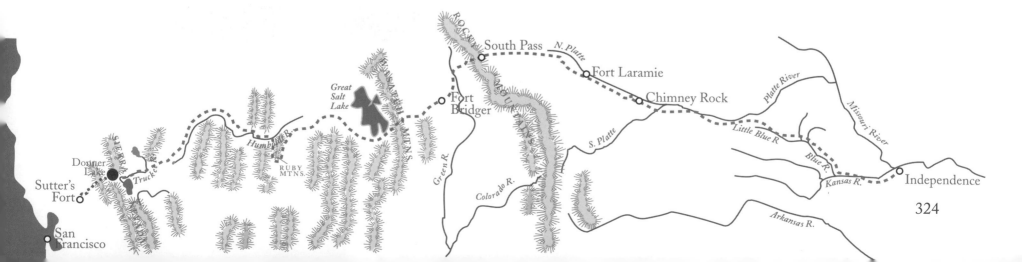

Sarah Graves — Emigrant Trails Museum

Sarah Foster — Emigrant Trails Museum

Mary Murphy — Emigrant Trails Museum

Leanna Donner — Bancroft Library

Lovina Graves — Bancroft Library

Elitha Donner — Bancroft Library

Mary Graves — Emigrant Trails Museum

Phillipine Keseberg — Bancroft Library

WOMEN FARED BETTER THEN THE MEN

Of the eighty-one members of the party that ascended the Sierra in October, one remains trapped, thirty-six are dead, and forty-four have reached the Sacramento Valley. The death toll includes Luis and Salvador, the Miwok Indians.

In the Donner tragedy, women generally fared better than men. Of the thirty-six who perished in the Sierra, twenty-seven were male and nine were female. In the Forlorn Hope party of fifteen, eight men died and two men and all five women survived the long walk to safety.

More than 140 years after the tragedy, Donald Grayson, a University of Washington anthropologist, will study the mortality of the Donner Party and of two Mormon handcart parties trapped in the Rocky Mountains in 1856. In the Mormon case, Grayson found that sixty-eight of 429 pioneers died in the snow — with the death rate among males being three times that of the females.

He will conclude that neither the greater work load among the men nor their gender roles can account for the higher male deaths. "Human biology determined who lived and who died," Grayson will write.

Other factors will suggest that age and family group size helped determine who would survive. "Males traveling alone or with small family groups died sooner than those who traveled with larger families. No females died until after fourteen males had already lost their lives."

The theme of women being stronger than men in extreme conditions will be embraced by many writers including feminist Eliza Farnham. Even at the time of the Donner Party, observers noted the survival rates were skewed.

At Sutter's, Sheriff George McKinstry is making jokes about "man-eating women" and lurid stories are spreading throughout California.

Already, the legends begin.

APRIL 6, 1847

Breens enjoying the paradise they set out for a year ago

Yesterday marked one year to the day that the Breen family set out from Keokuk, Iowa, toward Independence, Missouri, for the Missouri River crossing and the wilderness.

The nine Breens and their friend Patrick Dolan had three wagons, at least fourteen oxen, milk cow, and a horse. Patrick Breen had $500 in coin, hundreds of dollars worth of goods and provisions, and his dog, Towser.

The Breens arrived at Sutter's Fort last month with only their lives and the rags they wore.

Today the Breens are guests at the Martin Murphy Jr. Ranch on the Cosumnes River. Breen's sons are talking about going back up the mountains in the spring to salvage their goods.

To them, California appears the paradise they hoped for a year, a lifetime, ago.

"I will ever remember the appearance of the country about Johnson's Ranch," John Breen, who was 15 at the time of the entrapment, will write in his *Pioneer Memoirs* of 1877. "The grass was forward and many flowers mingled through it, the weather was warm and clear which gave the sensation to the true emigrant that I can not describe."

At Sutter's Fort, the youngster expected to see signs of the war with Mexico, but instead there were traders, Indian and Mexican cowboys, mountaineers and businessmen, a few Hawaiians, and a company of eighty Indian cavalry that drilled every day.

"There was no sign of war here; all was peace," John Breen will say.

Newspaper accounts of the 1840s ignore the heroism of John Stark, who brought most of the Breens out of the Sierra, but the Breens will remember.

"To his great bodily strength and his unexpected courage" we owe or lives, James Breen will write.

John Breen will remember: "He was what I call a perfect man, perfect in mind and body . . . all honor to your memory brave, generous, honest Stark."

John Stark— Bancroft Library

John Breen — Bancroft Library

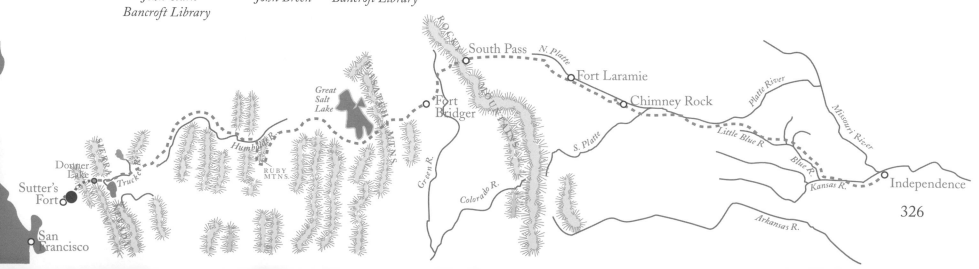

Edward Breen —
Bancroft Library

Simon Breen —
Bancroft Library

Peter Breen —
Bancroft Library

Patrick Breen, Sr.
— Emigrant
Trails Museum

John Breen —
Bancroft Library

James Breen —
Bancroft Library

The emigrants were bound here, Sutter's Fort.
— Marilyn Newton photo

APRIL 9, 1847

Keseberg plans scavenging trip; newspaper accounts create myths

April 10, 1847 California Star with a sensational account of the Donner Party's entrapment in the Sierra.

The storms have broken and the sun shines on the high camps.

Keseberg eats and sleeps in his cabin at the lake camp. His foot injury is healing. If this thaw continues, he plans to visit Alder Creek camp and see what there is to find. Maybe he is motivated by promises he said he made to Tamsen Donner. Others will say greed will drive him through the melting snow.

In California, the Donner tragedy is the subject of gossip in the saloons of San Francisco and the rooms at Sutter's Fort. A story in tomorrow's *California Star* newspaper in San Francisco — which takes the truth and adds wild imaginings — fans the fires of horror:

"A more shocking scene cannot be imagined . . . Bodies of men, women and children, with half the flesh torn from them, lay on every side. A woman sat by the side of the body of her husband, who had just died, cutting out his tongue; the heart she had already taken out, broiled and eat[en]! The daughter was seen eating the flesh of the father — the mother that of her children — children that of father and mother."

The account relates how normal people were turned into murderers (true in one case: William Foster killed Luis and Salvador) and mindless cannibals. Other incidents are blown out of proportion. The writer relates that survivors preferred "putrid human flesh" to the rescuers' food. Another legend — that Keseberg killed children — first sees print: "One of the emigrants took a child of about four years of age in bed with him, and devoured the whole before morning; and the next day [ate] another about the same age before noon."

The newspaper, which mistakenly says the "unfortunate emigrants" were principally from the neighborhood of Independence, Missouri, also incorrectly reports that they could have easily escaped if they had not been too greedy to leave their wagons and goods. This account and others to follow will spread throughout the nation. Eastern newspapers will add their own flourishes and the Donner Party will become a synonym for human depravity.

Thus, myths are born. In 150 years, they will still be repeated as history.

Tomorrow at Sutter's Fort, a meeting will set the stage for the final chapter in the Donner saga. A gruff mountain man will make a deal for salvage rights and the fourth relief party will be organized.

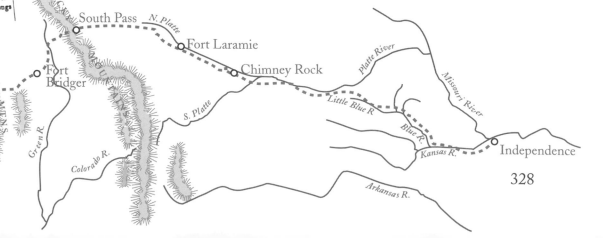

Winter at Donner Lake. — Tim Dunn photo

A more shocking scene cannot be imagined, than that witnessed by the party of men who went to the relief of the unfortunate emigrants in the California Mountains. The bones of those who had died and been devoured by the miserable ones that still survived, were lying around their tents and cabins. Bodies of men, women, and children, with half the flesh torn from them, lay on every side. A woman sat by the side of the body of her husband, who had just died, cutting out his tongue; the heart she had already taken out, broiled and eat! The daughter was seen eating the flesh of the father — the mother that of her children — children that of father and mother. The emaciated, wild, and ghastly appearance of the survivors, added to the horror of the scene. Language cannot describe the awful change that a few weeks of dire suffering had wrought in the minds of these wretched and pitiable beings. Those who but one month before would have shuddered and sickened at the thought of eating human flesh, or of killing their companions and relatives to preserve their own lives, now looked upon the opportunity by these acts afforded them of escaping the most dreadful of deaths, as a providential interference in their behalf. — Calculations were coldly made, as they sat gloomily around their gloomy camp fires, for the next and succeeding meals. Various expedients were devised to prevent the dreadful crime of murder, but they finally resolved to kill those who had the least claims to longer existence. Just at this moment however, as if by Divine interposition, some of them died, which afforded the rest temporary relief. Some sunk into the arms of death cursing God for their miserable fate, while the last whisperings of others were prayers and songs of praise to the Almighty.
— California Star, April 10, 1847

APRIL 11, 1847

Mountain man makes deal to salvage goods at camps

William O. "Le Gros" Fallon has made a bargain — to salvage the goods left at the Sierra camps of the Donner Party.

Fallon, a mountain man, got his nickname — Le Gros, meaning large — from French trappers. He's a well-known character around Sutter's Fort. Fallon is both tall and fat, but barrel-chested rather than pudgy. Reason P. Tucker's son, George, who helped with the relief efforts, will describe him as "a very large, stout, rough mountain man." Another pioneer will remember him as a crude fellow, always ready with a joke at others' expense and usually spoiling for a fight. He is the sort who might think it funny to spit tobacco juice on a man's boot and then grin at him. The era of mountain men is over, but Fallon will live the legend a while longer in front of an audience of pioneer greenhorns.

Le Gros made his deal with Alcalde John Sinclair, who took charge of the Donner children and wanted them to receive their inheritance before the high camps could be ransacked by scavengers. The agreement is signed by Fallon and by John Rhodes and Joseph Sels, veterans of the first relief expedition. It states that whatever property could be brought down the mountains would be divided in half. Half would go to the Donner children with the remainder being shared among the three men.

The document applies only to the goods and money of Jacob Donner because he and his wife Elizabeth are known to be dead. If George or Tamsen Donner remain alive, it is understood the rescuers would make arrangements with them in payment for transporting their property.

Fallon and the two others spent today gathering provisions and lining up recruits. Fallon is in a rare mood. This trip will be easier and more profitable than one of the beaver expeditions of his youth. The men of his party are in a hurry to start in order to take advantage of fair weather.

In two days, seven men will ride for the mountains. Some of them will hope Tamsen Donner and the three others will still be alive. Others among them will prefer a free hand to claim all the gold and valuables they can carry.

At the high camps lone survivor Lewis Keseberg is stirring. He limps around the lake camp in the snow, eager to begin a pilgrimage to Alder Creek.

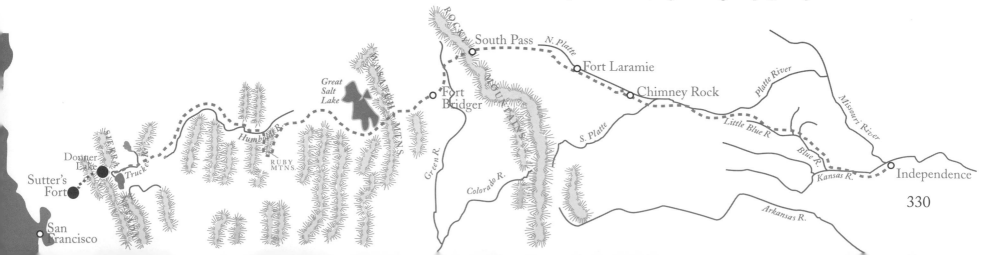

330

(Top left to bottom) A handbag, salt and pepper shakers, buckles from Donner Lake campsite, a button from the Murphy cabin, a U.S. Liberty penny dated 1830 and a 1839 British copper farthing both found at Alder Creek are some of the artifacts on display at the Emigrant Trails Museum in Truckee, California — Don Hardesty and Marilyn Newton photos

(Top right) Eyeglasses found at at Donner Lake, (Middle right) Pepper dish belonging to Tamsen Donner, (Bottom right) Brass military eagle emblem found at Alder Creek campsite are all on display at the Emigrant Trails Museum in Truckee, California — Marilyn Newton photos

APRIL 13, 1847

Fourth relief party leaves ranch and sets out for high camps

Late today the fourth relief party leaves Johnson's Ranch for the Sierra.

William Fallon, a self-styled "captain" and mountain man, leads the group. Accounts will disagree as to who was with him. Sources will say these men left: Fallon; William Foster, a Donner Party survivor; Joseph Sels, John Rhodes; Reason P. Tucker and his son, George; Joe Foster; Edward Coffeemeyer; "Keyster" and "Renar."

The weather holds; snow melts.

On this journey, the party will have a grisly landmark: the bones of John Denton, left behind by the first relief. Denton's body was examined earlier by William Eddy, who found a poem and his journal, apparently penned by the Englishman as he waited for death:

"O! After many roving years, how sweet it is to come/ Back to the dwelling place of youth, our first and dearest home/ To turn away our wearied eyes from proud ambition's towers/ and wander in those summer fields, the scenes of boyhood's hours."

The snow was fifteen feet deep as Denton wrote of summer fields, author George Stewart will remark.

Charles T. Stanton, who perished with the Forlorn Hope party on December 21, is still buried deep in snow. His bones will be found in June, the remains identified by the trappings of his life: a clay pipe, a pouch, pistols, and clothing.

George McKinstry will send Stanton's effects, presumably including his journal of the trip, to his family in Brooklyn. Charles's brother, Philip, will send McKinstry a letter describing one of the true heroes of the Donner saga:

"[Charles] was always noble and generous, even to a fault, always ready and willing to share his last cent with his less fortunate brothers and sisters. This characteristic he bore from earliest childhood. He was ever ready to sacrifice his own interest and means to the welfare of others, and hence it is not surprising" he gave his life to help his companions.

At the lake camp, Keseberg smokes his pipe, which is (as it was with many of the other men and women of the Donner Party) his only solace. He eats the only food he has. He thinks of gold. In a few days he'll take a walk.

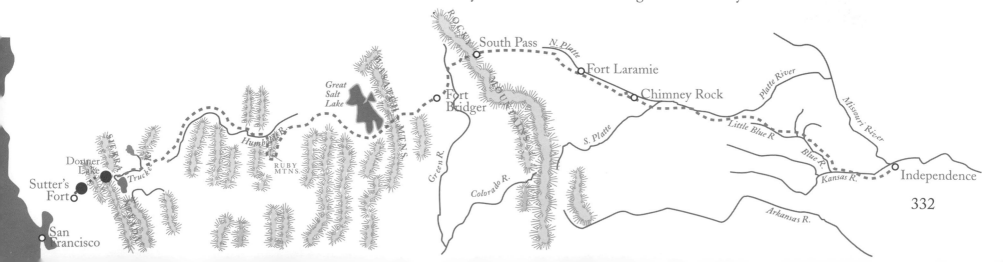

A pipe bowl found at the Murphy cabin site. The decorated pipe is made of clay. — from The Archaeology of the Donner Party *— Don Hardesty photo*

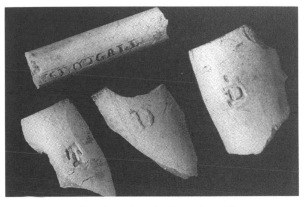

Clay tobacco pipes found at the Murphy cabin site. — from The Archaeology of the Donner Party *— Don Hardesty photo*

Stanton, an educated man, also wrote poetry. These are the first and final stanzas of the last poem he was known to have written:

Charles T. Stanton — Emigrant Trails Museum

Oh, how that word my soul inspires
With holy, fond, and pure desires!
Maternal love, how bright the flame!
For wealth of worlds I'd not profane
Nor idly breathe thy sacred name,
My mother.

When death shall close my sad career,
And I before my God appear —
There to receive His last decree —
My only prayer there will be
Forever to remain with thee,
My mother.

April 16, 1847

Rescuers nearing lake camps; Keseberg leaves for Alder Creek

Remnants of tree stumps, cut at the level of the snow, near Alder Creek.
— Nevada Historical Society

Today, the one-year anniversary of the Donners' and Reeds' first day of travel after leaving Springfield, Illinois, seven men make their way to the high camps to rescue the last Donner Party survivor still trapped in the snow.

The rescuers, led by mountain man William "Le Gros" Fallon, arrived at the lower end of Bear Valley yesterday. The men hung their saddles on trees and sent young George Tucker back with the horses. The snow was three feet deep as they shouldered packs containing ten days' provisions.

Today they travel twenty-three miles and flounder in the ten-foot-deep slushy snow. Sometime tomorrow they aim to reach Donner Lake where they think Tamsen Donner and Lewis Keseberg might be alive.

Even if there are no survivors, gold, silver, and valuables will be there — a fortune waiting to be picked out of the snow.

At the high camps, Lewis Keseberg, also thinking of money, makes his way to the deserted tent sites of the Donner family at Alder Creek.

As he leaves the lake, Washoe Indians stir among the pines. Tomorrow, three Indians will take a look at the place tribal members say shows the madness and unpredictability of the white emigrants.

Tomorrow, the curtain rises on the final scenes of the Donner tragedy. As usual, there will be more than one version of events.

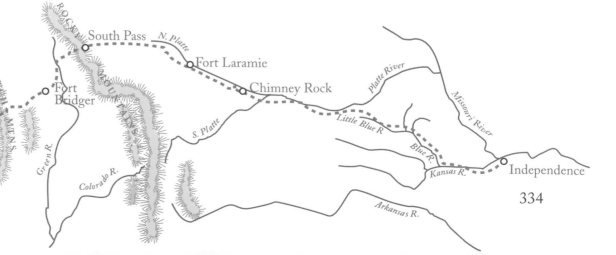

Washoe Indian basket — Emigrant Trails Museum

APRIL 18, 1847

Fourth relief party reaches camps, finds scenes of grisly horror

The seven rescuers reached the lake camp about noon yesterday.

The place looks as if an explosion has hit.

William Fallon will report that the cabins are full of scattered goods, severed body parts, cracked skulls, and two kettles of what appear to be blood.

The men called out for survivors and heard a shout. Three Indians bounded out of hiding and fled the camp, leaving their bows and arrows. The rescuers spent two hours searching the cabins.

"We were obliged to witness sights from which we would have fain turned away, and which are too dreadful to put on record," Fallon will say.

The men collected valuables, including jewelry and firearms, then walked the six miles (Fallon says eight or ten) to the Alder Creek camp.

They followed a fresh trail in the snow. The tracks were made by boots, not moccasins, but they do not meet whoever left them.

At Alder Creek, bolts of calico, pots and pans, books, smashed trunks, crates of tobacco and tea, shoes, ammunition, clothing, and other items are scattered. An iron kettle holds human flesh. Bodies are mutilated and skulls are split.

The meat of an ox, exposed by the thaw, has been placed on a chair but hasn't been used for food.

Today they dry the bolts of cloth and other items they found in puddles made by thawing snow.

Tonight, they again camp amid the carnage at Alder Creek. Tomorrow three men will leave for the lake camps where Lewis Keseberg, weighed down with plunder, already has returned.

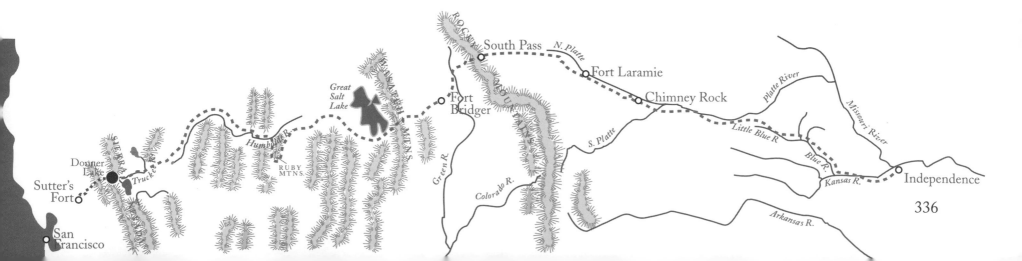

April 17th. Reached the Cabins between 12 and 1 o'clock. Expected to find some of the sufferers alive, Mrs. Donner and Kiesburg in particular. Entered the cabins and a horrible scene presented itself — human bodies terribly mutilated, legs, arms, and sculls scattered in every direction. One body, supposed to be that of Mrs. Eddy, lay near the entrance, the limbs severed off and a frightful gash in the scull. The flesh from the bones was nearly consumed and a painful stillness pervaded the place.

Knowing the Donners had a considerable sum of money, we searched dilligently but were unsuccessful. The party for the cabins were unable to keep the trail of the mysterious personage owing to the rapid melting of the snow, they therefore went direct for the cabins, and upon entering discovered Kiesburg lying down amidst the human bones and beside him a large pan full of fresh liver and lights. They asked him what had become of his companions, whether they were alive, and what had become of Mrs. Donner, he said, had in attempting to cross from one cabin to another, missed the trail, and slept out one night; that she came to his camp the next night very much fatigued, he made her a cup of coffee, placed her in bed and rolled her well in the blankets, but the next morning found her dead; he (ate) her body and found her flesh the best he had ever tasted! He further stated that he obtained from her body at least four pounds of fat! ...

— April 17 and 19th entries from "Captain Fellun's" journal as published in the *California Star* newspaper in San Francisco, June 5, 1847.

The California Star *newspaper for April 17, 1847*

APRIL 20, 1847

Keseberg is questioned, strangled, in attempt to discover Donner cash

Lewis Keseberg is being given the third degree.

Yesterday, William Foster, John Rhodes, and Joe Sels returned to the lake camps, where William Fallon will say Keseberg was found lying amid human bones next to a pan full of liver. The rescuers asked about other survivors.

"They were all dead," Fallon will write. "[Keseberg found Mrs. Donner] dead; he ate her body and found her flesh to be the best he ever tasted! He further stated that he obtained from her body four pounds of fat! No traces of her person could be found. . . ."

Keseberg will later deny he said those things, but won't deny eating Tamsen Donner.

The three men badger Keseberg for the Donners' money.

"I haven't it," he told them. "Nor the property of any person, living or dead!"

The men search Keseberg's bundle and find silks and jewelry taken from Alder Creek. They pull two pistols from his pockets which are marked as the property of George Donner. A lump in Keseberg's waistcoat is found to be $225 in gold coin.

They tell him that when Fallon arrives he'll hang the German from the nearest tree unless he comes up with the rest of the thousands in gold and silver believed to be carried by the Donner families.

Keseberg says the money in his vest is his and he doesn't know what gold they are talking about.

Fallon and the three other men visit Keseberg this morning.

"Keseberg, you know well where Donner's money is, and damn you, you shall tell me," Fallon says. "I am not going to multiply words with you, nor say but little about it. Bring me that rope!"

Fallon throws the German on the ground and loops a slipknot around his neck. The big mountain man pulls the rope, and Keseberg chokes out a few words: "I will tell," he says. "I will tell."

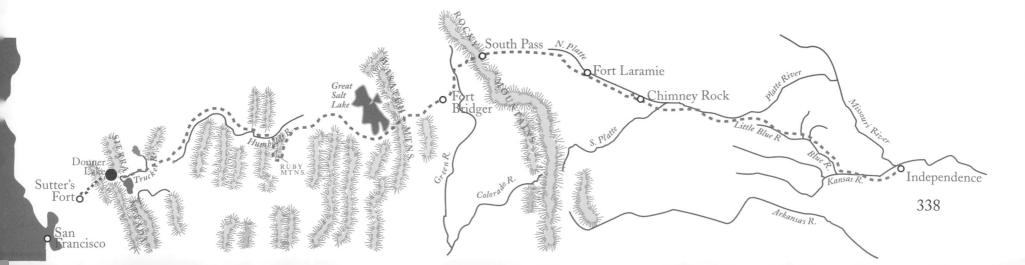

Lewis Keseberg — Bancroft Library

William Foster — Emigrant Trails Museum

April 23, 1847

Keseberg leads men to more coins; Fourth relief party descends Sierra

The last rescue party is in Bear Valley.

They left the high camps three days ago after Lewis Keseberg — nearly hanged by William Fallon — led them to an additional $273 in silver coin he had buried near the Donner camp. The money was cached beneath a pine tree. A branch pointed like a finger to the spot.

Fallon is not pleased. The Donners were believed to be carrying more than $10,000 in gold and silver, their savings and the profits of selling farms in Illinois. The rescuers have recovered $498 from Keseberg and were unable to find the rest. Most of the rescuers are in a foul mood.

"These men treated me with the greatest unkindness," Keseberg will tell author C. F. McGlashan. "Mr. [Reason P.] Tucker was the only one who took my part and befriended me."

Keseberg is so weak he lags behind the rescuers, even though they are burdened with a hundred pounds of goods including silks, calicos, and firearms. Each night he straggles into camp.

A day or two ago, Keseberg sat down to rest and absent-mindedly tugged on a piece of cloth sticking out from the snow. The cloth is the calico dress of his dead daughter Ada. Her body is accidentally exhumed. In this way, he learns of his infant daughter's death. Keseberg screams and shivers.

Today, just across the snow line, a grizzly bear comes into camp. "I knew I was too weak to escape, and so I remained where I sat, expecting at any moment he would devour me," Keseberg will say.

William Foster, who suspects Keseberg killed his own child, shoots the bear.

"I have been born under an evil star!" Keseberg will complain.

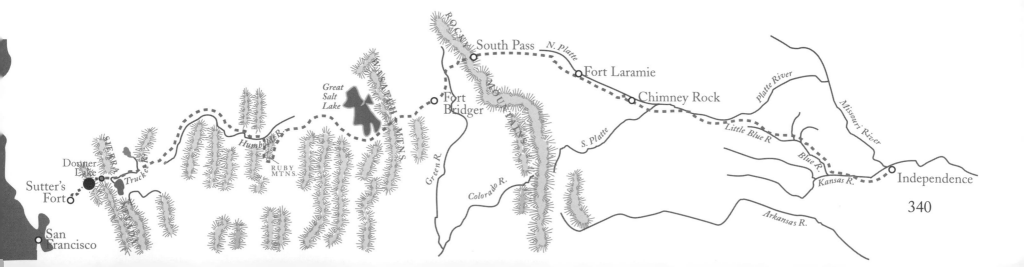

Trees, cut by the emigrants during the winter of 1846–47. — Nevada Historical Society

When they started over the mountains, each man carried two bales of goods. They had silks, calicoes, and delaines from the Donners, and other articles of great value. Each man would carry one bundle a little way, lay it down, and come back and get the other bundle. In this way they passed over the snow three times. I could not keep up with them because I was so weak, but managed to come up to their camp every night. One day I was dragging myself slowly along behind the party, when I came to a place which had evidently been used as a camping ground by some of the previous parties. Feeling very tired, I thought it would be a good place to make some coffee. Kindling a fire, I filled my coffee-pot with fresh snow and sat waiting for it to melt and get hot. Happening to cast my eyes carelessly around, I discovered a little piece of calico protruding from the snow. Half thoughtlessly, half out of idle curiosity, I caught hold of the cloth, and finding it did not come readily, I gave it a strong pull. I had in my hands the body of my dead child Ada! She had been buried in the snow, which, melting down, had disclosed a portion of her clothing. I Thought I should go frantic! It was the first intimation I had of her death, and it came with such a shock!
— Lewis Keseberg, to C. F. McGlashan

April 25, 1847

Keseberg reaches Johnson's; he's last emigrant of 1846

Lewis Keseberg, the last survivor of the Donner Party to come off the Sierra, today reaches Johnson's Ranch and safety.

Of the eighty-seven people who struggled through the Wasatch Mountains of Utah last August, five died before reaching the Sierra. Of the eighty-one people who ascended the mountains in October, including two Miwoks, thirty-six perished in the snow.

No other wagon train of 1846 suffered such casualties. The Donner tragedy — and the war with Mexico — will cast a pall on westward migration for two years. In 1848, the discovery of gold at a mill owned by John Sutter will send a sea of humanity surging over the California Trail.

Other dramas are already beginning: The Mormons are migrating. The Pioneer Camp of the Saints will use the trail blazed through the Wasatch by the Donner Party. Because of that road, they will arrive at the site of Salt Lake City early enough to plant crops and see their dreams bear fruit.

In Mexico, Capt. Robert E. Lee is with Gen. Winfield Scott's army, marching on Mexico City, which will fall to the Americans in September. Three months later, Abraham Lincoln will take his seat in Congress and join with the Whigs in blaming President James K. Polk for the war. Next year in Brooklyn, Walt Whitman will begin work on *Leaves of Grass* while in Hannibal, Missouri, Sam Clemens will be working as an apprentice in a printing firm.

Today at Johnson's Ranch, Keseberg is fed and cleaned up. Stories painting him as a monster already are spreading to Sutter's Fort and beyond.

William Fallon's journal, which author Joe King will suspect was ghost-written by Sheriff George McKinstry, will be published in the *California Star* newspaper in San Francisco on June 5. Other newspapers will reprint this account, and Keseberg will be reviled for the rest of his life.

Today, however, the mood is joyful. The last man is down. The crisis is over. The emigration of 1846, which sent more than five hundred wagons west, is ended.

The last party of that emigration now passes into history and legend.

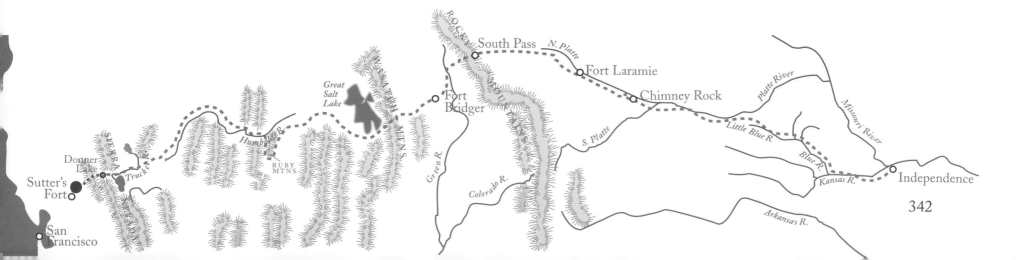

Tucker and Rhoads came back the next morning, bringing $273, that had been cached by Kiesburg, who after disclosing to them the spot, returned to the cabin. The money had been hidden directly underneath the projecting limb of a large tree, and the end of which seemed to point precisely to the treasure buried in the earth.-On their return and passing the cabin, they saw the unfortunate man within, devouring the remaining brains and liver, left from his morning repast! They hurried him away, but before leaving, he gathered together the bones and heaped them all in a box he used for the purpose, blessed them and the cabin, and said, 'I hope God will forgive me what I have done, I couldn't help it! and I hope I may get to heaven yet!

— William Fallon's Journal of April 20, as published in the *California Star* newspaper in San Francisco, June 5, 1847.

Artifacts found along the donner trail on the salt desert. They are now on display at the Donner- Reed Museum in Granstville, Utah. — Marilyn Newton photo

MAY, 1847

Part 4: Epilogue
California

*Never take no cutofs and hury along
as fast as you can.*

— Virginia Reed in a
letter to her cousin,
May 16, 1847

May 1, 1847

Hastings hangs lawyer's shingle; never accepts blame for tragedy

On the front page of yesterday's edition of the *California Star* newspaper, a reprint from the *New York Mirror* relates how Samuel Morse's invention, the telegraph, will someday send messages around the world in seconds.

Inside, among the bilingual announcements of San Francisco ordinances, ads for town lots (which sell for about $35), and the Mexican War news, there is an ad for an attorney: Lansford Warren Hastings Esq.

Hastings, a regular *Star* advertiser since February 20, specializes in land claims. The man who led the Donners to ruin will never admit any blame. All that was needed, he will say, were better roads and water in the desert.

Emigrant J. W. Harlan will chide the attorney about his "shortcut," but he will say he was doing the best he could. Hastings will later buy clothes for an orphan: San Francisco newsboy George Donner Jr.

Nearly fifteen decades after the ordeal at Donner Lake, historian and author Will Bagley will investigate the life of the Donners' guide. Noting that Hastings is painted as a scoundrel by most writers, he will try to see some good in the man. In an article for *Overland Journal*, the quarterly journal of the Oregon-California Trails Association, Bagley will explore the career and the character of Hastings, coming to regard him as a man consumed by ambition. He might have been involved in a covert operation during the James K. Polk administration to seize California from the Mexican government. It will be said he shot Indians for sport. He was a partner with John Sutter during the 1849 Gold Rush, an experience that Sutter summarized as, "The store made money but I did not." Empire-building was always on his mind.

In later years, Hastings will offer to open trade routes through deserts for the Mormons, ignoring such obstacles as the Grand Canyon. During the Civil War, he will hatch a plot to grab the West for the rebels. He will die aboard ship, aged about 50, sometime between 1868 and 1870, promoting emigration to Brazil, where Confederate veterans could set up a new nation.

He will still be dreaming of empire.

The May 1, 1847 issue of the California Star *featured bilingual advertisements selling San Francisco town lots and an ad that Lansford Hastings ran announcing his law practice.*

May 5, 1847

Keseberg brings slander suit; he'll later open restaurant

Tomorrow, a slander suit brought by Lewis Keseberg will go before a jury in Sutter's Fort.

Some members of the last relief party, including Ned Coffeemeyer, have been spreading tales about Keseberg. It is said he murdered Tamsen Donner. He is also implicated in the disappearance of Wolfinger on the trail in Nevada.

With the encouragement of Capt. John Sutter, Keseberg sues Coffeemeyer for defamation of character and demands damages of $1,000. Sutter presides over the court. John B. Rhoads, veteran of the first and fourth relief parties, is on the jury. Mrs. Wolfinger, among others, is called as a witness. The case is heard and the verdict delivered quickly: the jury agrees that Keseberg has been defamed, but limits damages to $1.

W. R. Grimshaw, whose notes are found in the Bancroft Library, will remark that Sutter had personal reasons for acquitting Keseberg. "What those reasons were partakes too much in the nature of gossip and scandal to be detailed here," he will write, beginning fifteen decades of speculation.

The verdict means little to the people in Sutter's fiefdom. Keseberg will be reviled; children will taunt him on the streets. However, Sutter apparently trusts Keseberg. He makes him captain of his schooner to San Francisco. Keseberg later runs businesses, including The Lady Adams Hotel, which contains a restaurant and gives birth to decades of ironic jokes.

His businesses will fail due to circumstances beyond his control. "I have been born under an evil star!" he will later complain.

Other pioneers of 1846, including Jacob W. Harlan and Heinrich Lienhard, will come to know and like Keseberg, judging him innocent of murder. Author C. F. McGlashan, who will interview Keseberg decades later, will come to the same conclusion, as will Eliza Donner Houghton, the youngest daughter of his supposed victim. A neighbor from his later years will recall Keseberg sitting on his porch mumbling about the cannibalism and the taste of human flesh.

Throughout his life he will be scorned. He will always claim innocence of wrongdoing and see himself as a victim of fate. He trusted that time would heal his wounds, yet more than thirty years later he will say, "My mind today recoils with undiminished horror as I endeavor to speak of this dreadful subject." It will always haunt him.

In 1879, he will tell C. F. McGlashan: "I have been treated with dreadful injustice."

Lewis Keseberg — Bancroft Library

Heinrich Lienhard — Marta Lienhard Vincent

I have been born under an evil star! Fate, misfortune, bad luck, compelled me to remain at Donner Lake. If God would decree that I should again pass through such an ordeal, I could not do otherwise than I did. My conscience is free from reproach. Yet that camp has been the one burden of my life. Wherever I have gone, people have cried, "Stone him! Stone him!" Even the little children in the streets have mocked me and thrown stones at me as I passed. Only a man conscious of his innocence, and clear in the sight of God, would not have succumbed to the terrible things which have been said of me — would not have committed suicide! Mortification, disgrace, disaster, and unheard-of misfortune have followed and overwhelmed me. I often think that the Almighty has singled me out, among all the men on the face of the earth, in order to see how much hardship, suffering, and misery a human being can bear!

— Lewis Keseberg

I have never believed in the truth of the terrible charges brought against this man, and I know that many of the old emigrants who, perhaps, knew the facts of his case better than myself, would give him the same verdict as myself — Not guilty.

— Jacob Wright Harlan

Appendices
End Notes
Bibliography
Index

In studying the Donner Party, I expected to find heroes and villains, monsters and saints. Instead, I found families and a cascade of events which swept them to disaster. They made mistakes; the biggest one was allowing the differences of class and race and national origin to keep them apart. Keseberg says they were born under a bad sign and what happened was predestined. It was not fate, but human failure that undid the Donners. The Donners are us, written very large.
— Frank Mullen Jr.,
Reno Gazette-Journal, June 15, 1997

We lived only three miles east of Donner Lake, the scene of the disaster, which every wild winter snowstorm brought naturally to mind . . . With no words spoken, I knew papa's thoughts were on the long-ago despair of a snowbound wagon train. My own thoughts turned to those doomed people whenever blizzards struck at night and witches danced on the whistling winds that rattled our many windows. And when I awoke on subzero mornings to a death-white world muffled in twenty-foot snowdrifts, I pictured the frozen cattle of the Donner Party buried standing.
— M. Nona McGlashan, granddaughter of
C. F. McGlashan in his biography
Give Me a Mountain Meadow

Survivors have mixed reactions to paradise

On May 16, 1847, Donner Party survivor Virginia Reed, 13, completed a letter.

"Oh, Mary I have wrote you half of the trouble we have had but I have wrote you enough to let you know that you don't know what trouble is," she told a cousin in Illinois.

"Thank the Good God we have all got through and the only family that did not eat human flesh. We have left everything but I don't care for that — we have got through."

After the ordeal, Virginia Reed went to school and married a Catholic, John M. Murphy, who had crossed the continent with the Stephens-Murphy-Townsend Party in 1844. This upset her father, James F. Reed, a Mason who mistrusted Catholics, but once she had children, grandpa Reed forgave all.

The Reeds prospered in California. The two girls seem to have made a quick recovery from the ordeal.

In her letter, Virginia encouraged her cousin to take the trip to California, where everything was beautiful and there were plenty of Mexican boys eager to marry. She reported Eliza Williams weighed 172 pounds and was going to marry a man named Armijo.

Survivor Mary Ann Graves, on the other hand, hated California even though she married there in May 1847.

In a May 22, 1847, letter to Levi Fosdick, Donner Party casualty Jay Fosdick's father, Graves wrote:

"I will now give you some good and friendly advice. Stay at home, — you are in a good place, where, if sick, you are not in danger of starving to death.

"It is a healthy country here, and when that is said all is said. . . . You can live without work if you are a complete rascal; for a rascal you must be to stand any chance at all."

Mary Ann's sister, Nancy Graves, who was eight during the disaster, carried the tragedy with her for many years.

She lost her mother, father, and a younger brother. Fellow survivor Eliza Donner Houghton noted how Nancy was once confronted about her frequent crying at a San Jose school.

"She told us of her being at 'Starved Camp' — how her mother died, how part of the flesh was prepared for food without her knowledge — and how she was told of it after she had partaken of it, and how perfectly heartbroken she had been ever since," Houghton wrote.

"We tried to soothe and comfort her but it seemed no use; for she would cry, 'How can I forget it; or forgive myself?'"

In 1852, Nancy Graves joined the Methodist church. Three years later, she married a minister, Richard W. Williamson, and they had nine children. They eventually settled near Sebastopol, California.

"I think she was severely traumatized, but was able to get on with her life by not dwelling on it," said Kristin Johnson of Salt Lake City, a Graves family historian. "I think she successfully closed the door on it."

She didn't talk about the tragedy as an adult and declined to help Truckee, California, newspaper editor C. F. McGlashan during his research for a book on it, said Nancy Lyons of Davis, a great-granddaughter.

Nancy Graves died in 1907 at age 69.

The Reed home in the 1850s in San Jose, California. From left are James Reed, Charles Reed, Patty Reed, unidentified child (barely visible), William Reed, James F. Reed Jr., Thomas Keyes Reed (also barely visible), Molly Murphy, Mary Donner, and Margaret Reed. —original daguerreotype in Sutter's Fort

Reeds, Breens destined to become prominent in northern California

The ordeal behind them, the families of James F. Reed and Patrick Breen are beginning to get on with their lives.

Their families were the only ones to survive the Donner Party ordeal intact. They will become leading figures in northern California.

Reed, 46, eventually will bring his family to San Jose, where he will become a miner, rancher, and land developer. He will be a member of the first town council of San Jose and serve as police chief. Reed took Mary Donner and later Frances into his home. Reed will donate land that will become the sites of San Jose State University and St. James Park.

"He was down and out by the time he got there, but I don't think he stayed down long," James Reed III of Edmonds, Washington, his great-great grandson, will tell Associated Press reporter Martin Griffith. "I would say absolutely he put [the tragedy] behind him . . . he lived a very successful life."

Reed will die in 1874 at age 74. To the end of his days, he will insist he was sent ahead for supplies and never will publicly mention killing John Snyder.

Breen, 51, will move his nine-member family to San Juan Bautista, where they will be the first Americans to settle there. He and his wife, Peggy, will have one more child. He will operate an inn, and become a rancher, school trustee, and postmaster. He will serve as a Monterey County supervisor.

Two of his sons, John and Edward, will serve as county supervisors; another son, James, will become a San Benito County superior court judge. In 1997, that judgeship will be held by Thomas Breen, great-great grandson of Patrick Breen. Patrick Breen will die in 1868 at age 73. He will leave an estate worth $110,000.

Margaret Breen — Emigrant Trails Museum

Margaret Reed, who had suffered from "sick headaches" in Illinois and during the ordeal in the mountains, will be free of migraines for the rest of her life. She will die on Nov. 25, 1861.

Margret Breen will die in 1874.

"She surely ranks as one of the greatest heroines of the old West," author Joseph King will remark.

John Sutter — Emigrant Trails Museum

John Sutter, savior of emigrants, will be ruined by gold discovery

It's raining again at Sutter's Fort, and around the fireplaces the talk is of the Donner Party, the horror of cannibalism, and why their trek turned into tragedy.

Theories abound: The Donners were too lazy in cutting their way through the Wasatch Mountains and too greedy to leave their wagons and proceed on foot before the snow trapped them, Sheriff George McKinstry says. Others offer their opinions. Some of those speculations will find their way into history books.

John Sutter is also a victim of the Donner Party and the other wagon trains of 1846. He will recover little of the money he selflessly spent on helping the ragged strangers who arrived at his gates.

Years later, McKinstry will petition Congress to make good on Sutter's outlays to emigrants. The request will be ignored.

Sutter is a Swiss national who came to the remote Sacramento Valley and began building his fort in 1839. In 1844 his settlement became the goal of western emigrants. He is lord of central California. His future seems secure.

"[He was] a fine looking man, attending to a large business," John Breen will remember. "He was a good friend to the emigrant in those days. Every member of the Donner Party has good reason to remember kindly, generous Captain Sutter."

Everything in Sutter's world will change after January 24, 1848, when gold will be discovered at one of his mills. His employees will desert for the gold fields; his businesses will close.

As Sacramento rises around what was once his fiefdom, his era will end. His reputation will endure. One hundred and fifty years after the Donner ordeal, a reenactment wagon train will climb the Sierra through Dog Valley. At a rest stop, three strangers — two passengers and a wagon driver — will introduce themselves.

The passengers: Bill Springer, a descendant of George Donner, and James Frazier Reed III, a descendant of his namesake. Their driver, John Schwartzler, counts Sutter among his ancestors. In the summer of 1996, in the shade of a Ponderosa pine, the two Donner Party descendants will thank Sutter's kin for the kindness his ancestor showed their starving families so long ago.

The fate of other Donner Party survivors

Lewis Keseberg was haunted by the tragedy for the rest of his life. Two of Keseberg's business ventures — a hotel and a brewery — ended in disaster. One burned down and the other was destroyed by flood.

He and his wife, Philippine, separated and none of their ten children lived past age thirty. Their first two children died in the tragedy.

Children taunted him and adults shunned him.

"It's unfair what happened to him," said Patricia Ramsey of Carmel, California, his great-great granddaughter and only known living direct descendant. "He died a pauper and didn't seem to have any friends."

Keseberg, then 32, was cast as a villain by sensational reports of his cannibalism. He was accused of murdering Tamsen Donner, wife of party captain George Donner, for her flesh at Donner Lake. The charge never was proved, but suspicion followed him the rest of his life.

"The man was unjustly accused," said Ramsey, a 68-year-old retired lawyer. "Nobody ever saw or heard him do anything. It [his cannibalism] was proper for the circumstances. We can't judge because we weren't there."

Some contemporaries said cannibalism forever changed Keseberg, the last survivor to leave the Sierra.

"He couldn't forget that orgy of flesh. . . . It was a nightmare that exerted a terrible fascination," recalled Dr. Victor Fourgeaud, an acquaintance. "Sometimes at night [I] would overhear him telling the crew of his horrible repasts, describing in minute detail the delicacy of what he considered the choicest bits."

Keseberg died in 1895 at age 81.

Jacob Donner's children, George, Mary, and Solomon Hook, stayed in California. Mary and Frances Donner were taken into the Reed home in San Jose. At one point, Hiram Miller acted as guardian for Frances, Georgia, and Eliza Donner. Georgia and Eliza were adopted by the Brunners, a couple from Switzerland. The citizens of San Francisco raised money to purchase town lots for George and Mary Donner, Jacob's children.

Harriet Pike, whose husband was killed by a pistol accident near the future site of Reno, married M. C. Nye at Sutter's Fort in 1847 and settled in Marysville, California, which was named for Mary Murphy, another Donner survivor, by her second husband.

Harriet's daughter, Naomi, three at the time of the ordeal, married a doctor and lived in Marysville. She later moved to Oregon and died in 1934, aged 90.

Patty Reed married in 1856 and had eight children. Tommy Reed never married. James Reed Jr. married in 1879,

had no children and died in 1901.

Eliza Williams, the Reed's maid, married and had two children.

William Murphy became a lawyer and practiced in Virginia City, Nevada, until 1866 and later became city attorney of Marysville.

Eleanor Graves married in 1849 and had nine children

William Eddy, who lost his wife and two children, remarried in 1848, had two more children and was divorced in 1854. He married again in 1856 and died in 1859. Some survivors called him a liar, but Georgia Donner, who was four at the high camps, said he was kind-hearted and that she owed him her life.

The Breen family of nine moved to San Juan Bautista, California, and had one more child. Patrick Breen and other family members became prominent figures in central California.

Sarah Graves Fosdick, who lost her husband in the escape of the Forlorn Hope party, married twice more. She died in 1871.

Dorris Wolfinger, whose husband was murdered at the Humboldt Sink, married 1846 pioneer George Zins, who came West with Heinrich Lienhard, and had two children. She died in 1861.

William C. Graves, who lost his father, mother, brother, and brother-in-law, became a blacksmith in Calistoga, California.

The five surviving children of George Donner were taken in by California families. All married and had their own children. Their descendants, and the descendants of many other Donner Party survivors, including the Breen, Murphy, and Graves families, gathered for a reunion at Donner Lake in the summer of 1996.

Mystery of the Donner gold remains after 150 years

Although the last survivor is off the mountains, many people plan to go back to the high camps.

The Breen family and others want to recover their wagons and their salvageable goods. William "Le Gros" Fallon will also return.

The Donner families — who sold their farms in Illinois — were said to be traveling with at least $10,000. In addition, Luke Halloran, who died near what will become Grantsville, Utah, willed more than $1,500 in coin to George Donner. Yet rescuers reported recovering only $498 of George and Tamsen's money. Did relief party members find other caches and secretly keep them?

Fallon will travel again — a log at Sutter's Fort shows his return from "the mountains" on May 29, 1847. If he found anything he kept the news to himself. Joseph King, author of *Winter of Entrapment*, will suggest researchers inventory land purchases made by members of rescue parties to discover any windfalls.

One hoard will surface: In 1891, two men will find gold coins — none dated after 1845 — hidden beneath a stump west of Donner Lake. Survivor William Graves will recognize one of the coins that had teeth marks and was used as a teething ring.

The coins were apparently cached by Elizabeth Graves during her escape. They will be distributed among Graves family members and the men who found the hoard.

In the 150 years since the tragedy, souvenir hunters, historians, archaeologists and metal-detector buffs will comb the sites without finding more gold. University of Nevada, Reno anthropology professor Don Hardesty will go over every inch of what he will believe is the Donner camp at Alder Creek, but his students will find only two small coins among the buttons, shards, and other artifacts.

Fifteen decades after the Donner's ordeal, the fate of their gold will remain a mystery.

Two men with the gold coins they found near a stump in 1891. — Bancroft Library

Over the decades,
evidence vanishes at the high camps
The high camps are deserted.

Among the lupine and Indian paintbrush at Alder Creek and Donner Lake, the ground is littered with household goods, bolts of fabric, crates of tobacco, tools, and the bones of oxen, horses, and humans.

John Breen and others will come to this place of tragedy and collect family goods and wagons. William Fallon will return, presumably to look for the missing Donner money. On June 22, General S. W. Kearny, leading a detachment of the Mormon Battalion back east with Fallon as guide, will do a quick cleanup at the camps. Human bones will be buried under a cabin floor.

The Murphy cabin will be listed as the location of the mass grave. University of Nevada, Reno anthropologist Donald Hardesty, who will publish *The Archaeology of the Donner Party* in April, 1997, will investigate the Murphy site in the 1980s but find no human bones.

He will speculate that the grave might be at the sit of one of the two other cabins, probably the Breen cabin, which C. F. McGlashan identified as the site now covered by the monument at Donner Lake State Park.

Over the years, tourists and authors will cart away ceramics, iron objects and other mementos. The high-cut tree stumps, marking the level of the snow, will rot and fall.

The Donner family name will become synonymous with cannibalism.

Nevada Governor Boyle, Martha (Patty) Reed Lewis, Eliza Donner Houghton, Frances Donner Wilde, and California Governor Stevens at the dedication of the monument at Donner Lake on June 6, 1918 — Bancroft Library

The story will spread throughout the country but it will be a different story everywhere. Even in Truckee, California, a few miles from the scene of the tragedy, author C.F. McGlashan, before his research into the story, will think the Donner Party consisted of three people eaten by a Dutchman.

Fifteen decades after the disaster, there will remain other clues. Some may be in the form of documents in attics or musty trunks; artifacts might still be sleeping in the ground. They might stay hidden forever, or come to light to provide further details on the death of a wagon train so long ago.

Descendants still debate what went wrong

Even today, Donner Party descendants analyze their ancestors' errors.

"They made mistake after mistake," said James Reed III of Edmonds, Washington, a great-great grandson of wagon train leader James F. Reed.

"Everything that could go wrong did."

"More than anything, I blame [Lansford] Hastings's misdirection for their problems," said Patricia Ramsey of Carmel, California, a great-great granddaughter of Lewis Keseberg. "I can't understand why he would say things, not knowing whether they were accurate or not."

Some descendants concede, however, that party members share the blame because of poor decisions made later in Utah and Nevada.

"It's hard to understand a lot of the things they did," Reed said.

The group was in over its head in what was then a wilderness under Mexican control. It also was plagued by personality conflicts, poor organization and a lack of leadership.

Reed faults the group for wasting three weeks in the Wasatch Range and a week in a fruitless search for lost oxen on the Great Salt Lake Desert. The delays in Utah played a major role in the final outcome.

Descendants defend their ancestors' decision to resort to cannibalism, saying it allowed many to survive.

"I have no doubt that it happened, but if we were in the same situation we would do it, too," said Barbara Wilder Politano of Rancho Cucamonga, California, a great-great granddaughter of party captain George Donner. "How much do you want to live?"

"My attitude is they did what they did to survive, and I wouldn't be here if they didn't," said Adam Breen of Hollister, California, a great-great-great grandson of Patrick Breen.

Some descendants complain that the cannibalism has made them a butt of jokes.

"It was kind of sad. As a kid, it was never a positive," Ann Donner-Simon said at a 1990 reunion of Jacob Donner descendants. "Kids used to say, 'Don't sit next to Ann; she'll eat your arm off.'"

Adam Breen said he has learned to take jokes about the party's cannibalism in stride. "I've heard all the bad jokes about finger foods and all that," he said. "When the world knows your family resorted to cannibalism to save themselves in the face of death, you'd better be able to laugh about it."

Patty Reed visits Donner Camp in 1918.
— Bancroft Library

Myths and facts of the Donner Party

For fifteen decades, myths have stalked the Donner Party.

"You had eighty-one people go up the mountain," said Bruce Turner, a Donner researcher who spends his summers in Truckee, California. "And if they all survived you would have had eighty-one different stories."

Some legends have dogged the accounts since 1847. No matter how many times they are questioned, disproven, denied, or debunked, the myths persist. Truth is elusive.

"How big was the Pioneer Palace Car?" asks Kristin Johnson, author of *Unfortunate Emigrants: Narratives of the Donner Party*.

"Was it the biggest wagon ever seen on the trail? Was it only the amenities that made it unusual? I've been researching it for a long time and I keep going back and forth."

Author Joseph King saw history's treatment of the Breen family as an injustice. In most accounts, Patrick Breen denies help, water, and food to other members of the party. He's branded "selfish."

"To people who travel Interstate 80 today in the comfort of their automobiles, some of the decisions the Breens and other members of the party made may seem harsh and uncharitable," King wrote. "[The party] members had to find answers to the most difficult of moral questions."

King, an English professor, would assign his students to read *Ordeal by Hunger* and then pose many questions: Should you give away food or water when they mean life or death to your own children? Should you loan a weakened horse in a doomed search for an old man? Should human flesh be devoured as food when the alternative is starvation?

Prejudice also affects Donner accounts. Much has been made of the impoverished condition of the Nevada Indians, yet most historians agree the tribes were doing just fine until the emigrants and their cattle badly damaged the river lifelines and shot Indians for sport.

Then there are the logistical questions. Some timetables and distances still don't add up 150 years later.

"There are so many accounts of events and places and so many contradictions," Turner said. "That's one of the neat things about the Donner story. You don't know if you can ever pin anything down."

Here's a look at some of the major myths, question marks, and facts of the Donner story.

Myth: The greatest myth of the pioneer wagon trains relates to the poverty and dishonesty of Nevada Indians. The emigrants crossing the continent from the 1840s onward characterized the desert tribes — now known as the Goshute, Paiute, Shoshone, Bannock, Washoe, and California Miwok — as shiftless, thieving beggars who were near starvation when the wagon trains crossed the desert.

Emigrants and writers like Mark Twain called these Indians "Diggers." Historian Bernard DeVoto defined the term: "Digger is an epithet, not a classification. It was properly applied to Indians who, being unskilled hunters or residing in country where game was scarce, lived on roots. But it came to mean certain degenerate bands of various tribes who were technologically unemployed. Unable to stand competition with hardier Indians, they had been pushed into the desert and ... lost their culture."

Fact: Far from losing their cultures, they created them in one of the most hostile environments in North America, University of Nevada archaeologist Don Fowler has said. They lived in small bands and made use of all the desert's resources. It was those resources — such as the grass along river banks — that the pioneers threatened. In addition, the Paiute, Shoshone, and Washoe bands that harassed the Donner Party wanted the emigrants' cattle, not their scalps. Even DeVoto sees some justice in this: "From [pioneers] Ewing Young and Joseph Walker on, they had massacred Diggers idly, for fun, or in punishment for theft. The Diggers remembered. If they had not, they might have succored the Donners."

Myth: Lewis Keseberg, a wife-beater and

Donner Party survivor, was a monster who exposed the whole wagon train to danger on the plains by stealing a buffalo robe from a Sioux grave. He also killed two people in the Nevada desert, murdered children in the party's lake camp, and killed Tamsen Donner for her money. In fiction, Keseberg is portrayed as an evil man, bent on surviving no matter what the cost to others, and quick to kill other members of the party.

Fact: Virginia Reed said Keseberg regularly beat his wife and that her father, J. F. Reed, warned him to stop. Keseberg did abandon an old man named Hardcoop on the trail, but surely Patrick Breen and Franklin Graves, who refused to loan William Eddy a horse to rescue Hardcoop, share some of the blame. Keseberg later defended himself by saying that everyone, his family included, had to get out of the wagons and walk and that's why he forced Hardcoop to do the same. The buffalo robe story was told years after the events by someone who claimed to have interviewed "Boonhelm the cannibal." The tale was used by George Stewart in *Ordeal by Hunger*. Yet none of the survivors, many of whom who hated Keseberg, ever mentioned Keseberg stealing from an Indian grave.

Jacob Wolfinger was murdered by others while Keseberg was miles away, even though at the lake camp Keseberg was known to have Wolfinger's rifle and W. C. Graves implicated him in a newspaper article years later. Graves, Kristin Johnson observed, apparently confused the abandoning of Hardcoop with the disappearance of Wolfinger.

There is no evidence Keseberg killed a child or murdered Tamsen Donner, although the entrapment apparently deranged him and the grisly events on the mountain haunted him for the rest of his life.

Myth: Mothers willingly ate their children and children ate their parents during the entrapment in the mountains. In time, all decency and morality broke down and each individual acted as an animal.

Fact: Such sensational accounts come from early newspaper articles about the tragedy, written by George McKinstry and possibly William "Le Gros" Fallon, who was the leader of the last rescue party. Survivors report they had rules about eating family members and did not do so knowingly. Nancy Graves was haunted by the belief that she had unknowingly devoured pieces of her mother during the "Starved Camp" ordeal. Other accounts, especially Eddy's version of arriving at Alder Creek as told to Thornton, emphasize the cannibalism and relate that Jacob Donner's children had their faces smeared with blood from eating their father's organs. Although this might have happened, it would have been a matter of necessity — there were no other bodies available to be cannibalized except that of their kin.

Myth: The wagon train members resorted to eating the dead as soon as people began dying. Cannibalism was a fast solution to hunger and people reverted to it without much guilt or grief. Today, the cannibalism stands as a depraved aspect of the Donner Party's entrapment.

Fact: The pioneers ate mules, pet dogs, glue made from boiled hides, the leather covers from books, shoes, and bone marrow in an effort to survive. It was only after no other food was available and death was certain that they resorted to cannibalism. The horror took its toll: The last rescue party reported the spring thaw had uncovered dead oxen, yet they said Keseberg was still eating human flesh when they arrived.

Myth: Wagon train leader James F. Reed killed teamster John Snyder at Gravelly Ford on the Humboldt River near present-day Beowawe, Nevada. Snyder is buried in one of two pioneer graves at the site. References for this can be found in C. F. McGlashan's *History of the Donner Party*, Irene Paden's *In the Wake of the Prairie Schooner*, *Fatal Decision* by Walter Stookey, and other accounts of the tragedy.

Fact: Those books do identify Gravelly Ford as the site of the killing, but it actually occurred about forty miles east of Beowawe between Iron Point and Golconda, Nevada. C. F. McGlashan, a newspaper editor in Truckee, California, in the 1870s, made the error when he misinterpreted what the survivors told him. Since then, the mistake was repeated in so many books — including an account by survivor Virginia Reed — that it keeps cropping up again and again. When the *Reno Gazette-Journal* published its sesquicentennial series in 1996-97, many readers disputed the location of the killing because they had read accounts naming Beowawe as the site of the homicide.

Myth: Tamsen Donner and others died because they were greedy and valued gold and goods before their own lives. This has become a favorite theme of fiction writers. Greed is sometimes seen as the main cause of the tragedy.

Fact: Tamsen refused to leave her dying husband and did not go with a rescue party. She was concerned about her children getting the family's gold, but did not die because she cared more for the treasure than for her life. Stories about people thinking more of their money than their safety could have been bolstered by the tale of Elizabeth Graves, who hid hundreds of dollars in gold during her escape from the camps with the first relief party.

Myth: John Baptise Trudeau (also spelled Trubode), a survivor, also killed children and bragged about eating them. He was, in author George Stewart's words, a half-breed "mongrel" who cared only about himself.

Fact: Trudeau, who was about 16 at the time, might have later bragged about eating human flesh. But he was well-liked by the Donner children whom he cared for at Alder Creek and then accompanied out of the snow. He re-

mained their friend years after the rescue. Author Joseph King (*Winter of Entrapment*) attacked Stewart's account of Trubode, claiming it was a symptom of prejudice against Mexicans. King also faults Stewart for bias against Indians, Irish, and "foreigners" in general. However, in his revisionist history, King apparently commits some of the same sins he ascribes to Stewart: He embraces accounts that fit his theories and discounts those which lend weight to the opposite side. His book does uncover some common inaccuracies and raises a great many questions about the facts of the Donners' trek.

Myth: Tamsen Donner's diary — which she kept as a reference for a book on botany and as a record of events on the trail — is the source for many books and plays.

Fact: To this day, the journal, filled with drawings and trail accounts written as they happened, has not been found. John Denton's journal, reportedly recovered by rescuers, also is missing and might have been sent to his relatives in England. Denton's journal could surface someday, doubtless causing more controversy among Donner scholars and rewriting of history.

Additional acknowledgments

Thanks to the Reno Gazette-Journal's audiotext actors who helped the series come alive with readings from pioneer diaries: The Legendary Big Gerry and His Pockets O' Gold Band; Cara Cudworth; William Tovell; Jim Stewart; Anne Marie Gangi; Bill Pugsley; Autumn Belnap; Echo Olsen; Bart Bevins; Bill Fisher; Jack Sutton; Fred Horlacher; Sue Kim Ping; Dan Haggarty; Jan Haggarty; Jason Machutta; Patricia McDowell Wing; Russ Lopez; Charlie Sierra; Theresa Feleciano; Emma Fulkerson; John Kupersmith; Shirley Adams; Norm Nielson; Natalie Ann Morningstar; Judy Friederich; Chris Friederich; Gunnar Freitag; Susan Scott; Russ Lopez; Susan Lynch; Leina Chang; Lois Elementary School students in teacher Barbara Snelgrove's class including Jeremy Wilson, Cassie Hester, Dwayne Jones, Faith Cherrito, Dina Wood, Rhonda Leach, Rebecca Kesner, and Jesse Welshonse; Mendive Elementary School students in Lisa Gorsalves' class including Anna Prior, Cameron Filer, Chris Friederich, Wyatt Robards and Kenneth Lin; Dan Danielson; Kris Wing; Karen Shrader; and Carol Brown Corbett.

Wagon train reenactors: H.B. McCay, Nancy McCay, Gene and Margaret Winters (and their grandchildren: Jonathon, Justin, Hollidai and Alan), Nancy Mueller, Ellie Lewis, Billy and Connie Custer, Gale Matteson, Joe Emmons, Connie Graham, Angela Cruz, Jason Hoke, Hedi Hoke, Mary Mallory, Jessica Eros, Andrea Columbia, Marie Wolf, Kathleen Fitzpatrick, Pat Fanelli, Larry Kerr, John Schwartzler, Red Baron, Elsie Olsen and Matt Carroll.

Special thanks to: The late author and historian Joseph King, who assisted in research for this presentation and was to participate in conferences during California Trails '96. King died April 29, 1996; Spencer and Jean Tryon of Minatare, Nebraska, for distributing the series each month to our friends in Nebraska; John Lacina of Lansdale, Pennsylvania; Jolene Kaufman, The Oregon Trail Museum Association, Scotts Bluff National Monument, Gering, Nebraska.; Frankye Craig, California Trail Days coordinator; Donner Memorial State Park; Nevada Historical Society; The Oregon–California Trails Association, Independence, Missouri; OCTA–Utah Crossroads Chapter; OCTA–California/Nevada Chapter; The University of Nevada, Reno; Chimney Rock State Historic Site, Bayard, Nebraska; The Washoe County (Nevada) Library; Sundance Books, Reno; The Nevada State Museum, Carson City; Krysta Tabuchi and Diana Frear Paschall of the Reno Gazette-Journal; Carlyn Moran; Sharon Genung; historians Phil Earl and Guy Rocha; teachers Joseph J. Brezina and Beverly Jones; Aviv Goldsmith Sensei and the students of the Reno Aikido Co-Op; The Swamp Gang, the Slob Family and the Metro Mafia.

End Notes

Details of the Donner narrative were primarily researched by comparing various pioneer journals, accounts and diaries of the 1846 emigrants. Many books — including C.F. McClashan's *History of the Donner Party: A Tragedy of the Sierra* and George R. Stewart's *Ordeal by Hunger* — were also consulted. The research was augmented by interviews with authors, educators, historians and others.

From Independence, Missouri on May 12, 1846 to Fort Bridger, where the Donner Party left on July 31, 1846, locations of the party were determined by comparing the journal of Edwin Bryant, published in 1848 as *What I Saw in California, Ordeal by Hunger,* and *The California Trail: An Epic With Many Heros* by George R. Stewart; and the journals, letters and diaries found in both volumes of *Overland in 1846: Diaries and Letters of the California Trail,* edited by Dale L. Morgan and J. Quinn Thornton's account with annotations found in *Unfortunate Emigrants: Narratives of the Donner Party* by Kristin Johnson.

Main source of the Donner's locations on the trail between July 31 and October 4, 1846 is the journal of James Frazier Reed, published in *Donner Miscellany,* edited by Carroll D. Hall, and the annotated version found in *West From Fort Bridger: Pioneering of the Imigrant Trails Across Utah, 1846-1850* edited by J. Roderic Korns and Dale Morgan, updated by Will Bagley and Harold Schindler; *Overland in 1846: Diaries and Letters of the California Trail,* edited by Dale L. Morgan, and J. Quinn Thornton's account found in *Unfortunate Emigrants: Narratives of the Donner Party* by Johnson; Stewart's *Ordeal by Hunger* and *Oregon and California in 1848* by J. Quinn Thornton.

After October 5, 1846, when J.F. Reed's diary ends, distances and timetables are based on Stewart's *Ordeal by Hunger* and *Oregon and California in 1848* by J. Quinn Thornton; Thornton's account in Johnson, and comparisons with other 1846 emigrant diaries including *From St. Louis to Sutter's Fort* by Heinrich Lienhard, kindly loaned to the author by Stanley Paher of Nevada Publications; journals and letters published in Morgan, and other primary sources. In addition, timetables along the Truckee River and up the east side of the Sierra Nevada were also checked by comparisons with available diaries of emigrants in the years following 1846.

Where timetables were a matter of dispute, discussions with historians, trail buffs, authors and others helped me come to my conclusions.

INTRODUCTION and MAY 12, 1846

Sources include: Stewart; DeVoto; Donald; Reynolds; Bryant; Morgan; Korns; Tamsen Donner letter published in Morgan; Harold Schindler's quote from "The Donner Party," a PBS documentary written and directed by Ric Burns (Steeplechase Films, New York, 1994); Eliza P. Donner Houghton; Ages of the Reed children in the first printing were based on Morgan, pg. 249. Morgan gives Virginia Blackenstoe Reed's birthdate as June 28, 1833; Martha Jane "Patty" on Feb. 26, 1837; James Jr. on March 26, 1840; Thomas Keyes on April 2, 1842. Another son, Dallas was born in July, 1844 but died in December 1845, two months before the Reeds began their trek. Two more sons will be born in California.

Ages of party members in this second printing come from Salt Lake City researcher Kristin Johnson (personal correspondence, April 8, 1998). Other ages of party members in the first printing came from a variety of sources, including Stewart and Joseph King. Johnson's age for Jacob Donner (56 as opposed to 65) is the most startling change.

MAY 15

Bryant; DeVoto; Virginia Reed; Stewart. Other sources found in Morgan, include *The Diary of Hiram Miller* (Miller-Reed Diary), who traveled as a teamster with the Reeds and Donners. The unannotated diary is also found in Hall. Frances Donner's quote is from *Pioneer Children on the Journey West* by Emmy E. Werner. The Donner Party portion of *Pioneer Children on the Journey West* has been produced as a radio play based on primary sources of the Donner Party and was presented live at California Trail Days, August, 1996 at Donner Lake State Park, Truckee, California. George Donner's advertisement is from a photocopy of the *Sangamo Journal,* March 26, 1846, kindly supplied by Maurice Simmons, Springfield, Ill. Documentation of Reed's service with Abe Lincoln in the Black Hawk War is found in Evelyn Wells' series on the Donner Party in the *San Francisco Call and Post,* commencing on June 11, 1919. The series includes a photo of Reed's copy of a muster roll in the Black Hawk, with Reed's and Lincoln's names listed one after another. Mountain man James Clyman and Lincoln's rival Stephen A. Douglas also served in the militia company. Douglas wrote a letter recommending Reed for a post as an Indian agent.

MAY 15

George Donner's ad also ran in April, 1846 in the same newspaper as above. Description of the trail is from Bryant and Miller.

MAY 17

Bryant; Miller; DeVoto.

MAY 19

Morgan; Thornton; Bryant; Miller. Virginia Reed's quote is from *Across the Plains In The Donner Party: A Personal Narrative of the Overland Trip to California, 1846-47* by Virginia Reed Murphy. Russell's letter of May 10, 1846 was published in Morgan, pg. 519. The information about Russell's personality is from Morgan, pgs. 460-461. The sketch of Russell originally appeared in *Dictionary of American Biography* and was written by W. J. Ghent.

MAY 22

Bryant. Reed's dogs' names from a letter by Virginia Reed, May 16, 1847, published in Morgan, pgs. 281-288. Frances Donner quote is from Werner, but it is a paraphrase of Eliza, not Frances, Donner. The original citation is Houghton, pg. 5.

MAY 24

McKinstry's journal published in Morgan, pg. 199-215; Morgan; Bryant.

MAY 26-29

McKinstry's diary is found in Morgan, as above. Thornton's quote as published in Johnson, pg. 18.

MAY 29

Journal of James Clyman as published in Korns, pgs. 23-45; Virginia Reed's letter published in Morgan, pg. 278; Miller quote from his diary published in Hall, pg. 13.

PIONEER PALACE CAR

The Pioneer Palace Car: Adventures in Western Mythmaking from *Crossroads,* the newsletter of the Utah Crossroads Chapter of the Oregon-California Trails Association, summer 1994; and *William B. Ide Describes the Pioneer Palace Car in 1845* by Johnson, published in *Crossroads,* summer 1994; The Emigrant Exhibition of the Tuolumne County Museum Sonora, Calif.; Eli Anderson, wainwright; Al Mulder, Crossroads Chapter of the Oregon-California Trails Assocation; Jolene Kaufman, the Oregon Trail Museum Association, Scotts Bluff National Monument, Gering, Neb.; Donner Memorial Museum, Donner Lake; Chimney Rock State Historic Site, Bayard, Neb.; Jean Tryon, Minetare, Neb.; Patricia McDowell Wing, reseacher, Reno; Stewart; Korns; *Bull Wagon* by Glen Dines; *Western Wagon Wheels* by Lambert Florin; *Carriage Terminology: A Historical Dictionary* by Don H. Berkebile. Additional research and compilation by artist Mark Bartley and Frank Mullen Jr., for the 1996 Donner Sesquicentennial Project. Thanks to wagon owners at the 1996 Reno Rodeo Cattle Drive, Wagonmaster H.B. McCay of Nevada, and to Mark Hirsch of Washington, D.C. for his help in locating relevant books.

MAY 31 to JUNE 5

Bryant; McKinstry journal quote published in Morgan, Vol. 1, pg. 209; Virginia Reed Murphy quote published in Century Illustrated Magazine, 1891; Keseberg quote from C.F. McGlashan, pg. 206.

JUNE 2

Bryant; Miller and McKinstry diaries in Morgan.

JUNE 5

Miller and McKinstry from Morgan; Morgan. Quote from Heinrich Lienhard, edited by Marguerite E. Wilbur from the German manuscript.

JUNE 7

Bryant; Morgan.

JUNE 9

The Great Platte River Road by Mattes, (Nebraska, 1969); Bryant; McKinstry quote published in Morgan, pg. 211-212.

JUNE 12

Diary of Hiram Miller published in Morgan, pgs. 199-218; Bryant; McKinstry in Morgan. *The Pioneer Memoirs of John Breen* by John Breen as quoted in *Fatal Decision: The Tragic Story of the Donner Party* by Dr. Walter M. Stookey. A photo, mistakenly labeled as Patrick and Margaret Breen, was removed in the second printing.

JUNE 14

Bryant; Virginia Reed Murphy; *The Journal of Nicolas Carriger* in Morgan, pgs. 143-158.

JUNE 16

Bryant; Morgan; Tamsen Donner's letter published in Morgan, pgs. 561-563.

JUNE 19-21

Bryant; Miller; Morgan; Hastings's quote from his *Emigrants Guide to Oregon and California,* pg. 137-138.

JUNE 23

Stewart; Morgan; The Oregon Trail Museum Association, Gering, Neb.; Chimney Rock State Historic Site Museum,

Bayard, Neb.; Miller diary quote from Hall, pgs. 14-15; McKinstry quote from his diary as published in Morgan, pg. 214.

JUNE 26
Fort Laramie and the Pageant of the West, 1834-1890 by LeRoy R. Hafen and Francis Marion Young, (Nebraska, 1938); Bryant; Morgan; Scotts Bluff National Monument, Oregon Trail Museum Association, Gering, Neb.; George Donner letter from Morgan, pgs. 576-577.

JUNE 28
Virginia Reed birth date information from Morgan, pg. 240; Stewart; Sutter's quote as published *in Lansford Warren Hastings: Scoundrel or Visionary* by Will Bagley, Overland Journal, Vol. 12, No. 1, (1994), pg. 18; Portions of *The Journal of James Clyman* are found in Korns, and *in The Controversial Career of Lansford Warren Hastings*, a doctoral dissertation by Thomas Franklin Andrews (1971). Andrews maintains Clyman's remarks about the meeting with Reed at the fort are suspect because the incident was related to a historian by Clyman in 1878, 32 years after the events. He believes Clyman may have made up or embellished the account in light of the latter importance of the Donner Party and their decision to travel Hastings's route. But in Clyman's journal (quoted in Morgan, pg. 58), which was wrtten as events unfolded, the mountain man notes on June 27: "...we met numerous squads of emigrants untill we reached fort Larrimie whare we met Ex govornor Boggs from Jackson County Misourie Bound for California and we camped with them several of us continued the conversation untill a late hour." Reed and the Donner brothers would have been in this group and surely Reed, whom Clyman remembers from "the Sauk War" would have pestered the mountain man with questions about the roads ahead. Clyman, having just scouted a cutoff with Hastings, could speak on this topic at length with Reed. So Clyman's later account is not only believeable, it's quite plausible in light of Clyman's feelings about the route and Reed's propensity to gather as much information as possible before deciding on a course, a trait he showed before leaving Springfield when he wrote many letters soliciting advice for his coming trek west. Reed, incidentally, at the time was warned by a friend to be sure to take enough food.

HASTINGS INTRODUCTION
Lansford Warren Hastings: Scoundrel or Visionary by Will Bagley, Overland Journal, Vol. 12, No. 1, 1994; Stewart; DeVoto; Morgan; Bryant; Andrews. The Bidwell story comes from Bagley's piece in the Overland Journal.

JUNE 30
Morgan; Bryant; *Basin and Range* by John McPhee (New York, 1980).

JULY 4-6
Morgan; Korns; Virginia Reed; astronomical research by Christopher Wing, with computer program from the Fleischmann Planetarium at the University of Nevada, Reno; excerpts from the Miller diary as published in Hall, pp. 15-16; McKinstry diary quotes from Morgan, pg. 215; V. Reed Murphy. Bryant; Flag research by the Flag Store, Sparks, Nevada.

JULY 10
Morgan; Bryant; Korns; source of the Putnam letter is Morgan, pg. 604.

JULY 12
Morgan; Stewart; Virginia Reed letter is from Morgan, pg. 278.

JULY 14
In *Ordeal by Hunger*, George Stewart writes that the Donners met Bonney and received Hastings's letter on July 17. But letters from members of the wagon train, included in Morgan's "Overland in 1846" show Bonney's visit as the afternoon of July 12. Stanton's letter of July 12 is published in Morgan, pg. 611.

JULY 17
Bryant; Morgan; Stanton letter noted above.

JULY 19
Morgan; Stewart; Thornton's journal published in Johnson. Interview with Bill Pugsley. Story on Pugsley in the *Reno Gazette-Journal*, July 18, 1996, pg. 1B.

JULY 24
Breen's assumed locations on the trail from King; Morgan; Korns; Stewart. Dr. T. Pope Long's letter of July 19, 1846 is published in Morgan, pg. 620-621.

JULY 26
Fort Bridger Museum; Morgan; Korns; Reed's letter of July 31 published in Morgan, pg. 279-280. Interviews with Martin Lammers and others, Fort Bridger Historic Site, PO Box 35, Fort Bridger, Wyo., 82933, (307) 782-3842. Interviews with Bill Pugsley.

FORT BRIDGER
This article by Mullen orginally appeared in the *Reno Gazette-Journal*, July 28, 1996, pg. 1B.

JULY 31
Fort Bridger Museum; Stewart; DeVoto; Morgan; King; excerpt from J.F. Reed's July 31, 1846 letter to James or Gersham Keyes as published in Morgan, pg. 279-280; Donner roster compiled from comparing King's and Stewart's accounts. As of July 31, 1846, the day they left Fort Bridger, the party consisted of 74 people and 19 wagons (George Stewart, author of 'Ordeal By Hunger" assigns a wagon to Spitzer and Reinhardt, but Joseph King and other authors dispute this). Ages given are primarily from Kristin Johnson (personal correspondence, April 8, 1998).

AUG. 2
Bryant; Korns; For more on the history of Luke Halloran, *see Luke Halloran*' by Kristin Johnson, *Crossroads* newsletter of the Oregon-California Trails Association, Spring/Summer 1996. The full Harry Breen account of his father's broken leg is published in Stookey, pg. 193-94 and is also mentioned in King, pg. 26.

AUG. 4
Stewart; Lienhard, pgs. 101-102; Korns; Morgan; Bryant; Thornton's account in Johnson; W.C. Graves account in the *Russian River Flag* newspaper, Thursday, April 26, 1877 (from a photocopy of the newspaper kindly provided by Kristin Johnson).

AUG. 7
Korns; Morgan; Bryant; interviews with Pugsley; W.C. Graves quote from the *Russian River Flag*, April 26, 1877. The number of wagons in Hastings' advance party has been variously described as 66 (J. Quinn Thornton), "nearly 100"

(Jim Bridger's comment to the Mormons the following year, a number which probably included the Donner's 22 wagons), "about eighty" (Edwin Bryant), and "some seventy-five" (George McKinstry in the California Star, Feb. 13, 1847). Historians believe there were more than 60 wagons ahead of the Donners on the cutoff.

AUG. 9-14
Morgan; Korns et al; Stewart; interviews with Pugsley. Portions of Leinhard's journal published and annotated in Korns, pg. 140; Pratt quote from Korns.

AUG 16
Morgan; Korns; King; Stewart. The date of the Graves family joining the Donner Party comes from Morgan. W.C. Graves apparently gives the date as Aug. 10, but Morgan, citing the many inaccuracies which pervade the Graves account, states that "he is entitled to no credence on this score." Kristin Johnson, in an article, "When Did The Graves Family Join the Donner Party?," published in the Spring/Summer edition of *Crossroads* magazine, cites problems with the Aug. 16 date and consults sources apparently unavailable to Morgan. She writes that other possible dates for the Graves' family's arrival are between Aug. 7 - 10. Looking at her source material, which indicates the Graves family was less than a week behind the Donners, then why, if the Aug. 16 date is correct, did it take so long for the Graves family to catch up? Since the answer remains unclear, I've stuck to Morgan's date in my narrative. W.C. Graves comments are from Johnson. Information about the Graves family from Ellsworth Spencer, "The Graves Tragedy," portions published in *Crossroads*, Spring/Summer 1996, pg. 22.

AUG. 18-23
Korns; Morgan; Johnson; Stewart; Stookey; Pugsley; V. Reed. Lienhard's journal and the annotated excerpts published in Korns, pg. 162.

AUG. 25
Korns; Morgan, et al.; Johnson, "Unfortunate Emigrants"; Interview with Bill Pugsley. Little is known about Luke Halloran, but "Luke Halloran" by Kristin Johnson, *Crossroads* newsletter of the Oregon-California Trails Association, Spring/Summer 1996, provides much information about the man and his possible burial site. Reed's quote is from his account in the Pacific Press. Pugsley came upon the OCTA commemoration of Halloran's grave by design, not accident. He was invited to attend and asked to walk in during the ceremonies.

AUG. 28
Korns; Johnson; Eliza Donner's quote from Houghton, pgs. 39-40. As Johnson observes, Houghton was only four years old at the time of the incident of the ripped up note, but probably had been told the story many times by the older children.

AUG. 30
Korns; Morgan; George Ivory of the Crossroads Chapter of the Oregon-California Trails Association, who assisted Bill Pugsley; Pugsley; Paul Sawyer; J.F. Reed quotes from Pacific Press account; V. Reed; Astronomical research by Chris Wing of Reno with the cooperation of the Fleischmann Planetarium of the University of Nevada, Reno.

SEPT. 4
Reed's account of the Salt Lake Desert trek from Johnson, pg. 189; Thornton; Stewart.

SEPT. 6
Although Patty and Virginia Reed later describe burying wagon boxes in the Great Salt Lake Desert, it is difficult to believe the wagon boxes were so elaborately hidden, given the difficulty in digging on the playa.

SEPT. 8
King; Korns; Morgan; V. Reed.

PALACE CAR
Excavation of the Donner-Reed Wagons by Bruce Hawkins and David Madsen, (University of Utah Press, Salt Lake City, 1990); "Pioneer Palace Car" by Kristin Johnson, OCTA *Crossroads* newsletter, Summer, 1994; Interviews with Kristin Johnson.

SEPT. 11
Korns; Morgan; Johnson; King. Information about the wagon cached at Big Springs comes from Thornton's account in Johnson, pg. 38. Greeley's quote from his *Overland Journey From New York to San Francisco in 1859*. By the time Greeley went west, the Humboldt was a wasteland. The river was in considerably better shape when the Donners traveled it in 1846, but compared to the Platte or even the Green River, the Humboldt was a poor water course with sparse vegetation and alkali banks.

SEPT. 13
Korns; Morgan; Bryant.

SEPT. 15-18
Pugsley; Korns; Morgan.

SEPT. 18
Lienhard.

SEPT. 22
Korns; Morgan; Johnson.

SEPT. 25
V. Reed; "Keseberg and the Buffalo Robe," by Kristin Johnson, published in *The Donner Party, An American Tragedy*, Utah *Crossroads*, Vol. 7, pgs. 2-3 a newsletter by Frankye Craig, Reno, Nevada, Spring 1997; Korns; Morgan; Thornton.

SEPT. 27
In Morgan; the Donners encampment of Sept. 27 is said to be on Susie Creek below Carlin Canyon (Moleen Canyon), pg. 439. The "hot springs" cited by Reed in his diary is apparently Carlin Springs, where J. Quinn Thornton indicates the party camped on Sept. 27, leaving the morning of Sept. 28. In Korns, the authors agree that the encampment of Sept. 27 was at Susie Creek below the canyon, although they admit the possibility that the creek may have been the present day Maggie Creek. In any case, as both these creeks are east of Carlin Springs, the Donners passed by that place on Sept. 28, even if they did not camp at the spot. The date for Carlin's commemorative postmark was based on the research cited.; Quotes from interviews at Carlin Nevada, Sept. 28, Thanks to Don and Carolyn Rose of Carlin, the people of Carlin, and Bill Pugsley.

SEPT. 29
When the newspaper ran the episode concerning the Donner Party at Gravelly Ford, the author received many letters and phone calls about the Snyder killing having happened there. Although several books say Gravelly Ford was the location of the tragedy and local Nevadans have long pointed out the "Donner graves" at the site, the killing took place near Gloconda, further up the trail. The mistake in geography was apparently made by C.F. McGlashan, who misinterpreted what survivors told him, and then repeated by other authors, including Walter Stookey in *Fatal Decision* and Irene Paden in *Prairie Schooner Detours*. Sources: Interviews with Kristin Johnson and Will Bagley; McGlashan; Korns; Morgan.

OCT. 2
Te-Moak band of Western Shoshones; Location of the party from Reed's diary, footnotes in Korns; Morgan; Pugsley.

OCT. 4
Korns; Morgan; Astronomy research by Christopher Wing of Reno.

OCT. 6
Interview with Martin Griffith, trail buff; Circumstances and eyewitness reports of the Reed-Snyder fight from Thornton; Korns; Morgan; John Breen; V. Reed; W.C. Graves.

OCT. 9
"The Snow-Bound, Starved Emigrants of 1846: Statement by Mr. Reed, One of the Donner Company"; "The Donner Tragedy-A Thrilling Chapter in Our Pioneer History," *Pacific Press* newspaper, Jan. 21, 1871; Johnson; V. Reed; Thornton; Korns; Morgan.

OCT. 11
Thornton, *Oregon and California in 1848*; Korns; Morgan publishes an article from the Oregon Spectator, Oregon City, Nov. 26, 1846, pg. 663, which mentions Sallie (Salee) of Carraway County, Mo., killed by the "Klamet Indians," although the tribe's base was Oregon and not Nevada. In his footnotes (pgs. 774-775) Morgan provides more information about William P. Sallee, who was traveling in "Capt. West's" company when he was killed by a poison arrow.

OCT. 13-16
Thornton; Johnson.

OCT. 18
Korns; Morgan; Stewart, *California Trail*; Johnson; *Life Among the Piutes: Their Wrongs and Claims* by Sarah Winnemucca Hopkins, edited by Mrs. Horace Mann, (1969, Sierra Media, Inc., Bishop, CA). Edition photographically reproduced from the 1883 original.

OCT. 20
Interviews with Kristin Johnson, Fred Horlacher; Will Bagley; Don Wiggins; John Clark; Howard Curran; Johnson; Thornton; the University of Nevada, Reno, Library, Special Collections for the T. H. Jefferson Map of 1846.

About Stanton's return to the party: Thornton (found in Johnson, pg. 42) states that Stanton and the two Indians met the party on the Truckee River on Oct. 19 at about 10 a.m. Stewart has Stanton rejoining the Donner Party after they labored up Truckee River Canyon for three days, putting the rondezvous near the future site of Reno.

But since Stanton is known to be at the vicinity of Johnson's ranch on this date (Morgan, pg. 444-445), the Thornton and Stewart accounts (McGlashan, who places the meeting at the current site of Wadsworth, Nevada) must be in error.

OCT. 25
Stanton rejoins the party near the head of the future site of Verdi on the Truckee River and the Sierra trail through Dog Valley. That estimate is based on the time it would have taken Stanton's mule train to reach the party from Johnson's. How could Wadsworth or the site of Reno have been confused with Verdi? In the memories of Donner Party survivors telling their tales more than three decades after the events, one small town on the Truckee River could easily have been confused with another. In any case, Oct. 20 is far too early for the event.

In addition, Stewart states that the emigrants remained in the Truckee Meadows for three or four days to recruit the cattle before attempting the steep climb up the Sierra. McGlashan has them "rest the cattle a few days" (pg. 55), but Thornton fails to mention the sojourn. In this book, I have the various groups of the party arriving and leaving the Truckee Meadows over a three- to four-day period, with the Breens the first to move west of the current site of Reno and the Donner families in the rear of the groups.

GHOST TRAILS
Interviews with Don Wiggins, Connie Stathes, John Clark, Howard Curran, Fred Horlacher; Connie Stathes, Nevada Historical Trails Association, PO Box 21238, Reno NV; The Oregon-California Trails Association, PO Box 1019, 524 Osage St., Independence, MO 64051-0519; and other sources listed in the story; T.H. Jefferson Map, UNR Library Special Collections. A copy of the map is also provided in a back pocket of the latest edition of Korns. "Ghost Trails" story orginally appeared in the *Reno Gazette-Journal* as part of a special section, OCT. 30, 1996.

OCT. 23
Thornton; Johnson; Donner Springs Elementary School, Reno; Interview with Fred Horlacher. In addition to the first edition of 1856, lengthy extracts of Eliza Farnham's narrative appear in McGlashan's *History of the Donner Party*, parts of which are reprinted in *History of San Benito County, California* (1881). A facsimile edition of Farnham's book was published by B.de Graaf in 1972; it also contains a biography of the author.

OCT. 25
Don Wiggins; King; Johnson; Farnham, *California, In-Doors and Out*; Stokey.

OCT. 27-30
Thornton; J. Breen; Wiggins; Thanks to Tony Shelton of KRNV Channel 4, Reno, for meteorological advice; Elitha Donner quote from Werner. Sarah Winnemucca quotes from Mann. Edition photographically reproduced from the 1883 original. Land petition published in Hall, pg. 32.

OCT. 31
Donner Memorial Museum, Donner Lake State Park; Thornton, Johnson, Pugsley completed his journey at Donner Lake State Park on October 31, 1996. He walked 900 miles.

NOV. 3
Main source of the events of this day are from Stewart; Elitha Donner quote from Werner. Notes for Milt Elliot from Hall, pg. 33.

NOV. 6-13
Mainly from Stewart; Comparison with Thornton's account in Johnson. Interview with Don Wiggins. Location of the three lake cabins is from Donald Hardesty, Archaeology of the Donner Party, (University of Nevada Press, Reno, 1997). The "big rock" at Donner Lake Memorial State Park is generally accepted as a wall of the Murphy cabin. The Breen/Schallenberger cabin site is said to be beneath the monument (deticated June 6, 1919) at the park. This location, identified by C. F. McGlashan after he toured the area with survivors, was called into question in 1920, when D.C. Chapman insisted the site was 30 yards away from the memorial. McGlashan fought against this notion and argued the remnants of a fire pit identified by Chapman were from campers who built fires there many years after the Donners. Despite compelling evidence supporting McGlashan's view, the Native Sons of the Golden West changed the plaque to read "near this site" instead of "at this site," a change McGlashan resented for the rest of his life. He refused to take visitors there anymore because "to him, that word 'near' made all the difference," according to his grandaughter, M. Nona McGlashan in Give Me A Mountain Meadow, a biography of her grandfather (Valley Publishers; Fresno, CA, 1977). In 1997, OCTA member Don Wiggins also called the Breen cabin site into question, stating that accounts of 1846 and later pioneers who stopped at the sites remember the Murphy and Breen cabins about a mile apart. The two sites as now marked are about 200 yards apart. The site of the Graves cabin is believed to be under Interstate 80 at about where the California Agricultural Inspection Station now stands, Hardesty said.

NOV. 15
Accounts of Eddy and the bear are found in Stewart and orginate in Thornton; Archaeology in Hardesty.

NOV. 17
Morgan; Thornton; Johnson.

NOV. 20
Breen Diary; Stewart; Thornton; Johnson.

NOV. 22-27
Thornton's account in Johnson; Stewart; P. Breen; George Donner's note is published in Hall, pg. 36.

NOV. 29
Stewart; Johnson; The Washoe Tribe of Nevada and California; The Autobiography of Mark Twain by Mark Twain, (Harper, NY, 1959); Mark Twain: A Biography: The Personal and Literary Life of Samuel Langhorne Clemens by Albert Bigelow Paine, (Harper and Brothers, New York, 1912). Walt Whitman's America by David S. Reynolds; Lincoln by David Herbert Donald.

DEC. 1-8
Baylis William's land grant petition published in Hall, pg. 38; Thornton; King; Stookey; Johnson; Farnham; V. Reed; main source for happenings at the camps is Stewart.

DEC. 11
Thornton's quote as published in Johnson.

DEC. 13
Stewart; P. Breen; Stanton's note from Hall, pg. 45.

DEC. 15
Stewart; In a letter, Mary Ann Graves gives a more generous inventory of "eight pounds of poor beef each" taken by the Forlorn Hope party. (Graves letter in Johnson, pg. 130.)

DEC. 18
Stewart.

DEC. 20-22
P. Breen; Stewart; Thornton.

DEC. 25
Stewart; V. Reed; P. Reed in Wells; Stookey; Farnham quotes from Johnson; Mary Murphy quote from Werner.

DEC. 27-29
P. Breen; Stewart; Thornton.

JAN 1-8
King; Stewart; Stookey; Johnson; Bryant; DeVoto. The account of Eddy shooting the deer is found. The book includes the Donner Party's entrapment narrative from Thornton's Oregon and California in 1848. Thorton was reprinted by Outbooks Inc., (Golden, Co., 1986).

JAN. 10
King; "Luis and Salvador: Unsung Heros of the Donner Party," by Joseph A. King, The Californians magazine, Vol. 13, No. 2.; Hastings shooting Indians is discussed in Bagley, "Lansford Warren Hastings: Scoundrel or Visionary" by Will Bagley, Overland Journal, Vol. 12, No. 1, 1994; and in The Controversial Career of Lansford Warren Hastings by Thomas Franklin Andrews (Andrews, 1971); Hastings.

JAN. 12
Stewart; Thornton; McGlashan; Johnson; Stookey; V. Reed.

JAN. 15
Stewart; King; Thornton.

JAN. 17
Stewart; Stookey; King; Reed's activities from Hall, pgs. 42, 46.

JAN.19
Stewart; Stookey; King.

JAN. 22
King; Stewart; V. Reed; Statement of Daniels and Stark from Hall, page 42.

JAN. 24
Thornton; Stewart; King; Hardesty; McGlashan.

JAN. 26
California Star; Stewart; King.

JAN. 29
Stewart; King; McCutchen's letter from Hall, pg. 50.

JAN. 31
P. Breen; Stewart; King; Thornton; Johnson.

FEB. 2
King; Stewart; P. Breen; Johnson.

FEB. 5
King; Stewart; P. Breen; Donner relief diary from Hall, pg. 52.

FEB. 7
California Star, Feb. 13, 1847, pg. 2; King; Stewart; Reed's diary of the Second Relief from Hall, pg. 62.

FEB. 9
King; Stewart.

FEB. 12
California Star newspaper, Feb. 13, 1847; Stewart; King. Partial list of provisions of second relief group from Hall, pgs. 48-49; Donner relief diary, Hall, pg. 52.

FEB. 14
Stewart; Stookey; King; P. Breen; Johnson; Hall, pg. 53

FEB. 16
Johnson; P. Breen; Stewart; King; Hall, pg. 53; pg. 62 for Reed's diary of the relief.

FEB. 19
Stewart; King; P. Breen; Hall, pg. 53-54.

FEB. 21
Stewart; King; P. Breen; Activities at Johnson's Ranch from Reed's diary of the relief, Hall, pg. 64. Roster of escapees from comparisons of Stewart, King and lists in Johnson and in Essential Aids For Understanding Donner Party Histories by Charles H. Dodd, which may be ordered from Dodd, Route 1, Box 9, Chilcoot, Ca 96105. Dodd's guide provides many lists of who was where when and a timeline of the Donner's trek.

FEB. 26
Georgia Donner quote from an 1879 letter to C.F. McGlashan as quoted in King, pg. 112; Reed's diary from Hall.

FEB. 28
P. Breen; Stewart; King; V. Reed; Thornton; Hall.

MARCH 2
Thornton quote from Thorton, pg. 58; Stewart; King discounts the "body parts" story, doubting that Cady and Clark could know which organs were being eaten, pg. 97.

MARCH 5
Stewart; King; P. Breen; V. Reed. King defends Woodworth, stating the passed midshipman personally went up the trail to meet three of the returning relief parties and that he did as much as he could have done to help the emigrants.

MARCH 7
Mrs. Breen's tongue-lashing of Reed and the others originates in Thornton, pg. 77. Thornton's account of her quotes is done in Irish dialect. The story is repeated in Stewart, pg. 226. Stewart has McCutchen uleasing a flurry of oaths at Breen to silence her. Joseph King, usually a staunch defender of the Breens, doesn't mention the incident. The remainder of the narrative is a result of comparing McGlashan, Reed's relief diary in Hall and his account in the Pacific Press; Stewart, Thornton and King accounts. Stewart and Thornton have the full party at Starved Camp for three nights and McGlashan reports a storm of "three days." The Reed diary, as King notes, supports only two nights of the storm. King questions Stewart's timetable and offers a more plausible version.

MARCH 9

Reed party's location and timetable from King. Account of the Breens at Starved Camp heavily relies on Margaret Breen's account to Farnham (Johnson, pgs. 160-163) with comparison to Stewart, Thornton and McGlashan. Incidents involving Cady and Stone are found in King, Thornton, Stewart and McGalshan.

MARCH 12

Account of Breens at Starved Camp from Farnham (Johnson, pgs. 163-165). Also, Stewart; King; McGlashan; Account of Patty Reed's doll from "The Tragedy of Donner Lake" by Evelyn Wells, *The San Francisco Call and Post*, Saturday, June 21, 1919; Patty's quote from a letter to C.F. McGlashan. King takes issue with Georgia Donner's statement about Georgie Foster being hung on a wall, writing that Georgia's memory and the recollections of the other small children were ``often refreshed and stimulated by lurid accounts of Keseberg'' (pg. 111).

MARCH 14

King; Stewart; Thornton; McGlashan. The "sunning themselves" comment orginates in Thornton and is repeated by Stewart. King notes that James Breen later called Eddy "Lying Eddy" and concludes that Eddy's account is "factually incongruous as well as unfair to the Breens." King questions several facts, including whether the sun could have reached the bottom of the snow pit, and attacks Eddy's statement that the Graves' child was fondling the body of its mutilated mother as having "the mark of pulp fiction." Whatever the true details, it is clear no one could have maintained perfect decorum under the circumstances faced at Starved Camp. Eddy's desire to kill Keseberg is mentioned in Thornton (pg. 83). An account in the *California Star* on April 10 closely follows Eddy's later statements to Thornton about Keseberg: that Foster's child was alive when Keseberg took him to bed and was dead in the morning. Thornton also repeats another anecdote found in the *Star*, that Keseberg ate another child (Eddy's) before noon the next day. Thornton, pg. 83. Keseberg quote from King, pg. 131.

MARCH 16

Johnson; King; Stewart. Note that John Breen remembers Mule Springs bare of snow, yet Woodworth in his *California Star* account of April 3, 1847, brags about camping in the snow for weeks. Quote from Houghton.

MARCH 18

Stewart; V. Reed; W.C. Graves, "Graves' Crossing the Plains in '46," *Hearldsburg Russian River Flag*, April 26 to May 17, 1877. Virginia Reed's May 16, 1847 letter to her cousin, Mary Keyes of Springfield, Ill., as published in Morgan, "Overland," Vol. I, pgs. 281-288.

MARCH 21

King; Stewart; Source for Keseberg quotes is an interview with C. F. McGlashan, pgs. 221-222. Keseberg said Tamsen Donner remarked that she had not turned to cannibalism at Alder Creek. However, given the rescue party members description of her as strong and her ability to not only survive at the camp but make trips to the lake, it's hard to believe she did not partake of the necessary food.

MARCH 23

Source for Keseberg quotes is McGlashan; V. Reed letter published in Morgan, pg. 281-288.

MARCH 26

Stewart; King; Stookey; Morgan.

MARCH 28

Keseberg as published in McGlashan; King; Stewart.

MARCH 30

King; David Galloway; Johnson. C. F. McGlashan, who met Keseberg, was convinced he was innocent of murder. When Eliza Donner Houghton met Keseberg, she took his hands in hers, looked into her eyes and said, "I did not kill your mother or harm her in any way." In *Give Me a Mountain Meadow*, a biography of C.F. McGlashan, his grandaughter, M. Nona McGlashan writes:

"Lewis Keseberg passed the ordeal which would have made a guilty man quake," Eliza (Donner Houghton) stated later. "Whatever slander accrued to Keseberg's name, Tamsen Donner's youngest daughter was convinced he did not murder her mother. Mac, too, was convinced of the man's innocence" (pg. 111).

APRIL 2

California Star, April 3, 1847; Stewart; King.

APRIL 4

McGlashan; King; Stewart. Grayson's mortality study is summarized in Hardesty, pgs. 125-132.

APRIL 6

Breen information from King; John Breen account published in Stookey; *California Star*, April 3, 1847.

APRIL 9

California Star, April 10, 1847; Stewart.

APRIL 11

King; Stewart; Fallon, "Extracts From a Journal Written By A Member of The Party Latest From The California Mountains," by Capt. Fellun (Fallon), *California Star*, San Francisco, June 5, 1847.

APRIL 13

Denton's poem from Stewart; Stanton's poem from McGlashan; Background on both men from Morgan and King. Denton's journal is referred to in the *Star* account, but the diary, probably sent to his relatives in Sheffield, has never been found.

APRIL 16

Fallon; Stewart; King.

APRIL 18-23

Fallon; King; Stewart; McGlashan.

APRIL 25

Fallon; King; Stewart; McGlashan.

APRIL 27

Lienhard; Stewart; J. Breen; Interviews by Frank Mullen Jr. during California Trail Days, August, 1996, *Reno Gazette-Journal*, Aug. 18, 1996.

APRIL 30

King; Interview with Kristin Johnson; Hardesty. Eliza Donner mentions that "an additional sum of ten thousand dollars" had been stitched into a quilt. This information comes from Alan Francis, editor of the *Springfield Journal* (Houghton, pg. 6).

MAY 2

California Star, San Francisco, May 1, 1847; *California Star*, Feb. 20, 1846 to May 1, 1847; Bagley, "Lansford Warren Hastings: Scoundrel or Visionary," *Crossroads*, the Quarterly Journal of the Oregon-California Trails Association," Vol. 12, No. 1, 1994; Interview with William Chrystal, scholar and Chatauquan performer, May 14, 1997, Galena Branch Library, Reno, Nevada.

MAY 4

Stewart; McGlashan; Johnson; King. J. W. Harlan quote from Jacob Wright Harlan, "California '46 to '88" (San Francisco, 1888) as published in King. King noted he was grateful to William K. Harlan of Walnut Creek for calling this testimony to his attention.

MAY 7

King; Interviews with descendants from Martin Griffith, trail buff and Associated Press reporter, Reno.

MAY 9

McGlashan; King; Stewart; Hardesty; J. Breen in Stookey.

EPILOGUE

Martin Griffith interviewed many Donner Party descendants prior to and during California Trail Days, August, 1996; Interviews with Donner Party descendants by Frank Mullen Jr. in 1990 and 1996; King; J. Breen in Stookey; Johnson; "Mary Ann Graves letter from California," edited by Kristin Johnson, published in *Crossroads*, the Quarterly Journal of the Utah Crossroads Chapter of OCTA, summer 1994.

Bibliography

Non-fiction books

Annals of San Francisco. Frank Soule, John H. Gihon and James Nisbet, editors. (Appleton, New York, 1855). (Authors and Newspapers Association, New York and London, 1906).

Bancroft, Hubert H. *History of California*. San Francisco, 1890. See Vol. 5.

Berkebile, Don H. *Carriage Terminology: An Historical Dictionary*. (Smithsonian University Press, Washington and London, 1978). Kindly located for the author by Mark Hirsch of Washington, D.C.

Breen, Harry J. Letter to Dr. Walter M. Stookey, Feb. 12, 1947. Printed in Stookey, *Fatal Decision*, pp. 189-94.

Breen, Margaret. Account of her experiences with Donner Party, as told to Mrs. Eliza W. Farnham in 1849 and published as an appendix (pp. 380-457) to Farnham, *California, In-Doors and Out*.

Breen, Patrick. Diary of Patrick Breen was published in *the California Star* (1847), and in Bryant's *What I Saw in California* (1848) and versions have appeared in many other books, including C. F. McGlashan's *History of the Donner Party* and Joseph *King's Winter of Entrapment*. The version of the diary used in this book is edited by Frederick J. Teggart from *Publications of the Academy of Pacific Coast History* (Vol. 1, No. 6) as reprinted by Vista Books; Dillon, Co.; 1991).

Brown, Dee. *The Gentle Tamers: Women of the Old Wild West*.

Bryant, Edwin, *What I Saw in California* (1848). (University of Nebraska Press, Lincoln and London, 1985). A reproduction of the 1848 edition. Bryant's journal set the standard for diaries of the overland trek.

Clayton, W. *The Latter Day Saints' Emigrants' Guide: Being a Table of Distances*. (Missouri Republican Steam Power Press, Chambers and Knapp, St. Louis, 1848). Kindly loaned to the author by Bart Bevins of Reno.

Croy, Homer. *Wheels West*. (Hastings House, New York , 1955)

DeVoto, Bernard. *Year of Decision: 1846*. (Houghton Mifflin Co.; Boston; 1942/1989 edition).

Dines, Glen. *Bull Wagon*.

Dodd, Charles. *Essential Aids For Understanding the Donner Party Histories*. (self-published, Chilcoot, Ca., 1996).

Donald, David Herbert. *Lincoln*. (Random House, London, 1995).

Eberstadt, Edward (editor). *A Transcript of the Fort Sutter Papers, Together With the Historical Commentaries Accompanying Them*. (De Vinne Press, New York, 1921).

Farnham, Eliza W. Narrative of the Emigration of the Donner Party to California in 1846, in *California, In-Doors and Out*. (New York, 1856).

Florin, Lambert. *Western Wagon Wheels*.

Franzwa, Gregory M. *The Oregon Trail Revisited*. (Patrice Press, Tucson, Arizona; 1972/1988).

Goetzmann, William H. *Exploration and Empire*. (The Norton Library, 1971).

Graydon, Charles K. *Trail of the First Wagons Over the Sierra Nevada*. (Patrice Press, Tucson, 1894).

Hafen, LeRoy R. and Young, Francis Marion. *Fort Laramie and the Pageant of the West, 1834-1890*. (University of Nebraska Press, Lincoln and London, 1938/Bison Book edition, 1984). Kindly loaned to the author by Bart Bevins of Reno.

Hall, Carroll D, editor. *The Donner Miscellany*. (California Book Club, San Francisco, 1947). A rare book with fewer than 300 copies printed. Books retail for $125 to $400, depending upon condition.

Hardesty, Donald L. *Archaeology of the Donner Party*. (University of Nevada Press, Reno, 1997).

Hastings, Lansford Warren. *The Emigrants' Guide to Oregon and California*. (Applewood Books; Bedford, Massachusetts; 1845.) An Applewood Books reprint edition.

Hawkins, Bruce and Madsen, David. *Excavation of the Donner-Reed Wagons*. (University of Utah Press, Salt Lake City, 1990).

Hillerman, Tony, editor. *The Best of the West: An Anthology of Classic Writing From the American West*. (Harper Collins, New York, 1991).

Hopkins, Sarah Winnemucca. *Life Among the Piutes: Their Wrongs and Claims*. edited by Mrs. Horace Mann. (1969, Sierra Media, Inc., Bishop, California). Edition photographically reproduced from the 1883 original.

Houghton, Eliza P. Donner. *The Expedition of the Donner Party and Its Tragic Fate*. (A. C. McKlurg & Co., Chicago, 1911). Reprint of the original edition by Sierra District of California State Parks, 1996, Sacramento, California.

Jonas, Gerald. *The Living Earth Book of North American Trees*. (Readers Digest Books, Pleasantville, New York, 1993).

Johnson, Kristin. editor. *Unfortunate Emigrants: Narratives of the Donner Party*. (Utah State University Press, Logan, Utah, 1996).

Johnson, Allen with malone, Dumas *Dictionary of American biography* (Charles Scribners and Sons, New York, 1931)

Kelly, Charles. *Salt Desert Trails*. (Wesstern Printing Co., Salt Lake City, 1930).

Kelly, Leslie A. *California's Gold Rush Country, 1848-1998*. (Les Kelly Publications; Huntington Beach, California; 1997).

Keseberg, Lewis. His statement to C. F. McGlashan in 1879 is published in *McGlashan's History of the Donner Party*, pp. 206-15 and in King, *Winter of Entrapment*, Chapter 10.

King, Joseph. *Winter of Entrapment: A New Look at the Donner Party*. (K&K Publications, Lafayette, California, 1992).

Korns, J. Roderic and Morgan, Dale; updated by Will Bagley and Harold Schindler. *West From Fort Bridger: Pioneering of the Immigrant Trails Across Utah, 1846-1850*. (Utah State University Press, Logan, Utah, 1994).

Lavender, David. *The Overland Migrations: Settlers to Oregon, California and Utah*. (Division of Publications, National Park Service, 1980).

Lavender, David. *Westward Vision: The Story of the Oregon Trail*. (University of Nebraska Press, Lincoln and London, 1963/Bison Book edition, 1985).

Lienhard, Heinrich. *From St. Louis to Sutter's Fort*. Translated and edited by Erwin G. and Elisabeth Gudde from the original German. (University of Oklahoma Press, Norman, 1961).

MacMahon, James A. *Deserts: A National Audubon Society Nature Guide*. (Alfred A. Knopf, New York, 1985/Ninth edition, 1997).

Mattes, Merrill J. *The Great Platte River Road*. (University of Nebraska Press, *Lincoln and London, 1969/ Bison Book printing, 1987)*.

McGlashan, C.F. *History of the Donner Party: A Tragedy of the Sierra*. (Stanford University Press; Stanford, California; 1947/1993). A reproduction of the 1880 second edition of McGlashan's classic work.

McGlashan, M. Nona. *Give Me a Mountain Meadow: A Biographical Account of a Remarkable Man*. (Valley Publishers, Fresno, 1977). Kindly loaned to the author by Carol Hines of Reno.

McGlashan, M. Nona and Betty H., editors. *From the Desk of Truckee's C. F. McGlashan*. (Truckee-Donner Historical Society; Truckee, California; 1986). Kindly loaned to the author by Jim and Marylee Glace of Truckee.

McFee, John. *Basin and Range*. (The Noonday Press; Farrar, Straus and Giroux; New York; 1980/1994 edition).

Miluck, Nancy Christian. *Nevada: This is Our*

Land. (Dragon Enterprises; Genoa, Nevada; 1994).

Morgan, Dale L. *Overland in 1846: Diaries and Letters of the California Trail*, Vols. I and II. (University of Nebraska Press, London and Lincoln, 1963).

Morgan, Dale L. *Jedediah Smith and the Opening of the West*. (University of Nebraska Press, Lincoln and London, 1953/Bison Book 1964.)

Murphey, Mary. "Mary Murphey's Story," a letter published in Jack Steed's *The Donner Party Rescue Site: Johnson's Ranch on Bear River*, pp. 15-18; Also in Steed's book on pp. 18-20, Mary Murphey's letter to "Dear Uncles, Aunts and Cousins" on May 25, 1847 is printed.

Murphy, Virginia Reed. *Across the Plains In The Donner Party: A Personal Narrative of the Overland Trip to California, 1846-47*. Originally published as a magazine article and then as a book. (1891 edition reprinted by Outbooks, Golden, Colorado, 1980).

Paden, Irene D. *In the Wake of the Prairie Schooner*. (The Patrice Press, St. Louis, 1990).

Paden, Irene D. *Prairie Schooner Detours*. (The Patrice Press, St. Louis, 1990).

Paine, Albert Bigelow. *Mark Twain: A Biography: The Personal and Literary Life of Samuel Langhorne Clemens*. (Harper and Brothers, New York, 1912).

Reed, Virginia. See Murphy, Virginia Reed.

Reynolds, David S.; *Walt Whitman's America*. (Alfred A. Knopf, New York, 1995).

Steed, Jack and Richard *Donner Party Rescue Site: Johnson's Ranch on The Bear River*, third edition. (self-published, Sacramento, 1993).

Stegner, Wallace. *When The Bluebird Sings To The Lemonade Springs*. (Penguin Books, New York, 1992).

Stewart, George R. *Ordeal by Hunger*. (Houghton Mifflin Co., Boston, 1963/1988).

Stewart, George R. *The California Trail: An Epic With Many Heroes*. (University of Nebraska Press, Lincoln and London, 1962/1983 Bison Book edition).

Stookey, Dr. Walter M. *Fatal Decision: The Tragic Story of the Donner Party*. (Deseret Book Co, Salt Lake City, 1950). Kindly loaned to the author by Jeannie Rasmussen of Sparks, Nevada, and later by Dr. Chuck Andrus of Reno.

Swan, John A. *A Trip to the Gold Mines of California in 1848*, ed. by John A. Hussey. (The Book Club of California, San Francisco, 1960).

Thornton, Jesse Quinn, *Oregon and California in 1848*, 2 vols. (Harper and Bros., New York, 1849).

Thornton, Jesse Quinn. *Camp of Death*. (Outbooks, Golden, Colorado).

Twain, Mark (Samuel L. Clemens). *The Autobiography of Mark Twain*. (Harper, New York, 1959).

Unruh, John D. Jr. *The Plains Across: The Overland Emigrants and the Trans-Mississippi West, 1840-60*. (University of Illinois Press, Urbana and Chicago, 1979/1993).

Werner, Emmy E. *Pioneer Children on the Journey West*. The Donner Party portion of the book was adapted by Werner into a radio play, performed at California Trail Days, August, 1996, under her direction and narration.

Wheeler, Sessions S. *The Nevada Desert*. (Caxton Printers Ltd.; Caldwell, Idaho, 1971).

Wild, Peter, editor. *The Desert Reader*. (University of Utah Press; Salt Lake City, 1991).

Wise, H.A. *Los Gringos, or an Inside View of Mexico and California, With Wanderings in Peru, Chili and Polynesia*. (Baker & Scribner, 1850).

Documents

Andrews, Thomas Franklin. "The Controversial Career of Lansford Warren Hastings: Pioneer California Promoter and Emigrant Guide." (University of Southern California Ph.D. dissertation, 1970, University Microfilms.) Kindly loaned to the author by William Chrystal of Reno.

The George McKinstry Papers, California State Library, Sacramento.

Fort Sutter Documents Collection, Reed Papers from the Patty Reed Lewis Estate, California State Department of Parks and Recreation, Sacramento.

The Bancroft Library collection, Berkeley, California.

Newspaper, magazine and newsletter articles

Bagley, Will. "Lansford Warren Hastings: Scoundrel or Visionary?" *Overland Journal* of the California Trail Association, Vol. 12, No. 1, (1994), p. 18.

Clark, Nicholas. "Nicholas Clark: One of the Rescuers of the Donner Party." *Truckee Republican*, October 24, 1885.

Graves, Mary Ann. "Letter from California," May 22, 1847, to Levi Fosdick. *Illinois Gazette* (Locon, Illinois), September 25, 1847, reprinted by Kristin Johnson in *Crossroads*, summer, 1994.

Grayson, Donald K. "Donner Party Deaths: A Demographic Assessment." *Journal of Anthropological Research*, (fall, 1990) pgs. 223-242.

Hoshide, Robert K. "Salt Desert Trails Revisited." *Crossroads*, the magazine of the Crossroads Chapter of the Oregon-California Trails Association, summer 1994.

Johnson, Kristin. "The Pioneer Palace Car: Adventures in Western Mythmaking." *Crossroads*, summer, 1994; and "William B. Ide Describes the Pioneer Palace Car in 1845." *Crossroads*, summer 1994.

Johnson, Kristin. "Luke Halloran" by Kristin Johnson, *Crossroads*, spring/summer 1996.

Laxalt, Robert. "Emigrants on the California Trail." *Reno Gazette-Journal*, October 31, 1995, p. 1A.

Mullen, Frank W. "On the Trail with the Donner Party, 1846-1996," a year-long, thrice-weekly newspaper series following the wagon train members day-by-day from May 12, 1846 (publication began May 12, 1996) to May 11, 1847 (the last episode ran May 11, 1997). *Reno Gazette-Journal*, Reno, Nevada, a Gannett newspaper. This book is based on the series.

Pigney, Joseph *For Fear We Shall Perish: The Story of the Donner Party Disaster*. (Dutton, New York, 1961).

Oregon-California Trails Association, P.O. Box 1019, Independence, Missouri 64051. Publishers of *Overland Journal* and *News of the Plains*.

Reed, James F. "The Snow-Bound Starved Emigrants of 1846." *Pacific Rural Press*, March 25, 1871 and April 1, 1871. A copy of Reed's manuscript is at the Bancroft Library; the original is in the Sutter's Fort Documents Collection.

Reed, James F. Letter written by Reed at Fort Bridger, July 31, 1846. *Sangamon Journal*, November 5, 1846. Photocopy of article provided by Maurice Simmons of Springfield. The letter is also reprinted in Morgan, *Overland in 1846*.

Reed, James F. Letter from Reed to his brother in law James W. Keyes of Springfield, May 20, 1847. Excerpts published in the *Illinois State Register*, Springfield Illinois, July 5, 1849. Photocopy provided by Maurice Simmons, Springfield. Also found in Morgan, *Overland in 1846*, *Surviving the Donner Party*, Discover magazine

Trudeau, John Baptiste. Statement given to a reporter of a St. Louis newspaper and reprinted in the San Francisco *Morning Call*, Sunday, October 11, 1891, p. 16. "One of the

Donners: A Chat with a Survivor of the Ill-Fated Donner Party."   Name cited as Juan Baptiste Truvido and Juan Baptiste Tuxido in this article.

Documentary videos and movies

Burns, Ric. "The Donner Party," a PBS video documentary written and directed by Ric Burns. (Steeplechase Films, New York, 1994).

"The Donner Party," produced for the series "The Real West," initially shown in January 1994, on A&E Cable TV, with host Kenny Rogers, narrators Roger McGrath of the University of California at Los Angeles, Martin Ridge of California Institute of Technology, and Joseph A. King. (Greystone Productions, Los Angeles).

Hardesty, Donald L. "On the Trail of the Tragedy," a documentary about the University of Nevada, Reno, archaeological work at the Donner camp near Alder Creek.

"One More Mountain," Disney Productions, a film shown on ABC-TV in March 1994, a fictional treatment.

Fiction books

Chapman, Mabel. *At Great Price*, a historical novel about Tamsen Donner.

Galloway, David. *Tamsen*, a novel about the woman and the trek. (San Diego, 1982).

Laurgaard, Rachel R. *Patty Reed's Doll*, a children's book.

Maino, Jeannette Gould. *Left Hand Turn: A Story of the Donner Party Women*. (Privately printed; Modesto, California; 1987).

Rhodes, Richard. *The Ungodly: A Novel of the Donner Party*. (New York, 1973).

Sutton, Margaret. *Palace Wagon Family*. New York, 1957. A children's book.

Whitman, Ruth. *A Woman's Journey*. (Cambridge, Massachusetts, 1985).

Index

Key: Names of Members of the Donner Party appear in SMALL CAPITALS; page numbers from books, diaries, journals, and other writings are shown in **boldface**; and all drawings, photographs, and other art are in *italics*.

Index of People in the Donner Party

Arranged by family or group
— name, age, and relationship to group.
Italics indicate those who died.
Some ages are approximate.

Name	Age	Relationship
James F. Reed	46	head of family, husband of Margaret Reed, left group 10/46
Margaret Reed	32	wife of James Reed
Sarah Keyes	70	*Margaret Reed's mother*
Virginia Reed	13	daughter of Margaret Reed by former marriage
Martha (Patty) Reed	8	daughter of Reeds
James Reed Jr.	5	son of Reeds
Thomas Reed	3	son of Reeds
Hiram Miller	29	teamster for Reeds, left group early
Walter Herron	27	teamster for Reeds, left group to join James Reed
Eliza Williams	31	sister of Baylis Williams, worked for Reeds
Baylis Williams	25	*worked for Reeds*
James Smith	25	*teamster for Reeds*
Milt Elliott	28	
William McCutcheon	30	husband of Amanda, went to Sutter's Fort with Stanton
Amanda McCutcheon	24	wife of William McCutcheon
Harriet McCutcheon	2	*daughter of McCutcheons*
Franklin W. Graves	57	*head of family*
Elizabeth Graves	45	*wife of Franklin W. Graves*
Sarah Graves Fosdick	21	wife of Jay Fosdick, daughter of Graves
Jay Fosdick	23	*husband of Sarah Graves Fosdick*
Mary Graves	19	daughter of Graves
William Graves	17	son of Graves
Eleanor Graves	14	daughter of Graves
Lovina Graves	12	daughter of Graves
Nancy Graves	9	daughter of Graves
Jonathan Graves	7	son of Graves
Franklin W. Graves Jr.	5	*son of Graves*
Elizabeth Graves	1	daughter of Graves
John Snyder	25	*teamster for Graves, killed by James Reed*
Lavinah Murphy	36	*widow, Murphy family*
Sarah Murphy Foster	19	daughter of Lavinah Murphy, wife of William Foster
William Foster	30	husband of Sarah Murphy Foster
George Foster	1	*son of Fosters*
Harriet Murphy Pike	18	daughter of Lavinah Murphy, wife of William Pike
William Pike	25	*husband of Harriet Pike, accidentally shot*
Naomi Pike	2	daughter of Pikes
Catherine Pike	1	*daughter of Pikes*
William Murphy	10	son of Lavinah Murphy
Landrum Murphy	16	*son of Lavinah Murphy*
Mary Murphy	14	daughter of Lavinah Murphy
Lemuel Murphy	12	*son of Lavinah Murphy*
Simon Murphy	8	son of Lavinah Murphy
William Eddy	28	head of family, only survivor of family
Eleanor Eddy	25	*wife of William Eddy*
James Eddy	3	*son of Eddys*
Margaret Eddy	1	*daughter of Eddys*

Jacob Donner	*56*	*head of family, brother of George Donner*
Elizabeth Donner	*45*	*wife of Jacob Donner*
Solomon Hook	13	son of Elizabeth Donner by former marriage
William Hook	*12*	*son of Elizabeth Donner by former marriage*
George Donner	8	son of Jacob Donners
Mary Donner	8	daughter of Jacob Donners
Isaac Donner	*5*	*son of Jacob Donners*
Samuel Donner	*4*	*son of Jacob Donners*
Lewis Donner	*3*	*son of Jacob Donners*
George Donner	62	*head of family, husband of Tamsen, wagon master*
Tamsen Donner	*44*	*wife of George Donner*
Elitha Donner	13	daughter of George Donner by former marriage
Leanna Donner	11	daughter of George Donner by former marriage
Frances Donner	6	daughter of George Donners
Georgia Donner	4	daughter of George Donners
Eliza Donner	3	daughter of George Donners
John Baptiste Trudeau	18	teamster for Donners
Noah James	16	teamster for Donners
Samuel Shoemaker	*25*	*teamster for Donners*
Milford (Milt) Elliot	*28*	*traveled with George Donners*
John Denton	*28*	*traveled with George Donners*
Luke Halloran	*25*	*invalid traveling with Donners*
Lewis Keseberg	32	head of family, husband of Philippine
Philippine Keseberg	23	wife of Lewis Keseberg
Ada Keseberg	*3*	*daughter of Kesebergs*
Lewis Keseberg Jr.	*1*	*son of Kesebergs*
Mr. Hardkoop	*60*	*friend of Keseberg*
Charles Burger	*30*	*teamster*
Wolfinger	*26*	*husband of Doris Wolfinger*
Doris Wolfinger	18	wife of Jacob Wolfinger
Patrick Breen	51	head of family, husband of Margaret Breen
Margaret Breen	40	wife of Patrick Breen
John Breen	14	son of Breens
Edward Breen	13	son of Breens
Patrick Breen Jr.	9	son of Breens
Simon Breen	8	son of Breens
James Breen	5	son of Breens
Peter Breen	3	son of Breens
Isabella Breen	1	daughter of Breens
Augustus Spitzer	*30*	*Reinhart's partner*
Joseph Reinhardt	*30*	*Spitzer's partner*
Antonio	*23*	*hired hand*
Patrick Dolan	*35*	*bachelor*
Luis	*?*	*Indian guide killed by William Foster*
Salvador	*?*	*Indian guide killed by William Foster*
Charles Stanton	*35*	*traveling without family*

JEN WILLIAMS started writing about pirates and dragons as a young girl and hasn't ever stopped. Her short stories have featured in numerous anthologies and her debut novel, *The Copper Promise*, was published in 2014 to huge acclaim. Jen was nominated in the Best Newcomer category at the 2015 British Fantasy Awards and her second novel, *The Iron Ghost*, was shortlisted for the 2016 British Fantasy Awards Novel of the Year award. All novels in the Copper Cat Trilogy, *The Copper Promise*, *The Iron Ghost*, and *The Silver Tide*, are available from Headline in the UK. *The Ninth Rain* is the first electrifying new novel of The Winnowing Flame Trilogy. Jen lives in London with her partner and their cat.

Praise for Jen Williams' Copper Cat Trilogy:

'A fresh take on classic tropes . . . 21st century fantasy at its best'
SFX magazine

'A highly inventive, vibrant high fantasy with a cast you can care about . . . There is never a dull moment'
The British Fantasy Society

'Williams has thrown out the rulebook and injected a fun tone into epic fantasy without lightening or watering down the excitement and adventure . . . Highly recommended'
Independent

'A fast-paced and original new voice in heroic fantasy'
Adrian Tchaikovsky

'Expect dead gods, mad magic, piracy on the high seas, peculiar turns and pure fantasy fun'
Starburst magazine

'The characterisation is second to none, and there are some great new innovations and interesting reworkings of old tropes . . . This book may have been based on the promise of copper but it delivers gold'   Quicksilver on Goodreads

'It is a *killer* of a fantasy novel that is indicative of how the classic genre of sword and sorcery is not only still very much alive, but also still the best the genre has to offer'
                              www.leocristea.wordpress.com

THE
NINTH
RAIN

JEN WILLIAMS

HEADLINE

HEADLINE PUBLISHING GROUP
An Hachette UK Company
Carmelite House
50 Victoria Embankment
London EC4Y 0DZ

www.headline.co.uk
www.hachette.co.uk

For Paul
(known to most as Wills)

With love from
Your skin & blister

You ask me to start at the beginning, Marin, my dear, but you do not know what you ask. Beginnings are very elusive things, almost as elusive as true endings. Where do I start? How to unpick a tapestry such as this? There was a thread that started it all, of course, but I will have to go back a good long way; beyond the scope of your young life, beyond the scope of even mine. Don't tell me I didn't warn you.

Extract from the private letters of Master Marin de Grazon, from Lady Vincenza 'Vintage' de Grazon

Prologue

Two hundred years ago

'Will we get into trouble?'

Hestillion took hold of the boy's hand and gave it a quick squeeze. When he looked up at her, his eyes were wide and glassy – he was afraid. The few humans who came to Ebora generally were. She favoured him with a smile and they walked a little faster down the echoing corridor. To either side of them enormous oil paintings hung on the walls, dusty and grey. A few of them had been covered with sheets, like corpses.

'Of course not, Louis. You are with me, aren't you? I can go anywhere in the palace I like, and you are my friend.'

'I've heard that people can go mad, just looking at it.' He paused, as if sensing that he might have said something wrong. 'Not Eborans, I mean. Other people, from outside.'

Hestillion smiled again, more genuinely this time. She had sensed this from the delegates' dreams. Ygseril sat at the centre of their night wanderings, usually unseen but always there, his roots creeping in at the corners. They were all afraid of him: bad dreams conjured by thousands of years' worth of the stories and rumours. Hestillion had kept herself carefully hidden

3

while exploring their nightmares. Humans did not care for the Eboran art of dream-walking.

'It is quite a startling sight, I promise you that, but it cannot harm you.' In truth, the boy would already have seen Ygseril, at least partly. The tree-god's great cloud of silvery branches burst up above the roof of the palace, and it was possible to see it from the Wall, and even the foothills of the mountains; or so she had been told. The boy and his father, the wine merchant, could hardly have missed it as they made their way into Ebora. They would have found themselves watching the tree-god as they rode their tough little mountain ponies down into the valley, wine sloshing rhythmically inside wooden casks. Hestillion had seen that in their dreams, too. 'Here we are, look.'

At the end of the corridor was a set of elaborately carved double doors. Once, the phoenixes and dragons etched into the wood would have been painted gold, their eyes burning bright and every tooth and claw and talon picked out in mother-of-pearl, but it had all peeled off or been worn away, left as dusty and as sad as everything else in Ebora. Hestillion leaned her weight on one of the doors and it creaked slowly open, showering them in a light rain of dust. Inside was the cavernous Hall of Roots. She waited for Louis to gather himself.

'I . . . oh, it's . . .' He reached up as if to take off his cap, then realised he had left it in his room. 'My lady Hestillion, this is the biggest place I've ever seen!'

Hestillion nodded. She didn't doubt that it was. The Hall of Roots sat at the centre of the palace, which itself sat in the centre of Ebora. The floor under their feet was pale green marble etched with gold – this, at least, had yet to be worn away – and above them the ceiling was a glittering lattice of crystal and finely spun lead, letting in the day's weak sunshine. And bursting out of the marble was Ygseril himself; ancient grey-green bark, rippled and twisted, a curling confusion of roots that sprawled in every direction, and branches, high above them, reaching through the circular hole in the roof, empty of leaves. Little pieces of blue sky glittered there, cut into shards by the arms of Ygseril. The bark on the trunk of the tree was wrinkled and ridged, like the skin of a desiccated corpse. Which was, she supposed, entirely appropriate.

'What do you think?' she pressed. 'What do you think of our god?'

Louis twisted his lips together, obviously trying to think of some answer that would please her. Hestillion held her impatience inside. Sometimes she felt like she could reach in and pluck the stuttering thoughts from the minds of these slow-witted visitors. Humans were just so *uncomplicated*.

'It is very fine, Lady Hestillion,' he said eventually. 'I've never seen anything like it, not even in the deepest vine forests, and my father says that's where the oldest trees in all of Sarn grow.'

'Well, strictly speaking, he is not really a tree.' Hestillion walked Louis across the marble floor, towards the place where the roots began. The boy's leather boots made odd flat notes of his footsteps, while her silk slippers gave only the faintest whisper. 'He is the heart, the protector, the mother and father of Ebora. The tree-god feeds us with his roots, he exalts us in his branches. When our enemy the Jure'lia came last, the Eighth Rain fell from his branches and the worm people were scoured from all of Sarn.' She paused, pursing her lips, not adding: *and then Ygseril died, and left us all to die too.*

'The Eighth Rain, when the last war-beasts were born!' Louis stared up at the vast breadth of the trunk looming above them, a smile on his round, honest face. 'The last great battle. My dad said that the Eboran warriors wore armour so bright no one could look at it, that they rode on the backs of snowy white griffins, and their swords blazed with fire. The great pestilence of the Jure'lia queen and the worm people was driven back and her Behemoths were scattered to pieces.' He stopped. In his enthusiasm for the old battle stories he had finally relaxed in her presence. 'The corpse moon frightens me,' he confided. 'My nan says that if you should catch it winking at you, you'll die by the next sunset.'

Peasant nonsense, thought Hestillion. The corpse moon was just another wrecked Behemoth, caught in the sky like a fly in amber. They had reached the edge of the marble now, capped with an obsidian ring. Beyond that the roots twisted and tangled, rising up like the curved backs of silver-green sea monsters. When Hestillion made to step out onto the roots, Louis stopped, pulling back sharply on her hand.

'We mustn't!'

She looked at his wide eyes, and smiled. She let her hair fall over one shoulder, a shimmering length of pale gold, and threw him the obvious bait. 'Are you scared?'

The boy frowned, briefly outraged, and they stepped over onto the roots together. He stumbled at first, his boots too stiff to accommodate the rippling texture of the bark, while Hestillion had been climbing these roots as soon as she could walk. Carefully, she guided him further in, until they were close to the enormous bulk of the trunk itself – it filled their vision, a grey-green wall of ridges and whorls. This close it was almost possible to imagine you saw faces in the bark; the sorrowful faces, perhaps, of all the Eborans who had died since the Eighth Rain. The roots under their feet were densely packed, spiralling down into the unseen dark below them. Hestillion knelt, gathering her silk robe to one side so that it wouldn't get too creased. She tugged her wide yellow belt free of her waist and then wound it around her right arm, covering her sleeve and tying the end under her armpit.

'Come, kneel next to me.'

Louis looked unsure again, and Hestillion found she could almost read the thoughts on his face. Part of him baulked at the idea of kneeling before a foreign god – even a dead one. She gave him her sunniest smile.

6

'Just for fun. Just for a moment.'

Nodding, he knelt on the roots next to her, with somewhat less grace than she had managed. He turned to her, perhaps to make some comment on the strangely slick texture of the wood under his hands, and Hestillion slipped the knife from within her robe, baring it to the subdued light of the Hall of Roots. It was so sharp that she merely had to press it to his throat – she doubted he even saw the blade, so quickly was it over – and in less than a moment the boy had fallen onto his back, blood bubbling thick and red against his fingers. He shivered and kicked, an expression of faint puzzlement on his face, and Hestillion leaned back as far as she could, looking up at the distant branches.

'Blood for you!' She took a slow breath. The blood had saturated the belt on her arm and it was rapidly sinking into the silk below – so much for keeping it clean. 'Life blood for your roots! I pledge you this and more!'

'Hest!'

The shout came from across the hall. She turned back to see her brother Tormalin standing by the half-open door, a slim shape in the dusty gloom, his black hair like ink against a page. Even from this distance she could see the expression of alarm on his face.

'Hestillion, what have you done?' He started to run to her. Hestillion looked down at the body of the wine merchant's boy, his blood black against the roots, and then up at the branches. There was no answering voice, no fresh buds or running sap. The god was still dead.

'Nothing,' she said bitterly. 'I've done nothing at all.'

'Sister.' He had reached the edge of the roots, and now she could see how he was trying to hide his horror at what she had done, his face carefully blank. It only made her angrier. 'Sister, they . . . they have already tried that.'

1

Fifty years ago

Tormalin shifted the pack on his back and adjusted his sword belt. He could hear, quite clearly, the sound of a carriage approaching him from behind, but for now he was content to ignore it and the inevitable confrontation it would bring with it. Instead, he looked at the deserted thoroughfare ahead of him, and the corpse moon hanging in the sky, silver in the early afternoon light.

Once this had been one of the greatest streets in the city. Almost all of Ebora's nobles would have kept a house or two here, and the road would have been filled with carriages and horses, with servants running errands, with carts selling goods from across Sarn, with Eboran ladies, their faces hidden by veils or their hair twisted into towering, elaborate shapes – depending on the fashion that week – and Eboran men clothed in silk, carrying exquisite swords. Now the road was broken, and weeds were growing up through the stone wherever you looked. There were no people here – those few still left alive had moved inward, towards the central palace – but there were wolves. Tormalin had already felt the presence of a couple, matching his stride just out of sight, a pair of yellow eyes glaring balefully from the shadows of a ruined mansion. Weeds and wolves – that was all that was left of glorious Ebora.

The carriage was closer now, the sharp clip of the horses' hooves painfully loud in the heavy silence. Tormalin sighed, still determined not to look. Far in the distance was the pale line of the Wall. When he reached it, he would spend the night in the sentry tower. When had the sentry towers last been manned? Certainly no one left in the palace would know. The crimson flux was their more immediate concern.

The carriage stopped, and the door clattered open. He didn't hear anyone step out, but then she had always walked silently.

'Tormalin!'

He turned, plastering a tight smile on his face. 'Sister.'

She wore yellow silk, embroidered with black dragons. It was the wrong colour for her – the yellow was too lurid against her pale golden hair, and her skin looked like parchment. Even so, she was the brightest thing on the blighted, wolf-infested road.

'I can't believe you are actually going to do this.' She walked swiftly over to him, holding her robe out of the way of her slippered feet, stepping gracefully over cracks. 'You have done some stupid, selfish things in your time, but this?'

Tormalin lifted his eyes to the carriage driver, who was very carefully not looking at them. He was a man from the plains, the ruddy skin of his face shadowed by a wide-brimmed cap. A human servant; one of a handful left in Ebora, surely. For a moment, Tormalin was struck by how strange he and his sister must look to him, how alien. Eborans were taller than humans, long-limbed but graceful with it, while their skin – whatever colour it happened to be – shone like finely grained wood. Humans looked so . . . dowdy in comparison. And then there were the eyes, of course. Humans were never keen on Eboran

10

eyes. Tormalin grimaced and turned his attention back to his sister.

'I've been talking about this for years, Hest. I've spent the last month putting my affairs in order, collecting maps, organising my travel. Have you really just turned up to express your surprise now?'

She stood in front of him, a full head shorter than him, her eyes blazing. Like his, they were the colour of dried blood, or old wine.

'You are running away,' she said. 'Abandoning us all here, to waste away to nothing.'

'I will do great good for Ebora,' he replied, clearing his throat. 'I intend to travel to all the great seats of power. I will open new trade routes, and spread word of our plight. Help will come to us, eventually.'

'That is not what you intend to do at all!' Somewhere in the distance, a wolf howled. 'Great seats of power? Whoring and drinking in disreputable taverns, more like.' She leaned closer. 'You do not intend to come back at all.'

'Thanks to you it's been decades since we've had any decent wine in the palace, and as for whoring . . .' He caught the expression on her face and looked away. 'Ah. Well. I thought I felt you in my dreams last night, little sister. You are getting very good. I didn't see you, not even once.'

This attempt at flattery only enraged her further. 'In the last three weeks, the final four members of the high council have come down with the flux. Lady Rellistin coughs her lungs into her handkerchief at every meeting, while her skin breaks and bleeds, and those that are left wander the palace, just watching us all die slowly, fading away into nothing. Aldasair, your own cousin, stopped speaking to anyone months ago, and Ygseril is a dead sentry, watching over the final years of—'

'And what do you expect me to do about it?' With some difficulty he lowered his voice, glancing at the carriage driver

11

again. 'What can I do, Hest? What can *you* do? I will not stay here and watch them all die. I do not want to witness everything falling apart. Does that make me a coward?' He raised his arms and dropped them. 'Then I will be a coward, gladly. I want to get out there, beyond the Wall, and see the world before the flux takes me too. I could have another hundred years to live yet, and I do not want to spend them here. Without Ygseril –' he paused, swallowing down a surge of sorrow so strong he could almost taste it – 'we'll fade away, become decrepit, broken, old.' He gestured at the deserted road and the ruined houses, their windows like empty eye sockets. 'What Ebora once was, Hestillion . . .' he softened his voice, not wanting to hurt her, not when this was already so hard – 'it doesn't exist any more. It is a memory, and it will not return. Our time is over, Hest. Old age or the flux will get us eventually. So come with me. There's so much to see, so many places where people are *living*. Come with me.'

'Tormalin the Oathless,' she spat, taking a step away from him. 'That's what they called you, because you were feckless and a layabout, and I thought, how dare they call my brother so? Even in jest. But they were right. You care about nothing but yourself, Oathless one.'

'I care about you, sister.' Tormalin suddenly felt very tired, and he had a long walk to find shelter before nightfall. He wished that she'd never followed him out here, that her stubbornness had let them avoid this conversation. 'But no, I don't care enough to stay here and watch you all die. I just can't do it, Hest.' He cleared his throat, trying to hide the shaking of his voice. 'I just can't.'

A desolate wind blew down the thoroughfare, filling the silence between them with the cold sound of dry leaves rustling against stone. For a moment Tormalin felt dizzy, as though he stood on the edge of a precipice, a great empty space pulling him forward. And then Hestillion turned away from him and walked back to the carriage. She climbed inside, and the last thing he saw of his sister was her delicate white foot encased in its yellow silk slipper. The driver brought the horses round – they were restless and glad to leave, clearly smelling wolves nearby – and the carriage left, moving at a fair clip.

He watched them go for a few moments; the only living thing in a dead landscape, the silver branches of Ygseril a frozen cloud behind them. And then he walked away.

Tormalin paused at the top of a low hill. He had long since left the last trailing ruins of the city behind him, and had been travelling through rough scrubland for a day or so. Here and there were the remains of old carts, abandoned lines of them like snake bones in the dust, or the occasional shack that had once served visitors to Ebora. Tor had been impressed to see them still standing, even if a strong wind might shatter them to pieces at any moment; they were remnants from before the Carrion Wars, when humans still made the long journey to Ebora voluntarily. He himself had been little more than a child. Now, a deep purple dusk had settled across the scrubland and at the very edge of Ebora's ruined petticoats, the Wall loomed above him, its white stones a drab lilac in the fading light.

Tor snorted. This was it. Once he was beyond the Wall he did not intend to come back – for all that he'd claimed to Hestillion, he was no fool. Ebora was a disease, and they were all infected. He had to get out while there were still some pleasures to be had, before he was the one slowly coughing himself to death in a finely appointed bedroom.

Far to the right, a watchtower sprouted from the Wall like a canine tooth, sharp and jagged against the shadow of the mountain. The windows were all dark, but it was still just light enough to see the steps carved there. Once he had a roof over his head he would make a fire and set himself up for the evening. He imagined how he might appear to an observer; the lone adventurer, heading off to places unknown, his storied sword sheathed against the night but ready to be released at the first hint of danger. He lifted his chin, and pictured the sharp angles of his face lit by the eerie glow of the sickle moon, his shining black hair a glossy slick even restrained in its tail. He almost wished he could see himself.

His spirits lifted at the thought of his own adventurousness, he made his way up the steps, finding a new burst of energy at the end of this long day. The tower door was wedged half open with piles of dry leaves and other debris from the forest. If he'd been paying attention, he'd have noted that the leaves had recently been pushed to one side, and that within the tower all was not as dark as it should have been, but Tor was thinking of the wineskin in his pack and the round of cheese wrapped in pale wax. He'd been saving them for the next time he had a roof over his head, and he'd decided that this ramshackle tower counted well enough.

He followed the circular steps up to the tower room. The door here was shut, but he elbowed it open easily enough, half falling through into the circular space beyond.

Movement, scuffling, and light. He had half drawn his sword before he recognised the scruffy shape by the far window as human – a man, his dark eyes bright in a dirty face. There was a small smoky fire in the middle of the room, the two windows covered over with broken boards and rags. A wave of irritation followed close on the back of his initial alarm; he had not expected to see humans in this place.

'What are you doing here?' Tor paused, and pushed his sword back into its scabbard. He looked around the tower room. There were signs that the place had been inhabited for a short time at least – the bones of small fowl littered the stone floor, their ends gnawed. Dirty rags and two small tin bowls,

14

crusted with something, and a half-empty bottle of some dark liquid. Tor cleared his throat.

'Well? Do you not speak?'

The man had greasy yellow hair and a suggestion of a yellow beard. He still stood pressed against the wall, but his shoulders abruptly drooped, as though the energy he'd been counting on to flee had left him.

'If you will not speak, I will have to share your fire.' Tor pushed away a pile of rags with his boot and carefully seated himself on the floor, his legs crossed. It occurred to him that if he got his wineskin out now he would feel compelled to share it with the man. He resolved to save it one more night. Instead, he shouldered off his pack and reached inside it for his small travel teapot. The fire was pathetic but with a handful of the dried leaves he had brought for the purpose, it was soon looking a little brighter. The water would boil eventually.

The man was still staring at him. Tor busied himself with emptying a small quantity of his water supply into a shallow tin bowl, and searching through his bag for one of the compact bags of tea he had packed.

'Eboran.' The man's voice was a rusted hinge, and he spoke a variety of plains speech Tor knew well. He wondered how long it had been since the man had spoken to anyone. 'Blood sucker. Murderer.'

Tor cleared his throat and switched to the man's plains dialect. 'It's like that, is it?' He sighed and sat back from the fire and his teapot. 'I was going to offer you tea, old man.'

'You call me old?' The man laughed. 'You? My grandfather told me stories of the Carrion Wars. You bloodsuckers. Eatin' people alive on the battlefield, that's what my grandfather said.'

Tor thought of the sword again. The man was trespassing on Eboran land, technically.

'Your grandfather would not have been alive. The Carrion Wars were over three hundred years ago.'

None of them would have been alive then, of course, yet they all still acted as though it were a personal insult. Why did they have to pass the memory on? Down through the years they passed on the stories, like they passed on brown eyes, or ears that stuck out. Why couldn't they just forget?

'It wasn't like that.' Tor poked at the tin bowl, annoyed with how tight his voice sounded. Abruptly, he wished that the windows weren't boarded up. He was stuck in here with the smell of the man. 'No one wanted . . . when Ygseril died . . . he had always fed us, nourished us. Without him, we were left with the death of our entire people. A slow fading into nothing.'

The man snorted with amusement. Amazingly, he came over to the fire and crouched there.

'Your tree-god died, aye, and took your precious sap away with it. Maybe you all should have died then, rather than getting a taste for our blood. Maybe that was what should have happened.'

The man settled himself, his dark eyes watching Tor closely, as though he expected an explanation of some sort. An explanation for generations of genocide.

'What are you doing up here? This is an outpost. Not a refuge for tramps.'

The man shrugged. From under a pile of rags he produced a grease-smeared silver bottle. He uncapped it and took a swig. Tor caught a whiff of strong alcohol.

'I'm going to see my daughter,' he said. 'Been away for years. Earning coin, and then losing it. Time to go home, see what's what. See who's still alive. My people had a settlement in the forest west of here. I'll be lucky if you Eborans have left anyone alive there, I suppose.'

'Your people live in a forest?' Tor raised his eyebrows. 'A quiet one, I hope?'

The man's dirty face creased into half a smile. 'Not as quiet as we'd like, but where is, now? This world is poisoned. Oh, we have thick strong walls, don't you worry about that. Or at least, we did.'

'Why leave your family for so long?' Tor was thinking of Hestillion. The faint scuff of yellow slippers, the scent of her weaving through his dreams. Dream-walking had always been her particular talent.

'Ah, I was a different man then,' he replied, as though that explained everything. 'Are you going to take my blood?'

Tor scowled. 'As I'm sure you know, human blood wasn't the boon it was thought to be. There is no true replacement for Ygseril's sap, after all. Those who overindulged . . . suffered for it. There are arrangements now. Agreements with humans, for whom we care.' He sat up a little straighter. If he'd chosen to walk to another watchtower, he could be drinking his wine now. 'They are compensated, and we continue to use the blood in . . . small doses.' He didn't add that it hardly mattered – the crimson flux seemed largely unconcerned with exactly *how* much blood you had consumed, after all. 'It's not very helpful when you try and make everything sound sordid.'

The man bellowed with laughter, rocking back and forth and clutching at his knees. Tor said nothing, letting the man wear himself out. He went back to preparing tea. When the man's laughs had died down to faint snifflings, Tor pulled out two clay cups from his bag and held them up.

'Will you drink tea with Eboran scum?'

For a moment the man said nothing at all, although his face grew very still. The small amount of water in the shallow tin bowl was hot, so Tor poured it into the pot, dousing the shrivelled leaves. A warm, spicy scent rose from the pot, almost immediately lost in the sour-sweat smell of the room.

'I saw your sword,' said the man. 'It's a fine one. You don't see swords like that any more. Where'd you get it?'

Tor frowned. Was he suggesting he'd stolen it? 'It was my

17

father's sword. Winnow-forged steel, if you must know. It's called the Ninth Rain.'

The man snorted at that. 'We haven't had the Ninth Rain yet. The last one was the eighth. I would have thought you'd remember that. Why call it the Ninth Rain?'

'It is a long and complicated story, one I do not wish to share with a random human who has already insulted me more than once.'

'I should kill you,' said the man quietly. 'One less Eboran. That would make the world safer for my daughter, wouldn't it?'

'You are quite welcome to try,' said Tor. 'Although I think having her father with her when she was growing through her tender years would have been a better effort at making the world safer for your daughter.'

The man grew quiet, then. When Tor offered him the tea he took it, nodding once in what might have been thanks, or perhaps acceptance. They drank in silence, and Tor watched the wisps of black smoke curling up near the ceiling, escaping through some crack up there. Eventually, the man lay down on his side of the fire with his back to Tor, and he supposed that was as much trust as he would get from a human. He pulled out his own bed roll, and made himself as comfortable as he could on the stony floor. There was a long way to travel yet, and likely worse places to sleep in the future.

Tor awoke to a stuffy darkness, a thin line of grey light leaking in at the edge of the window letting him know it was dawn. The man was still asleep next to the embers of their fire. Tor gathered his things, moving as silently as he could, and finally paused to stand over the man. The lines of his face looked impossibly deep, as if he'd lived a thousand lifetimes, instead of the laughably short amount of time allocated to humans. He wondered if the man would reach his daughter, or if he had a daughter at all. Would she even

18

want to know him? Some severed ties could not be mended. Not thinking too closely about what he was doing, he took a parcel of tea from his own pack and left it by the man's outflung arm, where he couldn't miss it when he woke. No doubt it would do him better than the evil substance in his silver bottle.

Outside, the world was silvered with faint light from the east, and his breath formed a cloud as he made his way down the steps – the steps on the far side of the Wall, this time. He tried to feel excited about this – he was walking beyond the border of Ebora, forever – but his back was stiff from a night sleeping on stone and all he could think was that he would be glad to be out of sight of the Wall. His dreams had been haunted by half-seen carved faces, made of delicate red stone, but he knew that inside they were hollow and rotten. It had not made for a restful sleep.

The far side of the Wall was blanketed with thick green forest, coming up to the very stones like a high tide. Quickly, Tor lost himself inside that forest, and once the Wall was out of sight he felt some of the tension leave his body. Walking steadily uphill, he knew that, eventually, he would meet the foothills of the Tarah-hut Mountains, and from there, he would find the western pass.

At around midday, the trees grew thinner and the ground rockier. Tor turned back, and was caught like a moon-mad hare by the sight of Ebora spread out below him. The crumbling buildings of the outer city were dust-grey and broken, the roads little more than a child's drawings in the dirt. Trees and scrubby bushes had colonised the walkways, dark patches of virulence, while over the distant palace the still form of Ygseril was a silver ghost, bare branches scratching at the sky.

'Why did you leave us?' Tor licked his lips, his mouth suddenly dry. 'Do you even see what you've done? Do you?'

Every bit as dead as the corpse moon hanging in the sky above him, the tree-god kept his silence. Tormalin the Oathless put his back to the great tree and walked away, sincerely hoping he would never look upon Ebora again.

2

Five years ago

You ask me, dear Marin, how I could get involved with so obvious a trouble-maker (with your usual tact, of course – I'm glad to see that my sister is still wasting money on your finishing school). I found him, if you must know, drunk as a lord outside a tavern, several empty bottles beside him in the dust. It was a sweltering day, and he had his face turned up to the sun, basking in it like a cat. Lying on the ground, a few inches from his long fingers, was the finest sword I had ever seen, thick with partially congealed blood. Well. You know how rare it is to see an Eboran, Marin, so I said to him, 'Darling, what by Sarn's blessed bones have you been up to?' He grinned up at me and said, 'Killing wild-touched monstrosities. Everyone here has bought me a drink for it. Will you buy me a drink?'

I ask you, how could you not love so obvious a trouble-maker? Sometimes I wonder that we are the same blood at all.

Extract from the private letters
of Master Marin de Grazon,
from Lady Vincenza 'Vintage' de Grazon

Vintage brought the crossbow up, relishing the familiar weight in her hands. She had, after some scuffling, secured a seat on a thick branch halfway up a tree and, some fifty feet away, she could see the pea-bug in the vine tree opposite, with no obstacles between it and her crossbow bolt. It was a big, slow-moving bastard; rather like an aphid, but the size of a tom-cat, with dark green blotches on its glistening skin – some Wild-touched abomination. It was hanging from the vine, translucent jaws busily tearing into the fat purple grape it had fixed between its forelegs. Her grape. One of the grapes she had spent, oh, only nearly thirty years cultivating and growing, refining and sorting, until her grapes and, more importantly, her wine, were considered the very best to come out of the vine forests.

And the little bastard was munching on it mindlessly. No appreciation at all.

Vintage took aim and squeezed the crossbow trigger, antici-pating the shudder and jump in her arms. The bolt flew true and easy, and the pea-bug burst like an over-filled water skin, pattering the tree and the vine with watery guts. Vintage grimaced, even as she felt a small flicker of satisfaction; the crossbow, designed by her brother so many years ago, still worked.

Vintage secured the weapon to her belt, before shimmying down the trunk with little concern for her patched leather trousers. She picked her way through the foliage to where the pea-bug had met its messy end. Judging from the damage to the plant around it, the creature had spent much of the day munching through her grapes, and had had a decent gnaw on the vine itself for good measure. This was gilly-vine, a particu-larly robust plant with branches as thick as her thigh in places, and grapes that grew to a full hand span across, but even it couldn't survive a sustained attack from pea-bugs.

'Trouble,' she murmured under her breath. 'That's what you are.'

There were no more pea-bugs that she could see, but even so, the sight of her decimated grapes had put a cold worm of worry in her gut. There shouldn't be any pea-bugs here, not in the untainted part of the vine forest. This was a quiet place, as free from danger as anywhere could be in Sarn – she had spent many years making sure of it.

Pushing her wide-brimmed hat on a little firmer, Vintage turned away and began to head to the west, where she knew a particular lookout tree to be located. She told herself that she was worrying too much, that she was getting more paranoid the older she got, but then she'd never been very good at resisting her impulses.

The forest was hot and green, and humming with life. She felt it on her skin and tasted it on her tongue – vital and always growing. The tall, fat trunks of the vine trees rose all around her, most of them wider than two men lying head to toe, their twisting branches curled around each other like drunken lords holding each other up after an especially hard night on the brandy. And the vines twisted around them all, huge, swollen fruit wherever she looked – purple and pink and red, pale green and deep yellow, some hidden in the shade and some basking in the shards of hot sun that made it down here, glowing like lamps.

She had just spied the looming shape of the lookout tree ahead, with the band of bright red paint round its middle, when she heard something crashing through the undergrowth towards her. Instinctively, her hand dropped to the crossbow at her belt, but the shape that emerged from the bushes to her right had a small white face, and blond hair stuck to a sweaty forehead. Vintage sighed.

'What are you doing out here, Bernhart?'

The boy boggled at her. He was, if she remembered correctly, around eleven years old and the youngest member of their staff. He wore soft brown and green linen, and there was a short bow slung over his back, but he'd forgotten to put his hat on.

'Lady Vincenza, Master Ezion asked me to come and find you.' He took a breath and wiped a hand across his sweaty forehead. 'They have business up at the house that they need you for.'

Vintage snorted. 'Business? Why would they need me for that? I told Ezi years ago that he could handle such things.' She narrowed her eyes at the lad. 'They don't want me out here in the vine forest. Isn't that right, my boy?'

His sweaty face turned faintly pink and when he spoke he stared fixedly at her right elbow. 'They said it was really important, m'lady.'

'Bernhart, on moon festival eve, who makes sure there are honey pastries on hand for all you little ruffians?'

Bernhart cleared his throat. 'They said you'd been out here for days now and it wasn't seemly for a lady of your years. M'lady.'

Vintage barked with laughter. 'Bernhart, promise me that when you're a grown man you'll have the good sense never to refer to a woman of forty with the phrase "a lady of your years". I promise it won't end well, my dear.' She sighed, looking at his pale face, already much too pink in the cheeks. 'Come on. I'm going to have a peek from the lookout tree. Will you accompany me, young man? It seems my *old* bones might require your assistance.'

Bernhart grinned lopsidedly. 'Can I have a go of your crossbow?'

'Don't push your luck.'

The lookout tree had a series of rough wooden planks fixed to its trunk, so climbing it was easier than her previous perch, although this one was much taller. When eventually they emerged onto the simple lookout bench, they could see far across the forest, the dark green of the canopy spreading out

24

below them like a rucked blanket and the distant mountains a grey shadow on the horizon. And in the midst of all that growth, a vast tract of twisted strangeness. Vintage didn't need to look at the boy to know he was looking at it too.

'Is it growing?' he said after a while.

'We go down to the border of it twice a year,' she said quietly. 'All together, our strongest and our brightest and our bravest, and we burn back the growth and we sow the soil with salt. Marin, gods love him, even brings his priest friends with him and they say blessings over the ground.' She sighed. 'But still it advances, every year.'

'It's dead though,' said Bernhart. 'It's a dead thing, nothing inside it could be alive now.' He paused, and Vintage wondered if this was what his mother had told him, perhaps after he'd had a particularly bad nightmare. The House wasn't close to the Wild section of the forest, but it was apparently close enough for bad dreams. 'It's just the broken shell of a Behemoth. Why does it make the forest –' He stopped, struggling for the right word. 'Why does it make the forest bad?'

'It attracts parasite spirits,' said Vintage. She slipped the seeing-glass from her belt and held it to her eye. The ruined section of forest suddenly loomed closer, and she frowned as she looked over the blackened branches and the shifting mists. 'It's long dead, Bernhart. Just the empty husk of a Jure'lia ship and that in pieces, but it's like a corpse attracting flies. The parasite spirits are drawn to it. If we knew why, or how, or what they really are . . .' She lowered the seeing-glass and bit her lip. 'I have always wanted to find out more about them, and what their connection is to the worm people. So little has been written about the Jure'lia, and gods know the Eborans have always been tight-lipped about their periodic scraps with them. All we have left are the remains of their Behemoths, and a lot of very unpleasant stories. If only Eborans were a little more . . . gregarious. But of course these days

25

they have no time for humans at all.' She pursed her lips as a face from the past rose up unbidden in her mind – eyes like dried blood, a sardonic smile, and the memory of her hands. Her touch had always been so warm. With difficulty she dragged her mind away from the pleasant memory.

'You must have every book written about it, m'lady. About the Wild, and the worm people, and the parasite spirits,' said Bernhart. 'In your library, I mean.'

Vintage smiled and briefly cupped her hand to the boy's face. Her fingers were a deep brown against his white cheek.

'There are bigger libraries than mine, Bernhart. And I suspect that what I want to know won't be found in one. In fact—'

They felt it as much as heard it; a low rumble that vibrated uncomfortably in their chests. Vintage looked back at the Wild part of the forest, half unwillingly. In the darkest part the canopy was trembling, blackened leaves rustling. It shouldn't have been possible for her to hear it from this distance, but she heard it all the same: a dry empty sound like the hissing of water across arid ground. A translucent shape, a deep dirty-yellow colour, briefly pushed its way up between the upper branches of the trees. It had multiple fronds that carried strange white lights at the ends, and darker stippled marks across its back. The parasite spirit twisted in the air for a moment, its fronds reaching out blindly to the bright sky above, and then it sank back out of sight. Its odd rumbling cry sank with it.

'Gods be damned, that hardly seems like a good omen.' Vintage looked at the boy, and saw that he was standing very still, his eyes wide. The blush of colour on his cheeks had vanished. Gently, she patted his shoulder, and he jumped as though he'd been dreaming. 'You know, I have a good mind to tan Ezion's hide for sending you out here by yourself. Come on, Bernhart, let us get you home. I'll have Cook make you some honey pastries.'

* * *

26

They were gathered in the dining room, the best silver and porcelain laid out on the vine-wood table, as if they were waiting for the Emperor himself to drop by for a currant bun. Vintage's family were wearing their best silks and satins, despite the heat. Vintage took a particular pleasure in watching their faces as she trooped up to the table, letting her solid boots sound noisily against the polished floor. She snatched off her hat and threw it on the table, her eyes already scanning the dishes the staff had laid out for supper. Just behind her, Bernhart loitered in the doorway, technically dismissed but reluctant to leave what might prove to be the scene of an argument.

'Is there any of the good cheese left?' she asked, dragging a plate towards her with dusty fingers. 'The one with the berries in?'

'Sister.' Ezion stood up slowly. He wore a deep blue silk jacket and a starched shirt collar, and his dark eyes were bright with impatience. 'I am glad to see you've returned to us. Perhaps you'd like to change for dinner?'

Vintage glanced around the table. Carla, Ezion's wife, met her eyes and gave her a look of barely restrained glee, and Vintage tipped her a wink. The woman was heavily pregnant again, her rounded belly straining at her exquisitely tailored dress, while Vintage's various nieces and nephews made a clatter of their cutlery and plates.

'I do believe I am fine as I am, Ezi.' She reached over and made a point of picking up one of the tiny pastries with her fingers, sticking out her little finger as she did so as though she held a fine porcelain cup. 'What were you thinking, exactly, by sending Bernhart out into the vines by himself?'

Ezion was frowning openly now. 'He is a servant, Vincenza. I was thinking that it is his job to do such things.'

Vintage frowned back at him, and, turning back to the door, held the tiny pastry out to the waiting boy. 'Here, Bernhart, take this and get on with your day. I'm sure you've arrows you could be fletching.'

Bernhart gave her a conflicted look, as though the brewing argument might interest him more than the cake, but in the end cream won out. He took the pastry from her fingers and left, decorously closing the door behind him.

'The boy will maintain the vines for us one day, it is his job to be out there, Vincenza, as well you know. If we don't—'

'The Wild is spreading.' She cut him off. 'And we saw a parasite spirit today, rising up above the canopy. It was very large indeed.'

For a few moments Ezion said nothing. His children were all watching them now, with wide eyes. They had grown up with tales of the tainted forest, although it wasn't something often discussed over dinner.

'It is contained,' he said eventually, his voice carefully even. 'It is watched. There is nothing to be concerned about. This is why you should stay at the House and not go gallivanting around the forest. You have got yourself all agitated.'

Vintage felt a wild stab of anger at that, but Carla was speaking.

'How can it be spreading, Vin? Do we need to check on the borders more often?'

Vintage pursed her lips. 'I don't know. This is the problem. We simply do not know enough about it.' She took a breath, preparing to rouse an old argument. 'I will go in the spring. I've waited too long already, but it's not too late. Ezion, dear, we need to do some research, need to get out into the world and find out what we can. There are Behemoth sites I could be learning from, out there beyond our own forests. We need to know more about the Wild, and the parasite spirits. Enough reading, enough peering at old books. *I* need to go.'

Ezion snorted with laughter. It didn't suit him. 'Not this again. It is ridiculous. You are a forty-year-old woman,

28

Vincenza, the head of this family, and I will not have you traipsing off across Sarn to gods only know where.'

'A forty-year-old woman who has spent her entire life running this place, growing these vines, and making this wine.' She gestured viciously at the glass goblets, all full of a pale golden wine – it was made from the grape called Farrah's Folly. She could tell from the colour. 'And I have had enough. All of this,' she lifted her arms wide, 'is your responsibility now, Ezion. And *I* am not.'

She plucked her hat up off the table, and, for the look of the thing, stuck it back on her head before stalking out of the room, slamming the door so hard that she heard the cutlery rattle.

Outside in the corridor, she leaned briefly against the wall, surprised at how wildly her heart was beating. It was the anger, she told herself. After a moment, Bernhart's head appeared from around the corner.

'Are you all right, m'lady?'

She paused. A slow tingling feeling was working its way up from her toes; some sense of a huge change coming, like the heaviness in the air when a storm was building. There would be no stopping her now.

'I am absolutely fine, Bernhart darling.' She grinned at him and was pleased to see the boy smiling back. 'Fetch my travel bags from storage, boy. I'm bloody well going now.'

3

Now

The drug akaris is produced by heating a certain combination of substances to extreme temperatures before being cooled, raked and sieved. Only winnowfire is capable of producing the temperatures required, and, indeed, seems to affect the substances in other, less obvious, ways. Akaris is produced in one place only: the Winnowry, on the island of Corineth, just off the coast of Mushenska. Other places have attempted to manufacture the drug, with their own, illegal fell-witches, but these operations have all, without fail, come to a somewhat abrupt and rather unpleasant end. The Winnowry, they say, are ruthless in protecting their own interests.

As for the drug itself: used in its pure state, it simply gives the user a deep and dreamless sleep (more valuable than you might think), but cut with various stimulants, of which Sarn has a vast variety, it brings on a waking-dream state. By all reports, the dreams experienced under the influence of adulterated akaris are vivid, wild and often unnerving.

Extract from the journals of Lady
Vincenza 'Vintage' de Grazon

Noon awoke to the sound of an argument echoing up from below. She slid out of her narrow bed, snatching a glance out the tiny smeared window – overcast again, a blanket of grey from top to bottom – and walked over to the bars of her cell. There was little to see. The vast emptiness that was the heart of the Winnowry hung just below, and on the far side, there was the northern wall of cells, all identical to hers; carved from dead black rock, the floors and the ceilings a grid of solid iron. It was always gloomy inside the Winnowry; the tiny windows were all thickly sealed with lead and wax, and the oil lamps wired to the walkways gave only a smoky, yellow light.

Noon leaned against the bars and listened. It was normally so quiet in the Winnowry, filled with the hush of a hundred women living in fear: of themselves, and each other.

'Lower your voice, Fell-Anya,' came the flat, oddly metallic voice of one of the sisters, edged with tension.

'I will not!' Anya was one of the older fell-witches, but her voice was cracked from more than age this morning. The woman had been here for nearly twenty years, twice as long as Noon. Noon could barely imagine what that was like, but she was afraid she would find out.

'What can you do? What *can* you do to me? I'd be better off dead – we all would.' The woman's voice echoed up and around the vast space, echoing like something trapped. Anya was from Reidn, a vast city state far to the east that Noon had never seen, and she spoke their oddly soothing, lilting language. Because fell-witches could be born anywhere, to

31

anyone, the Winnowry was full of women from all over Sarn, and over the last decade Noon had come to know something of all their languages. It was, she sourly noted, the only positive thing the place had given her.

'No one is going to kill you, Fell-Anya.' The sister who spoke to her used the plains-speak that was common to most of Sarn. She was forming her words slowly, calmly, perhaps hoping to convey the sense that everything was fine, that nothing could possibly be out of control here – and her use of plains-speak suggested she wanted everyone to know it.

'Oh no, I'm too useful! Kill me and you've one less slave to make your drug for you.' There was a crash and a rattle of iron. Fell-Anya was throwing herself against the bars. Noon glanced directly down, through the iron grid, and saw Fell-Marian's pale face looking up at her from the cell below. The bat-wing tattoo on her forehead looked stark, like something separate from her. Noon touched her own forehead unconsciously, knowing she carried the same mark branded onto her skin.

'What is she doing?' whispered Marian. Noon just shook her head.

'You will calm yourself, Fell-Anya. Calm yourself now, or I will take action.' From the other side of the Winnowry came a muttering of dismay. The whole place was awake now, and every fell-witch was listening to see what would happen.

Noon pushed herself against the bars. 'Oi! Leave her be!' Her voice, more used to whispers and low words, cracked as she shouted. 'Just leave her alone!'

'Calm myself? Calm myself!' Fell-Anya was shrieking, the rhythmic slamming of her body against the bars terribly loud in the vast space. Noon pressed her lips together, feeling her own heart beat faster. Such uncontrolled anger was not permitted in the Winnowry. It was one of the worst things they could do. And then, unbelievably, there was a blossom of greenish-blue light, impossibly bright in the gloom of their prison. Noon staggered back from the bars even as she heard Marian gasp below her.

'Fire and blood! Oh, she's done it now,' murmured Noon. 'She's fucking well done it.'

There were cries from the other cells, a bellowed shout from below, and someone somewhere must have pulled the lever, because one of the huge water tanks clustered above them tipped to one side. A great sheet of water, black and silver in the poor light, crashed down through the cells on the opposite side, churning and rushing through the iron grids so that every fell-witch on that side of the Winnowry was abruptly dripping wet. The women screamed – the water was icy cold – and the winnowfire that was just out of sight blinked out of existence. Noon shivered as a fine mist of water droplets gusted towards them, and took a few steps back. In the outraged cacophony of fifty suddenly soaked women, she didn't hear what happened to Fell-Anya, but she heard the clanging of a cell door from somewhere down below.

'It'll be a week before they get that tank filled up again,' said Marian, her voice low. 'It's so difficult to refill, they hate to use it. But it seems they're getting more difficult to please lately.'

'Touchy bastards,' agreed Noon. She stepped back up to the bars again. 'Bastards!' But her lone shout was lost in the echoes of dripping water. Noon stared out at the cells opposite, and the soaking, miserable women. She pressed her hand to her mouth, biting at a loose shred of skin on her thumb. It would likely take as long for the women on the far side to dry off as it would for them to refill the tank. They would be given no dry clothes, and the Winnowry was ever damp and cold, the tall black stones of its towers facing out to a cold and violent sea. The island it had been built on had been cleared of all trees, all grass – even the top layer of soil had been scraped away. Say anything about the sisters, say they were careful.

'How did she do it?' whispered Marian. Her voice was safely hidden under the moans of the other fell-witches, the constant dripping a quiet rain as the water worked its way through their cells.

'The sister must have been stupid enough to get within reach of the bars.'

They both knew that was unlikely. The wardens of the Winnowry wore long gloves and sleeves, with thick hoods holding their hair back. Over their faces they wore smooth silver masks, with narrow holes for their eyes and mouths. To let a fell-witch touch their bare skin would be a disaster, although Noon often wondered what good it would do the witch who took their life energy. You could take enough to drag them down into unconsciousness – *kill them*, a voice inside her whispered – but then what? Unless you were outside of your cell already, unless you were close to the way out . . .

Noon sat down on the grill floor, pushing her fingers between the gaps. Marian reached up to her, but as ever the grid was too deep for them to reach each other. It was simply a way of acknowledging that they weren't alone.

'She did it somehow,' Noon said quietly. 'Got close enough to take what she needed.' Her heart was still hammering in her chest. 'What do you think happened to her? Do you think she got out?'

Marian didn't answer immediately. When she did, she sounded worried. 'Of course not. You know that, Noon. They doused her and then they took her away. There's no way out of here. You know that.'

'I know that,' agreed Noon. She gnawed at her thumb again. 'I know that.'

'Fell-Noon. Off the floor, please.'

Noon scrambled to her feet. She recognised the voice of Sister Owain and looked up to see a tall figure at her cell door.

The woman's mask caught the subdued light of the cell, and not for the first time Noon half wondered if the sisters were real people at all, or just ghosts of metal and wool. Sister Owain's robes were the traditional dark blue of the Winnowry Sisters, and a heavy wooden cudgel hung at her belt, capped with dull metal.

'What?'

Sister Owain tipped her head, and all at once it was quite possible to see her eyes behind the metal mask. Not a ghost after all. 'It's time for your purging, Fell-Noon, as well you know. I hope you are not going to give us any trouble this morning, or perhaps you would like south block to have an early shower too?'

When Noon didn't reply, Sister Owain bent and pushed a tray through the slot near the bottom of the bars.

'Prepare yourself, witch.'

On the tray was a shallow bowl filled with pale grey ash, and next to it a length of sea-green silk and a pair of long grey gloves. Noon curled her hands into fists as her face flushed hot. Always this: a mixture of anticipation, and shame. Sister Owain tapped on the bars.

'Hurry up, witch. We do not delay purging, you know that.'

Noon knelt and picked up the silk scarf. She ran it through her fingers briefly, as she always did – there was nothing else this soft within the Winnowry – and then swept back her short black hair and covered it over with the scarf, winding it around her bare neck and tying a simple knot at the back. Then she pushed her hands into the powdery ash, getting a good coating on her palms and fingers; it looked almost white against her olive skin. Carefully, so that she wouldn't breathe it in and make herself cough, she patted the ash onto her face. Three times she repeated the process, until the fine grey powder covered her cheeks, her nose and lips. There was even a fine layer on her eyelids, and the mark of the Winnowry that was seared onto her forehead – the single bat's wing – was almost obliterated.

'Another layer, if you please, Fell-Noon. I am not in the mood for half-measures this morning.'

'Why? What's the point? What's it for?'

Sister Owain shook her head slightly. It was clear she knew Noon was being deliberately difficult, but even so, she couldn't quite resist trotting out the standard Winnowry tract.

'Penance, witch. We daub you with ashes to mark you for what you are, we cover your skin so that you should not come into contact with the world.'

Noon sighed, and patted more of the ash onto her face, feeling clumps of it falling away where it was already too thick. The smell of it in her nostrils was dry and strange, tickling at her throat. Not waiting to see if that was good enough for Sister Owain, she slipped on the long grey gloves.

'That's good,' said Sister Owain. 'Very good. Now, when I open your door, step outside. I know you're not foolish enough to try to ruin my day, Fell-Noon.'

Noon glanced down as the cell door was rattled to one side, and as she stepped outside the sister immediately slapped a pair of thick cuffs on her wrists – a steel loop tied with tough hessian straps. They *were* jumpier than usual.

Sister Owain urged her swiftly down the walkway, so quickly that Noon didn't have time to exchange glances with any of the other women imprisoned in south block. They went down several sets of stairs, through three sets of tall, locked doors, all made of thick ebony wood riveted with steel, and then abruptly they were outside. As ever, Noon caught her breath as the icy sea wind cut across her, stealing what little warmth she had gathered to herself inside her cell. The taste of salt on her tongue was like a slap, and her eyes watered with the shock of it. They were leaving behind the main Winnowry building, with its four scalpel-like towers that tore at the sky,

36

and heading towards the circle of white buildings that cupped the Winnowry like a pair of receiving hands. Tall alabaster chimneys sprouted from these buildings, their tops smeared with soot, and underfoot there was stony dirt, streaked here and there with bat guano.

Noon wrenched around to look behind her. It was possible, at just the right moment, to catch a glimpse of the far shore of the mainland, where the city of Mushenska festered and spread. Today, the sea was rough, throwing up mists and spray, but she did see it for a brief second; the harbour lamps had been lit, as had the big beacons over the market place. There was a smudge on the grey sky – the Tarah-hut Mountains – and somewhere below that, thankfully out of sight, the plains where she had been born. Much closer, on the Winnowry beach itself, was a small jetty with a narrow little merchant vessel tied up next to it. Noon caught a glimpse there of tightly caulked barrels being rolled on board, and a man with a salt-and-pepper beard talking to a tall woman wearing a sea-green travel shawl. There was enough time to catch the spiky shape of the bat tattoo on her forehead, and then Sister Owain yanked on Noon's arm, almost causing her to lose her footing.

'Was that an agent?' she asked, nodded towards the figures on the jetty. 'Selling your drugs on, is that it? A pet fell-witch to do your dirty business?'

'Keep it up, Fell-Noon, and I will make a special appointment with the Drowned One for you. How about that?'

Noon pursed her lips, feeling the ash crack and flake. She wanted to bite at the skin on her thumb again. The agent and the boat were already out of sight, lost behind the furnace buildings.

'What is the matter with you lot today?' Noon muttered. 'You've a face on you like a horse's arsehole.'

To her surprise, Sister Owain didn't even turn to glare at

her. Instead, she shook her head slightly, as though trying to clear it.

'Bad dreams,' she said. 'No one is sleeping properly.'

Noon found she had nothing to say to that. She didn't know where the sisters slept, but she was willing to bet it was more comfortable than the bunk in her cell. And then they were there, and Sister Owain was reaching up and yanking the length of rope that hung above the priest door. Somewhere inside, a bell rang. On either side of the door, carved deeply into the white stone, were the two figures of the order's founder, Tomas. In one depiction, he had his back to the viewer, walking away towards a stylised line that Noon knew was meant to be the sea. In the other, his face was turned outwards, wearing an expression that Noon supposed was meant to be a mixture of terror, awe and righteousness. To her, he mainly looked consti-pated. He wore garlands of seaweed about his shoulders, and in his hands were seashells.

'Just do as you're told,' muttered Owain. 'Everything will be fine. The evil in you must be purged. And all will be fine.'

Noon let her arm go slack. The woman was distracted, and they were outside. If she threw herself out of reach and ran, it was possible she could get down to the beach before the alarm was raised, and from there it was even possible that she might survive the swim to Mushenska. If she could get the cuffs off. Suddenly, the grip on her arm was like a vice.

'Don't think I can't see it in your eyes, fell-witch.' Owain no longer looked distracted. Through the narrow gaps in her mask her eyes were flinty.

'What happened to Fell-Anya?' The question was out before Noon knew she was going to ask it. 'Where is she now?'

Owain was unfazed. 'We give you a chance to live here, witch. A chance to burn away the evil that is in you.' She paused, and behind her mask Noon heard her lick her lips. 'You of all people should know where you belong. Murderer.'

Noon stood unmoving, the chill of her skin at odds with the visions of fire that filled her head. And then the priest door clattered open, and she was passed into the care of the men.

Inside the Furnace it was always hot, in such stark contrast to the damp Winnowry that it made Noon feel faintly dizzy. There was a scratchy, bitter scent, a mixture of smoke and the drug akaris, and a distant roaring as other fell-witches underwent their purging in other parts of the building. She was escorted by Father Wasten, a tall, thin man with a fringe of red hair about his ears and a carroty beard on the end of his chin. The men's robes were a lighter shade of blue, and the hem was stitched with a series of curling lines meant to represent the sea that had kept Tomas to its bosom for so long. They did not wear masks, but instead carried short, lethal blades on their belts.

'Why is it "sister" for the women, and "father" for the men?' Noon asked. The bare white walls shaded into brown at the tops, the result of decades of insidious smoke, and the floor was grey slate, faintly warm through her slippers.

'Fell-Noon, you ask the same question each time I see you.'

'Because you've never given a good answer.'

Father Wasten cleared his throat. 'The sisters are your keepers, brave women who dare to live close to the evil you carry. They dare to be close to you, like sisters.'

'"Close" is a funny word for it.'

'And Mother Cressin is the head of our family, as you know.'

'The Drowned One?'

Father Wasten pursed his lips, causing his carroty beard to stick out ahead of him as though it were leading the way. 'You should show more respect.'

'I'm evil, remember? And everyone calls her that.'

They arrived at the furnace itself. Wasten took off her cuffs and led her through the great iron doors into a narrow circular room, the soot-blackened walls rising out of sight. Another fell-witch that Noon did not know the name of was just being led out, her skin beaded with sweat and a faraway look in her eyes. She didn't look at Noon as she passed her, and she stumbled as though she had no bones in her legs.

'You know what you must do, so prepare yourself, Fell-Noon,' said Father Wasten, his voice solemn now. The other fell-witch left, and Noon walked into the centre of the circular room. She peeled off the gloves and threw them on the floor, and then pulled off the long-sleeved shirt and piled that on top, leaving her in her vest. Next, her soft slippers – she preferred to be barefoot. 'You are the weak place between worlds, you are the fracture that permits evil to enter. This is your penance.'

Noon coughed into her hand. 'Horseshit.'

Father Wasten left, clanging the iron door shut behind him. After a few seconds another door opened, and a slim young man stepped through. Noon looked away. It was Novice Lusk. She *hated* when it was Novice Lusk.

He was tall, with skin the colour of good cream, his shoulders and neck slightly pink from the outside work he was tasked with – clearing away any stray debris, scrubbing the bat guano from the stones – and his hair was like corn silk, so blond it shone. Noon remembered corn like that on the plains, whole sunny fields of it like a dream. His eyes were blue. He had already removed his shirt, and his chest was taut with muscles, the low band of his loose grey trousers riding on his hips.

Once, Noon had wondered why they didn't just use plants for the purging, or even animals of some sort, and she had asked, not the sisters or the priests, but another fell-witch who had been there longer than she had. *People get over it*, the witch had told her. *They have a rest, and come back. Have you ever taken life energy from grass? Dead straight away, isn't it? You could use pigs, maybe, or goats, but then you need someone to look after them, and you'd need a lot of goats. Men though – stupid men with nothing better to do – can look after themselves.*

Lusk came over to her and nodded, once.

'Are you ready, Fell-Noon?'

There were tiny creases at the corners of his eyes as he frowned in concern. Noon sighed.

'Let's get this over with.'

He nodded again, and went to his knees in front of her. 'As ever, it is my honour to assist you in your purging.'

She looked down at him and the top of his bowed head. Lusk's shoulders shone in the lamplight, smooth and lightly freckled. When everyone she saw was covered up lest they come into accidental contact with her, it was shocking to see so much bared flesh, so much skin uncovered, and part of her never tired of seeing it.

Lusk cleared his throat.

'Are you ready, Fell-Noon?'

She glanced up once, into the crowded darkness above them. There were more iron grids up there, and on top of them shallow pans full of the substances they used to make akaris. She walked behind him, and taking a small breath, placed her hands on his back, almost leaning on him. His skin was warm, and she could smell him now too – he smelled of soap and earnestness. A warm flush moved from the soles of her bare feet to the top of her head, and she sought a little deeper, seeking out his living energy. Lusk was murmuring a prayer of acceptance under his breath, and not for the first time she wondered what brought a man to a place like this, to take up this particular duty with all its risks, but the urgency of the winnowfire was growing and she pushed that thought to one side.

Her palms tingled, and with a shiver his energy flowed into

41

her. She took it eagerly, filling her and crowding out the darkness within, letting it pool and grow and surge. Lusk was trained for this, and she knew, more or less, how much was safe to take, but the more she could absorb in this first contact, the purer her winnowfire would be. And the moment was coming.

Noon lifted one hand and pointed up into the dark above them. A crackle in the air, and a bloom of blue-green flame curled from the end of her arm and shot up into the echoing chimney. A bare second later and she was wreathed in it, a glowing column of ethereal fire that surged up, crashing and rolling against the steel sides of the chasm above them. The roar of it filled her ears and everything was light. She could feel from the muscles in her face that she was grinning, and she savoured every moment. The fire poured from her like water from a broken dam, and she revelled in the power of it. Here, at least, for this brief time, she was free and powerful.

Lusk shifted under her hand slightly and she remembered to keep part of her consciousness monitoring the life energy she was taking from him. Already he was tiring, and she was surprised by how much she had taken. Somewhere above them the flat pans of chemicals would be cooking nicely, and the priests of Tomas would be waiting to harvest their precious akaris. She wondered how much she made for them, and who used it outside of the Winnowry.

Noon stood on the tips of her toes, reaching as high as she could for one final blast, and then abruptly the flames winked out. She sagged, half stumbling, and Lusk made to help her before catching himself. Contact outside of the purging was strictly forbidden. Noon shivered, her grey vest sticking to her back with sweat. Lusk was a shade paler than he'd been, and his forehead and chest were also beaded with moisture.

The steel door clanged open, and Father Wasten appeared.

He eyed them both warily, and nodded to her. 'Get dressed, Fell-Noon.'

Novice Lusk turned and left without looking at her, going through the other door, and Noon hastily pulled on her long shirt and soft slippers. She hated wearing them again when she was so covered in sweat, but she would not be permitted to go anywhere until she did. Once her hands were covered in the long gloves again, Father Wasten came fully into the room.

'Once again you are purged, Fell-Noon. You are, briefly, pure.'

Noon rubbed her hand over her face, grimacing as the ash there mixed with her sweat and turned into smears of dirt. She didn't feel pure. She felt sticky and dirty, and oddly ashamed. There was such a sense of release with the purge, and then, afterwards, guilt. The rush of the flames and the eerie light made it too easy to remember things she'd rather forget. Things she *had* to forget.

When she didn't say anything, Father Wasten held up a small fabric bag in his gloved hand, and placed it in her palm. Her small portion of the akaris, to give her a dreamless sleep. Not taken from what she had just made – it would be too hot, and would need raking and sifting – but an older supply. She pinched it between her fingers, feeling the grainy powder through her gloves. Under Wasten's careful watch, she pulled the drawstring open with a gloved finger and tipped the contents into her mouth. There was the familiar suffocating tickle as the drug coated her mouth, and then, on contact with her saliva, it turned slippery, oily almost. It tasted of nothing, and she swallowed it with a grimace before handing the bag back to Wasten. Many of the women chose not to consume akaris. She supposed that for them, their dreams were an escape from the Winnowry, bringing them sweet memories of their old lives. Not so for Noon.

'You know, Fell-Noon, why you are here, don't you?'

Noon looked up at him. His eyes were brown and watery, and could not disguise his disgust for her.

'Because I am too dangerous to be outside.'

He nodded. 'Evil works through you, girl. All of your kind are tainted, but here you have a purpose at least. You should be grateful. How many more could you have killed, if you were still free?'

Noon looked at him flatly until he turned back to the door, and they began the slow process of returning her to her cell.

4

In order to properly understand the Jure'lia and their queen, we have to know something of their opposite number. In recent times, the Eborans have been almost as hated and reviled as the invaders; their only saving grace perhaps the fact that they have, for thousands and thousands of years, held back attack after attack from the worm people.

What should we know of Ebora? For generations they were sustained in their glory by their god Ygseril, known more prosaically to outsiders as 'the tree-god'. The sap of their great tree, ingested orally, made them almost immortal – young forever, inhumanly strong, impervious to most wounds and diseases, and perhaps, to human eyes, beautiful.

And then at the end of the Eighth Rain, the last great war with the invaders, Ygseril suddenly died. There was no more sap. The Eborans began to grow old, they began to grow weak. They became ill, just as humans do, and succumbed to injuries and infections. Eborans do not have children at the drop of a hat like humans do, and without the sap, newly born children grew rarer and rarer. It was a disaster. Their great cities beyond the Wall began to fall into disrepair, and the Eboran people into despair.

In time it was discovered that human blood *could be used as a substitute (please see journal 73 on Lady Carmillion for the possibly apocryphal details of that incident). Blood was not nearly as powerful as the god-sap had been, of course, but it did slow their aging, and it gave them back their strength, their vitality, acting almost as a stimulant in small doses. Over a period of time, in sufficient quantities, it could even heal grievous injuries, to some extent.*

Unsurprisingly, relations between Ebora and their human neighbours deteriorated rapidly.

So began the years of the Carrion Wars. Ebora sporadically invaded the surrounding territories – the nomadic plains peoples taking the brunt of the attacks – stealing away human captives to be donors and, eventually, simply killing and 'harvesting' their human victims there on the battlefield. Out of desperation? Fear? Perhaps. Without their war-beasts born from Ygseril the Eborans were not as fearsome as they had been, but they were still stronger than the average human warrior, and could heal faster. It was carnage, and who knows where it would have ended? Except that human blood turned out not to be their saviour, but their curse.

The first recorded case of the crimson flux befell Lady Quinosta. Known for her prodigious consumption of human blood – bottle after bottle decanted at every meal, she would also bathe in the stuff – she awoke one day to find herself in terrible pain, her body stiff and unresponsive. Her white skin grew hard and cracked, revealing livid red flesh beneath. She developed a terrible cough, and her silk handkerchiefs were soon soaked with the strange fluid that passes for Eboran blood. She took to her bed, and spent six months dying in agony. Human blood did nothing to arrest the progress of the illness – it made it worse. And she was just the first.

Ebora was decimated. Those few who have so far survived the disease now keep to the land beyond the Tarah-hut Mountains, and many, it is said, still drink human blood in small, regular doses. Enough to keep old age and weakness at bay, but not enough to summon the crimson flux. They hope.

Extract from the journals of Lady Vincenza
'Vintage' de Grazon

There was half an inch of wine left in the bottom of the bottle. Untangling his arm from the sheets, Tormalin reached across and snatched it up. There were no glasses within reach of the bed, but he was no savage, so he poured it into one of Sareena's empty incense bowls instead. He took a sip and then spotted the tray of cheese and fruits she had left on the small table on the other side, so he rolled in that direction, narrowly avoiding tossing the wine over the sheets and falling out of the bed.

'What are you doing?'

Sareena had returned, a bottle of sweetly perfumed oil in her arms. She wore the purple silks he'd bought for her on a previous visit, and they shifted and swirled around her body as he'd known they would. He grinned at her.

'I am hungry, my sweet.'

She raised an eyebrow at him and came to sit on the bed, in the warm space left by the curve of his body. Tor drank the last of the wine and set the bowl on the table, before chasing a ball of cheese around the plate with his fingers. It kept getting away from him.

'I'm not surprised you are hungry,' said Sareena. She laid the bottle, still stoppered, on the bed, and smoothed some strands of hair away from his face. 'But does it always have to be cheese?' She wrinkled her nose, which Tor found delightful. 'And always the most pungent ones.'

Tor kicked his legs out and lay with one arm under his head, contemplating the cheese. 'There are few things as fine, Sareena, as a good piece of cheese and a decent glass of wine.'

'Except you are not even drinking it out of a glass.' She drew herself up, preparing to tease him. 'I am sure that the House of the Long Night does not whiff of strange cheeses, or keep ridiculous drinking vessels.'

Tor sat up and put the cheese to one side. He could feel the wine warming his blood and everything in the room was pleasantly hazy, but he attempted to focus. 'You are quite right, of course.' He took hold of both her hands, running the pads of his thumbs over the sensitive skin of her wrists. The Early Path: Spring's First Touch. 'It is a place of great serious-ness, and we have a contract, you and I. Forgive me, Sareena, for neglecting you.'

Her cheeks turned a little pink, and she even turned her smile away from him. He loved the fact that she was still bashful, could still blush at his words, even after all these months.

'If you knew how jealous my sisters are,' she said, 'you would know no forgiveness is needed.' Her smile was now wicked. 'Our arrangement is *very* satisfactory to me, Tormalin the Oathless.'

He kept his eyes on hers, and gently ran his fingers along the underside of her forearms. He felt rather than saw her shiver. The Early Path: The Rising Leaf.

'Do you want the oil?' she asked. Her eyes – a deep dark brown, just like her hair – were very wide, and as he smiled she bit the edge of her lip.

'In a little while.'

Tor knelt and slid one hand around her waist to rest on the

48

small of her back. Very gently, he pulled her to him, and he touched his lips to the smooth place where her neck met her shoulders. A line of kisses there, feather light. The Early Path: Spring's First Flight.

'*Mmm.*' Sareena swayed with him, and he could hear the smile in her voice. 'Do they really teach you all this at the House of the Long Night?'

'I studied . . .' he transferred his attention to the other side of her neck – 'for years.'

He followed the line of her jaw and then kissed her mouth, firmly at first, and then deeply. The Morning Sun: Dawn's Prayer. She responded eagerly, smoothing her hands along his arms and then his bare chest. Quickly, he gathered her up and lay her down in front of him, and she laughed a little – she was always caught unawares by how strong he was. Carefully, he pulled at one of the silk ties holding her outfit together, and the upper part began to unravel. She wriggled a little, and Tor smiled – he had known how the silk would feel against her skin, and had had the shift made specifically for this effect.

Leaning over her, he kissed the bare skin of her breastbone, and touched the tip of his tongue there. The Morning Sun: The Heart's Obeisance. She sighed, and when she spoke again her voice was huskier.

'That is very good, Tor, I can't even begin to tell you . . .'

He followed the line of her body down, smoothing away the ribbons of purple silk and tasting her skin as he went. She was apricots and smoke, and a faint curl of oil against his tongue, left over from their afternoon together. Her hands found his hair and pulled and pushed at it, running it through her fingers. She was making small noises now, taking small breaths. He should slow down. The High Sun: A Silk Flower.

Pulling back slightly, he slid his naked thigh along the inside of her own – The High Sun: Chasing Leaves – and was pleased as she shuddered amongst the sheets. The confection of purple silks had fallen completely away, and she was quite beautiful. He bent his head to her breasts, and caught her eye as he did so. 'You are a feast,' he told her, 'and I, my sweet, am ravenous—'

Something solid crashed against the chamber door and they both jumped. Tor lifted his head, his hair hanging in his face.

'Oh no.'

There was another crash. It sounded suspiciously like a large boot kicking the door.

'Oh *no*.'

'Tor!' The voice was remarkably loud. Tor winced. 'I know you're in there. I told you to meet me at sun down and it's already moon up!'

Tormalin sat up. 'I'll be with you in a little while, Vintage! There's no rush. Honestly, woman, we've been poking around these things for years and it's not as if they're going anywhere—'

There was another thump. 'Sareena, my dear,' the voice called, 'get back under the sheets for me, would you? There's a good girl.'

Sareena raised an eyebrow at Tor – he didn't miss the amusement in the quirk of her lips – and then shimmied over to the other side of the bed, where she swiftly wrapped herself in the bed covers. Abruptly, the door crashed open and an older woman with deep brown skin and a mass of tightly curled black hair stomped into the room.

'Vintage!' Tor put on his most outraged expression, and pulled the sheets around his waist. 'This really is unacceptable. Unacceptable. How dare you interrupt—'

'Darling, if I had to wait for you to voluntarily leave this good woman's bed, I'd be waiting until the Tenth Rain. And stop clutching at yourself like a maiden, you've nothing I haven't seen before.'

50

She smiled warmly at Sareena, who waved cheerfully enough.

Tor spluttered and did his best to look affronted, but it was difficult to retain the moral high ground when you were naked in front of a woman who you happened to know carried a crossbow on her belt. 'Really, Vintage, we haven't completed our transaction, and it is an insult to the teachings of the House of the Long Night.'

'Are you drunk?' Vintage stalked into the room and snatched up the empty bottle of wine, peering at the label. 'And on this swill?'

'Yes, I am quite drunk, which is exactly why I cannot accompany you on your latest ridiculous quest. It would be dangerous for both of us. And innocent bystanders, no doubt.'

'Nonsense.' Vintage put the bottle down and fixed him with a glare. 'Get back into your trousers, dear, or I will spend your wages on buying this girl some decent wine.'

Tor sank back, defeated. He needed what Sareena could give him, but he needed coin more.

'You are leaving Mushenska?' asked Sareena. 'You are going beyond the walls? Is that safe, Vin?'

Tor winked at her. 'Worry not, my sweet. What is out there holds no fears for an Eboran warrior and his fabled sword.'

'I'm sure the girl has heard quite enough about your fabled sword for one evening.' Vintage turned back to the door. 'You've got until I bring the horses round. Have a good night, Sareena my dear, and do send me the bill for the wine.'

Vintage went through her pack while she waited for Tor. The Frozen Moon Inn, where Sareena kept her suite of rooms, was on the very edge of Mushenska. From where she stood she could see the lanterns of the city wall, and the one great beacon that marked the northern gate. If the lad got a move on, they could reach the place before sunrise.

Notebooks, ink, spare crossbow quarrels. Oatcakes, ham,

water, cheese. A thick pair of leather gloves, a small collection of tiny glass jars, ready for any specimen she might be able to take. Knives, increasingly smaller blades for fine work. Sketching charcoal, grease, oil, a bundle of small sticks, some other odds and ends she hoped she would not have to use. With a sigh, she pulled the flap shut on her pack and secured it. She was as ready as she could be. Perhaps, this time, it might be worth all the preparation.

A polite cough alerted her to his presence. Tor could tread very quietly when he wanted to.

'You've dragged me out of a warm bed. I'm assuming you have spectacular reasons.'

Vintage tutted at him. 'My darling, when do I not have spectacular reasons?' She led him around the corner of the building into the stables where two young horses awaited them. There was a pack for Tor, already affixed to his saddle.

'More Behemoth bits, I assume? Well, I have had a full bottle of wine, so you might have to remind me of the specifics,' he said.

Vintage glanced up at his tall form. He did not look like a man recently rousted from bed with a bottle's worth of wine inside him. In the gentle lamplight his handsome face looked carved from fine marble, his long black hair tied and bound into a tail on the back of his head. His clear eyes, the irises a deep ruddy colour in this light, were bright and alert, and he was dressed in his infuriating manner – that was to say, he appeared to have thrown together a collection of silks, furs and worn leathers and somehow managed to look exquisitely elegant. In the years they had been travelling through Sarn together, Vintage had never seen him look anything less than composed, even when turfed out of someone's bed. The only sign that he'd had to rush was the lack of jewellery – he wore only a single silver earring in the shape of a leaf, and a silver ring with a fat red stone on his left hand; in the daylight, she knew, his eyes were the exact same colour as the stone. His sword belt was already in place, and his sword, the Ninth Rain, rested comfortably across his back. She grinned up at him.

'More Behemoth bits or, at least, the potential to find some. Let's get going. We'll ride and talk.'

Together, they mounted their horses and made their way through Mushenska's wide, cobbled streets. It was a large and crowded city, spilling over with lights on every corner and from every window; people felt safer when the shadows were kept at bay. Eventually, the great city wall loomed up ahead of them, and Vintage noted the beacons along it, the men and women armed with powerful longbows, and the solid black shapes of cauldrons. They would contain oil, which could be lit and tossed over the side at a moment's notice. She had never witnessed an incident while she had been staying in Mushenska – much to her annoyance – but she had returned from travelling once to see the smoking body of a great Wild bear, and the claw marks it had left on the walls. It had been twelve feet tall, its muscles so enormous it was misshapen. What it could possibly have been thinking to attack the wall, Vintage did not know – but the poisoned wildlife of Sarn did not always behave rationally.

At the thickly reinforced gates they met a trio of guards who expressed a great deal of concern about them leaving at night, until Vintage passed them each small bags of coins. Even so, the eldest, a stocky woman with a scar slashed across her blunt nose, fixed Vintage with a pained expression.

'If it can't wait until morning, then that's your lookout.' She glanced once at Tor, then looked away. 'But keep to the road. There are places further out that are getting overgrown, but it's still better than being out in the Wild.'

Vintage nodded seriously, touched by the woman's genuine

concern. The gates were opened for them and they passed through, riding their horses out into a balmy night. Ahead of them stretched the northern road out of Mushenska, a featureless stretch of brown beaten earth. Scrubby grassland flanked the road, and in the distance was the darker presence of the forest – or, as the guard had called it – the Wild. Vintage knew that the further they travelled from the city, the closer the Wild would get. The people of the city worked to keep it back, but their efforts only stretched so far, and the Wild was always growing. Vintage cleared her throat as the gates rumbled closed behind them. The road was utterly clear, with not a soul in sight, and it was eerily quiet.

'What's the story then, Vintage? What's the hurry? Surely this could have waited until the morning.'

Vintage touched her boot heels to her horse and they moved off smartly down the road. 'There is a settlement, not too far from here. Well, I say settlement. It's more a place where a few people bumped into each other and decided they were done travelling. A woman from there arrived early this morning, asking for aid. They have been visited. Half their livestock dead, and they've lost people, too.'

Tormalin snorted. 'What do they expect, living out in the Wild?'

'They expect to live their lives, just as all people do.' Vintage shifted in her saddle. 'Besides which, it is not the lively wildlife that is bothering them. It is a parasite spirit.'

Tor was quiet for a few moments. In the distance, the high and lonely call of some night bird rent the air.

'They've not been bothered by one before?'

'No. Which leads me to believe that there could be Behemoth remains nearby. Undiscovered ones.' She looked over at Tor and smiled. 'Can you imagine that, my dear?'

Tor didn't look nearly as pleased. 'Why now?'

'A shifting of the earth has uncovered them, perhaps. A tree

54

fallen in a storm has disturbed them, or perhaps just the rain. Or maybe something *large* has been digging.' She shrugged. 'Either way, it is worth a look. And the sooner we get there, the better chance we have of witnessing something ourselves. Besides which, we have decided that it is better to tackle these things in the dark, if we can. Have we not?'

Tor sighed. 'You are right, of course.'

Vintage nodded. A year ago, they had been investigating an eerie stretch of land known to its locals as the Thinny. It was a ravine, partially filled with rockfall and the usual explosion of plant life that was typical of the Wild, and the far end of it, the stories went, was haunted by parasite spirits. A local man had insisted on accompanying them. Berron, his name had been, and he had been kind – just like the guard on the gate, he had been genuinely concerned for them. Had wanted to help. They had spent hours clambering through the shadowy strangeness of the ravine, until they had come to an unexpected clear patch. The walls of the ravine had fallen there, letting in bright sunshine. The three of them had stood blinking for a moment, dazzled by the unexpected light, and that was when the parasite spirit had taken Berron. A being mostly made of light is harder to see in the daylight. It was as simple as that.

A comfortable silence settled over them, and they rode for some time with only the sound of their horses' hooves striking the dirt road. The night was still and the moon was as fat as a full tick, dusting the tops of the trees with a silver glow. In time, the Wild drew closer, eating up the scrubby grass and creeping towards the road.

'It stalks us,' pointed out Tor. Vintage felt a shiver of relief at the sound of his voice. 'Don't you think?'

'Nonsense, my dear.' She forced herself to smile. 'The Wild is not a living thing. Woods is woods, is what my father used to say.'

'Did you spend much time in the vine forest at night?'

'Not as such, no. The work we had to do there required daylight, but I did go walking after dark a few times. The night transforms a place like that. I grew up in between those trees, learned to walk and skinned my shins there, but at night it was like it no longer belonged to me.'

She could feel Tor's eyes on her now.

'Did it frighten you?'

'It exhilarated me. That even the familiar can have secrets. Here, look, that track ahead. We must take that, and then we shall be there in a few hours.'

The track cut off from the main road and headed straight into the dark trees. As they turned, it was possible to see how the trees had been cut back from this new, smaller road; tree trunks, their blunt ends like pale imitations of the moon, flanked it on both sides.

'Be on your guard, darling,' said Vintage. Here, the Wild pressed in to either side, a curtain of darkness trying to close over them. Her horse shuddered, a reflexive shivering of muscle, and she pressed her hand to its neck to calm it.

'You hardly need to tell me that.' Tor loosened his sword in its scabbard.

In the end they only had the one close call. Vintage had settled into her saddle, the rhythmic movements of the horse lulling her, when, abruptly, the animal skittered over to the far side of the path. She looked up to see Tor half rising from his saddle; on the far side of the road, on the very edge of the trees, were four hulking great wolves. In the shadows they were little more than lethal shapes, their eyes like pieces of yellow mirror. And beyond them, within the trees themselves, Vintage sensed the movement of others. Each of the wolves they could see was twice the size of a normal animal. Vintage had seen wolves – dark shapes trickling across the plains at night, and they were shy, wary animals – but these creatures watching them now had grown from puppies in the shadow of the Wild. Somewhere here, perhaps thousands of years ago, the remains of a Behemoth had disintegrated, seeping its subtle poisons into the soil until everything was tainted with it.

Tor drew his sword, a silent movement against the soft leather of his scabbard. The Ninth Rain ran liquid with moonlight, but Vintage shook her head at him.

'Wait. Wait.'

Vintage reached back to her pack and, without taking her eyes off the wolves, slipped her hand into the outer pocket. She brought out a handful of tiny white bulb-like objects, each twisted at the top. She passed these to Tor.

'Throw them. I know you can throw further than me.'

Tor raised his eyebrows, and then turned and threw the papery handful overarm towards the wolves. The bulbs landed on the dirt road with a series of surprisingly loud pops, and as one the animals skittered back from the noise. Vintage watched, her heart in her mouth, as the largest creature took one step forward, before shaking out his coat all over and slipping back into the tree line. After a moment, the others followed.

'We're lucky it has been a fine summer,' said Vintage quietly. 'Wolves, even ones from the Wild, are reluctant to approach humans unless they are really hungry.'

Tor grunted. 'You can't possibly know that for certain.'

'Of course not. What is familiar can always surprise us. Are you disappointed, my dear? Did you want to face down a pack of wolves in the dark?'

'I *have* had a very tiring day, Vintage.'

When they had ridden some distance from the dark space where the wolves had disappeared, Tor cleared his throat. 'These places give me the creeps.'

'So much of Sarn is like this now, we half think it's normal.'

57

Vintage sighed, trying to ignore the crawling of her own flesh. There could be hundreds of creatures like the worm-touched wolves close by, hidden beyond the tree line, watching them. 'We scuttle from one so-called settlement to the next, not questioning if this is how we should be living our lives. There are no places like this in Ebora?'

As usual, when Ebora was mentioned, Tor looked faintly pained.

'No, there are not.'

Vintage pursed her lips. 'Sarn has its safe places, the places that have not been poisoned. But once, before the Jure'lia began their relentless invasions . . . If we knew what the poison was exactly, if we could isolate and remove it . . .'

'Once, Sarn was safe, and the roots blessed us all.' Tor sighed. 'I'm not sure even my people remember that far back.'

They reached the settlement as the sky to the east was turning the expectant, bruised colour of the hours before dawn. The village was ringed with a wall made of thick tree trunks, and a pair of torches burned brightly at the open gates. Vintage could make out a trio of figures there, staring out into the dark.

'Do you see them?'

'I saw them half an hour ago, Vintage.'

'Be on your best behaviour. They're likely to be very twitchy.'

One of the men waved them down, and Vintage led them over towards the torches. There were two men, and a woman. They each wore short swords at their waists, and one of the men carried a long pitchfork. Beyond them, Vintage could see a ramshackle collection of huts and shacks, all unusually well lit with lamps and standing fires.

'Who are you? What do you want here?'

Vintage smiled down at the man who had spoken. His beard was scruffy, and he had the wide-eyed look of someone who hadn't been sleeping well lately.

'My colleague and I come on the word of one Cara Frostyear. She came to Mushenska seeking aid. With your current, uh, difficulties, my dear.'

The man looked confused. He glanced at his companions.

'But you are . . . forgive me, but you are a single woman. We hoped that Cara would bring back a host of the city guard.' His face creased with anger. 'It's all very well for them, safe inside their walls, but we're out here in the dark.'

Vintage pursed her lips. The city guard had their own problems. The men and women who chose to live out amongst the Wild were generally considered mad or foolish, and she could well imagine the reception Cara Frostyear had received.

'I am Lady Vincenza de Grazon, and your little problem just happens to be my speciality.'

Tor chose that moment to lead his horse into their circle of light. He drew his sword, twisting it so that the lamplight flashed along the blade.

'And I, Tormalin the Oathless, have come to slay your monster!'

As one, the three took a step back. The man with the pitchfork stood with his mouth hanging open.

'An Eboran? Here?' He moved the pitchfork in front of him. 'You bring a monster to kill a monster?'

Vintage heard Tor sigh noisily. She pointed to his sword.

'I well understand your caution, my good man, but do you see that? That is the Ninth Rain, a sword forged for a future battle, a sword forged in winnowfire!' When they didn't react, she cleared her throat. 'Steel forged in winnowfire is the only thing known to injure a parasite spirit.' When still they said nothing, she leaned forward in her saddle. 'You must know this?'

The woman stepped forward. She had a squarish, stern face, her black hair pulled back tightly into a bun. 'I know our swords have had no effect on it, and if you think you have a way of killing it, then I am very willing to listen. My name is Willa Evenhouse, and these are my cousins Dennen and Fera. This is a poor place, as I'm sure you can see, and I'm not sure what we'll be able to give you in return.' The woman took a breath, and abruptly Vintage could see how tired she was. It had been a long time since anyone had slept properly here. 'But we will gladly offer you what we can, if you can make this . . . this thing go away.'

'I want it dead,' said the man she'd named as Dennen, the one who'd spoken first. 'It killed Morin's boy, and Mother Sren. It must die.'

Tor sheathed his sword. 'Then let us talk of our fee—'

'Of which, there is none,' said Vintage hurriedly. 'Save for food, drink, a place to shelter our horses.'

Willa nodded. 'Come with me. Dennen, Fera, keep watch.'

Vintage and Tor dismounted and followed the woman into the village, leading their horses. It was quiet, the light from numerous lamps casting buttery light on the packed dirt ground. They passed a paddock filled with scrubby grass, and Vintage caught the mineral scent of old blood. There was a dark patch, difficult to make out in the colours of the night, but she was willing to bet that was where these people had lost most of their livestock. Likely, they had woken in the night to the sound of cattle screaming as their skins melted away, and then the first villagers had perished also. She had seen it before.

'Here.' Willa indicated a low, sturdy building, thick with the smell of horse. A young woman came out, her eyes wide in the gloom. When she caught sight of Tor she took a startled step backwards.

'Ma?'

'Take the horses in, Duana, have them made comfortable for the night.'

The girl looked as though she had a thousand questions,

but she did as she was told. When she was out of sight, Willa shook her head.

'We've heard of these parasites, of course we have. We might be in the middle of nowhere but we know some history. But never around here. We know what we risk, living out in the Wild, but these things – they shouldn't be here.'

Vintage reached within her pack and drew out a narrow silver flask. She passed it to the woman, who took it with a brief nod. 'I couldn't agree more. Tell us everything you can, my dear,' she said. 'Any small detail could help.'

Willa unscrewed the bottle and took three quick gulps of the strong brandy. When she began to speak, not looking at either of them, Vintage slipped the pencil and notebook from her bag and began to make hurried notes.

'It was four nights ago when it first came. I'd been dreaming. Some bad dream where I was trapped in the dark, and I could feel everything dying all around me. There was something terrible in the sky.' She looked up, glaring at them both. 'I know that sounds stupid, but I've never had a dream like it. It might be important.'

Vintage nodded. She liked this woman. 'You are quite right, my dear. Please, continue.'

'I woke up because Cara's goat was crying. I lay there listening to it and cursing it because it was still full dark, and I had a good three or four hours before I would have to be up. It was bleating, over and over, and then it was *shrieking*. Something about that noise . . . I leapt out of bed even as Duana came into my room, and I told her to stay where she was.' Willa took another gulp of brandy. 'Outside there was . . . there was a halo around Cara's place, yellow and blue and shifting. Looking at it, I felt unwell. Like perhaps I was still asleep. I ran down there anyway, and I was just in time to see—'

She stopped, and looked down at the straw-covered floor.

Next to her, Vintage could sense Tor becoming impatient, and she willed him not to say anything.

'I saw the goat. It was a stupid thing – what goats aren't? But I saw its eyes, and then I saw the thing standing over it. The thing ran its – hand – over the goat's flank and it just burst open. The skin peeled back and what was inside, what should have been inside . . .'

'Take a deep breath, Willa.' Vintage caught her eye and tried to hold her gaze. It was rare to have such a lucid witness, but they didn't need a description of what had happened to the goat. They had seen the aftermath of that often enough. 'What did you see standing over Cara's goat?'

Willa pressed her lips into a thin line. 'It was tall, taller than Cara's hut, and it looked like it was made of water.' She glanced at Tor, as if waiting for him to mock her. 'I can't think of another way of saying it. I could see through it, but not properly. Like looking through warped glass. And it was roughly shaped like a person, except that its arms were too long. And there were too many of them. There were lights inside it, blue and yellow pulsing lights. The ends of its arms had lots of fingers but no hands.' Willa visibly shuddered. 'It was its fingers it was using to peel back the goat's skin, and the flesh just seemed to boil away from it, like it couldn't bear for it to be touching—'

'Are there any Behemoth remains around this area, my dear?' Seeing the woman's blank expression, Vintage spoke again. 'Anything left behind by the worm people? Twisted pieces of strange metal, perhaps?'

'No, not that I know of.'

'Its face?' asked Tor. 'Did you see any of that?'

Willa shook her head. 'It was bent over the poor animal, I couldn't see it. Shen, Morin's boy, jumped over the fence and he had his da's sword with him, the young idiot.' Willa lifted a hand and pushed her fingers across her forehead.

They were trembling slightly. 'I told him to get away. I told him—'

There was a shout, and Willa stopped. They all turned to where it had come from, and a bare second later, there was another cry. The panic in it was as clear as sunrise.

'Willa my dear, go inside,' said Vintage quickly. 'Keep your daughter with you. We'll be back.'

Tor had his sword ready as they headed back the way they'd come. Halfway there and they saw it – the creature had come back to them, a beacon of strangeness on the edge of the village. As they watched, it moved through the tree-trunk wall as though it wasn't there, its translucent body oozing silently through the wood. The spirit was a good fifteen feet tall, and gently glowing fronds ringed it like petals on a deadly flower. The two men were below it now; one was scrambling away while the other, incredibly, was attempting to jab at the creature with his pitchfork.

'Ha! Well, it is a *touch* taller than the hut,' said Tor. 'Was that an elaborate joke of some sort, do you think?'

'Go, get between it and those idiots,' said Vintage. She had her crossbow in her hands, and was letting her fingers fit a new quarrel. She didn't take her eyes from the parasite spirit. 'If we can drive it back outside of the village, perhaps we can get a proper look at it.'

But it was too late. As they arrived, the spirit was bending down over the hapless Fera, who was still thrusting his pitchfork at it. Long tapered fingers closed over him – Vintage was struck briefly by how it looked like a child peering at a new bug on the ground – and then Fera was falling apart. He screamed as his body was unzipped, and Vintage saw a gout of blood and other fluids hit the dirt. The long transparent fingers were still moving though, and her stomach twisted as the man's skin rolled back like a carpet being peeled away from a floor.

'Damn it all.' She raised her crossbow, already knowing it was pointless. 'Ahoy! Lanky!'

She squeezed the trigger and one of her specially crafted quarrels sank home into the parasite spirit's uncertain flesh. It looked up, taking notice of them for the first time – as well it might. Each of Vintage's quarrels was tipped with shards of winnow-forged steel. Priceless, every single one. Inside the blurred glass of the creature's flesh, the quarrel grew faint, and then seemed to disintegrate, but the place where it had entered was a small blackened hole.

'Well, I think you have its attention.' Tor stepped up next to her, his handsome face creased with distaste. 'My undying gratitude, Lady de Grazon.'

'Shut up. See if you can push it back into the forest.'

He shot a look at her.

'Are you out of your mind? It just killed someone. The poor bastard's entrails are currently staining my boots.'

'Do as you're told.'

For a wonder, he did. Stepping lightly forward, Tor swept the long straight blade of his sword in front of him, directly challenging the parasite spirit. He didn't make contact, but the spirit took two large steps backwards, its focus on the blade. It knew what it was now.

Vintage stared at its face, for want of a better word. There were four circular white lights, that could have been eyes, swimming in its elongated head, while at the bottom a wide flap hung down, lined with gently glowing fronds.

'They are all different,' murmured Vintage under her breath. In her mind she was already sketching this beast into her notebook, taking care to capture the fronds, the oddly split feet, and the spidery hands . . .

'Do you have any further thoughts, Vintage?' Tor was yelling over his shoulder. 'On, for example, what we do once we get this bastard beyond the wall?'

64

'Just keep going!' She loaded another shot into her crossbow, fingers moving automatically. The spirit was stumbling slowly backwards now, its elongated head swinging slowly from one side to another, lighting up the night. She could hear shouting from behind her, and assumed that the villagers had come out of their homes; probably discovering the inside-out remains of their kinsman steaming on the ground. She had no time for them.

'Push it back gently,' she called to Tor. 'Perhaps if we just persuade it to leave, rather than chase it off, it will lead us back to the remains of a Behemoth.'

She could see from Tor's stance that he meant to reply with something quite rude, but then one of the creature's arms was sweeping down towards him. Tor jumped gracefully away, bringing the Ninth Rain down in a sweeping arc to sail through the parasite spirit's spindly arm, severing several waving fronds. Immediately, the creature's clouded-glass body turned darker and its head split open in the middle. A high-pitched keening noise filled the night, so loud that Vintage felt it reverberate against her eardrums. She winced even as the villagers screamed in response.

She sprinted over, keeping her crossbow trained on the monster and her eyes on the ground. There. Smoking pieces of what looked like glass lay on the grass, writhing like snakes, already growing still. One handed, she pulled a rag from her pack and threw it over the remains before scooping up what was left and stuffing it back into her bag. Above them both, the parasite spirit was howling; the cavernous hole in the centre of its head was sprouting dark tentacles like bloody tongues, and the four lights were blinking on and off furiously.

'Vintage!'

Tor was slicing madly at the parasite spirit, driving it back with abandon, while casting furious looks at her.

'Stop looking at me, you fool! Concentrate on getting that—'

There was a chorus of screams, quickly drowned out by an odd discordant bellowing. Vintage turned to see an alien shape burning in the night, all purple and green lights like a migraine. Another parasite spirit had melted out of the darkness, and it was heading right for them.

'Oh, well, that's just bloody marvellous.'

Tor ducked out of the way just as the first parasite spirit took another swing at him – it was still screaming, and the dark tentacles that had sprouted from its head were writhing maddeningly; meanwhile, the new creature was stomping along towards him with its head down. Vintage, her coat with its many pockets flaring out behind her, managed to jump out of its path just in time, and now it was bearing down on him. It was markedly different to the first creature; still formed of odd, twisted glass-flesh, it was squat, like a toad, with lots of tiny purple and green lights swarming and swirling at the ends of its appendages. It had a wide fleshy mouth, which fell open as it ran.

With one parasite in front of him, one about to arrive to his left, and the villagers behind him, he had very few options. Tor spun in a quick circle, letting the sword move like a thing made of water itself. Both parasites reared back, and Tor shouted in triumph. The sword of his ancestors would be too much for them.

Too soon. The tall parasite seemed to take sudden offence, swiping one long hand down at him while the toad creature lurched forward. All at once, Tor found he needed his blade in two places. Slashing at the shorter one's nose, he felt a surge of satisfaction as his blade met resistance, and then he was off his feet and crashing into the dirt. The taller one had caught him, and now his left arm was threaded with a weird combination of pain and numbness – it felt as though something had tried to twist the flesh off his bones.

'Die, beast!' One of the villagers had run forward brandishing a short sword, his ruddy face wild with terror.

'No, get back, you fool!'

The toad creature struck the man in the waist just as he stabbed downwards wildly. Rather than severing the flesh as the Ninth Rain had done, the man's sword became stuck, just as though he'd thrust it into a barrel of tar. He tugged at it once, and then, thinking the better of it, turned to run, but the toad parasite had hold of his tunic with its wide mouth and pulled him back easily enough. Long tapering fronds squeezed out the corners of its lips and slapped wetly around the man's neck. Tor, struggling to his feet, grabbed hold of the man's shoulder, hoping to yank him from the thing's grasp, but the fronds squeezed and the man's head burst like an overly ripe fruit. The strange appendages immediately slid into the wet mess where his neck had been, as though searching for something. Tor let go of the body, surrendering the useless flesh.

'That's quite enough.'

His words were quiet, but both the parasite spirits turned to regard him, lights spinning in their flesh like the stars after one too many glasses of wine. Tor bellowed and rushed at the toad-shaped creature, driving the Ninth Rain ahead of him with both hands on the pommel. His arm was still bright with pain but he kept it steady, and he had the satisfaction of watching the creature suddenly turn and scamper away. Tor struck, the long straight blade piercing the fleshy back deeply and then he flicked it up, tearing through the wobbly resistance. The torn area turned a cloudy grey, and the creature squealed and bellowed and fell onto its side. As it died, its form twisted and melted and re-formed, as if trying to find a shape where it was unhurt.

Tor stepped away, turning towards the tall parasite spirit – a moment too late. It was already bringing one of its long arms down, and again he was struck and this time thrown into a nearby fence. The touch of its glassy flesh trailed down his chest, and for a few horrible moments his breath was frozen where it was, a hard lozenge in his throat. Tor tried to sit up, his boots digging furrows in the mud, but a tide of weakness moved through him, holding him in place. Panic clutched at his throat – his sword was no longer in his hand – and with effort he forced himself to calm down. With his right hand, thankfully still responding to his commands, he slipped a glass vial from within his pocket. One-handed, he uncorked it and pressed it to his lips. Blood, salty and not as fresh as he'd like, flooded over his tongue and filled his mouth. He thought, briefly, of Sareena, and the sweet afternoon they'd spent together. It was pleasant to imagine that her blood tasted like her skin, of apricots and smoke, but it did not. It tasted of blood.

'Get up, lad!'

Vintage was sprinting towards him, waving the crossbow in a worrying manner. Tor stood up, feeling strength coming back to his arm, sensation coming back to his chest. He could breathe. He felt powerful. Behind Vintage, the tall parasite spirit was standing over the body of its kin, one arm blackened where Tor had severed some of its fronds, but when it saw Tor coming, something in his stance seemed to spook it and it began to take odd, lolloping strides backwards.

'Tor, remember, we may be able to follow it back to the Behemoth.'

Tor stalked past Vintage without looking at her. The creature had touched him, had hurt him. It had insulted him – had insulted Ebora itself. This would not stand.

But the creature was already leaving. Abruptly, it began to fade from view, vanishing like a deep shadow at sunrise. He had seen them do this before; seeping away into nothing, leaving their destruction behind. In a few moments it was gone completely, and the corpse of its brethren was mouldering where it lay, a pile of congealing jelly. The weird alien funk of it filled the air.

Tor sheathed his sword, watching the shadowed place where the tall parasite had vanished. Dimly, he was aware of shouting, of many complaints from Vintage and cries from the villagers, but the blood-fire was leaving him now and he felt oddly empty.

Hollow again.

5

In the dream, Noon was in the furnace room. Novice Lusk knelt in front of her, his broad back shining with sweat while the column of her flame danced above them. She felt the euphoria of the fire and treasured it, trying to hold it inside her forever; trying to remember what skin felt like under her touch, forever. And then the great chimney above them was torn to one side and the circular room was filled with daylight. As her flames spluttered and died, Noon looked up to see a nightmare hanging in the sky above them: it was the corpse moon come to life. This close, it was a fat segmented worm, the thicker bands of its centre studded with pulsing pustules, while the head was a writhing collection of finger-like growths. There were things pushing through that barrier, creatures new to the sky of Sarn being born into an unknown atmosphere, and she knew suddenly that if she looked on them, she would die.

Turning away, she was caught up in Lusk's arms. He pulled her close and peered at her, as if he didn't know what she was.

'Let go of me! We have to get out of here.'

He smiled, a weird twisting of his lips as though he had seen other people do it before and was trying it for the first time.

'You know, Fell-Noon, why you are here, don't you?'

She put her hands up and pushed at him, but when her fingers brushed his chin, his flesh fell back as though it were made of uncooked dough. She cried out in disgust as his pale skin came away in sticky strands, and then his entire face caved in, revealing an empty, hollow darkness. There was nothing inside him – no bones, no blood – yet somehow he was still speaking to her.

'You'll die in here with all the others.'

She yanked herself away and she was back inside the Winnowry itself, moving without moving, in the way of dreams. Everyone was outside of their cells, crowding onto the narrow walkways, and the walls were shaking, so that the air was filled with dust. Above them, the great water tanks swung from side to side, sloshing water onto the people below – and in the part of her that knew on some level that this was a dream, she wondered at the detail of that. The women were screaming and pushing against each other, trying to flee but not knowing where to go.

'Outside!' Noon cupped her hands around her mouth and shouted. 'We have to get outside! If we rush them all at once they can't stop us!'

Marian grabbed at her sleeve, and for a sickening moment Noon thought her face would collapse the way that Lusk's had, but instead the girl bit her lip, shaking her head.

'But *they* are outside, Noon! They're crawling all over the Winnowry.' She held up her arms – bare skin covered in brown freckles – and Noon saw fat creatures like black beetles scuttling down from her shoulders, climbing over her elbows with legs like tiny knives. As she watched, Marian screamed and the beetles rushed to her face, eager to run down her throat.

'They're in here!'

Noon didn't see who yelled, but panic spread like a fever. Now they were all running, all clamouring to flee down the steep steps. In their terror, some of them were taking life energy from the others, and Noon saw several fall down, weakened by their fellow prisoners before being trampled on by them. She saw one unfortunate woman tipped over the guardrail of the walkway, no doubt falling to her death. Rushing forward onto the dark staircase, Noon was pressed against so many bodies her breath seemed to lodge in her throat. There were cries in the dark, women sobbing and calling out to each other. Somewhere up ahead, someone was wailing that the doors were all locked, that they couldn't get out this way, but the press was relentless, pushing her forward. It was nearly pitch-black, yet somehow Noon could see bodies on the floor; women who had fallen and had been stamped on, and amongst them, like a terrible rippling tide, the black beetles that had swarmed inside Marian. They were everywhere. Flesh pressed against her on all sides, and perhaps it would be easier, quicker, if she summoned the flames and burned them all. One great typhoon of fire and it would be over; better than the hollow nightmare, better than the crawling death.

And then she was outside. The Behemoth that had once been the corpse moon had extended long insectile legs and they were breaking away pieces of the Winnowry, scattering black rock and white marble onto the desolate ground. Noon was on her own on the dirt, exposed to the busy sky. As she watched, the Behemoth, now dangerously alive, ripped off the top of one of the Winnowry's towers, and a host of bats flew out. Most of the giant creatures managed to fly away, but some were caught up by the Behemoth's legs and by the things that were crawling out of its pulsating mouth. Noon, who had occasionally glimpsed the great bats flying back and forth over her years in the Winnowry, had never heard any of them make the smallest sound. Now those that were caught were squealing, a terrible noise so high pitched she thought her ears might burst.

Without thinking about what she would do when she got there, Noon turned and fled for the beach, trying to ignore the corpses that littered the ground. However, as she lifted her head to look across the bay to the distant city, she saw that the sky was heavy with Behemoths. They hung below the clouds like terrible growths, and she knew that all the land beneath them was being harvested. The people of the city were being turned hollow, eaten inside out.

'We're coming back.'

The voice was soft, female, and just behind her right ear. In the way of dreams, Noon found she couldn't move or turn her head – instead, she stared across the bay as the city of Mushenska was turned into something slick and alien.

'We're coming back, and Sarn will be ours, finally. There is no one to stand against us, Noon.'

Except that wasn't true. There were those who would stand against the invaders, who had always stood against them. They were despised amongst the plains people, and cursed for the Carrion Wars, but her people had still sung songs and told stories about them.

Stumbling, she looked at the spaces between the terrible shapes in the sky. That was where they would be – it was where they were in every tale and song she remembered from her childhood. Great beasts of ivory feathers and silver scales. Mother Fast had chanted stories of the ancient battles, and her own mother had shown her pictures in books.

But there were no Eboran war-beasts in the skies over Mushenska, and no army of shining knights to be seen on the coast. There were just the dark shapes uncurling, and she knew that on the streets of the city – and in the shattered buildings behind her   men and women were dying, and then, worse than that, opening their eyes again . . .

There was a low chuckle from behind her, and she turned to see a humanoid shape walking across the sand. It was hard

73

to see properly – it blurred and shifted, as though it wasn't quite sure what shape it was – but the voice was female. It had to be their queen.

'We are coming back. And where is Ebora now?'

Noon woke with a start, not on her narrow bunk but on the iron grill of the floor. She had fallen out in her sleep, and then lain there long enough to imprint deep red lines in her skin where she had been in contact with the metal. She sat up, shaking with fright. The dream felt like it was still all around her, thick in her throat like fog. In it, she had known true despair; first, when she had been trapped in the dark, knowing that they would all die down there, and then at the sound of the woman's voice. There had been no speculation in the woman's voice, only certainty: they would all die, and Sarn would be lost.

Groaning, she rubbed her hands over her face, feeling tiny grains of ash under her fingers. Akaris was supposed to stop the dreams. She hadn't had such a vivid nightmare in years.

'Noon? Are you unwell?'

Marian's face was turned up to hers.

'I'm fine. I had a bad dream.'

Even in the gloom of dawn she saw the look of surprise on the other woman's face.

'The akaris didn't work. It was so real . . .'

Noon swallowed hard. Real was an understatement. Looking down at Marian she remembered how the beetles had scampered up her arms, eager to get inside and eat her away. Mostly, though, she remembered being trapped. All at once, being in the Winnowry was more than she could take, and the crushing terror of ten years caught like a spider under a pot rushed over her. She stood up, still shaking. It was difficult to breathe.

'If the akaris isn't working, you should tell one of the sisters.' Marian's voice floated up to her. It felt like it was coming from a great distance. 'Perhaps they could give you more.'

74

They might well do that. At the Winnowry, everyone was encouraged to be calm at all times. 'Unfortunate emotional states', as they were referred to by the sisters, were greatly discouraged, and a series of bad dreams could lead to unpleasantness. Noon, who had suffered from terrible nightmares when she had arrived at the Winnowry, took the akaris every day without fail, and valued her dreamless sleep. She took a deep, shaky breath. Her emotional state, she felt, could definitely be classified as unfortunate.

'Fell-Noon? What are you doing?'

Noon looked up to see one of the sisters peering in through her bars. Unusually, she held her silver mask between her gloved fingers, and she looked old; dark circles pulled at the bags below the woman's eyes, and her thin lips looked chapped. From her voice she recognised her as Sister Renier.

'Nothing. What does it look like I'm doing?' She spat the words so that the sister wouldn't hear how frightened she was. 'What else can I do in here?'

She expected a harsh reply, but Sister Renier just shook her head at her, and after a moment pulled her mask back on. When she spoke again, her voice had taken on its odd metallic twang. 'I don't have the energy for this, Fell-Noon. Get ready for your meditations.'

Noon blinked. Meditation. She had completely forgotten. Another method for avoiding 'unfortunate emotional states', of course – once every four days each fell-witch was required to complete a sequence of meditations with one of the priests.

The tray with the scarf, gloves and ash was pushed through the slot, and she knelt to receive them. Concentrating on preparing herself reduced the shaking to a tremble in her fingers. When her hands were concealed and her face was covered with the fine grey powder, the door of her cell was rattled back and she stepped out. Sister Renier pulled the cuffs around Noon's wrists and as she did so, her left-hand glove slipped down slightly on one side, exposing the skin of her forearm. Noon looked up, startled, but the old woman just yanked the sleeve back up and took hold of her arm to lead her towards the meditation chambers. The sleeve of the woman's robe had a loop at the end that was supposed to hook around her thumb, and then the long gloves were pulled right up over the sleeve. Sister Renier must have forgotten to do it when she dressed that day, but such a slip was unthinkable.

The woman walked her beyond the cells, and into the tightly wound warren of tunnels and staircases that riddled the Winnowry. They found a set of spiral stairs and headed up; at the end, Noon knew, they would come to a set of rooms with relatively large windows – all sealed shut, of course – that looked away from the mainland and out to sea. There was very little to look at, just waves the colour of steel, some clouds perhaps, and the occasional distant bird. The view was supposed to be relaxing, so it was easier for them to empty their minds, but today just the thought of looking out at the vastness of the ocean filled Noon with a chilly terror. It was too easy to imagine the empty sky populated with the bulbous forms of the Behemoths, and she would be trapped in here while the Winnowry was pulled down around them – there was too much stone above them, too much stone on all sides, like a tomb.

Above her somewhere was one of the chirot towers, where the Winnowry kept its giant bats. Noon had never been there or even anywhere close to it, but you didn't live in the same building for ten years without learning things about it. The idea popped into her head fully formed, and with an irresistible clarity. As Fell-Anya had said, what could they do to her? Kill her? Perhaps that would be a mercy.

'Sister Renier, is that a mouse on the step?'

It was a cheap trick, but the woman was tired and distracted. As she craned her head up to see ahead of them, her face creased with apprehension, Noon sharply tugged the glove off her right hand.

'What? I can't see anything.'

'You can't?'

Noon twisted round and grabbed hold of the woman's arm with both her hands – the bare one, she slipped under the end of Sister Renier's glove and she felt her fingers slide over bare skin.

'No!'

It was as easy as dipping her hand into water. Noon tore the old woman's life energy from her; she did not hold herself back as she did in the furnace, but let her own need dictate what she took. Sister Renier staggered on the steps, almost going to her knees.

'No . . .'

Surprised the old woman could talk at all, Noon glanced down the steps behind them, and then above, but no one was coming. Inside her, the swirling force of the woman's living energy was beginning to build to dangerous levels. She had to let it out in some form.

Keeping one hand on the woman's arm, Noon wrapped the other around the metal cuff that circled her wrist and, concentrating harder than she ever had in her life, focussed the winnowfire down to encompass the silver ring alone. There was a tense moment where Noon was half sure she was about to blow her own arm off, and then there was a blast of greenish light and the cuff shattered into pieces, throwing her and Renier back against the wall. The old woman moaned and pushed away from her.

'I'm not staying here to die,' said Noon. There was a roaring in her ears, a rising tide of panic. She let the woman go and she slumped bonelessly onto the steps. Noon bent down to speak directly into her ear. 'I could have burned you,' she hissed. 'Don't forget that.'

* * *

Lusk made his way down the central passage of the chirot chamber, walking silently from habit. To either side, the great bats of the Winnowry were hanging cosy in their alcoves. They were mostly hidden in the shadows, but here and there he could see a swatch of soft white or black fur, or the flap of a leathery wing. For the bats, this was the middle of their night, and they were all sound asleep – aside from the occasional squeak or huff, it was peaceful.

Tending the chirot tower was his favourite job. He would bring the bats their food – a strange mixture of fruit and dead mice – and he would clean up as best he could, scraping away guano and mopping the floors, tidying away snags of fur. Sometimes, if a bat came back from carrying a message while he was there, he would brush them down and scratch them behind the ears. The bats all knew him, and they also knew he was good for ear scratches and the occasional smuggled piece of red meat. Sometimes, very rarely, a patrol would return and he would nod to the fell-witches who dismounted with his eyes on the floor. These were the agents of the Winnowry – fell-witches who had proven themselves to be controlled enough to work for the Winnowry itself. They would fly across Sarn, seeking rumours of fell-witches out in the world, or they would take the akaris to the places where it was sold. Some of them, solo flyers, did jobs that were never spoken of openly. Lusk did not ask. It wasn't as if anyone would tell him, anyway. And the chirot tower was quiet. It gave him time and space to think; to concentrate on his meditation and the teachings of Tomas.

He was sitting at the small table repairing a piece of leather harness when he heard footsteps on the stairs outside. He rose, sure it must be someone coming to send a message – he would need to prepare a message tube.

'I will be right with you—'

The door flew open, and to his shock a fell-witch stumbled

78

in. Her arms were bare, and her eyes were wild in her ashes-dusted face.

For a moment they simply gawped at each other, and then Lusk remembered himself and rushed for the pulley on the far wall. It was attached to a bell system that would alert the entire Winnowry.

'Stop!' The woman held her hand up and a glove of green flame popped into existence around it, flickering wildly. 'Don't move. Not a bit.'

Lusk stopped. The woman was breathing hard. 'Fell-Noon?'

She came cautiously into the room, seeming to look all around her at once. She took in the bats sleeping peacefully in their alcoves and the wide strip of blue sky above them where they entered and exited the building.

'I still have plenty left,' she said, and as if to demonstrate this, the flames curling around her hand rose a few inches, eating up more of the air. 'I will use it.'

Lusk lifted his hands, palms out. 'Fell-Noon, you should be in your cell.'

'Oh, do you think so?' She glared at him, coming closer. Abruptly, she reached up and pulled the green scarf from her head and cast it onto the floor. Doing so seemed to give her a great deal of satisfaction. 'I have to get out of here. Now.' She swallowed. He got the impression that talking this much was hard. Without the scarf, her short black hair stuck up at all angles. 'I'm not dying in this place.'

'No one has to die. I can take you back downstairs.' Lusk kept his voice soft, trying not to think about how terrible it would be to burn to death. He had seen this woman many times in the furnace rooms, and while there had always been a contained anger about her, she had never seemed especially unstable. Now her eyes were wild, and her posture was that of an animal about to flee. Or attack. 'I'll tell them you got lost, and I'm sure it'll be fine. Just a misunderstanding.'

'No.' She came further into the room. The flames around her hand were starting to die down, and he knew that wherever she had stolen the living energy from, it would be running out now. Soon, he would be safe to try and overpower her, except that he was wearing only a loose work vest. If she got close, she could take his energy too – just as she did in the purging sessions. 'Get one of them ready.' She gestured to the bats.

'You cannot mean to leave here! Fell-Noon, it's not safe—'

'Not safe? Not safe for who?' She rubbed her forehead with her free hand, wiping away ashes to bare streaks of her own olive skin and the spidery lines of the bat-wing tattoo that marked all fell-witches. 'This *place* isn't bloody safe. Do it.' She suddenly advanced on him, holding her hands out. The green flame died, but there was still that wild look in her eye. 'Hurry up.'

He turned away from her and approached the nearest bat. It was a female with pearly white fur and a soft grey muzzle. He picked up the whistle at the base of her alcove and gave three short blasts. Each bat was trained to wake and obey on command. The bat shivered all over, and peeled back a wing to peer at him curiously. Eyes like pools of ink wrinkled at the edges.

'Morning, Fulcor,' he said softly. 'Come on down for me.' The bat scampered down, walking on her wing-feet until she stood in the middle of the chamber. She yawned hugely, revealing a bright pink mouth studded with alarming teeth. Lusk fetched the newly repaired harness and set about attaching the contraption. He could feel Fell-Noon watching him intently.

'Do that properly,' she said suddenly. 'I will know if you haven't. I used to ride horses.' She stopped and took a breath. 'When I was small, I had my own horse.' She ran her hands through her hair, making it even messier. 'I had a dream. I'm not supposed to have dreams in here, but I did. The worm

80

people came and tore this place apart. You were there, but you were empty inside.'

Lusk felt his skin grow cold. Surely she was mad, then. Ten years in this place, brought here at the age of eleven, and the monotony and the quiet had broken her, as it sometimes did – she wouldn't be the first fell-witch to have lost her mind. 'The Jure'lia? They haven't attacked for hundreds of years.' He pulled another strap home and patted Fulcor's furry forehead. 'I've heard some say the Eighth Rain will be the last.'

Fell-Noon shook her head. 'It was too real. It was dark, and everyone panicked, trying to get out of the doors. They suffocated. Fell-Marian had creatures inside her, eating her up.' She came over to him, looking at the bat. 'Is it ready? I have to get out of this place.'

But Lusk had stopped. Her words had unsettled something in his own mind. 'People fell, and they couldn't get up?'

'Yes,' she said irritably. 'And then I was outside. Their creatures were in the sky, floating over Mushenska.'

'And the dead littered the beach,' Lusk replied faintly. He had completely forgotten it. A terrible dream he'd had days ago, bad enough to have woken him in his small bunk, but then, on waking, it had fallen away into pieces, too vague to recall. 'There was a woman behind me, and she said they were coming back.'

'Their queen,' agreed Noon. She narrowed her eyes at him, her voice becoming softer. 'You had it too?'

Lusk ran his fingers through Fulcor's fur. He should jump for the pulley. He thought he could probably make it, now that she was distracted. But a terrible cold was keeping him in one place. 'How did you know?' he asked. 'How did you know it was them?'

'What else could they fucking be? And I've been looking at one my whole life, just like you have.' She gestured angrily at the strip of sky above them, and he knew she was talking

81

about the corpse moon. With a feeling like a cold finger down his back he remembered that it had been alive, in his dream.

'What does it mean?'

'What it means is, I'm bloody leaving this place. Before they get here. And destroy everything.'

Noon went around to the bat's hindquarters, where the animal was crouched lowest to the floor. She climbed on cautiously, pulling herself across Fulcor's muscled back to settle her legs into the saddle – riding a bat meant sitting with your legs bent at the knee and your own body thrown forward. Lusk still stood there unmoving, his chest filled with a weight of dread, until she gestured at him impatiently. He realised he was still holding the silver whistle, so he handed it over to her quickly. She was in contact with Fulcor now, and could choose to take the bat's energy if she wished.

'Her name is Fulcor,' he said, not sure why he was speaking at all. 'Three short blasts to wake her up, one long one to bring her to you, if she's close enough, and four blasts to dismiss her. She will stay with you, as long as you have the whistle, and she knows all the basic commands. They're trained that way. She's – she's a friendly sort, this one. Has a bit of an independent streak. Some of the agents, well, they prefer a more obedient bat, but . . .' He trailed off, aware that he was babbling now.

'What will you do?' she asked. Her voice was tense, her eyes bright with an emotion he couldn't read – they looked black, almost as black as Fulcor's.

'I will sound the alarm, of course. They will send agents after you, and I will be disciplined for letting this happen.'

For a moment she said nothing. She glanced up at the sky, biting her lip.

'Give me some time,' she said eventually. 'Just a little while. To get away.' She swallowed hard. 'I haven't killed anyone, not here. You could give me that much.'

They had both had the same dream. That had to mean

something – Tomas had written a great deal about looking for signs, and this was the only sign Lusk's life had ever seen fit to show him. Feeling as though perhaps he was trapped in another dream, Lusk met the woman's eyes and nodded once.

'Go. I'll give you as long as I can.'

Fell-Noon took the reins and tugged them. Fulcor shifted round on her wing-feet and scampered up to the platform on the far side of the room. The sky was a blue and grey plate above them.

'They will still come after you,' he called. 'The Winnowry doesn't let anyone walk away. They will chase you.'

'I'm sure they will. But I won't be in this fucking hole, and that's the main thing.' Fell-Noon leaned low over the bat and spoke softly into its large, crinkled ear. 'Fly!'

6

Feeling as though she'd left her stomach behind in the chirot tower, Noon lifted her face to the sun as the giant bat propelled them up into the empty sky. The cold wind stung her skin and forced tears to gather at the corners of her eyes. She was outside, finally – ten years of bars and silence and hopelessness, and already the Winnowry was falling away behind her. She felt caught between laughing and crying. Below her the strip of sea that separated the Winnowry from the mainland was streaking past, the colour of beaten steel, and she thought she'd never seen anything more beautiful. Beneath her bare hands she could feel the living force that was Fulcor; hot blood, thrumming muscles, a thundering heart. Freedom.

Faster than she would have believed possible, Mushenska was looming close, its busy port bristling with ships, the taste of sea spray in her mouth. With a lurch, she realised she hadn't thought about what she would do next at all. Her need to be outside of the Winnowry's walls had driven everything else from her mind, and now she had decisions to make that would likely mean her life or death. Abruptly, she was certain that Novice Lusk had sounded the alarm the very second she had left the chirot tower, and she twisted around in the saddle, squinting her eyes against the wind to peer at the Winnowry. It was as ugly as ever, the twisted black scalpels of its towers ripping at the sky, but all was still. Nothing flew in pursuit of her as yet, but even so, she needed to get out of sight while she decided what to do next.

Fulcor was taking them over roofs now, a confusing collection of brown and grey and black shapes, obscured here and there with smoke. Hoping she was doing the right thing, Noon leaned forward and spoke a single word into the bat's ear.

'Down.'

Fulcor dropped, causing Noon to press her thighs desperately to either side of the animal's back, and then, with a whirring of leathery wings, they were still. The bat had landed them on top of a surprisingly crowded flat roof – the place was littered with crates and there was a long, well-maintained garden. Noon unstrapped herself from the saddle, slipping off the bat while keeping her eyes on a small shed-like construction on the far side of the roof. It would lead, she guessed, to the interior of the building.

'I'm fine, I'm fine.'

She wasn't, though, and as she gained her feet her legs turned oddly boneless, tipping her into the dark dirt of the narrow garden. A smell so ancient she had half forgotten it, of deep rich earth and growing things, rose to engulf her. She made a choked noise, half a sob, and, as if in answer, Fulcor *chirruped*.

'I'm fine,' she said again, her whole body shaking. She reached out a hand to the plants growing in their neat rows and saw with wonder that she had slumped next to a tomato plant. There were tomatoes growing on it, tight in their skins and perfectly red. After a moment, she reached out a trembling hand and plucked one from its stem, jerking a little as she did so. She had entirely forgotten what it felt like to pick something from its branch, had entirely forgotten the smooth feeling of tomato skin under her fingers. There were no fresh fruit or vegetables in the Winnowry – too dangerous. Fell-witches only ate food that had been cooked and cooked into a hot grey paste.

Laughing quietly to herself, Noon raised the tomato to her lips and bit into it. Flesh and juices exploded onto her tongue and she jumped as though someone had pinched her. It tasted like . . . she had no words for how it tasted.

'Like life,' she murmured. 'It tastes like life.'

Oblivious now to the curious bat watching her, or the possibility of pursuit, Noon picked a small handful of tomatoes and slowly ate them all. After a little while, she realised she was crying as she did so, hot tears turning the pale ash on her face to sticky grit. With a hand covered in tomato juice she pulled up the bottom of her shirt and rubbed her face with it.

Shivering slightly against the chilly breeze blown straight in from the sea, Noon looked around, forcing herself to pay attention. Mushenska spread out in all directions, the confusion of roofs and chimneys completely alien to her. There was a great deal of noise too; a soft roar, not unlike the ocean at night, only this was punctuated with the shouts and cries of people living their everyday lives. Somewhere below, a man was shouting about fresh bread, and a woman was remonstrating with another woman about the shoddy work her son had done on a fence. Out here, beyond the towers of the Winnowry, people were getting on with their lives, in a city that was just waking up for the day. It seemed impossible.

And then, as if she'd summoned it, the door to the outhouse clattered open and a stout red-headed woman with sun-weathered skin stepped out onto the roof. She had an empty basket on one arm, and it occurred to Noon that the woman had probably come up here to harvest the tomatoes. For her breakfast. The woman's face jerked, first with surprise, and then with anger.

'Oi! What do you think you're bloody playing at?'

Noon fell back, her hands in the dirt, and, instinctively, she pulled the life energy from the plants behind her. The hot green flame kindled inside her for the briefest moment, and then it jumped from her hands in a bright blossom of fire. It passed harmlessly upwards, doing little more than adding an extra brightness to the morning, but the older woman let out a warbling shriek and fell back against the door, clutching at her considerable chest.

'Shut up.' Noon swallowed. It felt strange to be talking to someone who was neither a fell-witch nor a custodian of the Winnowry. The effort seemed to suck all command from her voice. 'Shut up, don't move. Just . . . stay there.'

The woman stood where she was. The fright on her face had rearranged itself back into anger. Slowly, Noon stood up, trying to act as though her legs didn't feel like they were made of water. She was very aware of the black dirt under her fingernails, and her dirty face.

'I own this place,' the woman said, holding her chin up. 'If you people want to come here and eat, you walk in the front door the same as everyone else. The Frog and Bluebell isn't your larder, missus.'

Noon blinked. The woman thought she was here on official Winnowry business. She must have seen the Winnowry agents flying over the city on their own bats, and she had assumed that Noon was an agent with a sudden taste for tomatoes.

'I am sorry.' Would a Winnowry agent apologise? Noon doubted it. She attempted to scowl at the woman. 'But I will take what I need, when on *official* Winnowry business. Is this place –' For a moment the word danced out of her reach – the plains people did not have such things, after all – but she had listened to the other fell-witches talk about them – 'a tavern?'

'Aye, it's a tavern.' The barkeep looked less angry now, and her eyes moved over Noon's face with more care, seeming to take special note of the bat-wing tattoo on her forehead. Noon resisted the temptation to cover it up with her hands.

'I am travelling north,' said Noon. Behind her, she could hear the snuffling of Fulcor. She suspected the bat was eating her own share of tomatoes now. 'Can you tell me what is north of this city?'

The barkeep frowned, pushing her jowly cheeks into loops of wrinkles. 'Nowt but Wild beyond Mushenska. Some small towns and settlements dotted here and there. Worm-touched in the head, the people who live out there, if you ask me. Give me good solid walls any day.' She tipped her head to one side. 'Surely you know that, witch?'

Noon lifted her chin slightly. 'Can you give me some food to take with me? I mean, you will give me food. The Winnowry will give you coin for it.'

For some moments, the barkeep just stared at her. The city around them was growing louder all the time – the roar was not like the sea after all, Noon realised. It was like a great beast; a slowly waking beast they were all living on.

'Wait here.'

With that, the barkeep disappeared back through the door. Noon stood rooted to the spot, feeling panic fill her like icy water flooding a well. The woman had gone to alert the Winnowry authorities, and she would lead them right here, where she would still be waiting, like an idiot, and then they would take her back – screaming, just as she had done when they had first captured her – but not to her cell. They would take her straight to the Drowned One, and she would face that pale, dripping horror and her tank, or perhaps they would burn her on the spot, not caring for the barkeep's precious garden . . .

The door opened and the woman stepped back through. She had a small hessian bag in her arms, which she thrust at Noon.

'Ale, some cheese. A nub of yesterday's bread. Take it, girl, and get away from here.'

The woman was close enough to touch, her brawny freckled arms bare of sleeves. It seemed impossible that someone should be so careless, and for a moment Noon couldn't breathe. *I could kill you now*, she thought. *In seconds.*

'What are you waiting for, you daft creature?' The woman scowled at her. 'Go!'

Noon hurried back to Fulcor, tugging on the animal's reins so that she left the remains of the plants alone, and swiftly strapped herself back into the saddle. She secured the sack the barkeep had given her behind her, and it really did seem to contain food and drink – she could hear the sloshing of the ale inside some sort of flask. It was only when they were back in the air, and heading to the outskirts of the city, that Noon realised that the barkeep hadn't believed her story at all, and why would she? A lone Winnowry agent on her knees in the woman's vegetable patch, scoffing tomatoes like she hadn't eaten anything in weeks, her face streaked with muddy tears – she was hardly convincing as a feared and respected agent of the Winnowry.

Why the woman would give her supplies regardless, she couldn't possibly guess.

Beyond the city of Mushenska the Wild spread out across the land like virulent mould. Even flying so far above it, Noon could see the difference between it and the normal patches of forest; the Wild was thicker, stranger. The shadows seemed deeper there, and she could see twisted sections of bare bark as trees curled around each other, fighting for space. It was late morning by then, and the sun was beating down on the top of her head, but something about the stretch of dark forest below made her feel cold. Her feet tingled, and she felt exposed. Even Fulcor seemed less comfortable, the small huffings and chirrups Noon had grown used to absent. Instead, the bat flew slightly faster, as though determined to get the Wild out from under them as swiftly as possible.

'We have to stop somewhere.' Noon's words were snatched away by the wind, and she grimaced. The very idea of landing somewhere within those worm-touched trees made her skin crawl, but the longer they were in the air, the more chance that the inevitable patrols – Winnowry bats carrying real Winnowry agents – would spot her. Besides which, her entire body was chilled and aching, and her eyes were sore from watering in the constant wind, which, in turn, was giving her a headache. 'I just need to sit for a while,' she told Fulcor. 'Eat this food, make a fire, and think what to do next.'

The bat gave no indication as to whether she thought this was a wise idea or not. Ahead of them, the landscape of twisted greenery gave away to a stretch of land so strange to Noon's eyes that she sat up in Fulcor's saddle, trying to see it more clearly. It looked to her almost like the surface of a pond crowded with lily pads, only the circular growths were huge, the size of the roofs they had passed over in Mushenska, and tall, on the same level as the tree canopy. Each circular mound was brown, or beige, or a pale cream with dark grey spots, and as they passed overhead and Noon caught a whiff of a deep, earthy and somehow *lively* scent, she realised that they were the caps of enormous fungi. It made no sense to her at all, but they were somehow less alarming than the clinging trees, so she leaned forward to speak into Fulcor's great crinkled ear again and the bat took them spiralling down through a chink in the caps. Beneath the surface of this strange, fleshy forest were more of the enormous toadstools, their caps smaller and in some cases more colourful; Noon saw pale pink, deep ochre and some examples of a dusty blue. White and grey stalks feathered with fringes of creamy white flesh twisted up all around, and the shadowed spaces were shot through here and there with shards of weak sunlight, dancing with motes of dust. It was all eerily quiet.

Fulcor landed on a craggy hill of black dirt, lifting her feet off it one at a time and making discontented squeaks. Noon unstrapped herself and her new hessian bag and just about had time to step down onto the damp ground before Fulcor flapped her leathery wings and was away again. Noon watched as the bat flew agitatedly from one stalk to another, looking for all the world like a moth battering a lamp, and then she found a space amongst the caps and was gone.

'Oh.'

Noon stood staring up at the place where the bat had vanished, trying not to feel the weight of shadows all around her. After a moment, she hesitantly blew on the silver whistle, feeling vaguely foolish, but the bat did not return.

'Fuck.'

Slowly, Noon realised that the place was neither as quiet nor as still as she'd initially thought. The shadows contained tiny points of movement, creatures native to this dank underworld skittering away from her intrusion, while a dry ticking, like bone dice being lightly thrown together, seemed to come from all around. Trying not to imagine what might live in this strange offshoot of the Wild, Noon swiftly gathered an armful of bracken and sticks, sucked the remaining life energy out of them, and built a small haphazard fire on top of a dirt mound. The sticks were still too damp, but she blasted them with winnowfire until she had a small, smoky blaze, and she crouched next to it, shivering.

'Here I am,' she said. The dry ticking noise had grown quieter, and she guessed that whatever had been making it had moved away. 'Here I am, then.'

It was strangely mild down under the fungi, and the air was thick, but the damp of the soil had quickly soaked through her Winnowry-issue slippers and a deeper kind of cold was seeping into her bones. Presently, she began to shake all over.

'I don't know where I am,' she said to the lively shadows. 'But I am free. I don't have much food, and I have no idea where I am, but I have escaped the Winnowry.' She picked up the hessian sack and clutched it to her chest, recalling the bustle and the noise of Mushenska. 'Free to starve to death under a fucking mushroom.'

7

Hestillion paused with her hand on the door, staring down the corridor at nothing. Nothing.

The slick wood was cold under her fingertips, but then, her fingertips these days were little beads of ice, a shivery reminder that everything was wrong. The end of the corridor was in shadow, with strained grey light falling across the threadbare carpet. It was an overcast day, and the windows were dirty. There was no one left to clean them – not unless Hestillion went and fetched a bucket from the cavernous servants' quarters, and she couldn't face that yet. Not yet.

There was nothing to look at down the corridor but, even so, Hestillion stared at it, letting herself fade into a kind of weary trance. Perhaps, if she stood here long enough, thinking very carefully about nothing, she could step outside of time. And then she would walk down this corridor and hear voices behind every door. The light would be the good, strong light of summer, and nobody would be dead at all. She would laugh with her brother, and this whole nightmare would seem so silly. Perhaps it was all a nightmare she had woven and made everyone dream for a time, and Tormalin would smile indulgently at her and suggest they toast her, a true master of dream-walking.

From inside the room came a high-pitched, wailing wheeze, snapping Hestillion out of her comfortable trance. Her fingers tightened around the clean linens she held in one hand as she listened for what came next. A wheeze, growing tighter and tighter as the lungs struggled to gather air, a few heartbeats of nothing – *was it over? Was this the end?* – and then the explosive rattle, a coarse tearing that made her wince. It was impossible to hear it without imagining soft tissues tearing deep inside, and the splatter of blood on sheets. Another whistling wheeze, another pause, and the thick avalanche that followed.

'Hold on,' she murmured, leaning on the door to open it. She wasn't sure if she was talking to herself or Moureni.

The room inside was dark save for the hazy rectangle of grey light that was the window. She could make out the great four-poster bed and a stormy sea of white sheets; the shape in the middle was a range of narrow mountains, twisted and treacherous. The air smelled of blood and dust, but then Hestillion was almost certain that Ebora had smelled of nothing else for the last hundred years.

'Good morning, Lord Moureni,' she said, gliding into the room and setting the linens on the corner of the bed, as if she were a maid and this were her job. 'How are we feeling today?'

Moureni answered with another rattling cough, one so severe that he went rigid under the sheets, his body caught in the violence of the spasm. Hestillion went to the window and pulled the sashes back as far as they would go. It barely made a difference.

'Girl,' croaked the figure in the bed. 'How do you think I am?'

'Do not call me that. I am no child, and I have a name.'

Moureni went back to coughing. As she turned back to the bed, Hestillion saw a dark patch spreading on the sheet near

94

the head of the bed. It was not the clear fluid that Eborans bled from a superficial wound, but the deep oily black blood they shed when death was near. By now, Lord Moureni would be leaking this black blood from cracks in his skin all over his body. It was near impossible to get out of white sheets.

'Good thing I brought fresh linen for you, isn't it?'

There was a candelabra on the small chest of drawers by the bed stuffed with fat white candles, half burned down to nothing, so she lit them quickly with the matches in her pocket. The warm yellow light that spread across the pillow was the brightest thing Hestillion had seen in months. Unfortunately, it also revealed the ravaged face of Lord Moureni, and that was less heartening.

He had once been a handsome man. The evidence of that was on the walls of this, his much-reduced suite in Ygseril's palace; enormous oil paintings of a striking man with broad shoulders, tightly curled dark hair and shining bronze skin, his clothes always a military uniform of some sort, and the setting often the top of some windswept hill, looking off across some newly conquered territory. The skies in these paintings were almost always stormy, as though Ebora's sprawling empire were itself an oncoming conflagration – or perhaps the artist had just liked painting clouds.

Now Lord Moureni was a wizened shell of a man; all that was wet and vital about him hollowed out and dry. His skin, once smooth and almost luminous, was now chalky and gritty to the touch, where it wasn't split and weeping. He looked up at her with eyes of yellow and red, and she had to look away. His darkly curling hair, once his pride and joy, was now a collection of half-hearted wisps, most stuck to his broad forehead with sweat. There was black blood on his chin.

'Here, I will change the sheets.' Hestillion took the edges of the soiled linen in between her frozen fingertips and yanked the sheet away. Moureni cried out, pulling his legs up to his chest and twisting his ragged nightshirt, but Hestillion ignored him. 'Stop whining.'

He opened his mouth to say something in reply, but instead he was coughing again, his whole body wracked with it. He pressed the backs of his wrists to his mouth but she still saw it: blood, thick and diseased, oozing through his teeth and the corners of his mouth.

I should just go, she thought. *Turn around now, close the door and start walking. Walk until Ebora is far behind me, and let Lord Moureni cough himself to death.* There was nothing she could do for him, nor for any of them, so she should just leave like her brother had and let it all fade into nothing – one endless corridor of shadows and memories and nothing else.

Instead, she threw the blood-stained sheet behind her, picked up the folded white linen and shook it out over the emaciated figure. The crimson flux was both merciless and slow. Those afflicted would feel tired at first, and then their muscles would feel sore. Next, they would start coughing, and that was the beginning of the true end. Skin became stiff and painful, flaking off in big pieces or splitting open to reveal raw flesh beneath, and the cough itself became a demon, a creature that attacked with razor claws and sharpened teeth. And they would live, in this half-life, for months, for years, some even for decades, until one day Hestillion would discover their husks – the last of their bodily fluids ejected out onto their clothes, their fingers twisted into tree roots with the final throes of death. That was the end that waited for most, if not all of them. That or a slow vanishing into decrepitude. This was what Tormalin had fled.

'There's no coming back from this.' Moureni's voice was a sour rasp. Hestillion was surprised he had a voice left at all. 'This is how I will be, until I die.'

Hestillion waited. Sometimes they would ask her to end it

for them, when the suffering became relentless. In the bed, Moureni clutched at the fresh sheet, pulling it up to his pointed chin, which now resembled a shrivelled root vegetable.

'I remember Ygseril,' continued Moureni. 'You probably don't, young creature like you, but I remember when the leaves were thick on the branch, and the sap ran. We were like children then. We had no idea of what fate was capable of. What a terrible lesson we have learned.' The old man – not old for an Eboran, not truly, but ancient now – wheezed and gasped in some parody of laughter. 'The Eighth Rain will be the last we'll see, and we, we will be dust and bones, just like everyone beyond the Wall. Just like the humans. Because we drank their blood.' Moureni stiffened as though he meant to sit up, but he didn't have the strength. Instead, he rolled over onto his side. 'This is their filthy disease! We've caught it from their dirty blood. That will be my last act. I will take my swords, my shining blades, and—'

To Hestillion's relief, coughing took him for a while then. It was a terrible, pained session, and for a few long moments Hestillion thought that he had lost all his breath, that he would simply choke to death in the middle of a rant, but although all the cracks in his powdery skin opened up and wept their oily fluid, he was still alive at the end of it. His eyes, like wet pebbles adrift on bone-white sand, stared up at the canopy of the bed.

'I must die killing them,' he whispered at last. 'The only way . . . the only way to cleanse this blood disease.'

'I went walking out across the city yesterday afternoon,' said Hestillion. She stood slowly and moved over to the dark wood cabinet. Behind the glass were various medals and trophies from Lord Moureni's glorious past. 'The doors to the old library were open, so I went inside. Hundreds of scrolls had been pulled out and torn to pieces, and in other places, an animal had made a nest of some sort. There were droppings.'

She paused, and took a heavy brass bowl from inside the cabinet. Gold coins rested in the bottom of it. 'I walked on from there, and was followed for a time by a pair of wolves. They were skinny things, and they must have been hungry, but they only watched me walk. I think even the wolves know what a diseased place this is now. They know better than to eat rotten meat.' She took the coins from the bowl and slipped them into her own pocket. 'If you left the sanctuary of Ygseril's palace, my Lord Moureni, you would perhaps have the energy to make it to the first flight of stairs. I promise you there are no nasty diseased humans waiting out there for you to kill, even if you had the strength to lift your sword.'

Moureni fell silent, and she returned to his bedside to pour a glass of water from the carafe on the side. The water swirled with motes of dust, but it hardly mattered. He would use it only to wash the taste of blood from his mouth – which struck her as ironic.

'There is water here for you. Can I get you anything else?'

Rather than answering, the emaciated figure in the bed turned his face away from her, staring into the shadows in the corner of the room. For a moment she looked where he was looking, wondering if he too found himself in a trance, looking for a past that wasn't there any more. Nothing left for Ebora but shadows and dust.

The man gurgled, preparing for another coughing fit, and Hestillion shook herself out of her funk. She snatched up the blood-stained sheets and closed the door quietly, before walking smartly down the corridor. On her right she came to a door that was half open, and without looking into its dark interior, she threw the dirty sheets inside.

There were no servants left to wash the linen, or indeed the windows or the crockery, but there were rooms and rooms full of things that had been made for people now dead: thousands of folded sheets, elegant glasses, delicate plates trimmed with gold, dresses and gowns unending. Much of it had been made or imported before the crimson flux began to make a serious dent on their population, and now Hestillion doubted she could possibly make use of all of it before it succumbed to mould, or rot, or simply crumbled away to nothing.

'Dust, dust, dust,' she murmured under her breath. She wiped her hands absently down her front, knowing that the feeling of grime would never quite go away. She wore a padded silk gown, a deep ochre embroidered with pale blue-and-white birds, and slippers with blue silk feathers, and these, at least, she did take care of. At the end of every day she would go to her own suite of rooms and brush the gown with the special brushes she had for the task – they were coated with a sort of powder that freshened the silk – and carefully put the gown back into her wardrobe with all the others. They were works of art, made years ago by Eboran men and women who had spent decades learning their craft, and she couldn't quite let them go to ruin along with everything else.

Following the corridors without needing to think about it, Hestillion made her way gradually to the centre of the complex. The palace was a warren, sprawling out from its heart like a knot of tangled roots – it had grown organically over the centuries, like the great god that sat in the midst of it. Halls intersected each other apparently at random; enormous rooms appeared suddenly with no warning, small chambers sprouted at corners, tiny courtyards appeared here and there, jewels in the midst of the confusion. Back when Ebora had been alive, there had never been any question of people becoming lost in this labyrinth – live anywhere for a hundred years and you will know its every nook and cranny.

There were other Eborans here, dotted throughout the palace, or out in the wider city. Little more than a handful now, and almost all of them were dying from the crimson flux, but they kept themselves to themselves, as though they had all made a joint decision that to watch each other die was too painful. Hestillion would see them sometimes; a hunched figure walking down an empty street, or a gaunt face at a window. A few of them, she knew, paid humans to come into the city and give them their blood. It made her cold to think of it. The sheer desperation of knowing that drinking human blood would only give the disease more strength, and then doing it anyway, because it made you feel better for a time. She thought of the humans, the disgust and the triumph that must move across their faces to see their old enemy so fallen, even as coins were pressed into their palms for their services.

She passed a room where a young man sat at a dining table. Spread in front of him were hundreds of paper cards, each about the size of the palm of his hand, each illustrated in bright inks. They were tarla cards. There was the Broken Moon, its yellow surface split like an egg; there the Just Warrior, depicted as a woman in shining silver armour; next to it was the Wise Woman, a smiling crone, her face half hidden within her hood. Tarla cards could be used for simple games of skill and chance, or they could be used to divine the future. Or so it was said; Hestillion had had a great aunt who had devoted decades of her life to studying the tarla, and she had foreseen nothing about Ebora's doom.

'Aldasair? What are you doing?'

The young man looked up, his eyes wide. His brown hair hung shaggy and unkempt over his shoulders, and his ruffled silk shirt had seen better days, but his deep-blue waistcoat still had its bright golden chain-watch at its pocket. It was etched with the image of a griffin.

'Hest. I'm reading the tarla, Hest.'

'Well, you have too many cards, then.' She came into the room. A good handful of the cards were scattered on the floor. 'How many decks do you have here? Three? You only need a dozen cards to read the tarla, cousin.'

Aldasair looked back at the cards spread before him, his brow creasing. 'No, I'm trying to read the whole future, Hest. I need to see *all* of it.'

Hestillion cleared her throat. 'So what have you seen?'

Aldasair sighed. 'Cards, mostly.' He had avoided the crimson flux so far – he was of an age with her, and had been too young to participate in the Carrion Wars – but that wasn't to say that he was well. 'Will I see Tormalin at dinner?'

There was a dead spider in the middle of the table, its legs curled up around itself. It looked quite dry. Hestillion wondered how long Aldasair had been sitting in here, trawling through his cards. Did she walk past this room yesterday? The day before? She couldn't remember.

'We've talked about this, Aldasair. Tormalin left years ago. Decades ago. He packed up all his things, and his fancy sword,' Hestillion reached across and flicked the dead spider off the table, 'and he took himself off beyond the Wall, and beyond the mountains. And now, no doubt, he spends his time getting drunk and keeping his bed warm. He was always very good at those things.'

Aldasair was nodding slowly, as though he didn't quite believe her but was trying to convince himself. 'Tormalin took the sword with him?'

'Why not? We hardly need it here any more, do we? The Ninth Rain will never happen, because Ygseril is dead.' She brushed her fingers over the cards, making them whisper across each other. 'I will be having dinner in the blue room tonight, if you want to join me, Aldasair.'

The young man nodded, but he was looking down at the cards again. 'Last night, I woke up in here, in the dark. I could hear wolves howling outside. Do you ever hear the wolves, Hest?'

'Oh yes, I hear them all the time.'

'In the dark I took cards from the pile. Four cards. And

101

when it was light enough I looked at them. The Poisoned Chalice – a bad decision. The Falling Star – something approaches that bears us ill. And the Bower Couple – a new path is uncovered.'

She had thought her lips too cold to smile, but she did anyway. 'Bad decisions and ill will. The tarla has never been so accurate.'

'And the fourth I was to give to you.' Aldasair held out a dusty card. On it, twisted green shapes like wizened fingers fumbled in the dark. The Roots. 'It was important you have it.'

Hestillion looked up at him sharply. 'Who told you that? Who told you to give this card to me?'

But Aldasair had gone back to the cards, spreading them out under his fingertips as though he were looking for something underneath.

'The blue room,' she reminded him, 'if you're hungry.'

Hestillion slid the dusty and creased card into the neck of her padded gown and left him to his confusion.

8

'Please come in, Agent Lin.'

Lin paused at the doorway to adjust her gloves. They were fine, calf-skin leather, soft and flexible, and they annoyed her. Outside of the Winnowry she didn't wear gloves at all, but these clucking hens would go spare if she didn't. At least, if she must wear gloves, they could be fine ones.

She looked up into the flat metallic face of the sister who had been sent to usher her in. Her tone was polite, but it was clear she was also trying to keep out of arm's reach. The trust between agents and the Winnowry was sometimes a very fragile thing.

'This way please.'

The heart of the Winnowry was located near the furnaces rather than the prison; Lin could never decide whether it was because the acolytes of Tomas wanted to be near the warmth on this chilly, damp island, or because they wanted walls between them and the women they imprisoned. Likely it was both. When she had been a prisoner, Lin had enjoyed her brief visits to the furnace simply to warm up, but the central receiving room was not especially welcoming; the floor of cold, grey flagstones radiated the chill up through her boots, and the large square windows were full of bright, cheerless daylight. The long, curved table the acolytes sat behind was made from stone too, and the single seat in front of it, for want of a better word, was a simple, polished boulder. There was a small padded matt on top of it. Lin stood next to it, her back straight and her eyes on the far window.

'Agent Lin,' began Father Stanz. He leaned forward on the stone table, linking his fingers together. 'I take it your last mission was successful?'

'The targets were eliminated,' said a short, stout woman to his left: Sister Resn. She looked furious for some reason, and her long blue gloves and silver mask lay on the table in front of her, as though she couldn't bear to be parted from them.

'Eliminated into some smears of soot and an unpleasant smell, as Sister Resn confirms,' said Lin. 'I had hoped for a rest before the next incident.'

'No chance of that, Fell-Lin.' This was Father Eranis, who always referred to Lin by her old title. She let her gaze fall on him, her face carefully blank. 'We've had a girl get loose.'

Lin raised an eyebrow. 'Loose?'

'Took one of the bats from the chirot tower,' continued Father Stanz. 'We're still looking into how she got that far in the first place, but as you can imagine, she needs to be brought back here as soon as possible. It is not safe for her to be outside of the Winnowry.'

'A novice may have helped her,' said Sister Resn. Her jowly cheeks were pink and trembled slightly with suppressed outrage. 'We think she . . . seduced him. And she drained Sister Renier almost to the point of death.'

Father Stanz cleared his throat. 'It is difficult to know exactly what happened, of course, but the alarms weren't raised for some time.'

'Who is the witch?'

'Fell-Noon, of the plains people. You remember . . .?'

104

Lin raised her other eyebrow. 'I do. I always said you should keep a special eye on that one. A great potential for . . . difficulties.' She let the sentence hang in mid-air, inviting them to fill in the rest for themselves.

'Not a problem for you, though, is it, Fell-Lin?' Eranis leaned forward slightly. He probably thought he was being intimidating. 'In fact, this particular case seems made for you. I'm sure a witch of – uh – your skills will have her back in no time. Crying and weeping and asking to be put back in her cell, no doubt.'

Lin ignored him. 'Is there anything else you can tell me?'

'You know her history. A murderer. And a liar too – her version of events never did add up.' Stanz looked down at a sheaf of paper in front of him. 'Mushenska is close enough to be a tempting hideout, of course.'

'How likely was it that she and this novice were in a relationship? Do you allow more fraternisation now between novices and fell-witches?'

'Of course not!' Sister Resn's cheeks turned even pinker. 'But the temptation could fester. The witches are the cracks through which sin seeps into the world, and even the most innocent can be corrupted. A boy like that could have had his head turned. It has happened in the past, as well you know.' She glared openly at Lin, almost as though daring her to say more.

'Any family or connections she could be returning to?'

Eranis chuckled quietly. 'The girl destroyed those herself a long time ago. I assume there will be no problems, Fell-Lin?' There was an edge to his tone.

'Of course not.' Lin kept half an eye on Sister Resn's outraged face, wondering if the woman would dare to say anything to her. When Lin had been a prisoner of the Winnowry, Sister Resn had patrolled the cells regularly, and Lin had frequently fantasised about boiling the skin off the woman, or simply ripping all of her life force from her in a brief, glorious second. She

105

kept her face calm as she considered it. She was only allowed to operate as a free agent in the name of the Winnowry because they believed her to be utterly under control. And she was. Control was everything. It was a simple choice, really – live as a prisoner for the rest of her life, or take the freedom she was offered. The consequences of rebellion were . . . unthinkable. 'I will find your runaway witch for you. If I should need to, do I have permission to remove the problem permanently?'

Father Stanz nodded solemnly. 'We would prefer otherwise, of course, but it's entirely possible she will be very dangerous to restrain. The Winnowry trusts your judgment.'

'As you should. You'll hear from me shortly.'

'One more thing, Fell-Lin.' Eranis was looking at the paper-work on the desk again, but couldn't quite hide the smirk. 'Mother Cressin wishes to have a word with you before you leave.'

Agent Lin held herself very still. Control. Always control. And then she nodded. 'I will go there now.'

Mother Cressin kept her rooms in the highest tower of the prison side of the Winnowry, meaning that anyone called upon to visit her had to walk up a near-endless spiral staircase. There were narrow windows on the way up, but Lin didn't bother to look through them. They only showed the featureless gloom of the sea, or the view across the bay to Mushenska, which was hidden within its own veil of fog.

The Drowned One.

That was what the fell-witches whispered to one another. Mother Cressin, rarely seen in the prison itself, would occasionally appear at purging sessions, her face hidden within a hood, or, if you were very unlucky and considered in need of further instruction in the ways of Tomas, you would be taken to her rooms.

At the top of the stairs was a driftwood door standing half

open. Inside, the circular room was gloomy, the thick swathes of old netting covering the windows doing a good job of keeping the light out and the cold in. There was one small, half-hearted fire in the grate and no rugs over the icy flagstones. To Agent Lin's right stood a tall figure, broad shoulders empha-sised rather than hidden under a dark cloak, her hair pulled back from a face like a slab of beaten meat. Agent Lin nodded to the woman.

'I am here to see Mother Cressin.'

The guard nodded to the back of the room, where the shadows were thickest. Fell-Mary, Mother Cressin's assistant and bodyguard, had never spoken more than a handful of words in Agent Lin's presence, which was something of a relief. Lin suspected that if Fell-Mary had a lot to say to you, you would be in serious trouble.

At the back of the room was an enormous, ornate tank. Sitting within a wrought-iron frame decorated with twisted metal shaped like seaweed, it was filled with what Lin knew to be seawater, and in the gloom she could just about make out a figure, sitting on its floor. Arms crossed, legs folded under her, Mother Cressin's head was bowed, her face hidden. Lin could make out the pale fronds of her white hair, moving in a ghostly fashion around her head. Every now and then, a silvery bubble of air would escape from her mouth or nose and make its wobbly way to the surface. The water was very still.

Agent Lin took a breath, and held it for a few seconds, before turning back to look at Fell-Mary. The big woman didn't move.

'I am to wait here until Mother Cressin is ready to receive me?'

No reply. Agent Lin cleared her throat. She didn't want to look at the woman in the tank, but her eyes were drawn back there all the same. She could hear the wind howling around the tower, and the sea-salt smell from the tank was thick in her nose. Slowly, slowly the cold was getting into her bones, and all the while she was too aware of her own breathing, strangely loud in the dismal room. It was always the same when you were summoned here; Mother Cressin's strange ritual never failed to be deeply unnerving, and Agent Lin found herself taking deeper and deeper breaths, as though fighting against the pressure of the water herself. Meanwhile, the figure in the tank was utterly still, her face hidden. Lin didn't want to think about how cold the water must be.

The Drowned One has the sea in her blood, the fell-witches whispered to each other, when the lights were out. Whatever Tomas and his disciples brought back from their own drowning, Mother Cressin had it still – some dark knowledge sifted from the lightless sands at the bottom of the ocean.

When she had been standing long enough to wonder if perhaps the old woman had finally died, peacefully expelling her last breath into the water, Mother Cressin unfolded her arms. The water swirled around her, a confusion of shadows and dust, and abruptly she pushed off the bottom and kicked to the top with precise, practised movements. Lin heard her break the water but thanks to the shadows saw only a glistening shape in the gloom. The old woman climbed down an unseen ladder and disappeared behind a screen. Fell-Mary crossed the room and retrieved an armful of dry clothes from a trunk, passing them swiftly behind the partition. From the small glance she got, Lin got the impression of black, salt-stained rags. She expected to wait until the Drowned One was dressed, but instead her voice floated up from behind the screen. It was quiet, the voice of someone who knew that those around her would rather strain their hearing than ask her to speak up.

'They've told you of our missing charge?'

'I have been briefed, Mother Cressin. I'll have the girl back with us in no time.'

There was a strangled noise, of someone expelling air in

disgust, or disbelief perhaps. 'Not a girl. An abomination. Do not forget what you are, Fell-Lin, just because we let you walk free in the world.'

Lin stared steadily at the screen. It would be very fine, she thought, to pick the scrap of a woman up and tip her back in her bloody tank. See how long she could really hold her breath for. Or throw her out the window of her own damn tower.

Control. Control at all times.

'I will not forget, Mother Cressin.'

'The creature Noon is the fracture through which evil enters our world, just as you are. She taints it, poisons it. She must be controlled.'

'Yes, Mother Cressin.' Lin's eyes shifted to Fell-Mary, but the woman was back to impassively staring at nothing. 'Control is everything.'

'Do you remember, Fell-Lin, when you were less than controlled?' The Drowned One emerged from behind the screen, wrapped from head to ankle in hessian, dyed black. A deep hood hid her face, and her feet, as white as the underbelly of a fish, were bare against the freezing flagstones. 'Do you remember the consequences of that?'

'I was very young,' said Lin. 'And the blame doesn't rest solely with me.'

Mother Cressin looked up sharply, and Lin caught a brief glimpse of a pale, round chin.

'You dare? You dare lay the blame at the feet of our priests? You?'

Agent Lin kept her eyes on the tank. It was important to remember that as useful as she was to the Winnowry, there were always plenty of women waiting to take her place.

'I am sorry, Mother Cressin. Truly, in Tomas's name. I only meant that the *consequence* that you spoke of, is as much priest as fell-witch, and I would hope that is remembered, when the future – when future decisions are made.'

109

Mother Cressin turned away, apparently too disgusted to look at her. 'It sits ill with me, Fell-Lin, that we must use your type at all. I would rest easier if every fell-witch were locked in a cell, or quietly taken from this world at birth. If there were a way to tell . . .' She paused by the tank and extended one pale hand to touch the glass. The ends of all her fingertips were deeply wrinkled. 'That way, we may start to *truly* cleanse Sarn.' She turned back. 'Until then, I am told I must suffer your continued existence. I want this cleared up quietly, the creature brought back. She will spend some time in the lower cells, and then she will begin a cycle of repeated purging.'

Agent Lin nodded. Repeated purging had been known to kill women before. It had the advantage of exhausting them beyond the capacity for thought, and providing a significant crop of the drug akaris.

'It will not be difficult, Mother Cressin. The . . . creature is young and alone, with no family left to run to.'

Cressin nodded and turned away. She gestured towards the door. 'Go. The sea calls me back.'

Agent Lin stood and watched the young man, letting the silence draw out between them. The Winnowry had stashed him away in a tiny cell somewhere in the bowels of the furnace, the only light from a pair of small oil lamps, high in the stone walls. He sat in its furthest corner, his head down. This was a punishment, of course, but also, she suspected, a neat way of preventing word of Fell-Noon's escape from travelling around the prison. She had to smile at that. As if anything were ever kept quiet in a prison. He was young, his body smoothly muscled, and his white-blond hair was plastered to his head with sweat. He was bigger than her, no doubt stronger too, but he made no move to overpower her. The boy knew better than that.

He cleared his throat, and dared himself to look up at her.

110

He clearly couldn't bear the silence any longer. 'Please,' he said. 'Who are you?'

In answer, she held her arms out to him, free of sleeves and gloves. He crossed his arms over his bare chest, a protective gesture. 'Novice Lusk, I am the woman who is going to ask you questions. Do you know what I am?'

'I've already told them.' He met her eyes then, trying to put a brave face on it. How delicious. 'The sisters have asked me over and over, and I told them exactly what happened.'

Lin nodded slightly, and began to rub her forearms together slowly. The soft rasp of skin against skin sounded loud in the tiny cell, and she saw his eyes flicker down to follow the movement. 'The sisters told me. You said that Fell-Noon appeared unexpectedly in the chirot tower while you were performing your duties. She took you unawares, and threatened to kill you and the bats if you raised the alarm, but she didn't actually drain you. Novice Lusk, you then saddled the bat for her yourself, and then stood by and watched as she made her merry way out into the wider world. Does that sound right to you? Does that sound like a thing that happened?'

'That was what happened!'

She took a few slow steps towards him, and he cringed back against the wall.

'What we're thinking, Novice Lusk, is that perhaps you'd had some sort of dalliance with the girl. That you were fucking her, in short.' She grinned at his shocked expression. 'Oh, it happens, even in this miserable place. You don't need very long really, and there were times when you were alone with Fell-Noon, unsupervised. Am I right?' She came over until she was standing over him. 'When I was still locked up in here, Lusk, you wouldn't believe the number of priests who were fucking the women. It's not natural, all of these people together in celibacy. I've always said so.'

Abruptly, she knelt and slid her arms around him, as if she

111

meant to kiss him, but instead, at the warm contact of his skin she *took*, ripping his life energy from him savagely. He cried out, falling against her, and she felt him attempting to marshal himself, to draw back from her – the priests were trained, after all, to take this sort of punishment. She snaked one hand up and took hold of his jaw, turning his frightened eyes to meet hers. 'You have so much to give, Novice Lusk. I can see why Fell-Noon was taken with you. Did you fuck her again before she left? Was that the price of her freedom?'

'No.' He forced the word out through lips that were rapidly losing their colour. 'We never . . .'

'How long can you hold out, do you think?' She was genuinely curious. The boy was remarkably strong, and his energy had a purity she had not tasted for a long time. After a while, you started to sense things about the people whose energy you took; she was beginning to believe that the boy didn't have a single lie in his head. It was remarkable. Meanwhile, his energy was gathering inside her, a storm with nowhere to go. Holding it steady within her – control, always control – Agent Lin pulled away just as the boy began to shake. Free of her, he slumped to the ground, shivering as though he were caught in a blizzard. That lovely warm skin of his would be cold now, she knew.

'One of the strongest I've tasted, if I'm honest,' she said to the room at large. She walked back towards the door and turned to face Novice Lusk, nursing the tide of stolen life energy within her. It would have to come out, and soon. Even the most skilled Fell-Witch couldn't hold on to it indefinitely. 'Did she tell you anything about where she intended to go, Novice Lusk?'

He lifted his head a touch, still shaking. His eyes were glazed, and the tips of his fingers had turned grey. She hadn't depleted him completely, but Lin thought he might die anyway – it was careless of her.

112

'Nothing,' he croaked. 'She said . . . nothing . . . to me.'

'Not even when you were fucking her, Lusk?'

He glanced up at that, his eyes widening, and she chose that moment to release the fire. Arms up, palms open, fingers spread; a blossom of winnowfire as green as fresh, new grass bloomed in the tiny cell, curling towards the shivering man on the floor. Agent Lin heard his abrupt, ragged scream and smiled to herself – with a gesture she increased the temperature of the flames, and his screams took on a panicked tone. The fire would be close – not close enough to kill him, not yet, but close enough to scorch. She closed her hands and folded her arms into her chest – enough – and the roar of green fire died instantly.

'Any more thoughts on that, Lusk?'

The boy was curled like a baby on the floor, his hands over his face. As she watched, he patted rapidly at the hair on his head, which was singed. It crisped away under his fingers. His knees and shins and the tops of his shoulders were a bright, shiny red, and his face looked a little like he'd been out under the hot sun all day.

'Please,' he gasped between blistered lips. 'Please.'

She chuckled to herself. 'Well, I can hardly resist.'

This time she turned her hands to face each other and funnelled a line of fire to the space next to the novice's feet. He shrieked, pulled his feet up and away, scrambling to push himself into the far corner, but she followed, sweeping the line of winnowfire up so that it brushed the delicate soles of his feet. The cell rang with the sound of screaming as the sweet scent of burned flesh filled the air. Agent Lin took a long, slow breath inwards, savouring it, before pulling her arms back to her chest and quieting the fire. The energy he had given her was nearly gone now, but she didn't think she would need more. The boy was crying, clutching at his ruined feet.

'The city,' he gibbered, tears streaming down his scorched face. 'When she took Fulcor, they flew towards the city. I watched them, I watched them fly, and it looked as though she landed there.'

'Of course,' said Agent Lin, cheerfully enough. She went to the door. 'Thank you, Novice Lusk. I'll tell them you weren't in collusion with the witch, of course. For what it's worth.'

The chirot tower was empty save for the bats. It was mid-afternoon, and the animals were all nestled snugly in their alcoves, soft rumbles and keenings in place of snores – all save for one. Lin walked over to the empty space and stood looking at it for a while. The white bat taken by Fell-Noon had not returned, suggesting that she still had it. This was good news for Lin, as a giant bat was hard to miss, particularly in the skies to the south of the mountains – however, it also meant that they could be almost anywhere. The Winnowry's giant bats were bred to be resilient and tough, and could fly continuously for almost an entire night.

Turning from the alcove, Lin walked to the roofless section of the tower, where the bat mount she had been assigned waited for her, ready to leave. The creature's leathery face was latticed with scars, and its black fur was streaked with grey behind its large crinkled ears, but its eyes watched her with bright intelligence. Smiling faintly, Lin sank her bare hands into the animal's fur.

'Ugly creature.' She took a touch of its life-force, just a touch – enough to warm her against the endless bloody damp of the Winnowry. The bat gave a high-pitched whine and shuddered under her fingers, while she felt the latent power curl inside her. She would be glad to be away from this cold, dead place and back in the land of the living. There was so much life to be taken, after all. 'Little Fell-Noon won't be lost for long.'

9

Well, yes, I did ask him about the blood, Marin, but just like Ebora itself and any family he might have there, it is a subject he is very reluctant to discuss. I know that he partakes of it in small doses, and carries small vials around with him in case it is required. When is it required, I hear you ask? Well.

From what I have observed, small amounts of blood act like a kind of pick-me-up. You remember that thick black drink from Reidn you were briefly obsessed with, the one that smelled like burning dog hair and made it impossible for you to sleep? I believe that very minor doses act almost like that on the Eboran system. Over time, the doses stop them aging like we do, and I have seen it written that large amounts can start to heal an injury, although, thankfully, I have not had to witness such. Tormalin is no creature of blood-thirst, ripping open throats and drinking his fill as the Eborans did in those woodcuts from that ancient book in the library – but he takes his doses steadily enough. More often than it is 'required', no doubt.

Will he catch the crimson flux? I do not know, my dear.

From everything I've read, and everything I've gleaned from Tor's tiny hints, I believe the onset of the disease is unpredictable – Eborans who sipped the occasional cup came down with it swiftly and died swifter, and those who drank lakes of the stuff are still living out their days in the city beyond the Bloodless Mountains, waiting for it to catch up with them. Only the handful who never touched a drop seem guaranteed to survive it, but they instead are taken by old age, and more prosaic illnesses. But for my sake, let's hope he has escaped it – having an Eboran bodyguard has done wonders for my reputation.

Extract from the private letters of
Master Marin de Grazon,
from Lady Vincenza 'Vintage' de Grazon

Vintage peered at the fibrous stalk. She had thought that it was just the shadows in this strange place, but no, it was there – a smear of something thick and glutinous and largely transparent ran across the length of the stalk and then the next one too, as though each of the towering toadstools had been brushed by something as it passed. Small white nodules, like blisters, clustered where the substance was thickest. She took her smallest scalpel and very carefully scraped away some of the affected tissue, pushing the flakes into the glass pot she had waiting. When she attempted to capture one of the nodules, it cracked open and a thin, pinkish fluid ran from it, smelling of old cheese. She wrinkled her nose.

'How charming,' said Tormalin. He was standing to one side, leaning against the towering stalk and watching her progress with a beautifully bored expression. 'I, for one, am more than glad to spend my time watching you root around in the mud.'

'Darling, will you kindly get out of what little light I have? Take your lanky arse off somewhere else please.'

Tor sighed noisily and moved back to where they had dumped their packs. A few moments later, she heard the unmistakeable noise of him liberating a bottle from her bag.

'I do not have an inexhaustible supply with me, Tormalin, my dear. You may want to go easy on that for now.' This time, she managed to lever off a piece of tissue big enough, leaving the nodule intact. She nodded with satisfaction. It was a small thing, but small things could be big clues.

'When I agreed to work with you, Vintage, you promised me "as much wine as I could drink". Good wine, too.'

'Yes, I did say that, didn't I?' Vintage stood up, wincing slightly at the ache in her back. Since the double attack on the village, they had been moving constantly, trying to follow the trail before it went cold. In truth, the trail hadn't been much more than a hunch and a hope for better luck, but here, finally, they had something solid. She had seen matter like this in her own vine forest, and now that she looked, it was clear that this patch of the Wild, with its monstrous fungi, had seen parasite activity. Aside from the glutinous smears and the blisters, the place just didn't feel right. It felt haunted.

'There's definitely something here.' She returned to the packs, where Tor was now examining packages wrapped in greased paper. 'We need to head deeper in.'

'I'm hungry. But the smell of this place makes everything unappetising.' He put the packages back, frowning slightly. 'If there's Behemoth wreckage around here somewhere, then why hasn't anyone found it before?'

Vintage shrugged and put the specimen jar back into one of the bags. 'Would you want to spend very long in this place? It's damp. It smells, as you say, appalling, and unless you have a deep and abiding hankering for mushrooms . . . It could be that the pieces of the Behemoth are very small, wreckage left over from one of the earliest rains, perhaps.' She smiled to herself. 'If that is the case, my dear, then this could be one of our best finds. A Behemoth site as yet undiscovered, and with pieces small enough to be studied properly. It might not even be that dangerous.'

Tor snorted. 'I love it when you say things like that, Vintage. It just makes it more delicious when you're wrong.' He paused, and put down the bag he was holding. In one smooth movement he pulled his sword free of its scabbard.

'What is it?' Vintage moved closer to the Eboran, one hand settling lightly on the crossbow at her hip.

'There's something beyond those stalks. Something moving.'

'A parasite?'

He waved at her to be quiet and moved off to where the shadows were at their thickest. Vintage ghosted along behind him, keeping her tread light. Now that they were closer, she could see it too – something pale moving between the giant stalks; flashes of black and grey.

'Not a parasite,' she whispered to Tor. 'There are no lights.'

'Could be someone trying to snatch the find out from under our noses,' he replied. 'Shall we have a look?'

Still moving silently, they slid themselves up between the stalks and looked down onto a stretch of black soil punctuated here and there with short, fat mushroom caps dotted and spattered with lurid colours, each big enough to sit on. After years of patrolling the vine forest, Vintage was reasonably good at moving quietly through foliage, but she felt their efforts were wasted on the young woman pacing in the clearing below them. She had her arms crossed tightly over her chest, and her short black hair stuck up at all angles. Her head was down, her narrow eyes glaring at the ground as though it had personally insulted her, and she wore thin grey leggings and a ragged long-sleeved top, more akin to nightwear than travel clothes. As Vintage watched, the woman raised her hands to her face and rubbed them across her cheeks, dislodging the remains of what looked like a pale powder. With a jolt, Vintage's eyes skipped to the woman's forehead – yes! There was the sigil of a bat's wing, tattooed onto her smooth olive skin and half hidden by her unruly hair. A fell-witch! What, by the bones of Sarn, was a fell-witch doing in the middle of a parasite-haunted stretch of Wild?

'What do we have here?'

Before she could snatch him back, Tor was stepping down onto the mud, skirting the thicker toadstools and sliding his sword away. The effect on the young woman was immediate. She scrambled backwards, reaching out for the twisted fungus behind her. Vintage opened her mouth to shout a proper greeting, thinking that the woman was trying to flee, when, abruptly, the space between her and the girl was filled with an enormous emerald fireball.

Vintage flew backwards, rolling awkwardly down a short incline of mud and coming to an abrupt halt at the foot of one of the giant toadstools. She lay there for a few moments, stunned and blinking away the bright after-image the light had left on her vision, while the quiet was shattered by Tormalin and this strange woman shouting at each other. She could smell singed hair. Gingerly, Vintage patted her head. Her hat was missing, but her own thicket of curly hair seemed intact. Groaning slightly, she climbed to her feet and brushed clods of wet mud from her trousers.

'Give me one reason why I shouldn't cut your throat!'

'Who are you? Why were you sneaking up on me?'

'Hold on, hold on,' Vintage hurried back to the clearing, holding her hands out in front of her. The young woman had her fist raised, a halo of bright green winnowfire dancing around it. The toadstool directly behind her had withered drastically, the pale column of its stalk now so twisted and dark that the fleshy cap had turned to one side as though avoiding a blow. Vintage tore her eyes away from that wonder

119

to see that Tor had his sword out again. 'Calm down now, my dears. Come along.'

The young woman dragged her eyes from Tor to stare at Vintage instead. She looked like one of the plains folk – Vintage had travelled back and forth over that region in the last few years – but, of course, all sense of identity was supposedly removed at the Winnowry. Vintage forced a bright smile onto her face. 'There's no need for fire here, fell-witch. We're just strangers stumbled onto the same path, isn't that right?' She paused to pull an errant twig from her hair. 'Let's exchange a few words before anyone kills anyone else.'

'You are with the Eboran?' The fell-witch lowered her burning hand a touch, although Vintage suspected it was from confusion rather than trust.

'Well, he is my employee, yes. Tormalin, my dearest, please put the sword away.'

Tor glared at her. 'This mad woman tried to blow you up!'

'I tried to blow both of you up.'

'Just a misunderstanding, I'm sure. Tor, please fetch our packs. This young woman looks like she could do with a glass of wine.'

'A . . . glass of wine?' The girl looked faintly stunned.

'Of course, darling. Meeting new people is always improved with a glass of wine, in my experience. Tor!'

Pausing to shoot one more poisonous look at the fell-witch, Tormalin moved back through the stalks to retrieve their packs. Vintage bustled over to the embers of the woman's fire, and made a cursory examination. No blankets to sleep on, a single bag of supplies, and now that she looked closer she could see that the young woman was wearing what appeared to be slippers, wet and stained with mud. Stranger and stranger.

'Now then. I am Lady Vincenza de Grazon, but you can call me Vintage. Tormalin the Oathless there, is, for want of a better phrase, my hired muscle.' She stopped and looked at

120

the girl, smiling in what she hoped was an encouraging manner. Behind her she could hear Tormalin dragging their packs down to the small camp fire, clearly making more of a hash of it than was necessary. The fell-witch cleared her throat.

'I am Fell-Noon, an agent of the Winnowry.' The green flames had winked out of existence, but from the woman's stance it was clear they could come back at any moment. Vintage sensed that hinged on whether she was prepared to believe such an obviously gigantic lie. 'I am on a . . . confidential mission.'

'In the middle of the stinking Wild?' Tor was now standing by their bags with his arms crossed over his chest. 'What possible mission could you have out here? Whatever it is, you are woefully underprepared for it.'

'I could ask what a blood-sucking Eboran is doing outside of your cursed city.' The girl lifted her chin, on the defensive again, and Vintage silently cursed Tor for it. 'I didn't expect to see your kind of monster in this place.'

Tor bared his teeth, clearly preparing to spit another insult, so Vintage stepped neatly in front of him. 'I do believe I promised you wine, yes? Here we are, look. Not my best, but not the worst we've produced either. Come on, I have some tin cups in here somewhere, I know it's not the same as proper crystal but I think we can make do. My dear Fell-Noon, would you mind perhaps building up the fire a touch? It's such a lovely trick and, well, you do look like you could do with some warming up.'

She bustled them into sitting around the fire, passing out cups and eventually a bottle of red, along with a broken piece of bread each and some cheese that had been squashed at the bottom of the pack. Fell-Noon still wore a guarded expression, although her obvious hunger had pushed that concern aside for one moment. Tormalin, as ever, looked as outraged as an insulted cat.

'How long have you been out here, my dear?'

121

Fell-Noon looked up from her piece of bread, which she was holding firmly in both hands. She had been nibbling the edges of it, as though savouring the texture.

'A day and a night.'

'Well. What a place to spend the night! I'm sure I don't know what the Winnowry's business could be out here, but there are aspects of Sarn's history that affect us all, no doubt.'

Fell-Noon kept her eyes on her bread, although Tor was giving Vintage a particularly sardonic look. She cleared her throat.

'That is to say, that perhaps there is much to learn from recent history, and perhaps this is one of the places where those lessons may be, uh, learned.'

Tor rolled his eyes at Vintage, and waved his cup of wine at the pair of them. 'What my employer is trying to ask you is, are you out here after the Behemoth remains too?'

'What?' The young woman half sat up, her black eyes suddenly full of alarm. 'A Behemoth, around here? Are we safe?'

'Well, yes and no.' Vintage stood up, sighing as the bones in her knees popped. 'We have reason to believe there are the remains of a Behemoth in the Shroom Flats somewhere – long dead, of course, likely the result of the Eighth Rain or perhaps an even earlier incursion, and therefore hundreds of years old – but thanks to the effects of such remains, no, we are not safe. We have encountered two parasite spirits on our way here, and we expect to encounter more before we find what we need. Here, look, the signs are all around us.' She walked around the fire to the ring of stalks immediately behind them. There were smears of the translucent substance on the trunks, complete with the clusters of white nodules. 'Do you see this? Parasite spirits can leave these markings behind when they brush against vegetation. They leave behind so little physical evidence, and we know so little about them.' Her lips turned down at the corners, recalling the devastation that crouched at the heart of the vine forest. 'I'm sure you've heard the stories, my darling. Parasite spirits are very dangerous indeed, and they are found in the vicinity of Behemoth remains.'

Fell-Noon looked haunted. 'Behemoths are dangerous. Why are you out here?'

'Everything worm-touched is a threat.' Vintage reached down and plucked up her tin cup. 'So much of Sarn is poisoned, twisted and strange, thanks to the influence of the Jure'lia. I want to find out why, Fell-Noon, and to stop it, if I can. How can we stop the Wild growing? What are the parasite spirits, and how can we live with them? The Wild, the worm people, the spirits – they're all linked, somehow, we just can't see the details. So I must learn as much about them as possible, which is why I spend my time, as Tor so expertly puts it, rooting around in the mud in dangerous places. Where I am from, Fell-Noon, we make wine from grapes that are worm-touched, and part of our land is slowly being consumed by the Wild. People have lost their lives trying to find out the truth.' She paused, remembering the first Eboran she had ever met: Nanthema with her useless spectacles and her quick mind. 'It's . . . a cause that's very dear to my heart.'

'And why is the bloodsucker here?'

'Charming,' muttered Tor.

'Your people slaughtered mine, for generations,' said Noon, her voice flat. Her eyes were bright with an unreadable emotion. 'What happened to you? Do you all still live in Ebora? Or did the crimson flux wipe you out?'

Tor sat very still. 'The fate of my people is of no concern to a witch.'

'Please, there's no need for us to argue,' said Vintage smoothly. 'It gets dark quickly in this place, and really, my dear, you shouldn't be out here by yourself. We are safer together. Tor, do you think there could be any game around here? Hot food would cheer us up, don't you think?'

Sighing heavily, Tor headed off into the shadows, his sword at the ready, while Vintage poured them some more wine.

'This doesn't look like the sort of place where you can chase down a couple of plump rabbits,' said Fell-Noon. She sat close to the fire, her arms wrapped around herself, not quite looking at Vintage.

'Oh, you'd be surprised. All sorts make their home in the Wild. Tor might appear to be little more than a pretty pain in my rear end, but he's unnaturally fast with that sword, and he sees very well in the dark. Now,' Vintage swallowed more wine, savouring the warmth it brought to her belly. 'Are you going to tell me what's really going on?'

For a long moment the girl did not move. She was so still that Vintage began to think she hadn't heard the question, but, eventually, she shook herself and touched her fingers, briefly, to the tattoo on her forehead.

'You shouldn't ask me questions,' she said, her voice so quiet it was almost lost under the crackle of the fire. 'You shouldn't talk to me at all.'

'What if I want to help you?'

The girl glanced up. The fire was reflected in her dark eyes, and her mouth was pressed into a thin line. 'I'm an agent of the Winnowry. Why would I need your help?'

'How did you get here? You can't have walked all the way from the Winnowry.'

Fell-Noon reached inside her sleeve and produced a long silver tube, which she held up to Vintage as though this answered the question. 'I flew here on a bat. That's how Winnowry agents travel.' She placed the tube, which was flattened at one end, into her mouth and mimed blowing on it. Then she put the whistle back into her sleeve, not quite meeting Vintage's eyes. 'Anyway. It's hunting at the moment. The bat. I sent it away.'

'Well.' Vintage stood up. 'One thing I do know – you will become ill, if you spend another night in this festering hole dressed as you are. Here.' Vintage went to Tor's pack and began pulling things out, holding them up to the firelight for a better look. The daylight, already weak under the canopy of mushroom caps, had turned to a velvet darkness. 'They will all be too big for you, of course, but you can roll the sleeves up. And I have a spare pair of boots.'

Fell-Noon's eyebrows shot up, creasing her tattoo.

'I can't take his stuff. Not *his* stuff. What if he—'

'Nonsense, dear, you'll freeze to death otherwise. Besides, Tor has an obscene number of shirts in here, I don't know why he feels the need to carry them around with him everywhere. Here, look, put that on, and this over the top. I know it looks thin, but Eboran silk is remarkably warming.' She thrust the shirt into the girl's arms and followed it with a jacket of stiff, black material with a high embroidered collar. While Fell-Noon sat looking at them in confusion, Vintage went to her own pack and yanked out a pair of battered leather boots with laces that went from the ankle right down to the toe. 'Here, put those on too. I don't for a moment think your little feet are the same size as mine, my dear, but you can pull the laces tight and here, stuff them with these socks.'

Noon looked at her for a long moment. She reminded Vintage of a half-feral cat that had hung around the House some years ago. Never quite tame enough to come into the kitchens, it would loiter on the broad stone steps outside. The animal would sun itself there, and if you left fish scraps on a plate, it would eat them, but if you tried to edge closer, it would watch you with careful eyes. Too close and it would run, every time.

'Thank you,' the young woman said, a little stiffly. She peeled off her sodden slippers and threw them behind her – with more than a touch of satisfaction, Vintage thought – and pulled on Vintage's big woollen socks.

'Makes my pack a bit lighter, dear.'

Fell-Noon pulled on the shirt and the jacket, before lacing up the boots.

Vintage sat herself down a couple of feet away from the girl – close, but not too close. She was still thinking of the cat. 'I haven't seen many fell-witches in my time, it's true.' She kept her voice casual. 'All those that I have seen wore scarves or hats, and their faces were all heavily powdered.'

She let the unasked question hang in the air. The fell-witch pulled a hand through her hair, not quite meeting her eyes. 'Customs change.'

'Well, if you should need a brush, my dear, just let me know.'

Tor appeared at the edge of their fire, moving in the unnervingly silent way that he had. There was something fat and wriggling on the end of his sword, which he tipped onto the dirt by Vintage's feet.

'It doesn't look like much, but it's actually pretty tasty, if you cook it for long enough. And douse it in wine. And drink lots of wine while you're eating it. And drink lots of wine afterwards, so you forget what you were just eating.'

Vintage kept her face as still as possible, but she couldn't help noticing Fell-Noon's horrified expression. Tor's catch appeared to be a huge woodlouse, some worm-touched creature that had grown fat and bloated in the crevices of the Shroom Flats. It was pale cream in colour, with an alarming multitude of stiff, grey legs.

'Is that what Eborans like to eat?' asked Noon. Her tone was suspiciously innocent, and Vintage opened her mouth to reply, but Tor was already stomping around the fire, his face like thunder.

'That's all there is to eat, but of course you are welcome to go hungry.' He stopped then and turned to Vintage, outrage quivering on every inch of his face. 'Vintage, I must be imagining things – perhaps my sight was damaged by the fireball this lunatic threw at us earlier – but it looks as though this

126

witch is wearing my clothes. How, by Ygseril's deepest roots, can that have happened?'

'Oh, do be quiet and help me spit this monstrosity you've brought back. Fell-Noon, I have eaten something like this myself, back when I was travelling across the Reidn delta, it's really not as bad as it looks—'

From above them came a scrabbling, shifting noise, and a pale shape dropped towards them from the canopy of mushroom caps. Vintage scrambled to her feet, her heart in her mouth, but the shape resolved itself into a pair of leathery wings and a blocky furred head. The bat swooped over their small camp, dropping something from its feet before flying up and away again, scrambling back up through the dark spaces between caps.

'Fulcor! That was Fulcor.' Noon was on her feet, and for the first time she was smiling. 'See? The bat I flew here on. Because I'm a Winnowry agent. And look.' She stepped around the fire and knelt by what the bat had dropped. It was a small goat-like creature, of the sort Vintage knew roamed in small herds through patches of the southern forests. 'Here is the dinner I told it to fetch for me.' The fell-witch stood up, a wild look in her eye. 'Agents of the Winnowry do not eat giant bugs.'

10

Of course, Marin, as I'm sure you will have heard from your dear mother over the years, and even Ezion, Tormalin the Oathless was not the first Eboran I ever knew. One, in fact, walked the halls of the House and even slept for a time in the room that would eventually belong to you. I hope that is thrilling for you in some way.

It was early summer and I was about to turn twenty. Your grandmother and grandfather were both still alive then, of course, and I had very few responsibilities save for not wandering off and getting killed in the vine forest if I could help it. One day, a delegation of merchants arrived to talk to us about potentially setting up a trade route with Ebora itself – it had, they explained, been years since any such thing existed, due to some sort of scandal that had occurred some time after the Carrion Wars had ended – and with them was an Eboran woman. Initially, I thought that she was there as a representative of her home, perhaps to ensure that their interests were properly taken care of and, nominally, she was, but as the weeks went by it became increasingly obvious that she was more interested in the forest, and the terrible secret that it held.

Eborans, Marin, are of course known for their ethereal beauty, and this woman was no exception. She was tall and solidly built, with skin like warm marble and hair blacker than night. She wore, I remember, these strange pleated trousers that puffed out over the tops of her leather boots, and a crimson velvet jacket that always seemed to be covered in a layer of dust, and she owned a delicate pair of spectacles that I am fairly sure she did not need at all. More than that, despite her cold beauty, she was funny and kind. She would wander off from the long discussions after dinner, where your grandfather was trying so hard to be impressive, and one could find her in the kitchens, eating pudding with the servants, asking them endless questions. She asked so many questions, and really listened to the answers; as you get older, Marin, you will begin to see how rare this truly is.

Her name was Nanthema, and she was beautiful.

What you will have heard from your mother, I am unsure, and what Ezion will have told you, I dread to think, but I— [the remainder of this page is torn away, leaving a ragged line]

Extract from the private letters of
Master Marin de Grazon
from Lady Vincenza 'Vintage' de Grazon

Morning in the Shroom Flats was unsettling. The place was still gloomy, and filled with the alarming funk of dirt and fungus, but the light that filtered down from between the caps was pale gold in colour, dancing with flecks of plant matter. Vintage sat on top of her pack and watched it, when she wasn't watching the sleeping girl. Noon was curled up by the extinguished fire, her knees pressed tightly to her chest, her hands covering her head. The girl was frightened, right down to her bones – when fear followed you that far into sleep, then you were in some serious trouble.

Vintage stood up, thinking to boil water for more tea, when the fell-witch jerked awake. For a few seconds, Vintage thought the girl might just stand up and run away, so alarmed did she look at her surroundings, but eventually she seemed to settle.

'Where is the other one?'

'Tor? I've sent him off to have a look around. I think we might be very close to what I'm looking for.'

'Pieces of a dead Behemoth.' Fell-Noon rubbed her hands over her face.

'Better than pieces of a live Behemoth, my darling.'

'I don't understand you. You travel with an Eboran, and you explore the Wild, and you're looking for things that might kill you. None of it makes sense.' Fell-Noon looked up, and Vintage noted the dark circles around her eyes. 'Explain the Eboran to me. You know what his people did? What they are?'

'I do, my dear. Do you?' Catching her look, Vintage sighed. 'Tormalin is very young for an Eboran, which means, of course, that he's nearly four hundred years old. He was too young to have had an active role in the Carrion Wars, but old enough to watch most of his people die from the crimson flux which followed. The dreadful stories that you have heard took place in a time when young Tormalin had yet to break his voice.'

'Does he drink human blood?'

Vintage blinked. The girl was blunt enough. 'I think that's really his business.'

'His *business*?'

Tormalin chose that moment to come stamping back into their camp, treading so heavily that Vintage was sure he must have heard their conversation.

'We're at the top of a small hill.' He didn't look at either of them, but came over to the remains of the fire and began picking at the carcass of the previous evening's dinner. 'I found

130

the edge of it, and below us there's a great deal of exposed earth.'

Vintage stood up. 'A landslide?'

Tor shrugged. 'Could be. Something has moved the ground around in a big way. A flood, perhaps.'

'Let's go and have a look, Tor,' said Vintage. 'That could be exactly what we're after.'

'I want to come,' said Noon. She stood up, wrapping the black jacket tighter around her waist. 'I want to see what it is you're so interested in out here.'

Vintage exchanged a look with Tor, but the Eboran turned away, leaving the decision up to her. She smiled at the witch.

'Of course, my dear.'

Leaving the remains of their makeshift camp, they followed Tor through the towering stalks of fungus. Vintage fell into step next to the girl, her eyes on the bulbous shapes that clustered to every side. 'Have you seen a parasite spirit before, my dear?'

For a long moment the young woman didn't answer. When she did, her voice was tight, as though she were recalling something she'd rather not. 'Once. When I was very small, and I only saw it from very far away. I used to live on the plains, and my people were moving for the spring. All of the carts and the tents and the caravans . . .' Her voice trailed off, and for a moment the strangest expression came over the young woman's face. Her eyes grew wide and glassy, and her mouth turned down at the corners, as though she were a child left suddenly alone in the dark.

'Are you quite well?' Vintage touched Noon's arm, and the fell-witch flinched as though something had scorched her.

'Fine. I just . . . we were travelling across the grasslands at dusk, and I saw something on the horizon. Lots of lights, dancing. I thought it was pretty, but Mother Fast came by on her own mount and she told everyone not to look at it. That if we looked at it, we'd be cursed.' She continued in a quieter voice. 'Maybe she was right.'

'A sighting on the plains.' Vintage frowned. 'The Behemoth remains discovered there were packed up and distributed eight or nine years ago. They were incredibly ancient, from the Third or Fourth Rain, we think.'

'You really study these things?' In the dim light the witch's face looked dirty, with its traces of ash. 'What for? I mean, really what for?'

'For the joy of knowing, of course!' She patted the girl's arm. 'It helps to understand things, don't you think? It makes them less alarming.'

Noon looked unconvinced. 'Things are less *alarming* when you put a lot of space between you and them. Hiding is easier.'

Vintage opened her mouth to reply, but ahead of them Tor had stopped. They had reached the place where the ground dropped away. Below, the dirt was black and exposed, riddled with pale roots grasping at the air like skeletal fingers. Looking at it, Vintage suspected an earth tremor rather than a flood; they weren't completely unheard of in this part of the world. Here, the shadows lay thick on the ground, gathering in pools where the earth was broken, but she thought she could make out something shiny catching the light within the crevice. Her heart skipped and thudded in her chest, and she took a slow breath to try and get it under control.

'Carefully now,' she said to them both. 'Let's go slowly.'

They half walked, half stumbled down the slope that circled the broken earth, until they were down in the mud and dirt. Vintage was glad of her tough boots. From this level, it was clear that there was a great rent in the ground; a meandering crack split the earth, and three large fungi had fallen back, exposing their strange roots to the air like a drunken woman's lacy skirts.

'There's something down here.' Tor, just ahead, had reached

the crack and was peering down into the dark. 'It looks like metal.'

Vintage hurried over. Far above them, pieces of blue sky like a shattered plate let in shards of light, and it was difficult to make out anything clear, but even so. The sheen of moon-metal was hard to mistake for anything else – not when you'd spent so many years hunting it.

'Move your lanky legs out of the way. That's it.' Vintage crouched by the edge. There was something down there; the last light of the day shone off a smooth, rounded surface, greenish gold in colour. Vintage bit her lip. The object was lodged in the ground some five feet below them, partially covered in loose dirt and twisted roots, but next to it the crack itself was much deeper – the darkness hid the hole's true depth.

'I think I might be able to reach it.' Vintage sat down on the cold damp earth, wincing as a root poked her in the back-side, and dangled her legs down into the hole. 'Tormalin, my dear, would you mind holding on to me? Just in case the edge is more fragile than it looks.'

Tormalin sighed. 'To excavate this safely, we need to get the ropes, even some ladders . . .' When she glared at him, he raised his eyebrows. 'I'm only repeating the various lectures you've given me over the years.'

'Nonsense. Come on, quickly now. It will be easy enough to grab, if I can just get in range.'

The Eboran came and knelt behind her and took hold of her elbow. Noon stood to the side of them, her arms crossed over her chest.

'There are other pieces,' she said. 'I can see more bits of shiny metal, all along this crack. Broken on impact with the ground, or just rotted away to fragments.' Awkwardly, Vintage leaned forward, reaching out with one hand. Tormalin's grip on her shirt increased. 'This one must be . . . very ancient . . . indeed . . . to have only come to light now.'

133

Her fingers brushed it, and she felt a tingle move up her arm. Definitely a Behemoth artefact. She grinned into the hole. 'Nearly there. Lower me down, just a little further, Tormalin, my dear, that's it—'

Behind them, Noon made a strangled sound, and several things happened at once. The dim patch of broken earth lit up with shifting pink lights, turning everything nightmarish; an undulating cry filled the air while Tormalin twisted round slightly, muttering under his breath; and the damp earth Vintage was sitting on fell away, dropping her into the darkness.

'Vintage!'

She fell, legs swinging through nothing, and then Tormalin had her arm. His white face hung above her, his mouth hanging open with shock. The little ledge containing the half-buried artefact was to her left, just out of reach. She swung her free arm at it, missing it by inches.

'Buggeration!'

Above her, a shimmering light-filled shape appeared behind Tormalin. It was an amorphous thing, shifting and melting while pink and white lights moved to cluster at what almost could have been a head.

'Tormalin, look out!'

The Eboran was already reaching awkwardly for the sword slung across his back, but Vintage's weight and the precariousness of his own footing made it impossible. He snorted with frustration and gave her a furious yank, intending to pull her up out of the hole, but the ground underneath him partially gave way, and he had to scramble back to avoid following her into the crevice.

The parasite spirit now seemed to fill the canopy above them. It spread to either side, fronds growing at its edges and curling in towards Tormalin, who could not reach his sword and was now in danger of falling into the crack with Vintage. *Well,* she thought, *how swiftly life shits in my face.*

'Let me drop!' she shouted at Tormalin. 'I'll climb back out!'

'Are you out of your mind?'

From her limited vantage point, Vintage saw Fell-Noon step into view. The young woman was staring up at the parasite spirit, apparently entranced. Her movements stiff and unnatural, the fell-witch took a step backwards, and, still with her eyes on the spirit, placed her hand on Tormalin's bare neck. Vintage saw the Eboran jerk as though he'd been touched with a hot poker, and he cried out – whether in pain or surprise she couldn't tell. For a moment, his eyes glazed over, and she wondered if perhaps he were about to pass out. That would end badly for both of them.

Instead, Noon lifted her other hand, almost dreamily, and from it erupted an enormous blossom of green fire. It floated up and exploded against the parasite spirit.

All was chaos. There was a flash of light so bright that, for a few moments, Vintage didn't know where she was, and then Tormalin was swinging her to the left. The warm presence of his hand on her arm vanished, and she crashed onto the muddy ledge, something hard striking her in the stomach. Vintage looked up to see a boiling nightmare made of flames staggering away from them, the silhouette of Noon caught against it like a tiny scrap of shadow.

'What . . .?'

It was the parasite spirit, consumed with winnowfire. Tormalin was staggering to his feet, one hand to his neck as though he were injured and the other brandishing his sword, but as they watched, the creature collapsed, falling to the ground and rolling in a very human gesture of desperation. Belatedly, Vintage realised that she had been hearing a high-pitched screaming since the explosion, which then stuttered and became a guttural howling. Despite everything she'd seen of the parasite spirits and the deaths she had witnessed, she felt a stab of pure horror at it.

135

Vintage stuck her boot on top of the metal artefact and used it to lever herself out of the hole. She scrambled out the rest of the way, her eyes riveted to the dying flames – they were turning a muddy yellow now, and a peculiar stench was filling the air.

'Roots curse you, what have you done to me?' Tormalin was gesturing at Noon's back with his sword, but the young woman was paying no attention. She was staring raptly at the burning form of the parasite spirit, which was shuddering on the ground now, still emitting terrible squawks of pain. After a moment, she raised her hands and placed them over her ears, and then she fell to her knees. The young fell-witch was shaking all over.

'I don't care what you're raving about, Vintage. This creature assaulted me!'

By the time they had beaten out the last of the fires the stench from the burned parasite spirit had been overwhelming, and they had retreated to their makeshift camp. Vintage had built up the fire again – she did not ask Noon for assistance this time – and now they were huddled round it. The fell-witch sat facing away from the flames, with her arms wrapped around herself. She appeared to be staring off into the spaces between the trees, although Vintage doubted she was seeing them at all. Tormalin had liberated a bottle of wine from the pack and was making short work of it, in between complaining. Every now and again his hand would sneak up to his neck and rub the skin there, as though it ached.

'That's right. You appear to have lost a couple of limbs, in fact. Whole pints of blood, no doubt.' Vintage rooted through her bags for her notebooks, trying to ignore how her fingers were trembling. A weapon. Finally, they had a formidable weapon. 'Oh no, what's that? You're absolutely fine? My darling, what a relief.'

Tor nearly spat his wine back into the cup. 'You don't know what she did! She tore the strength from me! She just . . . took it. Like a thief.'

'I am not a thief.' Noon's voice was soft. 'I just took what I needed. You'd both be dead now, otherwise.'

'We would have been fine!' Tor stiffened where he sat. 'Vintage and I have faced these monsters many times and have survived without your *assistance*.'

'What was that thing that . . . burned? What was it really?' Noon had turned back to the fire, her eyes on Vintage now. 'I know we call them spirits, but what *is* it?'

'No one really knows, my dear, and that's the problem. The information we have on these "parasite spirits" is so incredibly sparse. We know they've been around since the Eighth Rain, that there are no records of them appearing before that. We know that they haunt the remains of the old invader's ships. We know that they can attack and kill living beings – indeed, the touch of their flesh is extremely damaging – but they do not actually seem to seek out conflict. Living things get in their way, and so they are torn apart.' Vintage squeezed her notebook between her fingers, feeling the burn of a frustration that was decades old. 'We know nearly nothing about them or the invaders.' She cleared her throat. 'Which is why I would like to engage your services, Fell-Noon.'

Tormalin gave a short bark of laughter, while Noon seemed to break out of her fugue.

'What?'

'Of course, I understand that you're currently engaged in a very important and secret mission for the Winnowry,' Vintage paused to cough into her hand, 'but if you were able to put that to one side for a moment, I would be glad to pay you a wage to accompany us indefinitely. If anyone should have any queries as to your whereabouts, my dear, I would of course handle them personally.'

The girl looked startled now, and Vintage suppressed a smile. To be that young and so sure that your lies were subtle things.

'Listen to me. As far as we knew, winnowfire itself has little effect on parasite spirits. Winnow-forged steel, yes, but not the pure flames. Except *yours* did.' Vintage pursed her lips. She knew what she was about to say would not be received well, and yet she also felt instinctively that it was true. 'I think that was due to the energy you took. Eboran life energy. Together you have made something else. Something lethal to the spirits.'

'Vintage, did you suffer a blow to the head?' Tormalin was smiling faintly, but there was a stony look in his eyes. 'That little fireworks display back there nearly killed all of us, without even going into what this little thief did to me. And you are asking her to do it *again*?'

Vintage ignored him. 'Well, perhaps you could sleep on it, Fell-Noon. That's all I ask. I would like to return to the crevice in the morning, when, hopefully, the night's air will have dissipated the stench, and then we'll get you out of this gloomy worm-touched place. Plenty of time for you to consider my offer.'

Noon lay with her back to the fire. She was glad of the warmth, but she couldn't quite bring herself to look at it.

She felt exhausted to her very bones, but sleep was a distant prospect – her mind felt like a bird caught in a tent, bouncing from wall to wall in a panic, no way out. At the forefront of her mind was the fact that the woman *knew*. She knew she was no agent, that her story stank worse than horse dung. She had been kind, and polite, and hadn't come out and said directly that she knew Noon was lying, but it had been there in the hard glitter of her eyes when she had offered Noon the job. Noon had never met anyone like Vintage. Her cleverness was evident in her every word, in her assessing gaze. That could simply be because she was older than Noon, although it was difficult to guess her age; her warm brown skin was largely unlined, save for a handful of creases at the corners of her eyes, and a pair of laughter lines by her mouth. She had full hips and a thicket of dark curled hair, shot through here and there with a few touches of grey. Her eyes were kind, and to Noon she was beautiful. It made her more difficult to trust, somehow.

Noon pulled the collar of the jacket up to her chin. She needed to think, but whenever she closed her eyes she saw it all again, as if the image were still seared onto the inside of her eyelids: the strange creature made of lights, the soft way it had flowed around them, like a deadly flood. And then she had summoned her fire and it had lit up the night, an impossible torch, and she had been frozen with terror and exultation. The parasite spirit had burned, so wildly and so fast, and the noises it had made . . . She knew from the expressions on the faces of Vintage and the Eboran that they had never expected it to make such noises, but then they had never heard a living thing burn before. She was certain of it.

In the dark, Noon curled up as tightly as she could. Somewhere, deep inside her head, that noise went on forever.

Behind her, she could hear the small sounds of the others. Vintage was asleep, her hat – which she had insisted they retrieve – placed delicately over her face. The rhythmic fluting noise was her snoring. The Eboran was still awake, watching over them in the dark – she could hear him shifting every now and then, the occasional small sigh as he stood up to work the stiffness from his legs, the creak of his leather coat.

How strange to be here in the dark with such company. Ten years of nothing but the Winnowry and the witches, and now she made camp with an Eboran. It was like sleeping next to the bogey man, next to a monster out of one of Mother Fast's tales. He was everything she had said the Eborans were – beautiful, graceful, quick. His eyes were red and cruel, just as they were in all of Mother Fast's stories, and it was easy to imagine him on the battlefields of the Carrion Wars, tearing out the throats of men and women and drinking their blood while it was still hot.

And there was something else. In her fear and her panic, she had taken energy from him to fuel her winnowfire. Just a touch, and it had filled her in moments, something dark and old and unknowable – she had felt no other energy like it, and just like the winnowfire, it was frightening and glorious. She wanted to be far from here, to be alone so that she could never feel it again. She wanted to go to him now and place her hand against the smooth skin of his neck and taste it again. Take all of it, perhaps, and become someone else entirely.

Noon squeezed her eyes shut. Perhaps the Winnowry was right after all. She was too dangerous to be out in the world.

11

The story of Tomas the Drowned is an interesting, if ultimately tragic, one – tragic, mainly for the hundreds of women who have been imprisoned as a result of his unusual life.

Tomas was a fisherman, or so the tale tells us, and one night he was out alone in his fishing boat when a great storm came upon the reef. His boat was smashed into pieces and Tomas sank beneath the waves, supposedly lost forever.

(Interestingly, shards of his boat have been sold as holy relics for the last hundred years or so, collected by the faithful as they were washed up on the beach. How the faithful knew to collect those pieces when, as far as they knew, Tomas was just another drowned fisherman, I do not know, but it does not do to dwell too closely on the origins of 'holy' relics, I suspect.)

A hundred days later, Tomas walked out of the sea, followed by four men and three women. It must have been quite a sight, these bedraggled, soaking figures striding out of the waves and up the beach. Tomas claimed that he had been trapped beneath the sea within a vision of great evil; a terrible world, he said, existed elbow to elbow with our own. We were all in danger. There was a woman there, he said, a 'glowing woman', who 'burned with an eerie fire', and she was the 'heart and soul' of that evil place. The men and women who were with him corroborated his story, although, from what I gather, they were also quite confused by their time under the sea. (It is worth noting, however, that each one of them was traced as a person lost at sea; one had been lost nine years ago, yet he had aged not a day, and two others were from the same shipwreck.)

Tomas took himself to a remote part of the coast – for the rest of his life, he could never quite leave the sea behind – and along with his seven disciples, began to feverishly produce paintings and writings about his terrible experience, warning us of the burning woman who was the key to this evil landscape. (There is, it seems to me, a certain type of man who is terrified of the idea of a woman wielding power, of any sort; the type of man who is willing to dress up his terror in any sort of trappings to legitimise it.)

Word spread. People, the desperate, perhaps, or the rudderless, joined him at his lonely outpost, and eventually a woman called Milandra Parcs came to him. She had very good reasons to hate fell-witches, and she saw in Tomas's words and paintings a truth she already knew in her heart: the 'burning women'– to her mind, the fell-witches – were evil. Tomas died, finally, his body left in a high place to be eaten by birds and animals (only in death, it seemed, could he escape the sea) and Milandra created the Winnowry. It was sold as a refuge for these women at first – these were individuals, after all, who were often very frightened of their own extraordinary powers – but as the word spread of the fell-witches' *'corruption' (put about by the delightful Madam Parcs, no doubt), the Winnowry became a prison. Now the Winnowry come for any woman or girl who shows the 'corruption', and they live out their days in that pitiless place.*

What interests me is what actually happened to Tomas and the seven he led from the sea. Where were they during their missing days and months and years? Was Tomas simply mad, or had he seen part of a great revelation?

Extract from the journals of Lady Vincenza 'Vintage' de Grazon

The next morning the sky was overcast, and an alien stench still lingered in the Shroom Flats. Tor opened his mouth to complain about it to Vintage, before remembering what had caused it – the incinerated body of the parasite spirit. Vintage was already up and about, noisily packing bags and retrieving notebooks, while the fell-witch was curled up by the fire, still asleep. In the night she had turned over to face the flames, sleeping close enough that a stray spark could have set her on fire too. *Nothing less than she would deserve*, he thought, glaring down at her still form. The wave of weakness that had swept through him the moment her fingers touched his skin was all too easy to recall – he'd never felt anything like it, and he didn't care to ever feel it again. It had made him think of the crimson flux; your body an enemy, no longer obeying your commands.

'Wake up our friend there, would you, Tor?' Vintage was rooting around in bags and randomly pulling out glass jars, peering at them, and putting them back. 'If she's going to be helping us, she'll want to see this.'

'First, wake her up yourself. Second, are you truly persisting with this nonsense? She is clearly an escaped criminal of some sort.'

143

Vintage lowered her voice. 'An escaped criminal able to incapacitate a parasite spirit in seconds. Think how useful that could be to us. Do stop whining, Tormalin, my love, it doesn't suit you half as much as you think it does.'

'By incapacitate, do you mean set everything on fire?' However, he went over to the sleeping figure and rested his boot on her leg, giving her an experimental push. The girl gasped and scrambled backwards, the colour draining from her face. Tor frowned.

'There's no need to take on like that. Come on, we're going to look at the thing you destroyed last night, if there's anything left of it.'

The fell-witch was looking around at the towering mushrooms as if she were trying to figure out where she was. Tor crouched down and spoke to her quietly.

'Not used to the outside world, are we?'

She narrowed her eyes at him and scrambled to her feet, pulling the black jacket more tightly around her shoulders. *His* black jacket. 'Not used to waking up with a monster from a story standing over me.'

Vintage led them back to the crevice. Tormalin pulled the Ninth Rain free of its scabbard – there might have only been one parasite spirit, but it didn't hurt to be wary.

'Here, look,' Vintage marched down, pointing at the shattered ground, 'tiny pieces of the Behemoth's moon-metal scattered everywhere. This thing must have crashed in the Third or Fourth Rain, perhaps even the Second, and the Wild has grown over its ancient bones. And then an earth tremor, and it all gets shoved back up to the surface.'

'There's the remains of our parasite spirit,' said Tormalin, pointing with his sword. 'Worth scraping into a jar?'

It looked like a broken sheet of partially clouded jelly, marked here and there with dark craters. Tormalin reached down to poke it with the end of the Ninth Rain, but Vintage appeared

144

at his side, elbowing him out of the way none too gently. 'Don't touch it with winnow-forged steel! You'll only damage it more.'

She pulled a long-handled spoon from a pocket and carefully began to spoon the wobbly muck into a spare jar. As she touched it, the substance seemed to break up, falling apart into oddly fibrous lumps. Tormalin took a step back from the remains. Looking at those strange shapes made him feel uneasy.

'We've never recovered so much material!' Vintage was beaming with delight. 'I will need to purchase a whole new set of lenses to look at this. Now, I want to examine this hole again – don't give me that look, Tor, I will be more careful this time.'

The broken earth had partially covered up the artefact that Vintage had attempted to retrieve the previous evening, but it was still possible to see sections of it; greenish gold metal that looked oily in the daylight.

'I'll get it.' Tor stepped in front of Vintage, waving her back. 'Look, it's possible to see the edges of this thing now. I can climb down there.' After the violence of the previous day's attack the earth had settled again, revealing a rough path on the far side of the hole. Sheathing his sword, Tor lowered himself down and began to climb slowly towards the metal object.

'Be careful, my dear! We don't want to lose that sword of yours.' Tor glanced up to see Vintage smiling down at him. Noon stood at her back, her arms crossed over her chest and an uncertain look on her face.

'I'm touched by your concern, Vintage, as ever.'

When he laid his hands on the artefact he was surprised to find that it felt more like a piece of ceramic under his fingers – cool, but not cold as metal might be. He brushed the dirt and mud away to reveal its full shape; it was egg-like, with dimpled impressions in the wider half, but the top had been shattered. There was a thick substance leaking from inside. It was a deep gold in colour, but shimmering with a rainbow of other hues.

'What is it?' snapped Vintage. 'What can you see?'

'Hold on.'

He pulled the artefact away from the mud carefully, but, as he did so, more of it fell away to reveal an empty space where the oil from the artefact had obviously spilled – he could see the golden slick even against the dark mud – and in this tiny space was a riot of vegetation. A number of small plants had burst into life here, apparently underground and out of sight of the sun. There were thick branches with crowds of leaves, even flowers and the beginnings of fruit. He blinked at it in confusion.

'Tor, what *is* it?'

'Here, look for yourself.' Holding the artefact under one arm, Tor cleared away the rest of the mud and stepped back, revealing the vibrant and unexpected garden. It was an odd patch of colour amongst the black earth and pale roots. Above him, he heard Vintage catch her breath.

'The egg thing is broken at the top, and leaking some sort of golden fluid. And it appears to have led to this.' He gestured at the small riot of vegetation.

Vintage looked thunderstruck. 'Broken? It wasn't broken yesterday. Did we break it?'

'How can it have caused those plants?' asked Noon. 'That makes no sense.'

'Some sort of Jure'lia magic, my dear,' said Vintage. She had not taken her eyes from the unlikely garden. 'I will want samples of everything, Tor, and the whole object removed and taken back with us to Mushenska. I'll pass the jars down to you. And a pair of gloves. Can you get a sample of the fluid?'

It took Tor much of the rest of the morning to pack everything up as Vintage required. The egg-like artefact was put into a collapsible box Vintage had brought with her, packed

146

with sheep's wool, and many jars were filled with samples of the strange plants that had grown overnight in the dark. Of the golden fluid, he managed only to collect one vial's worth, being extremely careful not to get any on his hands. When, finally, he climbed out of the hole he felt dirty and tired, and he was certain part of that was down to what the fell-witch had done to him the night before. He wanted blood, and could feel the weight of the small glass vials in his own pack, but felt reluctant to get them out in front of the witch, with her watchful, dark eyes. *It's not even fresh*, he told himself. What Sareena had given him was days old now, and its effects would be greatly reduced.

'So this was part of a Behemoth? Like the corpse moon?'

The girl was crouched on a clump of exposed roots, her arms wrapped around herself again. To Tor she looked like a small dishevelled bird, ready to take flight at any moment. In the half-light of the morning the tattoo on her forehead was a dark smudge. Vintage was logging what they had found in one of her many notebooks, but she looked up with a smile at the girl's question.

'This thing was inside one once, yes. But my guess is that the Behemoth broke up in the skies over this forest, oh, a thousand years ago, and some of the wreckage landed here, only to be lost under the encroaching Wild. Even small pieces of a Behemoth are enough to attract a parasite spirit, it seems.'

'But there are whole ones. In places.'

Vintage nodded up at the sky. 'Our ever-present friend the corpse moon is one, my dear, trapped somehow on its way back out of our sky. And yes, there are others. Famous sites where Behemoths crashed. Three are no longer there, as they have been picked apart by scavengers or eroded away by time. One, on the coast of Kerakus, has been partly swallowed by the sea.' Vintage paused, a brief shadow passing over her face, and then she seemed to shake it off. 'Two others are now in pieces, on their way to being lost entirely themselves.' Vintage stood up, briskly rubbing her hands together. There was a damp chill between the toadstools, a mist that was lingering around the stalks. 'And three others. One somewhere in the vast tract of desert known as the Singing Eye. One on the heights of the Elru mountain, although it was said that last year it broke apart, the largest half falling into a chasm. And the last is on a piece of land owned by one Esiah Godwort. His family built walls all around it, and you can only enter the compound with his permission. He hoards it to himself like a dragon with gold, which is why I believe it to be the most intact example.' She cleared her throat. 'Which is *why* I believe we should refresh ourselves, gather our wits, and go there next.'

Tor laughed, ignoring the perplexed look Noon shot him. 'What makes you think Godwort will let you in this time? As opposed to the five other times you have asked? You know it's not about coin with that roots-addled fool.'

'It's not to do with coin, no, you are quite right, Tormalin, my dear. But now we have something quite different to barter with.'

For the briefest second Vintage's crafty gaze shifted to the fell-witch, but the girl was oblivious. Tor sighed; it seemed that Vintage really was intent on keeping the creature.

'Right. Fine. Can we get back to Mushenska now please?' He picked up the biggest pack, weighted now with various glass jars filled with dirt as well as the broken artefact, and settled it easily on his back. 'I'm thirsty.'

12

What do we know of the Jure'lia, then? Astonishingly little, given how long they have been haunting our history.

First, Jure'lia comes from the Kesenstan word for 'worm', or, more accurately, 'worm people'. As far as we can tell, Kesenstan would have been one of the first places to experience an invasion; artefacts dating back thousands of years have been found during mining operations in the country. We do not know what the Jure'lia call themselves.

Second, the Jure'lia are not from Sarn. Or, at least, not from any part of it we know about – not from the surface of Sarn . . . do you begin to see the problem? Every few centuries or so, they appear in our skies apparently from nowhere, and begin the relentless destruction of our lands, our cities, our people. I say 'our' here in the broadest sense – the Jure'lia focus their attacks on no particular country or nation, and send forth no diplomat to negotiate terms. Efforts have been made to communicate in the past, but it has always ended badly for our delegates.

We call the ships they arrive in Behemoths, and for

good reason. *Bigger than anything seen on Sarn, these flying contraptions are great, bulbous things, resembling, if anything, the humble woodlouse (for reference: Rolda de Grazon made a number of extraordinary sketches during the Eighth Rain, which are kept in the Grazon family archive, and these I have compared to other contemporary reports. Dear distant Cousin Rolda had a good eye). Within these Behemoths travel the seeds of their entire force. Behemoths that have been brought down and crashed into the surface of Sarn have proved difficult to explore, with most accounts of the interiors making little sense – the general assumption is that something within the broken ships causes humans to lose their sanity. It's not a comforting thought. In recent times, pieces of broken-up Behemoth, shards of their strange green or black 'moon-metal',* are known to generate or attract the beings known as 'parasite spirits' – no one knows why this is, whether they are from Sarn itself, or a direct fallout of this alien technology. The parasite spirits only started appearing after the Eighth Rain, for reasons we may never know. One theory I believe has merit is that they are some sort of 'sleeping weapon', left behind by the Jure'lia as a way of further poisoning our land while they themselves recuperate. It's a fascinating idea.*

Within each Behemoth will be several hundred 'mothers'. As ever, with the Jure'lia, we are uncertain whether or not these creatures are entirely organic, or

---

* *Moon-metal sounds like quite a romantic term, but in truth it's anything but. Simply put, the oily-looking greenish metal so often comprising Jure'lia artefacts is named for the corpse moon – it, too, shines with a greenish, coppery light when the sun hits it just so. And nothing about that dead creature speaks of romance.*

manufactured in some way. With six mobile legs coming together in a central 'cup', they mostly look like especially tall spiders, although without eyes or mandibles or even an abdomen. Instead, the cup holds a sac, pearlescent in colour, which generates, or gives birth to, thousands of 'burrowers', also referred to as 'bugs'. These creatures look a little like beetles with soft body casings. They are narrow, with multiple legs, and, unfortunately, that's about all I know as no organic material has ever survived from them. Infamously, burrowers are the true horror of the Jure'lia, and the method via which they threaten to conquer Sarn – burrowers will hide inside a human victim and 'eat' away their insides, leaving a hollow interior coated in a strange, black, viscous substance. Whatever this substance is, it is more than simple waste material, as it leaves the victim conscious and able to communicate to some extent – although, of course, all trace of their previous personality has been replaced with the Jure'lia hive. Such unfortunate souls are effectively dead – at least, to their families and friends.

When the burrowers have done their work, what we're left with are drones. They make up the vast majority of the Jure'lia force, and represent a terrible psychological toll on the survivors. Fight against the Jure'lia and you will be killing enemies with the faces of your neighbours, your friends, your family, your lover. We know from accounts of previous invasions that armies have suffered significant losses of morale, which in turn has been devastating.

Also contained within the Behemoths are 'maggots' (also referred to, rather colourfully, as the 'shitters', but I will stick to maggots for my purposes). Maggots are enormous living creatures, around sixty feet long and twenty feet wide. They move slowly, and seem to largely consist of a mouth at one end and an anus at the other, with a fat segmented middle section (for reference, again dear Cousin Rolda has done a series of drawings, from several angles. I must assume that because these things take a while to travel any distance, he was able to spend some time studying them). These creatures appear to have been entirely organic, with no interior skeleton and, consequently, no physical sign of them remains. These creatures made their slow way across Sarn, guarded by mothers and by drones, and consumed all the organic material in their paths. Trees, grass, plants, crops, animals, anything slower than them – and then excreted a vast amount of a thick, viscous slime, dark green in colour. This substance would then set, becoming harder than steel and smothering anything that came into contact with it.

It is possible to see evidence of this 'suffocation' at several locations around Sarn, most notably at the so-called 'abyssal fields' on the Wintertree plains – here you can experience a landscape so bleak and horrifying that I wouldn't recommend more than an hour's visit. It is possible, through the thick layer of vaguely trans-lucent green varnish, to see the lost earth beneath, with strands of lost grass frozen in time. And a fair few bodies too – some are almost certainly drones who did not get out of the maggots' way in time, and others were humans fleeing the invasion. It is a sad sight indeed, and deeply eerie – these men and women died hundreds of years ago, yet the maggot fluid has preserved them so well it looks like they have simply ducked their heads below the waters of a pond for a few brief moments.

There are similar sights at the Fon-sein Temple of the Lost, to the east of Brindlebrook in Reilans, the Iron

*Market Memorial in Mushenska, and in the Thousand
Tooth Valley, although that particular stretch of 'varnish',
as it has become known, has been built on top of and
has become something of an attraction for travellers. The
varnish has proved near impossible to move, which rather
raises the question: will the Jure'lia eventually win by
simply covering us over, piece by piece, however long it
takes? An alarming thought.*

Extract from the journals of
Lady Vincenza 'Vintage' de Grazon

As the dismal summer faded and autumn fell over Ebora,
Hestillion kept largely to the sprawling confines of Ygseril's
palace. What she had told Lord Moureni about the wolves
was true; they were normal wolves, not worm-touched creatures
half mad with the taint of the Wild, and they didn't seem
interested in her bony flesh, but that could well change as the
colder months drew in. Whoever was left outside the palace
would have to deal with that as they saw fit.

It was a cold, grey morning, chilly enough for her to see
her breath before her even as she walked the corridors of the
palace. It was just a cold snap – the true brutality of winter
was a way off yet – but it was a reminder that she would
need to start stockpiling firewood, and bring the warmer
gowns out of storage. This morning, though, she had set aside
for other concerns. She paused outside the Hall of Roots,
needlessly glancing over her shoulder in case there was anyone
there to observe her. The doors were as stiff and heavy as
they had ever been, and she had to lean her entire body
weight on them to squeeze her narrow frame through the
gap. Inside, the echoing hall was a forest of shadowed shapes,
ghostly in the muted light from the glass roof. A hundred
years ago, when he was still alive, Hestillion's uncle, Nourem,
had become convinced that the plains people on the other

side of the mountain were planning to band together to sack Ebora. He had been a sharp man in his day, but years of watching his people die and the early stages of the crimson flux had pushed him towards some teetering, paranoid edge. He had ordered all their valuables to be stored in the Hall of Roots, reasoning that it was the most defensible space in the entire city. Their artworks, their paintings, their sculptures and finest furniture had been brought into the hall and covered with sheets, and then allowed to moulder here in silence. Hestillion remembered watching the room fill up with their ancient treasures, and how the men and women moving the objects did not look at Ygseril, not even once. To them, the god was no longer there. It was just another piece of their lost history, gathering dust under the sky.

Hestillion wove her way between the shrouded statues of Eboran war-beasts and the towering blood-vial cabinets, heading towards the giant ghost in the centre of the room. Ygseril was a looming grey presence, his branches spread over her head like a cloud. Just as she had when she was a child, she climbed out onto the thick roots, feeling the solid cold press of their rippled bark through her slippers. It was so hard to get warm in this place. She promised herself a roaring fire when she was back in her suite.

'Hello, old man.' She sat down where the trunk met the roots, resting her back against the chilly bark. From here, Ygseril filled the whole world. 'Another quiet day.'

Silence hung in the Hall of Roots, an invisible shroud that Hestillion could almost imagine brushing against her skin – clammy and clinging, like death. Music was something else they had lost in the gradual collapse of Ebora. When was the last time she had listened to a song sung by someone else, or the playing of instruments? Ebora had once been full of men and women who were exceptionally skilled musicians and composers, having dedicated centuries of their lives to learning

154

their craft. Once, Ygseril's palace had echoed continually with music. Her brother had dedicated most of his years to sword-play and then to the more secretive disciplines practised in the House of the Long Night. He was very good at it, he never tired of telling her, and by all reports, he was right. Hestillion herself had never been drawn to music, instead studying painting and embroidery, but her greatest passion had been for dream-walking. Tormalin had always said that she was the finest dream-walker Ebora had produced, that she could hide herself within a dream as well as a grasshopper within a glade. Hestillion smiled bitterly to herself. Perhaps he had been right; it hardly mattered now.

Thinking of the dream-walking, she ran her hands over the cold bark underneath her. Once again, she looked around to make sure she was alone. Aldasair had not been in here in years, but that didn't mean he might not suddenly decide to make the trip – his mind was slowly spooling into chaos, after all.

Bowing her head, Hestillion closed her eyes, feeling her mind sink into the shadowy netherdarkness. It closed around her, as comforting to Hestillion as being held by a dear parent. She looked around. Darkness, almost entirely. There was a faint light that pulsed softly, which she knew to be Lord Moureni. Sleeping now, edging closer and closer to the point where he simply wouldn't wake up. She felt a brief stab of curiosity about the old Lord's dreams, wondering if he would be reliving past glories on the battlefield, but the possibility that he dreamed of misery, illness and a slow death was too great. She had no wish to share that with him. Another dreaming mind nearby was brighter. She was half surprised that Aldasair was still asleep when the sun had been up for hours, but then what else was there to do in this place now, but sleep? His dreaming mind was bright, a torch in the darkness. Allowing herself to feel briefly reassured by its presence, she turned her own mind

155

away. In the netherdarkness, Ygseril was a great grey blot, a shadow in the dreamspace.

'Ygseril. Are you there?'

There was no change in the grey shadow, no light to indicate a dreaming mind, not even a flicker. Just as it had been for hundreds of years.

'I still believe you are there, somehow. You sleep more deeply than any of us, that is all.'

Moving towards the shadow until it was all around her, Hestillion pushed her consciousness deep into the surrounding gloom, feeling for the resistance that would normally come before she entered a dream. It was like walking in the thickest fog. Once, when she and Tormalin had been small, they had gone exploring the ornamental forest that curled around the northern wall of the palace. It was an exquisitely beautiful place; every tree, every small hill, every plant and streamlet had been placed according to a design by Ebora's foremost gardener. In the summer months it was an island of greenery, thick with blossom and the scent of flowers, but they had gone walking in midwinter, and a swirling fog had grown up between the tree trunks. The white mist had made her think of forgetfulness, and as the trees and the plants vanished behind it, she had been filled with a terrible sense of loss. She had looked at her brother, and had seen the same misery on his face. Once, she and Tormalin had often shared the same feelings. That was a long time ago.

This was fog on a much grander scale. The shadow that was Ygseril was all around her, and although she searched with every fibre of her dreamself, there was nothing.

'Come back to us, Ygseril. Come back.'

Nothing. Hestillion swallowed hard, feeling an echo of that same loss and despair she had felt in the garden with Tormalin, so long ago. In desperation, she cast her awareness downwards, feeling along the complex labyrinth that was Ygseril's roots.

Down and down, into a darkness that rivalled the netherdarkness itself, until she felt lost, disconnected from herself. It was tempting to keep going, to keep pushing until whatever held her to her own body snapped, to sever that connection and stay lost in the fog forever. Better that than a slow death watching Ebora collapse into a horror of blood and empty corridors. But the truth was, she was too good at this. She had travelled further in the netherdark before, and survived, more than once.

Her heart stuttered. The tiniest blink of light had flickered on the edge of her awareness, just for a second. It had been there and gone so fast that she wasn't certain she hadn't imagined it, or if it had been an anomaly of her own vision – her brain trying to create light and colour when she had been in the darkness for so long. Without pausing to think further, Hestillion dived after it, seeking the space where it had been. The darkness pressed in around her, claustrophobic now, and she could almost feel the roots surrounding her, half unseen. Was it her imagination, or was the greyness lighter here? For a fleeting moment, it was almost as though she were standing in a dark room with someone beside her. If she reached out, without looking, she could touch them . . .

A hand curled around the top of her arm, and she was back in the Hall of Roots, her eyes wide open.

'Aldasair! What are you doing?'

The young man was crouched on the roots next to her, his tousled hair half falling over his face. He was still wearing his night robe, and his eyes were heavy with sleep. How long had she been in the netherdark, searching?

'You were asleep,' he said, a shade defensively. 'I wanted you to come and eat with me. And there's someone here.'

'You idiot.' Hestillion shook his hand away. Had she simply been sensing Aldasair's presence in the hall, or was it something else? 'What do you mean, there's someone here?'

157

'I wanted to have rala root with my lunch, so I went outside to see if it's still growing wild in the Red Singing Garden.' Hestillion raised her eyebrows. This was as lucid as she'd seen Aldasair in months. 'And I saw them, walking down the Great Street towards the palace. They were coming along very slowly, looking around at everything. They'll get eaten by wolves if they don't hurry up.'

Hestillion stood up, swaying slightly – she had been very deep in the netherdark when Aldasair had pulled her out of it, and the speed with which she had been drawn back was disorientating. She glanced up at the trunk of Ygseril, wondering if she'd imagined the light, but there was no time to think about it now. 'Aldasair, do you mean there are humans in Ebora?'

Aldasair brushed his hands down the front of his night gown. It was slightly dusty. 'That's precisely what I mean. All the rala root is dead, by the way.'

Hestillion hurried to the front gates, smoothing her hair back behind her ears while Aldasair followed her reluctantly. She had at least put on one of her finer padded gowns this morning – deep emerald green with a turquoise pattern of spiral serpents – and although she wore no jewellery her boots were studded with lesser gems. It would do, for meeting with surprise guests. She could see them already beyond the golden gates, a ragtag group of men and women standing very close together. From the shapes of their faces and the elaborate travelling tents they carried with them they were plains people, which was in itself a surprise. Since the Carrion Wars plains people had rarely come to Ebora voluntarily. Hestillion consciously smoothed her brow and put on her most welcoming smile before slipping out through the gates; they were always left open these days.

'Greetings!' she called. 'I cannot tell you how good it is to see visitors here. You must have come a long way.'

158

The small group were watching her with dark eyes. They wore soft deerskin leggings and heavy woollen garments that swept their shoulders with bright colours – reds, yellows, purples and greens – and hoods of horsehair circled their faces. As she watched, the men and women shuffled aside to reveal a sturdy wooden litter with a heavily padded seat at the centre. In it was a tiny, ancient woman, mostly concealed by blankets and her own horsehair hood. One long-fingered hand, leathery with exposure to weather, gripped the arm of the seat.

'You are in charge here, girl?' The woman's voice was cracked with age, but firm.

Hestillion came forward, her own hands folded into her sleeves against the cold. 'I suppose you could say that I am. Please, let me take you all inside. Whatever hospitality we have left will be yours.'

The figure in the litter raised her hand, beckoning.

'Let me have a look at you first. Been years since I've seen a real, live Eboran.'

Hestillion came forward slowly. She did not look at the men and women who stood with the litter, but she could feel the distrust radiating from them. As she drew closer, the old woman leaned forward, pushing her horsehair hood back. Hestillion's first instinct was to gasp, to look away, but she swallowed it down.

The woman must have been nearly a hundred years old, unspeakably ancient for a human. Her skin was as thin as a dried leaf and looked just as fragile, peppered all over with dark brownish age spots. This was not what had alarmed Hestillion though; at some point in the past, the old woman had been very badly burned. The skin on her face and neck was a raw, shiny pink, the flesh melted and twisted beyond all recognition. Her right eye was gone, a slippery pucker of scar tissue in its place, and her hair was reduced to a few scanty white braids on the left side of her head. Her mouth was little

159

more than a slit, and the eye that was left was a deep dark brown. It fixed Hestillion with a piercing gaze.

'I am Mother Fast, girl. I had a dream, and I've come to lend my aid to Ebora.'

13

There is one final figure in the Jure'lia force worth elaborating on: the Jure'lia queen. This appears to be a single entity who thinks independently for the hive; who appears to make decisions and issue commands. There can be little doubt that she is the heart of the Jure'lia invasion. And yet, very little is known about her and she remains, quite literally, a shadowy figure. She appears to be humanoid at least, with a head, two arms and two legs, and may even wear armour of a sort. But many questions remain. Is it the same figure each time or a new queen? What does she want? Why is she the only humanoid? Is she, in fact, a drone they have picked up previously elsewhere?

Rolda de Grazon appears to have only ever seen the queen from a great distance, and hence made some very rough sketches of something that appears to be a tall woman, standing just beyond a line of maggots and mothers. His hand, it is worth noting, is not as accurate as it has been in previous drawings, and indeed, all the pictures he brought back of the Jure'lia leader seem soaked in dread. I find them difficult to look at myself – the shadowy figure seems to shake and melt in front of my eyes, as though she cannot be pinned to paper – and so I put it away quickly, in a separate folio to the rest. Staring at it doesn't help, after all.

(I think of my brave and distant cousin often as I work my way through our precious archive. He returned from the Eighth Rain alive, something very few could say, and his diaries are full of praise for the brave Eboran warriors and their war-beasts who fought so valiantly against the invaders – I wonder privately if he had an affair of some sort during the war. There is a pair of silk gloves among his effects, with fine Eboran stitching. But he was a broken man, all the same. From his notes I know that he planned to write a book on the Eighth Rain on his return, but he appears to have made no progress on it in his later years, and eventually walked out into the vine forest one day and never came back. I imagine that he died out there somewhere, that his lonely bones rest under one of the giant trees. Poor old sod. His notes, and most importantly, his fine drawings, are the sturdy backbone of my own research.)

The final thing we know about the Jure'lia is, of course, that the Eborans were the only ones who could ever drive them off. The tall and graceful and lethal Eborans – with the curious magic of the strange beasts birthed to them by Ygseril, the tree-god. Time and again, the Jure'lia have come, and each time Ygseril has shed its extraordinary fruits, each silvery pod revealing an Eboran war-beast. They are, perhaps, an even greater mystery than the Jure'lia, and there is no doubt that Sarn would have been lost centuries ago without them.

Extract from the journals of Lady Vincenza 'Vintage' de Grazon

'What are we doing here? Vintage, would it not make more sense to return to your apartments? We've been travelling for days.'

Noon glanced at the Eboran, who was glaring around at the streets of Mushenska as if the city had done him a personal wrong. It was difficult to concentrate on his voice – there were so many, threatening to drown him out. She could barely think. Resisting the urge to place her hands over her ears, Noon took a slow breath. The city was overwhelming.

'I want to show you something.' Since the incident in the forest, Vintage had been full of energy, whisking them back to Mushenska with a fixed smile on her face and a steely glint in her eye. On some level, Noon felt it would be unwise to trust the scholar, but her options were limited. Once back on the road they had caught a postal carriage back, a heavily armoured vehicle pulled by sturdy horses, and in the crowded compartment Vintage had produced a small package and passed it to Noon. 'Just a gift,' she had said. 'I picked it up for my niece when I travelled through Jarlsbad last and have repeat-edly failed to post it to her, and, well, I believe the style is very fashionable in the big cities currently.' Noon had opened the package to find a soft black felt hat, with a lilac silk band that slipped down over her forehead. She opened her mouth to point out that the very first thing a runaway fell-witch would do would be to cover up the tattoo on her forehead, and that it would hardly hide her from Winnowry patrols in that case – but to say so would be to admit what she was. She closed her mouth and nodded her thanks awkwardly. Vintage knew what she was, and she was trying to help. Why? And now they were in Mushenska, a city Noon had only ever seen briefly from its rooftops. She tugged at the silk band on her hat, wondering at the noise and life around her.

'I think it would be instructional,' Vintage continued. She was leading them deeper into the city on a bright, hot day.

163

Men and women and children pressed in all around them, their heads and arms bare; so much skin, so many different colours – pale as cream and dotted with freckles, deep warm brown like polished wood, or a rich olive, like her own. The last time she had been around so many people, so close and so uncovered, was on the plains, with her mother and her people. It wasn't a comforting thought.

'What would be instructional, would be a good hot bath with a decent bottle of wine near to hand,' said Tormalin.

'We're going to the Iron Market Memorial,' Vintage carried on as if he hadn't spoken. 'Have you ever been, girl?'

'Me? No. No, of course not.'

Vintage nodded. She was as serious as Noon had seen her so far. 'I think it's something everyone should see, if they can.'

They wound deeper into the city, until they came to a set of tall walls of featureless black stone that stretched out to either side. Already the city was quieter here, and Noon felt a coil of dread unfurl in her stomach. She had heard of the Iron Market Memorial, she was sure of it, but couldn't say for certain what it was. She glanced at the hot blue sky above them, half fearing and half hoping to see Fulcor circling above them. The bat had been spotted twice, flying above them as they made their way back to Mushenska, and then it had disappeared again, apparently attending to bat business of its own; certainly it did not seem to feel that it had to obey her or the whistle. *Even the bat knows I'm not really a Winnowry agent*, thought Noon. She rolled her hands into fists. The urge to flee was still strong.

Vintage led them alongside the wall until they came to a simple, square archway. Here there was an inscription, in a language Noon could not read.

'What does it say?'

'The Sixth Rain. Let us not forget the lost, who can never leave this place.' Tor's voice was smooth and faintly amused, as though he found it funny that she couldn't read the inscription.

'How right they are,' murmured Vintage. 'Come on.'

Inside the walls, which Noon saw formed a simple square, was an odd, desolate oasis of calm. The grey cobbles of Mushenska ended, became brown dirt, which was then covered in a dark green substance, thick and hard like glass, shining under the hot sun. The slick substance covered the ground from wall to wall, and here and there it formed strange twisting shapes. These Noon found she had to look away from; there was something about the way they caught at your eyes that was unnerving. The place was empty of people.

'What is it? What is this stuff?'

Vintage led them out onto the slick ground. Under Noon's borrowed boots it felt slippery.

'How much do you know about the Jure'lia, my dear? About the *worm people*?'

'What everyone knows.' She frowned, thinking about her dream. The sense that it was real in a way other dreams were not hadn't left her. 'They're invaders that have tried to take Sarn. Each time, they've been stopped.'

'By my people,' put in Tormalin. 'Forced back by brave Eboran warriors and their war-beasts.'

'Well, what you're looking at here, my dear, is one part of how the Jure'lia have tried to make Sarn their own. We call it *varnish*, although that hardly does it justice.' She tapped her boot against it. Here, the roar of the city was a distant murmur. 'The Jure'lia, they bring their giant beasts, and they secrete *this*,' she gestured around at the memorial as a whole. 'They covered over great swathes of land with it, suffocating anything that might have been underneath, anything slow enough to be caught. Here, follow me.'

She led them out towards the centre of the square, still talking. 'There was indeed a market here once, before

Mushenska was Mushenska. In the time before the Sixth Rain, the Iron Market was the place you came to for your weapons and your armour.' Absently, Vintage patted the crossbow at her side. 'It was still quite a provincial place then, you must understand, a gathering of skilled blacksmiths and leather workers in the centre of a village. The village was called Fourtrees, for not especially imaginative reasons. And then the Jure'lia came. They landed a Behemoth to the east of what are now the outskirts of Mushenska, and they released one of their great maggots. The enormous worm creature and its helpers quickly consumed everything there was to Fourtrees, and then spread this glassy muck over what was left. Here. Look.'

Vintage pointed down at her feet. The translucent glassy substance was like looking down into a murky lake. The ground that had once been there had fallen away, leaving a hole, and in its greenish depths, objects were suspended, caught forever in the 'varnish'. Noon narrowed her eyes, trying to make out what they were.

'Really, Vintage?' Tor sighed and crossed his arms over his chest. 'This is what you delay my bath for?'

'There are swords down there,' said Noon. 'Just hanging there, in this stuff. They look as though they were made yesterday. And . . .' She stopped. What initially she had taken to be a bundle of clothes had, on closer inspection, revealed a round, pale shape at its centre. A woman's face, turned up to the light, her eyes open very wide, her mouth pressed shut as though she had tried to hold her breath. Her skin was clear and unblemished, and her hair, the colour of seaweed under the green, flared out around her like a woman caught mid-swim. Her hands, white exclamations in the dark, were reaching up to the surface. 'There are people in there.' Noon felt bile pushing at the back of her throat.

'Oh yes,' said Vintage. 'Men and women and children who

were not caught by the initial hunger of the worms were often caught by the varnish. Or fed to it by drones.'

'Drones?'

'Those that were taken by Jure'lia. You know what I speak of, my dear?'

Noon nodded slowly. In her dream, hundreds of black beetles had swarmed over Fell-Marian, rushing to fill her mouth and nose and eat her from the inside out.

There was a noise behind them, and a group of around ten children trooped diligently into the memorial. They wore expressions of barely checked fidgety boredom, and with them was a tall man with a fringe of white beard and dark eyebrows. He glanced over at the three of them as though surprised to see anyone else there, and then appeared to pick up a lecture he'd been giving outside.

'And here we have the Iron Market Memorial. The Iron Market was lost during the Sixth Rain, children, although much of this area was saved by the sudden intervention of the Eboran Empire.'

'Bloodsuckers,' one child whispered to another in an overly dramatic fashion. Next to her, Noon sensed Tormalin stiffen. 'They was monsters too, is what Mam said.'

'I'll show them how monstrous we are right now, if they would like,' muttered Tormalin.

'Tormalin, please try not to throw a tantrum over the comments of a child, there's a dear.'

'What are these weird things, sir?' asked another of the children. She was standing next to one of the strange spikey shapes formed by the varnish, leaning away from it slightly as if it smelled bad.

'No one knows. The Jure'lia were mindless monsters, who thought only of consumption and destruction. It is likely they mean nothing at all.'

Vintage narrowed her eyes at that.

167

'Luckily, the Jure'lia threat was ended . . . can anyone tell me?'

'At the Eighth Rain,' chorused a handful of the children.

'That's right. The Jure'lia queen was finally defeated at the great central city of Ebora itself, and all their creatures and all their ships died as one. The Eighth Rain was the last, the final invasion by Sarn's ancient enemy.' The tall man pointed up into the brilliant sky, where the corpse moon was a smear of greenish light. 'Their greatest ship tried to escape, but died before it could leave our atmosphere.'

One of the children began to jump up and down on the varnish, clearly meaning to attempt to break it, and a handful of his friends got the same idea. Noon watched their teacher take a deep breath – he, too, looked bored by the memorial – before ushering them back out through the simple archway.

'Look at that, would you?' muttered Vintage. 'One of the greatest and most terrible artefacts in Sarn history, and they were barely here a handful of moments.' She rounded on Noon, wagging a finger as though she were a reluctant student. 'And thinking of the Jure'lia as mindless monsters? Nonsense. Clearly, they were here for something, we just don't know what it was. Why won't people just *think*?'

'Was it the last invasion?' asked Noon, curious despite herself. She was thinking of the soft female voice in her dream, that presence unseen behind her. 'Was the Jure'lia queen really beaten in Ebora?'

To her surprise, Vintage turned to Tormalin. After a moment, he shrugged.

'No one truly knows what happened at the end of the Eighth Rain,' he said eventually, his voice dripping with reluctance. 'Even my people cannot be sure, because so many died at that battle. The Jure'lia queen was certainly there, and the lands beyond the Wall had swathes of this substance you call varnish.' He curled his lip as though tasting something sour. 'We built over it, preferring not to dwell on ugly things. We were fighting a battle on many fronts that day, our army spread across Sarn, but the queen was in Ebora. Warriors were dying, our war-beasts overwhelmed by drones. It looked like the end of all things. And then, suddenly,' he held his hands up and dropped them. 'The queen was there no longer, and all of her little toys stopped working. Just dropped dead in the middle of the fight. And when we had cleaned up the mess and finished congratu-lating each other, we found Ygseril cold and dead, his bark turned grey as ash.'

'Do you think . . .?'

'That the queen killed him before she was killed herself?' Tormalin's face was very still, very controlled, his maroon eyes dry. 'I, for one, do not care. It all comes to the same end either way.'

'Yes, well.' Vintage thinned her lips. For the first time since Noon had met her, she looked tired. 'We should not just forget. People were killed in their thousands, their insides eaten by the Jure'lia's pestilence – lives were destroyed. The effects of it are still being felt now.' She gestured down at the varnish again. Noon could make out more humanoid shapes down there. 'Look at those poor bastards. No graves for them, no way to retrieve their bodies without destroying them utterly, so they wait here forever, a frozen piece of history, while bored school children stomp around on their resting place. It shouldn't be forgotten. We can't just brush over it.' She shook her head. 'I need to know why these people died. We should *want* to solve this mystery, the mystery of the worm people. Not just pretend as though it never happened.'

There were a few moments' silence. Noon found herself glancing up at Tormalin, who gave the tiniest shrug.

'Come on, Vintage,' he said eventually. 'Let's get back to your rooms so you can find me some wine.'

14

One of the most well-documented facts about the Eborans is how remarkably long-lived they are. In the days when their tree-god Ygseril was mighty and running with sap, they were popularly thought to be immortal, although that was never quite the case. In their heyday, Eborans could expect to see more than 1,000 years of life, with the oldest recorded Eboran woman eventually shuffling off – no doubt exhausted – at the grand old age of 1,002. These days, with great Ygseril a sad husk of what it once was, Eborans often live for around 500 years, assuming the crimson flux doesn't strike them down first. For the rest of us, of course, such a lifetime seems unimaginable, and often I sense that this gulf is the true reason behind all the strife between our peoples – we just cannot understand each other.

With such centuries to fill, Eborans often chose to dedicate entire decades of their lives to mastering certain skills, meaning that the land beyond the Wall has produced many of Sarn's most extraordinary artists and composers. Great works of art, sculpture, music, dance and even cooking have all owed their genesis to Eboran men and women looking to fill in some time from one century to the next. One of the most notorious disciplines (one responsible for many of the most scandalous rumours about Eborans) is taught at the House of the Long Night – I talk about sex, of course.

It is treated as a priesthood of sorts. Men and women come to the House of the Long Night and swear to devote themselves to its teachings for no less than ten years. During this time, they learn as much as you can possibly imagine; they study the philosophy, the science, and the technique of pleasure. They learn which oils and which wines, which silks and which leathers, the dance of fingertips and tongues, the arts of abstinence and satiation. Sex is treated with the utmost respect in the House of the Long Night; it is regarded as the finest and most precious bond between people, even when that bond is for a single night, and the graduates of this academy regard the practice of their arts as a kind of worship.

As you can imagine, this has rather led to the assumption that all Eborans are ridiculously talented in bed, which is exactly the sort of assumption people make when they don't read enough books, or don't actually take time to talk to the people in question. Those few Eborans who ventured beyond the Wall before the crimson flux struck them down often did take human lovers, although from what I understand, the undertaking was never a frivolous one, given that sex was a form of worship for them – even when multiple partners were involved, the first teachings of the Long Night insist that everyone knows upfront what they are getting into. No doubt hearts have still been broken along the way, but it always struck me as an oddly respectful discipline.

My dear colleague Tormalin the Oathless himself entered into several such 'understandings' and despite

171

being of dubious morality in many areas, always behaved impeccably in this. He also claimed, of course, that a decade's study was not enough, and that he had dedicated half a century to his own 'pursuit of knowledge'. He was always, as he said, learning.

As a side note, very little is known about Eboran family names. Indeed, from what I gather it is considered 'illbred' to speak of them outside of Ebora, and it is an act of great trust to share a family name with someone who is not Eboran. I can hardly imagine my brother Ezion being so discreet – I'm sure he must drop the de Grazon name at the slightest provocation. (I have brought the matter up with Tormalin several times, and he simply changes the subject, the swine.)

Extract from the journals of Lady Vincenza
'Vintage' de Grazon

One of Tor's favourite things about working for Vintage was the free accommodation. The scholar had, for the last three years, taken over the top floor of the Sea-Heart Inn, a great sprawling building that nestled in the southern-most streets of Mushenska, on top of a small hill overlooking the coast. As sea views went, it wasn't the most attractive – the band of water they could see from their windows was steely grey much of the time, and far to the right was the distant spiky eyesore that was the Winnowry, sitting alone on its desolate island – but the service was exceptional, the food was decent, and the rooms were warm.

As they arrived at the rambling, wood-framed building, Vintage was already chattering about where she intended them to go next. Men and women peeled out of the back doors to take their bags, summoned by the familiar sound of Vintage ranting on about nonsense, while the owner of the inn, a Master Lucian, appeared at the door with his apron on – he supervised all of the cooking himself. He took one look at Vintage handing over bags and papers, and met Tormalin's gaze with a pair of raised eyebrows.

'Dinner will be required, m'lord Tormalin?'

'A light snack for me, Lucian, if you please.' He had asked the man not to refer to him in such grand terms, but it had never quite stuck. 'Your glazed-apple pudding with a round of your best cheese. Bring it straight to my room, please.' Tor glanced around and saw Noon, standing in the middle of the chaos like a stunned pigeon. She was gnawing on the skin of her thumb. 'Your best hot food for Lady Vintage and her new companion here though. Do you still have any of that . . . pigeon pie?'

Lucian dipped his head once. 'With the red-wine gravy, m'lord. Lady Vintage was kind enough to grace us with a new case.'

'That will be excellent. Enough for two, plenty of your creamed potatoes, hot vegetables, that sort of thing. We've had a tiring journey.'

Divested of her bags and trunks, Vintage was now making her way up the back stairs as the staff whisked her belongings to an interior lift operated by a pulley system. Noon had moved back to stand against the wall, her eyes trying to take everything in at once. Tor felt a brief stab of irritation at them both: at the girl for being so lost, and at Vintage for picking up a stray and then promptly forgetting about her. He went over to the girl.

'Come on, you'll get used to the chaos eventually, I promise. If we just go up after her—'

He touched her elbow lightly to turn her towards the stairs, and she jumped as though he had bitten her. She looked up at him, the expression in her dark eyes unreadable. Tor frowned.

'I'm not used to being touched,' she said. He watched her shoulders rise and fall as she took a breath, and when she spoke again her voice was softer. 'I'm not used to other people being . . . so close.'

He remembered the cool touch of her hand on his neck, and then the alarming dimming of his own strength as it was drained out of him. He was still feeling the effects of that, days later, and when he thought of it, it was the touch of her hand he remembered most clearly. Carefully, he put his hands behind his back and nodded brusquely to her.

'I expect Vintage intends for you to have the southerly bedroom. Follow me.'

He led her up the winding wooden stairs. The sounds of a busy inn echoed around them, and as they passed the first-floor corridor, he glimpsed a young couple dallying by a door, stealing a last kiss. On the second floor, a waft of strong liquor was followed by a barrage of cheers – someone was having a celebration – and then they reached the third floor, which belonged solely to Vintage. Tor did not know how much it cost to rent out the entire floor of the Sea-Heart Inn for a week, let alone for several years, but Vintage had never seemed to think it a ridiculous expense. Whoever sent her money did it regularly enough, and with no complaints. The thought of it stung a little, even now; as one of the last families of Ebora he was spectacularly wealthy, but claiming that wealth would mean opening communications with his sister. If she was even still alive. He shook his head briefly – dwelling on it didn't help.

'Down the end of the corridor Vintage has her bedroom, her study and a separate bathing room. My own bedchamber is here, alongside the shared dining room,' he nodded to an ornate door opposite, 'and your room will be this one, just across the way. We'll be sharing the same bathing chamber, I'm afraid.'

'And I will sleep here.' It was almost a question. The fell-witch was staring up the corridor, where a stream of staff were

174

depositing bags under the shouted supervision of Vintage. 'In this place – is it safe?'

'Safe?' Tor watched her face carefully. 'What do you have to fear? You are an agent of the Winnowry, on Winnowry business. Who would dare to challenge you?'

Her eyes snapped back to him, shining with sudden anger. She pursed her lips as though holding back some further comment, and then, without another word, opened the door to her room and slammed it behind her.

'And a goodnight to you too!'

Smiling to himself, Tor stepped into his own spacious room, finding it much tidier than he remembered. Lucian had had the place aired, so that it smelled of clean, sea air, and the empty wine bottles and dirty plates had been cleared away. He had just dropped his own bags and removed his sword belt when a soft knock at the door announced the repast he'd ordered. Nodding to the serving man, he took the plates to the table and sat, breaking the sugary crust on the pudding with his spoon, savouring the delicious smell of apples and spices.

And then he sat and looked at it.

When the witch had touched him, he'd never felt anything like it. To have so much of your strength snatched away in an instant, to be suddenly helpless. All at once he had felt the chill evening air against his skin, and every year of his long life had seemed to lie heavy on his bones. He wondered if that was what it felt like, when the crimson flux came. A sudden hollowing, an abrupt aging.

Tor stood up and crossed the room, where he pulled the bell to fetch hot water. He would wash the dust and grime from his skin, and then he would go out for the night. He was ravenous, but not for food.

The bed was enormous. Noon stared at it, not quite able to take it in. There were no less than three thick downy blankets

175

thrown across it, and an odd collection of pillows that did not match. She thought of the narrow bunk in her cell at the Winnowry, with its thin mattress of dried straw. Around the bed were piles of boxes, and more books than she had ever seen, randomly stacked as though they'd been put down for a moment and then forgotten. She suspected that Vintage had been using this as an extra storage room; there were dusty maps pinned to the walls, too, and papers strewn across a long table. Soft lamps had been lit in the corners, and there was a faint scent of angelwort in the room – her mother had used dried angelwort in small cloth bags to keep the tent smelling fresh.

The room began to spin. She sat heavily on the bed, placing her hands on either side of her head.

'They'll come for me,' she whispered to the room. From the street outside she could hear voices raised in cheery, everyday conversation. 'No one escapes the Winnowry and lives. I pretty much told them to go fuck themselves.'

It was the worst thing she could have done. By escaping, she had spat in the face of their precious Tomas, and in return she wouldn't just be killed. They would make her suffer.

Her hands turned into fists, pressing against the silky blankets.

'Let them fucking try.'

There was a clatter in the corridor and the door swung open to reveal Vintage, her arms covered in steaming plates.

'There you are, my darling, would you mind giving me a hand with these? I thought I'd bring dinner to you. The dining room is very pleasant but I've always thought this room was very cosy, and Tormalin has already flounced off somewhere. And I'll be honest with you, there's a pile of books on the dining-room table that I can't be bothered to find a home for right at this moment.'

Noon jumped up and together they wrestled the plates onto

the long table. There were thick slices of some sort of gamey-smelling pie, covered in hot gravy and roasted root vegetables, and a huge bowl of fluffy potato. Vintage had also managed to carry in a bottle of wine wedged under one arm and a handful of cutlery in her pocket. Noon stood back and watched as she set the table with practised ease, pouring them each a glass of wine in slightly dusty goblets. She then sat down and began to attack the pie with every sign of enjoyment.

'Ah, pigeon. Not my favourite, but it'll do. Well, my dear? Don't let it get cold.'

Noon sat down. The food was rich and hot, better than anything she'd eaten in years, and she had never tasted anything like the wine – it was a deep, dark purple, and she felt an overwhelming tiredness sweep over her after the first few mouthfuls. She resolved to keep an eye on how much she drank.

'You have been quiet, Fell-Noon, on our way back from the Shroom Flats. Quiet since we met you, really. Have you thought any more about my offer?'

Noon looked up. Vintage was watching her closely, her eyes bright with interest. She didn't look tired from their journey, or mollified by the wine. She looked alert.

'I'm used to being quiet. It's best to be quiet in the Winnowry.'

'You're safe here, you know. No one comes onto this floor but the staff I permit. I pay Lucian a significant amount of coin for that. You could try to relax.'

Noon put her fork down. 'If I am an agent of the Winnowry pursuing a secret mission, what reason do I have to worry about being safe?'

The corner of Vintage's mouth creased into a faint smile.

'Well, quite, my dear. Are you ready yet to talk about the truth?'

The sounds of a busy inn drifted up from below in the silence. 'I don't know you,' Noon said.

'This is true. We can continue, if you like, to pretend that

177

you are not alone, that you have not escaped the clutches of the Winnowry and are in desperate need of help. We can pretend that you are, in fact, what you claim to be – an exceptionally young fell-witch agent who is allowed to come and go as she pleases, with a mission so secret it required you sleep alone in a forest with no supplies and no decent shoes. Or, you can tell me, Noon, exactly what happened and I will do all I can to help you out of this mess.'

The woman's face was kindly but stern. Noon took another sip of the wine, playing for time.

'Why?' she said eventually. 'Why help me at all?'

'Well, there's a good question.' Vintage stood up, a glass of wine in one hand, and walked down the table towards her. 'For a start, my dear, I have been looking askance at the Winnowry for some years now – any institution that claims to keep women locked up for their own good should be watched very closely, in my opinion, but there is no one to do that. They are too powerful, too rich, and too feared. If helping you remain free causes them grief in any way, well, that's fine with me. Second, my interests are very singular, Noon, my dear. As you have already seen, I wish to solve the mystery of the Jure'lia – who they are, what they want, how they are poisoning our world – and I am willing to try anything to do so. Whether that's rooting around in the mud, hiring an Eboran layabout or assisting an escaped convict. Because that's what you are, isn't it?'

Noon looked up at the scholar steadily. 'What makes you think I can help you?'

Vintage's face broke into a true smile. 'Winnowfire, my darling. Your winnowfire, taken from Tor's energy. It could be a very unique weapon. No one has had this advantage before – think of the progress we could make!'

Noon looked away. 'You are being kind. It's a mistake. You don't know what I am, not really.'

'Kind, maybe. But self-serving? Always. I've spent my whole life being responsible for others, Fell-Noon, and now I would like to do whatever I buggering well like. It suits me. I think it'll suit you, too. Join me, and I'll keep the Winnowry from your back as long as I'm able, and believe me, my darling, I'm a wily old sod.' When Noon, didn't reply, she continued. 'What is it you need? A statement of trust? Very well. In my room, which is unlocked, there is a narrow chest shoved under the bed. In it are three cases of gold coins, in five different denominations, as well as bankers' marks for banks in Mushenska, Reidn, and Jarlsbad. With that little lot I think you'd have a decent chance of getting part the way across Sarn before the Winnowry caught up with you.' She held out her bare hand to Noon, as if she wanted to help her up from the table. 'Drain me. Leave me unconscious and take the lot. I can always get more. What else are you going to do?'

Vintage's hand was steady, the skin on her palm pale. There was a faint scar that swirled around her index finger. Noon stared at it.

'You don't know who I am,' she said again. 'You don't know what I've done.'

'Then tell me,' said Vintage, still holding out her hand. 'Take the money, or work for me. Let me be a friend to you, Fell-Noon.'

'Please, don't.' Unbidden, Noon remembered Mother Fast, her hands moving deftly with their needles, or the strings of her puppets. Her hands had been strong, too, and it hadn't saved her. 'You don't know what you're saying. Kindness won't—' She stopped, and looked up. 'I'll work for you, then, Lady Vintage. But I still might not say very much.'

Vintage grinned. 'That's fine with me, dear. Tormalin's endless complaining keeps me well enough entertained as it is.'

* * *

179

When Vintage left, Noon picked up the wine bottle and poured the last of it into her glass. It was getting on for the evening now, and the cluttered room was busy with shadows. There was a balcony beyond a pair of glass doors, so she stepped out into a still night. The thin band of the sea, a dark strip of grey-blue in the dying light, was a reminder that she wasn't so far from where she had started, and far to the west the Winnowry itself loomed – it crouched on the horizon like something jagged and broken. She could just make out tiny pinpricks of light there as the lamps were lit, and looking at it made her feel terribly exposed, as though the sisters who, no doubt, were now searching for her could look out and see her across the sea, homing in on her guilt like a beacon. Absently, her hand reached up to touch her hat.

'I'm free, until they catch me,' she said aloud. 'Until they kill me. I can't waste time being afraid of the landscape.'

Keeping her eyes on the distant prison, she lifted the glass to her lips and drank the rest of the wine, savouring the soft burn on the back of her throat and the spreading warmth in her stomach. When she had been a child, the plains people she had been born among had had a drink called stonefeet, which was made from fermented mare's milk. She had been too young to drink it, but had seen the effect it had had on their young men and women on festival days. They would be loud and boisterous, jumping from their horses or challenging each other to fights. Drunk as spring pigs, Mother Fast used to say. The effect of this wine was different, she thought. Like slowly sinking into hot water.

She wondered where Tormalin the Eboran had gone for the evening – perhaps even now he was reporting her presence to the Winnowry office in the city, hoping for a reward of some sort. Reluctantly, she recalled him standing next to her in the corridor, close enough for her to be able to smell the leather he wore. Up close, an Eboran did not look so different from her own people – the same narrow eyes, the same upward sweep of cheekbones – but his skin was like luminous stone, his eyes clear and blood-red. Mother Fast had owned puppets with the most delicate faces, carved from soft wood and then painted with fine brushes. There was a set of three that Noon remembered especially clearly; they depicted the three gods of Rain, Storm and Cloud. Their faces were beautiful, their lips painted into smiles, but their eyes were cruel. Tormalin, filling the corridor with his poise and calm confidence, had made her think of those puppets.

A piece of tile fell from the roof above and shattered on the balcony next to her, making her jump suddenly sideways. Reaching out blindly for any living thing near to hand with which to arm herself, she looked up to see a ghostly white shape peering down at her from the roof, huge liquid eyes shining in the last of the light.

'Fulcor!' she hissed, coming forward. 'What are you doing on the bloody roof?'

The bat tipped her head to one side, and scampered vertically down the wall towards Noon, thick leathery wings held out to either side.

'No, stop, stay where you are.' The bat paused, and then dropped something from her mouth. It was a dead rabbit. 'Fulcor, you don't have to. Well, I suppose the kitchens can use it.'

She reached up and stroked the velvety place between the bat's ears, watching as the animal's eyes crinkled shut. 'Why have you come back to me, you big daft thing? I thought you had abandoned me.' Noon pulled her fingers through the fur, considering. Perhaps this bat didn't like the Winnowry either. Perhaps she knew they had been running away. The giant bats were said to be intelligent. 'You have to listen to me, Fulcor. You can't just follow me around. They'll be looking for me, and you could lead them right here.' She glanced out across

181

the roofs below. None of them had a giant bat roosting for the night. 'You're pretty noticeable.'

Fulcor made a chirruping noise, the warmth of her blood and the faint patter of her heartbeat comforting against Noon's palm. What could the bat do? Go back to the Winnowry? Once there they might convince her to fly back to where she had last seen Noon. Or she could go to where her kind lived wild, but where was that? And how could she know? She had likely been raised at the Winnowry from birth.

'It's your hunting time,' Noon said, gesturing out at the darkening night. The clouds had broken, and a sliver of moon poked through like a peeking eye. 'Go get yourself something.'

Fulcor scrambled back up to the top of the roof and with an abrupt crack of wings, was a grey shape against the sky. Noon watched her go for a moment, before taking her empty wine glass and her dead rabbit back inside.

15

*The 'plains people' is a highly inaccurate term for the
great variety of communities living in the enormous stretch
of land that meanders its way from the eastern steppes
of Yuron-Kai to Jarlsbad in the far west, the Eboran
mountains looming to the north. This grassland is home
to numerous nomadic tribes as well as several more established settlements, and while most seem to share an ethnic
root, the sheer breadth of difference in language, culture,
religion, hunting practices, mythology, storytelling and
farming techniques is extraordinary, and, in my opinion,
long overdue a more exacting study.*

*Of the mobile tribes, most seem to move according to
the seasons or the migratory habits of the fleeten, a species
of goat hunted for their meat, skins and horns. Some,
however, have more mysterious methods; the Long-down
people, for example, seem to be following a gentle spiral,
inwards and then out again, through the generations, while
the Star Worm people – with whom I was lucky enough to
spend a few days – have a remarkable collection of telescopes,
more advanced than anything I've seen in Mushenska or
Reidn, and they use these to plot their own travels.*

While travelling with the Star Worm tribe, we spent one day at the Broken Rock sanctuary, a place that apparently acts as a neutral space for the various groups, and as a sort of ongoing seasonal market. If one group has a dispute with another, their representatives gather at Broken Rock and oaths are sworn that weapons won't be used. Often, I gather, large quantities of a liquor known as stonefeet are involved in negotiations. Otherwise, they bring their trade goods and their young people, and so the various tribes keep in touch, even forming closer alliances through marriage (meeting places with an abundance of available alcohol have the same consequences all over Sarn, after all).

A recent development will bear closer scrutiny, I feel. The newly constructed winnowline crosses the southernmost section of the plains, with two stations situated directly in what is, for want of a better term, plains-people territory. As mentioned previously, the tribes are by no means a single group and the fallout from this will vary greatly, I suspect, but, so far, I have witnessed a great deal of tentative curiosity regarding the line and its potential. Like most of Sarn's people, the tribes nurture many of their own superstitions about the so-called fell-witches, but I suspect the real test will come when the migratory groups need to cross the line. I would suggest that if the Winnowry feel like throwing their weight around in this regard, they may regret it. Or, at least, I hope they do.

Of course, it is difficult to talk about the region and the people who make their homes there without referencing the Carrion Wars, a dark period of history by anyone's reckoning. Still, my lamp is burning low and my fingers ache, so another time.

Extract from the journals of Lady Vincenza
'Vintage' de Grazon

184

Ainsel lived in the part of Mushenska known as the Downs, a shady and disreputable gang of streets that always looked like they were on the verge of either a civil war or falling down altogether. Unlike Sareena, she was not independently wealthy, and the cramped room at the top of the old house reflected that, but she was adept at making it cosy; whenever Tormalin visited, he found a room artfully lit with shaded lamps and full of the good, wholesome smell of bread and freshly washed skin.

'I did not hope to see you so soon!'

The frank pleasure on the woman's broad, honest face was a boon to Tor. He stepped through the doorway and placed the bottle of dark liquor on the simple table. Not wine, but a fiery drink called Gouron from Reidn – Ainsel made her living as a mercenary, and had a mercenary's tastes.

'My plans have changed, and I might be away from Mushenska for a little while. I thought you might be amenable to an unexpected visit?'

Ainsel grinned at him and picked up the bottle to examine the label. She was a tall woman, as thick with scars as she was with muscles, and her blond hair was tied back in a short braid. Ainsel nodded appreciatively at the Gouron; it was an expensive bottle.

'I'm always glad to see you, Tor, especially when you bring me such gifts. You're lucky to catch me, actually. Roland the Liar ships out with his Exacting Blades tomorrow, and I am to be aboard.'

'You're off to be one of his Blades?'

'For as long as the money lasts, at least.' Ainsel put the bottle down. She had brown eyes, which Tor had always found striking against her fair hair. 'Is it to be as it usually is?' Her voice turned ragged on the words. It had been a little while.

Tor nodded, feeling a wave of hunger blow through him again. 'The usual agreement.'

185

Ainsel came to him then and kissed him, and Tormalin slid his fingers, still chilled from the evening air, through the soft hair on the back of her neck. The First Step: The Rising Chorus.

Some hours later and they were a sweaty tangle of limbs on Ainsel's narrow but comfortable bed, most of the blankets long since thrown on the floor. They had both reached satiation twice now, and Tor sensed this would be their last climax. He shifted his body minutely, relishing the gasp of pleasure the small movement elicited from Ainsel; all was rhythm now – The Crashing Wave. With Ainsel's knee looped over his shoulder, he gently reached over and nipped her skin with his teeth.

'Yes,' gasped Ainsel. 'Take it now. Please, do it.'

On the bare mattress next to them was a long, slim bone-handled knife. Tor snatched it up and quickly, without losing his own momentum, cut a shallow wound in the skin just above Ainsel's knee. Immediately, he pressed his mouth to it, although this required lessening the pressure he was applying to other parts of her body for a few moments. Ainsel moaned, begging for final release, but Tor slid his hand up her thigh: the same message as always – *soon, my love.*

Blood. It filled his mouth with its salt and copper tang, and the feeling was indistinguishable from the knot of pleasure at the centre of his being. Ainsel was there in that taste, just as she was pressed beneath his skin now, vulnerable and so alive. The scent of sex in his nostrils and the taste of blood in his mouth, Tor let his tongue move across the torn skin, taking up the last of it, and then in one, smooth movement quickened his own pace. Water Across Sand: The Final Step. Beneath him, Ainsel caught her breath, gripping Tor's shoulder fiercely. A moment later, and Tor let go of his own control, carried on a tide of blood and memory and lust.

* * *

They lay together afterwards, the two of them almost falling out of the narrow bed. Tormalin stared up at the damp-stained ceiling, thinking, as he always did, that he should give Ainsel the money to buy a larger bed. She was already asleep, one arm stretched out for Tor to lean his head on, but Tor had never felt so far from sleep. It was the blood, so fresh it had been hot on his tongue, and now its heat was curling around his bones, making him stronger, healing all hurts. It was beautiful and intoxicating, so much so that it was almost possible to forget that it could eventually kill him.

Ainsel shifted slightly in her sleep, sighing heavily. Tor held himself still for a moment, sensing that she was close to waking, but she turned her face away, the sigh turning into a soft snore.

From somewhere down the street the sounds of an altercation drifted up to Ainsel's small window. The shutter was wedged half open, letting in the cool evening air that smelled of stale beer, smoke and the thick scent of the fat vats across the way. Tor stared at the window for a moment, wondering if people passing below had been able to hear them. Likely the whole street had. It never seemed to worry Ainsel.

The blood was still thick in Tor's throat. He should have a glass of the Gouron he'd brought to clear it out, but he was warm and comfortable and reluctant to move, and besides which, he savoured the taste of the blood. The rush of strength it brought him, the sense of power and rightness – and on the back of that, the taste of his own death. Did he enjoy that too? The danger of it, the inevitability. The blood, the sex, the strength, the dying. They were all tied up in each other.

Next to him, Ainsel moaned, her brow furrowing even as she slept.

Tor remembered clear, quiet nights in Ebora. When they were young, and long before the crimson flux swept their parents from their lives in a dark tide of misery and pain, sometimes their mother would extinguish all the lights and light the big lamp in the centre of the living room – it was longer than Tor's arm and shaped like an ear of corn – and then open the doors that led out onto the courtyard. He and Hest would wait, shifting and giggling, until tiny points of green light would begin to slip in through the open doors. They were moonflies, their rear ends filled with an emerald glow, and they loved the light of the lamp. They would swirl around the room in a great, excitable spiral. Tor and Hest would laugh and chase them, crashing into the furniture until Mother put out the lamp or Father would arrive and make them stop. Then the moonflies would leave in a stately procession, until all the light left the room. He thought of Ebora like that: a place where all the light had left, and all laughter had fallen silent. All save for his sister – the last, desperate moonfly.

Next to him, Ainsel gave a sharp gasp and Tor half sat up, thinking that something in the room had alarmed her, but all was still. Ainsel whipped her head from one side to the other, her eyes tightly closed, and Tor realised what it was: she was having a nightmare.

Tor propped himself up on one elbow, frowning down at the woman. Watching someone else have a nightmare was a uniquely unnerving experience. He watched his lover's face contract with fear, her eyelids twitching as her eyes rolled to watch something Tor couldn't see. The muscles across Ainsel's broad shoulders were tense. The blood tasted sour now. Lightly, Tor placed his fingertips on Ainsel's collarbone.

'Hey, Ainsel. You're having a bad dream. Wake up.'

Ainsel did not wake up. Instead, she drew her arm down to her chest sharply, nearly clouting Tor as she did so. Tor huffed with annoyance.

'Really, Ainsel, you'd have thought our evening would have brought you sweeter dreams.'

Ainsel went rigid, the cords on her thick neck bulging from

her skin. She began to shake, making tiny noises in the back of her throat.

'Shit. Shit. Ainsel? Ainsel, wake up!'

Nothing. Reluctantly, Tor sat up fully and knelt next to her. It was possible she was having a fit of some sort, he supposed, although she'd never mentioned suffering from such. Tor sighed and placed the palm of his hand against Ainsel's forehead. It was damp with a cold sweat – not, he thought, the result of their earlier exertions.

'It's been years,' he muttered. 'I'm not sure I even remember how.'

Even so, Tor closed his eyes and took a series of slow breaths. When Hestillion dream-walked, she described it as like being in a great shadowy realm, with distant lights all around. The dreaming minds were the lights, and you just had to find the right one. When the light shone on you too, she used to say, that was when you slipped into their dream. Tor pursed his lips and concentrated. It came back to him more easily than expected. In the darkness around him he could sense men and women sleeping – to him they felt like knots of warmth in a cold night – their minds either lost to the blankness of pure sleep, or caught in the intricate whirl of dream-sleep. There was a man somewhere on the floor below whose sleep carried the thick, pungent aroma of a day of drinking heavily, while a woman somewhere to the right of Ainsel's small room was lost in a dream that was repeating, over and over. If he wanted to, Tor could press closer to those minds, push through the soft barrier and step within, but he did not have time for sight-seeing.

Here was Ainsel's dreaming mind, the warmest of the lights surrounding him. Tor paused. What he was doing was, at best, impolite; at worst, a breach of trust. He knew from his own experience, and Hest's, that people generally did not want anyone poking around inside their sleeping heads without permission. Dreams were irrational, after all, and could suggest things about the dreamer that could shame them, no matter how untrue they were. More to the point, humans simply were not used to the art of dream-walking; in Ebora it might be a mildly diverting recreation with your closest friends, but to humans it was unfathomable.

Beneath him, Ainsel cried out, and Tor could feel the waves of fear emanating from her like a fever.

'Oh, damn it all. I will go quietly, at least.'

Gently, Tor reached for Ainsel's dreaming mind. He felt that odd mixture of light and warmth that was actually neither, and pushed through the faintly resisting barrier. For a few more seconds he was aware of himself kneeling on the bed, the breeze from the window chilling his uncovered skin, and then he was somewhere else. He opened his dreaming eyes.

He was standing on a beach. It was night-time, and somewhere off to his left there was the booming roar and hiss of the sea caressing the shoreline. Just ahead of him was a large camp fire, and a group of men and women sat around it in a circle. They were laughing and talking, and bottles and plates of meat were being passed around. Ainsel was there – she was difficult to miss, being nearly a head taller than everyone else at the fire. The flickering light danced off her blond hair, and she was smiling and nodding to a woman who was sitting next to her. She had auburn hair tied into many braids, and an eyepatch over one eye. Tor reminded himself that time was strange in a dreaming mind; dreams did not need to follow a linear pattern; they could skip back and forth over themselves. It was likely that Ainsel had already experienced this part of the dream, and he was still catching up. Tor frowned. Hestillion had always been so much better at this than him.

'To Lucky Ainsel!' A man at the fire raised his bottle, and

those next to him clinked their cups to his. 'Without her we'd all be at the bottom of the fucking sea.'

There was a ragged but enthusiastic cheer. Tor moved closer to the fire, taking care to stay out of the circle of its light.

'You should listen to me more often,' Ainsel was saying, grinning round at them all. 'Perhaps I should be your leader – we'd all be richer!'

There was another, slightly rowdier burst of laughter, and the auburn-haired woman next to Ainsel punched her on the arm, none too lightly.

'Less of your cheek, *Lucky* Ainsel, or I'll have you keel-hauled next time we take to the sea.'

Tor realised he had heard about this. When Ainsel had been working for the Broken Cage, a group of mercenaries operating out of Reidn, she had had a bad feeling about the ship they had been due to board for passage to Mushenska. Despite being ridiculed up and down by the rest of the crew, she had told Jessica Stormbones, their leader, about her misgivings – 'Don't get on that ship,' she'd told them. 'I get a cold feeling just looking at it.' As it happened, a bigger and better job had come up in the city state itself and so they had let the ship sail without them. A week later, news came back that it had been caught in a terrible storm in the midst of the Mariano Strait; all hands lost. After that, the Broken Cage mercenaries had taken to calling her Lucky Ainsel. So this was a good memory. What was it about this dream that had caused such a reaction in Ainsel?

'I'll be your lucky mascot, then,' Ainsel was saying now, grinning still. 'And I think the best way to keep that luck going would be to keep me in beer from now on. A small price to pay for your sorry lives.'

A solidly built man with a neat ginger beard laughed, slapping Ainsel on her meaty arm, and then his mouth seemed to droop open, as though his face were made of wet dough instead of skin and bone. He poked at his lower mouth in confusion, and his fingers sank into the doughy flesh. He tried to speak and, instead of words, a flurry of small black beetle-like creatures spewed from his mouth, running down his hairy chest. Next to him, Ainsel half scrambled away, an expression of dismay on her face.

Ah, thought Tor. *Here it is.*

'What's wrong with Bill?'

'There's nothing wrong with him,' said Jessica Stormbones. She looked at Ainsel and lifted her eyepatch to reveal a gaping hole. A handful of scuttling beetle creatures escaped it to run across her face. 'Just relax, *Lucky* Ainsel, and it'll be over soon.'

There was a hissing noise from all around, and Tor looked down to see a tide of thousands of the black-beetle creatures covering the sand. They ran over his boots, and he grimaced with displeasure. Ahead of him, Ainsel was on her feet, brushing away the beetle creatures from her shirt, her face pale.

Tor leaned down and, concentrating on the reality of the dream, concentrating on him being a part of it, picked up one of the creatures and held it up to the poor light. Its back flexed and twisted under his fingers, needle-like legs waved in the air.

'I think I know what this is. What an odd thing for you to dream about, Ainsel.'

Abruptly, the small beach was filled with a shifting, headache-inducing light. Wincing, Tor looked up to see a monster hanging in the sky above them, and despite himself, his heart skipped a beat in his chest.

It was a Behemoth. The harbinger of the ancient enemy of his people – a number of dim childhood memories surged to the surface, stories of war and monsters, half forgotten. It hung in the sky like a great segmented larva, the bulging plates of its body shiny with an oily brilliance. The bulbous lamps that hung from its lower section were pointed directly at the small group on the beach, while wet openings all along its side were peeling back to reveal creatures with six long, spindly legs. Tor felt a wave of dismay move through him. No wonder Ainsel was so afraid – very few humans had ever seen such a sight and lived. Disregarding all thought of being hidden, Tor marched over to the fire, determined now to bring Ainsel out of this dream before she saw any more, but as he looked up he saw that there were more of the spider-like creatures further up the beach, and among them were shambling humans, their eyes empty and their mouths twisted into vacant smiles. Drones.

'By the roots. This *is* an impressive nightmare you've concocted, Ainsel.'

He reached for her, meaning to drag her out, but the scene around him shifted and all at once the beach and the mercenaries were gone and they stood on the streets of a city, doused in daylight. It was not Mushenska – the buildings were of pale sandstone, with ornate conical roofs pointing towards the sky, and there were clusters of fruit trees lining the street – Jarlsbad perhaps?

'It's time to wake up, Ainsel.'

Ainsel took no notice of him. She was dressed now in loose white trousers with a billowing white smock covering her shoulders, and she was watching the building immediately in front of them. There was a tremor Tor felt through the soles of his feet, and an enormous writhing creature pushed its way through the building, smashing it to pieces as though it were made of dust. It looked like little more than a giant maggot, its blunt head a dark pearlescent grey against the creamy segmented flesh behind it. As Tor watched, the creature bent its head to the trees and, opening a wet, sticky mouth, it tore them up from the ground and ate them earth and all. Behind it, more of the long-legged creatures were coming, limbs skittering like spiders. Mothers, Tor remembered. That's what they were called in Vintage's extensive notebooks. Now there were men and women fleeing, their faces oddly unfinished – another strange aspect of dreams – but as they ran, they were being snatched up by the spindly arms of the mothers and fed directly into the maggot's pulsating maw.

'Roots be cursed. Did you eat something strange for dinner, Ainsel?'

The maggot pulsed, its fat body heaving itself towards them, and even though Tor knew this was a dream, he took a few hurried steps backwards. More mothers were coming, their grotesque shapes almost an insult against the delicate architecture of the city. The maggot pulsed again, and a thick tide of greenish fluid began to surge through the debris. Some of the men and women were caught in it, and they fell, faces filled with dismay as they found they couldn't escape it. Varnish.

'Ainsel, we must—'

An alien shape loomed up next to them; Tor had time to see the mother's spindly black arms loop around Ainsel's shoulders and they were somewhere else again, travelling in that dizzying instant that is the speciality of dreams. They were on the shores of a still lake, dark trees a thick line on the far side, the sky above grey. There was a presence behind them, and Tor felt himself caught in the sticky tendrils of Ainsel's dream terror – he could not turn to look at what was behind them; he was held as tightly frozen as Ainsel was. Inwardly, he cursed. Hestillion would never have been caught so.

The figure behind them approached. He could hear soft footfalls, the distant call of birds. What an idiot he had been. Not only had he failed to draw Ainsel from this nightmare, but it also seemed that he would be stuck to see it through to the end himself. Tor scowled at himself, and then he felt a breath on the back of his neck. He thought of Noon touching him there, then pushed the memory away.

'We're coming back, and finally Sarn will be ours.' The voice was soft, female, faintly amused. 'There is no one to stand against us.'

Using all his willpower, Tor commanded his dream self to turn and look at the owner of the voice, but he could not move an inch. A genuine shiver of terror curled up his spine.

'We're coming back,' continued the voice. 'And where is Ebora now?'

Tor felt his mouth drop open, whether in surprise or in protest he wasn't sure, and then he was awake, back in Ainsel's cramped room. He was still kneeling by her on the bed, his legs numb from sitting in an awkward position for so long and his flesh chilled to the bone. Ainsel was also awake, looking up at him with wide brown eyes; Tor thought he had never seen the mercenary look so young. Without speaking, Tor drew the blanket over them both and they lay together in silence, the first light of dawn seeping in through the shutters.

16

Perhaps the most extraordinary of the myriad legends and myths of Ebora are the war-beasts. It has been so long now since the Eighth Rain that the only living eyes to have seen them are Eboran, but to us they exist in art and sculpture, story and song. Perhaps this is why they seem so impossible to recent generations of humans – they are more story than truth now. Yet we know they did live and breathe, and indeed, without them, Sarn itself would have fallen to the Jure'lia centuries back. Given that it appears we will never see their like again, this isn't the comforting thought it once was.

   The war-beasts are inextricably linked to Ygseril, the Eborans' tree-god. At times of great peril to the Eboran empire, Ygseril would grow great silvery fruit, high up in its labyrinthine branches (the length of this process has never been agreed on – I have found writings that insist they sprouted from the buds of previous fruits, and spent centuries maturing, others say that the process was nearly instantaneous. Ebora, as ever, remains tight-lipped). When it was ripe, the fruit would fall, a miraculous 'rain', and the broken fruit revealed the most extraordinary menagerie of creatures, each ready to fight and die in defence of Ebora.

The date of the First Rain is not recorded, but the second we know took place at the time of the reign of Queen Erin of Triskenteth, when the city state of Reidn was in the grip of the Third Great Republic. There is a mural carved into the remains of the Triskenteth wall which dates from the period – it shows Ygseril, branches spread wide, and the silver fruit falling, the Eboran war-beasts leaping, fully formed, into the air. Further along, we see the war-beasts joining the Eboran knights and riding into battle together, while the Jure'lia are represented as great looming clouds, a host of the dead following on behind. See enclosed: rubbings taken directly from the remains of this incredible mural, which clearly show, I believe, that there was a significant connection between the war-beasts and their Eboran knight masters – each beast and knight wear similar insignia, and in some cases have been carved to resemble each other. The mural at Triskenteth was maintained beautifully for many, many centuries, but, sadly, the recent war with their Orleian neighbours has meant that it has disintegrated terribly, entirely blasted away in places by fell-mercenaries. I took what rubbings I could, and received many a dark look for my efforts. Triskenteth sees war everywhere these days.

And of the beasts themselves – they truly appear to have been creatures straight out of myth. The fruit of Ygseril produced not a single creature, like brown kittens born to a brown cat, but a wild collection of what, for want of a better word, I will call monsters. It's certain that some of those depicted in the paintings, sculptures and songs are fanciful creations, but I have seen repeated images of several types, and these I think we can safely

197

say were true forms of the Eboran war-beasts: dragons of all shapes and varieties, griffins with their snowy feathers flecked with black, giant birds and bat-like creatures with four legs, enormous armoured foxes, giant winged-wolves and cats.

Of course, the other thing that we know for certain about the Eboran war-beasts is also, in its way, the most significant: the Jure'lia always fell before them, eventually.

Extract from the journals of Lady Vincenza
'Vintage' de Grazon

Vintage pushed the heavy books as close to the edge of the table as she could without their falling off, and wiped down the section of table she'd been able to clear with a damp cloth. It was hardly the strictest of scientific methods, but needs must. On the far end of the table the breakfast the staff had brought up for them steamed away, untouched. Let the others have it. She couldn't wait any longer.

In the space she'd cleared she set up her vials and glasswear, her notebooks and inks, and then, finally, she unpacked the samples they'd taken from the forest. In one narrow glass tube she had the remains of the strange fluid that had seeped from the broken artefact she had found in the Shroom Flats – the fluid that had apparently grown a tiny garden overnight. She held it up to the light, turning it back and forth in front of her eyes; it had settled somewhat, leaving a yellowish liquid with a small storm of golden flecks. The Jure'lia had left many strange things behind them, all wondrous and strange, but few of them could be said to be beautiful. The liquid in this little vial appeared to be the exception.

She paused to make further notes – on the colour and viscosity, and, after uncorking it, on the smell. Using a pipette, she deposited the smallest amount on a glass slide, and slid this into the lens contraption her nephew Marin had sent her last year. The extraordinary thing magnified objects through a series of lenses, and must have cost the boy a fortune, but then he had always had good taste. Unfortunately, the lenses revealed very little, save for the oddly uniform shape of the golden flecks. Even so, Vintage paused to make a number of sketches, using a small box of watery paints to capture the colour as best she could.

'Hundreds of years old, and it hasn't dried up or turned to muck. Extraordinary.'

She looked back at the breakfast things. There was a bowl of fruit, with a bunch of tiny grapes. Vintage reached over and plucked them from the bowl; she was always faintly amused by the regular variety of grapes, so small and perfect. She set the bunch down on a porcelain plate, and then took from her own pocket a crumpled, dead leaf, picked up from the street that morning. She placed it next to the grapes and, using the pipette, placed the tiniest sample of the golden liquid on the cluster of tiny branches that the grapes sprouted from, as well as a single drop on the leaf. She was holding her breath and waiting for something to happen when Noon walked through the dining-room door.

'Oh, Noon, my dear, there you are.' Vintage didn't take her eyes from the grapes. 'There's breakfast, if you'd like it. Eat as much as you like. I'm not hungry and it seems Tor has yet to return from last night's escapades.'

Noon nodded and skirted the edge of the room like a wary cat, putting the table between them. The young witch stood for a moment, staring at the various foods, before cautiously taking a seat.

'What are you doing?'

'Having a proper look at what we've gathered. I've never seen anything like it, and certainly seen nothing that references it in all the studies I've read. Extraordinary.' She stared at it a little harder, willing something to happen. 'Extraordinary.'

'Why are you doing this? Really? There's a bigger reason.'

Vintage looked up. She blinked rapidly. 'I'm sorry, my dear?'

'A bigger reason for your interest in all this stuff.' The fell-witch tipped her head to one side. She had washed her hair and let it dry as it would, sticking up in black spikes, and she carried her new hat in her hands. 'You're not just curious. You're angry about it. All under the surface.'

Vintage straightened up. The girl was perceptive. She would do well to remember that. 'There are the remains of a Behemoth on land I own,' she said carefully. 'Land that has been in my family for generations. The vine forest there is the source of my family's wealth, but it is also incredibly dangerous, thanks to the presence of parasite spirits and the taint of the Wild. We monitor it, and we cordon off that section of the forest as best we can, but it is . . . a strain. I wish to know more about it, so we may neutralise it somehow.'

Noon was watching her closely even as she buttered her toast. 'And?'

Vintage felt her mouth twitch into a brief smile. Truly, this girl was worth watching.

'You said we should trust each other,' said Noon. She took a bite of toast, and her next words were muffled. 'If I'm helping you, I want to know why.'

'Pour me a cup of that tea.'

Noon did so, and Vintage took a sip, marshalling her thoughts.

'Do you find Tor charming?' she asked, and was amused to see the girl frown with annoyance. 'In his own strange way?'

'I find him . . . annoying. His people murdered my people. It's not easy to brush that aside because he . . .' the girl scowled at her toast – 'looks more like a sculpture than a real person.'

Vintage nodded. 'I was once charmed by an Eboran, long before I met Tormalin the Oathless. I couldn't have been much younger than you, I suppose, and she was beautiful and clever.

She came to my home to negotiate a trade agreement with a group of merchants, but really she was there to study the Behemoth remains on our land. A very dangerous pursuit, but she was full of curiosity and nothing would hold her back, certainly not the direst warnings of my father. She was full of fire, a need to know everything. I looked at her and an entire landscape opened up for me.'

Vintage shrugged.

'I went with her into the forest, against my father's wishes. When she talked about the Jure'lia and the parasite spirits, I realised how little we knew about them, and they became a source of wonder instead of terror. Through her eyes, I saw how much I had to learn and it was wonderful. She was generous, and kind, and— by all the bloody buggerations, would you look at that?'

Vintage put her teacup down on the table with a clatter and moved back to the grapes. The bunch was three times as big as it had been, and the new grapes were full and ripe to bursting. The leaf, previously brown and black and half crumbled to pieces, was now green and shining with health.

'Oh damn it all, I missed it!'

Noon appeared at her shoulder. 'What happened?'

'The substance we collected from the artefact, it has made the grapes grow in a matter of minutes and I've never seen anything like it. Damn and buggeration. Pass me that pencil, will you? I will need to get drawings of this. How do you feel about eating these grapes? I will need to know if they taste unusual.'

Tor chose this moment to arrive home. The tall Eboran looked strangely bedraggled, with dark circles under his eyes and his hair lying limp across his shoulders. It was a sight unusual enough to distract Vintage from the grapes; she had never seen him looking so unwell, even after a night consuming several bottles of her cheapest wine.

'Tor! What has happened to you?'

He went to the far end of the table and sat heavily in the chair nearest the food. 'Is there tea in this pot?'

'There is,' said Noon. He poured himself a cup, daubed a liberal spoonful of honey into it, and drank it down in one go. He poured himself another cup.

'Really, Tor.' Vintage placed her hands on her hips and gave him the look she normally reserved for her nieces and nephews.

'I've had a rough night,' he said. He was trying to summon his usual aloofness, but his eyes were moving restlessly around the room, lingering here and there on the books and maps, and the sketches of the Jure'lia fleet that adorned the walls. His fingers found a piece of bread, and he began to tear it into pieces.

'I was with Ainsel—'

'Who is Ainsel?' asked Noon.

'My lover.' Tor frowned at Noon as if he wasn't sure why she was still here. 'We have a pact under the Auspices of the House of the Long Night, and I . . .' He shook his head. 'Afterwards, she slept and it became obvious that she was having a nightmare. A particularly bad one, judging by the look on her face. So I dream-walked into it, thinking to bring her out.'

The witch raised her eyebrows. 'That's true, then? Eborans can see into your head?'

'Only sleeping minds, only when they're dreaming, and only those of us who are skilled at it.' He shook his head and grimaced slightly. 'I am mildly skilled at it, but not enough, it seems.'

'What was Ainsel dreaming of?' asked Vintage. There was a worm of worry in her gut now. She had never seen Tormalin so unnerved, even when facing down parasite spirits.

'She dreamed of the Jure'lia, Vintage.' His voice was almost plaintive now. 'A woman who could never have seen them, dreamed of the Jure'lia in such detail, that I . . . The colour and the noise, the smell of them. How could Ainsel, Lucky Ainsel from Reidn, whose grandfather wouldn't even have been born when the Eighth Rain fell, dream about the Jure'lia as if she had lived through every battle?'

'Well, you know, Tormalin, my dear, that dreams can seem very real, and perhaps you were caught up—'

'What happened? In the dream.' Leaning against the table with her arms crossed over her chest, Noon had gone very still. She was looking at Tor through the messy curtain of her hair, almost as if she couldn't quite bring herself to face him. 'What did you see?'

Tor took a breath. 'I saw her comrades consumed by the feeders, crawling like black beetles out of their mouths and eyes. I saw a Behemoth hanging in the sky above a beach, and then I saw one of their giant maggot creatures covering a city street in varnish. It ate people, and excreted this mess.' His mouth screwed up in disgust. 'And then we were somewhere else, and there was a figure behind us. It had a woman's voice, and it said, into my ear, "We're coming back".'

'And where is Ebora now?' Noon's voice was a dry husk. 'I've had this dream. I saw it too.'

There were a few long moments of silence. The sounds of the inn waking up for the day drifted up from below; the clattering of pans in the kitchen, someone emptying a bucket in the courtyard.

'How?' said Tor. 'How could you have the same dream?'

'I saw people I knew eaten all away inside by those black bugs, and I saw the corpse moon hanging over the Winnowry. And then the woman. It ends with the woman.' Noon reached over and picked up the cup of tea Vintage had discarded and curled her fingers around it, as though to warm them. 'It's why I ran away from the Winnowry. I couldn't just stay there. Not when I knew they were coming.'

'What do you mean, you knew they were coming?' Tor

was glaring at the girl as if the whole incident was her fault.

'Didn't you believe her?' asked Noon. Her voice was soft and faraway, as though she were talking to someone she'd known years ago, a memory. 'You listen to those words, in that voice, and you know. It's true.'

'Are you seriously suggesting . . .?'

Vintage held up her hand. 'Ainsel. Lucky Ainsel? Lucky because she sometimes has feelings about things. Isn't that right, Tor? It is she I am thinking of, is it not?'

Tor nodded reluctantly. 'She knew not to board the ship, and later it sank. If the company she's with want to ambush someone, they listen closely to her advice, because she always seems to know which way it will go. And no one will play cards with her.'

Vintage lowered her hand. 'A vision of the Jure'lia. What I wouldn't give to see such a thing.'

'But it doesn't mean anything.' The doubt in Tor's voice was terrible to hear, and she watched as his hand drifted down to the sword at his waist. 'It *can't* mean anything. It's just two people having very similar dreams. It happens.'

'You couldn't turn to look at her, could you?' When Tor didn't reply, Noon nodded. 'You know what it means. I can see it on your face.'

'The return of the worm people.' Vintage pressed the tips of her fingers to her forehead. 'Pray that it's not, my dears. Pray that it's not.'

17

My dearest Nanthema,

Many thanks for your last package. The soaps were exquisite, although I am afraid the bottle of bath oil had shattered in transit – everything smelled quite divine! Luckily, the pages you had hidden within the wooden box were unscathed, and I managed to retrieve them before anyone else saw them. They are now safely hidden in my rooms, the ribbon you gave me tying them securely. I've never been one for sentiment, but it seems you bring it out in me.

You have travelled so far in so short a time. I will have to ask you for more details of Jarlsbad. I know you only spent a few days there, but the scattering of lines you gave to the city have made it sound so bewitching. It will be one of the places we will visit together, I am sure of it. The bathing houses you mention I have read about in Father's library, although, if he caught me reading those books, I would be banned from the place.

Three days ago there was another sighting of a parasite spirit in the vine forest. I know that you wanted me to tell you if the remains were growing more lively, so I have started going along on the patrols – Father is livid but I *have pointed out to him that one day this will be my responsibility and I must learn. He is rather taken aback by my sudden interest, and the more wrong-footed he is, the easier it is to get what I want, and need. It was dusk, and we were making our way along the last section of the empty zone (we will need to burn back the foliage again soon, it grows so fast). The forest was dripping with shadows by then, and I was keeping my hand on my crossbow, quite glad that we were making our way back to the house, when the shadows stretched and vanished, and everything was lit up with pale blue light. We only saw it for a few seconds, my dear Nanthema – I don't think it even realised we were there – but I saw enough to know it was different to the one we observed while you were here. I have enclosed sketches I made as soon as we got back to the house. Please forgive my unskilled hand. I have tried to capture the colours as best I could, but, as you know, no watercolour could do them justice. It was an extraordinary sight. While everyone else was terrified, I could only think how much I long to be out there with you, solving this mystery. But my time will come. Soon Father must let me leave to attend further courses in Silia, and once I am on that road, Nanthema, he won't be able to stop me joining you.*

Copy of a private letter
from the records of Lady Vincenza
'Vintage' de Grazon

'Quickly, Aldasair, unfurl that rug and lay it in front of these chairs.'

Hestillion stepped back as Aldasair wrestled the rolled-up rug from where it was resting against the wall and rolled it across the marble floor. A cloud of dust rose up from it, and Aldasair grimaced.

206

'It'll have to do.' Hestillion stepped onto the rug and pushed some of the creases out with her slippered foot. It was a deep, dark blue, embroidered with a great silver stag, stars in its antlers, and if it was a little grey from years of disuse, it was still a beautiful thing. 'We just don't have time. Did you bring the food like I asked you?'

Aldasair moved to the corner of the chamber and picked up a linen sack.

'Good. Set it out on the table.'

The young Eboran stared at her blankly. 'I don't know how to do that. I'm not a servant.'

'Aldasair, this is hardly the time—'

'There are, there are proper ways, my mother used to insist on it, the right knives and the right forks in the right places, and nothing has been right for years, I can't.'

Hestillion forced herself to take a deep breath.

'It doesn't matter. These are people from the plains, Aldasair. Normally, they eat off their laps in tents; they won't know any better.'

Aldasair's eyes grew a little wider. 'Do they? Truly? Eat off their laps?'

'Quickly, come on. I'll help you.'

Hestillion emptied the bag onto the table, which was already covered in a snow-white tablecloth. The best foods they had to hand were preserves: jars of glass and clay that contained pickled fruits and salted meats, all sealed with cloth and wax. There was wine too, and spirits – she had raided anything that might look respectable – and she had already placed a large portion of what they had in Mother Fast's rooms. Hestillion had given the old woman and her people her mother's old suite; that had hurt, a little, but she had been keeping it clean for sentimental reasons, and they needed something workable, fast.

'Who are these people, Hestillion? Why are they here?'

Hestillion took a silver fork from his unresisting hand and laid it on the table. 'Go and fetch them, please. Can you do that for me, Aldasair?'

For a moment he looked at her uncomprehendingly, his dishevelled hair falling over his face. She had convinced him to put a brush through it, but he had refused to put it back in the traditional tail. Hestillion thought that perhaps he had forgotten how to do it.

'Aldasair?'

'Yes, I will.' He nodded. 'I will go and fetch them.'

He left, and Hestillion looked around the chamber. It would have to do. She had chosen someone's old study, a room with glass doors to one side that looked out across the gardens. It was a cold, bleak view on a day like this, and it made the palace feel all the more empty, but she felt it was better to have some daylight than to meet by candlelight. They had brought some of the paintings out of storage and had hung them hurriedly on the walls, beautiful expressive daubs of paint and ink that captured the wildness of surrounding Ebora and a few stirring portraits of war-beasts, long lost; a great snowy cat, dwarfing the Eboran that stood next to her; a dragon in flight with golden scales. The marble flooring was intact in here, at least. She looked down at herself, peering at her hands for remnants of dust. She had changed into a blue silk robe, simple and elegant, with a padded jacket of darker blue over the top; a white dragon, embroidered in white silk, clung to her left shoulder, and she had pushed a simple black comb into her hair to hold it away from her face. She could do nothing about her chalk-white skin or blood-red eyes, but she would do her best not to be intimidating.

There was a cough at the door, and Aldasair returned. He paused and gestured in what she suspected he thought was a welcoming way, and Mother Fast appeared. She was out of the chair she had been carried in, but there were two people at her elbow to support her: a burly woman with close-cropped hair, and a young man with flinty, watchful eyes.

'Please, do come in.' Hestillion bowed to the trio formally, and then gave them a moment to respond. When none of them moved, she forced a smile upon her face. 'I have food and drink here for you, and tea, if you wish it. But where is the remainder of your company?'

'They need more of a rest,' said Mother Fast. She looked at Hestillion with her one good eye, and then at the laden table. 'And I'm hungry enough to eat a scabby horse.'

'Please,' Hestillion came forward, half thinking to help the old woman to the table, but the man and the woman stepped around her and led Mother Fast to a thickly padded chair. She walked slowly, with one arm tucked away inside her jacket. She had removed the horsehair hood, as they all had, and it was possible to see that she wore a pair of silver chains around her neck, each with what looked like a carved wooden head hanging from them. *How charming*, thought Hestillion.

Seated in her chair, Mother Fast pulled a plate of salted sausage towards her, selected one, and chewed the end. For a few moments the only sound in the room was the old woman's determined chewing. By the door, Aldasair stood fiddling with the buttons on his frock coat, clearly wishing to be somewhere else, while the young man and the broad-shouldered woman stood behind their leader. Hestillion felt a brief wave of disorientation move through her, and all at once she wanted to be back in the empty corridors, waiting for the silence to claim her. It was too hard, all of this. Too desperate.

'I will have that tea, if you're offering.'

Hestillion nodded, glad of the distraction. She went to the brazier in the corner of the room where the pot of water was heating, and Mother Fast continued helping herself to the food on the plates.

'This is Frost –' she indicated the young man with a wave

of a sausage – 'and Yellowheart.' The stocky woman inclined her head. 'I do not travel well these days, and we are a travelling people, as you know, Mistress Hestillion. Frost and Yellowheart help me to get around, and they don't complain about it too much.'

Hestillion brought the pot over to the table, and poured the steaming water over the bowl of leaves. The familiar scent of tea, slightly stale but utterly welcome, filled the room. 'And I am very grateful that you have made such a journey, Mother Fast. A journey across the mountains at any time of the year is arduous.'

The unspoken question hovered in the air between them. Hestillion focussed her attention on mashing the leaves with a long silver spoon, wrought especially for the purpose. It was important, she felt, to let the old woman explain it in her own words. But it seemed Mother Fast wasn't to be so easily led.

'Our peoples have a shared history. You know that, Mistress Hestillion.'

Hestillion poured the tea into the cups. She had chosen a simple set; red-glazed clay with the lip outlined in gold. Abruptly, she wished she'd chosen another colour.

'A very long time ago,' she said, keeping her voice smooth. 'We call it history, for that is what it truly is.'

'You imagine we'd have forgotten, is that it?' Mother Fast grasped the cup between fingers like sticks, and glared at Hestillion with her single eye. 'Memories like that, girl, they get passed down in the bone. Your people swept down from the Bloodless Mountains and massacred mine. At first, you called it a border dispute. We had sent raiders to Ebora, you said, to steal away the treasures of your precious empire. Thieves and bandits. But, in the end, you had no time for excuses – you just came for our blood, and it didn't trouble your conscience *at all*.'

Hestillion took a sip of her own tea, savouring the burn

against her lip whilst keeping her eyes downcast. Let the old woman say her piece. In human terms she was teetering on the edge of death anyway. By the door, Aldasair was looking out into the corridor, his lips pressed into a thin line. She knew any mention of the Carrion Wars tended to upset him.

'Good tea.' Mother Fast cleared her throat. 'Anyway, I am not here to pick over old corpses with you. I don't have time for it, and, judging by the emptiness of your palace, neither do you. On the last full moon, I was troubled by a terrible dream.'

Hestillion looked up, settling her gaze on Mother Fast's ravaged face. She held herself very still.

'A dream?'

'The worm people.' Mother Fast spat the words, her lips twisted with distaste so that her burned cheeks stretched and puckered. 'The Jure'lia come again. I saw them as clearly as I see you now. By all the gods, I could *smell* them. They came again in force, and I saw the plains eaten up with their terrible excretions, and I saw my people eaten from the inside out.' For the first time, Mother Fast looked uncertain. The hand that had so far been hidden within her sleeve crept out and touched the carved heads at her throat; it was little more than a blackened claw. 'I've never had a dream like it, not one so real. There are very few of my people left, Mistress Hestillion, but we had seers. One or two. I never thought their blood had mixed with mine, but I cannot turn away from what this dream means. The Jure'lia are set to return. I woke screaming, the knowledge of that heavy in my bones.'

Frost and Yellowheart stood behind her still, their faces grim. Hestillion leaned forward slightly.

'And you have come to us?'

Mother Fast took a slow breath, rattling through her bony chest.

'You may have a monstrous past, and the gods know I have

211

no love for Ebora, but all know who stood against the Jure'lia, time and again. We all know it. Sarn knows it. For every invasion, a Rain.'

There was a brief silence. Aldasair was staring at the far wall now, his beautiful face blank. Hestillion let her eyes fill with unshed tears.

'Mother Fast, Ebora is not what it once was.'

'And all of Sarn knows that too.' The old woman leaned forward. In the cold daylight from the glass doors, the ruined landscape of her face was hard to look at. 'Whatever it is we can do to heal Ebora, we will do it. We must at least try.'

'But what can we do?' Hestillion lifted her hands once and dropped them, looking around the table as if the answer might be there amongst the jams and dried sausages. 'Our Ygseril, the giver of the Rains, sleeps and has not grown leaves in centuries, let alone the silver fruits. My people, Mother Fast, are dying. What can you do about that?'

'Whatever we can.' The young man called Frost stepped forward, one hand on the back of Mother Fast's chair. 'This is a problem we must open up to the world. Sarn has tried to forget Ebora, with its bloodlust and greed, but we don't have that option any more. As a people, you've always been closed off.' His eyes flashed, although whether with anger or passion Hestillion couldn't have said. 'But we will reopen trade routes. Bring people here again. We can start at the Broken Rock markets – we have riders already on their way – and work from there. Somewhere, there may be an answer to what has happened to your Ygseril, a cure even for your people, but you will not find it closed behind these walls.'

'A slower convoy is on its way here now.' Yellowheart's voice was deep and kind. 'Bringing supplies, medicines. It is a start.'

'Oh.' Hestillion stood up, her hands floating up to her face again, and she let a single tear fall down her cheek. 'Oh. Such kindness. I hardly know – Aldasair, did you hear? Help is coming. Help is coming for Ebora.'

Aldasair looked around the room as if he'd only just noticed the strangers there. His brow creased slightly.

'By the roots.'

Later, much later, when their guests were comfortably asleep and Hestillion could sense their dreaming minds like points of faint light, she went again to the Hall of Roots. It was dark, but the ghostly shapes of sculptures and furniture were so familiar she nearly danced around them, while sharp starlight fell on her through the glass ceiling.

She climbed out onto the roots without hesitating, feeling rather than seeing her way, until she sat once again underneath the enormous trunk. Mother Fast expected the convoy to arrive in the next few days – she had come on ahead with her closest people, to see that all was clear – and from there they could hope to start expecting other representatives. Frost and his riders had already started putting out the word to the other plains tribes, and from there word was expected to reach Mushenska, Reidn, even distant Jarlsbad. Trade would come again to Ebora, and perhaps, with it, the true cure for the crimson flux.

Laying her head against the cold bark, Hestillion closed her eyes and stepped easily into the netherdark. Ignoring the warm human minds, clustered close to each other in the south wing, she cast her mind down, down towards the roots again, searching for the light she was sure she had seen, just before Aldasair had interrupted her.

She went deep, perilously deep, far from any mind shaped like her own, feeling the press of cold roots against her dreaming self, squeezing down into the gaps. She imagined herself a drop of water, slipping down into the dark where her god might take her up and use her.

Ygseril? Ygseril, are you there?

There was a dull bloom of light – barely even light at all, more like the flash of colour that might blast someone's eyes if they were struck on the head. Hestillion shot towards it, letting herself be drawn.

Ygseril!

Now the light was constant, still dim like the light before dawn, but there was more to it than that. A mind hovered there, something so large and so alien Hestillion felt herself instinctively trying to retreat, but she held herself still, a hunted creature in open ground.

I knew it! I knew you lived!

It was fading already, sinking back away from her like water draining into sand, but she called after it, knowing that, next time, it would be easier to find.

They've fallen for it, Ygseril, exactly as I knew they would! Ebora will not die. Not while I live. They are like children, and they eat from my hands. I will see us live again, Ygseril!

18

Before Milandra Parcs, the organisation that was to become the Winnowry was a religious retreat of sorts – one with very strict rules, of course, and a great deal of time was spent studying the teachings (or ravings, depending on how you look at it) of Tomas. What Parcs did was to turn it into a prison, and perhaps more significantly, a business. And she was remarkably successful at that.

It helps, I think, to know some of the background of Parcs. She was born on the outskirts of Jarlsbad, scratching a living with her family in the terrefa fields. Terrefa, if you're not familiar with it, is a plant that can be smoked, producing a great sense of well-being and, from what I've smelled, a terrific stink. Terrefa is unusual – rather than harvesting the leaves of the plant and then drying them, they are left to die on the plant and then are carefully collected just before they start to drop. Jarlsbad is a region prone to forest fires and terrefa fields are carefully monitored leading up to the harvest period. Unbeknownst to Milandra, her sister – around seven years old at the time – was a fell-witch. One night, there was an argument between the smallest sister and her mother, and she ran out into some terrefa fields, letting forth a small barrage of winnowfire. The crop caught like tinder and was fiercely burning in seconds, flames sweeping across the entire field. Unfortunately, Milandra's father had been out in the fields, taking a walk in the evening air as he had a habit of doing, and he suffered severe burns to most of his body, and, after a few agonising weeks, died. With no father and no terrefa crop, the family was destroyed. Destitute, they moved into the city to beg on the streets. Milandra's official story was that her little sister ran away and was never seen again. I often wonder about that, myself.

The Milandra Parcs who came to the Winnowry was a woman who had vowed never to beg again – never to be destitute again. Under her guidance, winnow-forged steel and akaris became products that could only be purchased through the Winnowry (where else could you get it from, when all newly discovered fell-witches were immediately spirited away to the Winnowry?). Reluctant families were often paid off, a sum seen as an investment by Parcs. She developed the 'agent' scheme, trusted fell-witches who had been brainwashed enough to be trusted out in the world, who would be sent to perform special tasks for clients. They also formed groups of fell-mercenaries, women who could be hired to fight in wars and border disputes all across Sarn – for a very weighty sum.

Interestingly, there was one area when this particular money-making scheme failed. During the Sixth Rain, three countries paid for the fell-mercenaries to fight against the Jure'lia and protect their lands. It was, unexpectedly, a disaster. Winnowfire had little effect on the Behemoth ships or their roving 'maggots', although it was very

216

efficient at causing widespread damage to property. Additionally, the Eboran war-beasts had a particular aversion to the eldritch flame, often refusing to fight alongside the witches at all. The result was a great deal of resentment on both sides, as the Eborans found their carefully staged manoeuvres perpetually disrupted by unexpected explosions, fires and extremely agitated war-beasts. Meanwhile, the fell-witches were dying. Remember, usually there are only ever around a hundred to a hundred and fifty fell-witches at the Winnowry at any one time, and only a small percentage of those are ever trusted enough to become agents or mercenaries. During the Sixth Rain, almost all of them were wiped out.

(There is a stretch of varnish in western Reidn where an entire team of fell-mercenaries can be observed, trapped forever. A grisly souvenir from the Sixth Rain.)

Somewhat ungraciously, when eventually the Jure'lia were driven off by the Eborans, the Winnowry announced that it would henceforth leave the defeat of the worm people to their traditional enemies – the people of Ebora. I have never been able to find a record of the transaction, but I would be very interested to know what the Winnowry received for their services – and for the blood of the women they were supposed to be protecting.

Extract from the journals of Lady Vincenza
'Vintage' de Grazon

'What is it?'

Vintage had led them to the outskirts of Mushenska and through the northern gate. From there they had followed what appeared to be a long, freshly gravelled path, and now they stood amongst a crowd of people before a great steel contraption. Noon could only see pieces of it through the press of men, women and children around them – she caught glimpses of plates of metal, welded in place with studs as big as her fist, small glass windows glowing with orange light, and then green, and then orange again, and a fat chimney. Every now and then, a great gout of steam would escape from it. Around them, the crowd were full of excited chatter. Here, the Wild had been forced back until it was a thick dark band in the distance – much of it appeared to have been burned away, judging from the scorch marks and the faint smell of ash.

'How can you not know what it is?' said Tormalin. 'Your people made it. Your people run the thing.' The Eboran had not cracked a smile since he had told them of his lover's dream, and now he looked down at her with barely concealed impatience. He carried the heaviest pack, although it was slung easily over one shoulder with his sword belt. The blustery wind only served to tousle his hair into an attractive wave.

'The Winnowry are not my people.' Noon shifted the pack on her back, trying to get used to the weight. 'I don't have *a people.*' Vintage had given her new clothes, finely stitched and of the finest fabrics, and it was a day given to squalls of chilly rain, so she wore a coat of stiff black velvet, soft doe-skin leggings, and new black boots. Her new hat was firmly secured to her head with a series of cunning pins. Vintage had shown her how to do it.

'The winnowline, my dear, is one of the most extraordinary sights on Sarn.' Vintage was wearing her own wide-brimmed hat, pulled low against the intermittent bursts of rain, and she was cheerfully elbowing her way to the front of the crowd. Tor and Noon followed in her wake. 'Look at this lot, just come out to look at it. It will be a novelty for a while yet, no doubt. Here we are.'

The steel monster was revealed. Noon blinked rapidly, trying to take it in. Lights and steam and wheels. A confusion of metal tubes. And around the bulk of the thing, someone had etched a trio of enormous bats, their wings spread wide. Noon

218

felt her jaw clench tight. Of course. The Winnowry tradition-
ally travelled by their famous giant bats; how could they resist
putting them all over this thing?

'Marvellous, isn't it?' Vintage beamed at the contraption. 'A
steam-powered conveyance! The first on Sarn, as far as we
know. From what I understand, water is heated and turned
into steam, within a high-pressure boiler, then pushed on
through those pipes, which power pistons, which in turn, turn
the wheels.'

Noon glanced up at the puffs of steam escaping from the
chimney. 'When you say heated . . .'

'By winnowfire, my darling. A team of fell-witches and
novices heat the water tanks. From what I understand, the
heat provided is steady and constant, and there is less wastage
than what you might find from other fuels. You see the metal
lines set into the ground? Those are what it travels along.
Incredible. Years just to lay the track, and perfecting the engine
itself was no easy process, from what I've read. There were a
few accidents here and there, and there was that explosion
recently, but, largely, it's considered to be almost entirely safe.'

Noon was trying to shrink back into the crowd. There were
fell-witches here, which meant the Winnowry was here, and
she was standing right in front of them. The people at her
back, with all their living energy just within reach, were both
a terror and a temptation; she should just take what she needed,
kill them all, and run. A heavy hand settled on her shoulder.

'Not so fast, witch.'

Her heart turned over, but it was just Tormalin. 'You don't
want to draw attention to yourself just now, do you?'

His hand was a warm pressure through her coat, and it
made her think of the energy she had siphoned from him. She
half fancied that she could still feel it, hidden away inside her
somewhere.

'I know this is alarming for you, my dear,' Vintage was

219

saying in a low voice. Tor took his hand from Noon's shoulder. 'But it really is the fastest way. The track they have laid so far criss-crosses the Wild and the plains, and the easternmost stop is where we need to get to. It would take us weeks to get there otherwise, while the winnowline will get us there in days. I've booked us a private compartment. Keep our heads down, enjoy the view. We'll be there in no time. Come on.'

Vintage led them down past the great hissing beast that was the winnow-engine towards a series of ornate carriages that formed a line behind it. The doors were all open, and people were streaming on, carrying bags and children and the occasional chicken.

'We're down the end here, that's right. Last carriage, we'll have a good view of Mushenska as we rush away from it, won't that be wonderful?'

Noon followed, keeping her face down. Where were the fell-witches? All ahead with the winnow-engine, she hoped. There would be priests here too, men for the women to draw energy from. She thought of Novice Lusk, but of course he wouldn't be here; no doubt he was still being punished for failing to stop her escape. Noon closed her eyes for a moment, pushing that thought away. Were these fell-witches agents, allowed to operate independently, or would they have supervisors? Neither thought was very reassuring.

The final carriage had heavy curtains over the windows, and wooden panels carved from a grained wood the colour of good tea. As they reached the door, a heavy-set woman in patched trousers stepped down from it. Her skin was darker than Vintage's, and her curly hair was held back from her face in a yellow handkerchief. The shirt she wore had a number of tiny burn marks and she had a great smudge of soot across her cheek.

'Lady de Grazon?'

'Pamoz! There you are. The engine is looking in fine fettle this morning.'

220

The woman called Pamoz grinned hugely and pulled a rag from her pocket. She wiped absently at her face. 'We'll have you where you need to go in no time, Lady de Grazon. I just wanted to stop by and thank one of my best investors. Without you, the winnowline wouldn't exist at all.'

'Oh do give over, my dear. It all comes from your clever head. You know I can't resist seeing science in action. My colleagues here will be travelling with me.'

Noon detected a tiny tremor of surprise as Pamoz's eyes passed over Tormalin, but then she simply nodded to them both. Vintage must have paid a great deal of money for the private carriage – perhaps the coin paid for a lack of curiosity too. Pamoz stepped to one side and wished them a pleasant journey as they climbed up into the carriage.

'It's an honour to have you on board, Lady de Grazon. I'll be up front with the engine, but let me know if you should need anything further.'

Inside, the carriage was dark and cool, and filled with smoothly polished tables next to lavishly upholstered benches. There were even two pairs of narrow bunks, piled high with cushions and thick silky blankets. Noon ran her fingers over them, thinking of her bed in the Winnowry again, so close to the damp wall that it was never warm; the Winnowry apparently had different ideas about comfort, out in the wider world. She stood up and looked back towards the door, wondering again about the tame fell-witches that were powering this contraption. Did they have similar quarters on board? She turned back to look at Vintage.

'I thought you didn't like the Winnowry. But you throw your money at their projects?'

For the first time since she'd met her, the older woman looked uncomfortable.

'I do. I told you I was self-serving, didn't I, my dear? Well, the winnowline is useful. Faster travel across Sarn can only mean progress – a way for me to solve these mysteries, faster. Plus, the teams of women who power this thing get to breathe free air for a while. That is no small thing.'

Noon nodded and dropped her eyes. She was too unnerved by the presence of the Winnowry to argue the point, but she suspected from the uneasy expression on Vintage's face that she did not truly believe her own words.

Vintage cleared her throat. 'We'll open the curtains once we're on the move, Tor, but do pull the blind up at the back, will you? I want a bit of light to get my equipment sorted.'

With a few strides of his long legs Tormalin walked to the far end of the carriage and pulled the cord on the blind, revealing the bustling heap that was Mushenska behind them.

'That's it, lovely. Now, Noon, my dear, would you light the lamp on the main table? There are matches, don't give me that look. I would like to show you something.'

The lamp lit, Vintage wrestled a heavy scroll from one of her bags. She rolled it out on the table and Tor helped her weigh it down with a pair of wine bottles. The paper was clearly old but of excellent quality, thick and only slightly yellowed. It was covered from edge to edge in an ink-and-charcoal drawing that, at first, Noon could make no sense of. Whatever it was, it appeared to be split into roughly three pieces, with long trailing sections linking them, and there were gaping holes in the surface, like infirm mouths. She tipped her head slightly, narrowing her eyes, and saw that someone had drawn a tiny human figure standing amongst it all to give it some scale. Whatever it was, it was enormous.

'I give in.'

'This, Fell-Noon, is the Behemoth wreck that Esiah Godwort keeps on his land. Specifically, he keeps it in a compound, heavily guarded by a bunch of muscle-headed idiots.'

'Vintage had a disagreement with said muscle-headed idiots last time we visited,' added Tormalin.

Vintage scowled, and then abruptly the entire carriage shook. Noon straightened up, backing towards the wall in alarm, but Vintage waved a hand at her. 'We're just setting off on our way, girl, nothing to worry about.' Outside, a piercing whistle sounded. 'Tor, you can pull the curtains back now. We should get a decent head of steam on – Pamoz does like to show off.'

Tor threw back the curtains and, despite herself, Noon went over to the windows and pressed her hands against the glass. Outside, the people left behind were already streaky blurs, and the dark shape that was the Wild was streaming past, faster and faster. She thought of flying with Fulcor, but Fulcor was understandable; she had muscles and bones, and wings and claws. This was the winnowfire used for something useful. There was a bellowing, roaring *chufchufchuf* coming from somewhere ahead.

Tormalin joined her at the window, and for the first time in hours he smiled faintly. 'It's more comfortable than a horse, I'll give it that.'

'Eyes back here please.' Noon returned to the table, and Vintage tapped the sketch. 'This represents possibly the most intact Behemoth corpse we have on Sarn, an extraordinary artefact. With this, it's possible we could answer many questions about the Jure'lia and their queen.'

'Then why haven't you?'

'Because', Tormalin swapped one of the bottles of wine for the lamp, and pulled a corkscrew from his pocket, 'Esiah Godwort won't let her look at it.'

'Because Esiah Godwort is a stubborn, foolish, ignorant snob who wouldn't know true research if it reached up and poked his ridiculous, idiotic –' Vintage took a breath. 'Esiah is very protective of his property. He owns the land the buggering thing crashed onto, you see. It has been in his family for generations. From what I understand, his ancestors considered the land tainted, built a huge wall around it, and left it where it was – they

223

were rich enough to be able to afford to do that. Growing up, Esiah became obsessed with this secret place, this haunted wreck hidden behind the thickest walls he'd ever seen. His family tried to distract him, with work and wives and trips to distant lands, but always he'd come back to the compound. What did they expect? That's what I ask myself. You can't hide something that strange and expect people not to be curious.' She shrugged. 'When he inherited the land, when old man Godwort breathed his last, Esiah threw everything he had into gathering information on the Behemoths. He rebuilt the compound, thoroughly explored its haunted landscape. For a time, Esiah was the leading scholar on the subject, and very keen to keep it that way.' She coughed into her hand. 'Annoyingly. But then, earlier this year, he withdrew from academia, took back all the artefacts and writings he had brought out into the world, and retreated to the compound. He would not speak to anyone of it, would not speak to anyone at all. He became a recluse. All that knowledge, closed up behind those walls.' Vintage tapped her finger on the sketch. 'This drawing is one of the very few items remaining from Esiah's period of study. If we could just get inside it . . . we could learn more about the broken artefact we retrieved, I'm sure of it. Do all Behemoths carry such things? Where are they located?'

'What happened to him? To Godwort?' asked Noon.

'I have no idea, darling Noon. Rumours have flown around – that he's found himself a woman at last who is capable of distracting him. That he's ill, or mad. Or that he's discovered something so terrible within the Behemoth that it struck him immediately insensible.' Vintage paused. 'I quite like that one.'

The floor under their feet was thrumming slightly, and Noon found herself glancing towards the windows again and again, caught by the speed of the passing world. Tormalin had retrieved a goblet from a cabinet and poured himself a glass of wine the colour of rubies.

'Need I remind you, Vintage, that we have been here before, and Esiah Godwort wouldn't even speak to you?' Tor sipped his wine. 'He has no interest in sharing his compound with you.'

'Ah, yes, this is true, Tormalin, my dear, but this time I come ready with items to trade.' Vintage flapped a hand at the bags and cases piled in the corner. 'At the knock-down price of just-let-me-in-the-bloody-compound.'

'You're trading in your own collection?' Noon folded her arms over her chest. 'How do you even know that what's in this compound is worth seeing?'

Vintage accepted a glass from Tor. She was glaring at the sketch of the Behemoth. 'Because drawings and writings are not enough, and after what we saw in the forest, I am more convinced of that than ever. I need to see a Behemoth up close, and as intact as possible. Perhaps Esiah has also found samples of this golden fluid. It could be conclusive proof, finally, that the Jure'lia are responsible for the Wild.'

'But why? What do you get from it, in the end?'

Noon sensed Tormalin's eyes on her, giving her a warning glance perhaps, but she ignored it. Vintage took a long swallow of wine, not looking up. 'It's all in the spirit of scientific enquiry, my dear Noon. There is nothing finer than knowing the truth.'

There were a few moments of silence between them all, filled with the busy roar of the winnowline engine.

'Knowing the truth.' Noon nodded slightly. 'It's funny you should say that. Bringing me here, amongst all these fell-witches. What if they should find out the truth? About me?'

Tormalin looked up at her again, surprised perhaps that she was speaking so openly about what she was. She felt a prickle of irritation at that; it was none of his business – this was a pact agreed between herself and Vintage.

'You'll stay in here, keep to yourself. Don't set anything on fire. The witches here have a job to do, my dear, they aren't interested in finding you.'

225

'What if they've been told to look for someone like me? What if Fulcor is following me now, in the sky? She will lead them straight to me.'

'Fulcor?' asked Tormalin.

'The bat.' Noon frowned. 'She's following me. She seems to like me.'

'Someone has to, I suppose.'

Vintage flapped her hands at her. 'You worry too much, my dear. Stay here, be quiet, keep your head down. You'll be fine.'

Noon reached up and touched her fingers to the silk band that covered her forehead. 'I don't think you know what sort of people they'll have looking for me. I don't think you know at all.'

19

Dearest Marin,

Thank you for your most recent letter, you know I'm always thrilled to hear of life outside the vine forest – do not worry yourself about 'bothering me with childish tales of college life'. Truly, my dear, your letters are a highlight, especially as it's picking season and dear Ezion has a bigger pea-bug up his arse than usual.

I was particularly interested to hear of the 'incident' at your college. I am assuming that the young woman would have been around sixteen or seventeen years of age (if she shared classes with you). It is very unusual for a fell-witch to avoid detection for that long. She must have been very careful, and I can only imagine her despair when they finally caught up with her. Yes, I'm sure that your tutors have told you over and over how much safer you will all be now that the fell-witch is off to the Winnowry, but I ask you, Marin, did you feel in danger before you knew what she was? Were you, at any point, burned alive or did you have any part of you blown off? Of course not. I'm sure you would have mentioned it in your monthly letters.

I sense that you want my opinion on the Winnowry, Marin, but don't quite want to ask me. I suspect that their agents made quite an impression on you. Well, from what I can tell, they do a very good job of telling us that fell-witches are dangerous and must be controlled at all costs – there is good evidence for this, of course. We've all read the stories. It is like a terrible illness, they tell us. But in truth, we know very little about fell-witches – where the power comes from, why people are born with it, or why it only ever shows itself in humans (there have been no Eboran fell-witches). What I ask you to bear in mind, Marin my dear, is that when they have hurried these women off to their fortress in the south, do we believe they are treating them as victims of a terrible illness? Or are the more tractable ones used to keep the Winnowry powerful? They make their drug there, for one thing, via 'purging' (it seems awfully convenient to me that purging just happens to produce the most lucrative drug Sarn has ever seen); they hire the most controlled of their women out as mercenaries to any war or border dispute, and it seems to me that their agents – the same ones you will have seen whisking away your colleague – are the dangerous ones. Even the proposed winnowline (I sent you the sketches of the engine last year) relies on the indentured servitude of women who wouldn't see the outside world at all without it. What do I think of the Winnowry, Marin? I think we need to keep a beady eye on it – power and money, and not salvation, lie at the foundation of it.

Do burn this letter if you feel safer doing so, Marin. Not everyone is as critical of the Winnowry as I, and your college elders may be feeling a little twitchy.

Extract from the private letters of Master Marin de Grazon, from Lady Vincenza 'Vintage' de Grazon

Agent Lin hung suspended in the sky over the lights of Mushenska. The clouds and rain of earlier were gone, chased away by the incoming sea wind, and she was left with a clear night of stars and chill air. The bat she had been loaned for this mission was a source of warmth beneath her, its wings beating so fast that they were a blur. She had been told that its name was Gull, and indeed the name had been stitched into its leather harness. Someone cared for this creature enough to name it and personalise its belongings. She wondered if it had been the boy called Lusk – he had the look of sentiment about him. That was probably why he'd let Fell-Noon get away so easily. When she had left the Winnowry he had still been alive, although she didn't think he'd be stitching names into anything for a while.

'The rain will have washed away her scent by now, of course.'

She had been methodically sweeping the city for days, asking questions, looking for clues, and so far she hadn't turned up anything. Agent Lin tugged on the reins and they swept down low over the city. The smell of wood smoke and cooking food, old hay and wet stone enveloped them, and Lin smiled slightly to herself. It was a dirty business, being the Winnowry's attack dog, but you didn't get smells like this in a poky little cell, and you didn't get to feel the wind in your hair either. Most people, she suspected, didn't understand quite what a boon that was, but most people weren't wrestled from their crying mothers and locked up in a damp room for the majority of their lives. Fresh, clean rain was a thousand, thousand miles from the trickled moisture of damp down a rock wall.

'Let me know if you smell anything.' She leaned down close to the bat's great ears. 'I reckon you can smell your own kind better than anything else.'

She gave Gull the lead, letting the bat flitter back and forth over the city. She had never been particularly fond of flying with the creatures – they had a powerful odour all of their

229

own, and the bunching of muscles and flapping of wings meant it was hardly a restful experience – but it was useful, and generations of careful breeding meant that these giant bats were the best of their kind available: clever, obedient, strong. The Winnowry held the secret of their bloodline, of course. Something else they were very careful to keep to themselves.

Eventually, Gull made several tight circles over a certain roof, and she took him down, landing with a clatter of claws against clay tiles. It looked like the roof of a tavern of some sort, judging from the busy chimneys and the faint smell of food and ale. Climbing down from the saddle, she caught some laughter and the sound of several shouted conversations floating up to her. Laughter was something else you didn't hear much of in the Winnowry, of course. There was a small garden up here, she realised, where someone was growing vegetables and herbs, and a raised part of the roof revealed a small door. The scent of harla root and fever-leaf was faint, but Agent Lin had an appreciation for these things.

'Why have you brought me here, Gull?'

The giant bat was shuffling about with its head down, its huge ugly nose wrinkling and snuffling. Out of the sky, they were awkward, ungainly creatures, spindly arms reaching through the webbing of their wings like a child caught in a sack. Agent Lin frowned slightly.

'Do I need to remind you that Fell-Noon gets a little further away every moment we stand here?' She paused, pursing her lips. Why was she talking to a bat? There were many advantages to being an agent of the Winnowry, but they mostly worked alone. This is what it led to: talking to bats. Better, she reminded herself, than decades shut off from the world entirely.

At that moment, the small door behind them clattered open, and an older woman with wild red hair streaked with grey stepped out onto the roof, lit by lamps in the room behind her. A strange parade of emotions showed themselves across her tanned face: surprise, mild annoyance, and then a deep wariness.

'Here, what are you doing up on my bloody roof?'

Agent Lin stepped into the light, letting the woman see the bat-wing tattoo on her forehead and the green and grey travel tunic she wore. Winnowry colours.

'Nothing to concern yourself with. You can go about your business.'

The woman was watching her closely, and she looked a great deal more worried than Lin would necessarily expect from a civilian with nothing to hide. That was interesting.

'Huh.' The woman lifted her chin, attempting defiance. 'That's all very well, missus, but my business is those bloody herbs your giant bloody bat is stamping all over.'

Agent Lin looked back. Gull was busily nosing around in the far corner of the garden, huffing to itself. Ignoring the woman and her look of outrage, Agent Lin approached the bat and pushed his big head away from the earth. Splattered across the top of the thin layer of mud was a dried streak of bat guano, white and chalky in the dim light. Just next to it was a tomato plant, which was missing most of its fruit, and looked like it had been enthusiastically chewed on. She kicked at the guano with her boot, watching as it broke up into crumbling pieces. It was a few days old at least.

'The girl was here, then.' Agent Lin straightened up and turned back to the woman, who was watching her with her arms crossed over her chest. 'You own a tavern?'

'You're standing on it. The Frog and Bluebell. The ale's not bad but we do decent pies, which is what them herbs are for.'

'Any unusual visitors lately? A young woman, travelling alone, nervous?'

'Not that I've noticed.' The woman's face suggested that she could have an entire tavern full of nervous young women travelling alone and she wouldn't breathe a word of it to her.

231

Agent Lin turned away and looked across the city. Without another word, she walked back to Gull and climbed into the saddle, twitching the reins so that the bat tramped around in a circle twice before reaching the edge of the roof. She looked back, seeing with satisfaction that the plants were squashed into the mud, and then they took off.

Dawn had turned the sea to the south a beaten silver grey by the time they had found what they were looking for. Fresh guano, no more than half a day old, streaked across the balcony on the top floor of an expansive inn. The owner was already up, baking bread for his guests' breakfast, but his face was a closed book, and he would tell her nothing but generalities. Frustrating, perhaps, but his silence told her more than he could know: he had been paid to be quiet, and that was significant enough in itself. She had excused herself and hung around the alley behind the inn until the midday sun was high in the cloudless sky, and listened to the staff arriving for the day. As well as learning that Rufio had been out all night and had lost his shirt playing cards, and that Sara had a new bag of akaris ready for her week off, she also heard that one of their most eccentric guests had packed up her things and left, taking with her the Eboran bodyguard – the women took pains to describe his extreme beauty and to speculate on his prowess in bed – and a young woman who wore an unfashionable hat and didn't speak much. She was new, apparently.

Lin took the silver whistle from inside her tunic and summoned Gull. Within moments they were back in the air, northern Mushenska falling below them. The eccentric woman, one Lady de Grazon, was considered eccentric for her interest in the worm people, and because she had invested an outrageous amount of money in the winnowline, which the maids of the inn distrusted, partly because one of the engines had exploded not more than a moon's cycle ago, killing fifteen people. De Grazon had her own carriage on the contraption.

Gull circled around, and the lands north of Mushenska came into view, hazing into purple hills in the far distance. The land was dark with the Wild, and dividing it like a long silver spike was the winnowline. The bright midday sun caught it and danced along its edge, almost like a message from Tomas himself. Agent Lin smiled to herself. As if she believed in that old fraud.

Touching her hand to her side, where her pack sloshed with water and supplies, Agent Lin considered her options. Fell-Noon wasn't in Mushenska any more, she was fairly sure of that. It was the first place you might go on escaping the Winnowry – the nearest city, the closest place to get a hot meal – but if you were on the run, Agent Lin thought it unlikely that you would stay. You could attempt to lose yourself in the streets, perhaps, hope that your 'talent' was never noticed, and lead a quiet life. Or would you try to get as far away as possible? How far would you have to go before the Winnowry stopped chasing you? Sarn was very big, after all. Perhaps there was such a place.

But then, Agent Lin was a patient woman. She guided Gull up into the clear sky, the corpse moon hanging ghoulish to their right, and she began to follow the winnowline north.

20

My dearest Marin,

I have had several angry letters from your mother. She seems to think this latest idea of yours is my fault. Don't worry, I assured her that you are quite capable of coming up with your own dangerous nonsense and don't have to borrow any from me at all.

Even so, she is insisting that I write to you and tell you not to go. Obviously, my darling, I'm not going to tell you to do that. But I will tell you, quite firmly, with that look in my eye (you know the look) that you must research the expedition company thoroughly, preferably talking to customers who have made the journey previously. If you are unsure of them at all, go elsewhere. However well armed they are, take your own weapons, and keep your own supply of rations with you at all times. I know full well these ominous instructions will only add to your excitement, which is why you are my favourite nephew, but do keep this in mind, Marin: the Wild is more dangerous, and far stranger, than you could ever know. Our small patch of it in the vine forest is tame in comparison to what I've seen in my travels –

don't be swayed into complacency. And if you should see anything freakishly worm-touched write to me about it immediately.

Extract from the private letters of Master Marin de Grazon, from Lady Vincenza 'Vintage' de Grazon

Beyond the carriage window the tall grasses were a ghostly grey, like sea foam at night. Until he'd left Ebora, Tormalin had never seen the sea – it had been one of the first things he'd done, and he'd never tired of it. Even this, the grasses seen at night from a speeding carriage with the dark presence of the Wild beyond them, was something he could never have experienced at home. All that was waiting for him at home were bad memories and a slow death. It was important to remember that. He turned away from the window.

'Do we have any food here?'

Vintage was sitting at the long table, her legs stretched across an adjacent chair and a book on her lap. She waved a hand vaguely at the corner.

'There's dried meat and bread in one of the packs. Some fruit too.'

'I mean real food. Hot food. Food with sauce and gravy and cream.'

The witch was sitting in the corner at the back of the carriage, her knees drawn up to her chest and her new black coat wrapped around her, the hat pulled down low over her forehead. She met his eyes and raised a single eyebrow.

'There is a kitchen carriage two carriages down,' said Vintage, still not taking her eyes off her reading material. 'Try not to rouse the natives.'

Tor stood up, stretching out his back until the small bones there popped, and opened the door to the next carriage. Each carriage was linked with chains and metal tubes, and someone had helpfully covered the top of the gap with a thick roof of brown leather, but it was still possible to see the ground rushing away beneath your feet. Grimacing slightly, Tor stepped carefully onto the next platform and opened the adjoining carriage door.

Inside was a room even plusher than Vintage's carriage. The seats were upholstered with green velvet, and the curtains were yellow silk. Men and women were sitting around highly polished tables, drinking drinks and eating plates of steaming food. They were all well dressed, the elite of Mushenska: traders and politicians, criminals and merchants, with a few of the region's rare surviving aristocracy. He saw eyes jumping up from drinks and food to watch him pass; a few laden forks halted on the way to expectant mouths. He pushed a strand of hair behind his ear and nodded to a pair of young women playing a hand of cards between them, allowing the corner of his mouth to twitch into a speculative smile. They both turned faintly pink and, satisfied, he moved to the end of the compartment, enjoying for a moment how *apart* he was from them – a shark moving through still waters.

The next carriage was filled with steam and the smell of roasting meat. At a long polished counter he ordered a bowl of thick stew and a hot potato filled with melted cheese and flakes of a deliciously salty fish. There were tables in the carriage but they were all full, and on a whim Tor took his food through the door to the next. To his surprise, the dimly lit space was full of crates, boxes and sacks, although there were people there too, using the cargo as makeshift tables and chairs. These men and women did not wear fine clothes, and their faces had the pinched look of people who did not eat as often as they'd like. They had brought their own lamps, and sat in circles of their own light.

Tor stood for a moment, frozen. They did not look at him with awe or curiosity, but only with a flat acceptance; to these travellers, he realised, he was really no different to the people in the lushly furnished carriage. They only wanted to know if he was going to turf them out or not. He thought of the man in the watchtower, with his rags and his worn teeth. He had sat and shared tea with him all those years ago.

Carrying his food awkwardly, he sat on a sack and settled his things onto a crate. Far enough away from the others not to intrude, but close enough to suggest he wasn't insulted by their presence. With that done, he started to eat his food, trying not to think about the humans eyeing him cautiously. The stew was good, and the potato was even better, and he'd almost relaxed when a small hand clasped his sleeve. It was a human child, eyes enormous in a dirt-streaked face. He had a brown birthmark in the middle of his cheek. In his other hand was a slip of dirty paper.

'Are you an Eboran, sir?'

Tor put down his spoon and arranged his face into an expression of goodwill, preparing for the worst. He thought of the tramp in the tower again, how he had called him a murderer and told him that all of his people should have died.

'That I am.'

'I drew this.' The boy brandished the paper at him, and Tor saw that there was a rough sketch on it, half dirt and half charcoal. 'It's one of your war-beasts.'

'So it is.' Tor took the paper carefully and held it up to the dim light. There was a dragon there, looking rather like a large scaly dog, and a tall thin figure riding atop it with an oversized sword. Tor thought of the Ninth Rain, carefully stored back in the compartment with Vintage, and smiled. 'Is this what you imagined they looked like?'

The boy took the paper back, pushing his lower lip out slightly as he did so. ''Tis what they looked like. My grandpa told me. He saw 'em.'

'It is a fine drawing,' said Tor, even as he thought that the child's granddad was a fanciful liar.

'I thought you was all dead,' said the boy. His eyes kept wandering to the remains of Tor's potato. 'That maybe you wasn't real. But now I've seen you, so you can't all be dead.' He grinned suddenly. 'Wait until I tell my sister! She'll shit a brick.'

Tor fought to keep his face solemn. 'Sisters are like that, it's true.'

'So if the worm people come back again, the Eboran war-beasts will be there to tear 'em to bits.' The child gestured triumphantly with the paper. 'We thought you was all dead, but it's just a lie, like when I hide the best crusts from my dinner for later. You're just waiting, holding it back for later.'

Despite the warmth of the carriage, Tor felt cold. How to tell this boy, with his drawings and his easily shocked sister, that there were no Eboran war-beasts, that there never would be again? It was too easy to imagine the boy's mouth falling open, black beetles running over his tongue, his small body covered in a tide of green varnish. Ainsel's dream suddenly felt very close, as though he could look out the window now and see Behemoths hanging in the sky again. Tor felt his heart skip a beat in his chest. *We're all exposed and helpless*, he thought. *Not just Ebora, but all of Sarn. We are injured prey.*

'Here, kid, look, take this.' He picked up the plate with the remains of the potato on it, still swimming in hot butter. 'It's what you wanted anyway, isn't it?'

The boy took the plate, half crumpling his picture to do so, his face creased in confusion.

'I just wanted to—'

'Go away, kid. I'm sure your mother wouldn't want you talking to me anyway. Go on, go away.'

The boy backed off down between the boxes, his face hidden in shadows. Tor was glad.

* * *

Noon awoke to Tormalin stalking back into their compartment. Vintage had long since climbed into her own bunk, extinguishing all the lamps save one, but Noon had preferred to stay where she was, propped at the back of the carriage with her boots on. With fell-witches down the other end of this contraption, it felt safer.

The tall Eboran bumped into the table, and steadied himself by leaning on a wine bottle. His long black hair hung in his face, and she watched him gather his wits before moving again. Even drunk, he was capable of walking quietly when he wanted to, and he came towards her, stopping to drop himself into a chair. After a moment he rooted around in his pockets and came out with a glass vial, which he held up to the light. Noon could just make out the thick, crimson substance within.

'Having a good night?' she asked, her voice low. He didn't startle but he held his body very still for a moment, then he turned towards her.

'I thought you were asleep.'

'I don't sleep very deeply. Not without akaris, anyway.' She shifted in her seat, pulling her coat up to her shoulders as a makeshift blanket. 'Are you going to drink that?'

Tormalin looked at the vial of blood as though he'd forgotten it was there.

'This is old. It wouldn't be the same. Fresh is better.' He looked at her then, an expression she couldn't read on his face, and Noon felt her skin prickle all over. When he looked away again she was relieved, but she found herself thinking of his life energy, how it had filled every part of her. Tormalin cleared his throat.

'I would *feel* better,' he said, a sardonic edge to his voice. 'Old blood still carries that same euphoria, that sense of well-being, but it's a lie. A memory of something false.'

'Fresh blood heals you?'

He turned back to her, smiling, and it was like being in the

239

room with something impossible – the Eboran war-beasts of old, perhaps, or the storm gods Mother Fast used to talk about, their eyes full of sky-fire and hate. His skin was rare marble in the lamplight, and the finely boned hand that lay against his scuffed trousers was as exquisite as a snowflake. All around them, the winnowline rumbled on its journey through the Wild, and Noon tried to concentrate on that instead.

'It turns back the march of time, keeps me young, keeps me strong. If I am hurt, enough of it will close my flesh faster than true healing. Once, Ygseril's sap did this job, but I am almost too young to remember what that was like. Almost.' He looked down at the vial in his hand, and closed his fingers over it. 'Old blood, really, is no better and no worse than a decent bottle of wine.'

'And I reckon you've had a few of those this evening.'

He nodded. Noon glanced at the still form of Vintage. It was just possible to hear her soft snores.

'Vintage mentioned that you have an . . . arrangement. With people who give you blood.'

'I have sex with them for blood, yes. They seem to be very pleased with the trade actually.' He looked at her and she cursed herself for not being able to meet his eyes. 'Would you like to hear about how that works, Fell-Noon?'

'I know how sex works. Thanks all the same.' She kept her tone flippant, but her cheeks, curse them, were as hot as a brand. Tor was laughing softly, his shoulders shaking lightly with it.

'I have two lovers, carefully selected, who understand what I need – and I understand what they need, down to every last detail.' He sighed. 'With our little jaunt to Esiah Godwort's cursed compound, I will be going without for a little while. And so will they.'

'My heart bleeds for you,' said Noon. To her annoyance the memory of Novice Lusk's creamy skin had risen to the forefront

240

of her mind, followed closely by the memory of sliding her fingers across Tormalin's neck.

'Ah, Fell-Noon.' Tormalin stood up and swept an elaborate bow in her direction. 'If only it did. And please do not get all outraged on my account – as I said, my lovers are very carefully chosen.'

With that he walked over to the bunk on the far side of the carriage and fell gracefully onto the covers there. Within minutes his breathing evened out, while Noon sat rigid on her chair, glaring at nothing. The bastard was already asleep.

'Pay no attention to him, darling.' Vintage's voice was fuzzy with sleep. 'He enjoys your blushes too much to resist provoking them.'

21

Dear Nanthema,

*The box of artefacts I bought from the Rodelian
merchant arrived this week, and I am sad to say that they
are obvious forgeries – not even good ones! Half of them
are made from plaster and have broken to chalky pieces
on the journey, while the etching that claims to be the work
of Deridimas is laughable. I can, of course, imagine the
face you are pulling now, dear one, and you are completely
right. Dodgy dealings with merchants is no way to solve
the mysteries of the Jure'lia, but while Father keeps me
here that's all I have available to me. Once Mother has
recovered from the fainting fever I'm sure he will be more
amenable to letting me leave. Thank you again for the
crystal salts you sent, by the way – Mother tells me they
are of great comfort, when she is lucid, at least.*

*It has been a while since your last letter. I hope all is
well with you, my love.*

Copy of a private letter
from the records of Lady Vincenza
'Vintage' de Grazon

It was around mid-afternoon the next day when the chuffing contraption they were riding slowed abruptly, causing Noon to stagger up the carriage and Vintage's pile of papers to fly off the end of the table. Tor stood up, steadying himself against a bench.

'What was that?'

The carriage shuddered, and from somewhere ahead of them came the sound of squealing metal, followed by a chorus of shouts. The winnowline lurched again, and this time they came to a stop. Noon grasped the table, resisting the pull as the contraption fought against its own momentum, and then everything was still. As one, the three of them went to the carriage door, looking out the glass at an overcast day. It was, Noon thought immediately, a bad place to stop. The line here was carved directly into the side of a steep hill, curling around it like a belt, while above them and below them the Wild loomed, closer than ever. There was a scent, deep and earthy and somehow slightly wrong, just like there had been in the Shroom Flats – not quite disguised by the oil-and-hot-metal stench of the winnowline.

'Probably a technical problem,' said Vintage, climbing down onto the raw earth. There was a flat path next to the line, no more than twenty feet wide, scattered here and there with gravel. Not for the first time, Noon wondered at what an enormous undertaking this had been for the Winnowry, and all the while she and the other fell-witches had known nothing of it. And why should they? They were just the fuel for the Winnowry's wealth, after all. She stepped down after Vintage, touching her fingers to her head to check that the hat was still in place. Tormalin followed after, blinking at the subdued daylight.

'When you say technical problem, Vintage, are we talking about the sort of technical problem that results in the whole thing exploding? Like it did the other week?'

'I don't know.' Vintage pulled her own hat down over her bouncy hair. 'Let's go and have a look, shall we?'

'Of course,' said Tormalin. He had slipped his sword belt over his shoulder, and the hilt of the Ninth Rain looked dull in the grey light. 'Obviously, the clearest course of action is to get closer to the thing that might explode.'

Despite his dour tone, he followed Vintage as she began to walk to the front of the contraption, and Noon followed on behind, keeping her head down. Other passengers had come out of their carriages now, their faces rueful or worried, looking to the head of the contraption or out at the Wild that seemed to crouch below them like some waiting beast. Noon noticed a few heads turning to follow them curiously, so she hurried to catch up, putting Tormalin between her and the crowd.

'Pamoz! What's the problem?'

Vintage had reached the engine to find the engineer standing with her hands on her wide hips. She glanced at Vintage and gave her a wry smile.

'Come and have a look. It's big enough.'

Pamoz led them around to the front of the engine. Noon was so busy trying to keep an eye out for fell-witches or agents that she almost walked into the back of Tormalin, who had stopped. She ducked round him and winced. It *was* a pretty big problem.

A tree had fallen across the winnowline tracks, and this being the Wild, it was no ordinary tree; it was huge, a good sixty feet in length and wider across than the height of a human with her arms stretched above her. It was twisted and warped, the greyish bark bulbous and smooth, while the broken branches were still thick with dark, shiny green leaves. Pamoz was shaking her head.

'It's going to be a bastard to clear, Lady de Grazon. We'll have to take the engine back up the track aways, and then the witches can start burning it. They can do that – very controlled, focussed heat, take it to bits – but it's going to take a while. We'll have to go slow to avoid damaging the line underneath.

244

That's if it's not broken already.' Pamoz gave a sudden huge sigh. 'We'll need time to clear the debris too. This could put days on the journey.'

Vintage looked as serious as Noon had ever seen her; a deep line had formed between her eyebrows, and her mouth was turned down at the corners.

'I'd advise you to be careful burning it, Pamoz, my dear. The smoke from Wild wood can have strange effects, and this –' she paused, taking a few steps forward to look at the far end of the tree; an explosion of pale roots lay exposed to the sky, still thick with clods of mud – 'this isn't a dead tree. And nothing else has fallen on the track.' The frown deepened. 'I think this was placed here, Pamoz.'

'*Placed* here?' Pamoz laughed. 'What could possibly fucking lift it? I mean, I think it's a little large to be moved around easily, Lady de Grazon, is what I mean to say.'

There was nothing they could do here. Noon opened her mouth to tell Vintage that she was going back to their carriage to wait – she had no intention of being out in the open when the tame fell-witches came trooping out to deal with the tree – when there was a deafening crash, and the whole contraption rocked wildly towards them. For a moment, Noon was sure it would topple and fall on them, no doubt reducing them all to elaborate stains on the rough dirt, and then it fell back. The air was full of frightened shouts, and then they were all drowned out by a shattering, discordant roar.

'By the bones of Sarn, what—?'

A huge shape appeared around the front of the engine, shrouding them all in shadow. Noon felt her throat close up in fright – what it had been, or what its ancestors had been before it had been worm-touched, she did not know. Something like a bear, perhaps; it was bulky, with a thick midsection and four short but powerful legs, and a long, blocky head. But instead of fur it was covered in pale, fleshy pouches of skin,

245

which shivered and trembled as it moved, and Noon could see four circular black eyes along its head, clustered together and oddly spider-like. Its mouth, when it opened its jaws to roar again, was pink and wet and lined with hundreds of yellow needle-like teeth.

'Vines save us,' gasped Vintage. 'A horror from the deepest Wild!'

The monster reared up on its back legs and roared again, blasting them all with a hot stench of rot and green things. Long tendrils of drool dripped from its jaws, and Noon thought she could see things squirming in it. Behind them, the other passengers were screaming and running back down the track.

A few of the fell-witches piled out of the engine, their ash-covered faces slack with surprise. Instinctively, Noon tried to move away, but of course they weren't looking at her – as she watched, four of them formed a line and threw a swift barrage of green winnowfire at the monster. The creature reared up, the flames only licking at its strange, twisted flesh, and hitting instead the tree behind it. Small fires burst into life amongst its branches, while the monster roared again and leapt forward, directly at the fell-witches. The faster ones fell back, but one young woman was caught with its huge paw and she crashed to the ground, rolling in the gravel. The monster made to follow her when a short length of wood appeared suddenly in the side of its thick neck. Noon turned to see Vintage with her miniature crossbow raised, and then the monster was lumbering towards them, a thin line of crimson blood leaking from the hole she'd made.

'Did you mean to do that?' Noon was finding it difficult to catch her breath. She wanted to siphon energy, grab it from Tormalin or someone and then burn it, burn the monster, but if she did that, they would all see what she was. There would be no more hiding. 'Because now it's looking at us, Vintage, it's looking at us.'

246

Vintage was pressing another quarrel into her crossbow. 'Where's the boy?'

Noon looked around. Tormalin was standing over the fell-witch who had been thrown to the ground, but now he was drawing his sword, an outraged look on his face.

Later, when she would think of what happened, Noon was inevitably reminded of the stories Mother Fast had told them, and the books her mother had read with her. For all of the terror and the fear, she briefly saw a tale brought to life: when Tormalin the Oathless killed the worm-touched monster of the winnowline.

He brought the sword round in a series of elegant swipes, dancing the daylight along its length like sunlight on water, and the monster, dazzled for a moment, swept its great blocky head around to face him. With its attention solely on him, Tor stalked towards the creature, tall and steady, unafraid. Behind him, most of the passengers had fled, and the fell-witches were gathering their fallen colleague up and dragging her away, but a few people were left, watching with wide eyes. The monster roared and, still walking on its back legs, took a series of shuddering steps towards Tormalin, but, abruptly, the Eboran wasn't there. Noon blinked, and then he was back in sight, circling round the monster so that he was at its back. He ran, slashing his long sword low, across the back of the creature's legs. Bright blood spurted across the gravel and the animal *shrieked*. It tried to turn, but its legs were no longer obeying its commands, so instead it twisted the great bulk of its torso around, long jaws snapping at the thin form of Tormalin. For the strangest moment it looked to Noon as though Tormalin had chosen to leap to his own death – he reached up, putting himself within easy reach of the thing's teeth, and Noon was sure that he must now die, torn to shreds by the fangs of an abomination. But although the jaws seemed to close a hair's breadth away from his smooth neck, it was the monster's blood

247

that was shed; its throat burst open in a shower of red, a sudden second mouth where one hadn't been before. Belatedly Noon saw the silver line that was the Ninth Rain sliding through flesh like it was water – and then the monster was falling. Right on top of Tormalin.

Noon gasped and heard the watching crowd gasp behind her. The thing was enormous; it must surely have crushed the Eboran under its weight. But then the huge bulk of the thing rolled to one side, Tormalin the Oathless lifting it off as easily as a man discarding a horse-blanket, with the Ninth Rain still held firmly in his right hand. He stalked over towards them while a wide puddle of steaming blood grew from the body of the worm-touched creature. He looked aggrieved.

'Tormalin . . .' Vintage shook her head. 'Tor, my darling, are you all right?'

He pursed his lips at her, apparently oblivious to the watching crowd. 'Would you look at this?' He held up the cuff of his jacket, which was smudged with blood. 'Do you know how difficult it is to get blood out of Reidn silk? And now this.' He turned in a circle, revealing a huge patch of crimson on the back of his jacket. It was soaked in the monster's blood, as was much of his hair.

'Your clothes,' said Noon. She wasn't sure what else to say. 'Your . . . clothes?'

'I've had this jacket since I left Ebora, Vintage. There isn't another like it in Sarn. And, of course, this wouldn't be quite as much of an issue, if you hadn't started giving away my clothes to random women we meet in the woods.'

'Yes, dear,' Vintage patted his arm, smiling faintly, 'it is, indeed, a tragedy.' She turned away from him, looking back to the engine. 'Pamoz! You've another obstruction to burn, I'm afraid. Better get started.'

22

Evening had fallen over the hill, a deep purple dusk that chased the daylight to the west and left them with a clear sky and chilly winds, while at the front of the engine a great fire blazed on and on. The wind was taking most of the smoke away from them, although a low stink was still pervading the area, coating the back of Noon's throat so that she found herself swallowing repeatedly, as if she'd eaten something rotten. Many of the passengers had retreated back inside their carriages, while a few had made small campfires on the rocky strip of ground alongside the line, sitting and sharing food and stories. It was still dangerous to be this close to the Wild – even locked away for a decade, Noon knew that – but the defeat of the monster had emboldened them. Noon imagined they thought it something of an adventure; or, at least, those with fine clothes and the best food did. The men and women in the poorer carriage wore different expressions; the expressions of people for whom this was yet another crippling setback. They would be late for their promised jobs; the homes they were heading for might not be there any more; the food and drink they had packed might not be enough.

Noon kept herself apart from them all, staying near Vintage's rented carriage, while the scholar herself was gregariously moving from fire to fire, sharing her bottle of wine and chatting with everyone. Tormalin had attracted a small group of young women, who were cradling cups of wine in their hands and watching him with glittering eyes. None of them were sitting too close, but Noon thought that a sudden invasion by a pack of hungry worm-touched wolves wouldn't have been able to drag their eyes from his remarkable face.

She wandered towards the rear of the carriage. Vintage had insisted they light all the lamps inside and open the curtains, so that the winnowline became a series of beacons against the night. Above them, the clouds had mostly cleared and the stars were a layer of gaudy gauze while the hills merged into a single great beast in the growing dark. Far behind them was a soft blush of light against the horizon: Mushenska. So much space, so much air. It had been like this out on the plains, where the world had seemed limitless – when she had believed that the grasslands, and her way of life, would go on forever.

There was a dark shape on the ground just behind the end of the carriage. Noon paused. It looked like a bundle of clothes. Had something fallen from the winnowline when it had been struck by the creature? Noon walked over. The voices of the people by the fires grew quieter, the crunch of her boots on the gravelly ground louder than she would have liked. Her breath caught in her throat and she realised that the bundle on the ground was a person, their blank face turned up to the sky. There was another fallen shape just beyond it. Neither were moving. Noon knelt down next to the first one, holding her hand above the face, not quite daring to touch the bare skin. It was a boy, a small brown birthmark in the middle of his right cheek. His eyes were open. She pressed her fingers lightly to his chest, and was relieved to feel a heartbeat; faint, but very fast. Swallowing hard, Noon stepped over him to find a girl of around the same age, curled over onto her side as

250

though she had chosen to drop down and sleep on the steel rails. There had been a small group of children running around earlier, she remembered, chasing each other and entertaining themselves in the way that children did.

'What . . . hey, kid.' She gently shook the girl, but her head flopped back and forth, unresponsive. Noon stood up and walked back, trying to ignore the cold feeling of guilt that was uncurling in her stomach. She couldn't be blamed for this, it had nothing to do with her . . .

A figure stepped out of the shadows, moving silently. A tall white woman, wiry and contained. Her forearms were bare, and Noon could see the muscles standing out like cords. The woman's hair was grey and pushed back from her face in soft waves, but her face was unlined. There was a bat-wing tattoo on her forehead. As she looked at Noon she smiled, a thin tensing of her lips, and her eyes glittered.

'It seems I have found you, Fell-Noon. You did a pretty good job of running, I'll give you that. Will you come without a fuss?'

Noon stumbled backwards. Her heart was beating so fast her fingers were tingling.

'You would hurt children?'

'Don't be so dramatic. Just took enough to take you down, which I don't think will require very much at all. I am Agent Lin. It's time for you to come back to the Winnowry. Or die. I don't mind which.'

Out in front of the carriages, the other passengers were still sitting around their fires, laughing and talking. Noon opened her mouth to shout to them, and then felt fear close her throat. Agent Lin wasn't here for them, after all.

'Are you resisting me, Fell-Noon?' Agent Lin held up her hands, palms to the sky. 'Are you going to try to fight me?'

'I'm not going back,' said Noon. The words felt like tiny stones in her throat. They weren't strong enough. 'I'm not going back to that fucking hole.'

Two points of green light blossomed into being over Agent Lin's hands. As Noon watched they grew into two whirling pools of flame, painting the woman's face into a ghoulish mask. Frantically, she felt within herself for a scrap of winnow-fuel, but there was nothing. The terror and the frustration boiled up into her chest.

'I will fight you!'

At her shout, she heard a babble of confused voices rising behind her, but Agent Lin was already moving. The two fireballs she had summoned were in the air and flying towards her like comets, and she had to dive into the dirt to avoid being burned alive. The fireballs exploded onto the stones to her right, showering her with gravel. People were shouting now, yelling at each other to get back. Belatedly, Noon thought of the other fell-witches powering the engine. Surely they would join this fight, and then she would be dead within moments.

'Get away from me! I'm not going back!'

The woman continued to advance, smiling faintly. More green light was growing between her hands – she was building a single point of light now, curling it with her palms into a brightly glowing starburst.

'Do you really think you have a choice, Fell-Noon? You and I both know there are no choices when it comes to the Winnowry.'

Noon scrambled to her feet and ran around the side of the carriage, crashing through the door forcefully enough to bark her shins on the steps. Inside, she glared around the room at Vintage's belongings – the bags, the boxes of books, the crates of artefacts, the empty plates – before spotting a simple vase of flowers on a small side table. They had been placed there at the beginning of the trip and were past their best, but it was all she had. Noon grabbed the flowers out of the vase, water spattering over her shoes, and she drained the last of their life energy. It was a pitiful taste of what she needed, and the flowers wilted in her hands, black and dead and—

The windows on one side of the carriage blew out, showering her with glass as the whole contraption rocked wildly to one side. Everything was briefly filled with green light, and her ears popped. She had one brief thought – *How powerful is this woman?* – before she was thrown into the wall. The vase smashed to pieces under her.

'Had enough yet?'

Agent Lin was in the doorway, leaning there as though they were discussing the weather. Outside there were raised voices, and Noon thought she could hear Vintage shouting orders. Tormalin's sword was back in the carriage, she realised, carefully packed away again in its long leather case.

Noon jumped up and threw her hands forward, throwing a tiny blast of winnowfire, bright and almost entirely without heat. Lin flinched away from it, and while her head was turned, Noon ran through the door into the next carriage. There were people here, their faces blank with shock – some were already moving to the door, dragging children out by their cuffs. Noon lunged at the closest, a thick-set man with large oiled moustaches, and took his fat hand in both of hers. In her panic, she almost killed him. As it was, he dropped to the floor in a dead faint, his face grey, and Noon spun, conjuring the biggest fireball she could and throwing it behind her. Agent Lin was there, but the winnowfire exploded against the wall, missing the woman by a good two feet. Orange fire licked up the expensive silk curtains, and a section of blistered wall fell away.

'Very poor, Fell-Noon, very poor.'

Half falling over the man she'd drained, Noon made to run for the door, but Agent Lin flicked a hand and a bullet of green fire flew down the carriage, missing Noon's face by no more than an inch. She gasped, holding up her hands, feeling the winnowfire boiling up through her own fingertips, but another bullet of fire flew past her – she smelled burning hair – and her concentration fled. Agent Lin walked slowly forward, two daggers of green fire balanced on the ends of her fingertips. Noon dropped her hands and retreated.

'I'm doing what I can here to take you home in one piece,' Agent Lin advanced. She looked utterly calm, the daggers of fire seeming almost like solid objects. Noon could not take her eyes from them. She had never seen the winnowfire form such shapes. 'I don't know why I bother, really. You must have caught me in a good mood.'

'Home? That place isn't my home. I'll die before I go back there.'

'Oh, don't make it too easy for me. I have to have my fun somehow.'

The backs of Noon's heels knocked against solid wood, and she reached behind her for the door handle. Perhaps, if she could get into the next carriage, she could hide. It might be her only chance.

'Stay where you are!'

Lin threw the daggers and Noon dropped to the floor, narrowly avoiding their wicked points. They crashed into the door behind her, splitting the frame, a spreading pool of fire moving hungrily over the wood. She stood up and, ignoring the blisters that popped into existence on her hands, wrenched the door open, only to be met by the sight of Vintage, her crossbow held in front of her and a steely glint in her eye.

'Get down!'

Noon dropped to the floor in time to see Agent Lin thrown backwards by a crossbow bolt to the shoulder. The woman snarled with a mixture of pain and rage, but without hesitation she reached up and snapped the bolt away. There was blood on her shirt but it was just above her collar bone – Noon doubted she'd been seriously hurt. Then Vintage had hold of Noon and was dragging her to her feet and through into the next carriage.

'Run, girl!'

She ran.

Through the kitchen carriage into the next, dodging boxes and sacks, she could hear shouting and screaming from outside, and she wondered what had happened to Vintage. Surely the scholar wouldn't be foolish enough— there was an explosion from behind her, and more green light. The door had been blown off, but she was already at the next partition. The violence of the initial attack had torn the covering from the connecting space between the carriages. Noon took a breath and swallowed it down. She couldn't keep going forward – if she went forward far enough, she would just meet more fell-witches.

She scrambled up the side, using the door frame as leverage, until she pulled herself up onto the roof of the carriage. The late evening, which had seemed so peaceful only a few moments ago, was full of panic. Parts of the carriages behind her were on fire, and she could hear the confused shouts of men and women trying to retrieve their possessions and locate their children. She ran towards the engine and glanced over the side – she saw shocked faces looking up at her.

The slippery roof under her feet seemed to jump to one side, and she crashed to her knees. Looking up, she saw a sinister wave of green fire curl up at the space between the carriages, and then climbing up in its wake was Agent Lin. The left-hand sleeve of her shirt was crimson with blood.

'That's enough now.' The expression of faint amusement had vanished from her face. 'I've chased you for long enough, Fell-Noon. You come home, or you die. Last chance.'

'No!'

Gathering the last of what she had, Noon cupped her hands and pulled them apart, drawing the energy that stormed inside her into a maelstrom of green fire. It boiled in front of her, tongues of flame licking and flickering, growing bigger and bigger – the largest fireball she had ever attempted. She could feel the confines of it growing weaker as her control of it

255

lessened. The muscles in her arms singing with the effort, she shoved the ball of fire out, throwing it across the roof towards Agent Lin.

It was better than her first attempt, and it exploded with an impressive roar, but it was too large with too little winnow-fire energy within it. Agent Lin twisted her body away, her head down as she pulled up her cloak to cover herself – too late, Noon saw that it was made of heavy treated leather and it shone in the light – and the fire passed over her, as harmless as a blustery shower.

When she straightened up, the Winnowry agent was pin-wheeling her arms, faster and faster. Noon had a moment to wonder what she was doing when she saw the circles of green fire growing around the woman, bands of lethal flame. And then another figure appeared behind her, stumbling out of the dark, a long straight sword raised over his head.

Agent Lin must have seen something in Noon's face, or perhaps it was the simple tilt of her head, because the woman spun round and released one of the rings of fire towards Tormalin. It curled across the roof, licking sparks off the metal plates, and Tor was forced to jump out of its way, shouting with alarm and falling to his knees.

The second ring was for her. Noon staggered back, perilously close to the edge of the roof, and still she felt the heat crisping her clothes as it passed. She stumbled, falling onto her backside, and before she could get back up, Agent Lin was approaching, her hands full of fiery daggers again. As she spoke, she threw them. They landed to either side of the cowering Noon.

'I honestly don't know, Fell-Noon, whether I should kill you or not. I would *like* to, I would like to very much, but I suspect what they have waiting for you at home will be even worse.'

'Kill me, then. Because I'll kill you, first chance I get.'

The woman stood over her now. Her softly curling grey hair

was in disarray and there was a smudge of blood on her chin. Agent Lin raised her hand, summoning a long shard of brightly shining fire. Noon could already imagine how it would feel, plunged through her chest.

'Oh, well. If you insist.'

Agent Lin formed a fist, and a white ghost fell on her from above. It was Fulcor, her fur brilliant under the moonlight and her leathery wings filling the whole world. Noon heard Lin give a startled shout, and then the woman was gone, knocked from the side of the roof onto the dirt below.

'Fulcor?'

The bat rose up into the night, followed by a barrage of fireballs. Noon got to her feet to find Tormalin next to her, taking her arm.

'Quick, while that fiery lunatic is distracted. We have to get out of here.'

They ran to a ladder at the edge of the roof and descended into chaos. The passengers were crowded at the edge of the line, while Agent Lin fired knives of fire at the rapidly retreating shape of Fulcor. Vintage appeared out of the crowd; part of her coat was smoking and singed, but otherwise she appeared to be unharmed. The tar carriage, the one containing all of Vintage's supplies and the artefacts she hoped to trade with Esiah Godwort, was fully aflame, burning so brightly that Noon had to shield her eyes from it. Other parts of the winnowline looked like they would be in a similar situation shortly.

'Run, my dear, before she—'

Agent Lin screamed, a noise of combined rage and triumph, and an entire wall of green fire swept towards them. Noon saw it engulf a man and woman who didn't move out of the way fast enough, and in the next instant they were screaming horrors – the woman's hair flew up like a taper, and she saw the man press his fingers to a face that was already melting.

It burns so hot, thought Noon faintly. *Winnowfire burns so hot—*

Tormalin was barrelling her to the edge of the path and suddenly they were half falling, half scrambling down a steep incline, Vintage hot on their heels. The sky above their heads was rent with green fire, but the woods ahead of them were dark and thick. They ran between the trees, quickly losing themselves in the dark, and Noon thought she'd never been less afraid of the Wild.

23

My dearest Nanthema,

I'm hoping this letter reaches you safely and that, indeed, you yourself are safe. I am writing to you from the Goddestra Delta, where we arranged to meet, and I have been here now for the entire Fallen Moon festival. I have even made some discreet inquiries and listened very carefully to all the port gossip, but there has been no mention of an Eboran in these parts, and, as you can imagine, I'm sure it would have been remarked upon. I do hope you are safe.

I tell myself that I can't imagine what could have kept you from our long-awaited meeting, except, of course, that I am imagining everything – bandits on the road, a sudden illness (no, I will not name it here), a landslide, bad weather, or perhaps you took a shortcut through the Wild. You've probably been delayed by something terribly prosaic, and, of course, I shall wait. I have rooms at the Salted Anchor Inn and I have enough money to keep me here until the next moon (I have already written to my father asking for further funds. I concocted some story about college accommodation being pricier than expected. He will never question it).

I have sent this letter to the last address I have for you at Jarlsbad. It's likely that you'll never receive it, and tomorrow morning I'll spot you jumping up from the jetty, your face bright with adventure, but if not, then I hope these words find you well.

All my love, V.

Copy of a private letter from the records of
Lady Vincenza 'Vintage' de Grazon

'The dream you had—'

The fell-witch turned and glanced at Tormalin, before pulling her hat down further over her ears. The sun was a pale disc just above the treeline, watery and cold, and there was a chill mist between the trees. They had been walking through the night, moving steadily away from the winnowline. When Tor looked back behind them, he could still see a dense cloud of black smoke above the distant treeline. It made him uneasy.

'What about it?'

'You said you'd had the same dream as Lucky Ainsel. What did you make of it?'

Vintage was some way ahead of them, crashing through the undergrowth. She was, of the three of them, the most familiar with travelling through the Wild and had demanded that she scout ahead, but in truth, the scholar was in a foul mood. Noon was hanging back, much of the colour vanished from her cheeks, and there were dark circles around her eyes that hadn't been there yesterday.

'I knew I was in danger. I knew I had to get out of that death-trap.'

'But why? It was just a dream.'

Noon shook her head. 'No, it wasn't. And you know it wasn't, or you wouldn't be asking me. I saw the Winnowry crumble to bits, and all of us inside suffocating, and it was real.'

'You realise what you're saying? That you believe the Jure'lia are coming back?'

She stopped and turned to face him. There was a smudge of soot on her cheek. 'So?'

'Don't you see?' He stood close, lowering his voice, although he could not have said why. 'If they come back, then Sarn is – Sarn is fucked.'

She raised her eyebrows at him. 'The Winnowry sent someone after me to kill me. I don't give a single tiny shit about Sarn.'

That surprised a laugh out of him. 'You should, witch. Your feet are planted on it, are they not?'

'If they come back, then it's your problem.'

He shook his head, exasperated. 'Ygseril was the key to defeating them. He was the one who birthed the war-beasts. And he's dead.'

'I thought you didn't care. That you'd left those problems behind you.'

'Yes, well.' He took a breath, and then let it out in a sigh. 'I was rather hoping those problems wouldn't come and bite me on the arse.'

'Not until you've finished whoring your way around Sarn and drinking Vintage out of wine, at least?'

He looked down at her, ready to be affronted, but to his surprise she was smiling faintly – it looked as fragile as ice on a lake in late spring, but it was the first smile he'd seen her give in some time.

'You look a little more human when you're annoyed, Eboran.'

'Oh, I'm glad my countenance is more pleasing to you when I'm vexed, that bodes well.' A flock of birds passed overhead, and he looked up. There was more light in the sky than there had been, making it easier for them to find their way, and easier for them to be seen. 'About what happened at the winnowline . . .'

The smile dropped from her face, and she turned back to

261

the trees. After a moment she lifted her hand to her mouth and briefly gnawed at her thumb. The Wild pressed in all around them, quieter than any morning forest should be. 'What about it?'

'Are there likely to be more like her?' Tormalin scanned the sky for black fluttering shapes, for fiery death on wings. 'I'm not sure I'd like to see more than one.'

'Agents usually work alone,' said Noon. 'They are pretty rare – the Winnowry doesn't trust many fell-witches to control themselves – so they're in demand all over the place. They won't have many to send after me, and –' she cleared her throat – 'she was powerful.'

'She bent the winnowfire into all sorts of shapes. Can you do that?'

'No.'

'When she made rings from the fire and spun them around her arms – I have never seen such a thing. Can you do that?'

'No. You've seen what I can do already. I blow things up. Destroy things.' Her voice wavered, and Tormalin peered down at her curiously, but Vintage was stamping her way back towards them. If there were any worm-touched monsters around, Tormalin thought, they would be better off keeping out of Vintage's way.

'There's a settlement ahead. I should be able to buy us a roof to hide under for a few hours with what I've got left in my pockets.'

'A settlement, in the Wild?' Tor looked at the twisted trees ahead of them, trying to imagine living out here. 'Are they mad?'

'Vintage—' Noon started, but the scholar raised a hand, an expression of sheer weariness on her face.

'I am much too tired to talk about it, my dear, and there's very little to say as it is. If anything, it's my own fault. I'm no fool – I should have taken the threat of the Winnowry more seriously.'

'We lost all of your things,' said Noon, her voice flat. 'All of your papers and books, burned. And two people died.'

Vintage sighed heavily, leaning forward with her hands on her hips. 'It doesn't surprise me, if I'm honest, that the Winnowry would be so heavy-handed. Noon, those deaths are the fault of the unhinged woman they sent after you. Come along, I'm hoping we can get a stiff drink out of these people. They've already spotted us.'

Vintage led them down a slope, and once beyond the line of trees, they stood in front of an enormous thicket of monstrous thorns. It rose above them like a small hill, looking utterly impenetrable. It was a place full of ominous shadows and lethal spikes, but as they drew closer, Tor saw that at the very base of the thicket there was a way through the twisting foliage, and at the entrance stood a small, wizened old man. He was as pale as milk, and had tufts of silky blond hair behind a pair of protruding ears. The old man's eyes were lost in wrinkles, but he nodded to Vintage, and the two of them had a rapid conversation in a plains dialect Tor was not familiar with. He looked at Noon, and saw her eyebrows raised.

'Vintage has travelled a lot, even before she paid for my sword arm,' he said, by way of explanation. 'Also, she tells me she has a trustworthy face, although I'm quite sure I don't know what one of those looks like.'

'Why would you?'

He gave her a sharp look, but Vintage was beckoning. They followed her and the ancient man down the shadowy path – Tormalin had to crouch to avoid catching his head on the low-hanging briars – to find a curious little village sheltered within the enormous thicket of thorns. Above them was a circle of sky, pale blue now as the day got into its stride, while all around them rose a wild brown wall of monstrous thorn bushes; it was, Tor thought, rather like sitting at the bottom of a barrel. The space immediately in front of them contained a well and what appeared to be a small market place, while he could see men and women climbing in the thorn wall, looking like especially industrious ants amongst the twisted burs. Now that he looked closer, he could see rope ladders strung here and there like an elaborate web, and scraps of cloth hanging from thorns where people were drying their washing. They had burrows, he realised, tiny buried homes in the depths of the giant thorns. It was so different from the sweeping marble halls of Ebora that he wanted to laugh.

'What a miserable place,' he said, cheerily enough. 'Vintage, I do hope you have rented their very best rooms.'

'Be quiet, Tormalin, my darling, or I will waste one of my precious quarrels ventilating your beautiful throat. Here we are.'

The old man had led them to a hole in the thicket level with the ground. Inside was what appeared to be a communal resting place; the ground was covered in a pungent mixture of old leaves and grey feathers, and there were blankets everywhere, most of them occupied. Tor could see pale faces and bare feet here and there, could hear the soft sounds of snoring. He straightened up and looked at Vintage.

'Not on your life am I sleeping in there. On the floor. In rags.'

'Let me past, then.' Noon pushed past him, heading into the gloom of the den. She poked around until she found a free blanket and then dropped to the floor. In a moment she had her head tucked under her arm and her hat pulled down over her face. She seemed utterly unconcerned by all the warm bodies around her.

'Vintage, really. What *is* this place?'

'It's someone's home, like any other, so keep a civil tongue in your head. These are the Keshin people. There are little pockets of them all through these forests. They live and hunt out here, and occasionally trade. Their main source of meat

264

and fur are a particular type of nocturnal hare. They keep this room for the hunters who have been out all night and want to grab a nap.' She lowered her voice. 'Look, Tormalin, my darling, we need a rest, do we not? And we need it under cover.' She glanced up at the circle of sky, now the colour of a spring bird's egg. 'I don't want another visit from that fiery bitch.'

'Vintage,' said Tor, glancing at Noon's indistinct form, and lowering his voice, 'by all the roots, why didn't you just hand her in? We all make mistakes, and, as usual, yours has come from a place of kindness, but this waif is not worth getting us killed for.'

Vintage lifted her chin, her face stony. 'That *waif* saved our lives back in the Shroom Flats.'

'That's debatable.'

'And can you truly imagine me just handing her back to the filth that is the Winnowry?' Vintage sniffed. 'Tor, my dear, do you know me at all?'

Tor snorted in disgust. 'Well, at least if that fiery lunatic does find us, this place will go up like kindling, and it'll all be over swiftly enough.'

Vintage turned away from him in disgust. 'I'm going to bed. I suggest you do the same, if you can fit your lanky arse in here.'

She found her own space, whispering apologies to the sleeping men and women she stepped over, before disappearing into the shadows. Tor stood for a moment, at a loss. A quick glance around the so-called Keshin village was enough to tell him there wouldn't be anywhere to get a decent drink, so with little other choice, he crouched down and shuffled into the darkened chamber. It was warm inside, and filled with the unmistakeable odour of human bodies. Tor grimaced, looking around for an empty spot away from everyone else, but the only free section was next to Noon. He stepped over her – she was already asleep somehow, her breathing slow and deep – and settled himself between her and the twisted mat of twigs and branches that was the wall. From here, the entrance was a dull moon of yellow light, until someone pulled a gauze curtain over it. The whole place smelled strongly of rabbit.

'Just marvellous,' he murmured to himself. 'Absolutely marvellous.'

Someone from somewhere in the dark shushed him, so he lay back and closed his eyes. To cheer himself up he pictured Serena and Ainsel. They would be back in Mushenska now, going about their daily lives with no idea that their beloved Tormalin was currently sleeping in squalor. Serena and her skin that smelled of summer fruit, Ainsel and the smooth column of her neck. He pictured evenings they had spent together, lazy afternoons, and on the tail of that, he thought about the taste of their blood. Sex and blood: the two were always mingled, like a smell that brought back how it felt to be a child, or a song that holds the last memory of someone dear. The taste of their blood, the strength that it brought, and the touch of a willing hand. He was never quite sure which he craved the most – except that wasn't entirely true.

A small noise from beside him brought him back from his recollections. Noon had shifted in her sleep, her face turned up to the ceiling. In the dim light he could see that her eyes were squeezed shut, her mouth turned down at the corners, as though she were tasting something bitter. A cold hand walked down Tormalin's spine: she was having a nightmare. He thought of their conversation in the woods – could she be having the same dream again, the same one as Ainsel? If she was, that *had* to mean something. He had to know for certain.

Sitting up, he moved closer to the sleeping witch. He felt an odd pang of guilt, half expecting Vintage to appear and chastise him, and then he closed his eyes and slipped into the netherdark. Dreaming minds were pressed in closely all around him, but

266

Noon's was impossible to miss – she was the closest, and now that he knew her, it was almost familiar. He pushed away a brief memory of her warm hand on his neck and slipped through into her sleeping mind.

She was dreaming of a bright, sunlit day. White clouds daubed the horizon, and in all directions, there was grass as high as his waist; a tired, dusty green. There were large tents behind him, shaped like cones and draped with various animal skins and woven blankets and painted silks. There were horses here, and men and women with the horses. They were plains people, and they were going about their lives peaceably enough. He saw young men and women; warriors with horsehair vests and deer-skin trousers, with short, curving swords at their waists. He saw riders leading their horses to hunt, and a man turning a great side of meat over a fire. There was an old woman sitting amongst a crowd of children, and she was dancing a pair of puppets for them, telling them some story about the stars and the storm winds. It was a peaceful picture, full of the detail and warmth that told him it was a true memory, something cherished even. And then he remembered the distress on the fell-witch's face. He had not mistaken that.

Sensing a shape next to him, he looked down to see a child. She was around ten years old. Her black hair was tied back into a short, stubby tail and she carried a wooden sword in her hand. At once, all sense of peace and warmth vanished. Instead, Tor felt a wave of terror move through him, as sudden and as cold as a riptide. Threat was all around them, he realised, he just hadn't seen it before. Surely the Jure'lia would now arrive, coming from a blameless sky to kill them all.

'It's all connected.'

The girl's voice was soft, and she did not look at Tor when she spoke. Instead, she continued to stare keenly at the scene around her.

Tor waited, but there was nothing more. He stood for a

while with the child, making himself a shadow on the grass so that she would not notice him, but nothing came; no corpse moon, no wave of hungry black beetles, and she did not speak again. There were just the people, caught in this moment of living their lives, and this strange, serious girl, standing just beyond their circle, watching them. And the sense of a terrible calamity looming never lessened.

Quietly, a whisper on the breeze, Tor left. Whatever it was the girl faced, she would face it alone.

24

This was going to be bad.

Agent Lin knew it from the number of dark shapes against the evening sky. Six bats, their wings a blur, meant that they hadn't just sent a representative to deal with her – they had come themselves, with an entourage against the wilds of Sarn. Perhaps it was even the Drowned One herself. Wouldn't that be hideous?

She glanced at the wreckage of the winnowline beside her. They had had a brief rain shower earlier that day, which had filled the air with the smell of wet soot, and now parts of the thing were black and skeletal, while the corpse of the worm-touched monster that had delayed them merrily stank up the place. The main engine itself had been detached from the rest of the carriages in time and had survived more or less intact; the woman Pamoz was up there now, trying to get the thing moving again. She was, Agent Lin suspected, avoiding her, as were the small team of fell-witches who powered the contraption. Lin sneered to think of them. They were meek things, grateful for the tiny scraps of freedom thrown to them by the Winnowry, and, of course, now they were quietly furious that their precious winnowline was in jeopardy. Without it they might be forced to go back to their miserable cells.

There was a beating of wings and the bats were landing back down the line, kicking up dust. At the back, Lin noted one mount without a rider – her bat, the one she had sent back to the Winnowry, carrying her message.

'Fell-Lin.'

It was Father Eranis, his large hands held behind his back, his dark grey hair tossed around by the persistent wind. He was smirking, as he always was, but his eyes were cold. Behind him she could see the squat form of what was surely Sister Resn, her face a blank silver mask, and a fell-agent she did not know. The woman was short and stocky, her hair pulled back from her round face with a strip of blue material. She met Lin's eyes steadily, and Lin held herself very still. This agent was here to keep her in line, should she decide to misbehave. Not a good sign.

'Quite a mess, this, isn't it?' Father Eranis nodded at the remains of the carriages.

Lin pressed her lips together. 'I told you the girl was dangerous. She is very volatile. And how could I have predicted that she'd come to the winnowline as a means of escape?'

'Yes, that is quite unusual.' Father Eranis came alongside her. He smelled powerfully of soap. It made her nose itch. 'I had a hand in this project, you know, Fell-Lin. We had hoped that the winnowline would eventually encompass all of Sarn. Which is why I wanted to come and look at the ruins of it personally.' The smirk was gone from his face now, the lines at the corners of his mouth deep with displeasure. 'This is a significant setback. The passengers?'

Agent Lin briefly entertained the idea of burning him alive, but the other agent's eyes had not left her once. Control, always control. 'Before I sent the message to you, I got word to the next stop on this line. Men came with carts, and they were taken ahead.' She cleared her throat. 'Really, the damage is not so much—'

'It is not for you to say what the damage is, aberration.' The voice was a soft and dusty whisper, and at the sound of it, Agent Lin felt a genuine stab of dread. The Drowned One. She had not seen her alight from the bats. Father Eranis stepped to one side, his head lowered in respect, and the tiny figure came forward. Agent Lin saw her lined face, her wispy cap of hair, her grey skin. Everything of her spoke of great age and dust and despair. She wore the black wrappings of her order, stained grey in places with sea salt, and her hand – the fingers white and too soft – clasped the smooth end of her walking stick: a piece of carved driftwood. She was so pale that she looked powdered with the ash of the Fell-order – her pallor looked as though it might come away on your finger if you brushed the bony knob of her cheek. All colour, all joy had long since been washed away by her precious seawater. Behind her, Fell-Mary loomed.

'What do you know about the missing one, Fell-Lin?'

Agent Lin clasped her hands in front of her, feeling the soft friction of the calf-skin gloves. She dearly wanted to take them off, but to do so in front of Mother Cressin would be an insult bordering on a threat. At least she had knowledge to give the old crone – Pamoz the engineer had been reasonably helpful.

'The girl appears to be travelling with a woman called Lady de Grazon and an Eboran man.'

For the first time that Lin could remember, Mother Cressin looked faintly surprised. Near invisible eyebrows sent creases across her grey forehead.

'An Eboran? Out here?'

'He's a mercenary of sorts. I've heard all sorts of rumours about him in Mushenska, none of them savoury. It's de Grazon we should be taking notice of, Mother.' She paused. It was always difficult to call this woman by that title. She swallowed down her bile and continued. 'I think I know where she's going. According to Engineer Pamoz, the woman is a famous eccentric, obsessed with the Jure'lia, of all things.'

271

'Filth,' said Mother Cressin, mildly. 'A cancer from beyond this realm.'

'Yes, well. She was travelling to the Greenslick region, and it just so happens there's another Jure'lia-obsessed lunatic there. I've no idea why the witch is travelling with de Grazon, but Pamoz seemed to think she was working for the woman. It's a place to start.'

Mother Cressin nodded at the ground.

'Two people died in this mess, Fell-Lin. Eight more were injured. Two children – untainted children – were drained to a dead faint. You are one of our most controlled agents, I have been told. I see no evidence of control in this.' She gestured to the gutted carriages, and her voice became low and dangerous. 'Do you know why we don't send a whole army of agents after runaways, Fell-Lin?'

'Discretion, Mother.'

'The Winnowry performs a holy function. People trust us to keep them safe. All our movements out in the world must be quiet ones. To kill two innocents in pursuit of one fell-witch – tell me, what do you think the penalty should be?'

Lin stood very still. When she didn't answer, Mother Cressin cleared her dry throat.

'Of course, it's not you who pays the price, is it? I want you to know, Agent Lin, that it pains me that it is not you who suffers. You, after all, are the crack through which evil seeps into the world. What was the penalty last time you made a mistake such as this?'

Lin found that her mouth was clamped so tightly shut that she couldn't speak. With an effort, she forced herself to open her mouth, and her jaw popped audibly.

'It was a finger,' she said, and then, rushing on in the same breath, 'but he's just a child, Mother Cressin, please, for the mercy of Tomas—'

'A child born of forbidden copulation. Of evil. Of excrement.

272

We will, of course, make it look like an accident – he can never know how his life is used, we are not that cruel – but he might start to wonder at his luck. Ten years old, and missing two fingers. Perhaps we should make it an eye, just for the sake of variety.'

'No!' Lin almost reached for her, almost took hold of the tiny woman and wrenched the life force from her, but the other agent stepped forward, raising her arms slightly. Lin faltered.

'A finger, then, this time. Let's hope his mother is more careful in future.' The Drowned One raised her head, revealing eyes that were as colourless as her skin. 'Do your job, Fell-Lin. Fell-Noon belongs back at the Winnowry. Her living, breathing, traitorous self – or her ashes.'

Blood had dried on the bark, leaving it the colour of old meat. Oreon took hold of the squirrel's body, still flexible and slightly warm, and twisted it off the wickedly sharp thorn. She popped it in the basket tied to her back, and looked down to see her son doing the same with something she couldn't quite see.

''nother squirrel, Jaron?'

'Nah, Mum, bird. Red feather.' He briefly held up a small body, the scarlet slashes of the bird's flight feathers the brightest thing she could see. That was good. You didn't get a lot of meat off a red feather, not at this time of year, but they were tasty. Oreon took a handful of berries from a pouch at her waist and, leaning down carefully to avoid the bristling thorns, deposited a handful in the cup strapped to the intersection of branches. The animals in this forest were wild for these berries – over the years, she and her family had grown them in their tiny section of the Underthorn, cross-breeding varieties until they had a berry that was irresistible to the smaller forest creatures. So much so that they would force their bodies into these tiny, lethal spaces, and in their fervour would impale themselves. The Wild was strange – those words were with them always.

Jaron scrambled his way up and sat next to her. He was even better at moving through the thorns than she was. She patted his arm absently.

'You set your berries?'

'Aye.' He pulled off his gloves and fussed with his hair. 'Hey, who's that?'

They were on the very edge of the forest here, and high up, so that the plains fell away in front of them in a scrubby yellow-and-brown carpet and, far beyond that, the purple Bloodless Mountains were a jagged line. Three people were leaving the forest. They were riding the tough ponies that she often saw, making their way across the plains. She leaned forward, trying to get a better look.

'There were strangers in the Underthorn yesterday,' she said. 'I didn't see 'em, but they slept in the hunting den. Everyone was talking about it.'

They made a strange sight. In front was a shapely woman with dark brown skin and an explosion of black curly hair, hunched over her pony as though sheer determination could get them to their destination faster. In the middle was a young woman with a black hat, riding easily in her saddle but looking around continually. And at the end was the Eboran. Oreon sat up slightly, narrowing her eyes.

'Is he really one of those bloodsuckers, Mum?'

'It looks like it. Can't believe ol' Reen let them stay the night, whatever they was trading. Time was, an Eboran within miles of here was considered an act of war.'

'They're not dangerous any more, Mum, everyone knows that.' Jaron pushed his fingers through his hair, making it fall back from his forehead in a wave. He tried to oil it that way, sometimes. 'Blood lust killed 'em all out. And just one against all of us. He couldn't do nothing.'

Oreon pursed her lips. Oreon was too young to have heard the stories from his great-grandfather's own lips, but she remembered the look on the old man's face when he told them. He had been a gregarious man, more interested in his berry brews than on doing a proper day's work, but when he talked of the Carrion Wars all the good cheer would leave him; the stories of distant relatives slaughtered on battlefields and in their homes never seemed to fade with time. Those scars were deep for their people.

'He's very tall, isn't he?'

Oreon nodded. The Eboran, even lounging in his saddle, was an imposing figure. She could just make out his profile. As she watched, he pulled something from his belt and tipped it to his lips. Whatever it was, it was gone in one gulp. A shot of strong liquor, perhaps, or something else.

'Come on, my lad, let's get back to the Underthorn. I've seen enough blood for one day.'

The Wild was strange, but sometimes the world outside was stranger.

25

'And when will Mistress Hestillion be gracing us with her presence, exactly?'

Aldasair forced a smile on his face and transferred his attention to the old human woman with the melted face. Hestillion had told him to be polite at all times, particularly with more and more representatives from all over Sarn streaming into Ebora. Polite, but firm. It was inevitable, she had said, that the humans would see the terrible state of their people and home, but it wouldn't do to give the impression that they were desperate. They were still Ebora, they were still apart from the human rabble. It was important the human visitors did not lose sight of that fact.

However, Hestillion was increasingly absent from these uncomfortable conversations. She had been caught up by something he did not understand, and her face was lit from within with something he did not recognise, while he felt like he was being pulled out to sea by an invisible tide.

'She will be with us shortly, I'm sure,' he said, looking at his boots. 'As you can imagine, there is an awful lot for Hest – I mean, Lady Hestillion – to deal with at the moment.' He gestured around at the central plaza. For the first time in as long as he could remember, it was teeming with people: delegations from across Sarn, from Mushenska and Jarlsbad, Reidn and Finneral. A natural meeting place had grown here, sprouting from caravans and tents, while the officials from each gathering were given quarters inside the palace. Being one of the few Eborans left who wasn't bedridden, Aldasair had ended up with the task of finding them all places, of listening to their needs and making adjustments accordingly. At first he had been terrified. For the last few decades there had been only silence to deal with, the empty corridors of the palace, and the sense that everything was lost. He had gone weeks, months even, without having to talk to anyone, until the only person he saw with any regularity was Hestillion herself, and even then she was always too annoyed to talk to him for more than a few moments. Aldasair had been left to himself, and the tarla cards, and his days had been filled with the soft rasp of paper against paper, and a gentle cascade of images, weaving a web of inescapable doom. The cards had grown so familiar that even the frightening ones looked like old friends to him: The Broken Tower, with the tiny frightened figures falling from its windows; The Endless Death, featuring an old man bricked up inside his own tomb, still alive, his fingertips bloody stumps. The cards carried on their own infinite conversation, and Aldasair listened in, content that any role he had to play in the world had long since passed him by.

Only that wasn't the case any more. Almost, he could remember how it had been when he was very young, when he had had a sense of a future for himself. He had intended, he remembered now, to be an art merchant. He had loved painting, and paintings, very much. He was going to go out into the world and sell them, but that had been before everyone he knew had retreated to their rooms to cough out their lungs, and Aldasair had found himself suddenly alone. Answering the

277

irate questions of Mother Fast and the other diplomats was not what he had envisioned for himself, and it was frightening, but it was also something new. He had thought all new things forever lost to Ebora.

Mother Fast sniffed. 'It's all very well, boy, us being here and bringing our medicines and our knowledge, but if we are not permitted to see this god of yours, how are we supposed to help?'

And that puzzled him most of all. Despite all of these people coming to lend their aid, Hestillion had suddenly become incredibly protective of the Hall of Roots. No one was to see their god, she had told him. Not until she said so. The time, she said, was not right. Tell them to help the sick ones, she had told him, and so he did; healers now went to the Eborans suffering from the crimson flux, and sometimes they were even allowed to assist. And all the while, that strange light burned behind Hestillion's eyes.

Mother Fast was still glaring at him with her one good eye. He forgot, sometimes, that long gaps in conversations were considered rude. Aldasair opened his mouth to reply, when an imposing figure strode towards them from across the lawn. The man was a full head taller than Aldasair, which meant he towered over Mother Fast like a mountain. The hair on top of his head was yellow and wild, and he had a neat golden beard, braided here and there with tiny stone beads. He wore scuffed travelling leathers, festooned with more of the carved stone beads hanging from horsehair loops, and his bare arms were traced with ink. He had come in with the contingent from Finneral – Aldasair remembered, because even amongst that well-armed folk, this man's pair of war-axes had been formidable. He still wore them, slung at his belt, as easily as if they were made of leaves.

'You are in charge here, are you?' He spoke the plains language with a touch of an accent and looked Aldasair up and down with such an expression of frank concern on his face that Aldasair found himself quite unnerved.

For want of a better idea, Aldasair nodded.

'Stone knock me down. You're older than you look, I imagine?'

Aldasair blinked. The man looked no older than him, which meant that he was very young indeed, in Eboran terms.

'How old do I need to be?'

The man grinned, green eyes flashing. Aldasair had never seen a human with green eyes. 'Now, there's a bloody question. My name is Bern Finnkeeper. You are?'

Distantly, Aldasair was aware of Mother Fast's eye following them, her thin mouth twisted into a near invisible slash.

'I am Aldasair.'

'Good to meet you.' To his shock, Bern Finnkeeper took hold of his arm and gripped it fiercely. The strength in his long-fingered hands was surprising. 'There's no need for your people to die, Aldasair.' Bern Finnkeeper met his gaze steadily. 'No need for it. Now, what needs doing?' Then, before Aldasair could answer, the tall man had dropped his arm and was gesturing beyond the plaza. 'You've a lot of dead wood to the east, looks like it's been building up for decades, so you've got a deep layer of mulch under it. Once we've got that cleared, you'll have more space for these people and their nonsense.' He turned back, grinning happily. 'I'll start on that, shall I? I don't want to step on your stones, Aldasair, but I've a strong back and I'll be honest, days in a horse's saddle don't agree with me. I like to use my hands, if you understand me?'

'Uh . . .'

'I shall start there, then, but if you need any other heavy lifting done, you grab me. Go to my people, they're the ones trying to build a giant fire by your rockery – sorry about that – and ask for Bern. Actually, ask for Bern the Younger or you'll get a lot of funny looks. My father is a big man to my people.'

279

Aldasair swallowed and realised he'd been staring. He was trying to imagine a human man even bigger than this one, with his golden beard and green eyes.

'Thank you. I – anything you can do is much appreciated,' Aldasair took a deep breath. It was still dizzying to talk this much at once.

Mother Fast looked less impressed. 'We're not here to tidy your gardens, Eboran. We must heal your god. What good will a tidy garden do us when the worm people darken our skies again?'

'Our vision-singers had the same dream, Mother Fast,' said Bern the Younger. Aldasair did not ask how they already knew each other – Bern seemed to be the sort of person who became well known in a very short amount of time. 'And believe me, they've been shitting stones over it. But I am no healer!' He grinned again. 'There are more coming every day, and this city needs to be ready. I can help with that, at least. The healing of a god, well, I will leave that to your good self.'

Aldasair couldn't be sure, but he thought the look Bern shot Mother Fast was a challenging one, and certainly she pulled a face like she was chewing on something bitter. All at once keeping up with how the humans communicated with each other was too much to bear; he lifted a hand to rub at his forehead and saw that his fingers were trembling. He hoped that Bern hadn't noticed.

'Forgive me,' he said, straining to keep his voice steady. 'There are things I must see to in the palace.'

He turned away from them, his head down so that he might avoid being overwhelmed by their endless questions – but not quite fast enough to miss the concern in Bern the Younger's eyes. Keeping his back straight and walking slowly, Aldasair strode back across the plaza, promising himself a room full of silence, with just the tarla cards to read.

* * *

Hestillion was in the netherdark. The light was all around her, continually moving away and then back into her range, and she half pictured it as a startled bird, one not quite brave enough to settle on a permanent perch. She chased it, constantly trying to stay within its warmth and light; when she was there she could almost feel how Ebora had been. How it could be again.

'Talk to me, Ygseril,' she said, trying not to sound desperate or demanding. 'I know you are there. You do not have to hide from me.'

Silence. Hestillion was aware of the weight of the dream-roots around her, and very distantly, her physical body asleep next to the trunk of Ygseril. She had locked the doors from the inside, so that she could have this time alone. Aldasair hadn't understood why she wanted to be alone, but then it had been many decades since Aldasair had understood anything at all. For days now she had spent every spare moment here, chasing the light. The plan could change, and the humans could wait; Hestillion had important work to do.

'Ygseril. Please.'

The light grew, and Hestillion had the strangest sensation of something *pushing*, a membrane *breaking*, and then a cold wave that swept from her feet up to the top of her head.

You will not leave.

For a moment, Hestillion was lost. The shock was too great – she was a shed leaf, buffeted away from father-branch – and she thought she would be swallowed by it. Instead, she took hold of everything that she thought of as herself, and held it fast. The voice. The voice was real. It was soft and genderless, made more of thought than sound, existing as it did in the netherdark.

'No, Ygseril, I will not leave.' She swallowed down the tears. 'I will never leave you, not me. I knew, I knew you were not truly gone.'

What do you want?

Too many things to say. Hestillion was conscious of how delicate this connection was. Despite their physical proximity she was stretched to the very limit of her dream-walking, as deep as anyone could go without slipping into a permanent sleep, and the presence she felt was as soft as a shadow across skin. The smallest thing could break this link.

'To speak with you. To know how I can help.'

Help?

'Of course, Ygseril. Anything. Ebora –' Hestillion swallowed, aware this could be too much – 'Ebora needs you.'

Silence, and a shift in the tone of the light.

'Ygseril?'

You would give your help freely?

'Lord, in our ignorance we thought you had died. I would do anything to bring you back. Anything you require.'

Silence again. It was as if the great tree needed time to coalesce its thoughts after so many centuries of silence.

Dead. Was it her imagination, or did the god sound amused? *Not dead. Waiting.*

'Waiting for what?' asked Hestillion eagerly. Something was holding Ygseril back, she could tell that much. 'If I can give you what you need, I will.'

You are special. The shape of your mind. How it flits. Such a clever little shape.

Hestillion folded herself over, keeping the flare of joy inside lest it startle or embarrass Ygseril.

'I seek only to renew your glory for all of Ebora.'

A special child, continued the voice. It almost sounded dreamy now, distant. *So determined, so stubborn. You are willing to use everything you have, aren't you? Regardless of the cost, you would see your Ebora revived.*

Edging closer to the light-voice, Hestillion nodded. 'It is all I have dreamed of, great tree-god, all my long life.'

And yet my roots are still rigid with cold and death. For all your efforts, I am still a corpse.

Hestillion's stomach fluttered.

'Tell me what I can do.' She tried to sound confident, but a memory of how small she was here, and how dark it was, flickered at the edges of her mind. 'How can I bring you to life, great one?' More silence, so she tried a different approach. 'Perhaps, if you told me what happened at the end of the Eighth Rain – if you told me what did this to you, I could help.'

No. The voice was no longer a nervous bird; it was an iron door, closed tight. *Small flitting mind, let me sleep. Make my roots thirst and stretch again, if you can, but let me sleep.*

Hestillion let the silence grow. She did not want to go back to the palace, with all its problems of diplomacy and who was eating what where. Not yet.

'I have summoned the world to our gates to save you, Ygseril,' she said eventually. 'They have brought healers and mystics, men and women of alchemy. They are eager to help, all of them. Perhaps they can make your roots thirst again.'

Concentrating, aware that she was performing for her god, she dream-crafted the scene in the central plaza as it had been earlier that morning: the teeming caravans and tents, the long tables laden with food, the humans walking and talking and eating. She brought every inch of her dream-walker skill to the vision, crafting the watery sun in the pale sky, the mud from hundreds of boots that had been dragged across the shining stones.

'Ebora,' she said, 'has not been so lively in centuries.'

How did you make them come?

'I spun a lie for them, Ygseril, and I sent it out into the netherdark. A special dream, for especially receptive minds. I told them that the Jure'lia, the old enemy, were coming back, and without Ebora they would all perish. Without you and

283

the war-beasts born amongst your branches, Sarn will fall to the worm people in a single turn of the true moon.'

The voice did not reply immediately. Instead, the soft light increased in brightness, flickering oddly. Hestillion recoiled, holding fast to the netherdark to stop herself from jolting awake. When the voice did speak again, it sounded different.

You extraordinary creature, it said. *Such a thing to think, such a confection to craft.* The light faded, and then came back. It seemed to hang over Hestillion like a shroud, and for the first time she felt like she was being truly observed. *Tell me again, who you are.*

'I am your servant, the Lady Hestillion, of the Eskt family, born in the year of the green bird.'

Yes, but who are you? What holds you at your core, Lady Hestillion? All the tiny disparate pieces, what threads them together? What single thing?

Hestillion briefly found herself lost for an answer. Ygseril sounded strange – alert somehow, engaged in a way she hadn't felt before – but she hadn't the faintest idea what the god was getting at. She went for the obvious answer.

'You, my lord.' She collapsed the vision of the plaza, and instead summoned a vision of Ygseril himself, silver branches spreading over the palace roof. 'Your roots are what hold me together at my core.'

Only silence answered her.

'Ygseril? Are you there?'

As if her words were the catalyst, the god-light began to fade, moving so fast she could not follow it, and then she was alone in the netherdark, the cold press of dead roots all around her.

'But you are not dead,' she told herself. 'Not dead, after all.'

Slowly, she came back to herself. Her legs were numb from sitting curled on the hard roots, and there was a deep chill in her bones, but she hardly felt it. Ygseril was not dead, simply hiding. He might be inert, but he was reachable. Turning to face the door, she thought first of going to Aldasair, but would he even understand what she had discovered? And then she thought of the humans, swarming outside their gates, eager to help but also eager to help themselves. They brought trade, and life, and attention; these were valuable things. But perhaps . . . perhaps the salvation of Ygseril was her destiny after all. Who else had stayed? Who else had kept the small seed of hope?

'Only I,' she murmured through cold lips. 'And this shall be my own secret, a little longer. Just until I bring him back.'

26

It's possible to see, with a great deal of optimism and imagination, how the Greenslick region was once quite beautiful. There are the enormous scars in the landscape which were once the great lakes, some as deep as mountains are high, before the Jure'lia's so-called 'maggots' came and drained them dry (there is nothing at the bottom of these chasms, not a single fish bone – all living things were consumed) and if you close your eyes and squint, you can imagine that the great swathes of shining green are the grasses of picturesque valleys. But if you go and look closer, of course, and let go of your optimism, you will see that the greenish covering is hard as steel, and there are bodies suspended in it, carrying their final, terrified expressions as the varnish trapped and suffocated them.

Greenslick was once called Trisladen, and it was ancient and beautiful. A great many fanciful stories came out of Trisladen, with its kings and queens, and its heraldic knights. They were the sorts of stories I demanded from my nanny when I was a child. 'Tell me of brave Princess Guinne, and her quest for the enchanted jewels at the

286

bottom of Witch Lake.' You know the sort. In fact, there was a time when the mythology of Trisladen rivalled Ebora itself, and indeed, from what I can gather from the sources that are left, it was a place with a long and meandering history, and a great love of art and murals in particular. Even in recent times, it was a rich place, mining gold and copper from its hills and fish from its lakes. The Eighth Rain put a swift end to all of that. The Jure'lia found it very much to their tastes, I'm afraid, and that particular invasion put a great deal of its weight there. The maggots descended, the armies of Trisladen were eaten or hollowed out, and the magnificent castles were lost. It is a wasteland now, an eerie place fit only for the mad and the lost.

Greenslick does have one item of note: the lands of Esiah Godwort. His family lived on the very borders of Trisladen for generations, and it was on their lands that a Behemoth crashed at the very abrupt end of the Eighth Rain. I can imagine Godwort's ancestors, half afraid and half stubborn, refusing to leave lands poisoned and left ragged by the Jure'lia. And eventually, perhaps, they came to realise that there might be profit to be made from the gigantic corpse that happened to land in their back garden. At any rate, they built an enormous wall around the thing, and reinforced it over the generations until it truly is a fortress. I can no longer tell you if they hoped to keep the ghosts in, or keep pilferers out.

Extract from the journals of Lady Vincenza 'Vintage' de Grazon

Out from under the cover of the thorn forest it was an anxious journey. Tor found himself glancing at the sky frequently, expecting a flittering movement across the sky to herald their doom, while the landscape around them offered little else to look at. Vintage assured them that the border of Greenslick was no more than four days' ride, that the region was hidden from view by the elevation of the land, but that had been all the scholar was willing to say. She kept her own counsel, her eyes on the horizon. Tor sensed that she was now so focussed on reaching Godwort's compound that she had thrust all thought of the Winnowry's retribution to one side. She could be very wilful when she wanted to be. Which was all the time, in his experience.

The girl, at least, seemed to share his concern. More than once she caught his eye after they had both been scanning the clouds, and she had raised an eyebrow ruefully. That had surprised him. It was as though the further away they travelled from her old prison, the more she was becoming someone else. Finally becoming *herself*, perhaps. However, when they stopped for the night her sleep was always disturbed, tossing and turning as though tormented. Tor did not venture into her dreams again – not with Vintage so close at hand – but he did ask her about it one morning. She rubbed at her eyes, and shook her head.

'I've no more akaris,' she said. 'It was the only thing that kept the nightmares away. Well, most of them.'

'When you have bad dreams—'

'Not the one about the worm people. I've not had that since the Winnowry. These are just –' She lifted her hand to her mouth, and briefly touched her lips to a loose piece of skin on her thumb. 'When I have the nightmare, it's just the same memory over and over again. A broken one.'

Tor nodded, looking away. He thought of a small girl, a wooden sword in her hand, and a sense of impending doom. 'A memory of the thing that happened to you when you were a child.'

'It didn't happen to me. *I* happened to other people.' She

squeezed her eyes shut and when she opened them again, her expression was urgent, desperate almost. 'I can't remember what happened. Not all of it.'

'What do you mean, you can't remember?'

'I know what the conscquences were.' She lowered her voice. 'No avoiding those. But the rest of it. And it's really important I don't remember. It's dangerous to remember. Dangerous for everything.'

Tor frowned. 'If you can't remember, how do you know it's dangerous? Memories can't hurt you.'

'I just know.' Noon bit her lip, looking away to where Vintage rode ahead of them. 'And it's best if you don't ask me about it any more.'

As it turned out, they did not receive a visitor until the night before the valleys and empty lakes of Greenslick revealed itself. There was a crescent moon, blurred with fog as though seen through a misted window, and a cold wind was whipping across the grasses, filling the night with an unsettling wail. Tor pulled up his hood, and Vintage threw some more sticks on the fire. It appeared to be on the verge of going out.

'What I would really like now,' said Tor, 'is a very large glass of wine. Do you know, Vintage, that you promised me that I would have wine every night I was in your service? Do you remember that?'

'Did I?' Vintage clutched her chin and glared at the fire as though deep in thought. 'I am quite certain I would never promise anything as ridiculous as that, my darling.'

Tor narrowed his eyes at her, and held his hands out towards the sputtering fire. 'Wine, every bloody day. Did we write it down? I'm sure I have the paper somewhere.'

Noon leaned forward, her hand turned towards the fire, and it suddenly bloomed into emerald flames. Tor and Vintage both jumped back a little, and Noon shrugged.

'We don't have wine, but we don't have to be cold.'

'Well, yes, my dear, but I am also rather fond of my eyebrows.'

'What did you take the energy from to do that?'

Noon glanced at him from under her brow. 'From the grass under us. I lived on these plains as a kid. I always took from the grass.'

'There's certainly enough of it. So there will be a patch of dead, frozen grass where you're sitting now?'

'Would you rather a dead, frozen Eboran where you're sitting now?'

'Quiet, the both of you. Can you hear that?'

There was a sound, distant and growing closer. It made Tor think of a book falling downstairs, leather covers flapping. In a moment, he was on his feet, the Ninth Rain in his hands.

'Where is it? Can you see?'

The sky was black as slate, suddenly threatening. Vintage unhooked the crossbow from her waist. 'We should find shelter.'

'Oh yes, perhaps we could hide under the grass. Witch, you'd better gather some more of your winnowfire. If we can surprise her, we might have a better chance.'

'No, wait!' She had her hands cupped over her eyebrows, peering at the sky. 'I can see her. It's Fulcor, it's just Fulcor. Put your bloody sword away.'

'*Your* bat? Why is it still following us?'

'I don't bloody know, do I?'

The great creature landed a few feet away from them, leathery wings beating the grass flat. It shuffled towards the fire, moving in the ungainly way bats did when faced with horizontal ground. Their hobbled ponies snorted and shifted, edging away from the beast as best they could. Noon went to it, stroking its squashed velvety nose.

'That thing could lead the Winnowry straight to us.' Tor frowned at the bat. It had a pair of dead rabbits in its mouth, which it dropped at Noon's feet. 'Can't you make it go away?'

'I'd rather make *you* go away. Fulcor saved my life, and probably yours too.'

Vintage had approached the creature too, peering closely at its enormous crinkled ears. Fulcor made a snuffling noise, apparently enjoying the attention.

'The lad does have a point, Noon, my dear. This lovely girl is hardly inconspicuous, is she?'

'She doesn't seem to pay much attention to what I think.' Noon pulled the silver whistle from round her neck and gave four shrill blasts on it. The bat twitched her ears once, and shook herself all over, but did not move from her patch on the grass. 'See? I think she's like me. Fulcor wanted to be free all along, and now she does what she likes.' Noon bent down and picked up the rabbits, turning her face away from them, but Tor thought he caught a hint of blush around her cheeks. She was, he realised, embarrassed to have such a sentimental thought about an animal. 'Besides, Fulcor saves our skins and brings us dinner. That makes her more useful than most people I've ever met.'

Fulcor had gone by the time dawn spread its watery light across the plains. They cooked the rabbits, eating one for breakfast and parcelling the other away for later. From there the morning was filled with monotonous riding and featureless grass, but the weather had turned. The sky arched over them like a blue-glass bowl, and the sun was relentless, so that Tor soon found he had to remove his cloak and bundle it on his lap, and Noon took off her hat and fanned her face with it. There was no one out here to see the tattoo on her forehead, after all.

All morning they climbed a gradual incline until they stood at the summit of a hill, and falling away below them was the ruined landscape of Greenslick. Tor grimaced. He had been here before with Vintage, and the view had not improved.

'What is wrong with this place?' Noon looked paler than

she had a moment ago. She reached up and absently wiped the sweat from her forehead.

'The scars of the worm people,' said Vintage. Her mouth was turned down at the corners. 'Quite a sight, isn't it?'

Once a land of thickly wooded hills and bountiful lakes, Greenslick was a barren, broken place. The hills were raw heaps of stone and earth, mostly half collapsed – Tor could see the evidence of landslides everywhere – with many sporting thick swathes of the shining varnish. The lakes were dark holes, filled with shadows. In the distance, Tor could just make the scar that was the ruins of Trisladen's largest city, a confusion of rubble and varnish. On their last visit, Vintage had insisted they make a pilgrimage there. It was not a memory Tor looked back on with any fondness.

They moved off down the hill, travelling through the last vegetation they would see for some time, until they came to a stone obelisk, standing alone in the patchy grass. There were words carved on it.

'Do you remember what it says, Tormalin, my dear?'

Tor sighed. 'If I remember correctly, it says something incredibly cheery like, oh, "witness the graveyard of Trisladen" and "something something despair".'

'It also lists the number of people killed in the Eighth Rain, in this region alone,' said Vintage. 'It is a very sobering number.'

Through the sweltering afternoon they reached the bottom of the grassy hill and began to climb another. The difference was significant. Stripped of its trees and foliage the hill was a rubble of earth and stone, liable to shift underfoot at any moment. Repeatedly, Vintage told them to go carefully and slowly, stopping a few times to send Tor ahead to look for the safest path. Eventually, they crested this hill also and, finally, the home of Esiah Godwort was revealed, crouching on the very edge of Greenslick.

'It's so alone,' said Noon, genuine puzzlement in her voice. 'How can he exist out here by himself?'

The mansion sizzled under the wide sky. One look at it should have been enough, Tor would think later – the place already looked flyblown and finished, a mouldering corpse. It reminded him faintly of home, which should have been the biggest warning sign. It was built from dusty red brick, hazy in the heat, with flat black windows like blind eyes. They were dirty. Behind the sprawling house was a tall wall, and behind that, another so large that it resembled the hills that rose all around. It was impossible to see what was hidden behind it.

'Godwort is rich,' said Vintage, although she looked pained. 'When you are rich, it is possible to live how you want. You see that road?' She pointed to a stretch of bare track leading from the mansion to the east. 'A constant stream of goods comes up that road, bringing him and his son food, wine, building supplies, paper, ink, soap.' She shrugged. 'Years ago, he himself would travel, but these days, he prefers the isolation of Greenslick.'

'There's nothing on that road now,' Noon pointed out, and she was right. Nothing moved on the road. Nothing moved anywhere on the barren landscape.

Vintage frowned. 'Come on, let's get down to the gates.'

The house itself was also surrounded by an imposing granite wall – this was a family keen on walls – and on Vintage's previous visit there had been guards too, well-paid ones who took a keen interest in anyone unexpected approaching. Now, under the sweltering sun, there was no one to be seen. The tall wrought-iron gate stood open a few inches, and when Tor poked his head inside, he was met with an empty courtyard, flagstones dusted with rotting straw. Falling into silence, they led their ponies to the stables and made them as comfortable as they could. An empty bucket lay on its side in front of the empty guards' quarters. The silence was a weight hanging over their heads.

Tor cleared his throat. 'Perhaps he's dead,' he said. Silence rushed in again, and he almost imagined he could feel it, a pressure against his eardrums. He thought of the last vials of blood, hidden within his jacket. 'How old is he, Vintage? I never did get to see him the last time we were here.'

Vintage was staring up at the dark windows of the house as if she hoped to see a face looking out at them. Any human face would be a comfort at this point. 'Not so old. Besides which, he has a son, a full retinue of servants, a veritable army of guards . . .' She picked nervously at her shirt. 'We'll go up to the house. Come on.'

As they crossed the courtyard, Noon fell in next to Tor.

'What happened the last time you were here?'

'Well, Madam Vintage went up to the big house to conference with our recluse, while I was, uh, invited to wait in the guardhouse. As it happened, I won three rounds of cards before Vintage came stomping back, a look like thunder on her face. Esiah Godwort is very selective about who he opens his compound to.'

'He opens it to no one, my dear,' said Vintage, 'but I'm not taking no for an answer this time. Ah, here we are.'

The door was carved from a black wood and featured a pattern of leaping fish; no doubt once it had been very beautiful, but the varnish had mostly worn away and the wood had turned grey in patches. There was a huge ornate brass knocker, but it too had seen better days, and it had turned green at the edges. Rather than knocking, Vintage leaned her weight on the door and it slowly creaked open.

'Hello? Esiah?'

They stepped through into a blessedly cool foyer, thick with shadows. Dust danced in the light from the windows, and the room itself was dominated by an enormous painting hanging on one wall. It depicted, to Tor's surprise, a magnificent war-beast – a griffin stood poised on a jagged outcropping of rock, a bright slash of blue feathers at its throat, while a clouded, storm-tossed sky boiled in the distance. It was, in Tor's opinion, remarkable work, and he thought he even recognised the artist – the near legendary Micanal, who had vanished with his Golden Fox expedition – but its majesty was lessened somewhat by the squalor surrounding it. There were crumpled papers on the unswept floor, discarded sacks, a scattering of muddy footprints, long since dry. A set of stairs swept up to a darkened landing, while corridors leading away from the foyer were crowded with shadows and seemingly abandoned furniture. One corridor looked as though an attempt had been made to cordon it off – the space was filled with upended tables and chairs and cabinets.

'Can you hear that?' Noon was looking up the stairs.

'I can't hear anything,' said Tor. He was starting to feel irritable. 'Because the place is empty. All this way, all that trouble, to stand in an empty house. Perhaps we could find the kitchens? I want a decent meal before we go anywhere.'

'Be quiet,' snapped Vintage. 'What can you hear, Noon?'

'Something, so soft . . .' She closed her eyes for a moment, and then, in a much louder voice, called, 'Hello?'

Tor jumped, cursing himself. 'They're all dead and gone. Come on, Vintage, let's go—'

'Hello? Are you there?' Noon was walking towards the stairs, with Vintage following. Tor sighed and went after them, but he could also hear the sound now – a low muttering, constant and so quiet it was barely there. Noon led them to the top of the stairs and then across the landing. They passed a number of closed doors, and a few open rooms. Sunlight soured by dirty windows lay in pools on the thickly carpeted floors, and Tor had glimpses of furniture, of bookshelves, all covered in dust. The sense of desolation grew.

'There's someone down here.' Noon led them to the last room. It was large and spacious, with a great bank of windows across the far wall, but they had all been covered over with huge sheets of paper and parchment, filling the room with a strange yellowish glow. It had clearly been a study, with bookcases lining the walls to either side, but the desks and tables had been pushed up against the walls, covered as they were in open books, dirty plates and empty glasses. In the middle of the room was a thick rug, and on that were a number of oil lamps. Sitting amongst them was a man. Slowly he stood up.

'Esiah?'

He was, Tor guessed, middle-aged for a human, a handsome well-built man with thickly curling dark hair and a well-shaped beard that had only a dusting of grey across his cheeks. The man's eyes were hooded with thick eyelids – a lack of sleep, perhaps – and he had striking, expressive eyebrows. He wore a dusty red velvet coat which looked ridiculous, given the weather outside, and a stained shirt. The dun-coloured trousers he wore were smeared with dust.

He opened his mouth, but all that came out was a hoarse croak. He shook his head, and tried again.

'Who are you?'

Vintage strode into the room, a stricken expression of concern on her face. She went over to the man and smoothed down his lapels, blinking at the dust that came off him in little clouds.

'Esiah, what have you done? What's going on here?'

The man looked down at her, a perplexed expression on his face.

'Lady de Grazon? Is that you?' He patted her hands absently. 'It looks like you, but I told everyone to leave. Quite sure of it.'

'Master Godwort, why did you ask everyone to leave? Is there danger here?'

For a moment the man just stared at Tormalin, his mouth

working silently within his black beard. Then he shook his head. 'They told me you had an Eboran manservant, Vincenza, but I didn't believe them. Not even you, I said, could be so eccentric.'

Vintage opened her mouth to speak, but he waved her off, taking a step backwards into his circle of lamps and papers. He gestured at the ground. 'It's quieter when the house is empty, which is better. I can think. I still have so much to figure out.'

Noon had sidled further into the room, her eyes on the parchments pinned over the windows. They all featured elaborate pencil-and-ink drawings of the various forms of Jure'lia; close-ups of the burrowers, their sharp legs like blades, the bulbous bodies of the maggots, the mothers in a group, cresting a hill.

'Esiah, you don't even have guards on your front gate.' Vintage was frowning deeply now. 'Are you telling me the compound is unguarded too? What has happened here?'

'It's better when it's quiet,' said Esiah again. He was staring down at the papers on the floor. 'I need to think. There's so much to think about.'

Silence filled the room. Vintage seemed to be at a complete loss, taken aback by the scattered thoughts of her old colleague. Tormalin stepped from foot to foot. This was useless. They should leave and pretend this entire journey never happened.

'You need food.'

Tor looked up. Noon had approached Esiah Godwort, trying to catch his eye. 'Master Godwort? You need food, and so do we. Where are your kitchens?'

The man blinked at her for a moment, as if wondering why there was a young woman in his study, or perhaps he was trying to remember what the word kitchens meant.

'In the basement, under the central wing. Go back to the foyer, and go down the stairs behind the ones that led you up here.' Briefly he looked steadier, as though giving directions had cleared some of the fog from his mind, but then he looked away, staring at the corner of the room.

'Tormalin, let's have a look. See what food we can find for Master Godwort.'

Tor left the room just behind Noon, not troubling to lower his voice.

'Did Vintage give you permission to order me about? That would be just like her.'

'I'm hungry. Aren't you hungry?'

They passed a room with an open door, and Tor found his eyes caught by a flash of shiny metal. He paused and peered into the room. A moment later, Noon joined him.

It was a bedroom, dominated by a huge four-poster bed, the covers thrown back haphazardly and then left that way. There were pools of discarded shirts, trousers and underclothes all around, and a wardrobe standing open revealing an extensive collection of expensive clothes. To one side, by a window burning with daylight, was a partial suit of armour on a wooden stand – the metal had a greenish tinge, and the plates were joined with dark brown leather.

'That's winnow-forged metal,' said Tor softly. The armour was a thing of beauty – shining epaulets, greaves, a shirt of delicate-looking mail – and it appeared to be only half finished. A helmet stood atop it, an elaborate, fanned creation with a crosspiece to protect the nose and flared wings for the cheeks. 'Such a thing would cost a fortune. His guards have an impressive collection of winnow-forged swords, which they keep for venturing into the compound – I saw them the last time I was here – but an entire suit is an investment.'

'Godwort doesn't seem to be short on funds. Especially now he doesn't have to pay any servants.'

'This is his son's room.' Tor poked his boot into a pile of clothes on the floor. 'I recognise the smell of young, untidy man anywhere.'

Noon raised her eyebrows. 'I'll take your word for it.' She pressed her fingers to a dresser, and then stepped back towards the door. 'Everything in here is covered in dust. Thick dust.'

They exchanged a look, and then left without speaking. The kitchens were where Godwort had said they would be – his mind wasn't that addled, at least – and there they gathered a quick dinner of cheese and cured meats. All the bread was mouldy, but there were jars of preserves and several smoked fish hanging in a larder. When they took their finds back upstairs, they found Vintage and Esiah sitting on the floor together. Vintage still looked deeply concerned, but she was nodding encouragingly as Esiah spoke.

'Yes, Esiah, I agree that it would be a useful thing to know, but so few of these things survived.'

Godwort tapped a finger to a sheet of paper. It contained a drawing of what could only be a Behemoth, its shadowy form divided with notes and lines in a bright green ink.

'The heart of it. I need to solve the heart of it. What is it that lies in the heart of a Behemoth? How does it work?'

Vintage looked up at the two of them and gave the tiniest shrug.

'We have food,' said Noon. She put it down on the floor next to them, and began to peel one of the cheeses.

'But Esiah, my dear, surely the way to solve that problem would be to go and look at the thing. You do have one on your doorstep, after all.' Vintage laughed, a touch nervously, but Esiah lifted his hands to his head and grasped at his hair.

'No,' he said, very quietly. 'No no no. No no no.'

Tor found that he couldn't bring himself to sit with them. The sense of something wrong here was very strong. Where was everyone else? It reminded him of Noon's dream; the overpowering weight of doom, hovering just out of sight. He caught Vintage's eye; she looked stricken.

'Well, perhaps we could help you with that, my dear, if you

do not wish to re-enter the compound yourself.' Vintage cleared her throat. 'You know, of course, that I have longed to observe your extraordinary Behemoth specimen up close. Perhaps we could go and look at it for you, the heart of this beast. Bring back anything we find useful, make sketches, observations. You know I have a talent for this.'

Esiah Godwort made a strangled noise, and when he lifted his head his eyes were wet. Vintage continued.

'I know, Esiah, that you are very fond of your secrets, and that we have negotiated before and I have never got the better of you. Well, I have something new to offer. You see this girl I've brought with me?'

She gestured at Noon, who was busily munching her way through a slab of cheese liberally spread with jam. The fell-witch swallowed hard.

'What?'

'She's a fell-witch, Esiah,' said Vintage, pretending not to see Noon's raised eyebrows. 'She works for me now too, and she is quite capable of producing winnowfire. As soon as I saw it, I thought of you and Tyron's suit of armour. He is still collecting pieces for it, I assume?'

'The armour,' said Esiah, his voice utterly flat. 'The armour.'

'Yes, the armour of winnow-forged steel. I remember well your son's pride in all he had constructed so far, and just imagine, my darling, how his face will light up when you tell him—'

Abruptly Esiah Godwort was on his feet, scrambling back from the circle of lamps as though he feared to be bitten by something there. He bumped into the far wall and turned away from them, cowering as if from a blow.

'Go! You have to go! Get out, leave this place, get out of my sight, damn you.'

Vintage stood up. Her normally warm brown face had gone a milky grey, but as Tor watched he saw her gather herself.

Lady Vincenza 'Vintage' de Grazon was not to be so easily turned away from her path.

'Please, Esiah. Tell us what's wrong. How can we help?'

'There is no helping me. Nor any of us. This world is poisoned. Seeded with filth, death growing in the Wild.' The man took an agonised, watery breath that was half a sob. When he spoke again he sounded more awake and alert than he had since they'd arrived, but it was a voice heavy with sorrow too. 'It's the compound you want, isn't it? Go then. Go. The gate is unlocked and, the gods know, I can't look at it any more. Do what you must, but leave me alone. Now.'

27

The Winnowry's giant bats (or to give them their proper name, Targus Black-eye Bats) are originally from the mountainous region of Targ. It's a place that has long intrigued me, I must admit – all evidence points to a cataclysm taking place there millennia ago, long before even the very first visit from the Jure'lia – but its reputation as a cursed landscape means that it is absolutely impossible to book a passage there. No one travels to Targ, alas.

Except that wasn't always true. We know, of course, that when the early followers of Tomas were laying the foundations for their delightful prison for women, some of them did travel to Targ, and we know that they came back with a clutch of Targus Black-eye young. As a side note: I would dearly love to know why they travelled to Targ in the first place. With its bleak chasms and towering mountains you would need a very good reason to go. Perhaps the reason is hidden somewhere in Tomas's private writings; of the secrets he brought back from the sea, did one contain a reason to go to Targ? Or more intriguing still, does the region have a connection with winnowfire?

Either way, the young bats were raised at the Winnowry, as were their offspring, until they knew no other home, and generations of the creatures flew from the spindly chirot tower at the top of the Winnowry. They are carnivorous animals, hunting birds and smallish mammals, but they also enjoy fruit – on one memorable occasion I caught a fully grown Targus Black-eye feasting on the grapes in the vine forest. It must have been a rogue, having fled from the Winnowry – I can't imagine that even such a huge winged creature could fly all the way from Targus to my forest. I chased it off with a stick, the bugger.

By all accounts they are loyal, intelligent creatures, with a tendency to fixate on their keeper, or other close human.

Extract from the journals of Lady Vincenza
'Vintage' de Grazon

The day was swiftly dying, and the three of them stayed the night in Esiah Godwort's enormous empty house, each finding an abandoned room to bed down in. Tormalin woke in the early hours and went down to the kitchens, looking for food and a bottle of wine to ease him back to sleep. On his way back he noticed that there was a band of buttery light underneath the door of Esiah Godwort's study, and he could hear the dry noise of paper against paper; perhaps the man had been driven mad from a lack of sleep. From Noon's room he could hear small noises of distress, muffled with sleep, and he stood there for some time, one hand pressed lightly against the door. He was curious, but he was also tired.

Back in his own room, camped on a bed thick with dust, he opened the wine and found that he no longer wanted it. Instead, he reached into his bag and retrieved one of the last vials of blood – blood donated by Ainsel. Turning the glass between his fingers, he watched the crimson fluid swirling thickly by the light of his single candle. Years ago, when Ebora had only been a few years into its blood-lust, a coating had been developed for glass vessels that kept blood from growing thick too quickly, and he had made sure to pack several jars in his bags when he left the city. Tormalin unstopped the vial and pressed it quickly to his lips. The blood was no longer even in shouting distance of fresh, and it did little to alleviate his weariness, but the taste of Ainsel was still there, the memories of her warm skin sweet against his tongue. For a few moments the abandoned room felt less lonely.

Pinching out the light and crawling beneath the musty covers, Tormalin thought of Noon again, caught in the repeated nightmare that wasn't a nightmare, over and over. Eventually, he slept.

The girl wriggled deeper into the blankets, the horsehair rough against her bare feet. It was midday, and the walls of her mother's tent glowed faintly with captured sunlight. This was good. If it was bright outside, they would be less likely to see what she was up to.

She reached into the basket and pulled out the bushel of rala root her mother had harvested earlier that morning. It was dying fast, the long green leaves that sprouted above ground were already wilted and soft, but there was enough life left in them for what she needed – she could feel it through her fingertips, ticklish and alive and leaking.

The girl looked up to the entrance of the tent, checking again that her mother wasn't going to make a sudden appearance, but the flap was closed, and outside she could hear the gentle, everyday sounds of her people: voices raised in greeting, gossip and command, the huff and chuff of horses being tended, the faint sound of Mother Fast singing successful hunting to them all. There was the steady thump of axe against wood,

304

the sound of other children playing and calling to each other, but within the tent everything was still. This was her time, a brief moment alone where she could do what she wanted. And there was only ever one thing she wanted.

The girl wrapped the fingers of one hand around the rala root, and held her other hand out in front of her. The living greenness of the plant beat gently against her fingers, almost as though it wanted her to take it. In the sun-hazed gloom of the tent, the girl grinned.

The rala leaves crumpled and turned brown. The bulbous heart-shaped root, so good when cooked in stews, grew wrinkled and shrunken. After a few moments, the ends of the leaves turned black and curled up.

Almost triumphantly, the girl held up her other hand, her small fist clenched, and a ball of greenish-blue flame winked into life around it. The eldritch fire began at her wrist and formed a point above her closed fingers, flickering and dancing wildly.

Unable to help herself, the girl whooped with delight and the flames grew a little higher, filling the tent with shifting, other-worldly light. She no longer cared that someone might notice the light from outside; her chest was filled with a sense of floating, of *being apart*. There was nothing but the flame.

The inside of the tent was painted with light. The blankets, the bed rolls, her mother's cooking pots, her books, her scrolls, her precious bottles of ink, the girl's wooden toys, her wooden practice sword, the dirty cups and the crumpled clothes – they were all transformed, captured in a glow that made the girl think of the waters of the Sky Lake. She wondered if this was what it was like to live underwater.

Her hand did not burn, but the tent was filling with heat, and she could feel pinpricks of sweat under her hair and on her back. The rala root was a collection of soft, blackened sticks in her hand – there was a smell, like rot, like old mushrooms and

305

harvest – and the flames were dying now, sinking back towards her fingers. Desperate, the girl reached out without thinking, seeking more of that green life, and plunged her free hand into her mother's basket of greens.

The flames roared back into life, shooting towards the gathered ceiling of the tent in a wild plume of shimmering blue, and at that moment the tent flap was thrown back.

'Noon!'

Her mother shuffled rapidly into the tent, pulling the flap tight behind her. The flame swirled wildly for a moment as the girl tried to control it, licking against the dried flowers hanging above. They lit up like tapers, the blue-green light turning a more familiar orange as it came into contact with something to burn, and then her mother was cursing and shouting, snatching down the burning plants and smothering them quickly with blankets. The beautiful fire was gone, and the tent was thick with heat and the bitter stench of smoke. When the fires were out, her mother fixed her with a look. There was a smear of soot on her cheek, and her black hair was a tumbled mess.

'Noon! What have I told you about this?'

The girl hung her head, rubbing her fingers together to brush away the dead rala root. 'Not to do it.'

Her mother sat heavily across from her daughter. 'And?'

'That it is bad.'

'Noon. What have I raised? A little frog that croaks out words? Come on.'

Noon looked up. Her mother's face was a still shape in the gloom of the tent, her skin warm and alive. Her eyes glinted with exasperation, but the anger was already fading.

'That the winnowfire is dangerous. That I could burn myself, or other things. That I could burn the tent down.'

'You nearly did this time. Not to mention wasting an entire basket of decent food.' Her mother tipped the basket up so

306

that Noon could see the inside of it, revealing a sad pile of blackened vegetation. She sighed. 'Continue.'

'That no one must know I can do it. That if they find out –' Noon stopped, fidgeting – 'the Winnowry will come and take me away.'

'And they will, my sweet. I won't be able to stop them. Mother Fast won't be able to. None of us will. They'll take you far from the plains, and I won't see you again.'

Noon pushed the blankets away, sitting up properly. 'But how could they ever know, Mum? I will keep it secret, I promise. No one will ever see. I could use the winnowfire to be a proper warrior! I could protect us, keep us always warm when the snow comes!'

Her mother watched her for a few moments, saying nothing. 'What does it feel like?' she asked eventually. 'When you summon the fire?'

Noon paused, sensing a trap, but when her mother said no more, she shrugged. 'Like being alive. Like there is too much life in me, and I can do anything.'

Her mother's lips grew thin, and she looked away, her head bowing briefly so that her thick black hair covered her face. Then she looked back at her daughter, meeting her eyes steadily. 'I am sorry, Noon, but you must hide it. You are very small now, and you can't possibly – their witch spies are everywhere. You might be safe for a day or two, maybe even a week, or three, but eventually the Winnowry would come for you.' She shuffled over and gathered her daughter up into her arms, kissing the top of her head. 'I can't lose you, little frog.'

In her cold and dusty room in Esiah Godwort's grand house, Noon turned over and opened her eyes, pieces of the dream speeding away like leaves on the river. For a moment, she thought she could still smell her mother – the scents of wildflowers and horse – but it was just the stink of musty bedclothes, after all. Her hand trembling only slightly, she wiped her cheeks with the back of her hand and waited for the sky to lighten. Things would look better in the daylight.

It was the biggest wall Noon had ever seen. It was so big, in fact, that she hadn't realised it was a wall until she saw the enormous gate built into the side. If anything, it resembled an extremely steep hill, with unusually uniform sides. To complete the resemblance, the thing was covered all over with a brownish clay, and here and there small plants and trees had taken root. They should have been an encouraging sight in the barren landscape, but they were sad, twisted things; the poison of Greenslick seeped in everywhere, it seemed.

'He said the gate was open.' Vintage had her broad-brimmed hat pulled firmly down over her head, and had spent part of the previous day scavenging Godwort's house for supplies, so her pack was bulging. Tormalin stood next to her, his long sword slung over his back. He had been up before Noon, boiling water to wash in, and as usual he looked elegant and composed, his long black hair held in a liquid tail down his back, his skin shining. Looking at him, it was difficult to believe his people were a dying race.

'It is, but just a crack. Look.' Tor went to the enormous gate. It was constructed from oak trunks and riveted with iron, and it stood open about an inch. A thick blanket of shrivelled leaves and dirt had settled against it, but by leaning his whole weight against it Tor managed to open one door wide enough for them to squeeze through one by one. They filed in and stood, caught in silence for a moment.

'What a place.' Noon cleared her throat. 'I'd almost rather be back at the Winnowry.'

It was the Wild, festering behind gigantic walls. Enormous trees loomed over them, strange twisted things, their branches intertwining and spiralling around each other, as though they were blind and reaching out for their neighbours. Noon saw bark of grey, black and red, leaves of a diseased green, running with yellow spots. There were mushrooms too, bloated things like corpses left in the water too long, bursting from the trunks of the strange trees or erupting out of the black earth. It was already an overcast day, and dismal light within the compound was strained and jaundiced, almost as though it were an afterthought. A deep feeling of unease seemed to ooze from the deep shadows that pooled around every tree.

'Great, our own personal patch of Wild to get killed in,' said Tor. He unsheathed the Ninth Rain and held it loosely in one hand, his dark red eyes narrowed. 'This place is too quiet.'

'It's because there's no wind, that's all. Don't get jumpy before we've even started, my dear,' said Vintage dismissively, but she already had her crossbow held securely in both hands.

'Being jumpy in here might save our lives.' Tor started forward, sword at the ready. 'I'm assuming we just start walking, Vintage? The Behemoth remains will be hard to miss, I suspect.'

Within the shadows of the trees, Noon's sense of unease grew until it felt like a weight on her neck. She found herself looking back, seeking out the brown clay of the wall, but it was swiftly eaten up by the giant trees. She could see nothing moving.

'How big is this place?'

'It takes up over half of Esiah's land,' said Vintage. The scholar was trying to look everywhere at once, her eyes very wide. 'I can't believe I'm finally here. And he barely needed persuading at all.'

'Yes, because the fool has lost his mind,' said Tor, just ahead of them. 'Or have you politely chosen not to notice that, Vintage?'

Vintage ignored him, elbowing Noon instead. 'Try to remember as much of this as you can, my darling. Any strange

309

details, any odd thoughts that occur to you. I will be writing extensive notes afterwards.'

The Wild closed over them, and soon it was difficult to picture the outside world, or to believe that just an hour ago they had been standing in the hall of a great house, drinking slightly stale tea and packing their bags. In here, civilisation felt like a dream she had had once, now half forgotten. Noon was just starting to get used to the thick, alien stench of the place when a sonorous wailing sounded from nearby. Noon felt the hair on the back of her neck trying to stand up.

'A parasite spirit,' said Tor. 'Let's keep moving.'

It wasn't long before they saw their first one of those. A shimmering of lights lit up the gloom, and Noon found herself crouching behind a great mushroom the colour of cow's liver. The spirit passed around twenty feet away from them, a thing that looked like a shark with legs, blunt head fringed with yellow lamps, and it didn't appear to see them. Noon moved out of her crouch, only for Vintage to grab her arm.

'Stay there, my darling,' she whispered. 'Just a moment.'

Silence and gloom, and then an eerie brightening all around them. Blue light, then purple, then pink. Two more parasite spirits, passing by on either side of them. Noon shrank back against the fungus, her heart pounding. Another three hovered beyond that – she could make out glowing translucent flesh, fronds like oversized fingers, and dark, puckered holes. She had the absurd feeling that they were caught in a parade of parasite spirits – perhaps this was what they did for fun, alone in this forgotten place. Again, the sonorous wailing started up, much closer this time, and Noon remembered everything she had ever heard about the spirits; particularly the part about how, if they touched you, they could turn you inside out. She wished fervently that she could sink into the ground. Next to her, Vintage was speaking rapidly in a language she didn't know.

'I had no idea Catalen had so many swear words,' murmured

Tor, amused. 'Although I'm less than happy about offering up my own energy, perhaps we could get our witch to burn them, Vintage? Isn't that what she's here for?'

'Don't be absurd,' hissed Vintage. 'They will just move on past us. No sense in announcing our arrival.'

'Why are there bloody loads of them?' said Noon. Again, the spirits did not appear to notice them, and eventually their strange lights vanished back into the gloom of the Wild.

Vintage was grinning. 'Isn't it extraordinary? We are probably witnessing the largest population of spirits anywhere on Sarn.'

Noon blinked. 'Vintage, this is not a good thing. We could die. We really could.'

'Nonsense.' Vintage patted her sleeve. 'We have you, and Tor's sword arm. We'll be fine. Come along.'

They headed deeper into the compound, pausing every now and then as a parasite spirit lumbered silently past. Sounds like wailing and, once, a child laughing, echoed through the trees. On one of these occasions Tor stopped dead ahead of them, his entire body going very still. When he didn't move or speak, Noon went to him and tugged at his arm. His face was caught in the expression of someone desperately trying to remember something.

'Does that remind you of anything?' he said urgently, his red eyes meeting hers. Noon had never seen him look more unguarded.

'Does what remind me of what?'

'That sound, it's like music I heard, once . . .' He trailed off and shook his head. He turned away from her. 'Come on.'

When finally they saw the Behemoth, Noon thought they had come across some strange building in the midst of this overgrown forest, dark windows glinting under the overcast sky. Next to her, Vintage swore in another language again, her eyes wide.

'There it is. Look at the size of the bastard.'

As they stepped through the last fringe of trees, the remains of the Behemoth loomed into existence. At the Shroom Flats there had been tiny pieces of wreckage, and Noon had seen Vintage's drawings of the things, but nothing had prepared her for the physical reality of it. The thing rose above even the giant trees, dark green, grey and black in colour. It was made of what looked like softly curving sheets of metal, except that it didn't shine like metal – instead it looked greasy, like the skin of someone kept in bed with a fever for months. The surface was puckered here and there with round holes, some of which glinted darkly with what Noon assumed was glass. Hanging from one side was a strange, withered appendage, like an arm with too many joints, ending in a series of tapering claws.

'This is just the front piece,' said Vintage, her eyes shining. 'Its head, for want of a better word. This must be the most intact specimen on Sarn.' She took a deep breath. 'And, finally, I look upon it.'

They circled around and came to the ragged edges of the Behemoth's head – torn green plates tattered like skin, with fat pouches of some sort of grey material underneath. The interior of the thing was exposed to the air, and again Noon was reminded of looking at a building, only now it was one that had suffered a catastrophic disaster. She saw floors exposed, empty rooms with gently curving walls, the floors now covered with the debris of the forest. There were other shapes there hidden in the shadows. She couldn't even begin to guess what they were, but looking at them made her stomach turn over.

'The interior of a Behemoth,' breathed Vintage. 'By all the gods, it's more or less intact. I never thought I – it must have crashed at the end of the Eighth Rain with such violence that this entire section was torn off. Extraordinary.'

312

Noon caught Tor's eye. The corner of his mouth twitched into a smile, although there was no humour in it. 'Yes, we're very happy for you, Vintage. Shall we keep moving?'

Trees and fungus had grown up in the gap between the head of the Behemoth and its main body, which, Noon realised as they stepped through, was even larger than the front. Part of it had collapsed, the strange green-black material falling over the exposed innards like a flap of gangrenous skin, leaving a low, tunnel-like entrance to its insides. Vintage made straight for it.

'I'm not sure that that's a good idea,' said Noon. She glanced up at the sky, grey clouds indifferent over their heads.

'Nonsense. Esiah Godwort, remember, has been in and out of these ruins for years, gradually delving deeper and deeper, and he has always survived. It's probably safer in there than it is out here.' Vintage nodded back the way they had come. Noon turned to see the shifting amorphous form of a parasite spirit moving just beyond the trees in front of the Behemoth's head. The creature had six spindly legs, the bulk of its body suspended like a balloon over them, but its long neck twisted round, six glittering lights like eyes seeming to focus on their small group. It lifted one spindly leg, taking a step towards them.

'All right,' Tor waved them back, 'let's get inside and out of sight. Perhaps it will forget we're here at all.'

Glancing up at the sky once more, hoping it wouldn't be the last time she saw it, Noon ducked under the flap of oddly organic metal and followed Vintage into the interior of the Behemoth. The floor underfoot was soft and grey and somehow slightly warm, as though they walked across the living flesh of a giant. She supposed they did, in a way. They found themselves in a circular corridor, the walls streaked with a deep greenish substance that looked like a form of rust, next to strange geometric shapes etched in silver lines. There was a smell, sweet and sickly, like old meat, while nodules burst from the walls every few feet or so, twisted bunches of string-like membrane; each one glowing with a faint, yellow-white light.

'Interior lighting!' cried Vintage, peering closely at one such nodule. 'How long has this been burning? Can you imagine what sort of power source could be responsible for it? There is too much here, too much. I should have negotiated for a month in this place, or even a year's extended study.'

'For what it's worth, I don't believe Master Godwort would care much either way,' said Tor. This seemed to lessen some of Vintage's glee and they moved back off up the rounded corridor. The sound of their footfalls echoed strangely, becoming an odd discordant heartbeat, and, inevitably, Noon returned to the idea that they were walking around inside the body of a giant beast – not dead, despite all its torn pieces, but sleeping.

'Godwort and his team were studying here for years. Look at this.' The corridor had widened slightly and Vintage stopped by a piece of wall that was raised from the rest and covered with the silvery geometric patterns. Here, someone had constructed a wooden frame, on which rested several oil lamps, long since extinguished. They were covered in a thick layer of dust. Not sure what drove her to do it, Noon pressed her fingers into the dust and smoothed it between her finger pads. It was faintly greasy, and there was no life force to it at all. She didn't know why she had thought there might be. 'They wanted as much light as possible, do you see?' Vintage was saying. 'Some of these passages have only recently become accessible, you know, as parts of the Behemoth's body degraded and fell apart naturally. Godwort was always very keen that the thing be kept as intact as possible.'

'I don't know why we've bothered coming here, Vintage,' said Tor. He was peering at the oil lamps with a faint expression of distaste. 'You already know all there is to know about the place.'

Further up the corridor they came across more evidence that the space had been thoroughly explored: rope ladders led to empty alcoves in the ceiling; boot prints in the greasy dust; a single empty ink bottle. They reached a place where the corridor grew wider, and in the strange alcoves were several shining orbs, made of greenish-gold metal. Each had a clear section, like glass, and inside it was possible to see a viscous golden fluid.

'Look at this!' cried Vintage. 'This is what we found in the Shroom Flats, only intact.' She shook her head slowly. 'The substance that makes vegetation grow. Imagine what you could do with this much of it! Esiah Godwort is sitting on a fortune.'

'Do you want to take it with us?' asked Tor.

For the briefest moment, Vintage looked tempted, but then she shook her head.

'I could not break Esiah's trust so soon after gaining it.' She coughed lightly into her hand. 'Come on, there is much more to see.'

Eventually the corridor ended, and they were in a cavernous chamber, the shadowed ceiling stretching high above them, unseen. Here, there were more alcoves in the walls, all filled with strangely organic-looking tubes – Noon was reminded of the stringy roots on the bottom of the tubers her mother would boil for dinner when she was a child – and there was a persistent humming noise, just discordant enough to cause discomfort. Noon winced.

'This place is still alive,' she said, not wanting to speak the words aloud but unable to keep it in. She was thinking of her dream at the Winnowry, how the Behemoths had hung in the sky over Mushenska. Had she ever thought she would be walking around inside one? 'It's still alive, this thing. Can't you feel it?'

'Nonsense,' said Vintage firmly. 'This Behemoth crashed generations back and it has been rotting ever since. No, my

315

dear, you must think of it as a piece of clockwork still winding down, or a stone out under the sun all day that is gradually losing its heat.'

Noon nodded, but she crouched and briefly brushed her fingertips to the clammy floor, probing for a sense of life. There was nothing, but she didn't feel any safer for it.

'What's this in the centre here?' Tor led them across the floor. In the middle of the tall chamber there was a soft greyish mound rising from the ground. As they got closer, Noon saw that it was made from large, translucent lumps of material, all pressed in together to form the gently rounded structure. Some of the lumps, which were almost cube-like in shape, had more of the stringy tubes, like those in the alcoves.

'Fascinating,' said Vintage. She was trying to look everywhere at once, her eyes bright. 'Is this some sort of central control room? The heart of the system?'

'Whatever it is, it looks like Godwort has decided to see what's underneath.' Tor gestured from the far side, and Noon and Vintage joined him. He stood over a ragged hole in the greyish material, and it was clear that several of the lumps had been carefully prized away and put aside, forming a tunnel into the murk below, where a pinkish light glowed fitfully. Many of the tube-like appendages lay ragged and torn, blackening at the ends. Looking at it all made Noon feel strange – it was like staring at an open wound. And the smell of rotten flesh was stronger than ever.

'Well,' said Vintage, beaming at them both, 'I don't know about you, but I can't *wait* to get down there.'

A green flower of fire blossomed to life between her hands. Wincing slightly against the pain in her shoulder, Agent Lin laid the fire gently on the dry sticks she had collected, and watched as it spread, eating and consuming and growing bigger. Green turned to orange, and she felt the heat push against her face. This was still hers. This was still hers to control. There was always that.

She was camped some distance from Esiah Godwort's house, its red bricks just in sight. She and Gull had flown over it several times – had observed, from far away, the small figures of the fugitive Fell-Noon and her companions moving about its grounds. Of the owner, she had seen nothing, but it was well known, according to Pamoz the engineer at least, that Godwort was an eccentric recluse. The people she was looking for had headed into the compound behind the house some hours ago, and now she would wait. When they came out again – and they would, unless they were killed by the parasite spirits inside – she would kill them. As simple as that. She had rushed in before, too confident of her own efficiency. She had not taken into account the desperation of the girl, and that in itself was a ridiculous mistake. Had she forgotten already what it felt like to be that desperate? Or had she chosen to forget?

The problem with waiting, of course, was that it gave her too much time to think. To turn the Drowned One's words over in her mind, for example. To imagine the loss of her son's finger, to imagine the ways they would take it from him. How he might scream and cry.

When she had been a prisoner of the Winnowry, she had been wild and desperate enough to do anything. The need for the touch of another person was maddening after a while, and that had resulted in her boy, Keren. Not born of love, or affection, but a simple terrible need not to feel alone, just for a little while. It was incredible, the need for the sensation of skin against skin, and she had not been able to control it.

Sitting alone in the terrible landscape of Greenslick, Agent Lin summoned another ball of winnowfire and fed it to the flames already burning. And then another, of the exact same size and intensity. Control.

Keren had dark brown hair, like his father, and it had curled

317

against his skin, so soft. She hadn't believed such softness existed. His eyes, too, had been brown. He had been a warmth next to her chest, both better and deeper than the heat of the winnowfire, and they had let her keep him just long enough to name him. His fingers and toes had been tiny and perfect – but best not to think about that.

Fell-Noon would soon find out that there was no resisting the Winnowry. Just as she had.

Another ball of flame, identical in every way to the others, slid into the fire. Control. No more mistakes.

28

There was too much.

Vintage could barely move an inch without feeling the need to retrieve her notebooks and inks, to make quick sketches and observations. There was an extraordinary wealth of knowledge here, much more than she had expected – Godwort had made much deeper progress into the body of the Behemoth than he had reported, the old swine. There was too much, but every moment they were inside she was aware of the terrible danger they were in, and she had the distinct sense that her luck was now the thinnest piece of fragile ice, and they were edging out further and further over an abyss.

So as they climbed down into the ragged hole torn by Godwort's men, she didn't pause and make drawings, but held her breath, listening closely. She doubted even Tormalin – perhaps especially Tormalin – realised how much danger they were actually in.

Learn what you can and be quick, she told herself. *Gather your clues, take them with you. We can come back. Do not test your luck.* And on the back of that thought, as it was so often, was the memory of Nanthema. Did she die exploring a

Behemoth, just like this, or did she tire of her human companion and find some new bit of Sarn to explore?

'I don't like that smell,' said Noon. She was carrying Vintage's travel lamp, its small yellow flame lighting the girl's face more than the narrow tunnel. A curl of black hair had fallen from her cap to rest against her forehead.

'Yes,' agreed Tormalin. 'It smells rather like you did when we found you in the Shroom Flats.'

'Now then. It could simply be that Godwort's men left some food supplies down here before they left,' said Vintage. The greyish matter under her feet was springy, and faintly tacky. She kept expecting her boots to come away with a sucking noise. 'It's not necessarily something awful.'

'Hmm,' said Noon. Ahead of them, Tormalin stopped and raised his hand.

'Careful,' he said. 'It drops away sharply here.'

Vintage shuffled forward, keeping her centre of gravity low, and peered over the edge. They were hanging above what appeared to be an egg-shaped chamber, the smoothly curving walls formed of the greyish translucent blocks and lit with the dimly glowing nodules. There was a rope ladder next to them that ran all the way to the bottom, and there something sat, a shining something that was difficult to look at. It fluttered and pulsed with a sickly pink light, and for a frightening moment she thought it was a parasite spirit, but then she narrowed her eyes and saw that no, it was all sharp angles, and it was unmoving.

Reaching over, she tugged on the rope ladder. It was attached to a pair of wooden stakes that had been driven deeply into the yielding grey flesh.

'I'd say that looks sturdy enough, wouldn't you?'

Noon looked sick, the corners of her mouth turned down. Tormalin didn't look much happier.

'How much do you pay me again, Lady de Grazon?'

'Enough to get your bony arse down there, my darling.' Without waiting for an answer, Vintage took hold of the rope ladder and began to climb down, willing the thing not to fall to bits. She caught the look of exasperation on Tormalin's face, and then he was lost to sight.

'Fine. One at a time, though,' he said from above. 'We don't want to break this thing with all of us on it.'

Vintage made short work of the rope ladder – one didn't grow up next door to the vine forest without becoming an accomplished climber – and found herself standing in front of the light-filled object. It was a tall, jagged crystal, twice her height and wider at the base. It was pale pink in colour, but its smooth surfaces winked and slid reflected light around her, as though it were in motion. Looking at it made her feel mildly queasy. She glanced up to see Noon making her steady way down, her cap now pushed back from her eyes to reveal the bat-wing tattoo on her forehead.

'What is that?' she asked when she got to the floor.

'Well, that's quite the mystery, isn't it?' Vintage reached over and squeezed her hand briefly, noting the flicker of surprise that passed over the girl's face. This one wasn't used to human contact, she reminded herself, and felt a pang of sadness. 'I haven't seen anything like this on any of my own expeditions, and nothing in Godwort's sketches either. Tor? What are you doing?'

'Making bloody sure this ladder is secure before I come down there.' Moments later he climbed down, his long figure strangely awkward on the swinging rope. Noon had approached the giant crystal, her hands held cautiously in front of her as though she expected it to burn her, and then she gasped, taking an involuntary step backwards.

'Fire and blood, there's a whole world in there! What is this thing?'

'What?' Vintage jumped forward, peering closely at the

321

crystal. It was as if its clouded surface cleared – a hand wiped over a misted window – and an alien landscape was revealed, stretching off into the distance. She saw a night sky pocked with fiery stars she didn't recognise, and a desolate land of white rock and craters. Her stomach dropped away. There was another world in here with them, just beyond the surface of the crystal, and the effect was dizzying. She almost expected to feel cold air on her cheek, to hear the desolate howl of the wind, deep within the heart of the Behemoth. Nothing moved in that terrible landscape. She reached out one hand, meaning to push her fingers against the slick surface, but a hand settled heavily on her shoulder.

'Don't,' said Tormalin, his voice utterly serious for once. 'You know better than that, Vintage.'

She pursed her lips and nodded. Noon had walked off around the other side of the crystal, circling it like a wary animal. She disappeared from sight, and almost at once they heard her give a startled shout.

'What is it?' Tor was there before Vintage, one hand on the pommel of his sword, but she almost collided with him as, suddenly, he was brought up short. Noon stood staring at the crystal, her face drained of colour. There was a body standing half in and half out of the structure, and it was all wrong. Vintage pressed her fingers to her mouth, feeling her bile rising in her throat.

'By the roots,' cried Tormalin, his voice oddly breathless. The crystal continued to flash and flicker at them. 'What *is* this thing?'

The corpse had been a young man with unruly black hair and a comely face – they could tell this because the half of his body that stood in the alien landscape appeared to be untouched, his smooth skin clear and unblemished, his eyes so glassy they almost looked wet. The half of his body that was still in the chamber, however, was a terrible emaciated thing

322

of bones, and flesh turned soft and black. The boy's hand was curled against his thigh, and it looked like little more than a pile of brownish sticks, while his leg hung loose, at a strange angle inside his trousers.

'I think I'm going to be sick,' said Noon.

'Oh my dear,' said Vintage. Her voice didn't sound like her own voice. 'Me too, my dear.'

The boy had apparently been caught half in and half out of the crystal, as though he had been stepping into it at an angle and had been frozen in place. His head was entirely beyond the surface, as were his right arm and leg, while the line of the crystal ran from the left side of his neck – the ear there had only narrowly missed being left behind – down across his chest to bisect him neatly at the groin. Most of him was within the crystal. All of him was dead.

'It's his son,' said Noon flatly. 'Don't you see? It – his face looks like him.'

'Oh gods, Tyron, no.' Vintage took a startled breath, and all at once she was very close to losing the small breakfast she had eaten that morning. She had only met Tyron once, years back when he had been no older than four or five. He had been mischievous, she remembered, peering out from behind his father's legs, dark eyes full of curiosity. 'How is it – how is it holding him there? Some sort of trap?'

'Whatever it is,' said Noon, 'I think it's broken. Look at the way it's flashing. And there's this stuff on the floor.'

Barely able to tear herself away from the terrible sight of Tyron, Vintage looked where Noon was pointing. It was the remains of a camp. People had stayed here for days, perhaps, trying to get him out, and failing. The horror of it washed over her, and she felt a steadying hand on her arm. To her surprise, it was Noon.

'They found this chamber, and the extraordinary world in a crystal,' said Tor. He was staring at the corpse. 'Tyron

323

Godwort wanted to be the first to explore it, perhaps, but when he entered it, whatever magic powered the thing failed. Or started working? Either way, it trapped him there, half in and half out. Did he die immediately? I don't think so.' He gestured at the camp, still not looking at them. 'They thought it worth staying here, for days, in a hope of getting him free. Most of his body is on the other side – he would have been able to breathe, assuming there is something there to breathe, but not to eat or drink.'

Tor paused. Vintage felt a cold tingling sweeping up from her toes. Had he cried, and pleaded with them to help? Would they have been able to hear him, beyond the crystal?

'They tried to get him out, but nothing could break it.' There were hammers on the floor, several chisels. One of the hammers was broken, the head torn away from the shaft. 'So, what? They waited. Perhaps, they thought, the magic would change, or break, or release him randomly. They watched and waited as one half of his body wasted away. Perhaps he asked them to kill him towards the end, but they wouldn't have done that. There was still a chance.'

'Stop it,' said Noon. 'Just stop it.'

Tor turned to them, raising a single eyebrow. 'No wonder the old man can no longer bear to come out here. It is his son's tomb.'

They stayed in the chamber for another hour, Vintage taking the pencils from her bag, meticulously recording as much as she could, the strange walls of the chamber and the incredible crystal at its heart. She and Tor walked around the other side, away from the corpse, but Noon stayed, sitting amongst the remains of the camp. She couldn't help looking at the young man's face, his eyes open and his head lolling awkwardly on his shoulder. Whatever the place was beyond the surface of the crystal, it had held the boy outside of time. There was no

324

sign of corruption on that smooth face, no hint of the death that had claimed him – slowly, painfully – and yet he was dead. She wondered what that was like for Esiah Godwort; to know that his child was down here in the heart of the Behemoth. That he could come and look on his face any time he wanted, but that he would also have to face the terrible fact of his death. The bones and the running flesh. Tyron Godwort was a memory of himself, and his father was trapped by it.

Noon reached up and pulled off her cap, running her fingers through her hair. With some difficulty, she dragged her eyes from the still form of Tyron Godwort and looked at the strange landscape beyond him. A night sky, a desolate plain. Wherever it was, it wasn't on Sarn. The thought startled her with how true it felt. Fire and blood, she was hardly the most well-travelled fell-witch, but everything about the alien place beyond the crystal felt wrong to her. After a moment she stood up, thinking of the suit of winnow-forged armour in the young man's bedroom. She wished they had never gone in there; it felt like an invasion of a sort.

'I'm sorry,' she said quietly, before walking around the crystal to join Tor and Vintage.

'The place inside the crystal – I think it's where the worm people come from.' She cleared her throat. 'I think it's their home.'

Tor raised an eyebrow at her, but Vintage only nodded. 'I suspect you are right, Noon, my dear. It's no place on Sarn I've ever been and, of course, we've never known where the Jure'lia come from exactly.' She paused, clutching her notebook, and Noon noticed that her normally neat and steady hand-writing was wild and shaky. Noon pulled her hat back on. The room suddenly felt unbearable, a place of dead things and sorrow.

'We should go back,' she said.

To her surprise, Vintage agreed. The three of them climbed

out of the chamber in silence, leaving behind the flickering crystal shard and its prisoner. Tormalin led the way out, following the corridors without hesitation. The closer they got to the exit, the more Vintage seemed to recover, some of her usual cheer returning to her voice.

'We can come back,' she said, patting Noon on the arm as they walked. 'We've all had a shock, but we can rest, fortify ourselves. I want some time to think on the crystal, put it together with some other writings I've made over the years. I feel like it might be the key to the Jure'lia – who they are, what they want. That an unwary explorer can become trapped, stuck, in time. An overly curious person, perhaps, determined to find out –' Vintage paused, and seemed to trip over her own feet. Noon grabbed her and saved her from falling, but as she helped her up, she noticed that she was trembling all over.

'Vintage, what's wrong?'

'Oh my dear, I just had a thought, that's all.' Vintage smiled, but her face had gone an alarming shade of grey.

'We need to get out of here.' Noon looped her arm round the scholar's waist, taking most of her weight. 'Tor? Are we near the way out yet or what?'

Tor glanced back at them. He looked distracted himself, but he was standing in a ragged circle of dim daylight. 'We're so close we're here, in fact. Come on. I want a glass of wine and a hot bath, and another glass of wine, in that order.'

Noon and Vintage hurried forward, stepping out onto the dark earth. The shattered remains of the head of the Behemoth stood opposite them, and the air at least was fresher. For a moment Noon felt disorientated. How long had they been in there? It felt darker than it should; they had entered the compound in the early morning, and now it felt like the early evening.

She looked up and saw a huge amorphous shape hovering

over them, blocking out the sky. Baleful violet lights like diseased suns pocked its sides, and it turned its blunt head down towards them.

'Run!'

Tor turned at her shout, his eyes widening as he spotted the parasite spirit above them. He drew his sword.

Half running, half falling, Noon dragged Vintage away from the wreckage, only for another shifting shape to rise up from behind a piece of debris that had fallen away from the main section. It was sinuous and lizard-like, a clutch of brilliant blue fronds where its eyes should be, and it rushed at them, hissing. There was a thud, and a bolt hit the thing in the neck before Noon even realised that Vintage had wrestled her crossbow from her belt.

'There'll be more of them,' she muttered. 'We really *should* go, my darling.'

Noon turned, looking for Tor. The giant parasite spirit that hung over the entrance to the Behemoth was shaped a little like a great long-legged insect, the main bulk of it out of the Eboran's reach. Tor was pushing back a pair of parasite spirits with long, rabbit-like faces, multiple pink eyes shining brightly. The Ninth Rain flashed and danced, picking up and reflecting the eerie lights of the parasite spirits and driving them back.

'Tor! There're too many! We have to go!'

'Quick,' said Vintage, 'to the other side. Perhaps we can lose them in there.'

Tor glanced at them over his shoulder, his mouth moving, but the giant parasite spirit that hung over them all had begun to make a low, desolate wailing noise, drowning out everything else. Noon turned, and with Vintage's hand held firmly in hers, ran for the other half of the wreckage. More parasite spirits seemed to ooze out of the semi-dark, as if they were attracted by their movements. Barely thinking, she reached out and brushed the tips of her fingers across Tor's hand as he came alongside her, siphoning off energy from him even as he shouted with surprise. She turned and threw up her free hand towards the approaching spirits, feeling the churning energy she had stolen boiling in her chest, and threw *all* of it with as much force as she could muster. A fat blossom of winnowfire burst wildly from her palm. It dissipated long before it reached the parasites, but they reeled back all the same. Tor had stumbled at her touch, but his face was set in grim lines, and he was still moving.

'Good work, my dear!' gasped Vintage.

Just as they reached the other side of the wreckage a creature like a translucent snake boiled up out of the ground, fizzing and sparking with orange and green lights. Noon cried out and tried to push Vintage out of the way, but the tapering tail of the parasite spirit whipped around and caught the older woman across the hand. There was a terrible sharp tearing sound, and Vintage hollered with pain.

'What's happened?' Tor called, close behind them now.

'Get inside, get inside.' Noon pushed Vintage in front of her, almost throwing the woman into the shelter of the wreckage, before dragging her up a series of steps. More than anything she wanted to be away from the dirt – the spirit had just appeared from it, rising up like a flood water, and now nothing felt safe. 'Up, up!'

They scrambled up the steps, Tor's footfalls close behind them, until they found themselves on a platform looking back across at the other chunk of wreckage. This was the place where the two sections had once been joined, but now the walls ended in torn pieces. Below them, they could see around ten parasite spirits, writhing and wailing, obviously still searching for them.

'Fucking fire and blood, we're fucked.' Noon took a wild breath, willing her heart to stop hammering in her chest. 'Vintage, are you hurt?'

Vintage was leaning against the wall, her hand cradled to her chest. There was blood on her shirt. 'I'd say so, my darling, yes.'

'We should head deeper in,' said Tor. He had appeared behind them, his face in the shadows as serious as Noon had ever seen it. 'There could be a way out on the other side. Or we can cut our way out.'

He held up the sword, which was already caked in the oddly jelly-like blood of the parasite spirits – Noon had a moment to wonder when he had done that – when the narrow space behind him shimmered with ominous lights. He spun round, sword moving with precision despite the dark shadows under his eyes, and the parasite spirit that had followed them in screamed discordantly. Noon and Vintage took a few hurried steps back, taking them perilously close to the edge of the platform.

This time Noon saw Tormalin's sword at work: the thin blade cut through the writhing spirit like it was butter, and the screaming grew so loud she felt a pulse of pain deep in her head. Part of the creature fell away, followed by a shimmering cloud of what almost looked like smoke, but the long fronds that formed part of its head shot forward, barrelling past Tor towards where she crouched with Vintage. The pair of them scrambled backwards, only to find that the giant parasite spirit, the one that had hovered over them as they left the wreckage, was now waiting for them, its huge bulk blocking any view of the outside world. For a few alarming seconds, Noon was faced with the shifting, amorphous texture of its body; she could see tiny lights falling inside it, as though it were made of the night sky. She turned back, and saw Tor battling with the other creature; despite how badly he had wounded it, the spirit's fronds were filling the small space where they had taken shelter, writhing and whipping back and forth like a nest of angry snakes. They were trapped.

'Burn them!' Tor shot her a desperate look from beyond the fronds. One of them was sliding, tentacle-like, round his forearm, scorching the leather there.

'I can't!' Noon felt a surge of frustration. She'd already spent the energy she'd stripped from him in her useless fireball, and now Tor was out of reach, trapped behind a wall of shifting fronds. Vintage's energy would not be enough to harm the spirits.

Next to her, Vintage fired off one crossbow bolt after another, hitting a frond with every shot. Although each one she hit turned black and inert, the grasping appendages kept coming. Behind them, the giant spirit was pressing itself against the hole, and its body was slowly filling the space, like bread rising in the oven. The only light left was the light dancing inside the creatures just about to kill them. Noon thought of how they killed; of seeing Tor overwhelmed, of seeing Vintage turned inside out.

Reaching out behind her, she brushed her fingers over the smooth, yielding body of the giant parasite spirit, and she *took*. Ignoring how her hand turned cold and numb, she ripped the life energy from the creature with all her strength, and although she realised almost instantly what a terrible mistake she'd made, it was already too late. The energy slammed into her; at first at her summons, and then against her will. Bright light filled her, along with the sharp scent of sap and the sense of being high up, very high up, and surrounded by rustling and the feeling of breaking free, a terrible severing, *oh lost, we are lost*.

Noon stumbled away, breaking contact. Her body sang with a thousand voices, centuries of lost memories. It was too much. Dimly, through the cacophony that now inhabited her, she saw Vintage staring at her with horror, while Tor struggled, on his knees as the parasite spirit tried to tear him in half. Unable to do anything else, Noon raised her hand, feeling the winnowfire boiling into life inside her, and let it go.

The world was lost in green fire.

29

Tor remembered very little of what followed. For a brief time, everything was made of colour and pain. A boiling light had filled his vision, and then a skein of red covered all things. There had been a sense of falling, or flying, and a distant sound that, eventually, he realised was his own voice, broken and screaming. Then a blessed kind of darkness.

Beyond that were brief fragments of memory. He had an image of looking down at his own boots as the world spun around him. Noon's voice, shouting Vintage's name. The strange foliage looming all around them – it looked familiar, as if he'd seen it recently, but when he stopped to try and remember, someone tugged him fiercely in another direction. A time of lights and silence and fear. The gate to the compound – this he did remember, and he felt pleased with himself – and a man with a dark beard standing there, his eyes wide.

A knife near his throat. He had stiffened, pulling back, but it was cutting away his clothes, and all at once there was so much pain that he was gone again. Darkness.

Noon remembered it all.

A thousand voices shouting at once, or the same voice,

shouting a thousand times. The living energy of the parasite spirit overwhelmed her immediately, and the resulting explosion was a boiling green and white. She had been thrown backwards by it, through the space where the spirit had been until she'd absorbed it, and out into the air, where she crashed onto the black dirt. Debris from the Behemoth fell all around her, smoking and still aflame in places, while the roar of the greater fire in front of her reached up to the sky.

I've done it again.

The thought hit her harder than the explosion. She gasped, barely able to get air into her lungs, and it had nothing to do with the oily smoke roiling around her. *I've done it again.*

She scrambled to her feet and cupped her hands to her mouth, preparing to scream for Vintage, when she realised that one of the pieces of debris that had fallen around her was Tormalin.

'No. Tor! Tor!'

He had fallen face down, his leathers and silks scorched and spattered with mud. Reaching him she turned him over. Dimly she realised she'd lost her hat.

'Oh no. No.'

The blast of winnowfire had hit him from the left, it seemed. That side of his face – his beautiful face – was a red and black ruin, as was his neck, and from what she could see of his arm, it was in a similar state. The hair on that side of his head had been burned back from his forehead, and now hung in smoking clumps. Incredibly, he still held his sword loosely in one fist.

'Fire and blood, no.' She grabbed hold of his shoulders and shook him, not knowing what else to do, and to her surprise his eyes popped open. He seemed to focus on her for a moment, but his gaze was wild, skittering away from her face to the fires behind her. 'Tormalin! You have to get up, come on.'

He shook his head once, and she saw him shudder with the pain. He fought to stay conscious, however, and one long hand

332

came up to grip her arm. Standing up straight, she shook him off and looked around wildly. There was no sign of Vintage anywhere, and the smoke was thickening all the time. She took a few steps towards the wreckage.

'Vintage! Vintage, where are you?'

There was no reply. She stumbled first to the left, and then to the right, desperately searching for any sign, but everything was mud or twisted moon-metal – no sign of the scholar anywhere. Turning back, Tor was briefly lost in the smoke and she felt a fresh stab of panic, but then she spotted his pale hand against the dirt.

'Listen to me, Tor, we have to get out of here.' She slid his sword through the loop of his belt, and with more strength than she thought she possessed, yanked the tall Eboran to his feet, staggering as he stumbled against her. She felt the heat of his blood sinking into her coat, and she swallowed down a white-hot panic. Moving him might kill him, but if they stayed here, the parasite spirits would come again and they would surely be dead.

'Tor, have you seen Vintage?'

It occurred to her that he was probably in shock, might even have been deafened by the explosion. Pulling his arm over her shoulders, she yelled into the smoke.

'Vintage? Vintage!'

There was no reply. The blasted remains of the Behemoth carcase remained merrily aflame, pieces of it falling around them, while a shuddering groan from inside spoke of some deeper, more fatal collapse happening. She peered up at the Behemoth, trying to make sense of the mess even as the boiling fire stung her eyes. Was that a human shape in there? A shadow, something curled in on itself. Another crashing groan, and more pieces of fiery debris flitted down around them. They had very little time.

'Vintage!'

The parasite spirits had all fled, but at that very thought a surge of images she didn't recognise forced their way into her head. Noon cried out wordlessly, staggering under Tor's weight. She saw a man very like him, tall and beautiful, with hair like old, golden wine, wearing armour that appeared to be made of bright white scales. He smiled at her, and then the vision was gone. Noon shook her head.

'Vintage? Where are you? Fuck.'

A shimmering of lights appeared through the smoke. Noon didn't stick around to see what it was. Instead, she took hold of Tor as firmly as she could and walked him away from the wreckage and into the trees, hoping she remembered where the gate to the compound was. The sky was darker now, with the deep grey bruise that meant rain, sooner or later, and the shadows between the grotesque trees were long and deep.

The walk to the gate was nightmarish, and more than once Noon wondered if she was trapped in some terrible dream. She was walking too slowly, Tor was a silent weight, his blood soaking into her, and hidden things watched them from the dark places. Vintage was surely dead, and they would be turned inside out by a spirit before they ever reached the gate. When she did see the enormous doors, she almost fell to her knees with relief.

'Tor, we're nearly there. Stay with me.'

A figure stepped towards them out of the growing shadows, and Noon was surprised to see Esiah Godwort, his eyes wide with shock. Outside of the great house he looked wilder somehow, and lost. There were cobwebs caught in his hair.

'There is a fire,' he said.

Noon nodded. 'We were caught in it. Can you help me get him back to your home?'

'My boy is in there,' said Esiah, but he looked away from the forest and pulled Tor's other arm over his shoulder, and together they staggered back to the courtyard of the house. At the door, Esiah turned to go.

334

'Where are you going?' demanded Noon. She realised, faintly, that her voice sounded muffled to her own ears. 'I still need your help!'

'My boy is in there,' he said again, as though this were all the explanation required. He turned away from them and walked back across the courtyard. Noon called after him, telling him to look for Vintage while he was in there, but he didn't turn back. They didn't see him again.

Inside the house, Noon had an unsettling moment of light-headedness, black spots jumping at the edges of her vision, and she had to stand still, taking deep breaths. The chorus of voices she had heard at the moment of the explosion had not entirely gone; she could still hear them, a tide of whispers that gnawed at her every thought. Her head pounded sickeningly.

'Come on,' she said to Tor, trying to gather the last of her strength. 'You heavy bastard.'

She couldn't manage to drag him up the great sweep of stairs, so instead she found the servants' quarters by the kitchens and there she laid him down on a bed. He muttered to himself as he stretched out and started to tremble all over. Noon slumped against the wall and slid down to her knees.

'I got you here,' she said. 'I have to go back.'

Tor did not reply. She wondered how long this shock would last, and what would happen when he finally came back to himself; when he realised what had happened to him. When he realised what had happened to Vintage. Wincing, she pushed herself to her feet and went to his bedside again, forcing herself to look at him clearly.

She swallowed hard. The injuries were terrible. She knew from all of Mother Fast's stories that Eborans were fearsomely strong and healed quickly, but that was the Ebora of old, the one fed and nurtured by the sap of their tree-god. This Eboran was far from home, in a time when his people were weak and

335

dying. She doubted he would live to see the morning, and knowing that, she couldn't leave him.

'I walked away from them all before,' she said to him, although she knew he couldn't hear her. 'When I did this, before. I can't do that again.' Tor murmured, turning his head towards her. The bones on the burned part of his face jutted through raw flesh. 'How are you still alive?'

When she had lived on the plains with her mother, there had been a man living with her people called Cusp. When someone had a fever, or had broken a leg falling from their horse, or had received a bite from something hidden in the long grass, Cusp would come to them with his ointments and sticks, his ghost-stones and sure fingers, and he would help them if he could. He had been a serious-faced man, not old, his black hair shorn very close to his head. Cusp would have known what to do about Tor's terrible burns, but everything that Cusp had known had been lost along with everything else, ten years ago. In the Winnowry there had been a place where sick fell-witches had been taken, but Noon had never seen it. She knew precisely nothing about healing. Quite the opposite, really.

She straightened up, less than steady on her feet. 'I will make you comfortable. Hot water and clean linen. I can manage that much.'

At the door she staggered and cried out. She had tried to force the cloud of voices inside her into the background, but now it swarmed around her, overwhelming her as it had inside the Behemoth wreck. Her mouth flooded with the taste of something she didn't recognise, woody and almost tart, like old apples, and a booming voice in her head, speaking an unknown language. The voice sounded angry.

'Stop it, stop it.' She covered her ears with her hands, trying to block it out, and for a wonder, the sensation did retreat, although she could feel it, colouring the back of her mind like mould. 'Whatever this is, I don't have *time* for it.'

In the kitchens she didn't dare to use the winnowfire, not with the violence of the parasite spirit's energy still simmering inside, so she lit a fire the traditional way, as she'd once been taught by an unsuspecting Mother Fast a lifetime ago. When the water boiled, she tempered it with cold water from a jug, picked up a stack of dusty tablecloths from the side and went back to the room where Tor lay. She had just pushed the door open with her foot when that sense of an alien presence overcame her again and she dropped the pot of water, half soaking herself and the rug, before falling to her knees in a pile of linen.

The voice came again, although now it sounded joyful, exultant. The servants' quarters with the chest of drawers and brown curtains faded away, as though it were a particularly unconvincing dream, and she was flying, flying high above Sarn. Lakes like sapphires caught the sun and shattered it into gold, and the low slopes of a mountain revealed a pack of animals, running. The voice roared then, and, far below, the animals howled back; a shiver of recognition trickled down Noon's back even though she knew that the feelings were not her own. To her that lonely noise meant a night of extra fires around the tents and more warriors on watch through the dark hours, but to this other being it was . . . freedom? That wasn't the right word. Abruptly, the sense of flying was gone, and instead she was in a great plaza of white stone, dotted here and there with trees covered in pink blossom. Here there were tall men and women, beautiful in silk and silver plate, and then a child, running towards her. A small boy, his shining auburn hair pulled into a neat little bun atop his head, laughing as he came, his crimson eyes bright, and then he fell, chubby limbs crashing onto the smooth white stone. Noon winced, knowing the tantrum that would come, yet the child got back up onto his feet, still laughing, and continued running towards her. The palms of his hands were scraped and bleeding and she felt a moment's discomfort at that – *it will stain the feathers,* she thought, disjointedly – and then the child was wrapping his arms around her. Noon had a sense of *knowing*, of knowing she was much larger than the boy, much larger, and then she was lying on her back in a dowdy room, gasping for air. Her trousers and shirt were wet, and the empty pot lay beneath the chest of drawers.

'What is it?' she breathed. She held her own hands up in front of her, and for a second they looked the wrong shape. She squeezed her eyes shut, opened them again. 'What is happening to me?'

The only reply was Tor's ragged breathing. Cautiously, half sure that moving would bring the strange thoughts and sensations back, she got to her feet. Her heart was hammering in her chest as though she had been fighting, but as she looked down at Tor, something clicked into place. She thought of the little boy's bloodied hands.

'There is something I can do for you,' she said.

The knives in the kitchens were all well maintained, their edges keen. Noon selected three, cleaned them in a basin of hot water, and took them back to Tor's room. Trying not to notice the ruin of his face and neck, she carefully cut and peeled away the collar of his shirt. Instantly, he roared into consciousness, his eyes wild.

'What are you doing?' he demanded, in a tone so like his usual attitude that she was briefly too stunned to do anything. 'Do you know how much this shirt cost? I doubt—'

Noon saw the moment the pain hit him. He screamed, a high, broken sound, and then he passed out again, his head lolling against the pillow.

'You shouldn't have taken me with you,' she whispered, still gripping the knife. 'You should have left me. I told you to.'

She put the knife on a small bedside table and picked up another, smaller blade. Without thinking about it too closely,

338

she pressed its edge to the palm of her hand until a bright necklace of red beads grew there. It stung, and as she winced she thought she heard muttering from the tide of strange thoughts in her head, but she forced it away.

Taking hold of his jaw with her other hand so that his mouth was open, she squeezed her injured hand shut and a few drops of blood spattered onto his tongue. She squeezed again, a few more drops, and Tor swallowed hard, gasping as though he were drowning.

'Does it help?' She stared at his ruined face, trying to see some change. Perhaps it would heal him from the inside – either way, these few small drops of blood would not be enough. Taking hold of the sharp knife again she pressed the blade to the fleshy area just below her wrist, taking care to make a shallow cut. The blood this time flowed faster and trickled down her hand to the tips of her fingers. Grimacing slightly as spots of bright crimson appeared on the bedclothes, she leaned over and pressed the wound to Tor's mouth.

The response this time was immediate. His head shot up, his eyes still closed, and his mouth clamped down on the source of blood – she felt the hard pressure of his teeth on her skin, and for a moment she felt the room spin around her. Ten years of barely any physical contact, and now this. It was strange. His uninjured hand snaked up from his side and took hold of her arm gently. There hardly seemed to be any strength in him, but as she watched, the ruined side of his face began to subtly change. The charred and blackened skin began to flake away as new skin grew beneath, while the raw muscle and flesh began to knit itself anew. It was only in a few places, and it made little overall difference to the terrible damage she had inflicted, but it was something. Softly, he moaned under her, shifting in the bed.

'Tor? Are you awake? Speak to me, bloodsucker, come on.'

His eyes still shut, he slumped back to the pillow, a smear of crimson on his lips and chin. He did not speak.

'Tor?'

Working awkwardly with her injured hand, Noon tore off some strips of linen and bound the two cuts as best she could. In a little while, she would go back to the kitchens and wash her arm, but for now she felt oddly weak. With her good hand she pushed Tor's hair back from his forehead – what was left of it – and tried to slow her thundering heart. A little blood had given him strength, had started to heal his face and neck. She suspected it would take a lot more than that to save him, but whose price was that to pay if it wasn't hers?

Cradling her bleeding arm to her chest, she lay down next to him on the narrow bed, taking a brief and selfish comfort in the warmth of his body. She had a moment to consider that resting in such a way would have been unthinkable a short time ago, and then she was asleep.

30

The hot water stung on Noon's cuts, but it was a good pain. Alongside the heat of the water it was soothing, pushing away all her other thoughts and concerns.

She had dragged out a large tin bath and heated the water up in the kitchen. Sure that the house was empty save for her and a comatose Eboran, she had stripped off in front of the great oven, dropping her dirty smoke-stinking clothes onto the flagstone floor. Now the steam from the bath soaked her hair, and taking a nub of waxy soap she'd found by the sink, she methodically began to wash, taking comfort in the routine of it. Back at the Winnowry they had been allowed a cold bucket of water once every two days and a rough piece of cloth to rub themselves down. You learned quickly how to make the most of that, so this tin bath of hot water and the time to use it seemed an almost impossible luxury.

'I'm not at the Winnowry any more,' she told the swirling suds. 'And I won't go back. Not alive, anyway.'

Vintage was the reason she'd got so far from the Winnowry in the first place, and now Vintage – kind, eccentric Vintage – was almost certainly dead in the compound somewhere. She thought again of the shape she'd glimpsed against the fires, a blackened twisted thing, and bit at her thumb. Perhaps Godwort would find her body. Perhaps not. Perhaps even now Godwort was sitting in the strange chamber at the heart of the Behemoth, kneeling in front of his son's corpse, his mind finally broken.

Noon hunched over in the bath. Her hands under the water, she sought inside herself for the teeming parasite spirit energy. It was still there, like a banked fire, waiting to be poked into life. Cautiously, so cautiously, she summoned the winnowfire to her right hand, and saw a small green glow flicker into uncertain life under the water. The fire from this energy was strong.

'I could boil myself alive,' she said. Her voice was flat, her only audience the abandoned cutlery and the dusty shelves with their bags of oats and jars of spices. 'It wouldn't be quick, but who deserves a quick death less than me?'

Opening her hand, the swirling green flame grew a little brighter, and she felt a blush of extra heat against her legs. It would not take much to let the energy out – it would be easier than keeping it in, in fact.

Fool.

One word, spoken aloud in her head. Noon jerked with shock, the winnowfire winking out of existence.

'What are you?'

There was no answer, but she could sense that presence inside her again. Something alien, and old, so old. She could feel its disdain for her, its contempt for such a small and weak creature.

'Fuck you,' she said aloud, feeling vaguely stupid. 'You don't know. You don't know what I've been through.'

There was muttering now, in a language she didn't understand. Noon squeezed her eyes shut. It had to be the parasite spirit, there was little else it could be, but Vintage hadn't said anything about their being able to talk. Noon had thought of them as mindless animals of a sort, made of energy and light.

342

Standing up, Noon squeezed the last of the water out of her hair and stepped out of the bath, grabbing a linen sheet to dry herself with, but, as she did so, the ghostly presence elbowed its way to the front of her mind. The gloomy kitchens vanished, and she saw a battlefield. It was raining, the churned earth a slick of mud, and there were men and women all around her, dead or dying. A woman just in front of her was lying on her back, the elaborate armour she wore split open at the midriff. There were scurrying beetle-like creatures all around her, and the woman was trying to push them away, her movements becoming weaker. Noon felt a stab of alarm; the things she had seen in her nightmare, the insects that had been inside Fell-Marian, they were here too. Then the woman – she was Eboran, Noon realised belatedly, her beautiful eyes the colour of blood – looked up at her. She smiled crookedly, and shook her head. The black beetles surged then, slipping into the woman's open mouth, crawling eagerly inside her ears. Her body twitched with the violence of them.

Life is suffering. It was the voice again. *Life is war, and sacrifice. Life is victory.*

The muddy battlefield vanished, and Noon found herself lying naked on the cold flagstones, shivering all over. She felt chilled to the bone, but the presence had retreated. Grabbing the linen and wrapping it around herself, she staggered out of the kitchens.

'Yeah, well, fuck you,' she said to no one in particular.

Upstairs, she crept into Tyron Godwort's room and stood shivering, looking around at his abandoned belongings. Now that she knew what had happened to him, it seemed a sinister, lonely place, but she needed new clothes, and the boy had looked close to her height and size. She went to the wardrobe and began pulling out items of clothing and laying them on the bed – it seemed like Tyron had more outfits than anyone could ever possibly need, but then, Noon reminded herself, at the Winnowry she had only ever had the one. Perhaps this was a normal wardrobe, and everyone had more clothes than they could wear in a year.

She selected warm, woollen leggings and a long-sleeved silk shirt of pale green. She also picked up a maroon velvet jacket that was a little tight across the chest but had bright silver buttons she rather liked; this she stuffed into a bag with some other items, and went back downstairs. Tor was where she had left him, his long form stretched out in the dishevelled bed. His face was turned away from her, but she knew well what it looked like by now – the terrible raw landscape of it haunted her. She had managed, gradually, to cut away the shirt on the left-hand side of his body, so that the ruin of his arm was exposed to the light from the window. She had made small progress with his healing, but it was progress, nonetheless.

'Hey, bloodsucker, how do you feel today? You look a little, uh, peaky.'

She rolled up her sleeves, taking a brief pleasure in the sensation of silk against skin, and knelt on the bed next to him. Picking up one of the knives she now kept on the bedside table next to a bowl of water and soap, she sliced part of her arm open. She knew she was being less than careful now, but she also knew there was no stepping back from it.

Leaning over him, she pressed her wrist to his mouth and he moaned. His good arm came up around her, encircling her waist and pulling her forward so abruptly that she almost fell over him. Grimacing slightly, Noon held herself up with her other arm as he fed. There was strength in the arm that held her, and that gave her some hope.

'Easy, easy.' She tried to pull her arm away, to extract herself from him, but his grip on her intensified and a wave of light-headedness caused her to blink rapidly. It was too easy, she reflected, to let him take what he wanted – there was a close-ness to it that reminded her of the purging at the Winnowry, and the broad shoulders of Novice Lusk as he knelt before her. When you were denied all human contact, this moment of intimacy was powerful. For a few moments she allowed herself to enjoy that sense of closeness, the warmth of his mouth against her skin and the strength of his arm across her back, and then she remembered that she had yet to eat anything and to let this go on for too long would be dangerous for them both.

With more determination than before Noon pulled herself away from Tor's grip, noticing as she did so that the sheet that bunched around his waist was in more of a disarray than it had been. She stared at that a moment before she realised what it meant, and then she stumbled away from the bed, her cheeks suddenly hot.

'Oh. Fire and – oh.' Belatedly, she remembered that Tor usually received his blood donations from willing lovers. It made sense that he would associate the taste of blood with sex. She swallowed hard and left the room.

When she came back, she had eaten bread and cheese from the kitchens, fed their ponies with the oats left in the stables, and had downed a glass of wine. She felt unutterably tired, and Tor had turned over to one side, so that if he still had an erection, she couldn't see it.

'You know, I admire your dedication,' she said as she lay down on the bed next to him. The warmth of his body was a balm, her eyelids as heavy as rocks. 'Most people wouldn't be in the mood, but you –' she yawned cavernously – 'I guess what they say about Eborans . . .'

She slept.

In the dream she was by the Ember River. She had taken her boots off and she was sitting with her feet in the chill water, watching the moonlight glitter across it. Here and there she could just make out the red stones that gave the river its name,

345

and the dark clouds of the underwater plants that grew here. It was a mild night, but her feet were very cold indeed. Even so, she did not want to get up.

She remembered this place. The plains were dissected by two great rivers, the Trick, which was different depending on where you came to it, and the Ember River, which was wide and slow moving. Her people came here often, to wash and to collect water and to meet with the other people who came here. Rivers meant people, and they meant animals too, that was what her mother said. Water brought life.

Noon smiled, wondering dimly where her mother was, even as she looked at the shape of her legs as they dangled into the water. They were long and even shapely, the legs of an adult woman, and something about that and the memory of speaking to her mother didn't add up. Some piece of terrible knowledge seemed to loom over her at that, so she shook her head, backing away from it. Instead, she realised that there was someone else at the riverside.

'Greetings, witch,' said Tor. He was strolling along the bank, his hands behind his back. 'This is quite a picturesque spot. Somewhere you visited once, I assume?'

Noon scrambled to her feet. Tor's face and neck were unblemished, totally free from burns, and his skin seemed to glow under the moonlight. He wore an elaborate padded silk jacket she had not seen before. It was embroidered with silver leaves and his black hair was loose over his shoulders. He smiled at her expression.

'This old thing? It's a little extravagant, I will admit, but, occasionally, I do miss these comforts from home, and why shouldn't I wear them in dreams?'

'A dream.' Noon swayed on her feet. 'That's what this is. Shit.'

The river and the night sky wavered, becoming something false – like the sheets on which Mother Fast would paint scenery for her puppet shows.

346

'No, please, don't go.' Tor laid a hand on her arm. 'It would be good to have someone to talk to. Stay here for a little longer.'

He gestured and the river became a real place again, filling out at the edges and becoming a solid thing. Seeing her look of surprise, he grinned. 'My sister Hestillion was always better at shaping dreams, but I am not completely terrible at it. Don't think about the fact that this is a dream, just listen to my voice. Tell me about this place. About this memory.'

'How can you do that?' she demanded. 'What are you doing here?'

'Eborans can dream-walk,' he said mildly. 'Remember?'

'Yes, but . . .' She felt lost. His face, so close to hers, was calm and unconcerned. The last time she had seen it, that had not been the case. She took a breath. 'This is the Ember River. I came fishing here sometimes when I was small. In the deeper places there were pike, although I never caught one of those, I wasn't strong enough to pull them in.' She stopped. 'Is this really you I'm talking to, or a dream version of you I've made up?'

Tor laughed. 'That's a good question, witch. It's really me, for what it's worth, but then if I were a dream version, I would still say that, wouldn't I?'

Abruptly, Noon wanted to push him in the river. 'Leave me alone. This stuff is private.'

Tor made a point of looking around. 'This boring river is private? Very well, let me show you something, then. I'm not even sure if I can still do this . . .'

He took hold of her arm, and the balmy night and cold river swirled away, carried by something deeper than water, and they were standing in a grove of trees on a hot summer's day. Noon could feel the sun on the top of her head like a blessing, and she could even smell the blossom on the trees. Something about that was familiar, but she couldn't put her finger on it. Next to her, Tor was laughing.

347

'By the roots, I did it! You see this, witch? These are the sacred groves of Ebora as they were over two hundred years ago. No living human has ever seen such a sight, and here you are. Are you suitably honoured?'

'This is a memory of yours?'

'It is. A memory from before the worst times, before the crimson flux had truly decimated us. This orchard was grown in honour of Ygseril, and the trees were tended as honoured associates of the tree-god.' He paused, and Noon noticed that his clothes had changed again. He now wore a simple tunic of deep russet and ochre leggings. There was a bronze brooch at his throat. Somehow, the outfit made him look younger. 'When I left Ebora, of course, all of these trees had long since died. Of heartbreak, Hest was fond of saying, but they were just left unattended for too long. Delicate things like this require care.' He reached up and touched his fingers to the pale pink blossom clustered in the branches, causing a brief flurry of petals like snow. 'You should have seen Ebora in its glory, Noon. It was quite extraordinary.'

'Hest is your sister?'

Tor nodded. 'Lady Hestillion, born in the year of the green bird, mistress of dream-walking and ever my biggest critic.'

She didn't know what to say to that. She crossed her arms over her chest.

'This place is beautiful,' she said quietly. 'It's full of life here. I can feel it, even though it's not real.'

He looked back at her intently then, as if seeing her properly for the first time. It was unnerving, and she had to look away.

'Can you do this with any of your memories?' she said, hoping to distract him from his sudden examination of her.

'I have not tried, for a very long time.' His voice was soft. 'Tell me, witch, why is it I can feel you so clearly in this dream? You are closer to me than you were before. I can almost—' He stopped.

You drank my blood, Noon thought but did not say. A hot wind suddenly blew through the grove of trees, scattering blossom in a fairy blizzard. It smelled, Noon realised with horror, of burned flesh.

'What is that?' said Tor, looking across the neat avenue of trees. There was, Noon saw, a strange cloud hanging over the horizon, a silvery grey shape that she couldn't quite make out. 'Can you smell that? Perhaps something burned in the kitchens.'

'It's a dream, remember?' Noon stepped away, reaching up to pull her hat down over the tattoo on her forehead before remembering that she had lost it in the compound. 'I can't stay here with you, looking at your old Eboran crap. I have other things to do.'

She turned away, meaning to run back to the river somehow, when she lost her footing and fell, her stomach lurching uncomfortably. Noon woke, gasping, in the bed next to Tormalin. Thankfully, the tall Eboran was still asleep. Moving as carefully as possible, so as not to wake him, Noon turned over on her side and lay staring at the door, thinking of the river and the blossom, and the terrible smell of death that had come for them.

31

Aldasair stood on the far side of the gardens, looking down into the plaza. Already, there were more humans here, their tents and carriages clustered like colourful anthills. They had lit fires against the chill of the day. The smell of wood smoke and cooking was everywhere, and their voices were clear in the stillness, the babble of their feelings battering Aldasair like waves of pebbles: eager, angry, confused, calm, excited, uncertain. It was too much.

There were things he should be doing, but today it was so hard to remember how Ebora had been just a few short weeks ago, and that made him feel like he was a ghost of himself, so he turned away from the teeming plaza and walked, instead, further into the overgrown gardens. Bern the Younger had been hard at work on the other side, clearing away the debris of decades of neglect, burning it in huge piles outside the gates. Aldasair had nodded to him briefly the day before, not quite looking at the man's bare chest – the ink patterns on his arms swept across his skin there, too – but hadn't been able to speak. Instead, the human had nodded back, an expression of sympathy on his face that Aldasair had found deeply uncomfortable. He had avoided him since.

Here, the trees and bushes were thick, covering the narrow gravel paths and the rockeries. The small streams that had been carefully cut into the earth had either vanished entirely or been filled with a sludge of ancient dead leaves, and he passed two of the elegant enamelled bridges, hanging broken and skeletal over mud. The ground here grew steeper, and he quickened his pace, belatedly realising why he had come this way.

The Hill of Souls.

Eventually, he stumbled across the old path, the one that had been cut into the rising ground and paved with heavy black stones. These had mostly survived intact, although he took care to step over the piles of wet leaves that threatened to tip him back down to the plaza. He followed the path, up and up, looking over his shoulder once to see the palace spread below him; from here, the plaza and all its strange human activity was hidden, but Ygseril still spread its dead branches like a silver cloud. Like old times. The silent times.

Eventually, at the top of the hill, he came to the old orchard and the building that nestled at its heart. The ground was thick with grass and the puckered corpses of old apples. In the summer, he imagined this place would shake with the sound of wasps, but on this cold day it was silent, with just the half-hearted wind for company. Aldasair walked through the trees, stepping over fallen branches, until he stood at the door. This was a strange building, he had always thought; it did not match the organic, spiralling architecture of the palace, or even the sprawling houses that circled it. This place looked more like a beehive, rounded and simple, with large circular windows now thick with dirt. It was older than everything else. Aldasair looked down at his feet, his hand resting on the door. He couldn't remember how he knew that – some distant lesson or conversation, back when his people had lived.

The door was stiff to open, and he had to lean into it before

351

it stuttered across the stone floor, revealing a single, shadowed room. Circles of dirty light hung in a ring around him, while at the apex of the concave ceiling, the delicate pyramid of leaded glass that he remembered from his childhood had long since been smashed, leaving black twists of lead scratching at the sky. The circular room was ringed with long concentric steps, and that was where they were kept.

'I put mine on the highest platform I could.' Aldasair took a breath, smelling damp and rotten leaves. 'So they could see the moon at night.'

In his memory, the steps were polished stone, shining and clean. Now they were thick with mould and moss, dead leaves and even, he realised, the tiny skeletal remains of various small animals. They must have crept in through the broken skylight, seeking food and shelter, and then found they were unable to get out. It wasn't a reassuring thought.

His eyes adjusting to the gloom, Aldasair walked over to one of the steps. There were tiny mounds all over them, little pockets of shadow – it was almost possible to see what they had been, once, if you squinted.

He had just lifted his hand, daring himself to pick one of them up, when a footfall behind him caused his heart to leap into his throat. He spun round to see a figure blocking out the weak daylight coming in the door.

'Sorry!' Bern the Younger held up his hands. 'I didn't mean to startle you.'

Aldasair clenched his fists at his sides. 'What are you doing here?'

'I was curious. Not always my most useful trait, my father says, but there you go.' He stepped into the room fully, his head turning to try and take in everything at once. 'What is this place?'

'Did you follow me up the hill?'

Bern cleared his throat. His wild yellow hair had been tied

352

back in a tail, and despite the gloom, Aldasair could clearly see the faint blush that crept across his cheeks. 'You could say that. I mean, you could say that because it would be true. I saw you on the far side of the gardens, and you had such a look on your face—'

'I didn't hear you. I should have heard you coming.'

Bern the Younger grinned. It was such an incongruous expression in this broken, ancient place that Aldasair found he had to look away.

'I'm a hunter. It's my job to move quietly.'

'Are you saying you were hunting me?'

'By the stones, no!' Bern raised his hands again, looking genuinely alarmed. 'I am not good at this. Speaking to you people, I mean. I was curious, Aldasair. I didn't know what could be up this hill, that you were so determined to reach. Forgive me.' When Aldasair didn't answer, Bern nodded around at the steps. 'So, what is this place?'

'We called it the Hill of Souls.' Outside, the day brightened, filling the room with a soft glow. Dust danced in the shaft of light from the hole in the roof. 'It was—' Aldasair stopped. 'It's difficult to remember the words for these things, sometimes. It was something we did every season, and it was important.'

'A tradition,' said Bern. 'We have many of those in Finneral. Mostly, I'll be honest with you, to do with stones. Or drinking.'

'A tradition. Yes, that's what it was.' Aldasair closed his eyes, trying to remember. 'The youngest of us, the children. Those who were no more than fifty or sixty years old—' Bern made an odd noise, which Aldasair ignored. 'They would make charms in the shapes of the war-beasts, to honour them. Those who had fallen, their spirits returning to Ygseril. And then we would have a ceremony, with lights, and special food, and place them on the top of the Hill of Souls, so they could look from Ygseril's branches and see the lights burning here, and know they weren't forgotten. That they would never be forgotten.' Aldasair opened his eyes, his head spinning with the memories; he could taste the soul-cakes, could smell the fresh clay. It had all been yesterday, hadn't it?

'A festival day for your children.' Bern looked serious, one hand tugging at the stones in his beard.

'Yes,' Aldasair went back to the steps, smiling, 'when there were no spaces left for the charms, we would take them back and we would bury them somewhere so that they could return to Ygseril's roots. The place had to be secret.' Reaching out, he brushed away a clump of old leaves, revealing a small, misshapen lump of clay. 'There must be thousands of them, buried all over Ebora.'

'You have been doing this a long time?'

'For as long as anyone remembers.' Aldasair touched the twisted piece of clay. It crumbled under his finger, and his stomach turned over. 'Not any more, though, of course. Not for – not for a very long time.'

Bern joined him, and began sweeping away the debris with the side of one large hand, revealing more of the charms. Here was the snaking shape of a dragon, its horned head turned inwards to rest on its own flank; here was a great fox, its long snout chipped at the end; a griffin, one of its wings in pieces next to it. Others had not survived so well; damp had softened their edges and paint had flaked away, leaving suggestions of shapes, half-seen ghosts.

'Your children made these?'

'Yes, the youngest ones. I looked forward to it each season. We all did. Talking about which war-beast we would honour, and why. Some honoured the same war-beast every season, others made figures of those who had won the most battles, attained the most glory. Some of us just liked certain shapes.' He paused. It was difficult to talk this much at once. 'I remember the last time I came here. I was nearly too old to be included,

354

and the first instances of the crimson flux had started. I felt like it was the end of something, that day. I didn't realise it was the end of *everything*.'

Aldasair stopped, his face hot. He had said too much. Bern was looking thoughtfully at the charms, his green eyes serious for once, and then he turned to look at Aldasair.

'It's not the end. Things are changing already, don't you see?' One corner of his mouth lifted in a faintly bitter smile. 'You rarely see people working together as they are now, and stone of my heart, I think that means something. All of this,' he gestured at the room with its animal corpses and dead leaves, 'it can be what it was, again. There will be more Eboran children. We should tidy this up, so it is ready for them.'

Despite himself, Aldasair found himself smiling. 'The Hill of Souls is just a memory, and there are so many other things that need mending. But I appreciate the thought.'

Bern sighed. 'There is a lot of sadness here.' The look he gave Aldasair was so frank he had to turn away. 'All of you, so sad. But change is coming, my friend, I can feel it in the stone.'

Outside, the wind picked up, sweeping into the room and dancing dried leaves around their feet. Aldasair thought of the tarla cards and how they had spoken to him with words that had claimed to know the future – and how he no longer had time to listen to them.

'Change is coming,' he said. 'But what kind of change?'

Later, Aldasair found himself wandering the corridors of the palace again. He hadn't thought of the Hill of Souls in decades, but now that he had, random memories kept floating to the surface, like frogs disturbed on the bottom of a pond: himself and Tormalin arguing over which war-beast they would make, competing to see who could make the better one; the sight of the Hill when the lights had been lit, a beacon like a great eye,

355

looking out over Ebora; his mother burning the soul-cakes and laughing over it, even though he knew it embarrassed her.

The idea that it could all be as it was . . . Bern had seemed so earnest, but he was also human; humans were used to their lives being fast, everything changing overnight. No human had spent a hundred years in silence, watching as everything slowly fell apart.

Without realising it, Aldasair had walked to the doors of the Hall of Roots. It was the deep heart of the evening now, and outside in the plaza people were cooking food and talking, but inside the palace the silence was still as thick as fog. He raised his hand, meaning to knock at the door, or perhaps just rest his hand against it, when it suddenly swung open, revealing Hestillion's face. She stared at him as if she'd never seen him before, and then neatly stepped out into the corridor, slamming the door behind her.

'What do you want?'

Aldasair opened his mouth, and closed it again. Hestillion's eyes were wild, her mouth a thin colourless line, while the tops of her cheeks sported two bright blotches of pink. Seeing him struggling for words, she hissed with impatience.

'What are you doing here, Aldasair?'

'Our guests.' He cleared his throat. 'They want to know when they will see Ygseril. They are here to help, after all.'

She reached up and pushed a strand of hair away from her forehead. 'Of course. That is why they are here. And they will, they will help him, I'm sure of it. But I need more time.'

'More time? For what?'

She shook her head, irritated again, as though he had asked the wrong question.

'I must do all I can, first.'

Aldasair raised his eyebrows. He was thinking of the incident with the wine merchant's boy, so many years ago. 'What are you doing? What have you done?'

'Oh nothing, don't give me that look. Go and look after our guests, and let me do what I need to do. Please. Trust your cousin, Aldasair.'

With that, she opened the door and slipped back into the Hall of Roots, making certain to shut it firmly behind her. Aldasair stared at it for some time, trying to make sense of her words, and her mood. He had never seen Hestillion so flustered.

Eventually, he turned and walked away, heading towards the lights and noise of the plaza with what he would later identify as relief.

32

'Are they winnowfire?'

Tor laughed, and for a wonder, Noon wasn't annoyed. They were crouched inside the mouth of a dark cave, while outside a rain storm surged and thundered across a murky patch of marshland. The darkness wasn't complete, however: here and there floated great orbs of pale blue light, apparently unaffected by the rain. They cast eerie glowing patches onto the churning water and mud below them.

'Not winnowfire, no,' he said. He was staring out of the cave alongside her, looking pleased with himself. He enjoyed surprising her, she was starting to realise. 'I tried to poke one with my sword once, and it just skittered away. They're a type of gas, supposedly, but I met a hermit in this bog who claimed they were ghosts. I ask you, witch, what sort of gas jumps away from a sword?'

'What sort of ghost does?' she asked mildly, and he raised his eyebrows at her. 'Where did you say this was?'

'In Jarlsbad, some way north of their Broken River. I was here, oh, forty years ago. Isn't it a sight? I slept in this cave one night, and they all came and gathered at the entrance, like they were seeking an audience.'

As he spoke, the eerie blue orbs floated towards them out of the dark, filling the small cave with a glow that was somewhere between daylight and moonlight.

'I'm getting good at this.'

'Why were you out here, in the middle of nowhere? All your fine clothes, soaked. I dread to think what it would do to your hair.'

When he answered he didn't meet her eyes, looking instead out across the marsh. 'I was wandering. I wanted to see everything. I had spent so long looking at the same empty corridors, the same empty streets . . .' His voice trailed off, and then he took her arm, pointing with his other hand out into the dark. 'Look! There goes the hermit now, do you see?'

An oddly elongated figure was passing by in the distance, a black shape against the teeming rain. It took Noon a moment to realise that it was man on tapering stilts, picking his way across the marshes like a long-legged bird.

'Sorry,' Tor let go of her arm, and cleared his throat, 'I forgot that you prefer not to be touched.'

For a brief second Noon had a vision of crouching over him in the narrow bed, her bare arm pressed to his mouth, his hand pressing at the small of her back. She banished the memory – it was hazardous to think such things here.

'It's all right.' The rain was a soft curtain of sound, almost comforting. She hadn't thought of it that way in a long time. 'You have been to so many odd places. I've been nowhere.'

'You've been to the Winnowry. You've been to the Winnowry a lot, I think.'

She punched him on the arm.

'Fuck you.'

He cleared his throat again. 'I would be very curious to see it, actually. Up close. I've seen it from Mushenska, of course, ugly great spiky thing that it is, but the inside is a mystery that intrigues me.'

Noon pressed her lips together. There were times when she was sure he was about to mention Vintage, but he never quite managed it. She did not know if that were deliberate, or if in this odd, dreaming state, it did not occur to him.

'Mystery my arse.'

'Again, something I have seen from a distance and greatly wish to see up close—'

She hit him a little harder this time. 'Even if that shit hole were worth showing you, I can't just mess about with dreams like you can.'

'Of course you can. We're in your head, aren't we? You are dreaming and aware of it, yet you haven't woken up. That suggests to me that you have enough mastery of your own dreamspace to manipulate it.' He caught the look she was giving him and smirked. 'Just try it. Imagine being back at the Winnowry. Pick a memory of it, and concentrate on it.'

Noon sat back on her haunches, considering. She had lots of memories of the Winnowry – ten years of nothing else, in fact – but they were all more or less the same. Damp walls, narrow windows, grey food. There was one occasion when she had seen it differently, of course. She held her hands up in front of her, remembering that they had bound her hands and then wrapped them in thick black cloth, and during the journey they had covered her head with a heavy hood. When they had removed it and pulled her down from the back of the bat she had been surprised to land on wet sand. Confused, terrified and wracked with guilt, she had had no real idea where she was, and when she had looked up –

The cave and the grotty marshland were gone, and instead they were standing together on a beach. A bleak and featureless coast stretched away to either side of them, and, looming ahead, was the Winnowry.

'By the roots,' murmured Tor. 'The architect must have been having a really bad day.'

The black towers stretched towards an indifferent sky like broken knives. High above, tiny slivers of light burned from narrow windows, while just ahead a great iron door marked the entrance. On either side of it were a pair of torches, unlit now, above two pieces of bleached driftwood. Tomas's inscrutable face had been carved into both with little love for the subject, it seemed to Noon; the staring face looked blind. She remembered being dragged towards that door, boots pushing up furrows of sand. She remembered how she had screamed.

'I was eleven years old when they brought me here,' she said. 'They just snatched me up, bound me, and flew me to this miserable place. I wasn't allowed to bring anything with me. Not that I had anything left to bring.'

Tor didn't say anything, and she felt embarrassed that she had talked about it at all. She looked at him and noticed that his outfit had changed again – now he wore a dark maroon coat the same colour as his eyes, with a dove-grey silk shirt underneath. There was an elaborate earring hanging from his left ear, some confection of cloudy glass and spiralled silver.

'Why do you keep changing your clothes?'

He smiled at her 'Why not? I wear them so well.' He made a sweeping gesture as if presenting himself for inspection, and his earring spun, catching the muted light. Noon abruptly remembered that he barely had anything left that could be called an ear on that side of his face. She looked away.

'I never wanted to see this place again.'

'What's it like inside?'

As easy as that, they were there, standing too close together in the cramped cell Noon had lived in for ten years. The cold iron grid of the floor was the same, the narrow bunk untouched. It was smaller and darker than she remembered, but then it was a place from a nightmare – perhaps her own emotions were distorting it. Tor walked up to the bars and

361

looked out across the echoing chasm to the far side of the prison, where rows of identical cells waited. They were alone.

'I've never seen it empty,' she said. 'It's strange.'

'What a desolate hole,' remarked Tor. 'At least my prison was beautiful, if sad. No one should be kept in a place like this.'

'What do you mean, your prison?' asked Noon. She joined him at the bars. 'What did you get locked up for?'

'Oh. Forget I said it, I was being poetic.' Tor pushed the door and it swung open easily. Beyond Noon's cell the Winnowry was drowned in shadows, a place made of darkness and sorrow. Seeing it without the living, breathing women who had populated it was deeply frightening, she realised. Looking at the darkness and feeling the emptiness of the space between them, she didn't assume they had all escaped, like she had. She assumed they were all dead.

She turned to look back at her bunk, only to see the thin covers there boiling with movement.

'No!'

Hundreds of shining black beetle-like creatures erupted from the bedding, streaming towards her on needle-sharp legs. From somewhere outside and above them came a shattering roar, and the Winnowry trembled around them. She looked at Tor, who was staring at the beetles in bemusement.

'What is happening?'

'It's them! They're back, we'll all—'

There was another crash and Noon stumbled, trying to keep upright while the beetles surged around her feet. The Winnowry was now full of the sound of screaming women, and Noon knew that they were down in the shadows somewhere, crushing each other and suffocating in their panic to flee the building. The urge to summon the winnowfire was enormous, but if she did that, if she did that—

Tor was suddenly next to her, taking her hand firmly – she

was surprised that it was warm, when everything else here was cold – and they were back on the beach.

'Now, it really is quite rude of you to have a nightmare while I am accompanying you,' said Tor, in an entirely normal tone. 'It spoils the mood utterly.'

'Shut up, you idiot. Look!'

Above the Winnowry the sky was crowded with Behemoths, corpse coloured and teeming with tiny vessels pushing their way through the ships' shining skin. Things like giant spiders, their legs spread like grasping hands, were floating down towards them.

'Get control of it,' said Tor, sharply. 'This is your head, remember?'

'I can't! This thing, it – it comes from outside of me.' As soon as she said it, Noon knew it was true. 'This isn't my nightmare at all!'

The gates of the Winnowry were open, and thousands of the beetles were skittering towards them. In that way that only happens in dreams, she knew that there was someone behind them now, a figure with a low, feminine voice who would speak directly into her ear. She knew what it would say.

Tor spun round, looking towards the strip of iron-grey sea, and she knew that he had felt it too. 'There's no one there. No one there at all,' he said, his voice low. 'I've had enough of this.'

He took hold of her hand again, and this time Noon felt herself physically wrenched from the terrible scene around her. Caught between the feeling of falling down and being thrown up into the air, she stumbled to her knees, only to find herself on all fours on a thick, luxurious carpet.

'This is about as far from that miserable place as I could get,' said Tor in way of an explanation. 'Welcome to the Eskt family suite.'

Noon stood up. They were in a room more opulent than

any she'd ever seen; fancier than Vintage's carriage on the winnowline, larger than any of the rooms she'd seen in Esiah Godwort's rambling mansion. There were tall, lacquered screens everywhere, long, low seats spilling over with plush cushions, and elegant pieces of sculpture in each corner, stylised images of people with long faces. The walls were covered in patterned silk; blue herons against pale gold. She couldn't take it all in. Tor had sat down on one of the low seats. He was breathing hard and looking at the floor.

'What did you mean,' he asked, 'when you said that dream wasn't yours?'

'I meant what I said.' Noon pushed her hair back from her forehead. Her heart was still beating too fast. She half expected thousands of skittering beetles to come surging out from behind the screens, or for the ceiling to shake apart to reveal the fat belly of a Behemoth. 'I don't know where it came from. All my bad dreams, they've always involved what happened to me when I was a kid. I've never even thought about the Behemoths, they've all been gone for so long. They're just a story Mother Fast told us when she wanted to scare us.'

Tor made a pained face at that. 'What you dreamed was so similar to what Ainsel dreamed, I can't ignore it. What if—' he grunted and pressed his fingers to his forehead – 'it's still trying to push its way in. Maintaining this dreamscape is hard.' He looked up at her sharply. 'Stop it. Stop thinking about it.'

'Oh, that's great advice, thanks. I'll just stop *thinking* about it. Piece of piss.'

Tor stood up and stalked over to a low cabinet where a bottle of wine rested. Noon was sure it hadn't been there a moment ago. He picked up the bottle and poured himself a glass, draining it off in one go.

'Dream wine.' He put the glass down. 'Dream wine should be excellent, don't you think? But it's not. It's a ghost of the thing.' He took a breath. 'Don't you see, witch? What if these dreams mean something? What if they're a premonition?'

Noon looked at him. He was at ease here. There was an archway in the wall behind him, leading to another, equally beautiful room, and beyond that she could see glass doors leading out into a garden. She thought for a moment she could see figures out there, children running through the grass . . .

'You are pushing at the edges, Noon,' he said. 'Please desist.'

'When I escaped the Winnowry, it was because I fully believed the Jure'lia were coming,' she said. She paused, pressing her thumb to her lips before continuing. 'I didn't doubt it at all. And then I left, and all these other things happened. I've barely had time to think.' She took a breath. 'But if I think about it again, if I allow myself – yes, I think they're coming. I think the dreams are true.'

Tor picked up the bottle, and put it back down again. He laughed, a short, bitter sound. 'If that's true, witch, then we are all—'

There was a hand on her shoulder, shaking her. Noon turned to see who it was, and sat up in the narrow bed, nearly falling out of it.

'My darling,' said Vintage, 'look at the state of you both.'

33

Vintage wasn't in a great state herself, a fact of which she was well aware. Even so, she was gratified to see the girl's eyes widen in shock. She stumbled back as Noon jumped out of the bed and threw her arms around her, nearly knocking her into the wall.

'Vintage!' The girl broke the embrace and held her at arm's length, staring at her as though she'd never seen her before. For a moment her eyes brimmed with tears, and Vintage saw her struggle to control it: the sight broke Vintage's heart, a little. 'Fire and blood, Vintage, I thought you'd died, I thought you were dead, I would never have left you—'

'Take a breath, child, before you pass out.' Vintage patted Noon's face. She was gaunter than when Vintage had seen her last, her shining olive skin now washed out and pale. Her hair stuck up on end and her eyes were lost in shadows. 'It looks like you've had enough to deal with.' Before Noon could move away, she took hold of Noon's arms. They were crisscrossed with cuts, most of them looking painfully fresh. 'What have you been doing to yourself, my dear?'

Noon looked down at the cuts. She didn't seem ashamed or alarmed. 'Tormalin. He was nearly dead. It was all I could think to do.'

Vintage sighed. 'You probably saved his life, although I'm not sure he'll thank you for it, vain creature that he is.' Detaching herself from the fell-witch, Vintage approached the bed. Again, she felt her heart fracture. These children, how broken they were, and she had made it worse. The left-hand side of his beautiful face was a rippled mask of scar tissue, his hair seared away from his scalp. His left arm, which lay above the covers, was in a similar state. He appeared to be sleeping peacefully enough, at least.

'I don't know about you, my dear, but I could do with a hot dinner inside me.'

They bustled around the kitchens together, stoking up the oven and opening cupboards, searching through the cold larder. There was little planning to it, and Vintage suspected the girl wasn't capable of doing so; she seemed easily distracted, her hands trembling now and then. She would stop, as though listening to something only she could hear, before shaking her head and chopping the warty eyes off a potato. Vintage wondered how much blood she had given Tor in the time she had been gone. Too much could be dangerous, but having looked at the Eboran's terrible ravaged face, Vintage could well imagine making the same decision herself.

When finally they sat down at the table, it was to a hotch-potch meal of boiled potatoes with butter, thick slices of cured ham, pears poached in nutty ale, baked apples, and jars and jars of Esiah's best preserves. Vintage's stomach rumbled audibly at the sight of it. She caught Noon's eye and they both laughed.

'Vintage,' Noon said round a mouthful of potato, 'where have you been? What happened?'

'If I recall correctly, my dear, what happened was that everything erupted in a giant ball of winnowfire.' Seeing the expression on Noon's face, Vintage swiftly continued. 'I'm

367

not at all sure, but I believe I was blown free somehow. I awoke some distance from the wreckage of the Behemoth, with this delightful scorching on my face.' She dabbed her fingers lightly to her cheeks, which were still red and sore. 'And my clothes torn and burned. I had landed in a big puddle, luckily, and I believe that may have put any fires out. I don't know how long I was unconscious for, but the fire was down to its embers. Everything hurt.'

She paused, taking sips of the apple juice they had found in the larder. It was sweet and tart. 'I couldn't move for that first day, or the first night. I lay still and tried to figure out whether I'd broken anything. And I hoped that the parasite spirits didn't come across me.'

'I should have gone back.' Noon had stopped with a forkful of ham halfway to her mouth. 'I should have come looking for you.'

'The fact that you got Tor back here in that state is a feat in itself, Noon, my dear. Please do not be distressed. When finally I felt I could stand and walk, I started to make my way to the gate. I did not get far. I lay for another night in the hollow of a tree. It took me a long time to wake the following morning, and I knew I had to get some food.' She raised her eyebrows at Noon. 'Food heals, Noon, just as blood heals Eborans. More efficiently, in fact. I hope you have been eating?'

For a moment Noon looked confused by the question. 'I eat when I remember.'

'Good. Well, I foraged. You don't grow up with the vine forest as your backyard and not learn something about what you can and can't eat.' Vintage pursed her lips. 'Although it may be a while before I eat mushrooms again. Where is Esiah? He's not here?'

'We saw him as he came in the gate. He was worried, because there was a fire. He mentioned his son.' Noon grimaced. 'I don't think he was in his right mind.'

Vintage sighed. 'Poor man. He's not been in his right mind for some time. You don't need to know the endless details of my survival, Noon, my dear, save to say that it was unpleasant. I am more interested in what happened just before the Behemoth was blown into tiny bits. It was you, wasn't it? The green that I saw – it was winnowfire?'

The girl looked stricken, then angry, then lost. She pushed her hair back from her forehead – the bat tattoo there looked dark against her ashen skin. 'It was me. Again. I nearly killed you both. I –' she gasped, visibly keeping her distress under control – 'I took life energy from a parasite spirit.'

Vintage sat back, genuinely astonished. She put down her fork, and the clink of silver against the plate was very loud in the eerily quiet house. 'Well. Goodness me.'

'It was too much,' said Noon. 'It overwhelmed me. It was like filling a bucket from a river, but the river is running faster than you realise. Not only does it fill your bucket, but it also pulls it away from your hands, and it's lost. I couldn't control it.' Noon looked up, and now her eyes were dry and her voice was flat. 'It was too much for me, Vintage.'

And then, curiously, she gasped again, closing her eyes tight and bending over the table. Vintage stood up, ignoring the various aches and pains that clamoured for attention.

'My dear! What is it?'

Noon shook her head, half laughing. 'I don't know, I don't know what it is. Ever since the parasite spirit, everything has been slightly wrong. It doesn't follow me to my dreams, I know that much, but it's with me the rest of the time. The energy too – it's still there, it just . . . waits.' She looked down at her hands for a moment, and when she looked back up, her eyes were filled with a naked desperation. 'Why am I like this? Why am I this cursed thing? With all your reading, Vintage, you must know why fell-witches exist!'

'Oh my dear, I don't know. No one does.' Vintage sat back

down, chasing a potato across the plate with her knife. She had washed and bound her wound as soon as she'd got back to the house, but it was still awkward to eat with one of her hands injured. 'It's not passed down from mother to daughter, we do know that much. The children with this ability appear to be randomly chosen. There is no aptitude, no pattern across families that can be traced. It is an unknowable magic. It shows itself in all peoples, all across Sarn. Save for Ebora.' She paused. 'I did read something once. Did you have your own gods, amongst your people?'

'Yes. Gods of storms, the seasons. They were distant. They were just stories, really.'

'I read of a people once who believed that the winnowfire was a blessing rather than a curse. That it was a gift from a goddess.'

'A goddess?' Noon had picked up her fork, but now she put it back down again. 'Who were these people? What goddess?'

'I don't know, darling. All trace of that people are gone – hardly any writings about them exist. I suspect the Winnowry has rooted it all out and destroyed it. The idea of the winnowfire as a gift hardly fits with what they're selling, does it? But I remember they called the goddess "She Who Laughs".'

Noon shook her head. 'That means nothing to me.'

'No reason it should, my dear.'

For a time they were both quiet. Vintage concentrated on eating what was set in front of her, knowing that it was essential that she get her energy back. The girl was visibly struggling, her hands trembling, and not for the first time Vintage wondered about the terrible event in her past she was trying so hard to hide.

'I am sorry,' Noon said eventually. 'For what I have done to you, and to Tormalin. I can't control this, I've never been able to. I should never have left the Winnowry. It's true, what they say we are.'

'It is *not* true, and do not let me hear you say that ever again.' Noon's head snapped up, clearly startled by the venom in Vintage's voice. 'The Winnowry is a poison, a poison that has tainted all of Sarn, letting us think that certain women are inherently evil, through something that, as far as we know, is as natural as having freckles, or being left handed. It's easier to put these women out of our sight, of course, than to force ourselves to think of ways that we can help. All of that potential, all of those lives, curtailed because of the ravings of a sea-addled man –' Vintage took a sharp breath. 'Noon, my dear, we would have all died in that wreckage if you hadn't summoned your handy explosion, and that would have been my fault. I am always too willing to drag others into danger because of my own curiosity.' She thought of Nanthema then, her quick grin and her laughter, before firmly pushing the memories aside; there would be time to examine her own guilt later. The girl was looking at her uncertainly, her eyes too bright. Vintage took another sip of apple juice.

'Listen. There was an interesting case a while back. A boy was born in Finneral, who grew up to realise that, actually, he was not a boy, but a girl. This girl grew up wise, clever, able to see patterns in the movements of animals, warnings in the calls of birds, and the Finneral people venerated her. She became a "Stone Talker", which is their term for a wise person, or a spiritual leader. And then, one day, her winnowfire manifested.'

Noon blinked. 'She was a fell-witch?'

Vintage nodded. 'The Winnowry came for her, but the Finneral would not give her up. Stone talkers are rare, and she was beloved of them. The dispute became violent, and the fell-witch was killed in the conflict. The Winnowry and the Finneral have had a very icy relationship since.'

'That's terrible!'

'It is. But, you know, I have spoken to Finneral who insist that she is still alive. She was too wise, too canny, and she

371

made them think she was dead so she could escape. They insist she still lives now, somewhere in Finneral, a secret advisor to their leaders.' Vintage smiled. 'I hope that's true. But my point is, as you can see, that winnowfire isn't something we're even close to understanding. And there is so much potential, in all of you. Don't be afraid of who you are.'

'I don't know if I'm strong enough for that. I've already done too much damage, I—' Noon stood up, scraping the chair across the flagstones with a screech. 'It doesn't matter now, though, because you're here.' The cuts that traced a pattern up her arms were almost too red to look at. 'We'll get Tor better together, and it'll all be as it was.'

'I can't, Noon, my darling. I have to leave you. I have to go, immediately. There will be things I must pack, of course, and since it sounds to me like poor Esiah won't be coming back, well, I'm sure he won't mind if I avail myself of his supplies. But I have to go.'

Noon stood as if frozen. 'Leave us? What do you mean, leave us?'

'Listen.' Vintage stood up and went to the girl, taking hold of her arm. Her skin felt feverish. 'There was something I have missed, over all these long years. Something brought home to me by what we found inside the Behemoth remains. It's possible I have made an enormous mistake, and that someone I care about very much has paid the price. It has been so long, my darling, that I cannot possibly wait any longer. I have to go now.'

'What do you mean, a mistake? What are you talking about?'

Vintage sighed. 'It's probably best you don't know. I have already caused you and Tormalin enough pain, and besides which, neither of you are fit to travel. Take care of him, and yourself, and, hopefully, I will come back for you.'

Noon tipped her head, as if listening to some internal voice again. She winced as she did so. 'You really mean to go? Now?'

'I do.' Vintage patted her arm. 'I've got a way to go before I come to the first reasonable town, and I need to do it before the long rains come. Believe me, Greenslick is the most miserable place in the rainy season. Now, my dear, help me pack up some of this food. Thank goodness for Esiah's overly packed larder.'

Noon did what she could to talk Vintage out of it, following her from room to room, presenting her with reasons to stay, but the strange voice and alien images in her head kept intruding, causing her to stop mid-sentence, unsure of what her point had been. She saw that Vintage noticed her distress and confusion but did not comment on it. That in itself shook Noon – Vintage, always so kind and so nosy, had apparently decided she would have to cope with this, whatever it was, by herself. They stopped together at Tor's room, and Vintage went to his bedside, fussily plucking at his bedclothes until they were neater.

'He sleeps well, and deep,' she said. 'I believe that is a good sign. Sometimes the body just needs to rest, and by the vines, Eborans are tougher than most.'

'He moves when I . . . feed him,' said Noon. Vintage hadn't commented further on that either. 'But he doesn't talk or open his eyes. It's like he's closed himself down somehow, like a hibernating bear.' She wondered if she should mention their shared dreams, but that already seemed too personal somehow. And besides which, Vintage had made it very clear that she wasn't interested. She had other things to deal with. 'Vintage, have you ever heard of parasite spirits talking?'

The question was out before she'd thought to ask it. Vintage turned to her, her eyebrows raised. Her scorched skin looked tight and painful. 'I beg your pardon?'

'I mean, no one has ever spoken to them? That you know of?'

373

'No, no of course not.' Vintage was looking at her very closely now. 'Why do you ask that, my dear?'

'I just wondered. I mean, I thought I heard something in the compound, but it must have been shock, or my head being bashed around. I landed quite hard myself.'

Vintage looked like she might ask more, and then she nodded shortly. 'I'm sure that was what it is, my darling. It was a strange place. After all these years of waiting to explore it, I have to say, I shall be quite glad to leave it behind.'

With that she pushed Tor's hair back from his forehead, patted his face once, and left the room. When she took her leave of Esiah's house, she embraced Noon and kissed her firmly on the cheek. Noon blinked. Who had last kissed her like that? Her mother, probably. She had kissed her forehead when she served their breakfast, and then kissed her cheek when she was tucked up in bed for the night. She hadn't thought of that for years.

'Vintage, I . . . please keep yourself safe.'

The woman grinned at her. 'My darling, I have been keeping myself safe since before you were a twinkle in some rogue's eye. Stay here, get the pair of you better. This is as safe a place to hide as any.'

She took one of the ponies, which looked glad to leave. She rode out across the courtyard to the gates, a new hat – scavenged from Godwort's wardrobe – wedged jauntily on her head, and her crossbow bouncing at her hip. Noon watched her go through the gate, wondering if she would wave. She didn't. Overhead, the clouds were bruising, ready for more rain, and Noon felt goosebumps break out across her arms. To be alone in this broken landscape . . . She went back inside.

From her camp on the lonely hill, Agent Lin watched the black woman leave the gates, moving slowly but steadily up the road that led away from Greenslick. She waited, but her prey and her companion did not follow. Eventually, the rain that had been threatening all morning finally broke, and she moved into her makeshift tent, still sitting at the entrance so that she could watch the distant gates. Behind her, the bulky form of Gull made a muffled trilling noise. At first she had tried to chase the creature off, but the nights were cold in this miserable place, and the warmth of the bat filled the entire tent at night. Now he was asleep, his big ugly face tucked under a wing.

'Are they dead already? That's the question.' Lin squinted through the rain. There had been a fire in the compound, the smoke billowing up over it like a great cloud. Before it had been dispersed by the rain that came and went constantly, the smoke had briefly blotted the whole property from her view under a shifting veil of black and grey. The rain was so heavy now she could barely see the great house and its walls, and a worm of anxiety twisted in her stomach. When it rained, she could see very little. A teeming grey curtain stood between her and the mansion. 'Wounded in the compound, or killed outright. How would I know?'

Gull trilled again, as if he were answering her in his sleep. It was almost amusing to her that the bat responded to the sound of her voice.

'If they're already dead, I will have to go in and retrieve the body. Take it back to that bitch, and they'll have to leave me alone.' *Leave my boy alone*, she thought. 'You can bet I'll be fussier about what missions I'll do for them in future. Let some other agent deal with this nonsense.'

Fell-Noon could be leaving now. Sneaking out the gates under the cover of the rain, following on behind her friend. Lin would have to go right down to the gates themselves to check, and risk being uncovered. If she revealed herself too soon, all would be lost.

'I can't let them see me,' she said aloud. 'Not until I know I can take them. And in this weather . . .'

375

Winnowfire was unreliable in the rain. And she wanted everything to go smoothly. She needed everything to be under control.

'I will just have to be patient.'

Agent Lin shuffled backwards, never taking her eyes off the distant shadow that was the house, and lay back against Gull's warm mid-section. The bat gave a faint trill of protest, then went back to sleep.

34

'I am trying to help you.'

Nestled deep within the netherdark, Hestillion made herself small and pliant in an attempt to disguise her growing irritation. Ygseril's dreaming mind was brighter than ever, a great diffuse cloud of light that hung over her as the tree-god's branches once had, but his physical body remained inert – the grey bark did not grow warmer, no leaves grew, and most importantly, no sap flowed. She was no closer to understanding what had happened, and how it could be solved.

Why?

Ygseril had asked this before. No answer seemed sufficient.

'Because you are the god of my people,' she said evenly. 'Without you, we are dying.'

Living things die. Matter is consumed. Other things grow.

'Of course, my lord, but for an entire people to die? It is a tragedy.'

When the voice spoke again, the light was a little brighter. *Any people?*

If she had possessed her physical form, Hestillion would have bitten her lip. Conversations with Ygseril seemed to go nowhere, every attempt to extract information thrown off with incomprehensible questions.

'We are the god-touched, lord. You raised us above all the peoples of Sarn to be your glory.' Hestillion paused. Had Ygseril decided they were not worthy of saving? Did he no longer love his own creatures? That would explain the centuries of deathly silence. 'But without your sap, we wane.'

You are so determined. The voice sounded amused now. Hestillion swallowed down the surge of impatience that threatened to close her throat, but frustration shivered through her voice like the strings of a plucked instrument.

'I only wish to restore you, Ygseril. Please, tell me what you need and I shall see that it is done. My resources are so much greater than they were – I have much of Sarn dancing at my fingertips! Whatever it is you need, we can find it.'

Whatever it was, she needed to figure it out soon. The humans easily outnumbered them now, and she knew that if they truly wanted to enter the Hall of Roots, they could. And if that happened, any chance that Hestillion had to keep this secret – this incredible, this desperate secret – to herself would vanish, and with it her chance to be the one to save Ebora. She would never have the time alone with him, and she was sure that was the key.

It is so dark down here. We only seek the light.

Hestillion frowned. She had not heard Ygseril refer to himself as 'we' before.

'Do you require more light? Is that it?'

It couldn't be. They had tried that, more than once, over the long quiet years of slow death, and it had never made any difference. But Ygseril didn't answer, and as she waited, the soft cloud of light slowly faded away, until she was alone in the shadow roots.

It was intolerable.

Aldasair stood very still, feeling his discomfort prickle up his back like the legs of some great insect. There was no escaping. They were everywhere, blocking his every escape route.

'But there's nothing to do here!'

A small fist clutched at his cuff. It was probably a sticky fist. He looked down at the human child and attempted to arrange his features into something approaching affable, if not exactly friendly.

'Can you not amuse yourselves? When I was a child –' Aldasair cleared his throat. He hadn't been a child for hundreds of years. 'When I was a child we learned how to play musical instruments or paint pictures.'

The look the human child gave him made Aldasair realise that all the frustrated looks shot his way by Hestillion over the years had actually been remarkably polite.

'We don't *have* musical insraments.'

So many of Ebora's visitors had brought children with them that it had been decided that a particular place should be found for them – much of the city was still unsafe, after all, populated by hungry wolves, and dotted with buildings on the point of collapse; curious children exploring such a place could mean disaster. Aldasair had brought them to the old ballroom, thinking of long-ago evenings full of music and laughter, but of course there was no music any more, and it was a vast, lonely place despite the tall windows filled with light. Now, it smelled strongly of dust and mould, and the human children – around twenty of them so far – seemed distinctly unimpressed. They clustered around him, staring openly at his face with very little of the reticence of their parents.

'If you could, if you could just –' He took a slow breath. So much talking, after so many years of silence, and all these eyes watching. 'Please. Just –' He took a few steps backwards, and half of them shuffled with him. 'Whatever you would do, in your own homes, if you could—'

A tall figure swept into the room from behind him, picking

379

up the child at his sleeve and whipping him into the air as though he were made of feathers.

'I'm hungry,' declared Bern the Younger to the room at large. 'This rabbit looks about the right size for me.' He slung the child, who was shrieking with delight, over his shoulder. To Aldasair's amazement, the other small humans were grinning at him too. 'Or, let me check – not sure there's enough flesh on his bones.' He tickled the boy, who yowled and wriggled with laughter so violent that Bern swept him back down to the floor.

'Bern! Bern!' One of the smallest girls ran over and hugged his knee. 'It's so *boring*, Bern, will you play with us, Bern?'

'What's this chicken clucking at my leg? Are you laying an egg, little chicken?' Bern straightened up and looked around at the room. 'Well, this is certainly a big place. I am afraid, noisy chickens and skinny rabbits, that I have lots of important work to do, and so does Lord Aldasair here, but, I do have something for you.' He reached into a small leather bag at his belt and brought out a handful of perfectly round grey stones. They were all carved with symbols Aldasair didn't recognise.

'What's that, what's that?' The small girl threw herself at Bern's legs with all her might, not moving him in the slightest.

'These are Thump Stones.' He looked up and surveyed the room before gesturing to a lanky human boy with braided blond hair. 'I see you lurking at the back there, Raggn. Do you feel like teaching these smelly animals how to play Thump?' He reached back into the bag and retrieved two smaller bags made of yellow cloth. 'I have enough here to set up a tournament.'

The tall boy grinned lopsidedly.

'Aye, Bern, it's no trouble.'

The big man passed the stones to the boy, then looked at Aldasair for the first time. 'It's easy to learn, Thump. All Finneral

380

children learn how to play it as soon as they can hold a stone. You're not especially fond of those windows, are you?'

Aldasair blinked rapidly, trying to locate his voice. 'What?'

'Oh, and I've something to show you, if you don't mind?' Bern smiled, his eyes merry. 'Unless you'd like to stay here and learn Thump also?'

Aldasair followed Bern outside and across the palace grounds. It was a brighter day than they'd seen in some time, yellow tufts of clouds streaking across a blue sky.

'Thank you,' he said, fingering his sticky cuff. 'I did not know what to do with them.'

'Ah, well. I have eight brothers and sisters, all younger than me. I've always been good at controlling a crowd.'

They walked to the west, the ground growing steeper until they came to the black stone path of the Hill of Souls. It had been cleaned, Aldasair noticed, the foliage cut back from the path.

'You have been busy,' he ventured. Bern nodded. He wore a light tunic, his shirt sleeves rolled up to reveal his brawny arms, and he had discarded the fur-lined cloak Aldasair had so often seen him with, but his hefty axes were still slung on his belts. Seeing Aldasair looking at them, he patted the flats of their blades almost affectionately, as though they were faithful hounds.

'The Bitter Twins,' he said, smiling. 'My very own storied weapons. But here, they have been useful for clearing away some of the smaller trees. My father would have my guts for using them that way, but needs must.'

'You have great need of weapons in Finneral?'

Bern's normally merry face grew sombre. 'We have done, certainly. When I was a very young man, we were constantly involved in skirmishes with our neighbours, the Sown. Every girl and boy grew up knowing how to use a fighting axe then.

381

The Sown are a fearsome people.' He grimaced. 'We used to say that they raised their babies on cow's blood, to give them a lust for battle.'

'I have not heard of these wars.'

'No reason you should have. Not all conflict is with the worm people, my friend. Though our greatest warlord married his son into the family of their king, and now all is smooth as milk with the Sown. You'll have seen some of them ride in with us – they would have been the terrifically ugly people.'

Aldasair looked up, shocked, but Bern was grinning at him again. 'A jest. They are actually very similar to my own people, really, but with appalling taste in rum. Do not drink their rum. Look, here we are.'

The war-beast shrine still sat at the end of the grove of trees, but already Aldasair could see that it had been transformed. All the debris had been cleared away from beneath the trees, and one or two that were dead had been reduced to stumps. The rough clay of the shrine had been washed and rubbed down, shedding its crispy patina of old leaves and mud, and all of the windows had been cleaned. The path leading to it was clear, and for a moment Aldasair experienced a strange doubling of memory; he had stood here once, more than once, with his clay war-beast clutched in his hands, his friends all around him.

'Are you well?'

For all the strength in his arms, Bern's touch on his shoulder was light. Aldasair shook him off, and then vaguely regretted doing so.

'My apologies. It's just that I had thought this place lost, and you've brought it back.'

'Here. Let's go inside.'

Bern led him through the door – there was no creak, and it opened smoothly – and the room within gleamed. The stone benches, once lost under dirt and ancient animal corpses, now shone with polish, and the floor was covered with fresh rushes, lightly scented with something floral Aldasair couldn't place. There was a single lantern sitting on the lowest step, letting off a warm orange glow.

'You'll forgive me for the floor, I hope. The stones have cracked in several places – ice, I suspect – and it spoiled the impression I wanted to give. My mother insisted on clean rushes in the long hall, and I had some oils I use for me beard . . .' He trailed off, and cleared his throat. 'Not very Eboran, I know. As if you'd have rushes on your fancy marble floors! But they're easily taken away again. Oh, your skylight.'

Bern nodded to the ceiling and Aldasair looked up, belatedly realising that the tone of light was different. Where the broken glass and leading had been was now a clean stretch of a translucent skin of some sort, carefully caulked at the edges.

'I've no glass, of course, but we use these whale skins to let a little light into our tents when we're travelling. It'll keep the water out, for now.'

'Whale skin?' asked Aldasair weakly.

'Yes!' Bern's face lit up. 'Albino spear whales. They live in pods off our coast, and they have these extraordinary hides – pale, but strong, and water cannot get past them, yet they let the light in so well.' He shuffled his feet. 'Well, as you can see yourself.'

'Why?' said Aldasair eventually. He could not believe the change in this small room. Before it had been a sad, broken thing, a remnant of lost history, echoing with all the people who had gone. Now, it was cosy. Comforting even. 'By the roots, why have you done this?'

To his surprise, the parts of Bern's face not covered by his golden beard turned faintly pink. ''Tis a gift,' he said, his voice gruff now. 'A kindness. Ebora is –' he tugged at his beard once, twice – 'Ebora is a place of myth and story for my people, and by the stones, you can still see what it once was. You have been lost a long time, and no one should be left to wander alone.'

Aldasair looked up at the taller man. 'It is,' he said, with more feeling than he intended. 'It *is* a kindness. You cannot know . . .' He dipped his head once. 'Thank you for your kindness, Bern the Younger.'

'Here, look. There is another reason I wanted you to come up here.' Bern crossed quickly to the stone benches and picked up a wooden box. When he brought it over to Aldasair, he saw that it contained around twenty clay figurines, in varying states of completion.

'Most of them, I'm afraid, were all fallen to bits,' said Bern. He looked apologetic, which Aldasair found extraordinary. Humans were so strange. It was hardly Bern's fault that the Hill of Souls had been abandoned for so long, and yet there he was, looking sorry about it. 'A few were just sludge. But these ones were mostly intact. You can still sort of see what they were, I think.' He looked up at Aldasair, his expression uncertain now. 'I wondered if you wanted to put them into the earth. You said that's what you did with them, and I didn't want to just – well. Seems to me like these were special to someone once.'

For a moment the room seemed to spin around Aldasair, and Bern's face doubled, and then tripled. Aldasair thought of sitting at the long table of tarla cards, day after day after day, and the fat spider that had died in the middle of them all. Why hadn't he got rid of it?

'Yes,' he said. His voice sounded firmer than it ever had done to his own ear. 'We will take them, and find a good place for them to be.'

'Should it not be secret? Do you not wish to find other Eborans to do this with?'

'No.' In truth, he knew that to let a human participate in the rites of the Hill of Souls was unforgivable, but who was there now to oppose him? Should he go to the last Eborans, dying in their rooms, and ask their opinions? Or Hestillion? She wanted nothing to do with him. 'In a few days' time, it will be the turning of the half-season moon. Once, it was a sacred day. We had a lot of sacred days, but no one remembers them now. We should bury them then. The moon was always special to the war-beasts.' He cleared his throat. 'I would be very glad if you would come with me, Bern the Younger.'

35

One of the more intriguing footnotes I've come across in my research concerns that of the Golden Fox exodus. When the crimson flux truly took hold in Ebora, there were a group of people there who believed that perhaps they could outrun it. Led by an artist known as Micanal and his twin sister, Arnia, around fifty Eborans left their dying lands and travelled north to the Barren Sea, apparently sailing from there to – no one knows where.

The truth is, I suspect, more complicated. Little known to the world outside Ebora, there were two schools of thought regarding the origins of Ygseril. Many Eborans believed that the land in which the tree-god spread his roots was sacred, a place preordained to be the mighty Ebora. Others believed that a great seed was blown down from the north, brought to the central continent of Sarn by a lucky wind. Somewhere across the Barren Sea, they claimed, was a holy island, sacred to Ygseril and his warbeast children. No one has ever been able to say exactly where it is, however – as far as we know, there is nothing worth speaking of in the Barren Sea; hence its name.

There are so many juicy elements to this. First, Micanal

himself was a very interesting figure. He was known to be exceptionally beautiful even for an Eboran, a man with unheard of grace. There were multiple offers of marriage for him, but he turned them all down to concentrate on his own work. His paintings and sculptures still exist, most of them held in private collections, and I have had the privilege of viewing at least three pieces. They are exquisite, and all signed with his personal sigil, the golden fox.

He and his sister had a ship made on the Barren Coast, and sailed with a group of followers and believers, fans and lovers, hoping perhaps to rebuild Ebora far from the troubling corpse of Ygseril. They believed that the holy island existed somewhere to the north – although it should be noted that even war-beasts flying over the area have never found it – and perhaps they thought that the salvation of Ebora could be found there; perhaps they hoped to find a new seed, and birth a new tree-god on that distant coast. What became of them, we do not know. There is a notorious stretch of water known as the Assassin's Heart, twisting its way across the Barren Sea, and weather systems there do not usually let ships pass unscathed. So where did they go? Did they all die on the treacherous seas, or did they reach their mysterious destination? Did Micanal know something that we now do not? Everything I have read about him suggests a wise, careful man who did not make snap decisions. Why would he wilfully lead a group of his people to their doom? I don't believe he did, or at least, that he meant to. Clearly, he had other plans.

Personally, I believe the mystery of the golden fox exodus still has a few surprises waiting for us.

Extract from the journals of Lady Vincenza
'Vintage' de Grazon

Noon lay on her back looking up at a perfect blue sky. Indigo grass rose all around her, shifting and whispering in a mild breeze.

'This grass,' said Tor, who was lying next to her, 'is the same colour as the eastern sea. Was it truly this colour?'

'It was,' said Noon. 'There is an entire valley of it. Mother Fast called it "the god's eye". We never stayed here for long, though. Some people have a strange reaction to the grass. It makes them sleepy. Confused.'

Tor grunted. 'The plains, it seems, are much more interesting than I gave them credit for.'

'There are lots of strange places like this,' she said, remembering. 'Quiet, lonely places where people didn't go, and if they went, they didn't stay. All those memories I have, I can bring them back here, can't I?'

'I suppose you can.' Tor didn't sound particularly interested. He was brushing his fingertips across the blades of grass.

'I don't think you know what that means,' said Noon. She thought of her endless nightmare, the one that skirted around the hole in her memory, and then pushed it away. 'How dangerous that could be. To relive anything from your past.' She turned her head to look at him. 'You're too used to being able to do this. Do all Eborans dream-walk?'

Tor picked a blade of grass, twining the slim shaft around his fingers. 'We were all capable of it, to greater and lesser degrees, but not everyone was interested. My sister was the finest dream-walker Ebora ever had, I think.'

'And now I can do it too.'

'Well, no, actually. All you are doing is shaping your own dream. You have mastered dream awareness. All you can do is summon memories to experience. You can't, for example, enter my dreaming mind. You can't enter it, and you can't change things there. Whereas I . . .'

He gestured lazily and the blue grass turned a lurid shade

of pink. Noon elbowed him, and he laughed, turning to face her. Meeting her eyes, he seemed to grow suddenly serious.

'You are so clear to me,' he said. 'So close. In dreams, often other people, even the dreamer themselves, are mutable and shifting. But you are you. I can never not see exactly who you are. Why is that?'

Noon sat up, pulling away from the unsettling look in his eyes. Summoning the correct memories, she reached into the dense pink grass and pulled forth a shining greenish-golden vessel. It sloshed in her hands.

'What is that?' asked Tor, sitting up next to her. 'Is that . . .?'

Ignoring him, Noon peeled back the top from the throat of the vessel – part of her questioned how she knew how to do this – and tipped it towards the roots of the grass in front of her feet. The slow-moving golden liquid that trickled onto the ground smelled strange and alien; like the mineral silt of a river, and a sharper scent underneath that. There were a few moments of stillness, and then the ground erupted; shoots of blue and pink grass shot up from the dirt, while the grass already grown stretched towards the sky with an odd, whistling *whoosh*. Other plants were growing too, foliage with flat green leaves and dark red fruit, and bright orange toadstools; seeds and bulbs that had lain dormant under the ground forever. In moments they were surrounded by a strange chaotic forest, everything larger and wilder than it should be. Noon laughed aloud.

'All right, so you are quite adept at changing your own dreamscape,' said Tor, a touch sourly. He was finding the space where he had been lying suddenly very cramped. They crouched together under the extraordinary canopy. 'That was the substance Vintage found in the Shroom Flats, wasn't it? You have certainly replicated its effect—'

He stopped talking, and his face grew very still. *He will ask me about Vintage now*, thought Noon. *He will ask where she is, and then we will have to talk about this endless dreaming, and it will all come out. He will have to face it now.*

Instead, to her enormous shock, he snatched up her hand and kissed the palm of it. His eyes were wild. Seeing her expression, he grinned at her. 'Do you not see it, witch? You have given us the answer. The wild growth of these plants. When we spilled the substance, it reawakened dead plants, did it not? And it just so happens that I have a dead plant that is very much in need of healing.'

She blinked at him. 'What the fuck are you talking about?'

'Ygseril!' He scrambled to his feet, taking her hands and pulling her with him. 'So, the old god is slightly more than a plant, but don't you see? If we get enough of this substance and take it back to Ebora, there's a chance Ygseril can be saved. A chance for all of Ebora.' He grinned. 'I can see how it will all work now. We just have to wake up.'

'No,' said Noon immediately. 'We can't. Wait, you have to wait a little longer.'

He shook his head at her, still smiling. 'Why? It's all clear to me now. The answer has been sitting in front of us. Now we have access to so much of it . . . I don't know why I didn't think of it before. We've done enough sleeping.'

Noon grabbed his shoulders, trying to keep him with her, in this dream, this safe space that reality had yet to ruin, but he mistook her gesture and swept her into a hug.

'We can do it together, Noon,' he said into her ear. 'I know it.'

They woke up, Noon holding a scream of frustration deep in her chest.

There was something stuck to his face. Tor could feel it, thick and stiff and unyielding, partially gumming his left eye shut. Whatever it was, it also covered his left arm and part of his chest. He sat up, trying to get his bearings. He appeared to be

390

in a squalid little room, dirty light coming from a single window, partly obscured by a brown curtain. The place smelled of blood and wine, an oddly intoxicating mix, and he was lying shirtless on a narrow bed. Next to him, her body turned away, was Noon, curled up with her knees nearly up to her chest.

He smiled. 'Did I miss something?' He reached over to touch her shoulder, and that was when he saw what had become of his left arm. In the brief second before it all came back to him – the compound, the explosion, the agonising walk back to the house – he had a moment to regret the passing of that blissful, unknowing time. And then he was out of the bed, sprinting up the set of grand stairs to find a room with a mirror. On the upper landing he crashed into the wall, his legs weak and uncoordinated, and pain fell across his body like a clinging sheet. He cried out then, some wordless yell, and he heard Noon calling his name from below. Ignoring her he ran to the nearest bedchamber. There were boxes all over the floor, crates of jars and bundles of parchment, but there was also a tall standing mirror in the corner, covered in a film of milky dust.

'It won't be that bad,' he murmured as he wiped the mirror's surface. His fingers felt grimy and silky, like the powder from a moth's wing. 'It can't be.'

It was worse. The left side of his beautiful face was a purple mass of scar tissue, the cheekbone on that side too prominent, his eyebrow entirely missing. The fire had burned his hair away on that side so that his scalp showed through, livid and shining. The destruction continued, down his neck and shoulder and his left arm, and it was all the worse for the smooth perfection of the rest of his skin. He did not recognise himself, but those were his red eyes, wounded and frightened. Had he ever made that expression at a mirror before? He thought not.

'You nearly died.'

Noon was at the door. Her face looked too pale, her eyes

too dark, and for an alarming moment Tor believed that she had died in the explosion, and this was her ghost, hounding him. But then she stepped forward and the illusion was lost. Her arms were covered in cuts, and he suddenly knew why he had seen her so clearly in her dreams.

'I should have,' he said, his voice a rusty croak.

'Don't say that,' she said, anger in her voice. 'I gave you so much. You can't just give up.'

Tor looked back at the creature that was his reflection. Cautiously, he touched his fingers to his cheekbone. Painful, but not agonising.

'So much blood,' he said faintly. 'Enough to pull me back from death, and perhaps enough to summon the crimson flux. By the roots, what have you done?'

'What I had to do.' Noon crossed her arms over her chest. 'Do you even care what happened to Vintage?'

Tor looked at his feet for a moment. The room was swaying. 'Of course I do. Of course I bloody do.'

'She's alive,' Noon's voice wobbled and Tor looked up, but she had lifted her chin and was staring at him steadily. 'She made it out of the compound, but she's gone already. She said she had to go somewhere and that we couldn't come with her.'

'Vintage left?' Tor took a slow breath. His skin felt strange, too tight. 'She left me here, like this?'

'I told her not to, but she –' Noon stopped, shaking her head as though her ears were full of water, her eyes squeezed tightly shut. 'It won't leave me alone. I keep hearing it . . . why won't—' She pressed the heels of her hands to her fore-head, and staggered against the doorframe. Part of him – the part that knew the memory of the taste of her blood, the warmth of her slim shape on the bed next to him – wanted to go to her. But too much had happened.

'So here I am, grievously wounded, abandoned by my one friend to the company of the lunatic who nearly killed me.'

Noon seemed to collapse in on herself slightly at those words, but the look she threw him was defiant.

'You were just about to be turned inside out by a parasite spirit, or have you forgotten that bit? I dragged your lanky arse all the way back here, gave you my own blood to heal you when I could have left you to fester, when I could have gone back to find Vintage instead—' She stopped. 'I'm going to go and have a drink.' She went back out the door, pausing before slamming it. 'And you're welcome, by the way!'

36

Dear Lady de Grazon,

The work is slow and hazardous, as I'm sure you can imagine, but we have made some interesting progress with the outer sections of what I, for want of a better term, call the corridors of the Behemoth. As I have stated in the past, I strongly believe these beings are closer to being living, organic creatures than simple conveyances for the Jure'lia, and everything I have found so far only confirms this hypothesis.

I intend to publish my findings in the next two to three years. I have chosen to take your impatience over this as a compliment rather than the thinly veiled insult I suspect it actually is – I have no doubt that the great Lady de Grazon thinks she would have solved the mysteries of the Behemoth in half the time, but believe me when I say that there is more here than you can possibly imagine. Yes, my family have been investigating the site for generations, and they will continue to do so. My boy, Tyron, has all sorts of ideas as to how to make exploration of the compound less dangerous.

As I have said before – at length – I will not send you

*any maps or drawings or samples. There is nothing you
could trade that I would want. You will have to wait for
my book like everyone else. I do not wish to hear from
you again on this subject.*

With affection,
Your good friend, Esiah Godwort

Extract from the private letters of Lady Vincenza
'Vintage' de Grazon

Tor spent some time in front of the mirror, alternately unable to
look away from the ruin of his face, and unable to look at it,
staring instead at the richly woven carpet. Eventually, he stood
up, found a bathroom, and bathed slowly in cold water. He could
have gone down to the kitchens to heat it up, but then he would
have had to face the fell-witch, and he felt strongly that she had
seen him in this state for long enough. Soaping his hair and
carefully cupping water to his face, he watched as dark flakes
of dried blood fell away – it was black, the blood of a mortal
wound, but he had survived. When he was as clean as he could
manage, he went to Esiah Godwort's rooms and spent a good
hour scavenging an outfit he felt wasn't entirely abominable.

Dressed, with his hair pulled back into a simple tail, Tor
made his way down to the kitchens, where Noon was sitting
at the big scarred table, a goblet of wine in front of her. She
looked a little brighter than when he'd seen her last; her cheeks
were flushed – the wine, perhaps – and she was wearing a
scarlet velvet jacket with a high collar. It suited her.

'I will have that drink now, if you don't mind.'

Noon nodded once and filled the empty goblet that was
waiting on the table. Tor sat, too aware that he was moving
stiffly, that each movement pressed the tight skin of his shoulder
against his shirt.

'Ebora,' he said into the awkward silence. 'I still wish to
return there. With the Jure'lia fluid.'

395

Noon looked up at him, lacing her fingers around the goblet. 'The dreams, then. They were real?'

'What a question.' Tor half smiled, but feeling the way his face twisted strangely with the movement, he lost all urge to smile almost immediately. 'Yes, they were real, in so much as dreams can ever be real. The conversations we had there were, certainly.'

She looked away. Perhaps she was remembering how close they had been, in that dreaming place. How they had lain together in the grass. Tor knew now that part of that had been prompted by her blood; all that time it had been seeping through his own system, quietly repairing him. Or quietly summoning the crimson flux. It was an intimacy he normally only shared with lovers.

'The original sample of the fluid is gone,' she said. 'The Winnowry destroyed it along with Vintage's carriage on the winnowline. Even if we still had it, I doubt it would be enough to effect something as big as your tree-god.'

Tor took a sip of his wine. It was passable. 'Indeed. I will want to take as much of it as I can to Ebora, which is why we must go back inside the compound.'

Noon raised her eyebrows at him, crinkling the bat's wing on her forehead into a curious shape. 'Are you out of your actual mind? You really want to go back in there?'

Tor drank more of the wine. He was remembering brushing the dust from the tall mirror in the bedroom. How he had thought that it couldn't be that bad. 'I am saner and more observant than you will ever be, witch. We saw the containers in the Behemoth, remember? Golden orbs, just like the broken one we found in the Shroom Flats. Judging by everything Vintage said and wrote about him, Esiah Godwort was a cautious man. Those intact orbs will have been left in place so that he could observe them, get an idea of the bigger picture. There were several of them in the half of the Behemoth you didn't destroy. It could be enough.'

396

'Even so. We nearly died. All of us. To go back in there would be—' Noon stopped, pushing her hands back through her hair, making it stick up wildly. 'I can barely think with all this noise.'

Tor blinked at her. It was utterly silent in the house. 'What are you talking about?'

'Never mind. Look, the parasite spirits in that place were enormous, and aggressive.' She stopped again, wincing. 'It's not worth the risk.'

'Not worth the risk?' Tor slammed his goblet on the table, then took a slow breath. He would need the witch to watch his back inside the compound; it was important to remember that. 'Not worth the risk? How dare you say that to me?' He leaned forward over the table, meeting her eye. 'Because of you, I am stuck with this ruined mask of a face, possibly for the next few hundred years. Do you know what that means?'

'I saved your life.'

Tor laughed. There was a knot of nausea in his chest like a fist. 'Oh yes, thank you for that. I have a chance here, witch, to save not only my god, but my people. And if the sap of Ygseril runs again,' he pointed at the ruined side of his face, forcing her to look at it, 'then there's a chance it could heal this. Not worth the risk, you say?'

Noon finished the rest of the wine in her goblet, swallowing methodically until it was gone. When she put it down, Tor noticed that her hands were shaking, and for a moment he felt a brief spike of concern. He pushed it to one side.

'Fine,' she said eventually. 'Why not? Perhaps going back in there will sort everything out. Make everything clearer. I don't know.' She wiped the back of her hand across her mouth. 'Give it a few more days, until you're stronger, and we'll go back in.'

'We go back in immediately.' Tor stood up. 'It is a long way back to Ebora, and I have no intention of remaining in this – this *state* for a day longer than necessary.'

There was movement below.

Agent Lin stood up slowly, careful not to shift her gaze from the tiny figures moving in the distant courtyard. Her back was stiff from staying in one place for so long and there was a steady ache in the centre of her forehead from a lack of sleep, but there was no doubt her quarry had broken cover. The girl was there, her head uncovered, wearing a scarlet jacket, of all things.

'Doesn't she realise she's being hunted?'

Next to her, Gull shifted his enormous bulk and made a series of huffing noises. The bat had left to hunt periodically but had not gone far. Another figure had appeared in the courtyard: the Eboran who had dared to threaten her with his fancy sword. If she could kill him too – and she suspected she would have to, to get to the fell-witch – then Agent Lin decided she would keep the sword for herself. She deserved something out of all this mess, and there was little doubt that such a fine sword could be sold for an eye-watering amount of money. She wondered briefly if killing an Eboran could lead to any political trouble, but quickly she dismissed the thought. Mother Cressen preferred these things to be resolved without civilian deaths, of course, but this was a remote and lonely place with no witnesses, and besides which, the great empire of Ebora was a corpse now. Everyone knew that.

Gull chirruped, nudging her slightly with his great blunt head. She patted his nose lightly, still gazing down to the courtyard.

'Not much longer to wait, now. Not much longer at all.'

The flagstones in the courtyard were wet, turning the ground beneath her boots into a broken mirror, reflecting the dull grey sheen of the sky. Noon glared at the stones, putting one foot in front of the other and thinking only of that. If she lost concentration, part of her started to insist that she had four feet at her command, which made walking suddenly more confusing.

'What are you doing? Are you drunk?'

Tor was waiting for her at the compound gate. The Ninth Rain, which, against all odds, had not been lost on their flight from the fire, was slung over his back again, and he wore a deep hood that cast his face into shadow. Out here, in the daylight, the scars were especially hard to look at.

'Keep your hair on, bloodsucker.' Noon winced at her choice of words before continuing. 'I'm in no rush to get torn apart by parasite spirits.'

She had several empty sacks slung across her back, as did Tor, and a bag containing a pair of large empty jars they had found in the kitchens, just in case that was the only way they could transport the fluid, and two pairs of thick leather gloves. Neither of them wanted to find out what happened if you got the stuff on your skin.

'We'll move quickly,' said Tor, ignoring her tone. 'We know where we're going this time. We're not on one of Vintage's quaint sightseeing tours.'

Reaching him, Noon nodded. This close, she felt a flicker of the same awe she'd felt when she'd first seen him striding through the Shroom Flats towards her – only now he was an angry god, something half destroyed and vengeful. And on the edge of that, something else; a feeling she sensed came from the new presence inside her. It felt like longing.

'Let's get it over with.' She pulled the collar of her jacket up around her neck, glancing up at the bleak hills behind them as she did so. For a moment she thought she saw something moving amongst the rocks there, but dismissed it as the rushing shadows of clouds. There were enough immediate dangers without imagining new ones.

The gates to the compound were as they had left them, although a pile of old leaves had gathered against the door. Some of them, Noon noticed, were enormous; old brown and gold leaves as big as her head, twice as big. The cold presence inside her head shifted, and a new thought occurred to her.

'The Shroom Flats, and this place. They're both full of weird plants, aren't they?'

'Are you trying to impress me with your powers of observation now?'

Noon ignored him. 'The vine forest as well. Vintage said she makes her wine from giant grapes, and there is Behemoth wreckage there too, hidden deep within it. Look at these trees.' They had stepped inside the compound now, and the twisted, overgrown forest loomed all around them. The scent of smoke and wet ashes was a ghost on the edge of her senses. Noon lowered her voice. 'This is a yellow oak. They grow on the eastern side of the Trick. It just doesn't look like one, because the trunk is all swollen and twisted, and the leaves are three or four times bigger than normal.'

Tor had drawn his sword, and was moving slowly, the blade held at the ready. 'You know, when Vintage left us, I thought I might get a rest from this sort of scintillating conversation.'

'You really don't see it, do you, you massive idiot?' He shot an annoyed look at her for that. 'It's the fluid. The stuff we're going to collect for your big creepy tree-god. It must have soaked into the ground all around here, making all these trees and plants grow bigger and stranger than they should. I wouldn't be surprised if it happened wherever a Behemoth has crashed. Think. The fluid is what's responsible for the Wild.'

Tor stopped. He looked back at her, and the expression framed by his hood was one of genuine surprise. Noon felt her heart lighten slightly at the sight of it; it was the first time she'd seen him look anything other than angry or lost since he'd woken up.

400

'By the roots.' He looked around, as if seeing the strange vegetation for the first time. 'All Behemoths must carry this fluid. And perhaps when they crash, it spills out all over the ground. Or some of it is vaporised.'

They were moving again, creeping through the eerie forest. Water dripped from branches and trickled down trunks.

'In a place already densely populated by vegetation, like the vine forest,' said Tor, 'this Jure'lia fluid would have been carried even further. Dotted on the wings of birds, droplets on the wing-cases of beetles. I'm surprised Vintage didn't see it immediately.'

'There were so many pieces to the puzzle, that's what she said. And some of those pieces are trying to kill you.' Picturing the shimmering, light-spotted monsters, the presence inside her swarmed to the front of her mind. For a moment the dank forest floor was replaced by a shining riverbed of precious stones, glittering in sunlight – the water was cool on her claws, easing away the sting of hot sand. The world spun, and Noon stumbled back amongst the haunted trees. Tor was still stalking ahead and had not noticed her confusion. She cleared her throat. 'I bet she suspected it, though, when she saw what it could do. I think if she'd had a chance to sit and study it, she'd have seen it much faster than either of us.'

Tor grunted. 'But instead she rushed us halfway across Sarn to visit this lunatic and his hell hole. She always was too impatient.'

Noon didn't know what to say to that, and they walked in silence for some time. A light rain began to fall, and with it the temperature plummeted. Noon watched her breath turn to white vapour and she missed her warming scales, until she realised that made no sense at all. Shivering, she pushed her damp hair away from her forehead and retrieved a knitted cap she'd recovered from Tyron's bedroom. Ahead of her, Tor pulled his hood back, exposing his black hair and the livid skin on his face and neck.

401

'Aren't you cold?'

He shot her an irritated look. 'The hood already dampens my hearing. With the rain as well it is intolerable.' He took a breath. 'It's not as if you haven't already seen what I am.'

Noon opened her mouth to reply to that when, out of the dismal shadows just ahead, a limb covered in jelly-like fronds swept towards them, swiftly followed by a tall, oozing shape. It was lit all over with glowing points of purple light, and there was a dark, gaping hole near what Noon would be tempted to describe as its head. It made a ghostly, whooping sound as it came, dragging its lower limbs through the foliage.

'Quickly, let's go round it,' said Tor, skirting immediately to the right of the parasite spirit, moving nearly silently as he ran. Noon followed, horribly aware of how much noise her boots made crunching through the dead leaves. They quickly left the creature behind but Noon was certain she could feel it watching them go, that strange dark hole whooping after them as they left.

'We'll go faster now,' said Tor as she caught up. 'Where there's one, there will be others, and we don't want a repeat incident of you blowing anything up.'

Noon scowled. 'Believe me, I do not want anything—'

There was another swarm of lights, this time from their right. This parasite spirit had a great broad head and jaws that hung down onto its chest, and it reached towards them with translucent appendages like bear claws. Tor muttered several oaths under his breath, bringing the Ninth Rain around to meet it, but as Noon looked up at the parasite spirit, it stopped.

'That's right!' Tor shouted. Noon realised with some alarm that his voice was shaking. 'Step away!'

The parasite spirit cocked its head, in a gesture oddly like a hunting dog listening for a distant herd, and it let out a series of discordant wails. Noon cried out involuntarily – the noise seemed to stab at her ears, piercing her deep inside her head

– while at the same moment a great tide of sadness welled up inside her chest.

'Brave warrior,' she said through numb lips. 'You have been served a great injustice.'

'What?'

Tor took hold of her arm, pulling her away, and with some shock she realised she'd been reaching out for the thing, her fingertips outstretched. The feeling of sadness left her and they were running again, stumbling through the trees away from the parasite spirit. The smell of wet soot was growing stronger all the time.

'What, in the name of Ygseril's wisest roots, do you think you're playing at?' Tor glared at her. His skin was damp, although she couldn't tell whether it was the moisture in the air or sweat. 'You were reaching out to the thing like you wanted to pet it! Have you forgotten these things can turn you inside out?'

'We shouldn't have come back in here so soon,' she replied, shaking his hand off her arm. 'You're not ready. You're too afraid.'

From the corner of her eye she saw the expression of outrage on Tor's face, but a pair of parasite spirits were running towards them out of the gloom. Beyond them, she could see the shattered shape of the Behemoth wreck, black against the bright grey of the sky. Without thinking about what she was doing too closely, she called out to the cold presence in her mind while reaching towards the shimmering, changing shapes scampering towards them. All at once, Noon felt larger, more powerful. The creatures in front of her were not to be feared; they were to be pitied. Nothing so sorry could possibly harm her.

The parasite spirits stopped, wavering as though they were pieces of seaweed in a strong current. After a moment they turned away, and Noon was herself once more: small, reduced, no longer lethal.

Nonsense. The voice was like cold coins dropped into her mind. *You are a burning brand, child.*

'What happened?'

'I don't know.' Noon grabbed hold of Tor's arm this time, glad of the solidity of it. 'Come on, before more of them come.'

They ran together then, near arm in arm, until Tor's hand slipped down and took hold of hers. She squeezed it, and they ran faster; heads down, they were dark shapes slipping through the mutant forest.

'Here we are, witch. We're here.'

On their left stood the portion of the Behemoth that they had all been inside when Noon had set off the winnowfire explosion. It was not difficult to tell; it was a blasted, twisted wreck. Pieces of the greenish moon-metal were twisted, blackened shards, reaching up to the sky and out to the surrounding trees. It was hard to make out the interior structures that they had seen on their last visit; it was all broken and in pieces, the ground itself an inch thick with pale ashes and black soot. The place stank. Noon wondered what had happened to the parasite spirits that had been caught by the explosion itself. To their right was the half of the Behemoth that had contained the sad corpse of Tyron Godwort, and the metal orbs that, hopefully, would hold the Jure'lia fluid they had come for. Tor was already striding towards it, the Ninth Rain held out to one side, pointing at the ground.

'Go carefully,' she said to him. 'This is still a dangerous place.'

'We're nearly there.' The look he turned on her was wild. 'From here, to Ebora. Quickly now.'

The entrance they had used last time had collapsed further in on itself, but they could still just about squeeze through, Tor crouching so low that he was almost on his knees. Inside, they were lit with the same eerie lights, and Noon thought she could see their own boot marks in the dust. Coming back here felt like a further intrusion, and, unwillingly, she thought of Tyron Godwort, lost somewhere in a strange chamber below. She wondered if Esiah had reached him and was even now sitting by his son's body, his mind finally gone.

'It was this way. Keep close.'

Noon followed Tor up the corridor, glad that he remembered the way – to her this was a place of sly confusion, of alien directions – until they emerged into the widened section of the corridor where the orbs had been stored in alcoves in the walls. Here, part of the ceiling had fallen, and they had to climb over the twisted pieces of metal to reach the storage area. Leaning on one piece as she slid down another, the metal felt oddly warm under her fingertips and not for the first time Noon thought of clambering about in the entrails of a giant beast. She was so busy frowning over this and trying her best not to come into contact with the walls that Tor was some distance ahead of her, and his cry of dismay made her jump. She half stumbled, half fell the rest of the way until she was by his side.

'What is it? What's happened?'

The golden orbs had been shaken loose from the alcove, and all of them had shattered. Noon could see a shining wetness on the textured floor, and some of the curved pieces still held remnants of the miraculous fluid, but almost all of it was lost. Tor dropped to his knees and held his hands over the floor, as though hoping to scoop the fluid up somehow.

'No.' His voice was flat, and his hands were shaking. 'No, this cannot be.'

Noon could see how it had happened. Safe for hundreds of years, held in their delicate alcoves, until the enormous explosion just on the other side of the clearing – the same one that had brought down the ceiling – had shaken the orbs from their spaces and shattered them all across the floor.

'No!' Tor picked up one of the pieces and then threw it at

the wall. 'NO. This is all I have left, this is the last chance, I can't . . .'

He hid his face in his hands, his shoulders starting to shake. The contrast between the man she'd met in the Shroom Flats, so tall and confident, and this beaten person, wearing borrowed clothes and with his hair half burned away, suddenly cut her so deeply she could barely breathe. She went to him and gathered him to her, smoothing a hand over his hair.

'It will be all right,' she said.

'How?' He pressed his face to her stomach, and she held him there. After a moment, his arms circled her waist. She thought of how close they had been in her dreams; not all of that had vanished when he had woken them both. 'How can I do anything, like this? How can I live like this?'

'You are so dramatic.' Bending down and hesitating only slightly, she briefly pressed her lips to the top of his head. She felt some of the tension leave his body. 'This won't be the only chamber. It can't be. Remember what we figured out about this stuff? The Behemoths must carry lots of it – enough so that when they crash, the places around it are infected. We just need to look. It's worth looking, isn't it?'

All was quiet for a moment as he took this in.

'You are wiser than you look, witch.' Tor stood up, and to her surprise he took her hand and kissed the palm of it, just as he had within her dream. His eyes looked wet, but when he nodded at her she saw some of his old determination in the set of his shoulders. 'We will search for more. There is no need to despair yet.'

It took them hours. Narrow corridors led to cavernous spaces filled with shadowed, alien shapes; Noon could only guess at their function. They crawled through spaces where the walls were slick and yielding, climbed uneven sets of stairs, sought out each darkened corner. In one enormous chamber they found themselves walking on a suspended bridge, while below them something black and viscous shifted and moved. Noon knew that if Vintage had been with them, she would have insisted they explore further, but Tor took one look at it, grimacing slightly, and led them on. Noon was inclined to agree with him.

Eventually, they came to a long stretch of passageways where the strange lights had been damaged somehow, flickering and uncertain, until they died completely. For uncountable minutes they were in complete darkness, and Noon found herself wondering about the Jure'lia and whether they still existed somewhere in this giant corpse. Perhaps they were at the bottom of the evil liquid in the giant chamber; perhaps they had watched the trespassers with milky eyes, waiting for them to reach this place, where it was too dark and they were too lost to make it out alive . . .

'Noon,' came Tor's voice, 'you're breathing very rapidly. It's unnerving.'

She gave a strangled laugh. 'This whole place is fucking unnerving. Do you even know the way back?'

'Of course I do. I have an excellent sense of direction. Look, the lights are working again up ahead. Keep moving.'

Noon amused herself for the next few minutes by trying to decide whether she believed Tor's bravado, and then they were in a low ceilinged room. There were ragged black ropes hanging down, and a shallow pool in the centre. Something gold glittered there.

'Look!' Tor strode across the room, impatiently pushing the black ropes out of his way. There, in the shallow pool of what looked like water, were six of the orbs, entirely intact.

'Wait, shouldn't we figure out what that stuff is first? It could be dangerous.'

'What? You mean it might burn my flesh off?' Tor shot her a look before wading down into the pool, soaking himself to the knees. He paused for a moment, and then shrugged. 'It's just water. Here, I'll hand them to you. Be careful.'

Noon packed them carefully, swaddling the orbs in rags and cushioning them against each other. Each one felt heavy and full in her hands, and when she tipped them gently back and forth, she heard the liquid sloshing inside.

'Will it be enough?'

Tor took one of the bags from her and tied it carefully to his back. 'How could I possibly know that?' Then his voice softened. 'I think it will have to be. I barely have the energy to walk back out of this place, let alone continue searching. A few moments' rest, and we will hope that we can get out of here before nightfall.'

Noon looked closely at his face. His skin was grey, and there was sweat on his forehead now. He looked unwell.

'You look like you need more than a short rest.' After a moment, she reached into her pack and retrieved a short knife.

'Noon—'

'Do you think we'll make it back out of here if you're half dead on your feet? You'll lead us into some dead end, or we'll get outside and not be fast enough to avoid the spirits.'

'You don't know what it is you offer me.'

Noon grinned at him. The whispered voices in her head were quieter than they had ever been – she had the strangest idea that they did not like being inside the Behemoth – but even so, she felt half mad. 'I think it's a bit bloody late for that, don't you?' She held up the knife again, and this time he nodded, reluctantly. Sitting on the chamber floor, she cut a shallow wound in her arm and offered it to him, turning away as he bent his head over her – to save his privacy or hers, she wasn't sure. The warmth of Tor's mouth on her skin was shocking in this cold, alien place, and when he pulled away she was surprised by a sudden spike of desire for him. Dishevelled and vulnerable, his long hand resting against the skin of her arm, she thought she'd never seen him more beautiful.

408

'Thank you.' He stood up, and his movements already seemed smoother, stronger, and his eyes were brighter. 'Let's get out of here while the effect lasts.'

Their escape was much swifter. Without the need to stop and look for the orbs, they moved quickly through the narrow corridors and echoing chambers. Crossing the bridge again, Noon cast one glance over the edge, remembering how she had imagined the ancient Jure'lia lying in wait down there, but nothing looked back up at her as she passed. Eventually, they came to the broken exit, where a slash of grey daylight lit their way out.

'We'll leave tomorrow,' Tor was saying, adjusting his pack so that he had easy access to his sword again. 'Gather what we can in supplies and start making our way north. Vintage was right about the rains, it won't be pleasant, but there's no real sense in waiting—'

'Be quiet. I think I hear something.' Noon crouched and shuffled her way out, trying to see everywhere at once. Back out in the clearing, the sun was a lighter patch on the horizon, and the ground was steeped in shadows. The rain had stopped, but she could hear dripping everywhere, a disorientating sound.

'I can see no lights,' said Tor brusquely, emerging next to her.

'I said I heard something, not that I saw—'

A bulky shape dropped from the trees in front of them. It was a shadow against shadows, and then a flare of green light revealed the woman's face, caught in a snarl of rage. A moment later, Noon saw the ball of winnowfire suspended above her fist, and then the woman was jumping neatly from the back of her bat to land in the clearing in front of them.

'Shit! It's the Winnowry!'

Noon saw Tor draw his sword, the steel flashing green and white, and then a dart of green flame shot between them. Half falling, half running, Noon threw herself at the trees and then heard Tor's shout of alarm. She looked back to see that part of his jacket was on fire, and the woman who had called herself Agent Lin was advancing on him with her arms full of boiling flame. She intended to kill him; the intent on her face was as clear as the corpse moon in the morning sky.

'No!'

Before she really knew what she was doing, Noon was running back, already summoning the winnowfire from within her. The parasite-spirit energy, that slow-burning ember of power, suddenly flared back into life and green flames shot from her palms, coursing through the air towards the agent. The woman spat a curse and produced her own wall of flame, which dissipated Noon's own wild attack easily.

'Leave him alone! It's me you came for.'

The woman Lin raised her eyebrows. Tor was beating out the flames on his sleeve, an expression of sheer panic on his face.

'No loose ends,' the woman said. 'Besides which, he insulted me. And I'm in a bad mood.'

'A bad mood?' Noon gaped at the woman for a moment, and then shook her head. 'Why do this? Why work for them? You *know* what they really are.'

Agent Lin smiled. It was a brittle thing, and for the first time Noon noticed that the woman looked tired, careworn. Clearly she had not washed her hair for some time, and there was a layer of dirt on her skin.

'Oh, I know all about them, girl, which is exactly why I do this. Better to have the wolves on your side than at your throat.'

'Then you're a coward.'

Agent Lin smiled a little wider. 'If you're looking to distract me with insults, child, you will find that I am rather too thick-skinned for that.'

Noon reached inside her and found that swirling pool of

410

energy again. It threatened to overwhelm her, and Tor was too close. She moved towards the Winnowry agent, putting herself between the woman and Tor. She held her hands out in front of her.

'It is touching that you're defending the Eboran. You're of the plains people, aren't you? So you must know his people decimated your own, generation after generation. Are you a particularly forgiving soul, or are you also fucking him?'

'You should start running,' said Noon. The power was building inside, swirling into something explosive, but Agent Lin couldn't know that. 'Get back on your bat and fuck off.'

'Fell-Noon, that's cute, but I'm trained to do this.' The woman pushed a lock of grey hair away from her forehead. The bat wing there was cruder than Noon's, almost more a scar than a tattoo. 'I've seen you fight before, remember? You are no more than a child waving a torch.'

'Yeah, well, maybe my torch got bigger.' Noon thrust her hands forward and gave free rein to the parasite-spirit energy. A ball of flame erupted ahead of her, too bright to look at, and she heard Agent Lin give a startled shout. Noon felt a fierce moment of triumph, and then her ball of flame was torn to pieces, shards of emerald flame dicing it into tattered remnants. Noon threw herself to the ground to avoid the shards, landing in a squelch of mud and ash. Somewhere she could hear Tor shouting.

'Even *now*, even with *this*, I can't kill her.' There was mud in her eyes. She rubbed her face, desperately trying to see what was going on. 'I'm too weak.'

Nonsense. The voice in her head was back, stronger than it had ever been. Noon could almost feel the shape of the speaker, thundering through her blood. *You were crafted for war, just as I was.*

'Who are you? What are you?' Noon staggered to her feet.

The sounds of a fight drifted towards her, a woman laughing. There were flares of green light all around.

I am death and glory. Now, listen to me closely.

Noon listened.

Tor flicked the Ninth Rain up in front of him just in time to catch the narrow dagger of flame the winnowry agent had flung at him. The roll in the wet mud had extinguished the flames on his sleeve, but his heart was still beating too fast and his mouth was dry. He had thought that he had forgotten almost everything from Noon's explosion, but now he found that tiny memories were seeping back – the exquisite agony as the skin on his face was crisped away, the smell of his own flesh being instantly cooked, the searing pain as his shirt was consumed. He could not be burned again. He would not allow it.

The agent was advancing on him, and he couldn't see where Noon had ended up. He scrambled back, mud slipping through his free hand.

'I would normally have let you be,' the woman was saying in a conversational tone of voice. 'But this has turned out to be a particularly unpleasant experience for me, and I think someone else should pay for once. Someone other than me, other than my boy.'

'Lunatic,' Tor muttered under his breath.

'No one will know, anyway,' the woman was saying now. 'I'll leave your body here to rot in this haunted place. Your people are nearly all dead anyway, one more won't be a great loss.'

Noon appeared at the woman's right. Her black hair was standing on end, and she had an expression on her face Tor had not seen before. Without knowing why, he felt a cold trickle of dread move down his back.

The Winnowry agent shook her head as though dealing with

an errant puppy. 'You've not learned your lesson yet, Fell-Noon? Very well, I can't say it won't give me pleasure—'

Noon jumped and turned gracefully in the air, bringing down her arm in a sweeping motion, and with it several darts of fire, so bright that they were almost white, were born out of thin air. They shot across the clearing and exploded at the feet of Agent Lin, sending the woman flying up into the air, before she dropped, sprawled in the mud some distance away. To her credit, she was on her feet again immediately, flinging a barrage of fireballs at Noon's advancing figure, but the young fell-witch raised her arms and produced a shimmering wall of green flame; the fiery orbs were absorbed into it with barely a hiss. Dropping her arms, the fire was gone.

'What is this?' Agent Lin's face had gone white, speckled here and there with black mud. 'What have you done?'

Tor doubted the agent heard Noon's words, they were spoken so quietly, but he heard them clearly enough. They made him think of his childhood, the smell of clay and his cousin Aldasair, although he couldn't have said why.

'I am death and glory, tired one.'

Noon crouched, bracing herself on bent legs, before turning her upper torso in a slow circle, her arms outstretched. A bright shard of green fire formed there, which she gathered into a globe before pushing it towards the woman. It wasn't fast, but it expanded as it travelled, and the agent turned and started to run.

'Noon?'

Ignoring him, Noon swept her arms up and round, throwing a dart of green fire after the expanding cloud of flame. Like a stone thrown into a pond, the dart hit the cloud and it exploded, showering the agent and the area around her with a rain of emerald fire. There was no escaping it.

'Noon? Noon!'

She took no notice. She advanced on the woman, who was

413

writhing on the wet ground in a circle of fire, and, unconcerned by the flames, Noon reached down and seemed to pull something from around the agent's neck.

'Come on, before the spirits follow.'

They ran then, leaving the burning woman behind. Noon took a whistle from her pocket and blew a single sharp note. With a thunder of leathery wings, a dark shape rose above them and followed them. Noon caught Tor's eye, and the look on her face was one of quiet satisfaction.

'It will be faster to get to Ebora with two bats, wouldn't you say?'

37

I have asked Nanthema what she thinks about the Eboran war-beasts many times, of course, but I only get a few small pieces of information from her on each occasion. I think it makes her sad, to think about them. To her, of course, they are not distant mythical creatures that were only ever seen in paintings or depicted in poems, but living, breathing figures that were of enormous importance to her people. Nanthema herself was a child at the time of the Eighth Rain, and during that time of war her mother had seen fit to hide her away in a country estate – consequently, she did not witness the death of Ygseril, or the defeat of the Jure'lia. Before the invaders came, however, she often saw the war-beasts on their visits to and from the central city of Ebora. She describes them as impossible shapes in the sky, a thunder of laughter passing overhead. Once, there was a great celebration in the central plaza, and several of their number were honoured by the emperor of the time. Nanthema was there with her mother and brothers, a shy child peeking between cloaks and robes to get a better view. (It is difficult, I will admit, to imagine Nanthema as a shy child.)

She grows saddest when she relays this memory to me, however. She claims it is impossible to describe their glory to me, and I get frustrating snippets: the clack of a griffin's claws against the marble, scales like shining bone, an eye like an enormous opal, turning to watch the crowds with amusement. I have pressed her for more on the relationship between the beasts and the tree, but she will speak of this even less. The death of Ygseril, and the knowledge that there will be no more war-beasts, is a deep wound for the Eboran people. One that will not heal, it seems.

I have my suspicions. I believe that the war-beasts were essentially an extension of Ygseril, and therefore almost as sacred as the god itself. Usually, Nanthema will turn the tide of the conversation back to me, asking endless questions about things that she can't possibly find interesting, but I am flattered enough to give her what answers I can; about growing up in the vine forest, about my impossible father, my long-suffering mother, about my own favourite wine – even as she pours us another glass. And who could possibly resist the curiosity of a beautiful woman?

Extract from the journals of Lady Vincenza 'Vintage' de Grazon

'What is this place? It's remote enough.'

The moonlight had turned Bern's golden hair silver, and, standing on the summit of the small hill, he looked to Aldasair like some sort of unlikely statue – of an ancient human hero, perhaps. The Bitter Twins added to the illusion.

'I used to come here when I wanted to remember there were places other than Ebora.' Aldasair placed the box of figurines on the grass, and then turned to face the mountains. They were an ominous presence in the dark, more like a terrible absence than a great ruction in the earth. 'There, you see, is the Wall.' At this distance, it was little more than a pale line, scratched across the shadows of the night. 'When I saw the Wall, I could remember that there were people on the other side of it. Beyond the Tarah-hut Mountains, there were people living and talking and eating, and – not dying.'

'We call them the Bloodless Mountains,' said Bern. He sniffed. 'I was never sure if that was supposed to be a joke or not.'

'Because of the Carrion Wars?' Aldasair's heart dipped a little in his chest, but he forced himself to face Bern and keep talking. He would converse like a normal person. He could do this. 'A great many people died. A man I knew once, a relative of mine, jested that by the time we had dragged the humans as far as the mountains, they were certainly already bloodless. A poor joke.'

The expression on Bern's face was unreadable, much of his face hidden in shadow. 'Do you remember it?'

'Fragments. I remember the way Ebora felt, more than anything. There was such a frenzy. People seemed brittle, living on the edge of a life that could be taken away at any time. And then it was.'

He knelt on the grass, feeling the chill of the ground immediately soak into his trousers. From within his pack he took a pair of short-handled trowels, and passed one to Bern, who knelt across from him to take it. Finding those had been a challenge in itself; nothing seemed to be kept where he remembered.

'I attended a party at the height of it all.' Aldasair kept his eyes on the ground, watching as the edge of his trowel bit into the grass and lifted away a lump of turf. 'I was far too young to be there, really, but all the rules were looser, then. It was beautiful. All the lamps were lit, and there was music. I don't know if I've ever heard music like it since. The lady whose party it was, she wore red jewels at her throat and her ears, and I remember that was the fashion. For crimson.' Bern began shovelling dirt too, and the air filled with the good smell of wet earth. 'There was a human man there. He was pale, and I could smell his sweat, but he was smiling, smiling all the time. The lady told us all that he was our willing guest, and that for a life at the Eboran palace he would gladly give what he could. We knew he wasn't talking about money. As it grew later, the lady drank more and more, and, once, she caught hold of my sleeve and told me that I must serve her human. Fetch him food and drink, and attend him like a servant. I was, as I think I have said, very young, and I thought it a game. It was fun, to play at being a servant, so I brought him goblets of wine and platters of fruit, until it got very late and I was too tired for it all. I found a quiet room and slept there, very deeply. I didn't hear the rest of the party, and woke to full sunlight streaming in the windows.'

They had a reasonable-sized hole. Aldasair sat back on his haunches, looking away down the hill to the palace. The gardens were full of campfires. 'I remembered that I was supposed to be the human's serving man, and I wondered if I was supposed to serve him breakfast, so I got up and went back to the ball-room.' Aldasair lowered his head, looking only at the dirt. 'I couldn't find him. I found – other things. Later, I saw the lady who had thrown the party, and she was sitting in a corridor with her head in her hands, crying and crying. Her arms were bloody to the elbow.'

Bern the Younger had gone very still.

'Do you see what we are?' Aldasair asked softly. 'Do you see it, yet?'

For a long time, Bern didn't say anything. Somewhere, perhaps beyond the Wall, a wolf howled, and another wolf-voice joined it.

'Show me a people who don't have a bloody history.'

418

Aldasair sat for a moment in silence, his fingers clutching the edge of the box. Eventually, he reached inside and took out the first of the figures. Once, it had been something like a fox, with a great bushy tail. He held it up so that the light of the moon coloured its pitted surface, and then he placed it gently in the deepest part of the hole.

'Ebora thanks you for your service, mighty one. Return to the roots.'

By the time they had buried all the war-beast figures, the sky to the east was a watery pink, and the air was stiff with cold. Walking back together through the empty city, Aldasair felt an odd loosening in his chest – a tension he had been unaware of had lessened somehow, and although the empty buildings with their broken windows and overgrown gardens still looked ghostly, he found he could look on them without dread. Next to him, Bern seemed unconcerned by the chill of the dawn, even as his breath turned to puffs of white vapour.

When they reached the palace grounds, the humans camped on the lawns were rousing themselves; building cooking fires, fetching water, having their first conversations of the day. Aldasair looked at them with new eyes. To them, all of Sarn was in terrible danger, and the chances that Ebora could save them were so slim as to be impossible, but still they climbed out of their beds, cared for their children, cared for one another.

'Bern, I must thank you.'

They stopped on the edge of the main circle of tents. From somewhere nearby, a child was complaining loudly at being turfed out of warm blankets.

'It's a small thing,' said Bern. He seemed embarrassed somehow, and Aldasair thought again that he would never understand humans. 'By the stones, there are plenty of us who should have given thanks to your war-beasts long ago. There would be no Sarn at all, without them.'

419

'That's not the point, though, and you know it.'

Bern turned to him, his eyebrows raised in surprise, but at that moment there came a whiskering sound across the frigid grass. Aldasair jumped as though he'd been pinched and turned to see a pale figure bearing down on them. It took him a few seconds to see that it was Hestillion; she wore a padded robe, silvery white in the dawn light, but no cloak, and her yellow hair was loose over her shoulders. No, not just loose – tangled. Aldasair blinked. He had never seen Hestillion in such a state of disarray, not even when she was tending to the victims of the crimson flux. Striding towards them, it was possible to see that she wore soft silk slippers, shoes never meant to be worn outside the palace. She looked, if not angry, then only a heart-beat away from it.

'Aldasair, come inside with me. I need you to come to the Hall of Roots.' She didn't look at Bern the Younger. The tall man may as well have been invisible.

'I am a little busy at the moment, Hest.' He cleared his throat. 'You asked me to take care of the diplomacy, and that's what I'm doing.'

Hestillion's blood-red eyes flickered briefly to Bern, seeing him for the first time and dismissing him just as quickly. 'You can play with the humans later.'

'My lady Hestillion, we've not had time for much more than a few words, but I am glad to meet you.' Bern cleared his throat. 'I'd be glad to lend my arm, should you need anything.'

Hestillion shook her head quickly and turned back to Aldasair. 'By the roots, I do not have time for this.' Hestillion reached out and grabbed his sleeve, and he noticed that it was sewn all over interlocking tree branches, grey on cream. It made him think of the card he'd drawn for Hestillion in the room of dust and dead spiders, and for some reason he felt deeply uneasy. Without knowing why, he glanced up at the silvered shape of the corpse moon, hanging above them like a bloated egg sac.

'Bern, I am sorry,' he said, forcing his voice into the smooth tones he imagined fearless leaders used. 'This apparently requires my immediate attention. I must attend my cousin. We'll talk more later.'

Bern tugged at his beard, obviously concerned, but inclined his head. 'Soon, I hope.'

With no more than that, Hestillion was dragging him back across the gardens, her bare hand an icy cuff on his arm. He hissed questions at her, but she just shook her head, and eventually he simply let her lead him back to the Hall of Roots. Inside, there were lamps burning just around the thick trunk of Ygseril. As they approached the twisted landscape of the god's roots, Aldasair saw that there were some items spread out by the trunk – a thick embroidered blanket, a bowl full of something half congealed, a bottle of wine, mostly untouched. It looked as though Hestillion had made camp here. When he followed her up onto the roots, he noticed that the hem of her robe was stained, and again he felt that shiver of unease.

'Hestillion, you should leave it alone,' he said, glancing up at the branches as he spoke. The glass roof was full of lilac light as night shaded into day. 'I thought you wanted people to come here, so that we would get help. We have so many people here now, Hest, and they all have opinions and demands and they all want something else to eat or they don't want sleeping quarters near someone else, because their great-grandfathers were once on opposing sides of a battle, and they all want to know what's happening in here—'

'Be quiet. Do you remember dream-walking, Aldasair? Do you remember how to do it?'

'That's what you brought me here for?'

She took his hand suddenly, glaring at him, and squeezed it until he gasped with pain.

'You are so much brighter than you were, Aldasair. So much more aware. It's being around people that did that. Your mind was softening, being torn into shreds of rotting silk, but I brought people here and now you are getting better.' She squeezed his hand again. 'I did that for you. Now do this for me.'

He blinked and sat down next to her, looking carefully at his own feet. He remembered very well how he had once sat for hours, days even, without speaking. How the sun and the shadows chased each other through the window, and none of it mattered, and down the corridor somewhere there was the distant sound of someone coughing themselves to death. He did not want to go back to that silent place.

'I want to show you something,' Hestillion was saying. 'I wasn't going to yet, but I think perhaps, if there's more than one of us, he might respond better. That perhaps that is the key.' She took hold of his chin and made him look at her. 'Go into the netherdark, find me there, and follow me. Can you do that?'

Aldasair nodded solemnly, and closed his eyes. He had never been especially good at dream-walking, and hadn't cultivated an interest in it – dream-walking wasn't like painting, after all. The visions you conjured while dreaming were gone when you woke, never to be recovered. But he was certainly capable of the basics. Relaxing his body, he sent himself down, down into the netherdark, and quickly found Hestillion there. In that place she was more light than person; the sort of light that glitters on broken things.

Good, she said. *Now follow me down. We will have to go a long way, but you mustn't doubt me.*

She dived, slipping down away from him, and he followed after. Very soon he was aware of being in a place where the darkness pressed in around him, and although he couldn't see anything, the netherdark felt dense, thick with pressure. It was uncomfortable, but Hestillion kept slipping down, and so he

422

followed, wondering what she could possibly want to show him.

Once or twice, the light that was Hestillion stopped, turning and flitting, and Aldasair began to suspect that something was wrong. She put on a sudden burst of speed then, and he had to struggle to keep up with her, and then she stopped, rounding on him with a sudden flare of anger.

'Where is he?' she demanded. 'Why can I not find him again?' And then, before he could reply, 'It is your fault! You are not worthy!'

Aldasair opened his mouth to reply. He did not like to speak in the netherdark.

'But Hest—'

'No!' To his horror, Hestillion abruptly seemed on the verge of tears. She pushed at him with a force that wasn't quite physical, and suddenly they were both sitting on the roots again, the bottle of wine lying on its side next to them. 'Get out!'

'Hestillion—'

'I said get out! The Hall of Roots is not for you. If I have lost him because . . . Leave!'

Aldasair scrambled to his feet, more afraid of the naked sorrow on his cousin's face than her angry words. He stumbled across the roots, moving awkwardly on faintly numb legs, until the wine bottle sailed past him and smashed on the marble floor. He moved faster after that.

You would bring another to speak to me?

Hestillion's heart thundered in her chest, bringing her back to an awareness she had almost lost. She had been drifting in the netherdark for hours, convinced she had ruined everything, but the soft diffuse light of Ygseril's dreaming mind had returned. She let herself be warmed by it, almost ashamed at her childish joy.

423

'Aldasair is my cousin, Ygseril. He hasn't been well, but he has a kind soul. He would want only to help you. I thought – surely you wish to speak to your children once more?'

The light faded a touch. Hestillion held herself as still as she could, holding down the panic that threatened to flood her chest. But the presence of Ygseril stayed with her.

No. Only you. My special, strange child. There are things that I can trust only you with. We feel that strongly.

'I – Lord, I am honoured.' There were so many questions, but Hestillion forced them all from her mind. They had clearly done something to lose Ygseril's trust. It was now her responsibility to win it back. 'Whatever you wish of me.'

The light did fade then, but Hestillion felt a warmth from it that she hadn't felt before, and she knew that in some form, Ygseril had expressed his approval. Fighting back up through the netherdark, she awoke stiff and cold, crouched on the roots.

'My responsibility,' she said, stroking the twisted bark. 'My responsibility, alone.'

38

Tor stamped his feet on the ground, trying to force some warmth back into them while Noon began making their fire. It was certainly faster to travel by bat, he had to admit that, but it was neither comfortable nor warm. After several hours in the air his face felt like a rigid mask, the numbness all the worse on the damaged side, and his burned arm ached abominably from clutching at the reins. He shot a faintly resentful look at the great black bat they had retrieved from the Winnowry agent; it was snuffling and stretching its wings awkwardly, making ready to hunt for the night. Fulcor, the bat who had followed Noon from the Winnowry, and had been summoned once more by her whistle, had already gone.

There was a soft *whomph* of emerald flame that swiftly turned orange, and their fire was burning merrily. Noon no longer seemed to experience any discomfort over using her ability, and her face as she fed the fire sticks was calm and unconcerned. Tor found it vaguely alarming.

'Where are we now?' she asked.

Tor made a point of looking around, his hands on his hips. 'Judging by the constellations just starting to glint into life, the scent of the wind and the texture of the earth . . . I would say we're precisely in the middle of nowhere.'

She gave him a cool look. 'I am so glad you are in charge of navigation, oh great traveller.'

Tor went and crouched by the fire. In truth, he did vaguely recognise this place. The foothills of the Tarah-Hut Mountains had been the first place he had properly explored when finally he had left Ebora. Back then its twisting scrublands had seemed wild and gritty, just the place to start an adventure. Now it looked like a place where you couldn't expect to find a decent drink.

'If we were travelling by foot, we'd be about ten days away yet. With those creatures,' he nodded to the black bat, who chose that moment to launch itself up into the darkening sky, 'I'm really not sure.'

Noon shrugged, and began unpacking food from their bags. They had taken as much as they could carry from Esiah Godwort's mansion, along with blankets, water, wine and as many spare clothes as they could stuff into bags. Stopping each night was an exercise in unloading the bats so that they could go and hunt – fresh meat was very welcome – but in the last two weeks they had got it down to a fine art. The orbs were wrapped in thick furs, and kept as close as they dared to the fire. Tor unstrapped his sword from his back and set the kettle against the fire before retrieving the tin of tea leaves from his own pack.

After a moment he realised that Noon was staring at his sword. Her eyes had taken on an odd, almost silvery shine; he had seen it a few times since the incident in the compound. It seemed to go alongside her odd, quietly calm mood.

'Why is your sword called the Ninth Rain?'

Tor grimaced faintly. 'I'm sure I've already told you. Or Vintage must have told you.' He sighed, shaking tea leaves into a small clay pot. The scent made him think of Mushenska, which, in turn, made him think of Sareena. How long had it been since she had been in his thoughts at all? Feeling an

426

unwanted stab of guilt, he wedged the pot in the dirt to wait for the hot water. 'When the Jure'lia invaded, Ygseril would grow silver fruits in his branches, which would fall, hatching into the Eboran war-beasts. For each invasion, a silver rain.'

Noon tipped her head to one side, as though listening to a distant voice. The movement exposed the smooth skin of her neck, which looked creamy against the scarlet of her coat. Unbidden, the memory of the taste of her blood seemed to flood his mouth.

'I know that. I mean, why is it called the Ninth Rain? Wasn't the last one – the one where your god died – the Eighth Rain?'

'Oh,' said Tor. 'That.' The water in the kettle was boiling, so with his good hand he reached down and poured it into the clay pot, watching the leaves swirl darkly. 'That's a longer story. Quite a personal one, actually. And I hardly know you.'

She looked at him frankly again, smiling slightly now. For the briefest moment his chest felt tight, and he wondered if he were ill: a cold caught on the back of the blasted bat, or the crimson flux coming for him finally. *This woman burned your face*, he reminded himself.

'Fine. What else do I have to do on this lovely evening, but reveal painful family secrets?' He gestured around at the low hills, growing darker all the time.

'Stop complaining. Pour me some tea.'

'You have to let it steep longer than that, you barbarian.' Even so, he retrieved the small tin cups from his pack, and passed one to Noon. 'My people live for a very long time. If all goes well and we are not hacked to pieces in battle or eaten up by the crimson flux, we can live for hundreds of years. My father was still young during the Eighth Rain, and my mother had not long had me and my sister. At first, it seemed to be a smaller, almost half-hearted invasion by the Jure'lia. They landed near what is now Reidn, and started to consume that part of Sarn as swiftly as possible. Their Behemoths birthed their giant, hungry maggots, and the other scuttling creatures that are part of their charming company, and soon great stretches of that place were lost under a slick of their varnish.'

He paused to pour them both a cup of tea. The warmth was very welcome, particularly to his stiff, burned hand.

'My father and his older sister travelled there as part of the main force, wearing their shiny armour and happily carrying their lethal weapons. Back then, it was a matter of pride to repel a Jure'lia invasion, a rite of passage almost. My father had been anxious that the worm people might never return, and he would never get to face them on the battlefield. His younger sister was furious, as she didn't even get to leave Ebora.' Tor smiled slightly. 'What idiots they were. What idiots we are, especially if your dream turns out to be true.'

'Your father fought with the war-beasts?'

'Not directly alongside them,' he said. 'Only the most skilled warriors fought alongside the sacred beasts. There were those who had a special relationship with them, men and women who were heroes to the rest of us. My father and my aunt were not so important. Not then, anyway.'

'What do you mean?'

Tor grimaced, and took a sip of his tea to wash away the sudden bitter taste in his mouth. 'When the crimson flux came, it wiped out much of a generation. The old generals, the war leaders, the politicians and the royalty – all those who had been in power for centuries, in other words – all died of the curse. Those Eborans left behind suddenly found themselves with the reins of the kingdom – even if it was a doomed one. My family were largely untouched by the flux to begin with, and they rose in importance.' He snorted. 'Although all that really meant by that point was that you got the pick of the empty chambers in the palace.'

'And the sword?'

'Mm? Oh, yes.' Tor patted it absently where it lay on the

428

ground next to him. 'My aunt was the real warrior of the two of them. She had dedicated a full century of her life to the martial arts, while my father had only been training for a decade.'

'Only a decade, huh?'

'He was absolutely determined to go, despite his lack of experience, and in truth, my mother and my grandparents made no real attempt to stop him – as I said, fighting the Jure'lia was considered an honour, a rite of passage for any young Eboran. My aunt promised that she would keep a close eye on him, and off they went to Reidn.'

There was a flurry of leather wings nearby, and the flames of their fire danced wildly for a few seconds as Fulcor landed. The great bat scuffled over to them and dropped a dead hare at Noon's feet, before taking to the air again. Tor craned his neck to watch her go, but she was lost in the darkness almost immediately.

'Where do they go?' he asked.

'How should I know? Somewhere comfortable to sleep, I expect.' Noon had reached into her pack and retrieved her knife, now skinning the animal with swift, practised swipes of the blade. Feeling his eyes on her, she shrugged. 'It's odd how this stuff comes back. I didn't skin a single animal in the Winnowry, but put a knife in my hand and it seems as natural as breathing.'

'That's not exactly reassuring.'

She huffed laughter. 'The sword.'

'Right. When they got there, Reidn was a mess. The Jure'lia had more or less decimated it. What wasn't covered in varnish was scuttling with the burrowers – the beetle things you saw in your dreams – and the people . . .' He stared at the fire. 'My father was an unpleasant bully, much of the time, but whenever he talked about the Eighth Rain, he would go very quiet, and he would rub at his lips constantly.'

429

Tor demonstrated, frowning as he did so. 'Almost all the humans they found weren't human any more. You know what the Jure'lia do to captives?'

Noon shifted on the ground. 'If it's like what I saw in the dream . . .'

Tor smiled grimly, feeling the scar tissue on his face stretch as he did so. 'The burrowers get inside a victim and . . . hollow them out. What is left occupying that body is something else, some greater extension of the Jure'lia themselves.' He shook his head slightly. 'Vintage probably knows more about it than I do. But what my father said, what he told us, was that it must be incredibly painful to be eaten from the inside out like that, because the screaming deafened them, for days on end. None of them could sleep because of it.'

Noon had finished with the hare, and was busily skewering it to go over the fire. For the time being he watched her work, admiring how sure her hands were, even though they were covered in blood. Especially because they were covered in blood. He felt that tightness in his chest again, and breathed past it.

'So, they fought. It was a bloody and nasty fight, my father said, trying to cut a swathe through the occupied town. Mostly they were cutting down the bodies of the drones – that's what they called the humans who had been burrowed into – and it was dispiriting work. Above and in front of them, the war-beasts and their consorts tore into the maggots and the mothers.'

'Mothers?'

'The ones with spindly legs. They birth the burrowers out of their pulsating sacs.' Seeing the expression on her face, he grinned. 'Shall I go on? Would you like another bedtime story?'

'Get on with it.'

'Night came, and my father and aunt holed up in a deserted cottage. They had been separated from the rest of their unit

430

by that point, and they were both exhausted. My aunt, who had taken a shallow wound to her thigh, slept and my father took the first watch. It was quiet, he said. Eventually, the strain of listening to every single noise gave him a headache. He went to the kitchen of the cottage to see if he could find something to drink –'

'Like father, like son.'

'– when he heard a scratching at the back door, like a dog was out there, pawing for scraps, but then he heard a whimpering too, like a child crying. Needing to know what it was, he swept the door open and a small figure fell across the flagstones. It was a little human girl, covered in dirt, as though she'd been hiding for days.' Tor paused. 'You know, it's this part of the story I always find strange because, apparently, my father bent down automatically to pick her up, and the roots alone know how many times I fell over in front of my father as a child and not once did he—'

'Tor.'

'*Mmm*. Her head snapped up, and her eyes were gone. Just holes coated with the shiny black residue they fill their drones with. My father cried out and stumbled back, trying to get away. He was unarmed. Fortunately for him, my aunt appeared at that moment and ran the child through with her sword, but not before the girl had started to vomit up her burrowers. My father retrieved the sword and tried to get them off my aunt, or at least he said he did, but she was quickly overwhelmed. He left, before they could get him too, although he heard her screaming, all the way down the street.'

Silence grew between them for a time. The hare suspended over the fire popped as the fats started to cook.

'And the sword?'

'Oh. Yes.' Tormalin cleared his throat. 'My father had his sister's sword re-forged in winnowfire and renamed. When the Ninth Rain came, he used to claim, he would avenge her death. Unfortunately for him, the crimson flux carried him off before he ever got the chance, and the sword passed to me.' He touched the fingers of his good hand to the long thin scabbard. 'So he named the sword after the future war he hoped was coming, all so that he could assuage his own guilt about getting his sister killed. He was never a terribly complex man, my father.' Tor looked at the flames. These were things he had not thought about in a long time, and certainly he had not discussed them with anyone. To Vintage he had only ever given small hints; partly because he enjoyed frustrating her nosiness, but also because, he realised, he was ashamed. 'Once, when he was in his cups, my father told me that he did see his sister again, after the town had been reclaimed from the Jure'lia. He was leaving, preparing for a miserable march to the next battlefield, when he passed a giant pit that had been dug on the outskirts of the town. The last of the drones were being forced into it, where they were to be burned until they were nothing but ash.' He cleared his throat. 'What they carried inside them was considered a sort of pestilence, you see. My father saw his sister standing on the lip of the pit, her hair hanging down around her like a shroud and her eyes a pair of ragged holes. He said she looked at him, and then one of the soldiers pushed her down into the pit with the others.' Tor looked up at Noon, who was sitting with her teacup clutched in both hands, watching him closely. 'And then he left.'

'That's fucking awful.'

'It is, rather, isn't it? Doesn't show my family in the best light, certainly.'

'What was her name? Your aunt?'

For a terrible moment, Tor couldn't remember. He had no clear memories of her, had only seen her portrait in his family's apartments. She had been a striking woman: tall, with wide-set eyes and ebony hair, and in the painting she had looked faintly

432

angry, as if she already knew that her younger brother would cost her her life. And then it came to him, like a gift.

'Carpacia,' he said, wondering how many decades it had been since anyone had said her name. 'Carpacia the Strong.'

Noon nodded. 'Thank you for telling me the story. Eborans certainly have an – interesting history.'

'Well, don't go spreading it around.' He gestured at the empty landscape. 'I am choosing to trust you with this scurrilous information, since we're friends now.'

Noon raised an eyebrow. 'We are?'

Suddenly there was a tension in the air that hadn't been there before. Tor found that he couldn't read the expression on Noon's face. He remembered being on his knees inside the Behemoth, overcome with despair, and how she had held him to her, waiting for his pain to pass. He remembered the taste of her blood.

'After all we have been through together, witch, I should think so.' His tone felt too light, but he was powerless to change it.

Noon raised her cup, as if to toast him. 'I think you might be right, bloodsucker. So, friend, shall we eat this hare while it's still pink and juicy?'

The next few days were hard. A storm came down off the mountains, filling the skies with a thick powdery snow that turned the world into a blanket of white. Noon, awkwardly waving her arms and shouting at them, drove the bats off to find shelter until it had passed, and she and Tor had made their way as best they could on foot, dragging their bags along with them on a makeshift sledge. It was very slow work, and now that they were truly at the foot of the mountains shelter was scarce; it was all flinty rock and dead trees, the mountains rising to either side. They made camp in the shadow of a giant boulder, at least partly out of the winds, and Noon re-lit the fire every time it went out – it was, she joked to Tor, the one thing she was good at.

Despite the fire, the wolves came to them that night. They were dark, shifting shadows at a distance, eyes glinting yellow-green – not worm-touched, but very hungry. Noon could sense them circling, drawing slowly nearer, and neither of them got any sleep that night. The next day brought another blizzard and their progress was slower than ever, and as the sun set – a milky disc that looked painted on the grey patches between clouds – the wolves came for them again.

'Watch out!' She saw the first one slipping towards them out of the snow, as swift and as lethal as a thrown dagger, and Tor dropped the ropes of the sledge and turned, the Ninth Rain singing as he drew it from its scabbard. She saw him dance forward and there was a spray of crimson on the white, the brightest thing she had seen in days, but there were more coming, perhaps five or six narrow shapes closing in. Turning round she saw another three advancing directly behind her.

'Get these ones,' she shouted to Tor over the wind, gesturing behind her. Flakes of snow landed cold and biting on her tongue. 'I'll take those!'

He did not question her, only moved to take her place, and Noon reached for the presence inside her without hesitation. It had been quiet recently, assuaged, she suspected, by their fight with Agent Lin, but as she reached out it filled her again as it had before.

You fight with animals now?

The voice was cold, unimpressed.

'These animals want to eat us.'

It didn't matter. She felt strong, and the winnowfire was building within her. She pulled off her gloves and dropped them on the ground.

A wall of fire might startle them enough to leave, said the

434

voice. It sounded reluctant, and Noon knew why; startling something was not the same as fighting something. *No, I can see how hungry they are in the lines of their faces. Horizontal discs of your witch-fire. Swiftly now.*

Summoning the green flames, Noon held her arms out in front of her. The wolves were edging closer, and time was short. From behind her, she could hear Tor's grunts of effort as he held off the animals on his side. Holding her hands close but not touching, Noon swept downwards and to her right, feeling a surge of satisfaction as the ball of fire flattened and became a vertical disc, humming with its own energy. She let it build, even as the wolves crept nearer. They had been put off by the scent of wolf blood, but they were thin, and desperate.

What are you doing? Horizontal discs are what you need, several of them, and swiftly, to cover the widest area, snapped the voice in her head. *You are wasting time and energy.*

'It's snowing,' said Noon. Next to her, multiple discs had formed in the space between her hands, hovering and boiling with light. 'Winnowfire is weaker when it's wet. This shape will catch less of the snow.'

And then she swept her arms forward again, releasing the fiery discs. They shot outwards in a spray of green light, and four of the wolves were immediately aflame, their screams of pain sounding too human. Noon staggered, suddenly frightened again, *guilty*, but she felt the presence inside her step forward somehow, and her arms were moving again, dealing out sheaths of fire that skidded off into the shadows. The rest of the wolves fled, while the bodies of the others burned intermittently, the fire already being extinguished by the ever-present snow.

Noon sagged, exhausted, before turning to see where Tor was. The tall Eboran was leaning on the pile of bags. Three dead wolves lay in front of him, one of them perilously close. Seeing her look, he shouted across the wind.

'Bastard nearly got me. It seems I am not as fast as I once

435

was.' He was breathing heavily, and when she joined him at the sledge, she could see that his skin looked grey.

'Come on,' she said, retrieving her gloves. 'Let's get out of this fucking snow if we can.'

For once, they were lucky. Not far from where they were an old avalanche had created a deep cave, so deep that the floor was dry and the winds couldn't reach them. So tired now that spots of darkness were dancing at the edge of her vision, Noon helped Tor drag the sledge far enough inside so that the weather couldn't reach it, and then set about building a fire with the debris that had gathered in the corners. She built it as big as she could, glad to see that the smoke was filtering up and away from them through some unseen passage in the ceiling. Soon enough they both sat before it, for a time too tired to say anything.

'You were talking to yourself,' Tor said eventually. He had thrown back his hood and in the firelight his face looked gaunt. There were dark circles around his eyes, but the look he gave her was keen. 'When you were fighting the wolves.'

'Was I?' Noon busied herself with retrieving things from her pack, although she couldn't now think what it was she was looking for.

'Yes, you were. Like you were carrying on a conversation with someone who wasn't there.'

Noon shrugged. 'I spent ten years in a tiny cell by myself. It's not that weird for me to talk to myself sometimes, is it?'

'I've never known you to do it before.'

Giving up on her pack, Noon peeled off her scarlet coat and laid it by the fire. It was wet and cold.

'It must be the strain of putting up with you.'

Tor snorted at that, and then grimaced with pain.

'What's up with you?'

He shook his head at her. 'The burns. They're thawing out, as it were. Everything hurts.'

436

The wind howled outside, and Noon found herself listening for the voices of the wolves. She doubted they would come back tonight – surely they had established themselves as the greater predator. Blinking, she realised that thought had not come from her.

'Do you want to . . .?' Her voice trailed off awkwardly, and when Tor looked up at her he, too, looked faintly embarrassed. She held up her arm, the sleeve now rolled up to her elbow.

'Oh. That.'

'We've a long way to go yet, and the weather is shit. I don't want to be dragging that bloody sledge by myself.'

'This should not be the case,' said Tor. He turned his face away from her so that she could not see the scarred side, but not before she caught the look of hunger in his eyes. 'To need blood just to walk through snow – it shames me. This' – he gestured at his injuries – 'has taken more from me than I thought.'

Guilt again, a sore contraction in her chest, but she pushed it away. 'So you'd run the risk of getting stuck here for the sake of your pride?'

She expected him to get angry at that, but instead he nodded. 'You are quite correct. You have a pragmatic streak, just like Vintage did. Does.' He met her gaze now, and she thought she could almost sense the things he was hiding: fear, and a very stark need for what she was offering. 'Once we get to Ebora, all this will be solved. It is merely temporary.'

'That's the spirit.' She pulled a knife from her bag. 'Shall we?'

Rising, he came and sat next to her, facing away from the fire. She held up the knife, but he touched her hand.

'May I?' Seeing her look, he smiled slightly. 'I know where to cut so that it will bleed well, and cause you the least discomfort.'

For a long moment Noon didn't move. She thought of all the stories she had grown up with, of the inhuman enemy over the mountains, the monsters that came to steal their children and drink their blood.

'Do it,' she said, passing him the knife. He pressed the blade to her skin, and the sting was less than it usually was. He pressed his mouth to the cut before she even saw the blood, and she gasped a little – his lips were warm on her chilled skin. His other arm, the one not holding her hand, circled her waist, drawing her slightly closer whilst barely touching her. And this was what she hadn't told him, of course: that it was possible to become addicted to this closeness, the warmth of another body. She no longer felt cold at all. If anything, she felt feverish.

His tongue slid over the cut, and when he raised his head there was no blood on his lips at all.

'You've done this before,' she said, slightly shakily. He nodded, his eyes half closed. Already he looked brighter, his skin almost as luminous as it had once been. Without speaking, he held out her bare arm and touched his lips to the flesh of her forearm, tracing a path to her wrist. There he raked his teeth over the pale blue veins just under the skin, and Noon shivered, more violently than before.

'What was that?'

'The Early Path: Dawn's Awakening. One of the first levels attained at the House of the Long Night.'

'Will you do it again?'

His face split into a grin, and Noon saw several things happen one after another, like a stack of falling cards: genuine pleasure at her response, a flicker of that same hunger, and then, as his skin tightened on the burned side of his face, his smile faltered. She saw clearly, in the way he looked down and away, how he imagined she saw him – something ruined and broken.

'No,' she said, and she touched his face. 'No. I *want* you to.'

In the firelight his eyes were a deep maroon, warm and

uncertain. Without looking away from her, he pressed his mouth to her wrist again, kissing her skin and then biting, very softly. She had never seen him look so vulnerable, and it was that, more than anything, that made her shift forward and, as he raised his head, kiss him. He tasted of snow and apples and her blood, and then he moaned against her mouth, pulling her against him, his hands sliding up the back of her shirt.

Noon had not kissed anyone before. She quickly concluded that it was something she intended to do much more of.

'Wait.' Tor pulled away from her. He seemed to be searching her face for something. 'I am not what I once was.'

Noon blinked, for a moment completely uncertain of everything. Had there been an injury she had missed?

As if guessing her thoughts, Tor shook his head. 'I mean, I am – you can *see* what I am.'

'I do, I see what you are.' She took a slow breath. 'I see *who* you are, I think.'

This time he kissed her with an urgency that took her breath away, and banished all thoughts of their bleak situation; of the location of their friend; of the potential invasion; the alien voice in her head. She was lost in a silky warmth she had never guessed at.

They fell together onto the floor, Noon's hands seeming to search of their own accord for buttons, belts, fastenings. Tor tugged at her shirt and she yanked it off, revealing the tight undervest she wore against the cold. He murmured something in a language she didn't recognise and kissed her softly just under the ear, weaving a trail of kisses down her neck to the rise of her breasts. With a hand pressed on either side of her chest, he trailed his thumbs down to her midriff.

'What are you doing?'

'The Early Path: Morning's Music.' He paused. 'Can I take your trousers off?'

She kicked them off along with her boots and his hands

439

smoothed the skin along her thighs and the backs of her calves, curling around the soft roundness of her heel. It tickled slightly, and she laughed.

'The Morning Sun: A Bright Bird's Song,' he said, smiling.

'Take more of your clothes off.'

He hesitated only for a moment. Soon they lay together on the blanket, with only Noon's thin underclothes between them. She could feel every place that he had touched her with a special clarity, while at the centre of her was a deep rhythmic crashing, like the sea pounding the beach. Her hands were hungry devils, fascinated by the smooth, hard planes of his body, his luminous near-golden skin, like some exotic wood. Next to it, the tawny colour of her limbs was like silk.

'If the wolves come back now, we really are fucked.'

He gave a harsh bark of laughter. 'I refuse to rush.' Sliding his hand down the back of her underclothes, he pulled her close again. 'The Morning Sun: The Rushing of the Day.' His voice, she noticed, was less than steady, and under her hands his heart was beating rapidly.

She moaned and pressed her body to his; the crashing inside her was growing faster.

'The Afternoon's Awakening: The Turning Shadow –'

Her hands slipped around him, no longer thinking of anything coherent. He cried out a little, jerking against her, and with her free hand she pushed her underclothes to one side.

'Enough of your shadows and suns.' In another time and place she might have been amused by the sound of her voice – it was barely hers, so low and rough was it. Tor murmured something unintelligible to her neck, and then they were fully together.

A revelation. The crashing that had been inside her was now in both of them, tumbling them along in a riptide. Tor's hair hung over her face, she could taste his breath. He locked eyes with her and she remembered the touch of his tongue against her broken skin and that was when it took her. In the midst of the violence of it, she felt him shuddering over her and understood that he too had reached this final place.

For a time, the cave was full of the sound of their breathing, harsh at first and then gradually evening out. She became aware again of the howling blizzard outside, and it sounded different somehow. Everything did.

'Well,' said Tor, when he had his breath back. 'No wolves, at least.'

Noon laughed, and after a moment he joined her.

39

Vintage sat on the deck in a folding wooden chair, her wide-brimmed hat pulled low over her eyes to keep the hot sun off. Beyond the handrail the river tumbled past, and beyond it, the lush green fields. The winds were in their favour, the captain had told her, and indeed, from the maps she consulted in her room each night, they were making good progress. Still not swift enough for her liking, however.

She knew it was ludicrous, of course. If what she suspected was true, then in a very real sense it did not matter how fast she travelled. Even so, her own anxiety and guilt and yes, even terror, hung over her like a snow cloud ready to release its blizzard, and only the knowledge that she was travelling as fast as she could eased it in any way.

'Lady de Grazon?'

She looked up to see the ship's girl staring anxiously down at her, a creature of knees and freckles and unruly red hair desperately tamed in a series of over-worked ribbons.

'Yes, Marika, my dear, what can I do for you?'

'It's the captain, m'lady.' She stumbled over the honorific. They did not get much gentry travelling on the *Lucky Lizard*, and with her scruffy clothes and partly scorched face, Vintage did not much look like it either, but a bag full of coins and her own smooth confidence had bought her a berth easily enough. Not for the first time she thanked her past-self for having the foresight to have caches set up in so many towns and cities – even a backwater ditch like Hmar. 'We're coming up on something he thinks you might be interested to see. We can pause for a moment for you to have a look.'

Vintage pursed her lips, conflicted. She had to keep moving, *had to*, but the captain was a kind man who had taken a shine to her, and besides which, he was an intelligent fellow. If there was something he thought she would be interested in, it was probably worth taking a look at it.

Nanthema, she thought, *I am making my way to you, my darling. I promise.*

Gasping slightly as all her new aches and pains made themselves known, Vintage levered herself out the chair. Marika offered her arm but Vintage patted her away.

'My dear child, I am sore, not decrepit. Where is your handsome captain?'

The girl blushed furiously and led her to the prow of the neat little ship. All around them the crew were making themselves busy with all the mysterious activities that kept the vessel moving – to Vintage, who had lived much of her life in the middle of a dense forest, ships always seemed half made of magic.

'Lady de Grazon! I am sorry for interrupting your peaceful afternoon, but I thought you'd like to take a look at this. Seems like your sort of thing.'

Captain Arus was a stocky, weathered man, his skin deeply tanned from years spent sailing up and down the sun-locked Apitow River. He wore tough blue trousers sewn all over with pockets, and a pair of belts across his scarred chest. His shaven head was tattooed with a sprawling octopus, one of its tentacles curling around his ear.

'Always a pleasure, captain.' Vintage accepted his hand to

443

step up onto the platform – she didn't need it, but some men were charmed by such things – and she peered downriver, trying to see what all the fuss was about. 'Of course, I do not wish to cause you any inconvenience at all, but I am most dreadfully curious as to what dear Marika was talking about. You have something to show me?'

'It's no bother,' he said, beaming at her. 'We have to sail around it every time we come south, and sometimes I like to stop and take a look at it myself. It right gives me the chills.'

Vintage looked ahead of them again. All she could see was the wide and largely peaceful Apitow; nothing stirred on its teeming green expanse save for the occasional dragonfly. There weren't even any other ships that she could see, although . . . she narrowed her eyes. There was something – a flag of some sort, at the top of a tall thin pole. The scrap of material was red, its tapering tip the yellow of the sun.

'You've seen it,' said Captain Arus, obviously pleased. He turned away from her and shouted a series of commands to his crew. Almost immediately the *Lucky Lizard* began to slow, and she heard the splash as an anchor was thrown overboard.

'Indeed. It is a very fine flag, Captain Arus.'

He chuckled and beckoned her to join him at the rail. Peering over, at first she could only see the light dancing on the top of the water. It was unseasonably hot for the time of year, and the sun was a warm hand on the back of her head. She blinked at the light as it seared bright trails across her vision.

'My dear Arus, I'm not sure that I can—'

And then she saw it. At first she thought it was simply the natural green of the river itself, but then the light shifted and she saw the slick shimmer of it just below the surface of the water. There was varnish under the Apitow, a thick streak of it. She glanced around, but there was no evidence of such on the distant banks.

444

'It fair gives you a shudder, doesn't it?' said Arus, cheerily enough. 'It's 'cause it's hidden, I think. A little secret gift from the worm people. Everyone who sails down the Apitow knows about it, of course. If you're riding too low in the water, you're liable to rip your bottom out, or just get stuck, so we all have to go around it. That's what the flag is for.'

'What is that? I can make out shapes.' Vintage leaned right over the guardrail, leaning out as far as her balance would let her.

'Careful now, m'lady, unless you want an early bath.'

The water of the Apitow was famously clear, and there were shadows caught in the varnish: bodies, three or four of them – men and women or even children who had not moved fast enough to escape the Jure'lia – and something else as well. Vintage felt her heart turn over, and she began to climb up over the guardrail.

'Whoa, hold on!' Captain Arus sounded genuinely alarmed. 'What are you doing?'

'I must have a closer look, my good man. How deep is the water atop it? Can I stand on it?'

The captain looked bemused now. 'I reckon you could, m'lady, but you'll get your clothes all wet.'

She swatted at his arm. 'Wet clothes? Wet clothes? Do I look like I care about wet clothes?' Seeing his face, she relented slightly. 'My dear Captain Arus, I would be most grateful if you could take me down there. I would, of course, reimburse you for your trouble.'

Soon enough Vintage was bobbing on the river in the ship's small rowboat, the captain himself keeping it steady while she leaned over the side, peering down past the water at the grim scene beneath. It looked like two men and a woman, and they were tumbled every which way, as though a great tide of varnish had surged over them and caught them while they were fleeing. And it was as she thought – another figure caught down there in the green depths, something so rarely seen that it made her heart thump painfully in her chest.

'What is it, Lady de Grazon?' asked Captain Arus. 'You must have seen the varnish before? Those worm bastards have left their muck all over Sarn.'

'You probably won't have noticed it,' said Vintage softly. She had a sketchbook in her hands, her pencil moving feverishly across the page. 'It's down past the human bodies. We call them mothers, although it has always struck me as a wildly inappropriate phrase.'

It looked rather like a squashed spider seen from above, if spiders were the size of goats. From the drawings she had seen of them, she knew that there was an orb at the centre of those oddly muscled legs, a pale thing that pulsed and secreted the creatures they called burrowers. Not for the first time she felt a stab of frustration that the varnish was impenetrable, whilst simultaneously fighting a wave of horror that such a creature was so close. If they could extract it somehow, would it still be alive? They knew so little about the Jure'lia. Despite the heat of the day she felt a rash of goosebumps move across her arms. The captain was next to her now, peering down into the water too.

'I can see something dark.' He grimaced. 'I always thought that was a weird plant, or something.'

'This is incredible, captain.' She paused, and squeezed his arm. 'You could make a fortune bringing scholars such as myself up here to gawk at it. I cannot believe my luck, that I am the first to see it.' Her eye caught the pale shape of one of the human victims of the varnish, and her brief good mood seemed to evaporate. To be trapped like that, without even the simple dignity of being able to rot away to nothing. She swallowed hard. *Nanthema.* 'But I must keep moving, my dear Arus. I will be back one day to study this properly, I promise you.'

40

For Noon, her first sight of Ebora was an alarming doubling of images. Their bats flying almost wing to wing, she and Tor approached it as the sun was going down, the great clouds stacked on the horizon stained red and yellow like another world hanging in the sky. She saw the sprawling intricacy of the city, black and grey in the fading light, overgrown and broken down, and exploding from the very centre of it, the vast dead tree that was the Eboran god – all grey bark and twisted branches. The snow had not settled here. And yet at the same time, hanging over this first vision, she saw a city that sparkled with a thousand lights, that leaked spindles of smoke from a thousand inhabited homes, and in the centre of it crouched the silver glory that was Ygseril, its leaves shifting and stirring like a living thing. Because back then, it was.

She was aware that this second image was not her own, that for some reason the presence that was in her head had gifted it to her. It was so disorientating that she had to look away. Instead, she glanced over to Tor on the back of Gull, but his face was hidden within the scarf he'd wrapped around his head to keep off the chill, and what she could see of his expression was unreadable.

Following Gull's lead, they swept in lower, and the outskirts of the mythical city came up to meet them. Now they were closer, Noon could see the crumbling buildings, the flat red tiles of the roofs, the dark holes that had been windows, and the places where nature had started to claim the place as her own. She glimpsed a trio of sleek grey shapes flitting from one set of ruins to another, and she thought of the wolves that had surrounded them in the snow. Further ahead, just beneath the sprawling branches of the dead god-tree, she could see some lights – the flickering of campfires, and the steadier points of oil lamps.

Noon felt her heart begin to beat faster in her chest. The ancient city of Ebora, for centuries largely forbidden to humans, was now passing beneath her feet. Here were the homes of the rich and important; pale marble glinted in the peach fire of the sunset, and she saw pieces of richly carved architecture, cracked or covered in ivy. Once, armies had marched from this place and swept down across the plains, massacring her people as they went, drinking their blood and worse, according to the stories. Here she was, flying in to this place, a murderer herself, free for the first time in ten years and in the company of an Eboran to whom she had freely given her blood. An Eboran with whom she had shared more than her blood.

'Who am I?' she said aloud, but her words were scattered to the wind, and the voice inside her head was silent.

Gull was swooping in to land now, so she leaned close over Fulcor's head, murmuring into her cavernous ear, and they followed on down, wings beating a hectic wind along a deserted street. Tor dismounted, and she did the same, briefly hopping on legs that had grown used to not walking.

'We'll walk the rest of the way,' Tor said. He was already unstrapping his bags, taking extra care with those containing the Jure'lia orbs. 'I want to get a good idea of what we're walking into. I saw lights ahead. More lights than I was expecting.'

'What do you think it is?'

He unwound the scarf, and underneath it his face was tense. 'When I left fifty years or so ago, my sister was one of the few people still alive in this place.' He shrugged. 'She could be long dead. Perhaps they all are, and humans have crept in, looking to loot the place, or live in it.' He caught her eye, and his expression softened slightly. 'In truth, Noon, I don't know what we're about to face.'

'Are you all right?'

He smiled, the scarred side of his face creasing. Just lately he had seemed less conscious of it. 'I didn't think I would ever come back,' he said. 'Part of me is horrified that I have. It's a little unnerving.' He touched her face briefly, almost awkwardly. 'You must bear with me.'

Noon bent and picked up one of the bags containing the orbs, feeling the slosh of liquid as she shouldered it onto her back. They had tested it on one of their frequent stops, leaving an odd patch of bright foliage in the snowy mountain pass.

'There's only one way to find out, bloodsucker.' She gestured to the road ahead of them. The stones were cracked and riddled with weeds. 'Shall we?'

'Yes, let's.' Tor took a deep breath. 'Although, if my sister is still alive, you might want to refrain from that particular, uh, term of endearment.'

Little had changed, aside from the gentle slump into decay that had been ongoing for as long as he could remember. The buildings were shabbier, the trees and plants had encroached further. There was one quite sizeable tree growing in the centre of the main street, the street that led directly to the Palace of Roots. It had not been there when he left. At some point a storm had blown off all the tiles from the roof of what had once been a very fine house indeed, and now, as if that act had opened a lid, it was full to bursting with creepers and shrubs – they trickled out the windows like bloody tears.

'I can smell wolves,' said Noon next to him, making him jump.

'Can you? You can do that?'

'I can now,' she said, which was, in Tor's opinion, not really an answer at all.

They walked on, the sound of their boots too flat on the stones while shadows seemed to rush to meet them. Deep inside, Tor could feel a sense of dread gathering, as though they walked quietly towards their deaths. Because, of course, that was what Ebora had always meant to him – a quiet death in a dusty room somewhere, waiting endlessly for it to all be over. Why was he back here? What was he thinking? The plan had always been to run away, to run as far as possible and to have as much fun as possible before his body turned on him. His heart thudded sickly in his chest. What waited for him here? The giant corpse of a god that had abandoned them, or the skeletal remains of his sister, dead these fifty years and hidden in a room somewhere?

'Do you hear that?'

Tor grimaced. 'What?'

'Listen.'

He could hear only the wind, the quiet whisper of dead leaves being blown across their path. He glanced at Noon, but her face was intent, a crease between her brows that bisected the tattooed bat wing perfectly. For a moment, he remembered how much he enjoyed the stubborn set of her mouth, and how her narrow eyes creased with pleasure when he—

A pair of voices, chatting amiably enough – there and then gone. Noon met his eyes.

'You heard it.'

For one dizzying second he was seized with terror – the ghosts of his ancestors were here all along, waiting for the wanderer to return, Tormalin the Oathless, Tormalin the Walker on the Wall. And then the wind changed again and he heard

450

the soft babble of many people, gathered together somewhere ahead. A hidden crowd. They were nearing the outskirts of the palace and the public gardens that led to the inner gate.

'They're not Eboran, by the voices,' he said. This possibility too was frightening; not ghosts, but usurpers. Humans rattling around in the Palace of Roots, stealing all those things that had been hidden away or covered up, perhaps throwing out the long-dried corpses of his people into the gardens, to turn into mulch there.

'Tor?' Noon touched his arm, and he nodded once.

'Come on,' he said. 'Let's go quickly now. I need to know.'

Shortly they came to the small ring of buildings outside the palace, which in better times had been home to the men and women who kept the place running smoothly – servants, administrators, artisans. Tor led the way up the central street, skirting around a particularly dense thicket of thorn bushes, and suddenly it was in front of them – the great sweep of the welcome gardens, the gates shining in the distance, the low magnificence of the palace beyond that – and there were people camped on the grass. Tor stopped, and next to him he heard Noon catch her breath.

There were caravans and tents, great silk ones and smaller, cone-shaped ones, horses grazing on the now short-cropped grass, and several large campfires. Men and women were gathered around these, talking animatedly and cooking, while a handful of children ran around, shouting so that their words were caught in short bursts of white vapour. It was a cold night, and growing colder. The gates, he could finally see, stood partly open, and there was a steady stream of people wandering up and down the great path, even moving through the sacred gardens beyond. As he stared at them all, a few curious faces turned to look. He sensed more than saw Noon pulling her cap down over her forehead.

'There are lots of different people here, Noon,' he said, his

451

voice little more than a whisper. 'I see plains people, but there are also people from Reidn here, and Kesenstan and Jarlsbad, if I'm right. I recognise the languages, their caravans, their flags.' He blinked. 'What are they all doing here?'

'Plains people,' Noon croaked. Her eyes were riveted to a cluster of wide conical tents at the edges of the grass. 'I see them.'

Their arrival was causing some excitement now. Men and women leaned their heads close, staring, eyebrows raised as they speculated together. He stood up straight, and without waiting to see if Noon would follow, he began to stride towards the centre of the group. This was his home, after all.

He wasn't sure what he intended to do – stride up to the palace and then start shouting at everyone to get off his lawn? But instead, as he moved through a crowd that were all staring at him, Noon following on in his wake, he spotted a figure that caused an odd constriction around his heart. A slender young man with soft auburn curls, talking animatedly to a tall human man with a pair of axes at his waist. The last time Tor had seen the Eboran, he had been wandering away from him down a corridor, not listening as Tor tried to explain that he was going away, that they would not see each other again. He had had dust in his hair, he remembered, and his tattered shirt had been untucked. Aldasair had aged in the last fifty years, but only slightly.

'Aldasair?' Almost immediately he wanted to take the greeting back, half convinced that it wouldn't be his cousin after all, just some stranger with his face, and then he would find Aldasair's body somewhere in the labyrinthine palace, long dead of the crimson flux. But the young man was turning – Tor had a moment to admire the fine jacket he was wearing, not Eboran style at all – and he watched as the shock flitted across his face. Aldasair's eyes grew so wide that Tor thought they might fall out of his head.

452

'Tor? Tormalin?'

Around them, men and women were standing back, and Aldasair stumbled through them. When Tor had left, he had been certain that his young cousin's mind had been lost forever, but there was a brightness, an alertness in his face that hadn't been there before. The constriction in his chest grew tighter and he swallowed past it, feeling his mouth stretch in a grin he couldn't deny.

'It's me, Aldasair. I came back after all.'

Aldasair grabbed him and embraced him, and then held him back to stare at him closely. There was a glassy look to his eyes now, and Tor suspected that his mind had not healed entirely, after all.

'What happened to you?'

'That's a very long story, cousin, and I do want to tell you all about it, but first of all would you—'

'*Your face*, Tor, what happened to your face?'

For a second it was difficult to breathe, as though his lungs had turned to ice. He had forgotten. His cousin was reaching out well-meaning fingers, about to touch his scars. Tor stepped back lightly.

'That – is not something to be explained out here. Could we—?'

'And who is this?' Aldasair had stepped around him, peering at Noon, who was looking at him with a faintly amused expression.

'Ah. May I present Noon of the plains people, a companion of mine who has—'

'You travel with a human?'

Tor cleared his throat. 'Noon, this is my cousin Aldasair.'

'I figured that much out.'

The campsite was entirely silent now, watching their little scene. With faint desperation, Tor took Aldasair's arm. Only the tall man with the axes seemed to sense their need for privacy; he was carefully looking the other way, as though he'd spotted something incredibly interesting on the far side of the gardens.

'Please, Al. My sister. Is Hestillion still alive?' He wanted to follow up the question with, *and what are all these bloody humans doing here?* but it was so very quiet now. Only the crackling of the campfires accompanied their voices.

Aldasair jumped as though he'd been pinched.

'Your sister! Quickly, come with me.'

A thousand memories with every step. The palace gates were rusted in places but they did not screech as they once did when Aldasair led them through – someone had oiled them recently. The wide path that led to the palace had once shone with the brilliance of its polished white stones. Now many of them were shattered or lost, but someone had attempted to wash the rest – Tor could see dark streaks on some where a wet rag had been dragged across an accumulation of filth. Tiny details, but signs that Ebora was not quite as dead as when he had left it.

'This place,' said Noon, her voice low, 'I've never seen anything like it.'

Aldasair led them up the wide marble steps, through the gigantic lacquered doors – the elaborate golden trees had mostly broken or been chipped away, and these had not been repaired – and through into the palace itself. He took them down corridors, and here and there Tor heard human voices behind doors. It was difficult to concentrate.

'Where is she?' he asked finally, not able to keep it in any longer. 'Where is Hest?'

'Where else would she be?' said Aldasair. 'In the Hall of Roots.'

Faster than Tor had expected, they were standing outside another set of doors he remembered very well. The golden dragons and phoenixes looked dusty and tired. Aldasair paused then, looking at Noon.

454

'She may have to wait outside.'

'What? Why?'

His cousin looked uncomfortable, although Tor sensed it wasn't down to any embarrassment. There was something here that Aldasair didn't understand, or was afraid of. Looking at his face, it was easy to remember the vacant man Tor had left behind.

'Hestillion has yet to allow any of the diplomats into the Hall of Roots.' Aldasair blinked rapidly. 'Which I don't understand, because I thought that's why they were here. To see it. Him. To help bring him back.'

'Don't worry,' said Noon brightly. 'I'm not a diplomat. And given I've just flown over a mountain on a bat to get here, there's no way you're keeping me out of that room.'

'A bat, did you say?' Aldasair's eyebrows had disappeared up into his mop of hair.

'Enough.' Tor reached past them both and pushed the doors open. Inside, the Hall of Roots was a shadowy, cavernous space. Outside, the last of the sun's light had burned away to orange and purple, and all of the objects Tor remembered from this room, the paintings wrapped in parchment, the sculptures hidden in greying linens, had all been moved to the outer edges. Directly ahead of them, solid and dark and enormous, was the trunk of Ygseril. There was a collection of oil lamps, placed haphazardly on the roots, making it look as though a crowd of errant fireflies had decided to rest there, and amongst it all a slender figure sat, knees drawn up to her chest, her head to one side. Her yellow hair was loose, partially hiding her face.

A memory rose up in his mind, sharp and sick, and he was helpless against it; he remembered coming into this room, wondering where his sister had gone, only to find her perched on the roots, the body of a human child slumped before her. The human blood that had doomed them all already soaking into the dead roots of their god.

455

'Hest? Hest, it's me.' He shouted across the hall, too aware of how his words were eaten up by the space between them. Despite that, the head of the figure snapped up, as if roused violently from a deep sleep. As they watched, she stood up and walked across the roots, slowly at first and then with greater urgency until she nearly fell as she came to the edge. Instinctively, Tor began to trot towards her, until he found that he was running. And then she was running too. Tor had thought that nothing could have hurt him more than the cold fury she had shown him on the day he'd left, but as he looked at the desperate, unbelieving expression on her face, he felt that pain shrivel into nothing like parchment on a fire.

'Tormalin?' Her voice was hoarse, as though she hadn't spoken for years. 'Tormalin? Tormalin?'

She stumbled into his arms, muttering his name over and over again, her red eyes wide.

'It's me, Hest,' he said into her hair. 'I came home.'

She drew back from him, and seeing his face, all the strength seemed to rush out of her. He staggered as she fell to the floor, a sick tide of dread rising up in him as he saw the dirty cuffs of her robe, the way the hair on the back of her head was matted, as if she had been bedridden for months. There were dark circles under her eyes. She was alive, but where was his strong, unflappable sister?

'Your face,' she gasped. 'What happened to your face?' She took his hand, the one rippled with scars, and squeezed it as if checking it was real. 'Tormalin, what have you done?'

'There was an accident.' He forced a smile. Her fingers dug into his arm, her nails ragged and soft. 'But I am fine. I came back. Aren't you glad to see me?'

Out of the corner of his eye he could see Noon and Aldasair standing off to one side, having caught up with them. Noon had taken off her cap and was looking at Ygseril with an expression Tor couldn't fathom, but then his sister was grabbing at his arms, shaking him.

'You come back now, of course you do,' she said, moving her face into something that was more a grimace than a smile. 'If there is to be glory, you could not miss it. It is so like you to know, Tormalin. That you should come back precisely *now*, at this time.'

'Hest,' Tor took a slow breath, 'there is a lot we need to talk about, a lot to catch up on.' Carefully, he helped her to her feet. 'Hest, why are there humans in the city? What are they doing here?'

'They had dreams,' said Aldasair, in a matter-of-fact tone. 'Dreams that made them remember what Ebora was, and why they needed it.'

Hestillion looked up, seeming to see the other people in the hall for the first time. Tor saw her dismiss their cousin instantly, before her gaze snapped to Noon.

'Who is that?'

'Please, let me introduce you properly.' Tor cleared his throat. 'This is Fell-Noon of the, uh, plains. She has travelled here with me, Hest, because we found something important, which I need to tell you about.'

Noon was still staring at the tree-god, acknowledging none of them. Tor had the sudden dizzying sense that he was the only sane one in the room.

'A fell-witch?' Hestillion shook her head as if to clear it. 'No. No, not at all. This has never been a place for humans – I can't tell what effect that might have. What if he's insulted? What if the proximity of their blood taints him, as it does us?' She paused this strange diatribe as some sudden realisation washed over her, and Tor found that he knew what she was going to say before she said it. Hestillion the dream-walker, always too perceptive for anyone's comfort. 'Did she burn you? With winnowfire? She did this to you?' They were demands more than questions.

457

'It's a long story, Hest, please.' Tor took a slow breath. 'Let's go to one of the smaller rooms, sit down together and open a bottle of wine. We can talk about all of it, I promise. I would like to share a drink with my much-missed sister. You still have wine here, don't you?'

She was already shaking her head. 'No, I cannot leave here, and now that you are here, Tormalin, you will have to stay too. That one,' Hestillion pointed at Noon, as though gesturing to an offensive artwork she wished removed from her sight, 'must leave. Now. I will not have a human in the Hall of Roots.'

Finally, Noon seemed to hear what they were saying, and she turned, an imperious expression on her face that Tor had never seen before.

'You order me out? How dare you, small creature. I have more right than anyone to be here, in this place. Certainly more right than a child such as you.'

For a moment Tor was too stunned to move or speak. Dimly he was aware of Aldasair watching all this with a bemused expression.

'How *dare* I?' There was such a note of danger in Hestillion's voice that Tor felt a genuine surge of panic – again he remembered the small boy she had murdered, his throat cut open in honour of their god. Noon, meanwhile, stepped forward, her cap falling to the floor as her hands leapt with green fire, filling the Hall with eerie light.

'Noon, no!' He grabbed at her shoulder, turning her towards him, and whatever it was that had been in her face winked out like a candle. After a moment, the winnowfire vanished.

'Tor?'

'This is too much,' he said. 'This place, it's overwhelming. Aldasair, a quiet room where we can talk, please? A place where the stakes are not quite so apparent.'

Aldasair nodded. 'I know such a room. Hestillion, will you join us?'

Tor was surprised by the simple note of kindness in his cousin's voice, and even more surprised that Hest seemed to respond to it. Glaring once more at Noon, she pushed her hair back from her face and nodded.

'The Bellflower Room has recently been aired,' said Aldasair. 'And I've had wine put in there for future guests. Follow me.'

Tor knew where it was, but he was glad to follow his cousin from the Hall of Roots, and relieved to put the dead form of Ygseril behind him. For all the emotions that had rushed back to him at their arrival in Ebora, he felt only dread when he looked at the god-tree.

41

Noon sat with her hands pressed to the table top. It had been carved all over with a looping pattern of ivy and vines, with small creatures – bats, birds, mice – peeking from behind the leaves, and then it had been covered all over with a deep shining varnish. Looking at it, following the swirling shapes and imagining the skilled hand that made them, calmed her. It was difficult to stay afloat amid the thoughts and images streaming through her head.

'I then agreed to work for a Lady de Grazon, a human woman who owns property in the vine forest . . .'

Tor, she dimly understood, was giving his sister a swift account of his movements since he'd left Ebora. Noon caught pieces of story, unable to make sense of much of it, while the cold voice inside was suddenly hot, demanding to be taken back to the Hall of Roots, demanding to see the giant dead tree again. She blinked, pressing her hands to the table until her fingertips turned white.

'. . . She is an eccentric woman, with a frankly unreasonable obsession with the Jure'lia and their artefacts. Vintage employed mc as her hired sword and we explored certain areas of interest . . .'

The other Eboran, the one with long auburn hair, was staring at her from across the table. Just like Tor and his sister, he had deep crimson eyes and features as though carved from marble, but there was an openness to his face that she had not seen in his cousins.

He has been long lost, that one, said the voice in her head. *He feels the loss keenly, has been cut adrift. Is not capable of ignoring it, as your lover has, is not able to fathom taking action, like the sister.*

'. . . It was only when we explored the compound that we realised what had caused Godwort to lose his mind. Isn't that right, Noon?'

Her head snapped up, and she tried to recall what words had been said, in what order. 'Yes. That's right. The grief of it, the grief of it must have—'

Grief? Your human souls know nothing of real grief, nothing of what I and my kind have suffered.

Just like when she had entered the Hall of Roots, a confusion of sensations swept over Noon. *The taste of sap on her tongue, green and burning and alive. A sound that was both the whisper of a thousand voices and the rustle of leaves in all directions. New muscles used for the first time, the near-painful satisfaction of stretching wings, wet sap on pale feathers, drying from shining scales. An eagerness, knowing that your time was now, that you were a weapon, an instrument of a god – the presence that was always with you, that ran in your blood and was a warmth in the back of your mind. And then the terrible severing of that, like suddenly being blind, and having enough time to acknowledge that you would die and not return, that you would all die, now and forever. There would be no coming back. Feeling fear for the first time.*

Slumped at the table, Noon choked back a sob only to see everyone looking at her. Tor had half risen to his feet, an expression of alarm on his face.

'Noon . . .?'

'I'm fine. I'm fine. Pass me the wine, please.'

Aldasair poured her a fresh glass, and she took several loud gulps, ignoring the pointed look the blonde woman gave her. 'Thank you. That's better. Stop bloody looking at me and carry on.'

Tor cleared his throat. 'As I was saying, I think it's possible that something the Jure'lia left behind could help us revive Ygseril. It is a fluid that makes plant life grow very rapidly, even reviving dead plants, and reinvigorating seeds that are dormant in the ground. It is very powerful.'

'Ygseril is no mere plant,' said Hestillion. Her skin looked waxy, Noon thought, and she was holding herself very carefully. There was no doubt she was hiding something, but Noon was finding it very difficult to care. She drank some more of the wine, and filled the glass herself from the bottle.

'I think it is worth a try,' Tor was saying. 'We've never tried anything like this before, have never had access to anything like this before. Here, let me demonstrate it, what a small sample can do.' Tor began to rise from his chair again, turning towards where their bags had been placed by the wall, but Hestillion held up her hand.

'No. Do not waste it.'

Tor froze. 'You believe me, then?'

For the first time, a ghost of a smile touched Hestillion's lips. 'Why else would you return, dear brother? Only for something extraordinary, of course.'

Tor's movements became very stiff then. 'I had to leave. My reasons—'

'Your reasons are your own, Tormalin the Oathless, and that time is very far behind us. Circumstances have changed, as I'm sure you can see. Ebora has friends now, allies. Trade routes have reopened, the old road to the eastern forest has been cleared, and we are no longer alone. Now, you must excuse me. I must rest.' Hestillion rose from the table.

462

'You're going to bed?' Tor was frowning. 'But Hest, we may have the cure here! We could take the fluid there now, see what happens.'

The tall Eboran woman shook her head, her eyes downcast. 'Soon, Tormalin, I promise, but it must be the correct time. Do you not see? I would like some time to prepare. Aldasair will show you to your rooms.'

With that she left, not looking at the perplexed expression on her brother's face.

Hestillion hung suspended in the netherdark, waiting for Ygseril's response. After she had explained her brother's re-appearance and what he had brought back with him, the ghostly roots around her had seemed to grow closer, as though they were contracting somehow, but there had been only silence since. The glow that was the god's voice was a distant point of light. She knew that if she tried to move towards it, it would move away.

What day is it?

For a few moments, Hestillion couldn't make sense of the words.

'What day, my lord? I do not understand.'

Silence again. Hestillion thought she could sense a new tension around her though. What she had told the god had changed him, moved him somehow.

Where is the moon in the sky?

'Oh. It is the eighth day of the Sorrowing Month, my lord. The true moon is waning.'

The next new moon?

'In two days' time, my lord.'

Knowing it was foolish and even an insult, Hestillion reached out to the god, trying to get a better understanding of what he was feeling, but it was like placing your hands on a statue in a pitch-black room. She could only get a vague impression;

463

a sense of tightly held excitement, perhaps, of something being held back, but perhaps she was imagining it.

Do it then, said Ygseril. *On the new moon.*

'I don't understand, my lord. Do you believe it will work? Will you then come back to us? Why on this particular day?' She stopped. 'It is the Festival of New Lights on that day. An auspicious date, my lord?'

That is correct. The voice that wasn't a voice pulsed on and off in her head. *That day and no other.* There was a pause, and then, *You have done well, my remarkable child. Truly, an extraordinary mind you have.*

Despite the words Hestillion felt a brief stab of annoyance. It was her brother who had brought this solution, not her, and finally Ygseril was willing to cooperate.

As if sensing what she was feeling, Ygseril continued: *Do not worry, Hestillion the dream-walker. You will never be left behind again. We promise you that.*

And then the presence was gone and Hestillion was left in the dark, alone.

42

There could be few Behemoth sites more dangerous than this one.

Vintage had been camping on the beach for three days, just watching it, observing the distant glitter of parasite spirits slipping over the water. The wreckage itself was a jagged mess, salt blasted and covered in the white-grey shadow of barnacles, but still there, for all that, just far enough away from the shore to be a pain. The shape of it was hopelessly familiar, of course. She had been here, years ago, when finally it became apparent that Nanthema had vanished. Working back from her letters she had figured out that this was the wreck the Eboran woman had been on her way to when all communication had ceased, and so young Vintage – or younger, anyway – had travelled all the way here on her father's money, and she had spoken to the people of the nearby town. Yes, an Eboran woman had been here, she was difficult to forget. Yes, she had bought supplies and smiled graciously and tipped heavily. No, they didn't know where she was going. It didn't matter; Vintage knew well enough where she had been going.

So she had hired a boat and gone out there, rowing cautiously around the wreck, half terrified that her small vessel would have its bottom torn out by some unseen scrap of Behemoth metal, and half convinced that she would simply be caught by one of the parasite spirits that circled this lonely, artificial island. In the end, she had got as close as she could and called Nanthema's name for hours, feeling foolish and desperate all at once. She had never set foot on the wreck itself. It had been the first one she'd seen so close, and the alien sense of it closed her throat with fear.

Now, Vintage sat on the same beach with her crossbow next to her, the remains of a meal of fresh fish on a battered plate next to that. Down by the shoreline, the small boat she had purchased leaned slightly to one side, packed up and ready to go. She sighed.

'Dangerous or not, I am here now.'

As she watched, an elongated shape made of purple light rose shimmering from the waterlogged wreck, turning gracefully in the air as it sailed slowly from one side to the other. She missed Tormalin and his easy, cocksure confidence, and she even missed the strange forceful presence of the fell-witch Noon. But she could not have brought them to this particular wreck.

'I've put them through enough,' she said to the empty beach, to her half-eaten dinner. 'And they've already paid for my curiosity.' The guilt of leaving them was a heavy weight in her stomach.

Except that wasn't all of it, she well knew. The truth was that what this Behemoth might contain was much too personal, much too raw, to ever let anyone else see. Vintage stood up. It was a warm, balmy day but the breeze coming in off the Kerakus Sea was chilly. The scorching on her cheeks had finally healed, and the skin there felt tougher than it had before.

'Time to find out, either way,' she said aloud. 'Nanthema, if you're in there, I will be there soon, my darling.'

Kicking sand over the embers of her fire, Vintage slipped on her small pack – she would be travelling light today, no sample jars and no notebooks – and fastened her crossbow to her belt next to a newly sharpened hunting knife she'd bought in the seaside town. The boat was not easy to push into the sea, and she got a good soaking before she clambered into it, but the woman who'd sold it to her promised that once it was in the water it would be a dream to handle, and that much seemed to be true. Gathering up the oars, she leaned into the work with a grimace. Her back complained, but she could ignore that. It would complain all the more tomorrow.

'If I'm still alive, of course.'

The small boat bobbed and lurched, sunlight dancing across the water in blinding shards. The shattered Behemoth remains loomed closer, and she periodically reminded herself to keep an eye on the water as she went. The woman who had sold her the boat had told her that once they had tried to mark the areas where the Behemoth shards lurked just below the surface. A small party had come out here with specially made floats and chains, but three of their number had been turned inside out by parasite spirits and they hadn't tried again. Now people simply kept away from the bay entirely – it was easier that way. It wasn't a comforting thought.

As if she had summoned it, Vintage spotted a twisted point of oily-looking metal poking just above the waves ahead of her. Squinting so hard that she was sure she would get a head-ache, she steered the little boat away from it; as she went, she got a brief impression of the enormous piece of broken Behemoth hidden just below.

'I am a bloody fool,' she said, a touch breathlessly.

Ahead, the main section towered above her, cave-like and littered with shredded sections of what she now knew to be springy material that made up their corridors and walls. Now that she was closer, she could see thick wads of seaweed clinging to the places where the metal touched the water, as well as

467

sweeping colonies of barnacles and mussels. Giant crabs too – she saw their furtive sideways movements as they skittered into the dark. There was, she mused, a lot of food out here for someone willing to chance it, but no crab was tasty enough to risk having your innards exposed by a parasite spirit. Soon the Behemoth wreckage closed over her head, and the bright breezy day was lost to a shadowy quiet. It smelled strongly of salt here, and the other, unnameable smell she had come to associate with Jure'lia places.

'Here we go.'

Bringing the boat up as close as she could, she tied it up to a twisted piece of metal. Ten feet above her was a section like honeycomb, sheared in half by the violence of the impact; she was looking at the exposed ends of several passageways. They would be her way in, if she could get up there. Working quickly, all too aware that a parasite spirit could appear at any moment, Vintage slipped an augmented crossbow bolt from her pocket and fetched the length of rope from her pack. Tying one end to the bolt, she then fixed it firmly into the crossbow, and aimed it above her, trying to spot a good place to try. She only had five of these special bolts, each one tipped with an extra layer of steel.

It took three attempts before she got a bite she trusted, and then she was wriggling her way up the line, swearing violently under her breath and cursing her own stupidity, all the while hoping that a parasite spirit wasn't oozing out of the dark towards her. When she got her fingers hooked over the edge of the closest platform, she hauled herself up and over, and crouched where she was, listening and watching.

'Let's hope it stays this quiet.'

Satisfied that she wasn't in immediate danger, she began to move. From below she could hear the crash and slosh of seawater against the broken hull, and far, far above, the cries of seagulls. The sound cheered her a little. Reaching inside her

468

pack she retrieved and lit her travelling lamp. Its small, warm glow blossomed into life, and she grimaced at the walls of the passageway. The Behemoths were made of the most resilient material she had ever seen, but so many years in the water had taken its toll; moss and mould were in evidence here, and the place had a terrible, dying smell to it. Summoning what she remembered of the structure of Godwort's Behemoth, she walked down the passageway, boots echoing on the damp floor. All too quickly, her light was the only light.

'Nanthema,' she said to the walls streaked with mould and the encroaching darkness. 'I remember the first time I saw you, my darling.' Her voice was a whisper, keeping her company. 'I had never seen an Eboran before. I had never even seen anyone wearing spectacles before.' She found herself grinning reluctantly at the girl she had been. 'And there you were, larger than life in our drawing room, dazzling and frightening my father with your questions and your knowledge. You were a painting come to life. A figure from mythology walking around and eating our good cheese.'

The passageway curved and split. There was no way to know for sure where she was going, so she went left, deciding to trust her instincts.

'Soon it was me bothering you with questions, and you, I think, were glad to find someone finally interested in the ghosts in the vine forest. Nanthema, our time together was so short.' She took a slow breath. 'I do hope I am not about to trip over your skeleton in the dark. That would be dreadful. Unless I'm right about where you are . . .'

The smell of rot lessened, and the deeper she went the cleaner the walls were. Eventually, she came to a section where the strange pulsing lights were still working, casting a pinkish light over the empty corridors. She saw more of the strange tubes they had witnessed in the other wreck, and more alcoves, their meaning or use no clearer than before. Eventually, she came

469

to a section where the ceiling was lost in the darkness, and for a reason she couldn't pinpoint, this felt like progress.

She had raised the lamp to see the exit on the far side when a shifting pattern of light oozed through the wall to her left. Vintage gave a low cry and staggered away, reaching for her crossbow, but the thing was so fast. In moments, it was on her, a head like a bald skull made of light twisting down with its jaws open wide. The crossbow bucked in her hands and the bolt landed directly in the space between the holes she chose to believe were its eyes. The parasite spirit let out a high-pitched wail and floated up and away from her like a leaf caught in a strong wind. Not waiting to see what it would do next, Vintage snatched up her travelling lamp and sprinted across the chamber, a ball of terror heavy in her chest. Once through the exit she kept moving. Her hope was that she would lose it deeper inside, that it would be too pained and confused by the bolt in its head to come after her.

There followed a breathless, panicky run, the light from her lamp bouncing unevenly against the walls. When eventually she found what she was looking for, she did indeed nearly trip over it; a nerve centre of fleshy, greyish blocks rising in a low hill across the floor. Somewhere beneath that, she suspected, was the twin to the pink shard of crystal that had trapped Esiah's son and driven the old man mad. Her heart in her throat, she circled the protrusion, and when she found the hole she had known would be there, she felt a terrible mixture of hope and terror close over her heart. Someone had been here, someone had made it this far. And she had a pretty good idea of who that had been.

It was the morning of what the Eborans apparently called the Festival of New Lights. They were a people on the point of extinction, their city an empty husk with a dead god crouching at the heart of it, but despite this, Noon sensed an atmosphere

470

of hope about the place. It was a cold day, everything awash in sunlight that was bright and clean. Far above them, the corpse moon hung in the sky, a greenish smudge too bright to look at; it looked closer than she'd ever seen it, and very clear. Word of what was to be attempted had got about somehow, and the people camped on the lawns and the diplomats taking up residence in the rooms were all talking about it. Noon heard it on everyone's lips as she wandered around, speculation and gossip traded by people who looked worried, or excited, or bemused.

The ceremony was to take place at midday. Hestillion had wanted it closed off from the hordes, for them to try the worm people's magic privately and without an audience, but Aldasair had been besieged by interested parties desperate not only finally to see Ygseril, but also to see the use of an ancient Jure'lia artefact. And, of course, if this was to be the day that the tree-god came back to life, every one of them there wanted to be in the hall to witness it. What a thing to tell your children! What a thing to take back to your city or kingdom, a piece of prestige that would make you envied, famous, untouchable. Tormalin had given the word finally, a half-amused expression on his face, allowing the peoples of Sarn to be there to witness the revival of the great Ygseril. Noon thought only she had seen the expression that had flitted over his sister's face. She was worth keeping an eye on, that one, Noon felt instinctively, even as part of her felt calmer all the time; after the initial confusion, it seemed that the presence inside her was at peace here, and that, in turn, made her happier.

As she made her way back across the lawns she saw Aldasair sitting on the grass, a trio of children sitting cross-legged with him. He had a deck of cards covered in elaborate drawings, and he appeared to be teaching them a game of some sort. The children were laughing and elbowing each other, crowing at each victory, while a tall human man with a pair of shining axes stood over them. Noon smiled. Grass and laughter and the feeling of sun warming her through her clothes; it was all a long way from the Winnowry. Agent Lin was dead, and even the Winnowry would have to think twice about bringing their grievances to Ebora.

'Lady Noon, will you join us?'

Noon smirked. 'Just Noon is fine. What sort of cards are those?' She added herself to the circle, ignoring the brief puzzled glance one of the children gave the bat wing on her forehead. All behind her now.

'These are tarla cards.' Aldasair shuffled them skilfully, blending them between his fingers and making the children giggle. 'We used to use them to tell fortunes.' He nodded at a little girl with a snug fur collar and short black hair. 'They've already told us that Callio will grow up to ride a horse better than her brother, and Tris here,' he nodded to a small boy with a mess of ginger curls, 'Tris now knows that one day he will find a gold nugget as big as his fist. So we're going to try a game now.'

Aldasair began to deal the cards, but Noon shook her head. 'I'm happy to watch.'

And she was. Whatever happened this afternoon when Tor poured the golden fluid onto the roots of Ygseril, her past was behind her. The game went on around her and for the first time in as long as she could remember, she felt some of the tension go out of her shoulders. Deep inside, the presence that spoke to her so easily now seemed to stretch like an indolent cat.

Times of peace, it said, *should be savoured.*

She couldn't agree more.

Presently, a tall girl with scabby knees came running over to them, a flush of excitement on her cheeks.

'Callio, the lady is doing the puppets again! Come and look!'

The children immediately abandoned their card game, scrambling to their feet.

'I've heard the puppets are very good,' said the tall man with the axes on his belt. Bern. Aldasair, she remembered now, had introduced him to her the night they had arrived. 'Shall we go and have a look?'

Aldasair looked at her, and Noon shrugged. 'Why not?'

They followed the children as they weaved through the crowds. It *did* feel like a festival day out here – the smell of roasting meat, brightly coloured flags. There were lanterns and lamps everywhere – some already lit for the Festival of New Lights, others waiting for the evening. One tent had been covered in a piece of fabric sewn all over with pieces of broken mirror so that it winked and glittered like the sea under a summer sun; the people of Sarn were getting into the spirit of the thing. Presently they came to a small crowd of seated children. There was a young man wearing a bright blue hood – Noon noted absently that he looked like her, his black hair shining almost blue under the sunlight, his skin a warm olive colour – and he was dancing a figure on strings between his hands. The children were laughing, enjoying the show.

It was the puppet she recognised first.

Its face narrow and sly, its clothes made of tattered pieces of grey and blue silk so that they tugged and shivered in the slightest breeze. The god of the north wind had so often been the villain in the stories she'd heard as a child, so much so that they had booed him when he came on; arriving to chase the heroes into the sea, or trick the good warrior into giving up her best horse. Noon knew the hands that had made the puppet. She knew them very well.

'It can't be.'

Someone else had joined the man with the blue hood. The old woman moved slowly, because she had suffered a terrible injury in the past. That much was evident from the rippling of scars that covered her face and body, and from the awkward way she held one arm away under her coat, but her other hand

473

held the strings of a puppet, and despite her missing eye and the scars, it danced as nimbly as it ever had.

Horror crawled down Noon's back, holding her in place with an icy hand. Mother Fast was alive. It was impossible, impossible, she had seen the old woman burn. But she was alive, and here in this place, of all places.

Noon took a step backwards, filled with the powerful need to hide, but despite the cheerful shifting crowd around her, Mother Fast looked up and saw her immediately – she met her eyes and there was no looking away, no hiding. The old woman dropped the puppet – the only time Noon had ever seen her do so – and screamed.

It was a hoarse, angry sound. It silenced the crowd with a knife edge.

'You!'

Noon turned and tripped over her own feet, hitting the cold grass with enough force to wind her. Deep inside, the presence was reeling in confusion.

Why are you afraid? it demanded. *She is an old woman, half dead already. She is no threat at all.*

Noon moaned, squeezing her eyes shut against the flood of images that came. Not alien ones this time, but memories that were all too familiar: the grasses thick with smoke; a horse running into the distance, lit up like a torch; a woman's face, better known and dearer to her than even her own, melting and boiling away to bone. And after, the bones and the black ash, the smell of cooking meat.

'I mustn't remember. I *can't* remember, it would, it would—'

'You were sent away.'

Noon opened her eyes. The crowd had parted and Mother Fast stood over her, the man with the blue hood next to her. There were other plains people here now, she saw, crowded around them. Aldasair was standing to her back, looking perplexed.

'Is everything quite well?' he asked.

Mother Fast's one good eye flickered up to him, bright and black like a beetle.

'*Quite well*, Eboran? This girl here is a murderer. A murderer.' Her voice shook, and that was the worst of it. Mother Fast was angry, but she was also afraid.

Afraid of me, thought Noon. The smell of burning flesh would not leave her.

'I'm sure there must be a misunderstanding,' said Aldasair, mildly enough.

Mother Fast raised a trembling finger. It was a claw, Noon saw, a ruined cadaverous thing.

'This girl murdered her own mother, saw her burn up like a taper, like a pig on a spit, and she murdered a hundred and eight other souls too. Innocent people of her own kin, and she would have murdered me too, only I would not die.' Mother Fast gave a choked sob. 'Oh, I suffered and I burned like all the rest, but I would not die.'

Shaking now and unable to stop it, Noon climbed slowly to her feet.

'That's not who I am any more,' she said, her voice too quiet. Mother Fast was not listening. She had turned to the plains people at her back, shouting now, anger overpowering the fear in her voice.

'You all know the story!' she cried. 'The witch child who killed her own people. You all heard it, tribe to tribe. Passed the story around on icy nights to scare your children with, to scare them into behaving themselves. Well, here she is.' Mother Fast looked up. 'Here she is.'

'I'm not that person any more.' Noon took a slow breath. 'I'm not.'

'You should be in the Winnowry,' Mother Fast was leaning on the man with the blue hood now. 'They said that's where they were taking you. Why aren't you there, murderer?'

'The Winnowry is an abomination.' The words were bitter in Noon's mouth, and quite abruptly she wasn't afraid. Her own anger, slow to rise, was filling her chest. 'It's a place to punish women for something they have no control over. It's shameful. Listen to me. I am not who I was . . . that day. Not any more. Don't you understand?' Noon pushed past the roiling nausea in her stomach and nursed the flames of anger instead. 'I was a child. I was a fucking child!'

'I know what you are, well enough.' The flat hate in Mother Fast's voice was like a punch to her stomach. Noon gritted her teeth against it.

Kill her, said the voice in her head. *She is an enemy.*

'I was a child,' Noon repeated, but in her head all the memories were resurfacing, memories she had hoped had been forced down beneath everything else a long time ago. She remembered standing outside their tents, remembered the humming of the wind through the grass. Waiting for something, not knowing everything was about to change. Her mother's face, lost in green fire. She remembered, too, the terrible anger that had been born inside her that day, greater and more frightening than anything she'd ever known.

With a soft *whumph* both her hands were gloved in flame. There were cries of alarm all around, and she saw people stepping back from her.

Good, said the voice inside her. *You are a weapon, yet they admonish you for killing? Do they not see what you are?*

'No, I don't think they do,' she said. She felt light now, as though she were floating away. 'I don't think they know what I am at all.' Holding up her hands, the winnowfire grew stronger, brighter. There were people here, many of them moving away now, crying out to others to get away, but she could hear something else on the edge of that: shouting, the clash of swords, the screams of the dying. The Jure'lia must be stopped. Dimly she was aware that the old woman who had started all this had fallen back, her scarred face caught in a rictus of fear. Noon smiled slightly.

'Noon? Noon! What are you doing?'

It was Tor's voice, jerking her away from wherever she had been. She saw his face and the burn she had put there. The winnowfire winked out of existence.

'Tor?'

His arm came around her and she was being steered away from the crowd, back towards the palace. For a moment she resisted, in her confused state she felt that they must be taking her to the Winnowry – her mother had said that's what would happen if she summoned the fire, and finally it was happening.

'Noon, please, let's go inside. Listen to me.'

His face was close to hers and she could see his scars – the scars she had caused. The fight went out of her and she allowed herself to be steered inside, away from the crowds that were already recovering from their fright.

Inside the palace she seemed to lose track of time. Too many similar corridors, the bright squares of daylight on marble floors. And then they were in a room together, alone. Noon sat on a bed and ran her hands over her face.

'What happened?'

Tor was wearing the finest clothes she had ever seen him in, a long-sleeved robe of pale grey silk, tightened and shaped around his slim figure. The high collar was embroidered with black serpents, all twisted around each other, and there were smaller serpents at his cuffs too. His hair was shining, brushed back from his temples so that the scarred portion of his face was exposed, and he wore a silver earring in his unruined ear – a three-pronged leaf. She thought she had rarely seen him look more beautiful.

'Mother Fast was there.' Noon swallowed. 'I thought she had died. I thought I'd killed her, just like everyone else, when I was eleven.'

Tor stared at her, and, afraid of what she might see in his face, she looked away.

'What do you mean, everyone else? You killed everyone? Who?'

Noon looked down at her hands instead.

'I was born to the plains folk a fell-witch. You're supposed to be reported to the Winnowry straight away, but I hid it, and then my mother hid it. Not that it helped in the end. I'm a murderer, Tor. That's the truth. I killed a lot of people – people I knew, who I loved and who loved me – and then I was put inside a prison for it. And then I escaped, because I didn't want to die there, regardless of all the people I'd killed.'

For a long time, Tor said nothing. He went to a cabinet and retrieved a bottle and a glass, pouring wine and drinking it in silence. Noon found that she missed Vintage, except, of course, if Vintage was here, she would have learned the truth about her too.

'Noon.' Tor put the glass down, empty. 'Noon, I don't have time for this.' He turned to her and he looked faintly exasperated. 'We're trying the Jure'lia fluid in less than an hour, and I can't have any distractions. Hestillion won't stand for it.'

'Did you hear what I said?'

'I heard you. How is that woman here if you killed everyone?'

Noon blinked. It wasn't the question she'd been expecting.

'How should I know? She must have survived. Another tribe took her in and helped her to heal, I expect.'

'Well,' said Tor. 'That's unfortunate.'

Noon shook her head slightly. 'Unfortunate?'

'For her to be here now, in the middle of this. Never mind, it can be ignored for now, I think. People are too curious to see what will happen with Ygseril. We can continue as before, it's no matter.'

'No matter?' Noon curled her hands into fists, the bones popping like a knot of wood on the fire. 'That's all right, then.

478

I suppose, being a people so used to murdering to get what you need, my killings must seem like nothing to you.'

A flicker of anger crossed Tor's face. 'We're back to bloodsuckers, are we?'

'Isn't that what you are? Isn't that what I am to you – a handy vein?'

'Noon –' For a moment he looked stricken, and she remembered him on his knees inside the Behemoth wreck, how she had held him and kissed the top of his head. That same vulnerability was there in the set of his mouth and the cast of his eyes, but then she saw him visibly collect himself, pushing those feelings away. 'I am sorry for your past, Noon, but this is the future of my people I'm talking about here. It requires all of my attention.' With that, he went back to the door, turning to her just before he left. 'I'll let you know how it goes afterwards,' he said simply. 'Wish me luck.'

The door closed and, after a moment, Noon heard the rattle of a key turning and a lock tumbling into place. She stared at the spot where he'd been, a cold feeling settling over her like a shroud.

43

It was a slow process. All the time that Vintage worked, securing her own rope ladder to the soft cubes of greyish matter, she was all too aware that if she got this wrong – misjudged the length of the ladder or failed to secure it properly – then there was a good chance that she would die in this place, trapped inside the hidden chamber until she died of thirst or starvation. No one knew she was here, and no one would come looking for her. Not in time to save her life, anyway. And even worse – she could be trapped down there forever with the remains of her beloved Nanthema.

'Some people might call that romantic,' she muttered to herself as she gave her ties a final, experimental tug. 'Such people want their heads examined, of course.'

There was no more putting it off. Checking once more that her pack was secure across her shoulders and that the ladder could take her weight, she began to climb slowly down, the travel lamp hanging from her belt. It banged against her hip, sending confused shadows into the chamber below. It was tempting to look down, to glance over her shoulder, but she kept her observations to a minimum so that the ladder wouldn't twist about. Could she see the floor? Yes, and the ladder would be long enough. Bracing herself to take the impact on her knees, she dropped down carefully, staggering only slightly, and looked around. Down here, the soft nodules of light protruded from the place where the floor met the walls, so that everything was doused in a strange, dreamlike light – light that slid along the edge of the giant, jagged crystal.

'Well. Goodness me.'

Rather than pink, this crystal was yellow, sickly and off-putting, like jaundice. On the floor by her feet, Vintage saw some shrivelled pieces of fibre and a few sticks of splintered wood – the remains of the ladder brought by her predecessor, of course. Her heart thumping painfully in her throat, Vintage approached the shining surface of the crystal, and just as it had inside the Behemoth on Esiah Godwort's compound, the slick blankness of it vanished and instead she was looking at a vast, empty landscape, stretching from one horizon to another. It was like looking through a window at something entirely impossible.

'I don't think I'll ever get used to looking at this,' she said, her voice little more than a rushing sound in her ears. The landscape was different to the one at Godwort's compound. The sky was yellow and streaked with black clouds, while the stony ground was littered with all manner of strange, unlikely rocks. Boulders as big as houses perched precariously on top of each other, flat rocks with wide holes in their centres stood lined up together as though someone had thought to make a passageway somehow. Everywhere she looked, rocks stood in circles or in lines, or on top of each other. There were patterns everywhere, so many that they broke down, intersecting their neighbours and ruining the symmetry of it. As she watched, she realised that the clouds were moving, as if with a brisk wind.

'How can that be?' She moved closer to the crystal, until her fingertips threatened to brush its surface. Her breath

481

pillowed there, reminding her that she stood next to a solid object. 'The landscape was still at the other Behemoth, although I suppose it's possible there was nothing to move there, or we left before—'

A figure lurched out from behind one of the tall rocks and Vintage gave a breathy little scream, jumping backwards as she did so. A tall woman with a sheath of black hair falling untidily over her face stumbled towards her. She wore tight-fitting travelling leathers, functional and well used. There was a pair of wire-rimmed spectacles hooked over the collar of her shirt, and she looked no older than thirty, yet Vintage knew her to be much, much older than that.

'Nanthema?' Vintage found that she was gasping for air even as tears rolled silently down her cheeks. It was the damn spectacles, glinting in the light of an alien sky. Twenty-odd years later and she still had her damn spectacles.

The woman looked stunned, her eyes as round as moons as she approached the edge of the crystal. Vintage saw her lips move, saw her asking disbelieving questions, and then she broke into a grin. She was speaking faster and faster now, shaking her head.

'Nanthema, my darling, I can't hear you, I can't.' Vintage went back to the shard and without any thought for what it might do, pressed her hands flat to the surface. She did not fall through into the strange landscape, but when Nanthema placed her hands on the other side, her voice abruptly filled the chamber, tinny and strange, as though coming from a very great distance.

'– if anyone could find me, of course it would be you, of course it would, I don't know why I even worried for a moment –'

'Your voice!' blurted Vintage. She felt a wild impulse to crash her fists against the crystal, but controlled it. 'I can hear you!'

482

Nanthema looked down at where her hand was pressed against Vintage's, separated by a layer of crystal and an unknowable distance. Cautiously, she took it away, and Vintage saw her mouth move, asking a question. Then she put the hand back.

'Can you hear me now?'

'Yes, I can bloody hear you, what are you even doing in there?'

'It's the contact, somehow,' Nanthema was saying, peering at their hands. 'I would not have guessed that. Of course, I've had no way to find out.'

'Nanthema!' This time Vintage did knock slightly on the shard. 'You have been missing for twenty years! Do you have any idea what that has done to me? I thought you had run off, left me, decided I wasn't interesting enough . . .'

Vintage's words ran out. Nanthema was standing quietly, just watching her, in that way she had.

'Oh, Nanthema.' Vintage gave her a watery smile and they stood in silence for a moment, both pretending the other wasn't crying. Eventually, Vintage cleared her throat. 'How can I get you out of there?'

'As far as I know, you can't,' said Nanthema, shrugging slightly. 'The rest of the chamber is empty, if I remember correctly.'

'I will be back.' Vintage left the shard and did a slow circuit of the room, looking for something, anything – some sort of handy lever, perhaps, or a rope to pull. Aside from the remains of Nanthema's ladder, it was entirely empty. She returned to the shard and placed her hand against the crystal again. 'You're right, as ever, but that doesn't mean there's no way out of there. I will find it, even if I have to search this entire stinking wreck.' She took a breath. 'How did you even get in there in the first place?'

'Would you believe me if I told you I don't remember?' Nanthema looked rueful, an expression Vintage remembered

483

well. 'I was asleep, Vin, in this chamber. I had spent a good week inside this wreck, barely sleeping, trying to see as much of it as I could, and when I found this place – well.' She grinned. 'It's extraordinary, isn't it?'

Vintage glanced at the yellow sky above the other woman's head. 'It is certainly that.'

'It's also quite cosy, or as cosy at it gets in this place. I decided it was safe to have a nap. I woke up on my feet, walking through a crystal that I had previously thought to be entirely solid. By the time I was on the other side, it was too late. I couldn't get back through.'

'First of all, exploring this place for an entire week is utterly out of all realms of sense. Secondly, doing it alone it lunacy, actual lunacy. Third,' Vintage frowned slightly, 'I have missed you a great deal.'

Nanthema grinned. 'You haven't changed at all, Vin.'

At that, Vintage felt a surge of sorrow in her throat so thick that she could not swallow. Not changed at all, except that she had – she had grown older while Nanthema was trapped in here. Her skin had lost that deep burnished luminescence that the young take for granted and there were strands of grey in her hair. But Nanthema had not changed, not even the tiniest bit. Her crimson eyes were still clear, her black hair hadn't turned grey or fallen out. She blinked.

'Never mind that. How are you not dead? Is there food in that place? *Where* are you, exactly?'

'Vin, this place . . .' For the first time, Nanthema looked troubled. 'I'm not sure I can explain it to you, and I know you will hate that. I'm not dead, Vin, because I'm not hungry, or thirsty. I don't feel those things here. Time itself seems to have no meaning, and I don't really seem to feel that either. You said I've been in here for twenty years? I had no idea. Vin, if I had been sitting here in these rocks for twenty years, wouldn't I be a gibbering wreck by now?'

484

'But it *has* been that long,' Vintage insisted, feeling a fresh wave of sorrow at the thought. 'Look at my face, if you don't believe it.'

'I can't explain it to you.' With her free hand, Nanthema pushed her hair away from her face. 'It's like . . . like I am held in place, in here. Unchanging. This place, is unchanging.' She gestured behind her. 'You remember that chunk of amber I bought at the market in Jarlsbad, with the locust stuck inside it? That creature must have been ancient, but it looked like it could hop right away. That's how I feel, in here. Stuck in syrupy sap.'

'And have you explored it? This place?'

Nanthema snorted. 'What do you take me for? Of course I have. This place . . . I don't think it's real.' She shuffled her feet, real discomfort on her face at dealing with something she could not explain. 'There is an invisible boundary, and although it looks like there's more of this miserable landscape, you can't reach it. And if you look carefully at it, the rocks and the ground are blurred, out of focus.'

Vintage felt cold. 'Nanthema, none of that makes sense.'

'Oh, that's the least of it. It's also stuck in a loop.'

'You've lost me there, my darling.'

'It's like an unfinished book, but you can only get up to the third chapter and you must go back to the beginning, over and over. Look at the clouds.' She pointed upwards. Overhead, the black clouds scudded restlessly across the jaundice sky. 'I have seen those same clouds, a hundred thousand times. They pass over, drawn by a wind I can't feel, and then they start all over again.'

'Nanthema, how could you possibly tell?'

'Believe me, Vin, with nothing to look at but the clouds, you soon get to recognise them. It's like this place is someone's memory, or a dream, and I am stuck inside.'

She stopped talking, and for a moment the only thing Vintage could hear was her own breathing. They were so deep within the Behemoth that even the sea was silent. A thought occurred to her.

'So what are you looking at now? What does the chamber look like to you?'

Nanthema grinned, although there was little humour in it. 'It looks like a great shard of crystal, with my dear Vintage sitting within it.'

'*Hmph.*' Vintage shook her head. 'What is this thing, then? What is it to the Jure'lia? Why would they need such chambers at the heart of their vessels? What does it do?'

Nanthema smiled lopsidedly. 'That's my Vin, always two steps ahead. And what do you mean, chambers? Have you seen another like this?'

'I have.' Vintage did not want to describe what they had found in Esiah Godwort's Behemoth wreck – it would be like admitting that Nanthema must stay trapped forever – so she spoke quickly before she could ask more questions. 'What else can you tell me about it?'

In answer, Nanthema shifted closer to the crystal, bowing her head as though she were going to whisper in Vintage's ear. 'I hear voices in here sometimes.' The Eboran woman swallowed hard, and Vintage realised that she was frightened. 'You will now declare me a lunatic, I expect, but it's true. Whispers carried on the wind, drifting . . .' Nanthema's eyes rolled back to the rocks behind her, and Vintage had to swallow down a surge of fright. What if she had been driven mad, after all? 'I think this crystal and the memory it contains, Vin, are integral to the Jure'lia in some way. Something deep, in the bones of what they are. And there's something else.'

Nanthema turned back, and now she looked very young indeed, her face that of a child waking from a nightmare. 'Vintage, the Jure'lia never went away. They're still here.'

*   *   *

Tor had never seen so many people in the Hall of Roots. The sight made him deeply uneasy for reasons he couldn't quite pinpoint, but he kept an easy smile on his face as he moved among them. All of the diplomats were here, the minor royalty from far-off kingdoms, the representatives of a dozen republics, the men and women from less defined places, the traders and the merchants, eager to see what coin could be made from Ebora's corpse, no doubt. Aldasair had introduced him to them all, rattling off names and honorifics and locations in a manner that quietly stunned Tor – his cousin had rarely been so collected – and the people he met eyed him curiously, no doubt fascinated to talk to another living artefact from this mausoleum.

Except that wasn't quite the case. There were a handful of Eborans here too, the last haggard survivors of the crimson flux, flushed out of their rooms and hiding places to be here. Hestillion had insisted that they be seated separately, away from the sharp eyes of the humans, and they were clustered to the east of the room. There Tor saw faces he hadn't seen in decades, the faces of people he had been sure were long dead. It was unsettling, like sharing air with the ghosts of your ancestors, and mostly they looked like they might die at any moment anyway; he saw skin turned dusty and broken, riddled with the tell-tale red cracks of the crimson flux, and on some faces, the simple signs of old age. He felt a mild trickle of disgust down the back of his throat. They should not be here. *For their own health*, he added silently to himself.

But of course, who could stop them? Today might see the resurrection of their god, and if Ygseril lived again, his sap would restore them all. Crimson flux would be banished, his scars would be healed, and Ebora would rise from the ashes.

He suddenly realised what was bothering him. He leaned over to speak directly into his sister's ear.

'Where are all the paintings? The sculptures and cabinets and so on?'

487

'We have moved them.' Hestillion had washed and brushed her hair and her skin was shining. She wore a white silk wrap over a pale blue dress, but there was a feverish energy about her that he did not like. Her eyes moved too often, and were too wet. Once, Ainsel had come down with a sweating sickness and Tor had moved into her rooms for a few days to nurse her. She had been outraged at first, horrified that he should see her in such a state, but he had insisted. Human illnesses were not the crimson flux, after all. At the height of the sickness she had been fidgety, would not stay in bed, and her eyes had had the same restless brightness of Hestillion's. 'The artworks are now stored in some of the outer rooms. We still have plenty of empty ones, after all.'

'Hmm.' Tor realised that deep in the back of his mind he had thought the strangers had stolen them. Just spirited away thousands of years' worth of Eboran artefacts; hidden them under their tunics, perhaps. He pursed his lips. It seemed that Hestillion wasn't the only one who was nervous.

'Where is your human pet?'

Tor raised his eyebrows at that. 'Noon is resting. How do you want to do this?'

Hestillion looked up, and Tor followed her gaze. Above them, the glass roof of the Hall of Roots was filled with bright sunlight. The dead branches of Ygseril hung there, as they ever did, and beyond that Tor could see the ghostly smudge that was the corpse moon.

'We just do it,' said Hestillion. 'We've all waited long enough.'

'I couldn't agree more.' Tor raised a hand to Aldasair, who had been standing with a tall man with green eyes, and his cousin came over. Of the three of them, Tor noted, he looked the least nervous – Aldasair looked better than he'd ever done. Together, they went to the edge of the roots, where the Jure'lia artefacts had been set, and they each picked up two of the orbs, one under each arm. A hush fell across the Hall, and Tor knew suddenly that this was right. No elaborate speeches, no declarations or promises. They were simply the children of Ebora, doing what they could for the tree-god. There would be witnesses, whatever happened, and that was good.

The three of them stepped up onto the roots together and walked slowly apart. There had been some discussion about this – they would pour the fluid over the widest possible area, and slowly. Tor stumbled slightly and felt a rush of heat to his cheeks. It had been a long time since he had walked the roots. He looked over at Hestillion for support, but she was staring straight ahead, her pale face as expressionless as a plate. Abruptly, he wished that Noon was here; she would have rolled her eyes at the solemnness of it all, and told them to get on with it.

Eventually, he came to the appointed place. With numb fingers he set one of the orbs down, and then removed the other's seal. Wincing slightly, he knelt directly on the roots.

'Please work,' he murmured. 'Please just . . . fucking *work*.'

He glanced up to see Hestillion and Aldasair to either side of him, performing the same slow actions. Ahead of him now he could see the crowd of humans and the handful of Eborans, watching closely. Some had their hands clasped over their mouths.

He tipped the orb, and the shimmering golden fluid poured from the opening. It was thick and slow, like syrup, and it pooled at first on top of the gnarled root he was perched on, before slipping to either side and moving down into the dark. Tor felt tension thrumming in all of his muscles – it was like the pent-up feeling you got just before cramp seized your leg.

Nothing was happening.

Glancing up again, he could see Hestillion to one side of him, her head bent gracefully over her work. To the other side, Aldasair was gently shaking the orb up and down to encourage the fluid out. The crowd were still silent, but he could see one or two people moving from one foot to the other, craning their necks to get a better look, and he knew they were thinking the same as he was. Nothing was happening, and this was a waste of time. Worse than that, it was a humiliation. Fumbling for the next orb, he tore the seal from it with more violence than was necessary, and hurriedly shook the contents over the roots. Still, that terrible silence.

As the last of the syrupy fluid dribbled from the orb he stood up, already thinking of how swiftly they could leave. He would grab Noon, several cases of wine, and he wouldn't even need to look at his sister again. He had just taken his first step when he lost his footing; the roots under his feet had shifted, and he scrambled to stay upright. There was a chorus of cries from all around the room, a mixture of wonder and fear.

The roots were moving – not quickly or violently, but enough to make it difficult to stand on them. Tor looked up at the branches spreading above the glass roof, and they were moving too, as though a strong wind had suddenly blown up on this sunny, peaceful day. Tor ran for the edge, his heart beating sickly in his chest. Of all the things he had expected to feel if this happened, he had not expected to feel so afraid. He half fell, half jumped onto the marble floor and turned back to look. Aldasair and Hest had had the same thought and joined him moments later, Hestillion's empty orb slipping through her fingers to smash into brittle pieces. Behind them, the murmur of the crowd was growing into a roar.

'By the roots,' breathed Aldasair. 'We did it!'

'We did something,' said Tor. Why was he so afraid?

Ygseril's bark, grey and silver for as long as Tor could remember, was changing colour before their eyes. The roots were darkening, growing plump and dark, steel warming to a deep burnished copper, and then a dark, reddish brown. The warmth flowed up from the roots to the enormous girth of the trunk, rising rapidly like a tide line. The newly ripened

490

bark shone with health. There was a crackling noise, like a blazing fire on a cold night.

By now, the crowd of observers were shouting, some of them even whooping with joy, and reluctantly Tor felt his face split into a grin. Out of the corner of his eye he could see that several of the ill Eborans had climbed out of their chairs and were staggering towards the roots. Next to him, Hestillion was murmuring under her breath, words that he couldn't catch, but he did not look at her; he couldn't take his eyes from the glory of Ygseril.

Up and up the new colour spread, making them all lean back, craning their necks to watch as it flooded up and through the branches, and it was moving faster now, racing to the tips and flooding them with health.

Someone was crying. Tor could hear their breathless sobs, and he didn't blame them. His own throat was tight with unshed tears.

'We will be healed,' he said, his voice thick, and Aldasair took his hand and squeezed it. His cousin was grinning.

'It wasn't the end after all,' he said brightly.

There was movement in the branches high overhead. At first Tor thought that it was light in his eyes, perhaps reflecting off his own tears, but new points of brightness were appearing there; silver leaves were unfurling.

'He lives!'

The cry came from one of the Eborans, an ancient man with broken skin and his crimson eyes sunk deep into his skull. He had reached the edge of the roots and had knelt to lay his hands on them, his ruined face split into a beatific smile. 'He has come back to us!'

Tor grinned, turning to his sister with the thought that he would embrace her – not something they had ever made a habit of, but if any occasion merited it, surely this was it – when abruptly he was filled with a sense of enormous sorrow.

It had come from outside himself, he was certain of it, and it nearly felled him like a blow to the stomach. He gasped, staggering, and saw Aldasair do the same, the pleasure on his face replaced with dismay. There was such sadness everywhere, such regret. It was hard to breathe, under that blanket of despair.

'Oh no,' said Hestillion. 'Oh please, no.'

His sister was so pale now she looked almost translucent, as though he might see the shifting of her blood under her skin, and for a frightening moment Tor thought she would faint dead away, but then she was pointing at the roots. At what was boiling up through the gaps between the roots.

A black, viscous liquid was seeping up, surging everywhere between the healthy roots, like a dark oily sea coming into shore. Tor took a step backwards, confused. Was it the golden fluid? Had it been corrupted somehow? The cheers and chatter behind them stuttered and died.

The black liquid leapt and spread, moving not like a liquid at all, but like a living thing. Wet fingers of fluid danced and came together, weaving a form in the centre of the roots, a figure of sorts, something taller than an Eboran, something formed of sticky strands and seething wetness. Arms and legs appeared, a torso, a sleek head garlanded with tendrils of the shifting black substance. And a face surfaced there – beautiful, terrible. Pleased.

'You have freed me. Remarkable child.'

'It can't be!'

For a moment Tor couldn't think who was screaming until he saw Hest advancing on the roots, her hands knotted into fists at her sides. She was glaring at the creature standing on the roots as though it had done her a personal insult, and more alarmingly, the creature was looking back at her with something like fondness.

'You lied to me!' Hestillion's voice was ragged with rage. Tor made an attempt to snatch her back but she shook him off. All around them now he could hear the men and women of their audience panicking, shouting in alarm. Someone had thrown open the big doors and some of them were leaving, but not actually that many. Despite themselves, most of them were still curious. The thing that had formed from the black substance under the roots was still shifting, changing as though forming itself; long hands with fingers like talons, hips like thorns, narrow clawed feet, all sculpted in oily darkness.

'It is good to see the light,' said the figure. Its voice was soft and yet still carried to every corner of the room. The voice, Tor realised, and the figure, were female. It stepped forward a little, holding up its hands to look at them. 'To smell something other than dirt.'

'You lied to me!' With a start, Tor saw that his sister was crying. He had never seen her cry; not when their parents died, and not when he left. 'I would have died for you!'

'Dear Hestillion, special child,' said the figure. It smiled. 'A remarkable mind.'

'Hest, how does it know your name?' All at once this seemed like the most important question he'd ever asked. 'Why does it know your name, Hest?'

He didn't expect an answer, but his sister spoke without looking at him. 'I spoke to her,' she said, her voice soft and dreaming now, as though half asleep. 'I believed she was our god, but she was a prisoner within his roots, whispering through the cracks.'

'*What* is she, Hest? What is this?'

The woman on the roots turned – she hadn't formed completely, he saw then, there were ragged holes in her fore-arms and calves, bisected with slimy strings of matter – and gestured, almost lazily. The remaining ooze in the roots surged into busy life again and split into thousands of tiny scurrying things, a tide of them moving out of the shadow of Ygseril and towards them, the people on the marble floor.

493

Burrowers had come to Ebora, and the figure that stood on the sprawling roots of his god was the Jure'lia queen.

'Get away!' He turned and began running for the back of the room. 'Everyone, get out!' Most of the guests had got the idea already and were crashing through the doors, but in their panic, many of the chairs had been overturned. He saw people falling, being trampled underfoot, and then he saw them being overtaken by the beetle-like creatures. In moments, the Hall of Roots was filled with screams, and with a wave of horror that was almost like fainting he realised that he had left his sword back in his room.

He looked back, seeking his sister. What he saw was the old Eboran who had knelt by Ygseril's roots. The old man was writhing as the burrowers surged down his throat and nibbled busily at his eyes; they were inside him already, eating away at his soft organs and flesh and leaving behind their own excreta – black lines of it dribbled from his mouth. Beyond that he could see the rest of the Eboran contingent – some of them had had the sense to get up and were making for the doors, but most were too weak to move. He saw one woman stamping weakly at the beetle-like creatures underfoot, but they were already in her hair, their mandibles slicing easy holes into her flesh. Aldasair's friend, the big one with the axes – he remembered, his name was Bern and he was from Finneral – had his axes in his hands now. Although they were little use against such a small, fast moving enemy, he stood in front of his cousin as though he meant to protect him.

'Hestillion!'

His sister jerked at the mention of her name, but she did not turn – she merely shook her head, as if disbelieving. The old Eboran had stopped writhing, and now he was standing up calmly, moving with more grace than he had in centuries. His eyes were empty holes, and he was smiling.

'Hest! We'll die if we stay in here! Come away from there!' Tor shouted.

A crowd of burrowers swerved towards him then and Tor danced back, his heart in his throat. One of them got a purchase on the soft material of his boots and he felt a series of pinpricks in his skin as it scrambled up his leg. Grimacing, he smacked it away, but there were already two more in its place.

'We have to run,' he said, although he no longer knew who he was talking to. The Jure'lia were back, they had released the queen, and it would all end here after all; just faster than expected. A bitter laugh twisted in his throat.

And then there came a voice. There were no words, but a series of feelings, impressions – it came, he knew instinctively, from the same source as the great sense of sorrow he had felt moments before. Something enormous was speaking, although it had no mouth or throat, and with a shudder Tor knew what it was saying.

A gift. A final gift.

High above them, in Ygseril's newly living branches, something silver was growing.

44

Noon lay on her back on the enormous bed, staring up at the ceiling. There was a painting there – Eborans were keen on paintings everywhere, it seemed – and if she looked at it, following the lines and guessing at the story it told, she didn't have to think about Mother Fast, and her missing eye or her melted face. She didn't have to think about how even the lush grass, full of spring juices, had caught fire, or the look on her mother's face when she had realised what was happening, or how people smelled when they were burning, the noises they made.

Noon cleared her throat, and narrowed her eyes at the ceiling.

The painting showed tall, elegant figures leaving on a ship, taking a route north, into an unknown sea. The ship had an elegant golden fox at the prow, and the artist had populated the ocean with wild sea monsters; giant squids with grasping tentacles, a thing like a great armoured crab, and women who were half fish, their mouths open to reveal pointy teeth. It was dangerous, their journey, but the artist had painted a tall man with brown skin leading the people, and he looked wise. You looked at him and you believed that he knew the paths around the monsters.

AWAKE.

The voice in her head obliterated all thought, and Noon squirmed on the bed as if she were drowning. She could taste blood in the back of her throat.

'What is it?'

War, said the voice. It sounded both exulted and afraid. *War has come for us again, my friend. Move! Quickly now!*

Noon swung her legs off the bed. 'What are you talking about, war? And where are you expecting me to go? The door is locked.'

But the voice was gone. Noon stood up, feeling warily for the stirring of energy within her. It was still there, banked down to embers now but ready to be called on. She walked over to the door and rattled the handle, just in case, but it was still firmly locked. Leaning against it, she grew still. What was that noise? She held her breath, and it came again: distant screaming. Her skin grew cold all over.

'What's happening?'

The voice rushed back into her head, and for the first time it did not sound calm or in control – it was panicked, wild and desperate.

Go! it cried. *You have to go now, or you will miss it. You will miss me!*

'You have to tell me what you're talking about. Talk some sense!'

The Hall of Roots. Please. You must go there, for me.

It was the note of pleading in the normally arrogant voice that got Noon moving. She grabbed her jacket and pulled on her boots, her heart thudding painfully in her chest. The screaming was louder now, and she thought she could hear the thunder of people running. She went back to the door and crashed her fists against it.

'What's happening? Let me out!'

There was no reply. Noon turned back to the room. There

497

was a feeling now, a rushing tightness in her chest that had nothing to do with the screams outside or even the voice inside her. There was somewhere else she needed to be. This room was all wrong.

'I'm stuck in here,' she said aloud. 'I can't get out.'

The bitter amusement of the voice spread through her, making the ends of her fingers tingle.

You believe that this place can hold you?

It was a good point. Noon raised her arms in a slow graceful movement, summoning a churning ball of winnowfire between her hands. She swept it back and forth, feeding it the energy it needed to grow slowly, calling on the discipline of the presence inside her to do so. Eventually, the globe of fire hummed between her arms, a pot waiting to boil over. She ran towards the window and threw it. The fireball crashed into the window and it exploded in a shower of wood and glass. Noon covered her head with her arms, an expression on her face caught somewhere between fright and joy as the debris pattered down all around her. There were cuts on her forearms, stings like kisses over her flesh, but she barely noticed them. Now there was a hole in the wall rather than a window, and through it she could see bright daylight and the embers of her own fire. A way out. It seemed she was pretty good at finding those, after all.

As an afterthought, she picked up Tor's sword before she left.

The distance between Ygseril and the doors had never seemed so far.

Behind Tor, the Jure'lia queen still hung suspended over the tree-god's roots, held in place by the stringy black material that seemed to be both a part of her and something she could control. Hestillion had dropped to her knees where she stood, but the burrowers were ignoring her, splitting around her still

498

form like the sea around a rock. He had lost track of Aldasair, somewhere in the midst of the panic, and now Tor was climbing over a mass of overturned chairs, pausing to stamp on the burrowers underfoot or brush them from his clothing. Everywhere he looked, humans were falling to the scurrying creatures, and the great hall rang with the sound of their screams as they were eaten alive. A figure lurched in front of him – a man with a trim black beard, now his face was lined with scratches from the busy feet of burrowers, and his eyes were holes lined with the same black substance oozing out from the roots. He grinned at Tor, and reached for him as though they were old friends.

Tor pushed him away, and then, thinking better of it, punched him solidly in the jaw. The man went down like a sack of potatoes but as Tor stepped over him, he saw that he was still grinning. Tor remembered something from Vintage's many notes: it was difficult to knock a drone unconscious, because they had no brain left to damage.

'I need to get my damn sword.'

Ahead of him he saw a pair of drones – they were easier to identify than he'd ever have imagined because they all moved in the same slick and boneless way – standing over a human, an older woman with a red scarf over her hair. The drones were holding her down while the burrowers flowed all over her, seeking their way in, and the poor woman was screaming and kicking. Tor vaulted over the fallen chairs, in the grip of a horror so great that it seemed to fill his throat with a painful heat, but as he reached them he saw two burrowers busily forcing their way down the woman's throat, and her screams were abruptly muffled. He turned away. There was nothing he could do.

There was another woman on the floor ahead, struggling to get to her feet, and he recognised Mother Fast, the representative of the plains people who had so unsettled Noon. For now, the burrowers had missed her, and he scooped her up by her elbow. She met his eyes with her one working eye.

'I believe it is time for us to leave, Mother Fast.'

'And go where, boy? The worm people are back, and there are a handful of Eborans left to face them. We may as well lie down here, and have an end to it.'

'You're a barrel of laughs, aren't you?' Tor steered her round a pile of chairs, while all around them the screaming went on. 'I have no intention of dying today, so if you'll just—'

Ahead of them, the doors to the Hall of Roots blew off their hinges in a crash of green fire. Noon stepped into view, her black hair a corkscrewed mess and a teeming glove of green fire around her right arm. Next to him, Tor felt Mother Fast recoil.

'That's it, she's come to kill us all now.' Her voice was breathy, on the verge of hysteria. 'I should have known, should have known that's how it would end.'

'Oh, do get a grip.' Tor stamped heavily on a pair of burrowers skirting around Mother Fast's feet. At the sight of Noon he had felt his heart lighten, and now he waved at her. 'Noon!' And she had his sword.

They met each other by a pile of broken chairs. Most of the audience had fled, with the remainder either drones or in the process of being made into them.

'I don't know what's happened,' he said quickly, although he suspected that wasn't entirely true. Hadn't it always been a mystery, what had happened to the Jure'lia at the end of the Eighth Rain? Hadn't the question now been answered? 'We have to get out of here.'

Noon pushed his sword into his hand. There was no confusion on her face now, no uncertainty. She didn't even appear to be upset by the presence of Mother Fast; she gave the old woman one appraising glance and looked away.

'Are you out of your mind?' she said. Around them everything was terror and chaos, with the screaming of the people being eaten alive, the desperate scrabble for escape, and, underneath it all somewhere, the quiet and impossible sound of his sister weeping. But he looked into Noon's face and he saw quiet amusement, and something else: a challenge. 'Tor, if we can kill her here, all of this will end, now. Don't you see?'

With the familiar weight of the Ninth Rain in his hands, he did see. 'Will you cover me?'

Noon grinned, and he remembered the sweet taste of her blood.

Noon ran ahead of Tor, letting her instincts take over. The voice within her was a steadying presence, keeping her focussed, while a deeper inner voice moved her body. Spinning and sweeping her right hand down towards the floor, her fingertips brushing the marble surface, she built a great swathe of winnowfire around her, a bright green tunnel of vertical light powered by the alien energy inside. When she had been very small, the plains had once witnessed violent storms that looked like her tunnel of fire. Mother Fast – whom Tor had carefully pushed towards the door – had called them 'gods' fingers', tall wavering columns of darkness that would eat up the land. Now Noon was her very own storm, and outside of it she could sense the figures of those already consumed by the Jure'lia, and beyond them the towering shape of the queen.

The drones fell back as her flames licked their spiral of destruction around her. Next to her, Tor was a blur, his sword slicing through the air with precise movements; drones fell to the floor, their heads severed from their necks, their happy smiles still in place.

'Keep moving forward, don't look back!'

A flood of burrowers swarmed towards them in an arrow-shape, a direct attack from the queen herself, no doubt. In response, Noon released some of the energy from the green storm circling her, and a curl of fire swept across the marble floor. Scores of burrowers exploded with yellow hisses of flame, and a strange, acrid smell filled the Hall of Roots.

Halfway there now. More drones came, their faces full of an empty contentment, and Noon lit them up like tapers, noting as she did so that the smell of burning flesh no longer bothered her.

Because you are a soldier, came the voice in her head. And then, *I am close now. Look for me.*

She glanced at Tor. He was heading towards his sister who was still sitting in a crumpled heap at the edge of the roots. His face was caught in profile, his fine brows drawn down in an expression of faintly annoyed concentration as he bloodied his sword again and again – although, in truth, it wasn't blood that spurted from the bodies of the drones, but the same thick black substance that formed the body of the queen. It was likely that they would both die here, she reflected, as a cold sense of calm filled her chest. Too late to tell him anything, too late to express her particular affection for how his face looked right now – angry, indignant, desperate.

Concentrate on your task, soldier.

'What is this? The very last warriors Ebora has to offer?' The queen had walked to the edge of roots, and Noon caught a glimpse of her face; masklike and beautiful, it hung suspended in the shifting black matter of her body like a leaf floating downstream. In response, Noon released the energy of the storm surrounding her to swirl across the remainder of the hall, but the queen gestured and a wall of oily black liquid rose in front of her. The fire hissed against it, and Noon sensed rather than saw the queen flinch. The wall of black fluid dropped.

'The last, and the best,' called Tor. He met Noon's eyes briefly, and she grinned at the reckless good humour she saw there. 'You can crawl back to the dirt if you like, your majesty, and we can all carry on with our day.'

502

'Manners, I like that.' The queen turned her head to address Hestillion. 'This one is blood to you, yes?'

Noon saw Hestillion's shoulders move as she answered but within the roaring of the winnowfire she could not make out the words, and then a flower of pain blossomed on her leg, distracting her. She looked down to see a burrower making its way up her boot. Noon reached down and grasped it in her palm, summoning the fire to crush the creature in a short explosive gasp.

'We'll rush her,' Tor was saying, his voice pitched only for her. 'Throw what you've got up there for as long as you can, and I'll circle around. This sword should do the trick, don't you think? This is what it was re-forged for, after all.'

'The Ninth Rain,' said Noon in agreement, but she was thinking of something else now. There was some other factor, something else they had forgotten about, that they shouldn't forget about. As if moving by itself, her head tipped up and, far above them, she saw the branches of Ygseril, spreading out over the great glass roof. Nestled there were silver shapes, bulbous and strange, surely too large and heavy to stay where they were. And when they dropped, they would crash onto the glass roof. Perhaps they would break through, lacerated on the way down by shards of glass, or perhaps they would roll away to land elsewhere in the palace grounds.

Noon stopped.

'What are you doing?'

Ignoring Tor, Noon summoned the winnowfire once more, knowing that now more than ever she needed to be in control, and control had never been her defining trait. Briefly, she thought of Agent Lin, her steely expression of determination as Noon fled, frightened and weak.

That isn't you any more.

'I am a weapon.' Noon thrust her arms up, and with it went a column of green fire that briefly turned the inside of the Hall of Roots as bright as a summer's midday on the plains. Meeting the ceiling of glass, it blossomed, curling out in all directions.

'What have you—?'

Noon threw herself at Tor, knocking him to the floor and into a pile of broken chairs. At almost the very same moment, the glass ceiling above them shattered with an ear-bruising explosion. The noise was extraordinary, and a deadly rain of glass and twisted iron followed it. Pressing her body to Tor's, she waited for it to be over even as she tensed her body for what had to come next.

'Did you just destroy the Hall of Roots?' Tor's voice was a hot gasp in her ear.

'Just the glass,' she replied, 'not the branches. Can't touch those.'

'What?'

But Noon was already moving. Distantly she was aware that, again, she had been cut in various places, but, blotting out everything else was the sense that something was about to happen that she couldn't miss. A quick glance told her that the queen had retreated behind her wall of ooze again, and that Hestillion was still alive, her slim arms held over her head. They were shaking. Noon looked up. The glass roof was gone, the edges of it smouldering, and Ygseril's branches were swaying back and forth.

'What – what did you do that for?'

Tor was by her side again. A piece of glass had caught him and a sheet of transparent blood had slicked his hair to his scalp, but he held his sword as steadily as ever. Noon pointed upwards. The clutch of silver pods were shivering now, high in the branches, nearly ready to fall.

'It's their time, Tor.'

She had spoken quietly, but the Jure'lia queen had heard her anyway.

'You are wrong,' she said, her colourless lips peeling back from perfect, gumless teeth. 'It is finally *our* time.'

The branches of Ygseril were shaking, and the strange silver fruits were beginning to fall.

'Nothing you're saying makes any sense, my darling.'

Vintage sat with her legs out in front of her, one hand pressed to the crystal. Next to her Nanthema crouched on the other side of an impossible divide. She was being insufferably calm.

'Think about it, Vin. Where do they go when they're not attacking us? They must come from somewhere.'

'If we knew that . . .'

'Yes, so many other questions would be answered.' Nanthema sighed, a short puffing of air between her lips that Vintage remembered very well. It was the sound of her putting a difficult problem to one side. 'I'm telling you, I hear them, Vin. I can't make out what they're saying, of course, it's like a distant room where a lot of people are talking a language I don't speak. But every now and then another voice will come, and all the other voices become quiet. Or they all become the same voice.' Vintage could see her frowning now. 'But they are not far. Not far at all.'

'None of this sinister speculation gets us any closer to freeing you.'

'No, and you will need to go back soon. How much food did you bring with you? How much water?'

Vintage snorted. 'What do you take me for? Some green-kneed child fresh out of the nursery? My dear, in my pack—'

At that moment the entire chamber shuddered violently. Vintage yelped, falling away from the crystal, and Nanthema's startled query was cut off mid-sentence.

'What the . . .?'

At first Vintage thought it must be the wreck finally falling apart – a big wave had loosened it, perhaps, preparing to shake

505

its old bones onto the seabed at last. But the shuddering vibration was too constant, too regular. She turned back to the crystal and pressed her hand to it.

'Get out now, before it all collapses! You fool, start climbing!'

Vintage shook her head. 'I'm not leaving here without you, my dear.' Behind Nanthema the clouds were racing faster across the sky, and a wind began to tug at her hair.

'It smells like a storm here,' said Nanthema, her eyes very wide. 'It has never smelled of anything here before.'

Vintage opened her mouth to reply and a ring of bright white light travelled down the length of the chamber, from the very top to the very bottom. For a few seconds the light burned on the crystal, too bright to look at, and then Nanthema was falling through it, into her arms.

They both screamed.

Vintage recovered herself first. 'This bloody place is waking up!' She struggled to her feet, pulling the taller woman with her. She was delightfully solid, warm against her hands.

'Then I think it's best we are not here when it stretches its legs.'

Climbing out of the chamber, with the rope ladder swinging wildly back and forth with the vibrations, was, Vintage would reflect later, the hardest thing she had ever done. Knowing that Nanthema was alive and free, knowing that if she didn't get her arse up the ladder swiftly enough she would doom them both, made her knees turn to water and her fingers turn into numb sticks. She gulped down air, desperate not to panic, and then they were out of the chamber and in the larger room. All around them, lights behind the fleshy material of the walls were bleeding into life, and the shuddering underfoot went on and on.

'Can you find the way out, Vin?'

'Of course I bloody well can.' Vintage grabbed Nanthema's hand. 'Stay close to me.'

506

They ran.

To her surprise and enormous relief, Vintage found that she did indeed remember the way out. It was her observer's eye, honed all these years on the strangeness of the Jure'lia artefacts. She could get them out, if the whole place didn't fall to pieces around them, or they weren't turned inside out by a stray parasite spirit, or they went too quickly and fell down some unseen chasm.

'What was that?' Nanthema squeezed her hand hard, forcing her to stop. They stood together in a darkened corridor, breathing hard.

'Nanthema, we really need to—'

'*Shhh!* Listen.'

Vintage stopped. There was the shuddering all around them, and she could hear the distant hiss of the sea now – they were close. And then, from somewhere deeper within the Behemoth, a soft voice, calling. It was female, that voice, and something about it caused Vintage's insides to fill with ice.

'How can that be?' she hissed at Nanthema. 'How can there be someone in here?'

'It's the voice I heard inside the crystal,' said Nanthema. There were two points of colour high on her cheeks, and her crimson eyes were too bright in her pale face.

'Come on, we're nearly there.'

They heard the voice again and again as they ran, seeming to come from all over the broken Behemoth. It was soft, teasing almost, as though they were playing a game, and Vintage felt as though it was coming after them, seeping through the dark places wherever they ran.

Eventually, they saw a splash of daylight ahead, washed out and dappled with the shifting shape of the water, but as they approached it, a thick black substance began to ooze from the walls there. Nanthema skidded to a stop, and Vintage collided with the wall to her right.

'What is it doing?'

The black substance appeared to be alive. It reached up with tar fingers and seeped towards the broken ceiling. As they watched, it flowed around the panels and tubes there, gently pushing them back into place. Further down, more of the black ooze was smoothing over the yielding material of the floor, healing it in some way that Vintage couldn't understand.

'It's mending itself.' Vintage blinked. She had an urge to pinch her own arm, sure that this must be some sort of nightmare – surely she must be back at Esiah Godwort's compound, unconscious on the dirt, her face scorched with winnowfire – but then she heard the soft, cajoling voice again.

'I'm not going through it,' she said firmly, tugging at Nanthema's arm. 'Let's go around.'

Edging around the corner they found another corridor leading to daylight, but it, too, was dripping with the substance. It was growing livelier all the time, as if it were gaining strength at the sound of the strange distant voice. The entire structure was groaning now, creaking as things that had not moved for centuries were shifted and eased into new positions. Vintage and Nanthema moved on, still seeking a clear way out, but the stuff was starting to ooze up from the floor, sticking to their boots and slowing them down.

'It's no good, Vin. We'll just have to force our way out.'

Vintage nodded grimly. She unhooked the crossbow from her belt – although what good that would do against the oozing substance, she did not know – and they moved as quickly as they could down the nearest corridor. Vintage kept her eyes on the circle of weak daylight ahead while the walls to either side teemed with busy life. Once, a tendril of the stuff curled out towards her, exactly like a curious finger, and she had to bite her lip to keep from yelping as it brushed her curly hair. It was like being within the busy bowels of a gigantic creature:

all the vital systems that kept it alive were churning on, and Vintage was a small piece of food, waiting to be digested. She pushed the image away hurriedly.

'There, look!'

They had come to the end of the corridor, and from there she could see the rope she had used to climb up into the belly of the Behemoth, and, bobbing below it, her small boat. It was being tossed back and forth violently, as the waves were teased into action by the simmering movement of the wreck. It was around fifteen feet away, across a section of jagged wall.

'We'll have to climb it,' said Nanthema. As soon as she finished speaking, the whole section they stood on tipped abruptly, nearly dumping them both straight into the water. Just above their heads, a smooth piece of greenish metal was being twisted back into place, and further up, similar parts were moving, the pieces of some giant jigsaw puzzle.

'And bloody quickly. You go first, go!'

Nanthema scrambled down and across, taking fistfuls of the fleshy material and using it to yank herself along; she moved, if not with grace, then at least with strength. Vintage followed on behind, the muscles in her arms still numb with fright. She gritted her teeth against her panic. It would not do to fall now and drown in the black water below, drowned or crushed in the mysterious shifting of the Behemoth.

Ahead of her, Nanthema cried out. At first Vintage couldn't see what had caused her to do so, and then a series of bright points of light slid through the wall around a hand's breadth from Nanthema's head. They looked like the sharp fingers of a glowing hand, filled with blue light. A parasite spirit – perhaps they were leaving like rats deserting a sinking ship? Nanthema cringed away from it and, holding on with one hand and her boots wedged into the Behemoth's broad side, Vintage yanked her crossbow from her belt again and fired off a shot without pausing to think about it. The bolt struck the creature and it retreated instantly, the bolt itself snapping off and falling past Nanthema to be lost in the water.

'Keep moving!'

They made it to the small boat, although it was bucking and dipping so wildly that Vintage felt they should be no drier than in the water. Nanthema took up the oars and began trying to manoeuvre them out of the shadowed space within the wreckage, while Vintage used a small pot to bail them out; the waves were slapping at them, threatening to toss them over as the Behemoth shifted and murmured to all sides, a long sleeping beast now awakening. The black substance was running down the walls, up and down and in all directions, and everywhere it went the skin of the creature repaired itself, pulling its scattered innards back from the corrosive seawater and unkind daylight; an uncanny healing.

As they left the main section of the Behemoth behind, the whole thing started to shift forward, meeting the section that stood stranded from it. Black tendrils reached out for it like grasping hands, and identical limbs met them from the other side. Vintage and Nanthema narrowly avoided both capsizing and being crushed between them, and then they were out, the overcast sky a blessed space over their heads.

'Careful,' said Vintage. She was still bailing out the boat, although she could barely tear her eyes away from the Behemoth. 'There's wreckage under the sea where we can't see it, and knowing our luck that'll be moving too.'

'Right. Keep an eye out, Vin.' Nanthema's black hair was stuck to her cheeks with sweat.

The small boat tossed and lurched, and more than once Vintage was sure that they must be turfed out into the unkind sea, but Nanthema kept them moving and they didn't stop until the shore was dusting their hull. Then, without speaking, they both turned and looked at the wreck they had just escaped.

'By the roots,' murmured Nanthema. 'By the blessed roots.'

As they watched, the Behemoth – and it was a wreck no longer, there could be no doubt about that – began to rise out of its grave. Water gushed from it, a deafening roar as places that had been waterlogged for centuries were suddenly cleared. Portals opened in the side of it and more seawater was expelled, so much that Vintage thought it would never stop. The whole thing rose, clearing the sea in a great dripping mass. To Vintage, who had never truly expected to see a complete specimen of the things she had studied all her adult life, it looked like an impossibly fat woodlouse, segmented and swollen, covered all over in pulsing pores. Tendrils of the black material were still crawling over it, like flies over – well, flies over something very unpleasant.

The Behemoth, nearly whole and newly alive, rose slowly into the sky.

'What is happening?' Vintage took hold of Nanthema's hand and the Eboran woman covered it with her own. They both stared at the vast creature, eyes wide like frightened children. 'What is *happening*?'

45

The question is: what broke our world?

Better yet: what poisoned it? They did *of course. Every place they touch is broken and strange, and everything they leave behind sinks into the very flesh of Sarn to spread its tendrils of poison.*

It poisons the world, but where do you put it? It's not refuse that can be dumped in a distant ravine – the ravine will become poisonous, and the poison will spread. Put it in the sea, and the sea will also be poisoned. Attempts have been made to move the broken pieces of Behemoth, over the generations. They always result in people dying, one way or another. Even my beloved vine forest, and the grapes I have cultivated my whole life, are just as poisoned as anywhere else that has been touched by the Jure'lia.

So, instead, we build walls around our cities, the edges of towns are closely watched, and travel is a dangerous occupation, fit only for the mad and the desperate.

Extract from the journals of Lady Vincenza
'Vintage' de Grazon

The silver pods, high in the branches of Ygseril, were trembling slightly all over. Noon could see perhaps fifteen of them, and under the smooth silver skins living things were moving sluggishly. She had a moment to wonder if the fall would just kill them outright, and then they were falling, dropping one by one like overripe autumn apples.

'The Ninth Rain,' Tor breathed next to her. 'But it's so fast . . .'

The pods fell, and, belatedly, Noon realised exactly how large they were – the biggest was the size of a fully loaded cart. She yanked Tor back, looking too late for cover, and then they were crashing to the marble floor all around them, bouncing and rolling in sudden chaos, hitting with deep sullen thuds that Noon felt through her boots. She and Tor danced out of their way while Hestillion cringed against the roots, but miraculously none of them were struck.

'I never thought I'd see it.' Tor looked bewildered, and much younger than he had a moment ago. 'I never thought I'd see *them*.'

Noon glanced around at the pods, her heart in her mouth. Something was wrong here, terribly wrong, but there was no time . . . she knew which one as soon as she laid her eyes on it, as clear to her as the full moon in an empty summer sky. It was the largest of them all, taller than she was, and the pull towards it was impossible to ignore.

'Now you have to cover me, my friend.'

Tor blinked at her, utter confusion on his face, but then his sister was standing up and shouting questions at the queen, her voice strong and faintly outraged.

'This is holy ground you walk upon, creature. What do you think gives you the right to be here?'

Noon saw the mask-like face that hung within the teeming mass of the queen's body turn towards Hestillion, its perfect eyebrows raised in genuine surprise, but then the pod seemed to summon her again. She walked towards it, no more able to

513

stop than she was able to float up into the sky. Inside her there was a fluttering sensation, as though she were a glass jar with a moth trapped inside.

'I am here, I am here,' she murmured. Placing her hands on the smooth skin of the pod, she wasn't surprised to find that it was hot to the touch, fevered almost. Beneath the taut covering something was shifting, pushing and straining. Distantly, she was aware of both Tor and Hestillion remonstrating with the queen – they were distracting the Jure'lia creature, but she wouldn't play along for long.

'Everything hangs in the balance,' she said to the pod. 'Here, at the time of your new birth.' The words weren't hers, and as each one left her mouth she felt dizzier and dizzier.

Help me, said the voice in her head. *You will have to help me. This is too soon.*

Noon was momentarily lost. She had no knife, nothing to cut this smooth surface with. Dimly she was aware that Aldasair and the big man, Bern, were somewhere amongst the fallen pods, and she briefly considered asking the Finneral man to let her use his axes; but instinctively she flinched away from this idea. Human steel at such a birthing was wrong. Instead, she knelt by the pod and pressed her hands flat to it, summoning the swirling energy to her as she did so. Not flames, but heat; not the sun, but the fine building of summer within the sun-soaked stone. She poured it into the pod, feeling the surface beginning to blister under her fingers, and then it split, suddenly, like a nut on a fire. Noon pushed her fingers under the edges and pulled, revealing a membranous white material, a little like lace, and then that tore and she was looking into a huge, violet eye, the pupil a black slash down the middle, narrowing at the sight of her.

VOSTOK.

It was like being punched between the eyes. Noon reeled, struggling to stay conscious, and then she was tearing at the pod, and inside it something huge was battering its way out. Pieces of the pod came away in her hands easily now, slippery with an oily fluid, and the lace-like substance disintegrated in her hands. A scaled snout thrust its way through the gap, blasting hot breath into her face, and then an entire head appeared, shaking off scraps of pod material before collapsing heavily onto her lap.

'Vostok?'

Bigger than a horse's head, it was reptilian in nature, a long snout studded with pearly white scales, some as big as medallions, some as small as the nail on Noon's smallest finger. The creature – Vostok, thought Noon feverishly, her name is Vostok – opened her long jaws and panted, revealing lines of wickedly sharp teeth and a dark purple tongue. The top of her sleek head bristled with curling horns, bone-white and tapering to points, while on the bony nubs protruding from beneath the violet eyes, tiny white feathers sprouted, damp and stuck together. A long, sinuous neck led back inside the pod, where Noon could just make out a body, curled and compact but already moving to be free. Noon cradled the head in her arms as best she could. The fluid of the pod had soaked into her clothes, and there was a bright, clean smell everywhere, like sap.

Child, you birthed me in your witch fire.

Noon nodded. The voice was echoing strangely.

You understand I have to take back what was taken.

Noon nodded again. She understood. She welcomed it.

The great reptilian body inside the pod – *dragon*, exulted Noon, *dragon* – flexed and the last of its cocoon burst and fell aside. The head rose from Noon's lap and the snout rested against Noon's forehead for a moment. The scales felt cool now, like a blessing.

There was a brief impression of movement and bulk – Noon saw great white wings, still wet and pressed to the dragon's

515

back – and then a long talon pierced her, in the soft place below her ribs.

Pain, and a rushing sensation. The presence within her, and its boiling energy, flowed away, rushing out and leaving her stranded, a piece of debris on the shore. And then on the tail of that, her blood, soaking the front of her jacket. In confusion she thought of Tor. Couldn't she hear him shouting something now? Wasn't it her name?

'Thank you, child.' The voice that had been carried inside her for so long was now issuing from the dragon. Noon didn't understand how that could be, but it was. Vostok's long jaws hung open, panting like a dog. 'But your service is not over.'

Vostok withdrew her talon. Noon screamed, unable not to – the taking away was somehow worse than being pierced – yet when she looked down she saw her torn jacket, her blood, but no wound; just a ragged silver scar. She pressed her fingers against it wonderingly.

'No time.' Vostok thrust her head against her, nearly knocking her over. 'Get up and fight.'

A war-beast. A real living war-beast, born from Ygseril's branches.

Tor could hardly drag his eyes from it. The creature was glorious, a confection of pearly white scales and silvered claws. It had wings like an eagle, but each feather was as white as snow, and as yet still wet with the fluid it had been birthed in. Noon was talking to it, her hands pressed to either side of its long mouth, heedless of the teeth and the power in that jaw—

Hestillion's elbow caught him in the rib and he dragged his attention back to their current problem.

'This is unprecedented,' Hestillion was saying. Her voice now was level, control in every word as she spoke to the

Jure'lia queen. And, for a wonder, the queen was listening. 'Our peoples have never spoken before, as far as I know?'

'Peoples.' The Jure'lia queen seemed to find this amusing.

'Why is that? You are clearly intelligent, you can communicate with us.' Hestillion cleared her throat and held her head up. Her face was still much too pale for Tor's liking, but there was a stubborn set about her mouth that he remembered well. 'What I'm saying is, surely an agreement can be reached.'

'Hestillion . . .'

She elbowed him in the ribs again. She didn't want his opinion; she wanted his attention.

'Such a remarkable mind,' said the queen. Her mask-like face split into a wide smile. Slightly too wide. It made Tor think of hands making her face move; hands that did not truly understand how human faces worked. 'Always thinking of solutions. You never rest, seeking it. Remarkable. I have so enjoyed our talks.'

Hestillion seemed to ignore this. 'There is no need to re-live this war over and over again, as we have done for generations. You want land? You can have it. We can agree on land for you to have. Then you will stay there, and we will stay here. In time, we may . . . reach out to each other. Or, if you prefer, we could never speak again.'

The dripping black mass that made up the body of the queen shivered all over, like a breeze across the calm surface of a lake, and then she made an odd, hissing sound. It took Tor a moment to realise she was laughing, or whatever the Jure'lia equivalent was.

'Your bright little mind does not know everything,' said the queen, baring her gumless teeth. 'All must be consumed, for us to live. We do not make agreements with food. You have no idea how close to the end you are.'

The queen gestured up, to the bright sky overhead. Within it, the corpse moon hung like a green shadow and – Tor felt his heart lurch in his chest – it was larger than he had ever seen it. The corpse moon, the long-dead Behemoth in the sky, was coming towards them. Now that he looked, he could see movement on the surface of the thing. Too distant yet to identify, but patches of it that had been in shadow as long as he could remember were growing bright again.

'No!' Hestillion took an angry step towards the roots. 'Why won't you listen to me? I know you're not an idiot!'

'Enough, little morsels,' said the queen, almost kindly. 'Ebora ends here, now, forever. And Sarn will follow.'

'*Never.*'

At the sound of that voice, Tor felt all the hair on the back of his neck stand up. He turned round to see the dragon stalking towards them, Noon sitting on its back, just ahead of where its wings began.

'Oh, old enemy,' said the queen. 'You have been turned out of your womb too early. You are but a babe in arms, and your brothers and sisters still sleep.' She pouted. 'I am sad for you.'

'My wings may be wet and my fire unkindled, but I can still kill you, parasite. I am not alone.'

The dragon lowered its head as Noon sat up, her hands in front of her. A bright point of green light appeared there, and then Noon seemed to strike it, sending a ball of roaring fire across the hall straight at the Jure'lia queen. The wall of black ooze rose to meet it in a teeming curtain, but the fire exploded against it like acid, blowing it to tatters. The Jure'lia queen shrieked, twisting the black slime around her like a cloak. All around them, the drones and the burrowers that had been still lurched into sudden life.

It was the strangest, and perhaps shortest, battle of Tor's life. There were around fifteen drones left, men and women with holes for eyes and dreamily blank expressions. Three of them rushed him, trying to overpower him at once, but none of them carried weapons and his sword made short work of

518

them. Two of them went for Hestillion, who produced a short dagger from the folds of her dress, and then she was lost to view as another three came for him. He heard a bellow and a series of thumps and spotted the warrior Bern, his axes flying as he took down the drones on that side of the hall, an expression of horrified disgust on his face. Aldasair was there with him, weaponless but refusing to leave the bigger man's side.

Tor raised his sword again and was almost knocked flying as the dragon leapt past him, crashing into the group of drones. Tor caught a glimpse of Noon, her hands and arms working furiously as she generated ball after ball of winnowfire. Her face wasn't just calm; it was exalted. The dragon swept its long tail across the floor, knocking a handful of the drones onto their backs, before Noon drenched them all in dragon-fuelled winnowfire. They went up like tapers, as though being hollow inside made them easier to burn.

Another drone lurched at Tor. This one he recognised; once, it had been Thadeous, an Eboran who had been a good friend of his father's. When Tor had trained for the sword, Thadeous had been there too; the man had been a legend amongst those who trained with weapons, practising relentlessly, decades of skill endlessly honed. For the ceremony, he had dressed in his old military uniform, despite the ravages of the crimson flux turning his face into a cracked mask, and his sword still hung at his side. Now, his eyes were empty black holes.

'Thadeous,' Tor nodded formally, 'I don't suppose those creatures ate away your skill at using a sword, by any chance?'

The drone bared its teeth at him and lunged, the blade suddenly in its hands. Tor met it easily enough but found himself pushed away, wrong footed, and narrowly avoided being run through. He staggered, aware now that there were burrowers all around, scuttering across his boots and dividing his attention. Thadeous leapt at him again, and they fought bitterly for a few moments, Tor gradually being pushed back away from his sister and the roots. The burrowers may have eaten the man's brain, but it seemed that his body remembered his years of training, and Tor found himself at a distinct disadvantage.

'Too many years,' he gasped, 'fighting off – giant bears and – bloody parasite – spirits.'

The old man got in under his guard; too close for a killing wound, but the drone brought up his fist and punched him on the scarred part of his face. Tor felt the skin across his cheekbone split, a bright slither of pain, and that somehow was too much. This day had started so well, with its sunshine and its hope, and now he was here, about to be killed by one of his father's oldest friends while the Jure'lia spread their filth over Ebora. Enough.

With a bellow of rage he brought his elbow up and crashed it into Thadeous's throat, half collapsing it in one blow. The drone fell back and Tor swept the Ninth Rain up and round, severing its head from its neck so swiftly it turned a full somersault in the air before falling to the marble floor with a hollow thud.

'You always were a tedious old fart, Thadeous.'

The joy of battle.

Vostok had spoken of it to her in the quiet moments between dreams, but Noon had not understood. Now, with one hand pressed to the dragon's smooth scales and the other carving elegant shapes in the air – shapes that summoned flames more precise and powerful than she'd ever imagined – she saw their enemies falling before them and she was filled with a sense of *rightness*. No question here of what was right or wrong, no concerns over guilt. There was just the joy of battle, of believing utterly in the fight.

Together they had edged closer to the Jure'lia queen, burning or breaking the drones she sent towards them, and now they were on the edge of the roots. To Noon's surprise, Vostok stepped lightly over them, her enormous serrated talons not leaving a scratch, and the queen retreated, slithering back to the bulk of the trunk. There was a building of excitement in Noon's chest as the queen threw up wall after wall of her strange black substance, and again and again she burned it away.

'Bite her or burn her?' she murmured to Vostok. The dragon's amusement washed over her.

'I would not bite such as she. I will be picking it out of my teeth for weeks.' Vostok shook herself, like a dog in the rain. 'No, you must burn her, child.'

Noon grinned. 'Gladly.'

At that moment, the Hall of Roots filled with a desolate roaring. Hot, fetid air was blasted on them from above, and a great shadow fell over them. Noon looked up and saw the corpse moon hanging now not in the distant sky but just above them. Scuttling shapes like six-legged spiders moved busily across its surface, and at the blunt head of the thing, a dark mouth was opening. All joy and certainty fled, and instead she was left with the eerie sense that her dream had come back – the nightmare that had caused her to flee the Winnowry had followed her and here it was. Perhaps everything had been a dream, after all.

'Pay attention!' Vostok shook her, tossing her back and forth like a doll. 'Are you a warrior or not?'

'But that thing—'

'That thing is a distraction. Will you look at what is happening here?'

Dragging her eyes away from the rapidly approaching corpse moon, Noon saw that Tor was fighting for his life. With them distracted, the queen had sent the burrowers in a thick wave towards him, and now he was thrashing on the floor, trying to keep them from crawling inside his mouth.

'Tor!'

'Leave him. Now is our chance to take the queen. Take what you need from me—'

'No.' Noon could feel Vostok's will pressing on her like a physical weight, but she threw it off. 'You can't ask me to do that. Not him. I will not—'

'Humans! You are more foolish even than Eborans.' But the dragon turned and leapt, crashing down to stand over Tor protectively. Noon slipped easily from her back and released a wide cloud of green flame, a burst of near-heatless energy that doused Tor from head to foot. Each of the burrowers burst into flame but the Eboran was left unscathed. Dragging him to his feet, Noon shoved him towards Vostok.

'Thank you, I think. Did you mean to burn just them?'

'Shut up and get up there.'

Together they scrambled up onto Vostok's back, but it was too late. The corpse moon now blocked out all daylight, and a thin line of the wet black fluid had descended from the gaping hole in its front end like a rope, and the Jure'lia queen had extended her arm to reach it – the two were one now, a glistening black line from one to the other. She smiled at them.

'You are running away?' bellowed Vostok. The dragon reared back in frustration and Tor and Noon had to grasp onto her shoulders to keep from falling off. 'Coward! Noon, burn her!'

Noon scrambled up, holding on with her thighs only, and threw a barrage of winnowfire at the queen, but she swept away from it, closer to the waiting Behemoth.

'You will get your fight soon enough, relic.' Her face changed, becoming, to Noon's mind, almost conflicted. 'I said, did I not, that you would not be left behind again?'

Noon frowned, belatedly realising that the queen wasn't talking to them. She looked up to see Hestillion standing on the roots, her dress ragged and torn but otherwise untouched. In her arms she held the smallest of the war-beast pods.

'You did say that, yes,' she said. Her face was very still and pale.

The Jure'lia queen nodded once, and Hestillion and the pod were swept up in a wave of black fluid, borne past them and up, up towards the broken ceiling of the Hall of Roots. There she joined the queen and then they were lost to view, spirited up to the waiting Behemoth at an uncanny speed. Vostok leapt forward, her wet wings beating once, twice against her sides before giving up. The gaping mouth at the front of the corpse moon sealed over in silence, and a dozen spidery creatures crawled over it, smoothing it into place before the whole thing shuddered and roared again, turning slowly away from them.

Noon watched as the Behemoth moved south, edging out of their field of vision until the blameless blue sky filled the hole in the roof again. Small fires burned everywhere in the Hall of Roots, and bodies were strewn amongst the broken chairs. The place stank of smoke and death.

Tor was the first to break the silence.

'Did the Jure'lia just steal my sister?'

Noon opened her mouth to tell him that she didn't think 'steal' was the right word, but looking at his stricken, bleeding face, she found that she could not.

Instead she took his hand and kissed the palm of it. She tasted blood.

46

Of all the places in the palace, Tor had always considered the Hatchery to be the saddest. Even Hestillion, in her passion to keep things running as though the Eboran empire still lived, could not face the Hatchery, and the place had not been opened in at least a hundred years. It was a beautiful, long room, lined with windows on both sides so that the warm sunlight could gently heat the fruits of Ygseril, but the windows were blind with dust now, and the padded silk nests that had been built to house each of the silver pods were half rotted, the silk peeling away like old skin. In truth, Tor had felt embarrassed, particularly under the unnerving violet gaze of the dragon, Vostok. Looking at this room, you could not ignore the fact that Ebora had admitted defeat.

Nonetheless, it was all they had. One by one, he and Aldasair and the big man, Bern, had carried the pods in here, settling them into the musty silk nests. There had been fourteen in all, not including Vostok, but a number of them were small, and cold to the touch. This had been one of many things they had resolutely not spoken of as they set about their work – along with the return of the Jure'lia, where the queen had been exactly all these years, and what had happened to his sister.

It was the next day. The sky was overcast now, and the palace was inordinately quiet. Tor had grown used to the people on the lawns, the gentle noise that you barely noticed, and now most of them were gone. Aldasair had told him that some had left when the corpse moon had charged down out of the sky towards them – Tor could hardly blame them for that – although a few had remained, perhaps out of curiosity, perhaps out of the slightly desperate belief that Ebora could still protect them in some way. Or perhaps the newly birthed pods were a symbol of hope. Tor frowned and touched his fingers to the cut on his burned cheek. *We can hardly protect ourselves.*

'This will be the next to hatch, I think.'

Aldasair was at one of the nests. He had a fine purple bruise on his cheek, and a lot of his confidence appeared to have ebbed away again, but he spoke quietly and firmly, with little of the absentness of the old days. The pod that he stood in front of was very large, the size of a small cart, and heat came off it in waves.

'I think you are right,' Tor squeezed his cousin's shoulder. 'We will be here when they are born, all of them. For what it's worth.'

'Vostok said – Vostok said that those that are dead should be given to her, to eat. To bolster her strength.' Aldasair patted the surface of the pod lightly. 'She said she can feel them growing, some of them, but that others are absent. They were just the start of something, unfinished.'

'Is that what she said?'

Tor looked down the other end of the long room. The dragon who called herself Vostok was there, her great bulk curled around on itself, her long head lying on the thick carpet. Noon was there too, also sleeping, curled up against the dragon like a baby lamb with its mother. She had no fear of the dragon – had not been apart from it since the battle, in fact.

'She also said . . . some other things.' Aldasair straightened up, grimacing. 'I think you should talk to her, Tormalin.'

Tor sighed. 'I expect you're right.'

'You have questions, son of Ebora?'

There was no ignoring the summons in that voice. Tor turned away from the pod and walked down to the far end of the room. Noon had woken up too, and the look she gave him was uncannily like that of the dragon – piercing, confident. Certain.

'More to the point, do you have answers?' Tor paused, shaking his head. There was too much he needed to know. 'The other war-beasts. Why have they not grown properly? What will happen to them?'

Vostok grunted, raising her head on its long serpentine neck so that it was on a level with Tor. Noon stood up and leaned against the dragon's great bulky shoulders.

'A short question with a long answer. My brothers and sisters and I, we are born from Ygseril, and we go back to Ygseril when we die. Our spirit returns to him, and eventually, our souls move up from the roots, through the trunk, and into his branches, where we are born again. When we are needed.'

Tor realised he was blushing slightly. 'You have to understand. Ebora is not what it once was. The knowledge we had . . . it has died, with our people. You must forgive my ignorance.'

The dragon tipped her head slightly to one side; it did not matter.

'The Eighth Rain. New war-beasts were born, and we went to do battle, as is our purpose. There were hundreds of us then, and we flew out across Sarn to drive the invaders back, as we always did. But this time, mistakes were made.' Vostok's eyes flashed, with anger or some other emotion, Tor could not tell. 'The Jure'lia encroached deep into Eboran territory. They came here. The queen herself came here.' Scaly lips peeled back

526

to reveal shining teeth; there was no mistaking a sneer, thought Tor, even on a dragon's face. 'Ygseril took it upon himself to end the war. When the queen sank into his roots, seeking his power and knowledge, he let himself die, trapping her down there in the icy web of his own death. As long as he was dead, the queen could not escape. And she has always been the very heart of what the Jure'lia are. Without her, the Behemoths failed, and all her little creatures died.'

Noon caught Tor's eye then. 'When we see Vintage next, we'll have to tell her this. Can you imagine the look on her face?'

She was smiling, just slightly, and Tor was filled with a terrible urge to kiss her, to take her to him and— he looked away. The blush hadn't left his face.

'Unfortunately, when Ygseril died, it left us stranded,' Vostok continued. 'We are as deeply connected to him as the queen is to her minions. We died too, yet this time, our souls were lost. With no comprehension of what we were, we wandered, unknowing things of light and sorrow. I . . .'

Vostok trailed off, and Noon carried on for her. It was impossible to miss the connection between them now.

'They were the parasite spirits, Tor. All along, they were the souls of your war-beasts, cut adrift from their home. Their souls couldn't return to Ygseril.'

'Even we did not know what we were. All we had was a sense that the Behemoths were important somehow, dangerous, that we should be . . . near them. We felt a great loneliness, and a need to be within living flesh. Something we could never achieve.'

Tor felt his stomach lurch. That was why the spirits turned people inside out; they were seeking their physical bodies.

'And this is important, son of Ebora,' said Vostok. When the dragon spoke, her mouth hung open and the words were there, although Tor did not understand how – she had no human lips and tongue to form them. 'I am here because Noon carried me back inside her. I know who I am and our history. These others, my brothers and sisters that remain alive in their pods. They will not have their true voices. They will not have their root-memories. In short, they will not be complete. It is important you understand this.'

Tor blinked. 'Noon carried you back here? What do you mean?'

'It was in Esiah's compound, Tor.' For the first time, Noon looked mildly uncomfortable. 'When I absorbed the parasite spirit, that was Vostok. I took her inside me, and she has been with me since.'

Tor raised his eyebrows. 'You didn't think this was worth mentioning at the time?'

'I don't know if you remember, Tor, but you weren't in much of a state for deep discussions.' But she turned her head away as she said it, and Tor thought he wasn't the only one feeling wrong-footed.

'Hundreds of war-beasts flew to fight in the Eighth Rain, you said,' Tor continued. 'We have only fourteen. Fifteen, including you.'

'You don't even have that,' Vostok's tone was sour. 'The newly revived Ygseril was far too weak to produce the pods that he did, but he did it anyway, out of desperation for his children. We were not ready. Rightly, we should have had days to gestate upon the tree, but we fell too early.' Vostok shrugged, a strange movement that travelled down her entire body. Pearly scales caught the subdued light and winked like moonlight on water. 'You are lucky that I live, and that I was present enough, thanks to Noon, to fight. The others . . . time will tell. If you have more luck, son of Ebora, they will live, and although they may not have their true voices, their root-memories, they will choose warriors to bond with, as I have. Then we may have a chance.'

528

'You have bonded? Already?'

An uncomfortable silence pooled between them, Vostok and Noon both looking at him steadily. Eventually, he shook his head, half laughing.

'I may not know enough about Eboran history, but I do know that no *human* has ever bonded to a war-beast . . .'

He trailed off. Noon tipped her head to one side, still looking at him, and he cleared his throat. Vostok chuckled.

'Yes, it is unusual. Particularly as my kind has never had any love for the green witch fire . . . however, having lived inside it for a time, I see it anew. It is a fine weapon, of a sort. And son of Ebora, we can hardly afford to be choosey. How many of you live, now? Bearing in mind that your sister has left you.'

It was painful to hear that. 'A few live. If we can throw the crimson flux off, there is a chance for us. Speaking of which, this must mean Ygseril lives?'

Now Vostok looked uncomfortable, turning her long head away. 'He lingers,' she said. 'Being dead for so long, waiting with the poison of the Jure'lia suffusing his roots . . . it has left him greatly weakened.'

Tor took a slow breath against the thudding of his heart. 'Then, the sap? Will he be able to produce it? Will my people be healed of the crimson flux?' He felt a terrible urge to touch his scarred cheek, and fought it down with difficulty.

'You must wait, son of Ebora. Ygseril fights – he fights to live. For now, it is taking all of his essence to sustain his link with us, his war-beasts, and as I said before, without that link, we are nothing. I cannot say if he will be able to heal Ebora. You will have a small and weakened force here, Tormalin the Oathless, and a terrible war is about to begin. You will have to *fight*.'

Aldasair's shout echoed down the room, the excitement and anxiety impossible to miss.

'It's hatching! It's coming, quickly now!'

Heedless of the dragon, Tor turned and ran back down the chamber. Aldasair was kneeling in front of the pod, his face flushed. The silvery surface was already breached, and behind a thick lacy membrane something alive was moving. Tor knelt next to him and together they began to break away pieces of the pod, scattering them to the floor. Vostok and Noon came up behind them.

'Will this be another dragon?' asked Noon as the pieces fell away. Tor glanced up at her, and saw the same anxious excitement on her face as he felt on his own.

Vostok rumbled a response. 'I cannot say, child. We are all of us different.'

Be strong, thought Tor. The oily fluid inside the pod coated his hands and forearms now. The smell of it was a good thing, clean and sharp, like apples. *Be strong, be a weapon for us to use in this war. Help us to survive, at least.*

The lacy material split and a huge paw burst through, covered in wet grey fur and studded with four long black claws, wickedly curved like hooks. It landed on Tor's hand, and a moment later a great blunt head forced its way through the hole – it was an enormous cat, eyes bright and yellow, like lamps, ears folded back against its head. It stared, it seemed to Tor, directly into his soul, and then the thing hissed, digging its claws into his arm. Tor yelped.

'Looks like you've been chosen,' said Noon, from behind him. He could hear the smile in her voice. 'I would recommend leather gloves. Elbow-length ones.'

On the third day, they camped in the hills, some distance above the small seaside town. They had been there briefly, attempted to warn who they could, but what could you say, other than run? The people there had been disbelieving, and then they had seen it for themselves, rising like a bad moon over them.

Vintage and Nanthema had fled with heavy hearts – the risen Behemoth had moved slowly in the first couple of days, still juddering and uncertain, but despite the gaping holes it still sported in its side, the thing appeared to have recovered some of its appetite.

Now Vintage poked their fire, her eyes returning again and again to what was left of the little town. In the purple light of dusk it was difficult to tell that it had ever been a town at all. Now it was a confusion of thick green varnish, a collection of broken buildings under it somewhere. The Jure'lia had moved on, but not before the Behemoth had birthed one of its terrible maggot-like creatures, a thing that consumed everything before it and excreted the viscous substance they called varnish. Vintage thought that she would never forget the sight of that hideous, wriggling thing being birthed from the side of the Behemoth. She thought it would probably haunt her dreams nightly, for however long she had left.

'I never really thought I'd live to see the Ninth Rain,' said Nanthema. She had made a rough sort of stew from their supplies and was pushing it around the bottom of her bowl. 'I don't think any of us did, really.'

Vintage felt the corners of her mouth turn up, against her will.

'What is it?'

'Oh, an Eboran friend of mine had a sword named the Ninth Rain. I wonder how he's getting on.'

'You had an Eboran friend besides me?' Nanthema had injected a note of outrage into her voice, but Vintage didn't feel much like laughing.

'I think you'd like him. We have a lot to talk about, Nanthema.'

'We do.' The humour faded from the Eboran's face, and for the first time she did look older. 'I need to go home, don't I?'

At that moment, the wind changed, and, carried on it, they

531

heard a distant, eerie crying. At first Vintage thought it must be an animal, hurt in the forest somewhere, but the wind blew stronger and it became clearer. It was the sound of a great number of people crying out in horror and pain; another town, somewhere near, had discovered that the worm people were back.

'Yes. But let's not talk about it tonight.' Vintage looked up at the sky, deepening towards night all the time. The stars were just coming out, a scattering of shining dust in the heavens, but she found them no comfort. The Jure'lia had returned, and she had lived to see a war that could end them all. Reaching across, she pulled a bottle of wine from her pack, and ferreted out a pair of tin cups. 'Drink with me, my darling, and let's keep the darkness at bay for one more night, at least.'

Acknowledgements

This book was a journey through strange seas, with no familiar stars to navigate by . . . save for those people, stars every one, who helped me point the ship in the right direction and bail out water when necessary.

My everlasting gratitude to my brilliant editors, Emily Griffin and Claire Baldwin, who took to Vintage instantly and provided endless advice and support through what was a fairly long and tricky process. Ladies, you rock. Big thanks also to Katie Bradburn who managed to get me, the world's least organised person, to various conventions this past year, even when *The Ninth Rain* had more or less melted my brain. And as ever, wild applause for Patrick Insole and the design team at Headline, who gave this rather difficult to classify book a cover.

I have the best agent. Thank you, Juliet Mushens, for loving this book and sending me excitable texts about it; for teaching me what to order in Wahaca; for being a bezzer mate. Thanks must also go, as usual, to the whole of Team Mushens for general support and excellence. Specifically, I must thank Andrew Reid for continuing to be one of the best people I've had the good fortune to know and exchange terrible jokes with, and Den Patrick (now technically more Team Mushens

533

than all of us), who not only continues to sail the good ship Super Relaxed Fantasy Club with me, but also, by the time this is printed, will have taught me how to play X-Wing miniatures. Thanks also to Pete Newman, exchanger of bemused looks on con panels and Scarborough buddy – a friend who knows when to listen to your problems, and when to send outraged-on-your-behalf emails. Thanks, as ever, to Adam Christopher, my oldest writing buddy, who gave me a cheerful shove towards the writing life. Writers are a fragile bunch in many ways, and I feel very lucky to have such a great bunch of writer mates to cling to when the stories are sticky and I've forgotten how to word.

This time round I also wanted to give a shout out to Laura, Blighty, Lee, Christian, Herc, Jonesy, Leslie, Uncle Badger and the rest of the Hard Core Krew (and occupants of the Inappropriate Corner). I'm aware that I've been barely present this year, for various reasons, but the sight of your faces and posts online has been a boon when things were tough. Big thanks also to the readers who supported my previous series, The Copper Cat trilogy – thanks to you, I get to write another.

This book is dedicated to my brother, Paul, who was my first hero and the person I continue to look up to. As a kid, I decided I wanted my handwriting to look as cool as my brother's, so I spent some time copying it – my cheerfully messy scrawl still bears the marks of this. Sorry for stealing your handwriting, bro. As usual, I must mention my mum, unerringly kind and tolerant despite my being a massive pain in the arse, and my dear friend Jenni, a quiet source of strength and wisdom since I was ten, if you can believe it.

Lastly, thanks and love in stupendous quantities to Marty, my partner/best friend/soul mate/fellow cat wrangler. We continue to laugh every day and that's why we're the best, Harvey.